THE COMPLETE ENCYCLOPEDIA OF ILLUSTRATION

THE COMPLETE ENCYCLOPEDIA OF
ILLUSTRATION

by J. G. HECK

TRANSLATED BY SPENCER F. BAIRD, A.M., M.D.

CONTAINING ALL THE ORIGINAL ILLUSTRATIONS FROM THE 1851 EDITION OF
The Iconographic Encyclopedia of Science, Literature and Art
WITH EDITORIAL REVISIONS FOR EASIER REFERENCE

MATHEMATICS AND ASTRONOMY
NATURAL SCIENCES
MILITARY SCIENCES
NAVAL SCIENCES
ARCHITECTURE
GEOGRAPHY
HISTORY AND ETHNOLOGY
MYTHOLOGY AND RELIGION
FINE ARTS
TECHNOLOGY

FOREWORD BY PAUL BACON

PARK LANE
NEW YORK

Originally published in 1851 as *Iconographic Encyclopaedia of Science, Literature, and Art.*

This edition is published by Park Lane,
a division of Crown Publishers, Inc.
a b c d e f g h
1979
Manufactured in the United States of America

Library of Congress Cataloging in Publication Data

Heck, Johann Georg.
The complete encyclopedia of illustration.

Reprint of the 2 vols. of plates originally published by R. Garrigue, New York in 1851 as part of the author's 4 vol. work entitled: Iconographic encyclopaedia of science, literature, and art.
1. Illustration of books. I. Title.
NC960.H4 1979 769 79-84864
ISBN 0-517-27889-8

FOREWORD

The idea of using old engravings as a basis for current design—whole, in fragments, whatever—is probably as old as design itself. I first became aware of the process in the late 1940s, especially because of Bradbury Thompson's work in *Inspirations for Printers,* a publication of the West Virginia Pulp and Paper Company. At first, it didn't occur to me to wonder about where exactly Thompson got those things, but the stuff looked good, with a strange harmony: in the abstract and transparent color shapes that Thompson used, the old steel engravings looked peculiarly at home.

The designer I was then apprenticed to, Hal Zamboni, had a collection of old illustrated encyclopedias, I discovered, and we pored over them occasionally for some apt application; there were jealous mentions (in precisely the style of record collectors) of the lucky so-and-so who had this or that crumbling but priceless set. I thought then, and still think, that the craftsmanship and the sheer output of those steel engravers were sobering to contemplate. Sometimes completely straightforward, sometimes romantic, they showed what was known about the appearance of things: real, mystical, practical, ancient, new, preposterous, scientific, or sacred. And, in the case of this book, encyclopedic in the truest sense.

These images are wonderful to look at and to think about; so many of the extraordinarily detailed engravings show us the things that were obsolete before the Civil War—yet here they are, awesome devices we can't even imagine in operation, in flawless detail.

In the Naval Sciences plates, for instance, note the quality of the seas and skies; they are only there as background, but they are done with a painter's eye, so that a ship's rigging is seen in its own environment. And there are innumerable other examples: faint buildings in the distance behind depicted animals, buildings which suggest college or church spires and are not necessary, but which are there because the engraver wanted them to be.

You want to know what *Corvus corax*, the raven, looks like? Well, here is what he looks like—and what a bevel gear looks like, and a nasal cleft, and the *Arc de Triomphe*—lovingly detailed, cross-hatched, and, luckily for us, splendidly reproducible.

Paul Bacon

ACKNOWLEDGMENTS

The publisher wishes to acknowledge, with gratitude, the help of Andrew Yockers in researching and securing the captions to the plates, and the cooperation of Mrs. Martha C. Slotten, of the Library at Dickinson College, Carlisle, Pennsylvania in providing that material. Catherine Riley created plate titles from figure captions where they were missing from the original edition.

INTRODUCTION

In the mid-nineteenth century, when this book was first published, a man was not considered fully educated unless he had a broad, deep, and detailed knowledge of all areas of culture and human endeavor. This was expected to include a solid grounding in the scientific disciplines, an appreciation of art in all its manifestations, a store of mythological references and tales, considerable knowledge of geological wonders and oddities, plus curiosity about technological developments that were changing the face of society at that time.

To such a many-faceted man, this encyclopedia could well have been his greatest treasure. He would have spent hours browsing through its richly adorned pages, expanding his knowledge and increasing his perception of every area of human achievement by coming in contact with illustrations of such realism, beauty, and detail that their impact would be lasting. Today this work can be viewed with that same fascination, expecially since it emphasizes how we have to place much of scientific knowledge and instrumentation in historic context.

Originally published in 1851 as *The Iconographic Encyclopaedia of Science, Literature, and Art,* this work was based on the famed *Bilderatlas*, by Friedrich Arnold Brockhaus, one of the finest encyclopedias of its day. Spencer Baird translated the captions and text from the original German, and those captions have been included here, although the text has not, since it would now be thoroughly outdated.

This edition, at the most modern level, reproduces the entire body of plates by means of fine-line offset lithography, which will enable their most successful use by artists, designers, and others; and this is also the only edition to place complete captions and translations of all German terms for convenient reference within the same section as their respective plates.

The physical and intellectual world of the nineteenth century has been captured and categorized in this volume in ten major divisions representing the various areas of scientific knowledge and artistic achievement of the age.

In *Mathematics and Astronomy,* the extraordinarily complex mathematical and geometrical drawings are painstakingly precise, and the astronomical illustrations give the views of the planets and the heavens a startling beauty.

In the *Natural Sciences,* graphic representations of the principles and instruments of Physics, Meteorology, and Chemistry provide a virtual history of these sciences; in the subsection on Mineralogy, there are drawings of minerals in exquisite crystalline forms.

Geognosy and Geology spread before the viewer the interior of the earth, its many strata and substrata, and the earth's exterior formations from the Coral Islands of the Pacific to the grottoes of France, to a volcanic crater in Iceland. The Meteorology section includes diagrams and displays of nature's climatic phenomena—the common as well as the more unusual, such as air hurricanes, mirages at sea, or the aurora borealis. In the sections on Botany and Zoology, the scientific accuracy of the drawings is rivaled only by the diversity and beauty of the subjects. Depicted in their natural habitats, whether jungle, desert, seashore, or countryside, the birds, animals, fish, and snakes have a lifelike quality and power that make them seem ready to spring off the page. The surgical drawings in the Anthropology and Surgery section, with the expertise and comprehensiveness of a classical anatomy text, can instruct or simply please the eye.

Geography and Planography: An immense range of subject exists in this section—from atlases of the continents to maps of mountain and river systems, from a map of the world according to Ptolemy to a plan of Paris in the nineteenth century.

History and Ethnology: Of the divisions, this is one of the most variegated and informative of all areas of culture, containing drama, tragedy, surprising facts, and a multitude of costumes and customs. Scenes of antiquity include a terrifying view of the Roman Coliseum with lions and an elephant attacking the Christian martyrs; there are numerous plans, drawings, and diagrams of catacombs, early churches, and chapels. Illustrations of medieval life cover the range of emotions, from the ceremony bestowing knighthood, an exhilarating scene, to plates portraying the horrors of the Inquisition. Crowns and shields appear in rich profusion, followed by histories, in graphic form, of the various religious orders and communities. The nineteenth century section presents life in every area of the world, from earthy scenes of Russian peasant life to the pomp and splendor of an Oriental court, from views of the Brazilian slave trade to an elegant masked ball in Paris.

Military and Naval Sciences: The review of *Military Sciences* begins with the simple hand-held weapons of the Egyptians, Medes, and Persians; advances through the growing complexity of instruments and armor of the Middle Ages; then proceeds to a complete study of all aspects of military life in the nineteenth century: cavalry, infantry, officer dress, fencing positions, tactics and battle formations, medals and military orders, and finally, military structures, engines, and fortifications.

Naval Sciences contains some of the most beautiful plates in the book. The artistry of the engravers captured the lilting movement of the ships at sea almost in three dimensions, and the excitement of the era of the immense sailing ships. Ships of all nations are shown: cutters, frigates, fishing smacks, barques, coasters, sloops, schooners, and steamships. There are quaint scenes of shipboard life, of naval officers and sailors in full dress and at ease.

Architecture: In pictures of extraordinary clarity garnered from every corner of the globe, we marvel at the Egyptian pyramids, the purity of line of the classic Greek and Roman styles, the intricacies of pre-Columbian temples in Central America, the ornateness of Islamic architecture, and some of the most stunning examples of European cathedrals built through the centuries: the magnificent Cologne and Rouen Cathedrals, the Minster at York, the gloomy but intriguing interior of the Cathedral at Milan. This tour ends with a review of the architecture of palaces.

Mythology and Religious Rites: This is not only a comprehensive survey of religious customs, ceremonies, deities, and artifacts through the ages, but also an assemblage of many intriguing curiosa: penitents, ascetics, and fanatics, statues of Indian idols, the funeral of the Dalai Lama, Persian Magi, and the amazing plethora of gods and symbols that the Egyptians worshiped.

The *Fine Arts* section is a treasure trove of painting, sculpture, and other decorative arts from ancient, classical, Renaissance, Baroque, Mannerist, and Neoclassic periods. There are numerous illustrations on the theory of drawing, including life studies and the graphic arts, and the section ends with an intriguing collection, "Alphabets of Various Languages for the Use of Engravers."

Technology documents the rapid industrialization of the 1850s incorporating all the new and exciting technological innovations that were then radically changing the nature of life. Although it illustrates innumerable constructions—streets, tunnels, dams, bridges, canals, aqueducts, cranes, pumps—the highlights inevitably are those inventions or processes that were to have the greatest repercussions on society: the locomotive, the cotton gin, the industrial weaving looms, and the minting, mining, and metal-mill equipment.

In this extraordinary compilation, with the completeness and variety of its subject matter, the delicacy and precision of the engravings, and the authoritativeness of the treatment, we see mirrored the meticulously cultivated mind of the nineteenth century. In fact, it is a cultural ideal for all times, but even more so today, when technological advances give man the impression that he can forsake the meticulous and leave those details to machines. This volume demonstrates to the modern reader the importance of delving knowingly and lovingly into the past to discover, preserve, and re-create the art and artifacts of old.

These illustrations are the realizations, in every sense, of an earlier age, which will gratify the appetite of people in our society for information, history, and the craftsmanship of another day.

CLAIRE BOOSS

NOTE: On certain of the plate titles, only the principal elements have been named, as the subjects are sometimes too many and too diverse to enumerate. Complete descriptions can be found in the figure captions that precede each major section of the book. There are some figures which have no captions, these having been omitted from the original edition, and there the reader must rely on the general information provided by the plate titles.

TABLE OF CONTENTS

TRANSLATIONS OF GERMAN NAMES AND TERMS USED IN THE PLATES WILL BE FOUND IN THE GLOSSARIES IN EACH CAPTION SECTION.

MATHEMATICS AND ASTRONOMY

NATURAL SCIENCES

PHYSICS AND METEOROLOGY

CHEMISTRY, MINERALOGY, AND GEOLOGY

BOTANY

ZOOLOGY

ANTHROPOLOGY AND SURGERY

GEOGRAPHY AND PLANOGRAPHY

HISTORY AND ETHNOLOGY

ANCIENT TIMES AND MIDDLE AGES

ETHNOLOGY OF THE NINETEENTH CENTURY

MILITARY SCIENCES

NAVAL SCIENCES

ARCHITECTURE

MYTHOLOGY AND RELIGIOUS RITES

THE FINE ARTS

TECHNOLOGY

THE COMPLETE ENCYCLOPEDIA OF ILLUSTRATION

MATHEMATICS AND ASTRONOMY

Captions to the Mathematics and Astronomy Plates, 1–15

PLATES 1 and 2.
Mathematical and Geometrical Problems

Figures 1–91.

PLATE 3.
Mathematical and Geometrical Problems

Figures 1–142.

GLOSSARY

Milchstrasse, Milky Way

PLATE 4.
Problems in Geodesy or Surveying, and Projection in Vertical and Horizontal Planes

Figures 1–68.

PLATE 5.
Mathematical and Surveying Instruments

Figure
1, 2. Hair compasses
3, 4. Proportional compasses
5. Proportional compasses with micrometer screw
6, 7. Beam compasses
8, 8*a*. Triangular compasses
9, 10. Elliptograph
11–13. Farey's elliptograph
14. Excentric compasses
15. Pantograph
16. Wallace's eidograph
17. Spring compasses
18, 19. Parallel ruler
20. Lehman's plane table
21. Mayer's plane table
22. Mayer's fork and plummet
23, 24. Tubular level
25. Diopter ruler
26. Diopter ruler with telescope
27. Measuring chain
28. Measuring staff
29. Arrow or picket
30. Zollman's instrument for measuring angles
31. Astrolabe
32. Hadley's sextant
33, 34. Compass and telescope
35, 36. Schmalkalder's prismatic compass
37. Graphometer
38. Theodolite
39. Borda's reflecting circle
40, 41. Water level and movable diopter
42–44. Keith's mercurial level
45. Level and compass
46. Levelling telescope
47. Levelling compass
48. Levelling circle
49, 50. Explanation of the vernier
51, 52. Levelling staves
53, 54. Target of levelling stave
55. Plate compasses
56. Mason's level
57. Application of plane table
58–60. Lehman's method of topographical drawing

GLOSSARY

a = der Projection des Bergstriches, a = Projection of the mountain tract
b = der Höhe der horizontalen Schicht, b = Height of the horizontal stratum
c = wahre Länge des Bergstriches, c = True length of the mountain tract

PLATE 6.
Illustrating Theories, Forces, and Phenomena of the Solar System

Figure
1, 2. The armillary sphere
3. Illustrating the properties of the circle
4. Illustrating the properties of the ellipse
5. Illustrating the parallax
6. Illustrating the centrifugal force of the earth
7. Illustrating the rotation of the earth
8, 9. Illustrating the proof of the earth's being of spherical shape and an elliptical spheroid
10. Illustrating the local variation of gravity
11. The parallelogram of forces
12. Illustrating the points, circles, and terms of the terrestrial sphere
13. Illustrating the apparent rotation of the celestial sphere
14. Illustrating the heliocentric and geocentric place of the planets
15. Illustrating the perihelion distance
16, 17. Illustrating refraction
18. Illustrating the theory of eclipses of the sun and moon
19. Illustrating the phases of the moon
20. Illustrating the moon's nodes
21. Illustrating the apparent course of Venus
22. Illustrating the theory of twilight
23. Illustrating the theory of ebb and flow
24, 25. Illustrating the apparent course of superior and inferior planets
26. Illustrating the resistance of the ether

PLATE 7.
Various Planetary Systems

Figure
1. Planetary system of Ptolemy
2. Planetary system of the Egyptians
3. Planetary system of Tycho de Brahe
4, 5. Planetary system of Copernicus
6. Illustrating the velocity of planets
7. Illustrating the inclination of the planetary orbits to that of the earth

PLATE 8.
Celestial Bodies

Figure
1. Group of stars in Hercules
2. Group of stars in Aquarius
3, 4. Group of stars fan shaped
5. Nebula in Ursa
6. Nebula in Gemini
7. Nebula in Leo Major
8, 9. Nebulæ in Monoceros
10. Nebula in Canes Venatici
11. Nebula in Sagittarius
12, 13. Nebula in Auriga
14. Nebula in Andromeda
15. Comet of 1819
16, 17. Comet of 1811
18. Surface of Mars
19. Surface of Jupiter
20. Surface and rings of Saturn

PLATE 9.
Seasons and Other Phenomena of the Spheres

Figure
1. Illustrating the seasons
2, 3. Daily and yearly motion of the earth
4. Illustrating the parallel sphere
5. Illustrating the right sphere
6. Illustrating the 13 transits of Mercury in the 19th century
7, 8. Illustrating the phenomena of the transit of Mercury, May 4, 1786
9–13.The sun's spots

PLATE 10.
Illustrating Phases of the Earth's Moon and Orbits of the Earth and Various Moons

Figure
1. Illustrating the determination of longitude and latitude
2. Illustrating the theory of the elliptical orbit of the earth
3. Illustrating the duration of a revolution of the moon
4. Illustrating the daily revolution of the moon around the earth
5. Illustrating the phases of the moon
6. Orbits of the moons of Jupiter
7. Orbits of the moons of Saturn
8. Orbits of the moons of Uranus
9. Orbit of the earth's moon
10. Serpentine projection of the moon's course on the plane of the earth's orbit

GLOSSARY

Abend, Evening; *—stern*, Evening star
Abnehmender Mond, Decreasing moon
Aphelium, Aphelion
Apsidenlinie, Line of Apsides
Aufsteigender Knoten, Ascending node
Austritt beim Aufgang der Sonne, Emersion at sunrise; *—beim Untergang der Sonne*, Emersion at sunset
Axe der Ekliptik, Axis of the Ecliptic
Bahn des Merkur, Orbit of Mercury; *—der Venus*, Orbit of Venus
Colur des Frühlings-Æquinoxiums, Colure of the vernal equinox; *—des Herbst-Æquinoxiums*, Colure of the Autumnal equinox; *—der Nachtgleichen*, Colure of the equinoxes; *—des Sommersolstitiums*, Colure of the Summer solstice; *—des Wintersolstitiums*, Colure of the Winter solstice
Comet von 1811 *vor seiner Erscheinung. Projectirt auf die Ekliptik am* 25 *März* 1811. *Neigung der Bahn* 75° 5′, Comet of 1811 before its

appearance. Projected on the ecliptic March 25, 1811, Inclination of the orbit 75° 5′.—*von* 1811 *nach seiner Erscheinung b am* 1 *März* 1812, Comet of 1811 after its appearance until March 1, 1812

Dauer der längsten Nächte, Duration of the longest nights; *—des längsten Tages,* Duration of the longest day

Dichteres Medium, Denser medium

Drei Uhr Morgens, 3 o'clock A.M.; *—Nachmittag,* 3 o'clock P.M.

Dritter Octant, Third octant

Dünneres Medium, Rarer medium

Ebene der Pallas, d. Juno, etc., Planes of the orbits of Pallas, Juno, etc.

Eintritt beim Aufgang der Sonne, Entrance at sunrise; *—beim Untergang d. Sonne,* Entrance at sunset

Ekliptik, Ecliptic

Erdaxe, Axis of the earth

Erdbahn, Orbit of the earth

Erde, Earth

Erster Octant, First octant

Erstes Viertel, First quarter

Excentricität, Eccentricity

Frühling, Spring

Frühlingsnachtgleiche, Vernal equinox

Gemässigte Zone, Temperate zone

Grosse Axe, Axis of the heavens

Halley'scher Comet v. 1759 *u.* 1835, *Neigung seiner Bahn,* Halley's Comet of 1759 and 1835, inclination of its orbit

Heisse Zone, Torrid zone

Herbst, Autumn

Herbstnachtgleiche, Autumnal equinox

Horizont, Horizon

Kalte Zone, Frigid zone

Kometenbahn, Orbit of a comet

Letztes Viertel, Last quarter

Millionen Meilen, Millions of miles

Mittag, Noon

Mittelkraft, Mean force

Mitternacht, Midnight

Monate, Months

Mond, Moon; — *-bahn,* Orbit of the moon; — *-finsterniss,* Eclipse of the moon

Morgen, Morning; — *-stern,* Morning star

Neumond, New moon

Neun Uhr Abends, 9 P.M.; *—Morgens,* 9 A.M.

Niedersteigender Knoten, Descending node

Nord, North; — *-pol,* Northpole

Nördliche Declination der Sonne, Northern declination of the sun

Nördlicher Polarkreis, Arctic circle

Obere Conjunction, Superior conjunction

Œstliche Digression, East digression

Ost, East

Perihelium, Perihelion

Polarstern, Polar star

Polhöhe über dem Horizont, Elevation of the pole above the horizon

Richtung des Schattens um Mittag, Direction of the shadow at noon

Rotationsaxe, Axis of rotation

Scheinbarer Himmelsbogen, Apparent arch of the heavens; *—Horizont,* visible horizon

Sechs Uhr Abends, 6 P.M.; *—Morgens,* 6 A.M.

Solstitial oder Wendepunktlinie, Solstitial colure

Sommer, Summer; — *-Sonnenwende,* Summer solstice

Sonne, Sun; *—Sonnen-Æquator,* Sun's equator; — *-finsterniss,* Eclipse of the sun; — *-scheibe im Grössenverhältniss zu den Planeten,* The sun's disk; its size compared to the diameters of the planets

Stunden, Hours; *—Entfernung,* Hours' distance; — *-ring,* Hour-circle

Süd, South; — *-pol,* South pole

Südliche Declination der Sonne, Southern declination of the sun

Südlicher Polarkreis, Antarctic circle

Südwestlicher Sonnenrand, Southwestern edge of the sun

Trabanten des Jupiter; —des Saturn; —des Uranus, Satellites of Jupiter, Saturn, and Uranus

Untere Conjunction, inferior conjunction

Vierter Octant, Fourth octant

Vollmond, Full moon

Vom Pol bis zum Zenith, From pole to zenith; *—Zenith biz zum Æquator,* From zenith to equator

Wahrer Horizont, True horizon

Wendekreis des Krebses, Tropic of Cancer; *—des Steinbocks,* Tropic of Capricorn

Westliche Digression, West digression

Winter-Sonnenwende, Winter solstice

Zoll, Digit, inch

Zunehmender Mond, Increasing moon

Zweites Octant, Second octant

PLATE 11.
Beer and Mädler's Map of the Moon

PLATE 12.
Map of the Northern Heavens

PLATE 13.
Map of the Southern Heavens

PLATE 14.
Planet Sizes and Various Phenomena

Figure

1–11. Relative sizes of the planets with respect to the sun's diameter

12–15. Positions of Saturn and its ring with respect to the earth

16–35. Apparent size of the planets in their perigee and apogee

36–45. Apparent size of the sun as seen from the planets

46–54. Comparison of the diameters of the moon and the planets to the diameter of the earth

55. Mode of observing a transit of Venus

56. Total eclipse of the sun

57. Aurora borealis

58. Aurora australis

59. Mock suns

GLOSSARY

Anfang bei Sonnenaufgang, Beginning at sunrise; *—bei Sonnenuntergang,* beginning at sunset

Arabien, Arabia

Atlantischer Ocean, Atlantic Ocean

Azorische Inseln, the Azores

Berberey, Barbary

Berührung des Sonnen-, und Mondrandes, Contact of the edges of sun and moon

Canarische Inseln, Canary Islands

Capverdische Inseln, Cape Verd Islands

Centrale oder totale Verfinsterung, Central or total eclipse

Drei Zoll Verfinsterung, Three digits eclipsed

Ende bei Sonnenaufgang, End at sunrise; *—bei Sonnenuntergang,* End at sunset

Grönland, Greenland

Grossbritanien, Great Britain

Grosser Ocean, Pacific Ocean

Indisches Meer, Indian Sea

Island, Iceland

Mittel bie Sonnenaufgang, Middle at sunrise; *—bei Sonnenuntergang,* Middle at sunset

Mittelländisches Meer, Mediterranean Sea

Mongolei, Mongolia

Neun Zoll Verfinsterung, Nine digits eclipsed

Nordpol, North pole

Norwegen, Norway

Nubien, Nubia

Ost Indien, East Indies

Russland, Russia

Sechs Zoll Verfinsterung, Six digits eclipsed

Sibirien, Siberia

PLATE 15.
Astronomical Instruments

Figure

1. Herschel's reflecting telescope

2. Fraunhofer's achromatic refractor at Dorpat

3–10. Meridian circle at Pulkowa

11, 12. Meridian circle at Hamburg

13. Roemer's transit instrument

14. Dollond's repeating circle

15–17. Repsold's Equatorial at Hamburg

18. Troughton's quadrant

19. Tycho's mural quadrant

20. Clockwork of Fraunhofer's refractor

21. Ptolemy's triquetrum

22. Portable transit instrument

23. Reflecting sextant

24. Reflecting sector

25–34. Repsold's small transit instrument at St. Petersburg

35–37. Ertel's theodolite

38. Henderson's planetarium

39. Henderson's explanation of the seasons

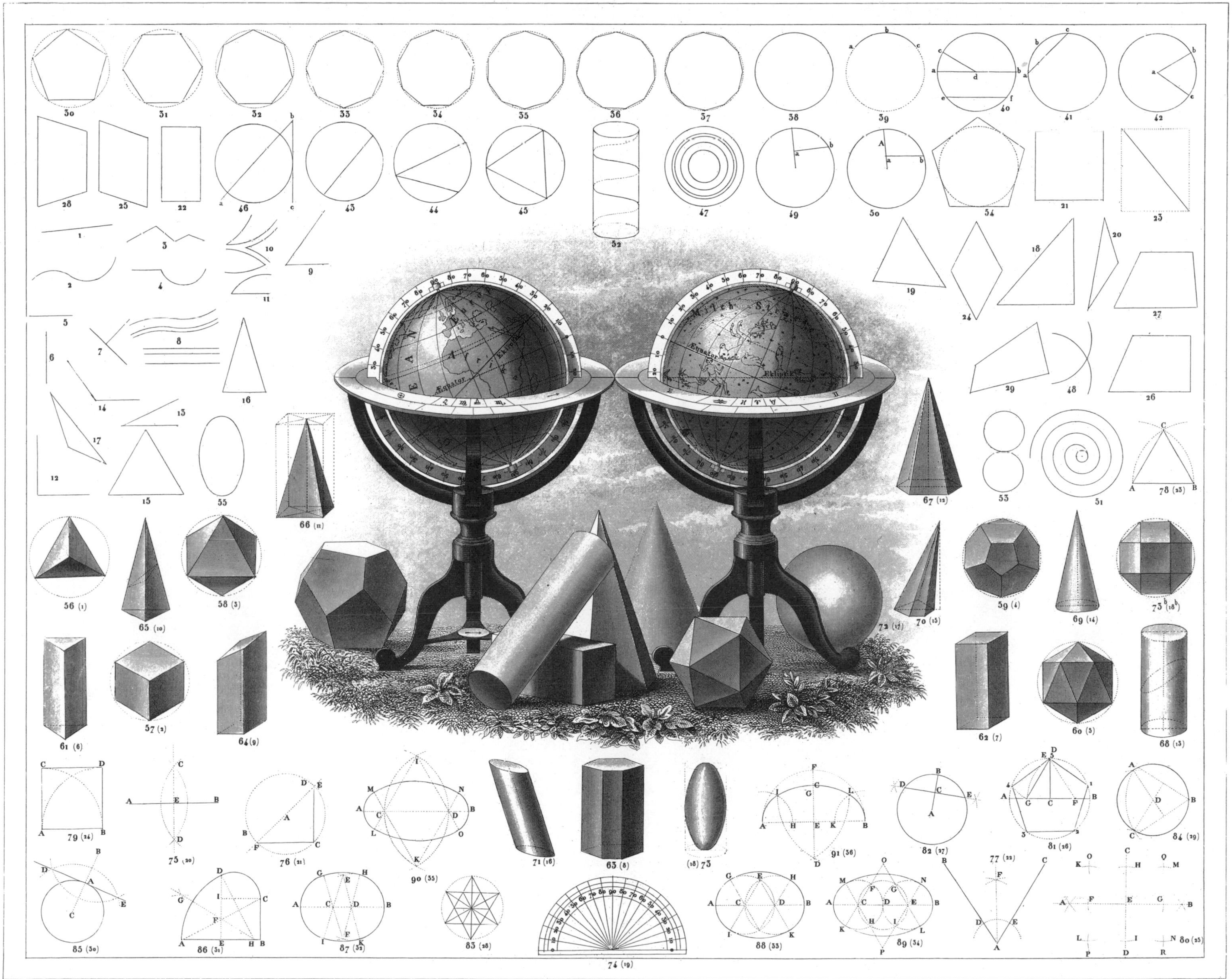

G. Heck dir.t *Henry Winkles sculp.t*

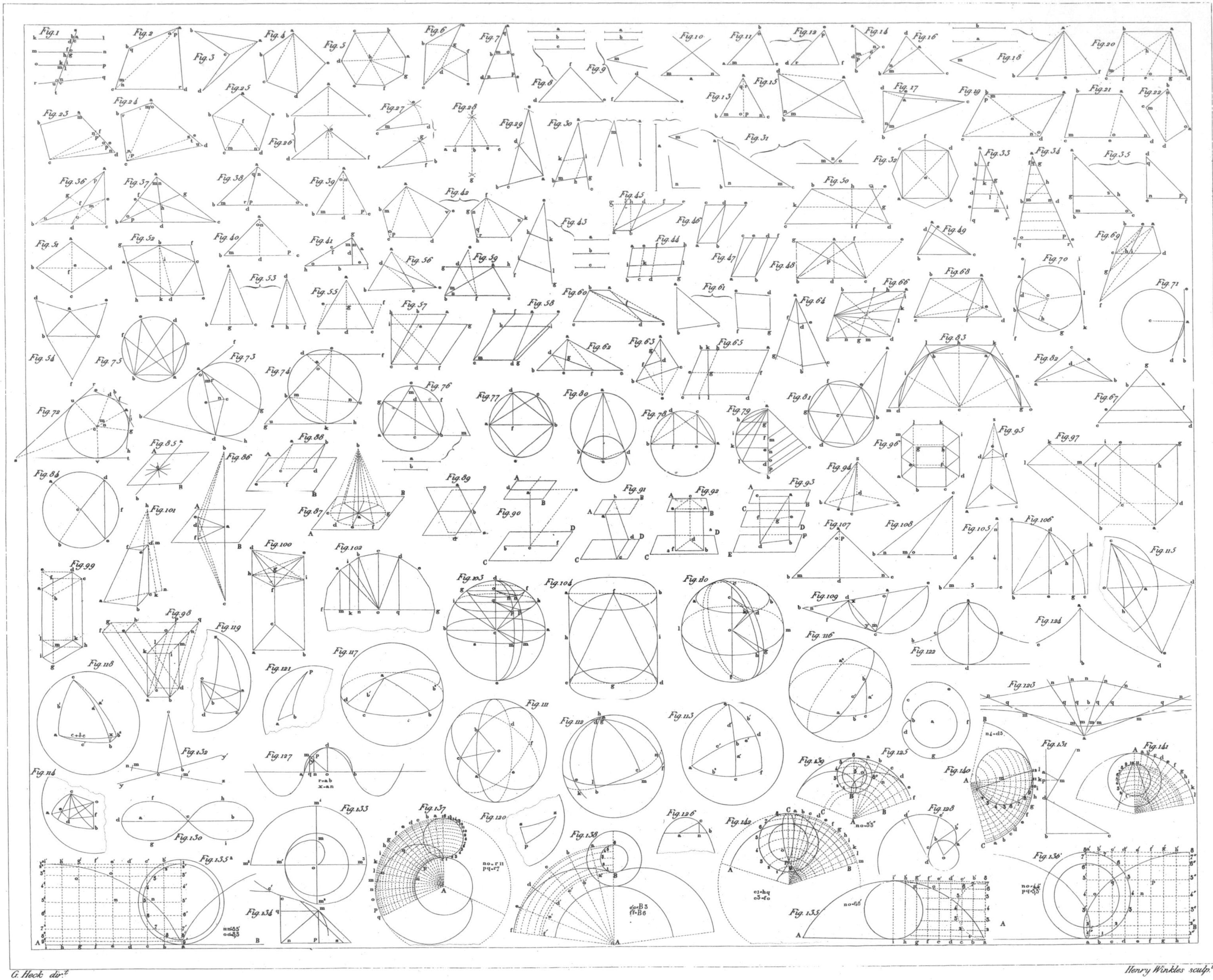

G. Heck dir.t

Henry Winkles sculp.t

PLATE 3. MATHEMATICAL AND GEOMETRICAL PROBLEMS

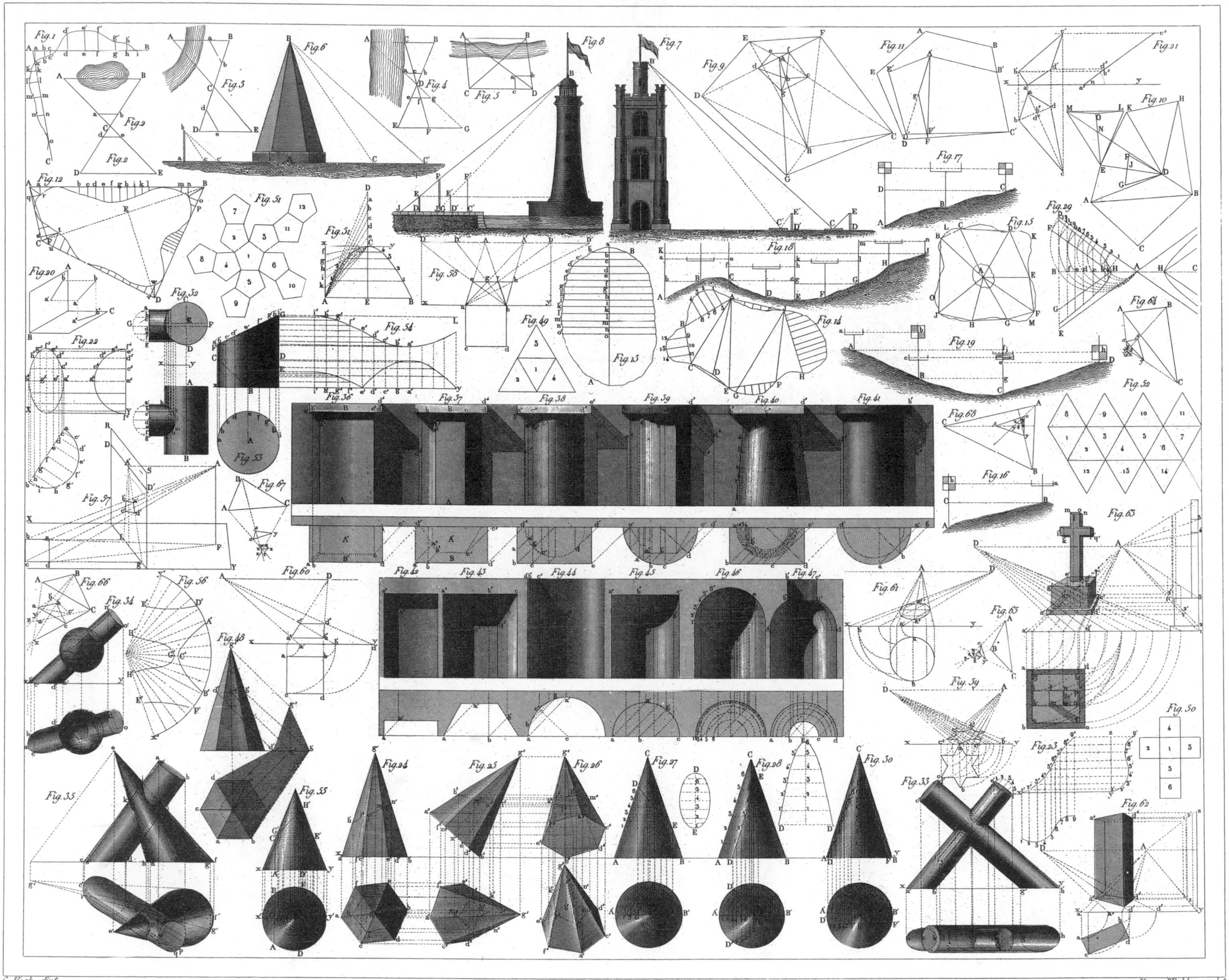

G. Heck dir.t Henry Winkles sculp.t

PLATE 4. PROBLEMS IN GEODESY OR SURVEYING, AND PROJECTION IN VERTICAL AND HORIZONTAL PLANES

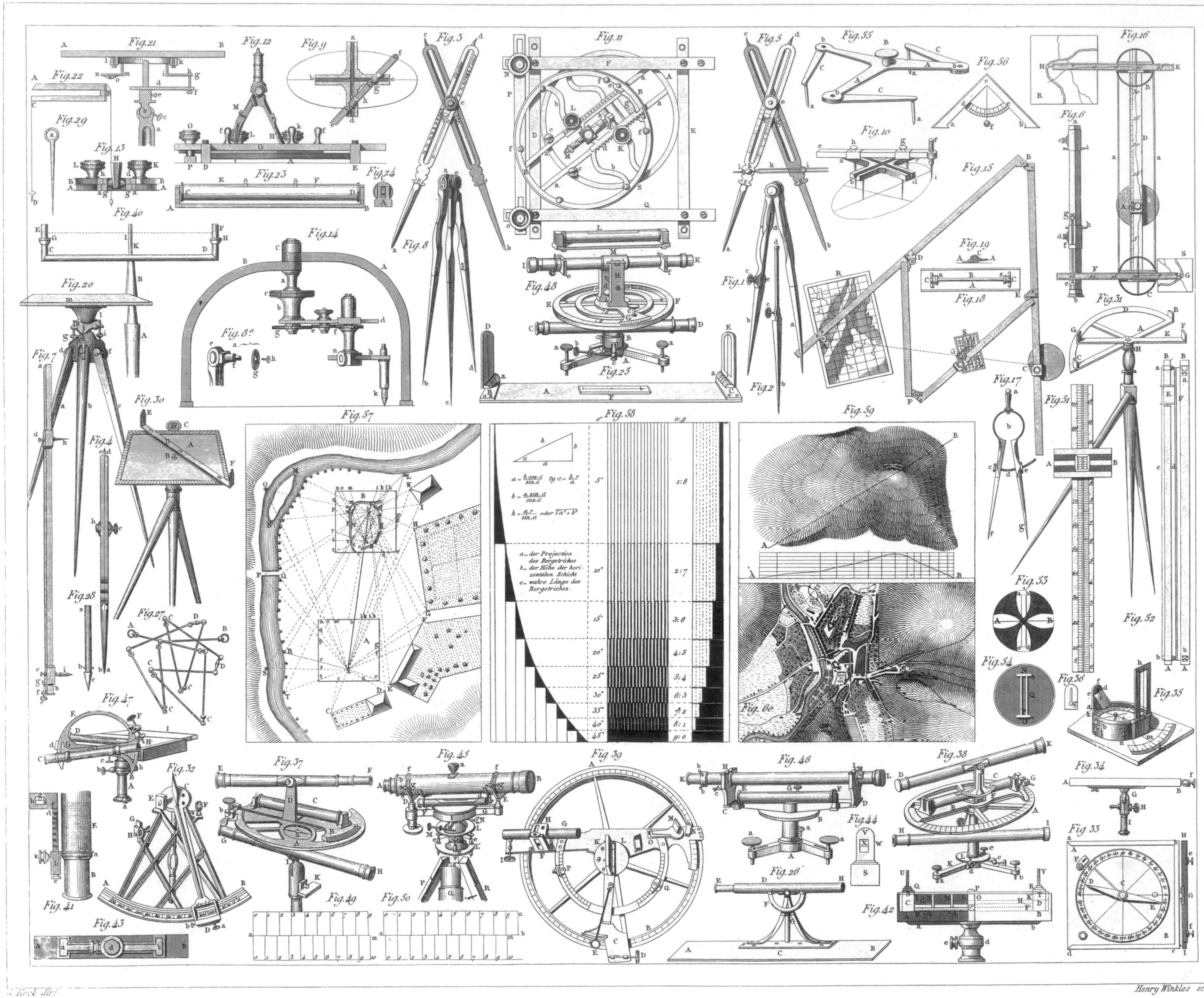

Heck dir. Henry Winkles sculp.

 PLATE 5. MATHEMATICAL AND SURVEYING INSTRUMENTS

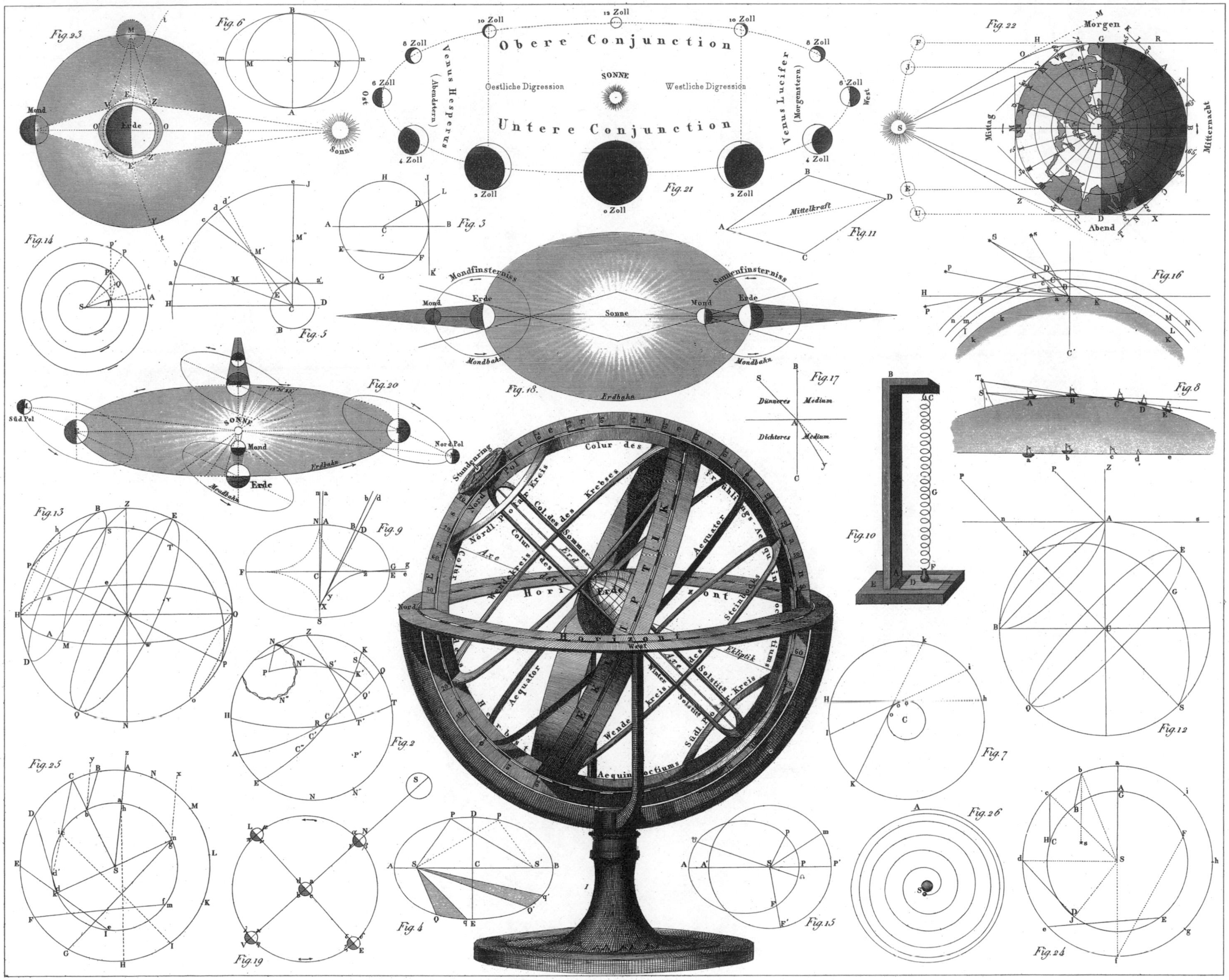

G. Heck dir.t

Maschinenschrift von E. Kretzschmar. Leipz.

Henry Winkles sculp.t

PLATE 6. ILLUSTRATING THEORIES, FORCES, AND PHENOMENA OF THE SOLAR SYSTEM

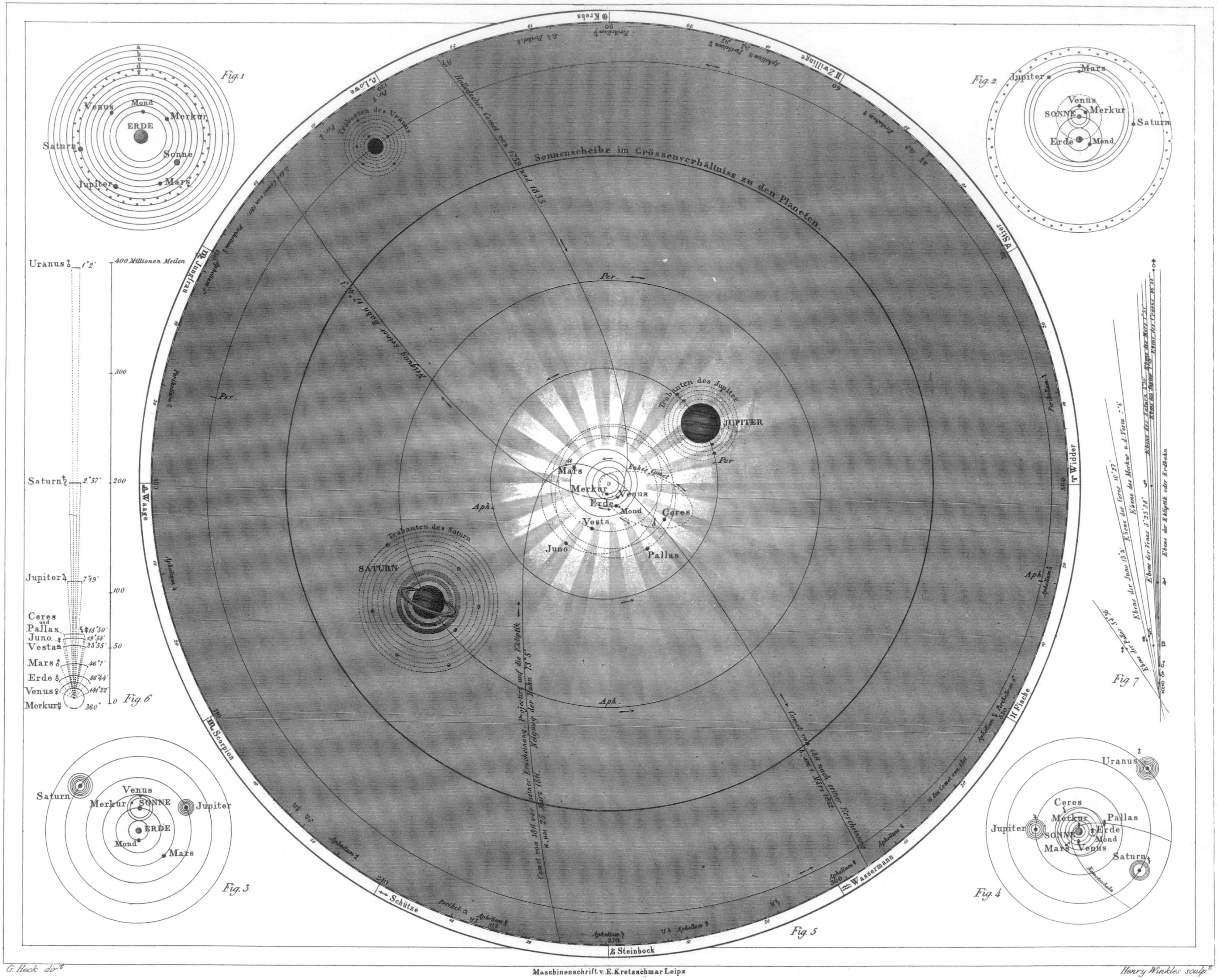

Fig. 1
Venus
Mond
Merkur
ERDE
Saturn
Sonne
Jupiter
Mars
Fig. 2.
Jupiter
Mars
Venus
SONNE
Merkur
Saturn
Erde
Mond
Uranus
400 Millionen Meilen
300
Saturn
200
Jupiter
100
Ceres
und
Pallas
Juno
Vesta
50
Mars
Erde
Venus
Merkur
0
Fig. 6
Saturn
Venus
Merkur
SONNE
Jupiter
ERDE
Mond
Mars
Fig. 3.
Uranus
Ceres
Pallas
Jupiter
Merkur
Erde
SONNE
Mond
Mars
Venus
Saturn
Fig. 4
Fig. 7
Fig. 5
Krebs
Zwillinge
Stier
Widder
Fische
Wassermann
Steinbock
Schütze
Scorpion
Waage
Jungfrau
Löwe
Sonnenscheibe im Grössenverhältniss zu den Planeten.
Trabanten des Uranus
Trabanten des Jupiter
JUPITER
Trabanten des Saturn
SATURN
Mars
Merkur
Venus
Erde
Mond
Ceres
Vesta
Juno
Pallas
Per.
Aph.
G. Heck dir.
Maschinenschrift v. E. Kretzschmar Leipz
Henry Winkles sculp.

PLATE 7. VARIOUS PLANETARY SYSTEMS

G. Heck dir.

R. Schmidt et Madel M. sc.

PLATE 8. CELESTIAL BODIES

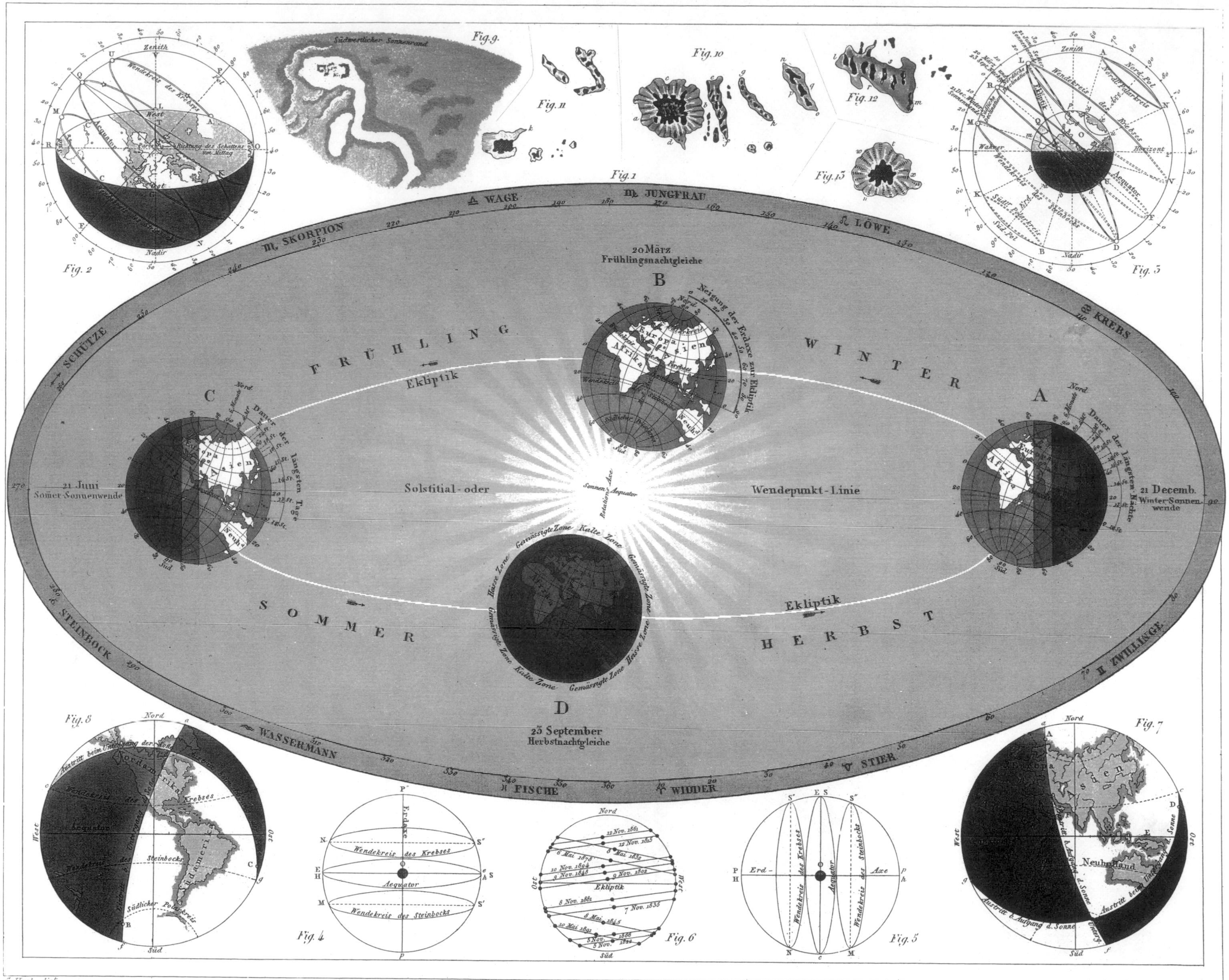

G. Heck dir.

Henry Winkles sculp.

PLATE 9. SEASONS AND OTHER PHENOMENA OF THE SPHERES

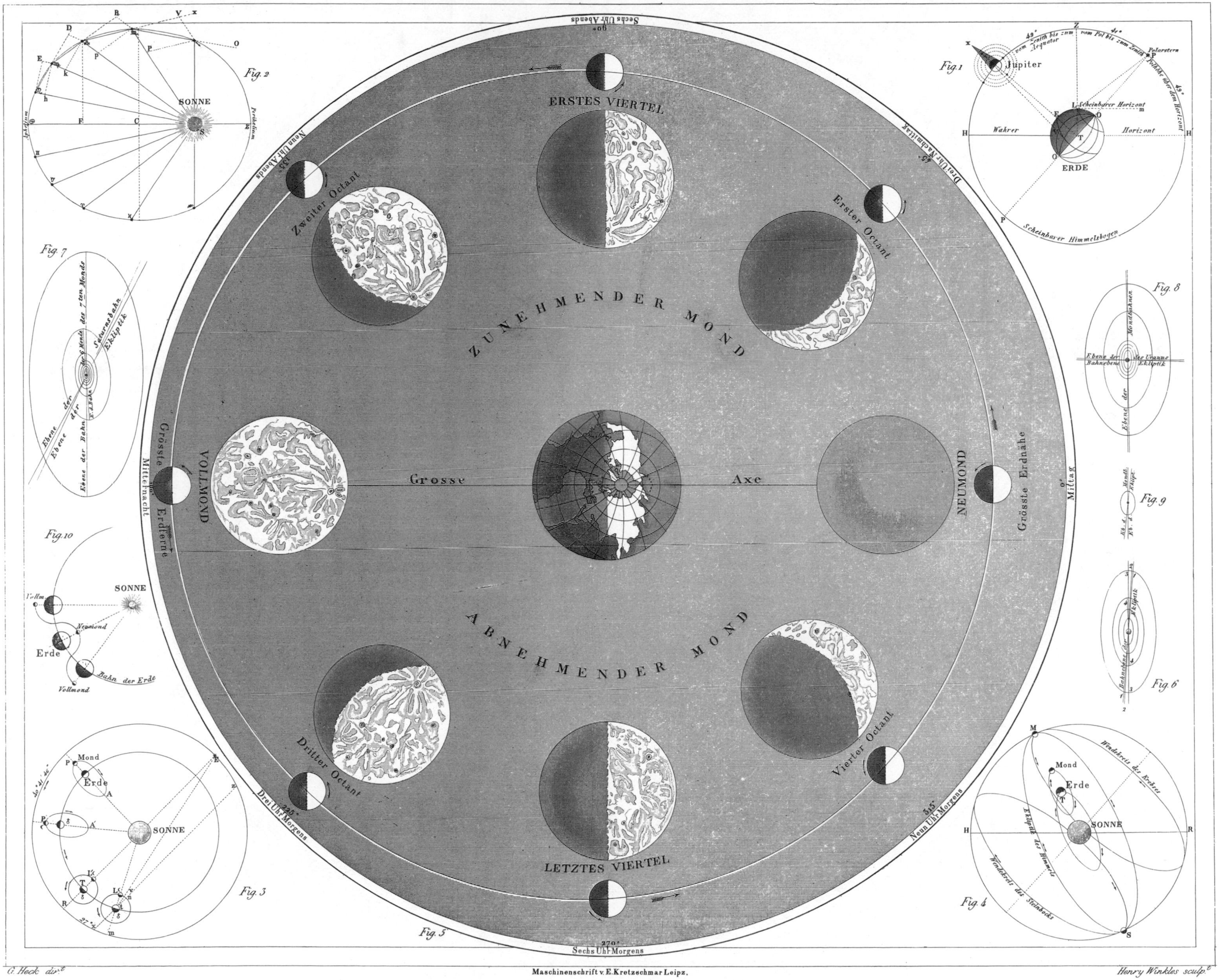

PLATE 10. ILLUSTRATING PHASES OF THE EARTH'S MOON AND ORBITS OF THE EARTH AND VARIOUS MOONS

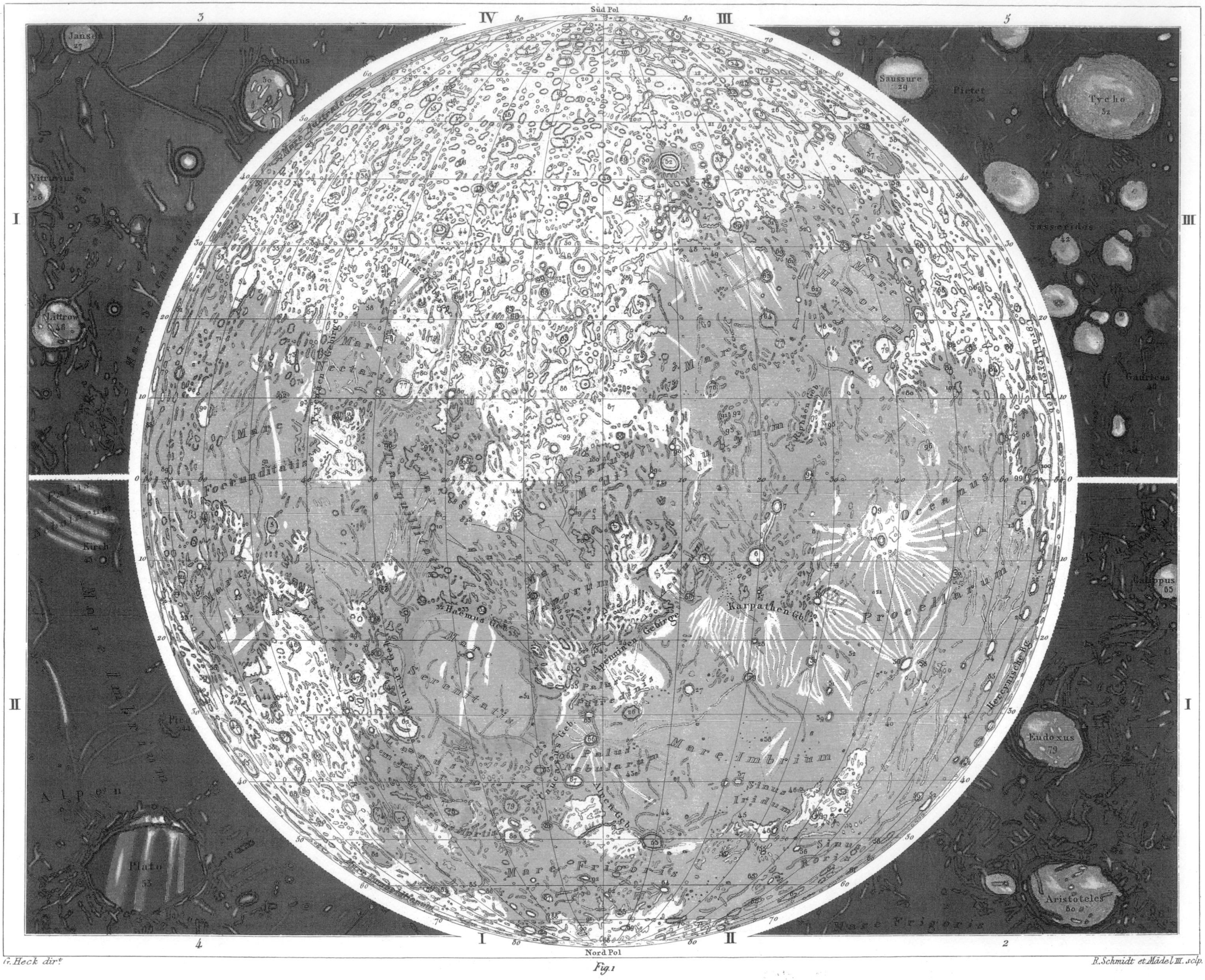
Süd Pol
Nord Pol
Jansen
27
Vitruvius
28
Littrow
48
Kirch
43
Alpen
Plato
55
Saussure
29
Pictet
30
Tycho
32
Sasserides
42
Gauricus
40
Calippus
65
Eudoxus
79
Aristoteles
80
Mare Foecunditatis
Mare Nectaris
Mare Humorum
Mare Nubium
Oceanus Procellarum
Karpathen Gb.
Hercynisches Gb.
Haemus Gb.
Apenninen Gebirge
Mare Serenitatis
Palus Putredinis
Palus Nebularum
Mare Imbrium
Sinus Iridum
Sinus Roris
Mare Frigoris
G. Heck dir.
R. Schmidt et Mädel III. sclp.
Fig. 1

PLATE 11. BEER AND MÄDLER'S MAP OF THE MOON

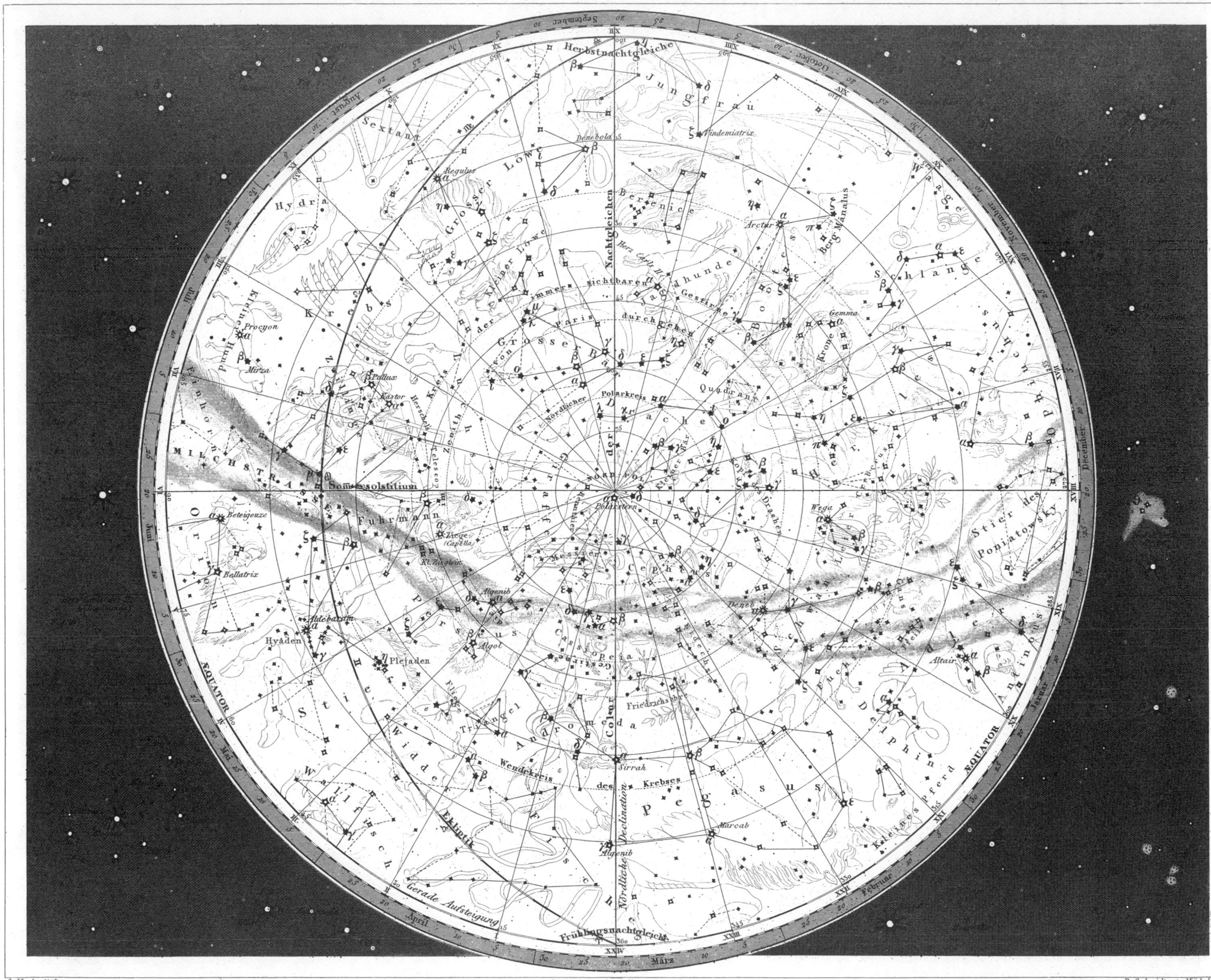

G. Heck dir.

R. Schmidt et Mädel M.sc.

1te 2te 3te 4te 5te 6te
Sterngrösse

PLATE 12. MAP OF THE NORTHERN HEAVENS

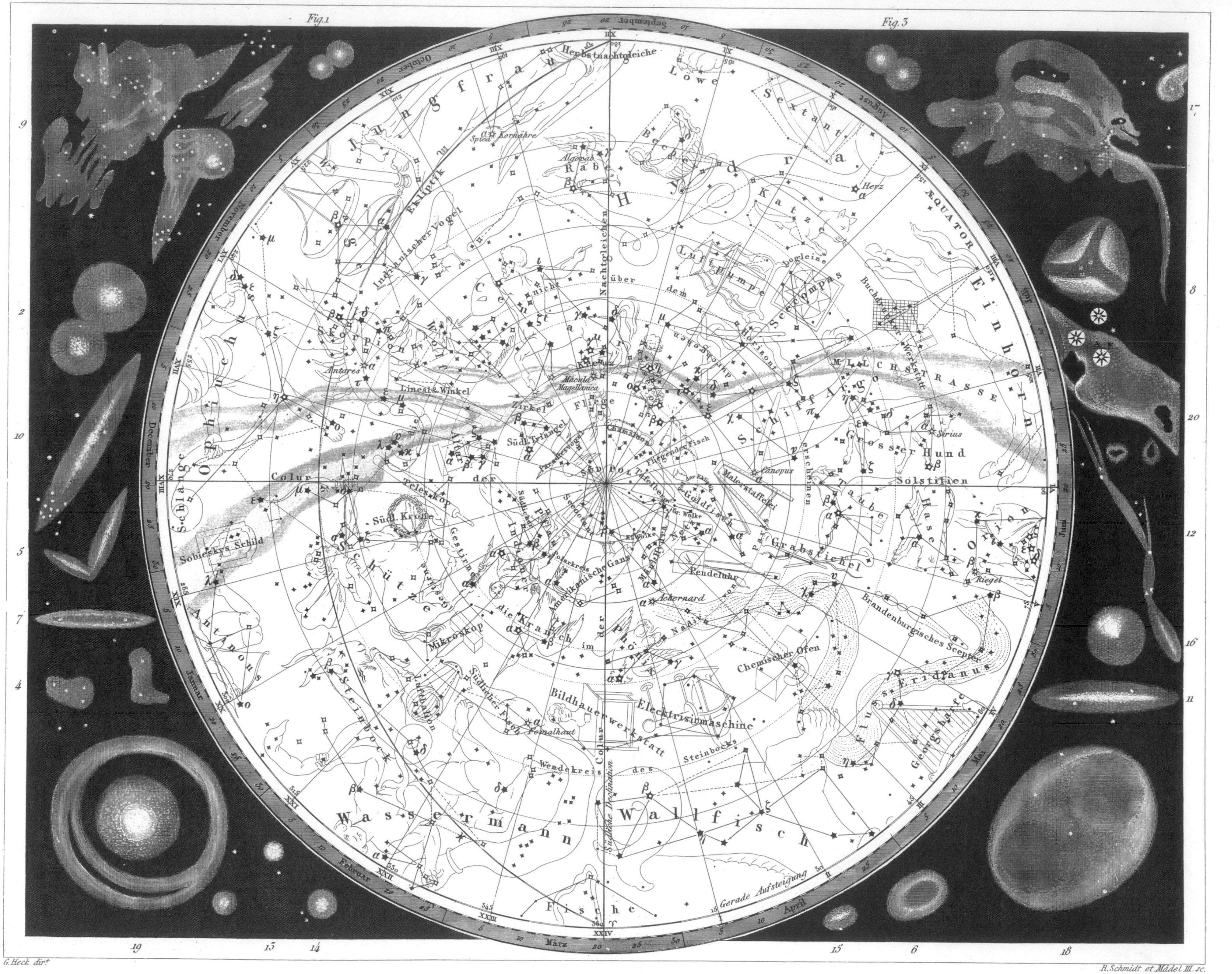

G. Heck dir.

R. Schmidt et Mädel III. sc.

PLATE 13. MAP OF THE SOUTHERN HEAVENS

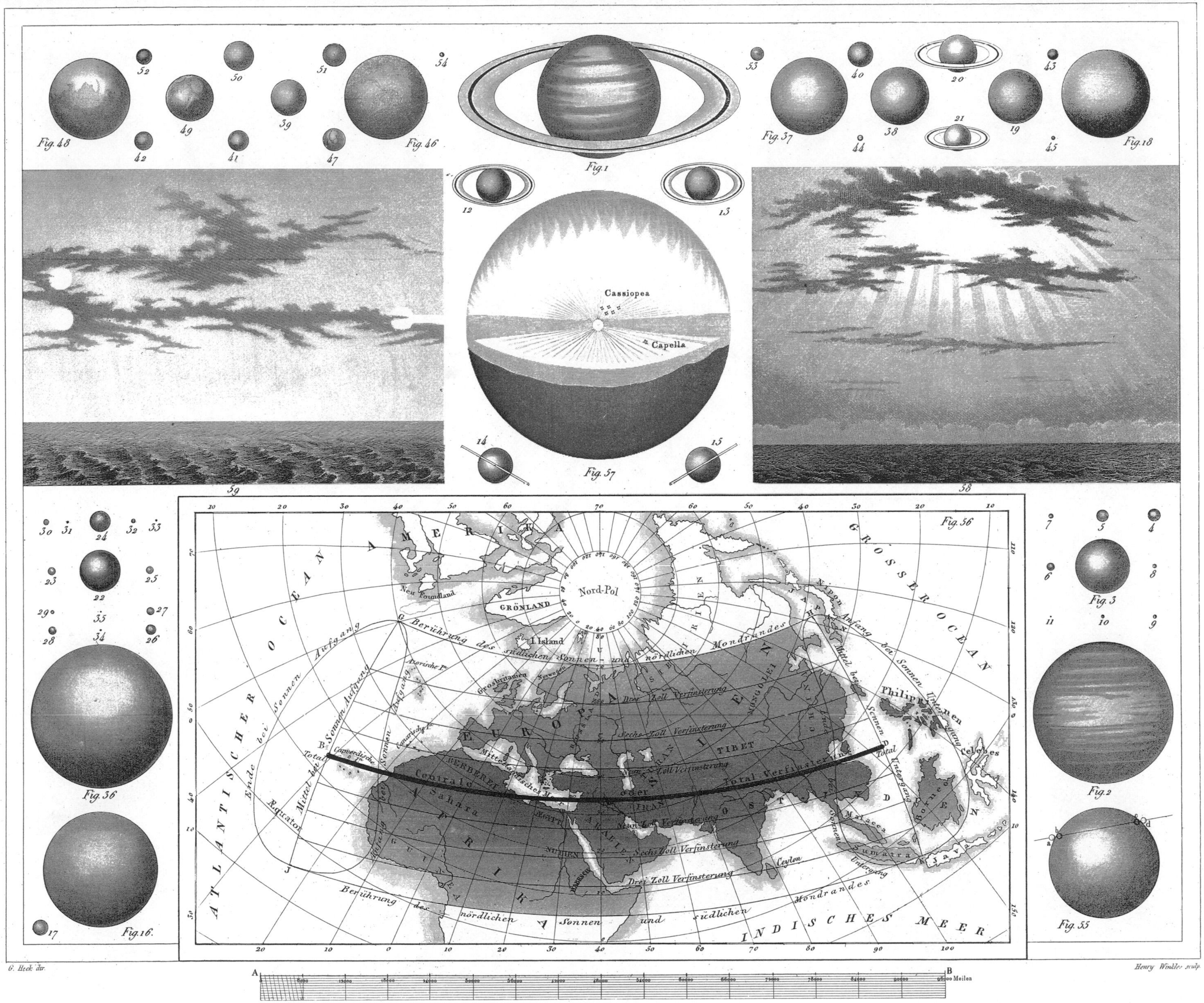
Fig. 48
Fig. 46
Fig. 1
Fig. 37
Fig. 18
Cassiopea
Capella
Fig. 57
Fig. 56
Nord-Pol
GRÖNLAND
Island
EUROPA
TIBET
Philippinen
Celebes
Borneo
Sumatra
Java
Ceylon
Malacca
Sahara
Fig. 3
Fig. 36
Fig. 16.
Fig. 2
Fig. 55
G. Heck dir.
Henry Winkles sculp.
Meilen

PLATE 14. PLANET SIZES AND VARIOUS PHENOMENA

G. Heck dir.[t]

Henry Winkles sculp.[t]

PLATE 15. ASTRONOMICAL INSTRUMENTS

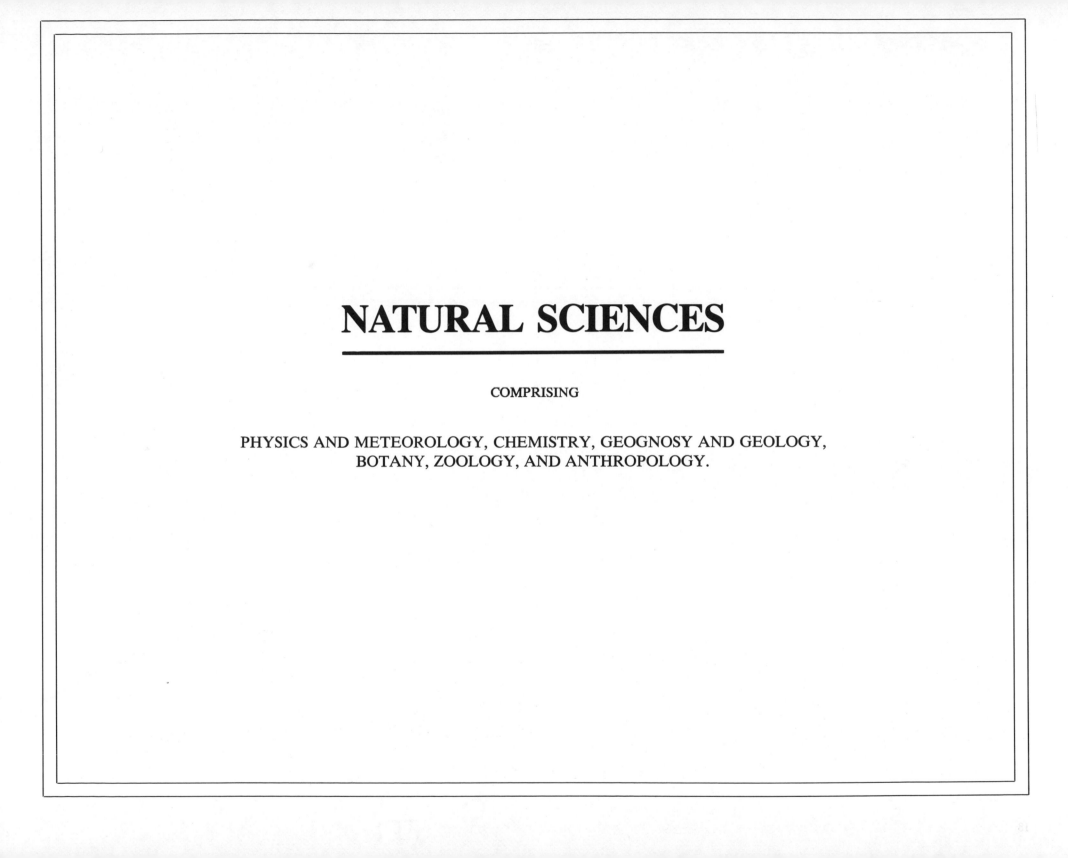

NATURAL SCIENCES

COMPRISING

PHYSICS AND METEOROLOGY, CHEMISTRY, GEOGNOSY AND GEOLOGY,
BOTANY, ZOOLOGY, AND ANTHROPOLOGY.

Captions to the Natural Sciences Plates, 16–141

PHYSICS AND METEOROLOGY

PLATE 16.
Theories of Force and Gravity; Demonstrations of These and Other Physical Laws

Figure
1. Parallelogram of forces
2. Triangle of forces
3. Polygon of forces
4. Parallelopipedon of forces
5. Center of gravity of a line
6. Center of gravity of a triangle
7. Center of gravity of a polygon
8. Center of gravity of a parallelogram
9. Center of gravity of irregular surfaces
10. Center of gravity of a cube
11. Center of gravity of a parallelopipedon
12. Center of gravity of a pyramid
13. Center of gravity of two different bodies
14. Illustrating Varignon's funicular machine
15, 16. Illustrating the theory of the pulley
17, 18. Atwood's machine for demonstrating the laws of freely falling bodies
19. The fixed pulley
20. Illustrating the oscillation of the pendulum
21. The gridiron pendulum
22. The mercurial pendulum
23. Lever of the first class
24. Application of the same in the steelyard
25. Lever of the second class
26. Lever of the third class
27, 28. Illustrating the theory of equilibrium
29. Lever and pulley
30. Bent lever
31. Compound lever
32, 33. Wheel and axle
34. Endless screw attached to windlass
35. Wheel and axle with pulley
36–40. Movable pulleys
41, 42. White's pulley
43. Pulley with cords working obliquely
44–46. Inclined plane
47, 48. The wedge
49–52. Illustrating theory of strength and stress of materials

PLATE 17.
Illustrating Theories of Dynamics and Other Physical Laws

Figure
1–3. Illustrating the theory of the screw
4. Hunter's differential screw
5–21. Illustrating the theory of strength and stress of materials
22. Illustrating the theory of uniformly varying motion
23. Illustrating the theory of unequably accelerated motion
24. Illustrating the influence of gravitation on the motion of projectiles
25–28. Illustrating the theory of projectiles
29. Illustrating the centrifugal force
30. Illustrating the lateral pressure of moving liquids
31–33. Illustrating the velocity of efflux
34. Illustrating the forcing pump
35. Prony's swimmer, a contrivance to regulate the velocity of efflux
36. Illustrating the hydraulic ram
37, 38. Illustrating the ballistic pendulum
39, 40. Valve and parachute of the Hampton balloon
41. Henson's flying machine
42–48. Illustrating the pneumodrome of Partridge

PLATE 18.
Theories and Instruments of Hydraulics and Aerodynamics

Figure
1–8. Illustrating the pressure of liquids
9, 10. Illustrating the law of Archimedes
11. The Cartesian devils
12–14. Hydrostatic balance
15. Nicholson's areometer
16. The scale areometer
17–19. Illustrating capillary attraction
20–30. Illustrating phenomena of attraction of liquids and solids
31. Dutrochet's endosmometer
32. Common barometer
33–35. Gay Lussac's syphon barometer
36–38. Fortin's barometer
39–41. Arago and Dulong's apparatus for proving Mariotte's law
42. Kopp's differential barometer
43. Kopp's volumeter
44. Gay Lussac's hand air-pump
45, 46. Larger air-pump
47. Two-cylindered air-pump
48–50. Babinet's cock for obtaining the greatest rarefaction
51–53. The condensing pump
54–56. The syphon
57, 58. Apparatus involving the theory of the syphon
59. Cup of Tantalus
60. Fountain involving the syphon
61. Hero's ball
62. Intermitting spring
63, 64. Hero's fountain
65–71. Hydraulic press
72. Apparatus to measure the pressure of falling water
73. Ordinary air balloon
74. Marey Monge's copper balloon
93 see 43. [The figure is marked 93 by mistake of the engraver.]

PLATE 19.
Theories and Instruments of Mechanics, Thermodynamics, and Acoustics

Figure
1. Gasometer
2, 3. Cylindrical blower
4. Water regulator
5. Wind measurer
6. Common bellows
7. Mercurial thermometer
8. Apparatus for measuring the expansion of solids
9–11. Apparatus for measuring higher temperatures
12. Metal or quadrant thermometer
13. Breguet's thermometer
14. Air thermometer
15. Pneumatic apparatus
16. Illustrating the relative expansion of mercury, water, and alcohol
17. Illustrating the laws of vaporization
18. Illustrating the tension of vapor in unequally heated places
19, 20. Apparatus for measuring the elasticity of vapor
21. Apparatus for ascertaining the density of watery vapor
22. Apparatus for mixing vapors with gases
23. Apparatus for measuring the tension of this mixture
24. Apparatus for boiling water by the condensation of vapor
25. Papin's digester
26. Papin's first steam-engine
27–34. Watt's steam-engine
35. Illustrating the transmission of heat
36. Rumford's differential thermometer
37, *a*, *b*. Melloni's thermo-multiplier
38–40. Locatelli lamp, etc.
41. Illustrating the refraction of heat rays
42. Apparatus for ascertaining the laws of cooling
43. Calorimeter of Lavoisier and Laplace
44, 45. Apparatus for determining the specific heat of bodies
46. Apparatus for determining the specific heat of gases
47. Cooling tube
48. Cooling vessel
49. Apparatus for measuring latent heat
49, *a*. Illustrating the transmission of sound
50. Savart's monochord
51, 52. Vibration of strings
53–58. Illustrating the construction of organs
59–61. Cagniard de la Tour's system of determining the number of vibrations in a tone
62. Apparatus for causing plates to vibrate
63–90. Figures produced by the vibration of plates, bells, etc.
91. Apparatus for producing tones by the combustion of hydrogen gas
92. Illustrating the manner of communicating vibrations to the air
93. Illustrating the echo in arched rooms
94. Hearing tube
95. Illustrating the metal tongue
96, 97. Tongue work of the organ
98. Illustrating the nature of the human voice

PLATE 20.
Theories and Instruments of Electricity and Magnetics

Figure
1. Attraction of a natural magnet
2. Attraction of an artificial magnet
3. Curves of filings over a magnet
4. Influence of a magnet on an iron rod
5. The same without contact
6. Magnetic needle
7. The various poles of a magnet
8. Compass
9. Variation of the compass
10. Inclination of the compass
11. Action of the earth upon the magnetic needle
12. Intensity compass of Gambey
13, 14. Coulomb's torsion balance
15. Coulomb's determination of the strength of the magnet at various distances from its pole
16, 17. Duhamel's method of preparing artificial magnets
18. Œpinus's method of doing the same
19. Horse-shoe magnet
20, 21. Armature of natural magnets
22. Electrical pendulum
23. Coulomb's electroscope
24. Pith ball electroscopes
25. Electric pistol
26. Volta's straw electrometer
27, 28. The electrophorus
29. Plate electric machine
30, 30*a*. Rubbers of the same
31. Van Marum's electric machine
32. Nairne's electric machine
33. Franklin plate
34. Discharging rod
35, 36. Leyden jars
37. Electrical battery
38. Henley's universal discharger
39. Electrical mortar
40. Kinnersley's thermometer
41. Leyden jar with movable coatings
42. Lightning plate
43. Lightning tube
44. Electrical light
45. Wheatstone's apparatus for determining the velocity of electricity
46. Electric wheel [By mistake of the engraver this figure is numbered 76. It stands in the center of the plate.]
47. Influence of Galvanism
48. Volta's galvanic double plate
49. Voltaic pile
50, 51. Fechner's improvement of Bohnenberger's electrometer
52. Trough apparatus
53–55. Wollaston's battery
56. Volta's simple galvanic series
57. Hare's calorimeter
58. Becquerel's constant battery
59, 60. Daniel's constant battery
61. Grove's battery
62, 63. Bunsen's carbon battery
64, 65. Apparatus for decomposing water
66. Apparatus for decomposing salts
67. Becquerel's galvanoplastic apparatus
68. Influence of the galvanic current on the magnetic needle
69. Schweigger's galvanometer
70. Nobili's improved galvanometer
71–74. Tangent compass
75. Sine compass
76. [See 46.]
76–78. Magnetic action of the galvanic current
79–81. Electro-magnets
82. Rotation of the magnet under the influence of the galvanic current
83–85. Ampère's apparatus for determining the influence of terrestrial magnetism on the galvanic current
86. Neutralization of terrestrial magnetism
87. Rotation of vertical currents
88. De la Rive's apparatus showing that feeble currents are affected by magnetism
89, 90. Disconnecting and severing of magnetic currents

PLATE 21.
Theories and Instruments of Optics

Figure
1. Refraction of light in its passage from water into air
2, 3. Full shadow and half shadow
4. Inverted image caused by a ray of light entering a dark room through a small aperture
5. Angle of reflection of light
6. Apparatus to prove the equality of the angles of reflection and of incidence
7. Proof of the symmetry of images reflected by plane mirrors
8. Construction of reflected images
9. Mirrors placed together at an angle
10–12. Wollaston's reflecting goniometer
13. Gambey's goniometer
14, 15. Reflecting sextant
16–18. Concave mirror
19, 20. Nature of images formed in concave mirrors
21. Spherical convex mirror
22. Image formed on the same
23. Caustic curve
24. Angle of refraction
25. Laws of refraction
26. Total reflection
27. Prism stand
28. Solar spectrum
29. Prismatic refraction
30. Hollow prism
31. Dulong's apparatus for determining the refractive powers of gases
32. The six kinds of lenses
33. Refraction by lenses
34. Focus of lenses
35. Divergence of rays in concave lenses
36. Secondary axis of lenses
37–39. Images formed in lenses
40. Aperture of the lens necessary to unite all rays in one point
41, 42. Fresnel's polyzonal lens
43, 44. Decomposition of light into various colored rays
45. Composition of white light from various colored rays
46. Decomposition of the natural colors of bodies by the prism
47. Achromatic prism
48. Achromatic lens
49. Mosaic composite eye
50. Simple human eye
51. Illustrating double sight
52. Illustrating the possibility of seeing various objects at once
53, 54. Irradiation
55. The phenakistoscope
56. Wollaston's camera lucida
57, 58. Camera obscura
59. Solar microscope
60, 61. Compound microscope
62. Gregorian telescope
63. Cassegrainian telescope
64. Newtonian telescope
65. Galilean telescope
66. Astronomical telescope
67. Determination of the magnifying power of telescopes
68. Fresnel's apparatus for determining the interference of light
69. Nörremberg's polariscope
70. Angle of polarization
71, 72. Rochon's micrometer
73. Soleil's apparatus for measuring the rings of polarization
74–76. Daguerreotype apparatus
77. Reflexion by spherical concave mirrors
78. Refraction in water
79. Common prism
80. Refraction by prisms
81. Construction of the hollow prism
82. The direction of emerging rays shown to be parallel with that of entering ones
83. Divergence of rays emerging from lenses
84. Convergence of rays emerging from lenses
85. Angle of vision
86. Vanishing of small objects on the punctum cœcum
87. Apparatus for exhibiting the duration of an impression on the retina
88. Apparatus for experiments on the interference of light
89. Undulation of rays
90. Illustrating the theory of interference
91. Illustrative of the explanation of reflexion by the undulatory theory
92. The law of refraction similarly illustrated
93–99. Fraunhofer's spectra
100, 101. Polarization of light
102, 103. The magic lantern
104. Camera lucida
105, 106. Brewster's kaleidoscope

PLATE 22.
Phenomena and Apparatus of Electricity and Magnetics

Figure
1. Apparatus for observing the action of terrestrial magnetism on vertical currents
2, 3. Faraday's apparatus for observing the rotative action of terrestrial magnetism on horizontal currents
4. Action of parallel currents upon each other
5, 6. Apparatus to show the action of crossing currents upon each other
7. Apparatus for determining the plane of the terrestrial currents
8. Declination spiral wire
9, 10. Ampère's apparatus for explaining the rotation of the magnet
11. Thermo-electric currents
12. Thermo-electric multiplier
13. Apparatus to show the development of electricity by combustion
14. Illustrating induction currents
15–17. Neef and Wagner's induction coil
18. Apparatus to show the production of electrical currents by magnetism

19. Induction coil in connection with magnets
20–22. Ettinghausen's magneto-electric rotating machine
23–27. Stöhrer's triple magneto-electric machine
28. Differential galvanometer
29. Apparatus for determining the conducting powers of metals
30. Apparatus for determining the requisite qualities of conducting wires
31, 32. Apparatus for obtaining an unalterable thermo-electric current
33–35. Thermo-electric pile
36–38. Stöhrer's improvement of Daniel's electro-magnetic machine
39. Ritchie's improved machine
40. Wheatstone's telegraph
41, 42. Steinheil's telegraph
43–47. Illustrating Ampère's theory of the rotation of magnets
48, 49. Astatic multiplier
50, 51. Weber's apparatus for demonstrating the laws of magnetism
52, 53, 53*a*. Arago's apparatus for investigating phenomena in rotation magnetism
54. Illustrating the intensity of electricity in combined elements
55–58. Clarke's magneto-electric machine
59. Henley's quadrant electrometer
60. Apparatus for proving that free electricity is confined to the surface of bodies
61. Gold leaf electrometer
62. Buff's apparatus for determining the kind of electricity in a body
63. Apparatus to show the separation of the combined electricities when an electrified body is brought near
64. Apparatus to show that the connection of two similar electroscopes by an insulated conductor will separate their electricities
65. Construction of the electrometer
66, 67. Different windings around the electro-magnet
68. Rotation of the magnet around its own axis
69. The voltaic pile
70. Illustrating the action of electrical currents
71. Production of electric light in a vacuum
72. Electric dance
73–75. Eisenlohr's hydro-electric machine

PLATE 23.
Sun Rays, Winds, Precipitation, and Condensation Phenomena

Figure
1. Howard's diagram to elucidate the action of the sun's rays on the earth
2. Illustrating the snow line
3. Curvature of the Alpine snow line
4–23. Forms of snow crystals
24–35. Forms of hailstones
36–38. Illustrating the amount of dew on trees and herbs
39, 40. Illustrating the amount of dew on differently inclined surfaces
41–43. Illustrating the greatest deposit of dew on the highest points of an object
44–47. Illustrating the increase of dewdrops
48. Illustrating that an object rolled up in a ball receives less dew than if spread out flat
49–52. Illustrating that gilt paper is bedewed only when its unmetallic side is in contact with wood
53, *ab*. Zone of dew deposited in the cavity of a watch-glass
54. Regular deposit of dew *around* wafers on a glass plate, not *on* them
55. Deposit of dew on a window
56, 57. Deposit of dew on spiders' webs
58. Perpendiculars from the widest boughs of a tree marking the limits of the formation of frost
59. Curious formation of frost on the chiselled star of a tombstone
60, 61. Curious formation of frost on leaves
62. Illustrating the theory of winds
63. Illustrating the theory of whirlwinds
64. Rain gauge

GLOSSARY

Februar, February
Fische, Pisces
Frühling 90 *Tage*, Spring 90 days
Heisseste Temperatur, Hottest temperature
Herbst 90 *Tage*, Autumn 90 days
Januar, January
Juli, July
Jungfrau, Virgo
Juni, June
Kälteste Temperatur, Coldest temperature
Krebs, Cancer
Löwe, Leo
Mai, May
März, March
Mittlere Temperatur, Medium temperature
Schütze, Sagittarius
Skorpion, Scorpio
Sommer 93 *Tage*, Summer 93 days
Steinbock, Capricornus
Stier, Taurus
Waage, Libra
Wassermann, Aquarius
Widder, Aries
Winter 93 *Tage*, Winter 93 days
Zwillinge, Gemini

PLATE 24.
Phenomena of Condensation and Air Currents

Figure
1. Peculiar crystallization on the window of a drug store
2. Two trees trained on a wall, only in part exposed to frost
3–6. Ice flowers
7. Formation of fog over rivers
8. Overtopping of trees by fog
9. Formation of fog over rivers enclosed by hills
10. Illustrating the different appearance of clouds to observers at different places
11. Illustrating the difference of shape of clouds according to their elevation
12. Illustrating the difference of currents of air at different heights
13–18. Different formations of fog near the harbor of Plymouth (England)
19. Mirage in Lower Egypt
20, 21. Mirages at sea
22. Theory of mirages
23. Mirage on the lake of Geneva

PLATE 25.
Cloud Formation and Light Refraction

Figure
1–8. Forms of clouds
9. Halo around the sun
10, 11. Haloes around the moon
12. Halo and colored ring
13–20. Mock suns

PLATE 26.
Phenomena of Clouds and Light

Figure
1–9. Illustrating phenomena in clouds
10–12. Rainbows
13. Aurora borealis
14. Midnight sun in the polar regions

PLATE 27.
Meteorological Elements and Instruments

Figure
1. Whirlwind and waterspout
2, 3. The sun behind clouds
4. The drawing of water
5. Converging in the east, of the shadow of the setting sun
6. Illustrating that objects on earth can throw shadows into space
7. Shadows thrown on a bank of fog
8, 9. Coloring of clouds by the sun
10, 11. Phenomena of the sun's apparent contact with clouds
12. Apparent contact of clouds
13. Zodiacal light
14–19. Lightning rod
20–26. Magnetic observatory at Greenwich

PLATE 28.
Climate and Weather Charts

Figure
1, *ab*. Inclination charts
2, *ab*. Isodynamic charts
3 (center). Chart of magnetic declinations
4, *ab*. Barometrical wind rosettes
5, *ab*. Thermometrical wind rosettes [For Glossary see after Plate 29.]

PLATE 29.
Rainfall and Temperature Map; Temperature Charts

Figure
1. Map of Humboldt's isothermal lines showing the distribution of heat and rain on the earth
2. Diagram of the mean annual temperature at various places
3. The mean decennial temperature of various places
4. Comparison of temperature

GLOSSARY

Ægypten, Egypt
Æquator-Grenze des Schneefalls, Equatorial boundary of the snow region
Aleuten, Aleutian Islands
Arabien, Arabia
Asien, Asia
Barometer steigt,—fällt, Barometer rises,—falls
Berberei, Barbary
Beständiger Regen, Perpetual rain
C. der guten Hoffnung, Cape of Good Hope

Canarische Inseln, Canary Islands
Capverdische Inseln, Cape Verd Islands
Deutschland, Germany
Erd-Æquator, Terrestrial equator
Europa, Europe
Frankreich, France
Freundschafts Inseln, Friendly Islands
Gebiet der Monsun Regen, Region of the Monsoons
Gesellschafts Inseln, Society Islands
Grönland, Greenland
Grossbritanien, Great Britain
Grosser Ocean, Pacific Ocean
Herbst und Winter Regen, Autumn and winter rains
Indisches Meer, Indian Sea
Italien, Italy
Kopenhagen, Copenhagen
Kurve von Leith, Br., Curve of Leith, latitude
Kurve von Padua, Br., Curve of Padua, latitude
Linie ohne Inclination, Line without inclination
Magnetischer Æquator, Magnetic equator
Manschurei, Mandshoo territory
Maximum der magnet, Kraft, Maximum of magnetic power
Mittlere Tageswärme, Medium daily temperature
Mongolei, Mongolia
N. O., N. E.
Neufundland, Newfoundland
Neu Guinea, New Guinea
Neu Sealand, New Zealand
Niedrige Inseln, Low Islands
Nord Amerika, North America
Nördlicher Gürtel der beständigen Niederschläge, Northern zone of perpetual deposits
Nördliche Hemisphäre, Northern Hemisphere
Nördlicher Polarkreis, Arctic Circle
Nördliches Eismeer, Arctic Sea
Nordpol, North pole
Nord See, North sea
Norwegen, Norway
Nubien, Nubia
Oceanien, Oceania
Ost Indien, the East Indies
Ostseite, East side
Persien, Persia
Provinz des Herbstregens;—des Sommerregens;—des Winterregens, Region of autumnal, of summer, and of winter rains
Regenloses Gebiet, Rainless region
Russland, Russia
Schwacher Sommerregen, Light summer rain
Sibirien, Siberia
S. O., S. E.
S. O. Monsun im Apr.–Oct., N. W. Monsun im Oct.–Apr., S. E. Monsoon from April to October, N. W. Monsoon from October to April
Spanien, Spain
Süd Amerika, South America
Südpol, South pole
Südlicher Continent, Southern continent
Südlicher Gürtel der beständigen Niederschläge, Southern zone of perpetual deposits
Südliche Hemisphäre, Southern Hemisphere
S. W. Monsun im Apr.–Oct., N. O. Monsun im Oct.–Apr., S. W. Monsoon from April to October, N. E. Monsoon from October to April
Thermometer steigt,—fällt, Thermometer rises,—falls
Turkei, Turkey
Vereinigte Staaten, United States
Wärme-Æquator, Equator of heat
Wendekreis des Krebses; —des Steinbocks, Tropic of Cancer; —of Capricorn
West Indien, the West Indies
Westseite, West side
Winterregen, Winter rains
Wüste Schamo oder Gobi, Desert of Shamo, or Gobi
Zone häufiger, fast beständiger Niederschläge, stets mit electrischen Explosionen, Zone of frequent, nearly perpetual deposits, always accompanied by electrical explosions

CHEMISTRY, MINERALOGY, AND GEOLOGY

PLATE 30.
Chemical Laboratory, Apparatus, and Equipment

Figure
1. Ground-plan of the chemical laboratory at Giessen
2. Perspective view of part of the analytical laboratory at Giessen
3, *3a*. Portable wind furnace
4, 5. Portable distilling apparatus
6, 7. Fixed furnace
8, 9. Sand bath furnace
10. Small table for raising or lowering receivers
11, 12. Small alembic
13. Pharmaceutical steam apparatus
14–20. Pharmaceutical steam apparatus with its utensils
21, 22. Crucible furnace
23. Tongs for handling hot crucibles
24. Splitting iron
25, 26. Retorts
27–29. Globes or matrasses
30–34. Hessian crucible
35, 36. Evaporating dishes
37–41. Thermometers
42. Separating funnel
43. Bent tube with bulb
44, 45. Walter's safety tube
46. Filtering funnel
47. Separating funnel
48. Special funnel
49. Washing bottle
50. Measure
51–54. Florentine flasks
55. Pneumatic tub
56, 57. Wolff apparatus
58, 59. Gasometer
60, 61. Davy's apparatus for investigating earths
62. Apparatus for generating prussic acid.
63. Apparatus for producing small quantities of illuminating gas from various substances
64. Argand's oil lamp
65–68. Pharmaceutical extract presses
69–73. Chemical balance

PLATE 31.
Chemical Apparatus and Equipment

Figure
1, 2. Oxy-ethereal lamp
3. Distilling apparatus
4, 5. Gasometer
6, 7. Apparatus for rendering carbonic acid liquid
8. Apparatus for obtaining phosphorus
9. Furnace for obtaining caustic soda
10. Furnace for heating matrasses
11. Berzelius lamp
12. Triangle of iron wire
13. Apparatus for obtaining the gaseous elements
14. Apparatus for obtaining chlorine
15–23. Drying apparatus
24. Air pump
25. Calcium tube
26. Chloride of calcium tube
27–29. Combustion tubes
30–32. Combustion furnace
33. Apparatus for elementary analysis with application of oxygen
34–38. Apparatus for determining the nitrogen in organic substances
39. Apparatus for filling the potash apparatus
40, 41. Apparatus for determining the specific gravity of vapor
42. Muffle furnace
43. Cupel
44. Muffle
45, 46. Apparatus for generating carbonic acid gas
47. Two-branched tube for washing precipitates
48, 49. Washing bottles
50–52. Filtering apparatus
53. Suction tube
54. Washing bottle
55. Galley furnace
56. Gas generator
57. Crucible
58. Apparatus for ascertaining the amount of pure metal in oxydes
59. Davy's safety lamp
60. Apparatus for procuring oxygen
61. Safety tube
62, 63. Blowpipe
64. Iron pincers for handling heated vessels
65. Apparatus for obtaining nitrogenous substances from organic matter
66. Eudiometer

PLATE 32.
Forms of Crystallization; Various Instruments

Figure
1. Blowpipe
2. Attenuated point of flame caused by the blowpipe
3. Forceps
4. Berzelius blowpipe
5. Nicholson areometer
6. Magnetic needle
7, *ab*. Instrument for detecting electricity in minerals
8. Common goniometer
9. Gambay's goniometer
10. Wollaston's goniometer

Forms of Crystallization

11, 12. Regular octahedron
13. Octahedron abbreviated to a six sided plate
14. Cube
15. Relation of the cube and octahedron
16, 17. Cubic octahedron
18. Rhombic dodecahedron
19. Relation of the rhombic dodecahedron and cube
20. Pyramidal cube
21, 24. Cube with dodecahedral faces replacing its edges
22. Octahedron with dodecahedral faces
23. Octahedron passing into a dodecahedron
24. See 21
25. Combination of cube faces and those of the pyramidal cube
26. Tetrahedron

27. Octahedron passing into a tetrahedron
28. Cube with its edges replaced by three faces
29. Pentagonal dodecahedron
30. Trapezohedron
31. Octahedron passing into a trapezohedron
32. Obtuse square octahedron
33. Acute square octahedron
34. Square octahedron with two corners truncated
35. Right square prism
36. Regular eight sided prism
37. Right square prism with its corners truncated
38. Square octahedron with truncated basal edges
39. Square octahedron with truncated lateral edges
40. Eight sided pyramid
41. Twelve sided prism
42. Six sided prism with bevelled edges
43. Right square prism with basal edges truncated
44. Rectangular octahedron
45. Rectangular octahedron truncated
46. Square octahedron with bevelled lateral edges
47, *a*. Obtuse rhombic octahedron
b. Acute rhombic octahedron
c. Rectangular octahedron
48. Rhombic octahedron with two corners bevelled
49. Octahedron with the corners of the vertical axis replaced by four plane faces
50. Right rhombic prism
51. Right rhombic prism with obtuse edges truncated
52. Irregular eight sided prism
53–55. Combination of prisms belonging to the trimetric system
56. Rectangular prism
57, 58. Modified octahedrons
59, 60. Oblique six sided prism
61. Octahedron with half the edges truncated
62. Prism with half the basal edges truncated
63–65. Oblique rhomboidal prism
66. Oblique six sided prism
67. Double six sided pyramid
68. Pyramidal six sided prism
69. Modified rhombic octahedron
70. Regular six sided prism
71. Regular six sided prism with truncated basal edges
72. Regular six sided prism with truncated corners
73. Obtuse double six sided pyramid
74. Scalene octahedron
75. Rhombohedron
76. Six sided prism with four edges bevelled
77, 78. Natural situation of two rhombohedrons
79. Grouping of crystallizations
80–87, 90, 91. Forms of ground jewels
88, 89. Crystalline formations
90, 91. See 80, etc.
92, 93. Crystalline structure

PLATE 33.
Minerals and Their Crystalline Forms

Figure
1. Meteoric iron
2. Iron pyrites
3, 4. Sulphur
5–10. Native bismuth
6–11. Galena
7. Weidmannstedtian figures
8. Sulphate of lead
9. Native silver
10. See 5
11. See 6
12. Arborescent native silver
13. Native copper
14. Native gold
15. Pyrites in calcareous spar
16. Filiform native silver
17. Galena on quartz
18. Arsenical pyrites
19. Galena on calcareous spar
20. Galena in cubes
21. Selenid of mercury
22. Crystallization of iron pyrites
23. Molybdenite
24. Native copper
25. Native antimony
26–29. Sulphur
30. Native silver
31. Antimony
32–36. Gold, galena, etc.
37. Sulphuret of copper
38. Antimony
39, 47. Antimonial silver
40–45. Gold, 40 and 42, Silver, 42, 43, Diamond
46. Diamond
47. See 39
48. Copper pyrites
49, 50. Glance cobalt
51. Diamond, Grey copper ore
52, 53, 56, 59. Grey copper ore
54, 55. Glance cobalt
56. See 52
57, 58, 60. Glance cobalt
59. See 52
60. See 57
61–63. Native mercury
64. Glance cobalt

PLATE 34.
Minerals and Their Crystalline Forms

Figure
1. Micaceous iron ore
2, 3. Quartz
4. Tourmaline
5. Hematite
6. Datholite
7. Pyrolusite
8. Tin ore
9. Fibrous brown hematite
10. Rutile
11. Scaly hematite
12. Andalusite
13. Asbestos
14. Stilbite
15. Analcime
16. Mesotype
17. Apophyllite
18. Chabazite
19. Tin ore in granite
20. Reniform hematite
21, 22. Silica
23, 25. Oxyde of iron
24. Manganite
25. See 23
26. Braunite
27. Red copper ore
28. Apophyllite
29. Hausmannite
30. Sapphire
31. Oxyde of iron
32. Anatase
33. Red copper ore
34. Tourmaline
35. Augite
36. Quartz
37. Oxyde of tin
38. Corundum
39, 40. Arsenious acid
41. Picrosmine
42. Oxyde of tin
43. Rutile
44. Oxyde of copper
45. Nepheline
46. Scapolite
47. Staurotide
48, 53. Idocrase
49. Beryl
50. Thomsonite
51. Silica
52. Augite
53. See 48
54. Chondrotite
55. Humboldtite
56. Various silicates
57. Emerald
58. Euclase
59. Natrolite
60. Dichroite
61. Oxyde of copper
62. Prehnite
63. Epistilbite
64. Garnet
65. Albite
66. Chabazite
67. Pyroxene
68, 69. Beryl
70. Staurotide
71. Iolite
72. Silica
73. Datholite
74. Olivine
75. Hornblende
76. Feldspar

PLATE 35.
Minerals and Their Crystalline Forms

Figure
1. Spodumene
2. Feldspar twin crystal
3. Sphærosiderite
4. Natrolite
5. Harmotome
6. Green garnet
7. Strontianite
8, 10, 11, 14, 16–22, 24, 25, 27–29, 31–37, 40, 41, 43–47, 49. Various forms of arragonite and calcareous spar
9. Topaz
10, 11. See 8
12, 30, 38, 39, 42, 48. Boracite
13, 23. Stalactite
14. See 8
15. Opake beryl
16–22. See 8
23. See 13
24, 25. See 8
26. Feldspar
27–29. See 8
30. See 12
31–37. See 8
38, 39. See 12
40, 41. See 8
42. See 12
43–47. See 8
48. See 12
49. See 8

PLATE 36.
Minerals and Their Crystalline Forms

Figure
1, 2, 4, 6, 8–10, 13. Sulphate of baryta
3. Double spar
4. See 1
5. Wavellite
6. See 1
7, 20. Strontianite
8–10. See 1
11. Thorns coated with salt
12. Gypsum
13. See 1
14. Spathic iron
15. Wolfram
16, 24, 25. Alum
17. Sulphate of soda
18. Sulphate of ammonia
19, 34, 35. Copperas
20. See 7
21. White lead ore
22. Yellow lead ore
23. Sulphate of zinc
24, 25. See 16
26, 36, 41, 43, 47, 48. Saltpetre
27. Green vitriol
28. Sulphate of potassa
29, 37. Calcareous spar
30. Rocksalt

31. Karstenite
32. Fluor spar
33, 40. Sulphates of alkalies
34, 35. See 19
36. See 26
37. See 29
38, 39, 42, 44, 46, 49. Phosphates of alkalies
40. See 33
41. See 26
42. See 38
43. See 26
44. See 38
45 Sulphate of iron
46. See 38
47, 48. See 26
49. See 38

PLATE 37.
Fossils and Representation of Animals of the Lias

Figure
1–59. Fossils of the transition slate
60–72. Fossils of the carboniferous period
a–f. Buckland's representation of animals of the Lias

PLATE 38.
Section of the Wirksworth Cave and Fossils

Figure
1, 2. Fossils of the Copper Slate Formation
3–11. Fossils of the Rock Salt Formation
12–67. Fossils of the Jura
68. Section of the Wirksworth cave

PLATE 39.
Fossils, a Skeleton, and Veins of Ore

Figure
1–45. Fossils of the Cretaceous System
46–50. Fossils of the Tertiary Period
51–80. Skeleton of Hydrarchos harlani
81–87. Illustrating the formations of veins of ores

PLATE 40.
Fossils and Skeletons

Figure
1–3, 11–22. Fossils of the Tertiary Period
4–9. Fossils of the Rock Salt Formation
10. Plesiosaurus macrocephalus (Jura)
11–22. See 1

PLATE 41.
Fossils, Skeletons, and Tracks

Figure
1–10. Fossil remains of Arachnida, etc. (Tertiary)
11–27. Fossils of the Jura
28. Fossil Irish elk (Tertiary)
29. Dinotherium giganteum (Tert.)
30. Missourium theristocaulodon (Tert.)
31, *ab.* Batrachoid tracks (Rock Salt)
32. Birds' tracks in Connecticut (Rock Salt)
33. Skull of Hyæna spelæa (Tert.)
34. Skull of Ursus spelæus (Tert.)
35. Pterodactylus crassirostris (Jura)
36. Human skeleton from Guadaloupe (fossil in Limestone)

PLATE 42.
Fossils from Various Periods

Figure
1–12. Fossils of the Tertiary
13–23. Fossils of the Cretaceous
24–31. Fossils of the Jura
32–40. Fossils of the Rock Salt
41–56. Fossils of the Carboniferous
57–66. Fossils of the Transition Slate

PLATE 43.
Rock and Valley Formations and Stratification

Figure
1–3. Illustrating the formation of valleys
4–6. Illustrating the formation of rock beds
7–9, 12. Illustrating stratification
10, 11. Penetration of various rocks in volcanic regions
12. See 7.
13–15. Illustrating the relation of stratification to mountain masses
16–19. Illustrating subordinate strata
20, 21. Illustrating disseminated and imbedded ores
22–25. Illustrating the cleavage of rocks
26. Table mountain at the Cape of Good Hope

PLATE 44.
Stratification in Mountains and Basins; Fissures and Craters

Figure
1. The valley of Pyrmont
2–5, 12–14. Illustrating the relation of stratification to mountain masses
6, 7. Tertiary basin of Paris
8. Dunes on the sea shore
9. Section of a volcanic cone
10. Mont Blanc chain
11. Mountains in the vicinity of Bärschwyl
12–14. See 2
15. Fissures in the earth in Calabria
16. Circular cavities in the plain of Rosarno
17. Crater of the Geyser in Iceland
18. Volcano of Eyafiël in Iceland

PLATE 45.
Volcanoes and Volcanic Formations

Figure
1. Illustrating valleys of disruption
2. Extinct volcanic district in Auvergne
3. Section of Judæa and the Dead Sea
4. Vesuvius in the time of Pliny
5. Vesuvius as seen at present
6. Mount Etna
7. Campi Phlegræi near Naples
8. Chart of the Bay of Naples
9. Volcanic chart of Etna
10. Volcanic chart of Iceland
11. Map of the vicinity of Lake Titicaca, in Peru
12. Section of the mountains around the lake

GLOSSARY

Basalt Boden, Basaltic soil
Bugt, Bay
Busen von Neapel, —von Salerno, Bay of Naples, —of Salerno
Cyclopen Inseln, Cyclops Islands
Die Flegreischen Felder, The Phlegræan fields
Fiorden, the inlet
Island, Iceland
Längenthal im Trachyt, Long valley in the trachyte formation
Lava Ströme, Lava streams
Neapel, Naples
Nord Cap, North Cape
Œ, Island
Passhöhe, Height of the pass
Polarkreis, Arctic circle
See, Lake
Vesuv, Vesuvius

PLATE 46.
Special Geognosy

Figure
1–3. Silurian system
4–6. Devonian system
7, 8. Carboniferous group
9, 10. Copper slate formation
11. Rock salt formation
12–16. Jura formation
17. Cretaceous system
18. Upper tertiary
19. Erratic boulder

GLOSSARY

Aufgeschw. Land, Deposited ground
Braunschweig, Brunswick
Bunter Sandstein, Variegated sandstone
Donau, Danube
Ebbe Geb., Ebbe Mountains
Egge Geb., Egge Mountains
Geb. v. Charolais, Mountains of Charolais
Harz Gebirge, Hartz Mountains; *—und Thüringer Wald,* Hartz and Thuringian Mountains
Hochwald, High forest (mountain tract)
Jura Gebirg, Jura Mountains; *— -kalk,* Jurassic Limestone
Kohlengebirge, Carboniferous formation
Kohlenkalk, Carboniferous limestone
Kohlensandstein, Carboniferous sandstone
Kreide, Chalk
Laacher See, Lake Laach
Porphyr, Porphyry
Quadersandstein, Freestone
Rhein, Rhine
Rheinisches Uebergangsgebirg, Rhenish transition rock
Rothhaar Geb., Rothhaar Mountains
Schuttland, Conglomerate
Steink. Gebilde, Carboniferous formation
Tertiär, Tertiary
Teutoburger Wald, Teutoburg forest
Todtliegendes, Red sandstone
Trias, Rock salt formation
Trier, Treves
Uebergangskalk, Transition limestone
Vogel Geb., Vogel Mountains
Vogesen sandstein, Vosges sandstone
Vulcan Gebilde; —Gerölle, Volcanic formation; —rubble
Weser Geb., Weser Mountains

PLATE 47.
Volcanic and Hurricane Charts; Mountain Profiles; Craters; and Antarctica

Figure
1. Volcanic chart of the world, [Also chart of the winds; Glossary at Plate 29.]
2. Chart of European volcanoes
3. Volcanic chart of Lower Italy
4. Crater of Kirauea
5. Crater on the Island of Hawaii
6. Landscape from the Southern Continent

7. Profile of mountains in the Old World
8. Profile of mountains in the New World
9, 10. Charts of hurricanes

GLOSSARY

Ægatische In., Ægatian Islands
Atlantischer Ocean, Atlantic Ocean
Canal von Malta, Maltese Channel
Deutschland, Germany
Frankreich, France
Grosse Antillen, The larger West India Islands
Indischer Ocean, Indian Ocean
Kleine Antillen, the smaller West India Islands
Liparische In., Liparian Islands
Lissabon, Lisbon
Meerb. v. Taranto, Bay of Taranto
Mittelländisches Meer, Mediterranean Sea
Mozambique Kanal, Mozambique Channel
Neapel, Naples
Nord Amerika, North America
Sicilien, Sicily
Spanien, Spain
Str. von Messina, Strait of Messina
Türkei, Turkey
Tyrrhenisches Meer, Tyrrhenian Sea
Venedig, Venice
Vesuv, Vesuvius
Wien, Vienna

PLATE 48.
Boring Equipment; Stratification and Artesian Wells

Figure
1. *Coup d'œil* of the normal masses
2. Illustrating the theory of springs and Artesian wells
3. Section of the Artesian well of Grenoble
4. Interior of a boring shed
5–14. Boring tools

PLATE 49.
Notable Geological Formations

Figure
1. Interior of the crater on the Island of Hawaii
2. Coral island in the Pacific Ocean
3. Rock groups on the Faroe Islands
4. Natural bridge of Icomonzo in Columbia
5. Glacier sources of the Rhine
6. Trachyte columns in the Siebengebirge
7. Basaltic groups on the Island of Staffa
8. Fissured clay slate on the Lahn
9. Cleft variegated sandstone near Kreuznach, Germany

PLATE 50.
Volcanoes, Geysers, and Water Falls

Figure
1. The Geyser of Iceland
2. Submarine volcanic eruption
3. Air volcano of Turbaso in Columbia
4. The volcanic Island of Ferdinandea
5. Crater of the same
6. Crater of the Krabla in Iceland
7. Crater of Etna in Sicily
8. Niagara Falls
9. The Dal Elf Fall in Sweden

PLATE 51.
Forests, Lakes, Caves, and Unusual Rock Formations

Figure
1. Primitive forest of Brazil
2. Lake of Keswick, Cumberland, England
3. Arch of rock on Cape Parry
4. The fresh water cave, Isle of Wight, England
5. The Blackgang cave on the Isle of Wight
6. Basalt rocks on the Island of Tahiti
7. The Grotto del Cane near Naples
8. The grotto of Jupiter on the Island of Naxos, Greece

PLATE 52.
Caves, Icebergs, Lava, and Rock Formations

Figure
1. Icebergs of the Antarctic regions
2. Sandstone cave in Sicily
3. Lava arch in Iceland
4. Burning mountain near Duttweiler
5. Cascade of Teverone near Tivoli
6. Basalt columns on the Island of Staffa
7. Upright tree stems found in carboniferous formations
8. Island of Staffa with Fingal's cave
9. Section of the cavern of Gailenreuth in the Hartz

PLATE 53.
Caves and Rock Formations

Figure
1. The Grotte des Demoiselles in France
2. The Dunold Mill Cave, Lancashire, England
3. The cave of Montserrat in Catalonia, Spain
4. Porphyry mountain near Kreuznach, Germany
5. The Lurley rock on the Rhine
6. The Rhonetrichter (*Perte du Rhone*), France
7. Serpentine rocks near Lizard Point, Cornwall, England
8. Clay slate strata on the coast of Scotland
9. Submarine section of the Straits of Gibraltar
10. Submarine section between Tarifa and Alcazar, Spain
11–13. Illustrating the cleavage of rocks
14. Illustrating subordinate beds

BOTANY

PLATE 54.
Representatives of the Algae, Fungi, Bryophyta, Polypodiophyta and Other Nonflowering Plants

Figure
1–15. Jussieu's Classification of Plants, types of classes
16. Ustilago segetum
17. Uredo phaseoli
18. Tuber cibarium, truffle
19. Bovista gigantea
20. Morchella esculenta, morel
21. Polyporus perennis
22*a*. Boletus umbellatus
22*b*. Boletus edulis, edible mushroom
23. Hydnum auriscalpium
24. Cantharellus cibarius
25. Agaricus fimetarius
26. Agaricus campestris, champignon
27. Agaricus procerus
28. Agaricus muscarius, toadstool
29. Cladonia pyxidata
30. Parmelia parietina
31. Cetraria islandica, Iceland moss
32. Rochella tinctoria
33. Usnea florida
34. *a*, Conferva bombycina; *b*, C. rivularis; *c*, C. flaccida; *d*, C. glomerata
35. Sphærococcus coronopifolius
36. Laminaria digitata
37. Laminaria saccharina
38. Fucus vesiculosus
39. Spagnum acutifolium, Peat-moss
40. Polytrichum juniperinum
41. Climacium dendroides
42. Anthoceros punctatus
43. Gymnoscyphus repens
44. Marchantia polymorpha
45. Pilularia globulifera
46. Salvinia natans
47. Marsilea quadrifolia
48. Ceterach leptophylla
49*a*. Polypodium vulgare
49*b*. Ceterach officinarum
50. Aspidium filix mas
51. Asplenium trichomanes
52. Scolopendrium officinarum
53. Lomaria spicans
54. Adiantum capillus veneris
55. Osmunda regalis
56. Botrychium lunaris
57. Ophioglossum vulgatum
58. Lycopodium clavatum
59. Equisetum limosum

PLATE 55.
Fig tree, Aquatic Flowering Plants, and Representatives of the Families Gramineae and Cyperaceae

Figure
1. Potamogeton natans
2. Arum maculatum, wake robin
3. Zostera marina
4. Acorus calamus
5. Typha latifolia, cat-tail
6. Eriophorum angustifolium
7. Cyperus officinalis
8. Saccharum officinale, sugar cane
9. Oryza sativa, rice
10. Bambusa arundinacea, bamboo-cane

Center figure: Musa sapientum, banana tree (German: *Banana oder Feigenbaum*)

PLATE 56.
Habitat Grouping and Reproductive Parts of Various Woody Monocots, Especially Palms and Cycads

Figure
1. Cocos nucifera, cocoa palm
2. Phœnix dactylifera, date palm
3. Sagus farinifera, sago palm
4. Cycas circinalis, sago tree
5. Dracæna braziliensis
6. Aloë arborescens
7. Areca catechu, areca palm
8. Zamia elliptica
9. Papyrus antiquorum

PLATE 57.
Representatives of the Monocot Order Liliales

Figure
1. Dracæna draco, dragon's blood
2. Luzula pilosa, woodrush
3. Commelyna tuberosa

4. Colchicum autumnale
5. Veratrum album, sneezewort
6. Fritillaria imperialis, crown imperial
7. Erythronium dens canis, dog's tooth
8. Agave americana, century plant
9. Phormium tenax, New Zealand flax
10. Scilla maritima, squill

PLATES 58 and 59.
Aromatic Plants

Figure
1. Amaryllis formosissima, daffodil lily
2. Narcissus pseudo-narcissus, daffodil
3. Crocus sativus, saffron
4. Iris germanica, iris
5. Musa paradisiaca, plantain
6. Curcuma zedoaria, turmeric
7. Zingiber officinale, ginger
8. Vanilla aromatica, vanilla
9. Nymphæa lotus
10. Aristolochia clematis, birthwort
11. Aristolochia sipho, Dutchman's pipe
12. Aristolochia serpentaria, Virginia snake root
13. Elæagnus angustifolia
14. Daphne mezereum, mezereon
15. Camphora officinarum, camphor tree
16. Cinnamomum zeylanicum, cinnamon tree
17. Laurus nobilis, victor's laurel
18. Cinnamomum cassia, cassia tree

PLATES 60 and 61.
Cultivated Plants from Diverse Families: Ornamental, Edible, or Medicinal

Figure
1. Protea speciosa, sugar-bush
2. Banksia serrata
3. Myristica moschata, nutmeg
4. Rheum palmatum, rhubarb
5. Beta vulgaris, common beet
6. Celosia cristata, cock's comb
7. Plantago major, common plantain
8. Mirabilis longifolia
9. Plumbago europæa, toothwort
10. Anagallis arvensis, pimpernel
11. Dodecatheon integrifolium, American cowslip
12. Cyclamen europæum, sow-bread
13. Lysimachia vulgaris, loose-strife
14. Veronica officinalis, speedwell
15. Pedicularis palustris, lousewort
16. Lathræa squamaria, tooth-wort

PLATE 62.
Members of the Acanthus, Olive, Verbena, Mint, Figwort and Nightshade Families

Figure
1. Ruellia formosa
2. Acanthus mollis, bear's claw
3. Olea europæa, olive
4. Jasminum officinale
5. Vitex agnus castus
6. Betonica officinalis, betony
7. Galeopsis tetrahit, hemp nettle
8. Digitalis purpurea, purple foxglove
9. Calceolaria corymbosa, slipperwort
10. Verbascum thapsus, mullein
11. Nicotiana tabacum, tobacco

PLATE 63.
Plants of Several Families Which Contain Toxic Compounds, Especially of the Order Polemoniales

Figure
1. Hyoscyamus niger, henbane
2. Datura stramonium, jimson weed
3. Atropa belladonna, belladonna
4. Solanum dulcamara, climbing nightshade
5. Capsicum annuum, cayenne pepper
6. Borago officinalis, borage
7. Exogonium purga, jalap plant
8. Polemonium cœruleum, Jacob's ladder
9. Jacaranda tomentosa
10. Bignonia leucoxylon
11. Gentiana pneumonanthe, common gentian
12. Spigelia marilandica, pinkroot
13. Nerium oleander, oleander

PLATE 64.
Plants with a Resinous or Milky Sap

Figure
1. Cynanchum vincetoxicum, celandine
2. Asclepias cornuti, swallowwort
3. Mimusops dissecta
4. Styrax benzoin, benzoin tree
5. Ledum palustre, marsh tea
6. Erica filamentosa, cape heath
7. Campanula trachelium
8. Lobelia fulgens
9. Lactuca virosa, poison lettuce
10. Cynara scolymus, artichoke
11. Carthamus tinctorius, safflower
12. Serratula tinctoria, saw wort
13. Tanacetum vulgare, tansy

PLATE 65.
Plants Brewed as Teas and Representatives of the Umbelliferae, Some Poisonous

Figure
1. Artemisia absinthum, wormwood
2. Dipsacus fallonum, cardoon
3. Rubia tinctoria, madder
4. Coffea arabica, coffee
5. Lonicera caprifolium, woodbine
6. Aralia nudicaulis, sarsaparilla
7. Œnanthe fistulosa, dead tongue
8. Cicuta virosa, water hemlock
9. Æthusa cynapium, fool's parsley
10. Chærophyllum temulum, cow parsley
11. Conium maculatum, hemlock
12. Sium latifolium, water parsley

PLATE 66.
Cultivated Plants of the Ranunculaceae and Other Families

Figure
1. Clematis erecta, creeping climber
2. Anemone hortensis, garden anemone
3. Pulsatilla fratensis, pasque flower
4. Ranunculus acris, crowfoot
5. Adonis vernalis, bird's eye
6. Helleborus niger, black hellebore
7. Aquilegia vulgaris, columbine
8. Aconitum stœrkianum, helmet flower
9. Papaver somniferum, poppy
10. Chelidonium majus, celandine
11. Sinapis alba, white mustard
12. Capparis spinosa, caper plant
13. Reseda luteola, dyer's rocket
14. Paullinia pinnata, paulinia
15. Æsculus pavia, small buckeye

PLATE 67.
Various Plants of Economic Importance, including Tea, Wine Grape, Cotton and Cacao

Figure
1. Acer pseudo-platanus, white maple
2. Malpighia urens
3. Hypericum perforatum
4. Garcinia cambogia
5. Citrus medica, citron
6. Thea chinensis, tea plant
7. Swietenia mahogoni, mahogany tree
8. Vitis vinifera, wine grape
9. Geranium sanguineum, cranesbill
10. Oxalis acetocella, wood-sorrel
11. Gossipium herbaceum, cotton plant
12. Theobroma cacao, cacao tree

PLATE 68.
Cultivated Plants of Many Families, Mostly Ornamental

Figure
1. Magnolia grandiflora
2. Illicium anisatum, star anise
3. Anona squamosa, anona
4. Cocculus lacunosus
5. Berberis vulgaris, barberry
6. Tilia grandiflora, lime tree
7. Bixa orellana, arnotto tree
8. Helianthemum vulgaris
9. Guaiacum officinale
10. Diptamus albus, white dittany
11. Dianthus caryophyllus, carnation
12. Saponaria officinalis, soapwort
13. Camellia japonica, camelia

PLATE 69.
Plants Indigenous to Sandy or Rocky Soil, a Sandalwood, and Representatives of the Order Myrtales

Figure
1. Sedum acre, stone crop
2. Saxifraga granulata, stone-break
3. Cereus hexagonus, six-edged cactus
4. Tamarix germanica, tamarisk
5. Mesembryanthemum rubrocinctum, fig-marigold
6. Œnothera biennis, evening primrose
7. Epilobium angustifolium, willow-herb
8. Santalum myrtifolium
9. Melaleuca cajeput, cajeput tree
10. Melaleuca fulgens, fiery cajeput
11. Eugenia pimenta, allspice
12. Caryophyllus aromaticus, clove-tree
13. Melastoma malabathricum

PLATE 70.
Lythrum and Representatives of the Order Rosales

Figure
1. Lythrum salicaria
2. Mespilus germanicus, medlar
3. Rosa moscata, musk rose
4. Potentilla anserina, silver weed
5. Amygdalus communis, sweet almond
6. Acacia vera, gum arabic tree
7. Cassia lanceolata, senna

8. Tamarindus indica, tamarind tree
9. Hæmatoxylon campechianum, logwood
10. Coronilla varia, sicklewort
11. Phaseolus vulgaris, kidney bean
12. Genista tinctoria, dyer's greenwood
13. Indigofera anil, anil
14. Glycyrrhiza glabra

PLATE 71.
Various plants, Including Members of the Sumac, Spurge and Gourd Families

Figure
1. Anacardium occidentale, cashew nut
2. Rhus cotinus, smoke tree
3. Pistacia terebinthus, turpentine tree
4. Juglans regia, English walnut
5. Euonymus europæus, spindle tree
6. Ilex aquifolium, European holly
7. Rhamnus catharticus, buckthorn
8. Euphorbia cyparissias, wolf's milk
9. Euphorbia officinarum, spurge
10. Siphonia elastica, caoutchouc tree
11. Cucumis citrullus, water melon
12. Momordica balsamina, balsam apple
13. Bryonia alba, white bryony
14. Carica papaya, West Indian pawpaw
15. Cucumis melo

PLATE 72.
Coniferous Gymnosperms, and Angiosperms of the Mulberry, Pepper, Beech and Witch Hazel Families

Figure
1. Ficus carica, fig tree
2. Artocarpus incisa, breadfruit
3. Morus nigra, black mulberry
4. Humulus lupulus, hops
5. Cannabis sativa, hemp
6. Piper nigrum, black pepper
7. Castanea vesca, chestnut
8. Quercus tinctoria, black oak
9. Liquidambar styraciflua, sweet gum
10. Taxus baccata, European yew
11. Juniperus communis, common juniper
12. Cupressus sempervirens, European cypress
13. Larix cedrus, European cedar

PLATE 73.
Maps and Charts of Plant Distribution

Figure
1. Botanical chart
2. Chart of the Chinese and Indian cotton region
3. Chart of the American region of the sugar cane, coffee, etc.
4. Chart of the *vertical* distribution of plants in Asia
5. The same of America
6. The same of Europe
7. The same of the Canary Islands
8. The same of the frigid zone of Europe

GLOSSARY

Ægypten, Egypt
Aleuten, Aleutian Islands
Algerien, Algeria
Amazonenstrom, Amazon River
Anden Gebirge, the Andes
Arabien, Arabia
Aral S., Lake Aral
Asien, Asia
Atlantischer Ocean, Atlantic Ocean
Australien, Australia
Azorische In., the Azores
Bahama In., Bahama Islands
Baumwolle, Cotton
Bonin In., Bonin Islands
Brasilien, Brazil
Californien, California
Canarische In., Canary Islands
Cap der guten Hoffnung, Cape of Good Hope
Cap Horn, Cape Horn
Cap Verdische In., Cape Verde Islands
Caraibisches M., Caribbean Sea
Carolinen In., Caroline Islands
Caspisches M., Caspian Sea
Chinawälder, Bathbark forests
Deutschland, Germany
Falklands In., Falkland Islands
Feuerland, Terra del Fuego
Frankreich, France
Freundschafts In., Friendly Islands
Gallopagos In., Gallopagos Islands
Gerste u. Hafer, Barley and oats
Gewürznelken, Cloves
Grönland, Greenland
Grossbritannien, Great Britain
Grosser oder Stiller Ocean, Pacific Ocean
Habesch, Habesch
Himmalaya Geb., Himmalaya Mountains
I. Island, Iceland
I. Karafta oder Sachalin, Island of Karafta or Sachalin
Indisches Meer, Indian Ocean
Irland, Ireland
Kaffee, Coffee
Kaschmir, Cashmere
Kurilen, Kurile Islands
Ladronen In., Marian Islands
Mais, Indian corn
Malediven In., Maldive Islands
Mandschurei, Manchooria
Marañon od. Amazonenstrom, Amazon River
Marianen od. Ladronen In., Marian Islands
Mb. v. Mexico, Gulf of Mexico
Mendana's Arch., Mendana's Archipelago
Mittel Amer, Central America
Mittelländisches Meer, Mediterranean Sea
Mongolei, Mongolia
Moskau, Moscow
Muscatbaum, Nutmeg tree
N. Gran., New Grenada
Neufundland, Newfoundland
Neu Guinea, New Guinea
Neu Seeland, New Zealand
Nord Amerika, North America
Norwegen, Norway
Nubien, Nubia
Ost Indien, East India
Patagonien, Patagonia
Pfeffer, Pepper
Reis, Rice
Roggen, Rye
Russisches Amerika, Russian America
Russland, Russia
Sandwichs In., Sandwich Islands
Schiffer In., Navigators' Islands
Schwarzes M., Black Sea
Schweden, Sweden
Sibirien, Siberia
Sklaven S., Slave Lake
Spanien, Spain
Süd Amerika, South America
Thee, Tea
Toisen, Toises (1t. = 6 feet.)
Türkei, Turkey
Vanille, Vanilla
Vereinigte Staaten, United States
Vulc. v. Aconcagua, Volcano of Aconcagua
Weitzen, Wheat
West Indien, West Indies
Wüste Sahara, Desert of Sahara
Wüste Schamo oder Gobi, Desert of Shamo or Gobi
Zeichenerklärung für fig. 1, 2, *u.* 3, Explanation of the marks in figs. 1, 2, and 3
Zimmt, Cinnamon
Zucker, Sugar

ZOOLOGY

NOTE: The names used in the plate titles are the currently used scientific names for the groups of animals recognized in 1979. Many of the names for the species (figure captions) are out of date, some for over 100 years. Many of the common names are also out of date or are names used for groups of species.

PLATE 74.
Classification

Figure
1. Monas, animalcule
2. Monocerca, animalcule
3. Spongia, sponge
4. Hydra, naked polypi
5. Diphies, medusa
6. Velella, nautilus
7. Sipunculus, tube worm
8. Holothuria, sea jelly
9. Ligula, strapworm
10. Nemertes, cordworm
11. Botryllus, sea grape
12. Ostrea, oyster
13. Chiton, sea cockroach
14. Fissurella, fissure shell
15. Vermetus, worm shell
16. Strombus, screw shell
17. Carina, keel shell
18. Bulla, wood digger
19. Phyllidium, leaf shell
20. Tritonium, triton
21. Limnæus, mud shell
22. Clio, whale louse
23. Octopus, polypus
24. Hirudo, leech
25. Aphrodite, sea mouse
26. Amphitrite
27. Anatifa, duck mussel
28. Cancer, crab
29. Squilla, shrimp
30. Talitrus, sea flea
31. Cyamus, whale louse
32. Oniscus, cheslip
33. Cyclops, water flea
34. Caligus, fish louse
35. Aranea, spider
36. Chelifer
37. Scolopendra
38. Lepisma, book worm
39. Pediculus, louse
40. Pulex, flea
41. Carabus, ground beetle
42. Forficula, earwig
43. Cimex, bedbug
44. Libellula, dragon fly
45. Tenthredo, tailed wasp
46. Vanessa, butterfly
47. Stomoxys, autumn fly
48. Petromyzon, lamprey eel
49. Squalus, shark
50. Raja, ray
51. Acipenser, sturgeon
52. Orthagoriscus, moon fish
53. Hippocampus, sea horse
54. Anguilla, eel
55. Pleuronectes, sole
56. Merlangus, whiting
57. Cyprinus, chub
58. Xiphias, swordfish
59. Salamandra, salamander
60. Rana, frog
61. Vipera, viper
62. Boa, boa constrictor
63. Anguis, adder
64. Ophisaurus
65. Chirotes

66, 67. Chalcides
68. Bipes
69. Anolis
70. Scincus
71. Tilicua
72. Chamæleo, chameleon
73. Ptyodactylus
74. Basiliscus, basilisk
75. Iguana, guana
76. Draco, dragon
77. Agama
78. Stellio, stellion
79. Lacerta, lizard
80. Tejus
81. Crocodilus, crocodile
82. Plesiosaurus
83. Ichthyosaurus
84. Chelonia, sea tortoise
85. Testudo, land tortoise
86. Anas, duck
87. Sula, dodo
88. Pelecanus, pelican
89. Procellaria, petrel
90. Podiceps, diver
91. Phœnicopterus, flamingo
92. Rallus, water rail
93. Scolopax, snipe
94. Ardea, heron
95. Grus, crane
96. Otis, bustard
97. Struthio, ostrich
98. Gallus, cock
99. Crax, curassow
100. Columba, pigeon
101. Psittacus, parrot
102. Picus, woodpecker
103. Buceros, rhinoceros bird
104. Merops, bee-eater
105. Sitta, nut-pecker
106. Alauda, lark
107. Cypselus, sea swallow
108. Pica, magpie
109. Otus, owl
110. Vultur, vulture
111. Milvus, kite
112. Balæna, whale
113. Cervus, deer
114. Bos, ox
115. Camelus, camel
116. Equus, horse
117. Sus, hog
118. Elephas, elephant
119. Ornithorhynchus, duckbilled platypus
120. Manis, pangolin
121. Bradypus, sloth
122. Lepus, rabbit
123. Sciurus, squirrel
124. Castor, beaver
125. Mus, mouse
126. Didelphys, kangaroo
127. Phoca, seal
128. Mustela, marten
129. Viverra, civet
130. Felis, cat
131. Hyæna, hyena
132. Canis, dog
133. Ursus, bear
134. Erinaceus, hedgehog
135. Vespertilio, bat
136. Pteropus, rousset
137. Lemur, maki
138. Hapale, ouistiti
139. Simia, monkey
140. Homo, man

PLATE 75.

Representatives of the Phyla Protozoa, Porifera, Coelenterata, and Mollusca

Figure
1. Monas lens
2. Proteus diffluens
3. Bursaria vesiculosa
4. Cryptomonas ovata
5. Trachelocerca olor
6. Trachelocerca viridis
7. Vibrio anguillula
8. Cyclidium glaucoma
9. Paramecium compressum
10. Chilodon cucullatus
11. Gonium pectorale
12. Bursaria truncatella
13. Urocentrum turbo
14. Trichodina cometa
15. Volvox globator
16. Rotifer vulgaris
17. Opercularia articulata
18. Stentor mylleri
19. Melicerta ringens
20. Carchesium polypinum
21. Hydra grisea
22. Hydra fusca
23. Hydra viridis
24. Virgularia juncea
25. Pennatula granulosa
26. Pennatula phosphorea
27. Pennatula grisea
28, 29. Tubularia coronata
30. Sertularia polyzonalis
31. Sertularia falcata
32. Thuaria thuia
33. Sertularia abietina
34. Sertularia operculata
35. Corallina rubens
36. Flabellaria opuntia
37. Penecillus penecillus
38. Corallina officinalis
39. Tubularia sultana
40. Tubularia campanularia
41. Acetabulum mediterraneum
42. Tubularia indivisa
43. Flustra foliacea
44. Spongia fistularis
45. Spongia officinalis
46. Alcyonium ficiforme
47. Alcyonium palmatum
48. Gorgonia flabellum
49. Gorgonia verrucosa
50. Gorgonia cerataphyta
51. Antipathes spiralis
52. Coralium nobile
53. Isis hippuris
54. Flustra
55. Pocillopora polymorpha
56. Retepora
57. Eschara
58. Oculina virginea
59. Oculina gemmascens
60. Madrepora prolifera
61. Porites porites
62. Astrea astroites
63. Explanaria ananas
64. Meandrina labyrinthica
65. Fungia fungites
66. Tubipora musica
67. Teredo navalis
68. Sabella ventilabrum
69. Vermetus lumbricalis
70. Serpula glomerata
71. Aspergillum javanum
72. Serpula arenaria
73. Dentalium elephantinum
74. Dentalium politum
75. Dentalium entalis
76. Patella granatina
77. Patella saccharina
78. Calyptræa sinensis
79. Patella laciniosa
80. Fissurella græca
81. Ancylus lacustris
82. Emarginula fissura
83. Pileopsis hungarica (Trochidæ)
84. Neritina crepidularia
85. Patella vulgata
86. Haliotis tuberculata
87. Neritina fluviatilis
88. Natica canrena
89. Sigaretus haliotideus
90. Melania amarula
91. Limnea auricularia
92. Limnea stagnalis
93. Bulimus decollatus fasciatus
94. Bulimus decollatus albus
95. Paludina vivipara
96. Janthina ianthina
97. Helix memoralis
98. Helix pomathia
99. Turbo nautileus
100. Clausilia perversa
101. Scalaria dathrus
102. Scalaria scalaris
103. Turbo cochlus
104. Delphinula delphinus
105. Telescopium indicator
106. Trochus solaris
107. Trochus magus
108. Solarium perspectivum
109. Cerithium vertagus
110. Pleurotoma babylonia
111. Murex ramosa
112. Murex haustellum
113. Murex tribulus
114. Strombus lentiginosus
115. Pterocera chiragra
116. Rostellaria rectirostris
117. Terebra maculata
118. Purpura lapillus
119. Harpa ventricosa
120. Baccinum undatum
121. Cassidoria echinophora
122. Oliva ispidula
123. Mitra episcopalis
124. Mitra papalis
125. Oliva porphyria
126. Oliva maura

PLATE 76.

Representatives of the Phyla Mollusca, Echinodermata, Ctenophora, and Arthropoda

Figure
1. Auricula midæ
2. Ovula volva
3. Bulla physis
4. Ovula ovum
5. Cypræa moneta
6. Cypræa mauritiana
7. Cypræa arabica
8. Conus aurantiacus
9. Conus summus
10. Conus cedo nulli
11. Conus textillis
12. Conus marmoreus
13. Spirula spirula
14. Nautilus beccari
15. Nautilus calcar
16. Nautilus pompilius
17. Argonauta argo
18. Pinna obeliscus
19. Pinna rudis
20. Avicula margaritifera
21. Mytilus cygneus
22. Mytilus bidens
23. Terebrata caput serpentis
24. Crania craniolaris
25. Ostrea cristigalli
26. Malleus malleus
27. Pecten corallinus
28. Pecten pallium ducale
29. Pecten maximus
30. Perna ephippium
31. Arca senilis
32. Arca noæ
33. Tridacna gigas
34. Isocardia corallina
35. Spondylus gæderopus
36. Venus mercenaria
37. Cytherea dione
38. Donax rugosa
39. Donax scripta
40. Mactra solidissima
41. Hemicardium cardissa
42. Cardium echinatum
43. Cyclas
44. Tellina radiata
45. Solen vagina
46. Solen siliqua
47. Unio complanatus
48. Mya pictorum
49. Pholas pusillus
50. Pholas dactylus
51. Pollicipes mitella
52. Lepas anatifa
53. Coronula
54. Balanus psittacus
55. Chiton squamosus
56. Holopus rangii
57. Encrinus radiatus
58. Pentacrinus osteria
59. Oreaster turritus
60. Asterias aurantiaca
61. Astrogonium granulare
62. Ophiolepis scolopendrina

63. Astrophyton caput medusæ
64. Ophiurus asterias
65. Stellonia rubens
66. Solaster papposa
67. Spatangus purpureus
68. Clypeaster rosacea
69. Echinus cidaris
70. Cidaris diadema
71. Cidaris esculentus
72. Lucernaria quadricornis
73. Thaumantias cymbaloidea
74. Aurelia aurita
75. Octopus octopodius
76. Loligo loligo
77. Sepia officinalis
78. Clio borealis
79. Scyllæa pelagica (Tritoniidæ)
80. Lernæa branchialis
81. Lernæa cyprinacea
82. Terebella conchilega
83. Porpita nuda
84. Velella spirans
85. Cucumaria frondosa

PLATE 77.

Representatives of the Phyla Coelenterata, Chordata, Mollusca, Platyhelminthes, and Arthropoda

Figure
1. Physalia physalis
2. Thetis fimbria
3. Salpa maxima
4. Pedicellaria
5. Actinia undata
6. Actinia senilis
7. Ascidia lepadiformis
8. Ascidia venosa
9. Nais serpentina
10. Nais proboscidea
11. Phyllodoce stellifera
12. Nereis tubicola
13. Amphitrite reniformis
14. Spio filicornis
15. Aphrodite aculeata
16. Doris papillosa
17. Doris argo
18. Aplysia depilans
19. Limax agrestis
20. Limax empiricorum
21. Limax fuscus
22. Malacobdella grossa
23. Nephelis octoculata (Hirudinidæ)
24. Clepsina complanata
25. Hæmopis vorax
26. Hirudo officinalis
27. Sipunculus saccatus
28. Sipunculus nudus
29. Echinococcus veterinorum suis
30. Cysticercus cellulosæ
31. Tænia cateniformis
32. Bothriocephalus latus
33. Tænia solium
34. Ligula cingulum
35. Planaria cornuta
36. Distoma hepaticum
37. Lumbricus variegatus
38. Lumbricus terrestris
39. Echinorhynchus gigas
40. Trichocephalus dispar
41. Ascaris lumbricoides
42. Oxyuris vermicolaris
43. Filaria medinensis
44. Lumbricus aquaticus
45. Filaria papillosa
46. Argas fischeri
47. Argas savignii
48. Chelifer beauvoisii
49. Galeodes phalangium
50. Galeodes araneoides
51. Scorpio europæus
52. Buthus afer
53. Epeira imperialis
54. Tetragnatha argyra
55. Theridion denticulatum
56. Argyroneta aquatica
57*a*. Uloborus walcnærius
57*b*. Gasteracantha armata
58. Mygale avicularia
59. Epeira diadema
60. Pallene brevirostris (Pycnogonidæ)
61. Chelifer cancroides
62. Phalangium opilio
63. Phalangium ægyptiacum
64. Hydrachna abstergens
65. Hydrachna despiciens
66. Ixodes annulatus
67. Ixodes americanus
68. Sarcoptes scabiei
69. Gamasus coleopterorum
70. Acarus siro
71. Ixodes orbiculatus
72. Pulex penetrans
73. Pulex irritans
74, 75. Nirmidæ
76. Phthirius pubis
77. Pediculus capitis
78. Lodura nivicola
79. Podura villosa
80. Smynthurus fimetarius
81, 84. Machilus polypoda
82, 83. Lepisma saccharina
84. See 81
85. Melophagus ovis
86. Hippobosca equina
87. Bombylius major
88. Dioctria ater
89. Asilus cabroniformis
90. Conops macrocephala
91. Stomoxis calcitrans
92, 93. Empidæ
94. Anopheles bifurcatus
95. Culex nemorosus
96. Culex pipiens
97. Tabanus tropicus
98. Tabanus bovinus
99–109. Muscidæ
110. Clitellaria ephippium
111. Volucella pellucens
112. Scæva pyrastri
113. Crysotoxum vospiformis
114. Eristalis tenax
115. Helophilus pendulus
116. Leptis vermileo
117. Stratiomys chamæleon
118. Chironomus plumosus
119. Anisomera nigra
120. Ctenophora elegans
121. Psychoda phalænoides
122. Mycetophila cericea
123. Bibio marci
124. Mycetophila mirabilis
125. Cephalemyia ovis
126, 127. Gasterophilus equi
128. Œstrus tarandi
129. Œstrus bovis

PLATE 78.

Representatives of the Phylum Arthropoda: Classes Crustacea and Arachnida

Figure
1, 2. Cancerinæ
3. Thalamita natator
4. Gecarcinus lateralis
5. Gelasimus annulipes
6. Ocypoda arenaria
7. Philyra scabriuscula
8. Dorippe sima
9. Ranina serrata
10. Pagurus diogenes
11. Palinurus guttatus
12. Seyllarus æquinoctialis
13. Stenopus hispidus
14. Callianassa uncinatta
15. Squilla maculata
16. Gonodactylus stylifer
17. Phyllosoma stylicornis
18. Orchestia fischeri
19. Ancylomera hunteri
20. Cymadocea armata
21. Sphæroma serratum
22. Porcellio granulatus
23. Caprella acuminifera
24. Cyamus ovalis
25. Aprus cancriformis
26. Branchipus pisciformis
27. Cyclops communis
28. Phyllophora cornuta
29. Ergasilus sieboldi
30. Lernæa polycolpus
31. Achtheres percarum
32. Pycnogonum litterale
33. Nymphon gracile
34. Limullus moluccanus
35. Nemesia cellicola
36. Segestria perfida
37. Lycosa tarentula
38. Lycosa melanogaster
39. Hersilia caudata
40. Chersis savinii
41. Salticus formicanus
42. Eripus heterogaster
43. Arcys lanceolarius
44. Latrodectus malmignatus
45. Nyssa timida
46. Tegenaria domestica
47. Lachesis perversa
48. Uloborus walcnærius
49. Argyroneta aquatica

PLATE 79.

Insects of the Orders Hymenoptera, Diptera, Lepidoptera, and Odonata

Figure
1. Mutilla europæa
2. Apterogyna occidentalis
3–9. Formicidæ
10. Bombus lapidarius
11. Bombus muscorum
12. Megachile sementaria
13. Bombus terrestris
14. Xylocopa violacea
15. Nomada variegata
16. Eucera longicornis
17. Megachile centuncularis
18. Apis mellifica
19. Vespa maculata
20. Polistes paritum
21. Vespa vulgaris
22. Vespa crabro
23. Leucospis dorsigera
24. Chrysis cyanea
25. Chrysis aurata
26. Chrysis ignita
27. Pompilus cœruleus
28. Pompilus viaticus
29. Crabro cribarius
30. Pelopæus spirifex
31. Ammophila sabulosa
32, 33, 36–39. Ichneumonidæ
34, 35. Chalcididæ
36–39. See 32
40. Rhyssa persuasoria (Ichneumonidæ)
41. Urocerus spectrum
42. Urocerus gigas
43. Lophyrus juniperi
44. Nematus capreæ
45. Cimbex americana
46. Tenthredinidæ
47. Cimbex variabilis
48–53. Cinipidæ
54. Mantispa pagana
55. Raphidia ophiopsis
56. Termes fatalis
57. Bittacus tipularia
58. Panorpa communis
59. Ascalaphus barbarus
60. Myrmeleon libelluloides
61. Myrmeleon formicarius
62–64. Hermerobiidæ
65. Hydropsyche plumosa
66. Phryganea striata
67. Perla bicaudata
68. Limnophilus rhombica
69. Phryganea grandis
70–72. Ephemeridæ
73. Agrion puella
74. Calepteryx virgo
75. Libellula depressa
76. Æschna grandis
77. Pterophorus pentadactyla
78. Coccyx resinosa
79. Carpocapsa pomonella
80. Hercyna paliotalis
81. Tinea granella
82. Plutella xylostella
83. Gallerea cereana
84. Tinea pellionella
85. Lemmatophila salicella
86. Hyponomeuta evonymella

87. Hyponomeuta pedella
88. Hypena rostralis
89. Botys verticalis
90. Sciaphila literata
91. Tortrix viridana
92. Halias prasinana
93–102. Geometridæ
103–123, 129, 136. Noctuidæ
124. Callimorpha jacobææ
125. Arctia fuliginosa
126. Arctia matronula
127. Arctia dominula
128. Pygæra bucephala
129. See 103
130–135, 137–151. Bombycidæ
136. See 103

PLATE 80.
Insects of the Orders Lepidoptera, Orthoptera, and Hemiptera Mantedea, and Hemiptera

Figure
1. Lasiocampa quercus
2. Dendrolimus pini
3. Odonestis potatoria
4–7. Bombycidæ
8. Zygæna filipendula
9. Sesia fuciformis
10–21. Sphingidæ
22. Hesperia malvarum
23–50. Papilionidæ
51. Thrips phisapus
52. Lecanium illicis
53. Lecanium hesperidum
54. Coccus cacti
55. Psylla alni
56. Dorthesia urticea
57, 59. Aphidæ
58. Chermes ulmi
59. See 57
60. Pyrrhocoris apterus
61. Coryzus hyoscyami
62. Cydnus biguttatus
63. Pentatoma juniperinus
64. Pentatoma baccarum
65. Acanthosoma hæmorrhoidalis
66. Cimex rufipes
67. Acanthia lectularia
68. Ranatra linearis
69. Nepa cinerea
70. Neucoris cimicoides
71. Belostoma grandis
72. Corixa striata
73. Notonecta glauca
74. Aphrophora spumaria
75. Cicada fraxini
76. Fulgora candelaria
77. Fulgoria laternaria
78. Œdipoda stridula
79. Œdipoda cærulescens
80. Œdipoda migratoria
81. Acridium cristatum
82–85. Locustidæ
86–88. Gryllidæ
89. Phyllium siccifolium
90. Mantis religiosa
91. Empusa gongylodes
92. Cyphocrana gigas
93. Blatta orientalis

PLATE 81.
Members of the Insect Order Coleoptera; and the Chordate Classes Chondrichthyes, Osteichthyes, Amphibia, and Reptilia

Upper Division

Figure
1–3. Forficulidæ
4–6. Brachelytra
7. Meloë proscarabæus
8. Lytta vesicatoria
9. Blaps mortisaga
10. Tenebrio molitor
11–16. Carabidæ
17. Dyticus marginalis
18. Hydrophilus piceus
19–21. Mordellidæ
22. Buprestis mariana
23. Euchroma gigas
24. Buprestis chrysostigma
25. Elaphrus riparius (Carabidæ)
26–29. Cicindela
30–33. Elateridæ
34. Malachius æneus
35–38. Cantharis
39. Lycus sanguineus
40. Pyrochroa coccinea
41, 42. Lampyridæ
43. Necydalis cærulea
44–61. Longicornia
62–64. Clerida
65–76. Rhincophora
77–79. Bruchus
80–101. Trimera
102, 103. Nitidulidæ
104. Silpha thoracica
105, 106. Necrophorus
107, 108. Anthrenus
109. Byrrhus pilula (Byrrhidæ)
110. Gyrinus natator
111. Ptinus fur
112. Anobium pertinax
113. Apate capucinus
114. Hylesinus piniperda
115, 116. Bostrichus
117, 118. Dermestes
119–123. Hister
124. Lucanus
125–127. Cetoniadæ
128–131. Melolonthidæ
132, 136–144. Scarabæidæ
133–135. Aphodiidæ
136–144. See 132
145–148. Dynastidæ

Lower Division

Figure
1. Alosa vulgaris, shad
2. Clupea harengus, herring
3. Engraulisencrasicholus, anchovy
4. Harengula sprattus, sprat
5. Thymallus vulgaris, greyling
6. Cobitis fossilis, mudfish
7. Exoglossum barbatula, groundling
8. Rhombus vulgaris, brill
9. Platessa flesus, fluke
10. Zeus faber, dory
11. Lota vulgaris, burbot
12. Trachinus draco, sea cat
13. Xiphias gladius, swordfish
14. Amodytes tobianus, sand-eel
15. Syngnathus ophidion, sea serpent
16. Syngnathus acus, sea-needle
17. Pegasus draco, sea-dragon
18. Lumpus anglorum, lump sucker
19. Diodon punctatus, sticklebag
20. Tetraodon lagocephalus, star belly
21. Centriscus scolopax, trumpet fish
22. Aluteres monoceros, unicorn fish
23. Lophius piscatorius, widegap
24. Acipenser ruthenus, caviar sturgeon
25. Acipenser sturio, sturgeon
26. Sphyrna malleus, hammer-headed shark
27. Spinax acanthias, thorn-hound
28. Petromyzon fluviatilis, lamprey
29. Seps chalcides, bronze colored lizard
30. Scincus cyanurus, scink
31. Plestiodon aldrovandii
32. Triton cristatum, eft
33. Draco dandini, flying dragon
34. Rana temporaria, yellow frog
35. Hyla viridis, tree or green frog
36. Bufo calamita, toad
37. Bombinator igneus, glistering toad
38. Pelobatus fuscus, water toad
39. Testudo geometrica, tortoise
40. Testudo græca, mosaic tortoise
41. Cistudo europæa, European tortoise
42. Emys picta, terrapin
43. Sphargis coriacea, leather turtle

PLATE 82.
Chordates of the Classes Chondrichthyes and Osteichthyes

Figure
1. Aspidophorus cataphractus, pogge
2. Pristis antiquorum, saw fish
3. Esox lucius, pike
4. Perca fluviatilis, perch
5. Anguilla vulgaris, eel
6. Gasterosteus aculeatus, stickleback
7. Salmo fario, salmon trout
8. Holocanthus tricolor, tricolor
9. Synanceia horrida, dragon's head
10. Labrax lupus, bass
11. Solea vulgaris, sole
12. Platessa limanda, dab

PLATE 83.
Osteichthyes of the Orders Perciformes, Scorpæinformes, Beryciformes, and Dactylopteriformes

Figure
1. Holocentrum longipinne, red perch
2. Acanthurus gemmatus, gem fish
3. Amphacanthus corallinus, coral perch
4. Sphyræna spet, barracuda pike
5. Scorpæna scropha, dragon's head
6. Naucrates ductor, pilot fish
7. Trigla lyra, piper
8. Thynnus vulgaris, tunny
9. Scomber vulgaris, mackerel
10. Acerina cornua, ruffe
11. Cepola rubescens, band fish
12. Dactylopterus volitans, flying fish

PLATE 84.
Members of the Classes Chondrichthyes, and Osteichthyes

Figure
1. Carcharius verus, shark
2. Coryphæna hippuris, dolphin
3. Echineis remora, sucking fish
4. Chondrostoma nasus, broad snout
5. Cottus gobio, bullhead
6. Gobio fluviatilis, gresling
7. Alburnus lucidus, bleak
8. Acanthurus chirurgus, lancettail
9. Chætodon auriga, angel
10. Barbus vulgaris, barbel
11. Cyprinus carpio, carp
12. Tinca vulgaris, tench
13. Anabas scandens, climbing perch

PLATE 85.
Representatives of the Classes Chondrichthyes and Osteichthyes

Figure
1. Morrhua vulgaris, codfish
2. Merlangus vulgaris, whiting
3. Raia batis, skate
4. Trachinus vividus, weever
5. Blennius viviparus, guffer
6. Ophiocephalus striatus, ophidion
7. Mullus barbatus, mullet
8. Dipterodon capensis, Cape-dipterodon
9. Amphiprion bifasciatus, amphiprion
10. Scolopsides vosmari
11. Trachypterus spinolæ, trachypterus
12. Cyprinus auratus, gold-fish

PLATE 86.
Reptiles of the Suborders Sauria and Serpentes

Figure
1. Deirodon nasutus, green snake
2. Tropidonotus natrix, ringed snake
3. Trigonocephalus lanceolatus, copperhead
4. Naia tripudians, cobra di capello
5. Boa constrictor
6. Phrynosoma cornuta, horned frog

PLATE 87.
Reptiles of the Suborders Sauria and Serpentes

Figure
1. Anguis fragilis, slow worm
2. Vipera berus, viper
3. Cerastes cornutus, horned viper
4. Xiphosoma caninum, dog boa
5. Crotalus horridus, rattlesnake
6. Seps chalcides, scink

PLATE 88.
Amphibians of the Order Urodela and Reptiles of the Orders Squamata and Crocodylia

Figure
1. Siren lacertina, siren
2. Necturus lateralis, water puppy
3. Chamæleo vulgaris, chamæleon
4. Platydactylus guttatus, gecko
5. Uroplatus fimbriatus, flat headed salamander
6. Lophyrus furcata, lophyrus
7. Crocodilus lucius, alligator
8. Crocodilus vulgaris, crocodile

PLATE 89.
Amphibians of the Order Urodela and Reptiles of the Suborder Sauria

Figure
1. Salamandra maculata, salamander
2. Triton tœniatum, brook salamander
3. Draco dandini, flying dragon
4. Scincus officinalis, scink
5. Basiliscus mitratus, basilisk
6. Iguana tuberculata, guana
7. Lacerta viridis, lizard

PLATE 90.
Members of the Classes Reptilia and Amphibia

Figure
1. Bufo viridis, green toad
2. Engystoma ovale, S. Amer. toad
3. Dactelythra capensis, Cape toad
4. Pipa americana, Guiana toad
5. Rana esculenta, frog
6. Hyla viridis, tree or green frog
7. Achrochordus javanica, Java snake
8. Platurus laticaudis, India water snake
9. Elaps corallinus, coral snake
10. Typhline cuvierii, blind scink
11. Chelonia mydas, green turtle
12. Cistudo europæa, land tortoise
13. Testudo geometrica, India tortoise

PLATE 91.
Aves of the Orders Podicipediformes, Pelecaniformes, Sphenisciformes, and Gaviiformes

Figure
1. Podiceps cristatus, crested grebe
2. Podiceps minor, little grebe
3. Colymbus glacialis, loon
4. Sterna nigra, sooty tern
5. Larus eburneus, ivory gull
6. Pelecanus crispus, hairy pelican
7. Cygnus olor, mute swan
8. Cygnus ferus, hooper swan
9. Oidemia americana, scoter
10. Anas crecca, teal
11. Procellaria capensis, Cape pigeon
12. Diomedia exulans, white albatross
13. Aptenodytes patagonica, Patagonian penguin
14. Fratercula arctica, puffin
15. Alca torda, razor-billed auk

PLATE 92.
Members of the Orders Anseriformes, Pelecaniformes, Charadriiformes, and Sphenisciformes

Figure
1. Carbo cormoranus, cormorant
2. Eudytes cristatus, crested penguin
3. Tachypetes aquilus, frigate pelican
4. Phæton æthereus, tropic bird
5. Plotus anhinga, snake bird
6. Sula bassana, booby
7. Anser segetum, bean goose
8. Anas boschas, mallard
9. Anas galericulata, mandarin duck
10. Merges cucullatus, hooded merganser
11. Larus argentatus, herring gull
12. Sterna hirundo, sea swallow

PLATE 93.
Members of the Orders Ciconiiformes, Gruiformes, and Charadriiformes

Figure
1. Charadius auratus, plover
2. Vanellus cristatus, lapwing
3. Grus cinerea, crane
4. Platalea leucorrhodia, roseate spoon-bill
5. Ardea purpurea, purple heron
6. Egretta candidissima, snowy heron
7. Ciconia alba, white stork
8. Gallinago major, snipe
9. Limosa rufa, rufous godwit
10. Recurvirostra avocetta, avocet
11. Phænicopterus ruber, scarlet flamingo
12. Ardea ralloides, pigmy heron

PLATE 94.
Members of the Orders Struthioniformes, Gruiformes, Ciconiiformes, and Charadriiformes

Figure
1. Struthio camelus, ostrich
2. Otis tarda, great bustard
3. Otis tetrax, smaller bustard
4. Balearica pavonina, crowned crane
5. Botaurus stellaris, bittern
6. Ibis alba, white ibis
7. Numenius arcuatus, curlew
8. Totanus calidris, sandpiper
9. Parra indica, Indian jacana
10. Fulica americana, coot
11. Porphyrio hyacinthinus, hyacinth gallinule
12. Heliornis surinamensis, sun bird
13. Totanus ochropus, green sandpiper

PLATE 95.
Aves of the Orders Casuariiformes, Anseriformes, Charadriiformes, Galliformes, and Gruiformes

Figure
1. Casuarius galeatus, cassowary
2. Palamedea cornuta, horned screamer
3. Ibis cristatus, crested ibis
4. Tringa rufescens, rufous sandpiper
5. Glareola torquata, pratincole
6. Himantopus albicollis, stilt
7. Cinclus interpras, turnstone
8. Rallus aquaticus, dusky rail
9. Rallus crex, corn crake

10, 11. Gallus domesticus, common fowl

12. Meleagris gallopavo, turkey
13. Numida meleagris, guinea fowl
14. Pterocles alchata, desert grouse
15. Turnix dactylisonans, quail

PLATE 96.
Members of the Orders Galliformes and Columbiformes

Figure
1. Tetrao urogallus, cock of the woods
2. Tetrao tetrix, moor cock
3. Perdix cinerea, grey partridge
4. Perdix rubra, red partridge
5. Pavo cristatus, peacock
6. Phasianus colchicus, pheasant
7. Phasianus pictus, golden pheasant
8. Argus giganteus, argus pheasant
9. Tragopan hastingsii, golden breasted horned pheasant
10. Crax rubra, red curassow
11. Lophortyx californicus, California partridge
12. Columba livia, rock pigeon
13. Columba œnas, blue-backed dove
14. Goura cruenta, ground pigeon
15. Columba turtur, turtle dove

PLATE 97.
Representatives of the Orders Psittaciformes, Piciformes, and Trogoniformes

Figure
1. Cacatua sulphurea, yellow-crested cockatoo
2. Psittacus erythacus, grey African parrot
3. Palæornis malaccensis, Malacca parrot
4. Palæornis alexandri, redheaded parrot
5. Psittacus melanocephalus, black-headed parrot
6. Trogon curucui, curucui
7. Trogon viridis, green curucui
8. Bucco macrorhynchus, puff-bird
9. Monasa tranquilla, S. Amer.
10. Capito viridiauranthius, green and orange barbet
11. Pogonias sulcirostris, grooved-bill barbet
12. Pteroglossus aracari, long-tailed aracari
13. Ramphastus tucanus, largebilled toucan

PLATE 98.
Members of the Orders Psittaciformes, Piciformes, and Passeriformes

Figure
1. Platycercus viridis, green parrot
2. Ara ararauna, blue and yellow maccaw

3. Ara militaris, military maccaw
4. Lorius domicellus, lory
5. Picus villosus, hairy woodpecker
6. Picus cayennensis, Cayenne woodpecker
7. Gecinus viridis, green woodpecker
8. Picus major, large woodpecker
9. Yunx torquilla, wry neck
10. Pica caudata, magpie
11. Corvus monedula, jackdaw
12. Corvus corax, raven
13. Corvus cornix, hooded crow

PLATE 99.
Members of the Orders Apopodiformes and Passeriformes

Figure
1, 3. Garrulus glandarius, jay
2. Nucifraga caryocatactus, nutcracker
3. See 1
4. Paradisea minor, bird of paradise
5. Paradisea regia, king paradise bird
6. Paradisea superba, superb paradise bird
7. Paradisea sexsetacea, six shafted paradise bird
8. Trochilus moschitus, ruby topaz hummingbird
9a. Trochilus ornatus, magnificent hummingbird
9b. Trochilus colubris, humming-bird
10. Trochilus delalandii, De Lalande's hummingbird
11. Trochilus minimus, smallest humming bird
12. Trochilus cristatus, crested hummingbird
13. Trochilus macrourus, swallow tailed hummingbird
14. Buphaga africana, beefeater
15. Sturnella ludoviciana, American lark
16. Icterus baltimore, Baltimore oriole

PLATE 100.
Representatives of the Order Passeriformes

Figure
1. Sturnus vulgaris, starling
2. Loxia pityopsittacus, parrot crossbill
3. Coccothraustes vulgaris, hawfinch
4ab. Fringilla canaria, canary bird
5. Fringilla cannabina, red poll
6. Fringilla domestica, house-sparrow
7. Sylvia hippolais, willow wren
8. Oriolus galbula, oriole
9. Merula vulgaris, blackbird
10. Merula saxatilis, rock thrush
11. Pastor roseus, rose colored starling
12. Merula viscivorus, missel thrush
13. Merula iliaca, redwing
14. Merula musica, song thrush

PLATE 101.
Members of the Orders Passeriformes, and Apopodiformes

Figure
1. Trochilus granatinus, garnet humming bird
2. Pyrrhula europea, bullfinch
3. Spermophila crassirostris, thick-billed finch
4. Coccothraustes chloris, green finch
5. Fringilla senegala, senegal finch
6. Fringilla amaduva, amaduvat
7. Vidua regia, king widow bird
8. Vidua erythrorhynchus, red-billed widow bird
9. Carduelis spinus, siskin
10. Carduelis elegans, goldfinch
11. Calliste tatao, seven-colored tanager
12. Fringilla cœlebs, chaffinch
13. Emberiza hortulana, ortolan
14. Emberiza schœniculus, reed bunting
15. Emberiza citrinella, yellowhammer
16. Rupicola aurantia, cock of the rock
17. Muscicapa grisola, grey flycatcher
18. Muscicapa albicollis, white-necked flycatcher
19. Muscicapa regia, king of the flycatchers
20. Ampelis carnifex, scarlet-crested chatterer
21. Ampelis cortinga, banded chatterer

PLATE 102.
Representatives of the Orders Passeriformes and Apopodiformes

Figure
1. Trochilus albicollis, white-necked humming bird
2. Certhia familiaris, brown creeper
3. Parus cristatus, crested tit
4. Parus major, titmouse
5. Alauda calandria, field lark
6. Alauda cristata, crested lark
7. Alauda arvensis, skylark
8. Acanthiza campestris, hedge warbler
9. Cæreba cyanea, blue creeper
10, 11. Phœnicura, redstarts
12. Phœnicura suecica, blue throated Swedish redstart
13. Erythaca rubecula, robin
14. Menura superba, lyre bird
15. Dicrurus forficatus, fork-tailed drongo
16. Cracticus varius, black and white shrike
17. Vauga curvirostris, hooked-bill shrike
18. Laniarius barbarus, Barbary shrike
19. Laniarius collurio, red-backed shrike
20. Laniarius exubitor, butcher bird

PLATE 103.
Members of the Orders Passeriformes, Coraciiformes, and Caprimulgiformes

Figure
1. Buceros erythrorhynchus, red-billed hornbill
2. Buceros rhinoceros, rhinoceros hornbill
3. Halcyon atricapilla, black capped kingfisher
4. Ceryle javanicus, Java kingfisher
5. Alcido ispida, common kingfisher
6. Caprimulgus europæus, goatsucker
7. Hirundo rustica, swallow
8. Cypselus melba, black martin
9. Tyrannus severus, Cayenne flycatcher
10. Milvulus forficatus, South Amer. flycatcher
11. Parus ater, pine tit
12. Regulus auricapillus, golden crested wren
13. Philomela luscinia, nightingale
14. Curruca hortensis, garden warbler
15. Curruca atricapilla, blackcap warbler
16. Phœnicura ruticilla, common redstart
17. Motacilla boarula, grey wagtail
18. Saxicola œnanthe, wheatear

PLATE 104.
Members of the Orders Strigiformes and Falconiformes

Figure
1. Strix flammea, European barn owl
2. Otus brachyotus, short eared owl
3. Otus wilsonianus, long-eared owl
4. Bubo maximus, grand duke
5. Falco peregrinus, wandering falcon
6. Falco œsalon, merlin
7. Milvus regalis, kite
8. Buteo vulgaris, common buzzard
9. Gyps fulvus, griffin vulture
10. Sarcoramphus papa, king vulture
11. Sarcoramphus gryphus, condor

PLATE 105.
Members of the Order Falconiformes

Figure
1. Aquila chrysaëtos, golden eagle
2. Archibuteo niger, black buzzard
3. Pandion ossifragus, osprey
4. Haliaëtus albicilla, sea eagle
5. Astur palumbarius, goshawk
6. Accipiter nisus, sparrow hawk
7. Falco subutes, hobby
8. Falco alaudarius, kestril

PLATE 106.
Chart of the Migrations of Fishes and Birds

GLOSSARY

Aleuten In., Aleutian Islands
Amazonenstrom, Amazon River
Arabien, Arabia
Arabisches M., Arabian Sea
Asien, Asia
Atlantischer Ocean, Atlantic Ocean
Behringsstrasse, Behring's Straits
Baffins Meer, Baffin's Bay
Californien, California
Canarische In., Canary Islands
Cap der guten Hoffnung, Cape of Good Hope
Capstadt, Capetown
Cap Verds In., Cape Verde Islands
Caspisches Meer, Caspian Sea
Donau, Danube
Felsen Geb., Rocky Mountains
Fensterschwalben, Domestic swallows
Feuerland, Terra del Fuego
Freundschafts In., Friendly Islands
Gesellschafts In., Society Islands
Gr. Bären See, Great Bear Lake
Grönland, Greenland
Grossbritannien, Great Britain
Grosser Ocean, Pacific
Häringe, Herrings
Hudsons Meer, Hudson's Bay
I. Melville, Melville Island
Indisches Meer, Indian Ocean

Lissabon, Lisbon
Makrelen, Mackerel
Meerb. v. Bengalen, Bay of Bengal
Meerb. v. Mexico, Bay of Mexico
Mongolei, Mongolia
Neuseeland, New Zealand
Neu Sibirien, New Siberia
Nord Amerika, North America
Nördliches Eismeer, Arctic Sea
Patagonien, Patagonia
Raben u. Krähen, Ravens and crows
Rauchschwalben, Barn swallows
Russisch Amerika, Russian America
Schiffer In., Navigators' Islands
Schleiereulen, Barn owls
Schwarzes Meer, Black Sea
Sibirien, Siberia
Sklavensee, Slave Lake
Stadre u. Amseln, Starlings and blackbirds
Sud Amerika, South America
Uferschwalben, Bank swallows
Verrinigte Staaten, United States
Versammlungs u. Abzugspunkt, Place of meeting and departure
Wachteln, Quails
Warschau, Warsaw
West Indien, West Indies
Wien, Vienna
Wüste Sahara, Desert of Sahara
Zeichenerklärung, Explanation of the marks

PLATE 107.
Mammals of the Order Cetacea: Suborders Odontoceti and Mysteceti

Figure
1. Balæna mysticetus, Greenland whale
2, 3. Physeter macrocephalus, sperm whale
4. Delphinus delphis, dolphin

PLATE 108.
Representatives of the Orders Artiodactyla, Lagomorpha, and Rodentia

Figure
1, 2. Cervus elaphus, stag
3. Cervus dama, fallow deer
4. Cervus capreolus, roebuck
5. Lepus timidus, hare
6. Lepus cuniculus, rabbit
7, 8. Bos taurus, common ox
9. Ovis aries, sheep
10. Capra hircus, goat
11. Sciurus vulgaris, squirrel

PLATE 109.
Representatives of the Order Artiodactyla: Suborders Tylopoda and Ruminantia

Figure
1. Camelus bactrianus, two-humped camel
2. Camelus dromedarius, dromedary
3. Camelopardalis girafa, giraffe
4. Moschus moschiferus, musk
5. Antilope dorcas, gazelle
6. Antilope redunca, antilope of Senegal

PLATE 110.
Members of the Orders Artiodactyla and Perissodactyla

Figure
1. Bison americanus, buffalo
2. Bos bubalus, Indian buffalo
3. Rupicapra tragus, chamois
4. Antilope scripta, Cape-elk
5. Auchenia alpaca, paco
6. Auchenia lama, lama
7. Auchenia vicunna, vicunna
8, 9. Tarandus furcifer, reindeer
10. Cervus alces, eland
11. Siberian horse

PLATE 111.
Members of the Order Perissodactyla: Family Equidae

Figure
1. Equus zebra, zebra
2. Equus asinus, ass
3. Equus mulus, mule
4. Equus caballus, horse
5. Norman team horse
6. Arabian mare and colt
7. Arabian stallion

PLATE 112.
Representatives of the Orders Artiodactyla, Perissodactyla, Hyracoidea, and Proboscidea

Figure
1. Tapir indicus, tapir
2. Hyrax syriacus, daman
3. Dicotyle labiatus, peccary
4. Porcus babyrussa, Asiatic hog
5. Sus domesticus, domestic hog
6. Sus scropha, wild hog
7. Phacochœrus æthiopicus, wart hog
8. Hippopotamus amphibius, hippopotamus
9. Elephas indicus, Indian elephant

PLATE 113.
Representatives of the Orders Edentata, Marsupialia, Pholidota, Carnivora, and Monotremata

Figure
1. Ornithorhynchus anatinus, duck-billed platypus
2. Echidna aculeata, porcupine ant-eater
3. Manis pentadactyla, pangolin
4. Myrmecophaga didactyla, two-toed ant-eater
5. Myrmecophaga jubata, great ant-eater
6. Chlamydophorus truncatus, Chili armadillo
7. Dasypus sexcinctus, six-girdled armadillo
8. Dasypus novemcinctus, nine-girdled armadillo
9. Bradypus didactylus, sloth
10. Bradypus tridactylus, aï
11*ab*. Halmaturus laniger, rufous kangaroo
12*ab*. Halmaturus dorsalis, ashy kangaroo
13. Didelphys murina, Brazilian opossum
14. Didelphys virginiana, Virginia opossum
15. Nasua rufa, brown coati

PLATE 114.
Representatives of the Orders Insectivora Carnivora, Rodentia and Lagomorpha

Figure
1. Chinchilla lanigera, chinchilla
2*a*. Cavia cobaya, Guinea pig
2*b*. Lagomys alpinus, pika
3*a*. Cercolabes villosus, Brazil porcupine
3*b*. See 16 [mistake of the engraver]
4. Hystrix cristatus, European porcupine
5. Halamys caffer, Cape jerboa
6. Mus sylvaticus, field mouse
7. Mus rattus, black rat
8. Mus musculus, common mouse
9. Cricetus vulgaris, hamster
10. Myoxus glis, dormouse
11. Arctomys alpinus, marmot
12, 13. Pteromys volucella, flying squirrel
14. Sciurus carolinensis, grey squirrel
15. Sciurus maximus, Malabar squirrel
16. Lutra vulgaris, European otter
17. Talpa europæa, European mole
18. Erinaceus europæus, European hedgehog

PLATE 115.
Representatives of the Orders Rodentia and Carnivora

Figure
1. Castor fiber americanus, beaver
2. Phoca vitulina, seal
3. Trichechus rosmarus, walrus
4. Felis domesticus, cat
5. Felis domesticus angorensis, Angora cat
6. Hyæna striata, striped hyena
7. Canis aureus, jackal
8. Canis lupus, wolf
9. Canis familiaris pastoreus, shepherd's dog
10. Lutra canadensis, Canada otter
11. Ursus maritimus, white polar bear

PLATE 116.
Members of the Order Carnivora: Family Felidae

Figure
1. Felis leo, lion
2. Felis tigris, tiger
3. Felis leopardus, leopard
4. Felis onca, jaguar
5. Felis pardus, panther
6. Lynx europæus, lynx

PLATE 117.
Representatives of the Order Carnivora: Families Canidae, Ursidae, and Mustelidae

Figure
1. Vulpes fulvus, red fox
2. Meles vulgaris, badger
3. Mustela martes, marten
4. Mustela foina, beech marten
5. Mustela putorius, polecat
6. Putorius furo, ferret
7. Putorius vulgaris, weasel
8. Putorius erminea, ermine
9. Ursus arctos, brown bear
10. Ursus americanus, black bear
11. Canis familiaris sibericus, Siberian dog
12. Canis familiaris, domestic dog
13. Canis familiaris molossus, bull dog
14. Canis familiaris leporarius, greyhound
15. Canis familiaris normanus, chase dog
16. Canis familiaris vertagus, badger dog

PLATE 118.
Representatives of the Orders Chiroptera and Primates

Figure
1. Galeopithecus rufus, flying lemur
2. Plecotus timoriensis, long-eared bat
3. Vespertilio noctula, common bat
4. Vespertilio serotinus, serotine bat
5. Vespertilio murinus, European bat
6. Rhinolophus ferrum equinum, horse-shoe bat
7. Megaderma lyra, broadwinged bat
8. Vampyrus spectrum, vampire
9. Pteropus vulgaris, roussette
10. Otolicnus senegalensis, galago
11. Lemur pusillus, fox-nosed maki

12. Lemur macao, maki
13. Cynocephalus maimon, mandrill
14. Cercopithecus diana, holoway
15. Hylobates agilis, agile gibbon

PLATE 119.
Representatives of the Orders Perissodactyla and Primates

Figure
1. Rhinocerus indicus, Indian rhinoceros
2, 3. Cebus capucinus, capucin
4. Macacus cynomolgus, hare-lipped monkey
5. Cercopithecus ruber, patras
6. Cercopithecus griseus, grey patras
7. Macacus silenus, maned macaque
8. Cynocephalus sphinx, baboon
9. Inuus ecaudatus, Barbary ape
10. Troglodytes niger, chimpanse
11. Pithecus satyrus, orang outang

ANTHROPOLOGY AND SURGERY

PLATE 120.
Varieties of Mankind

Figure
1–9. Varieties of mankind
10–12. Facial angles
Center figure. Chart of the five races of Blumenbach

GLOSSARY

I. *Kaukasische oder Weisse Race*, Caucasian or White Race
II. *Mongolische oder Gelbe Race*, Mongolian or Yellow Race
III. *Æthiopische oder Schwarze Race*, Ethiopian or Black Race
IV. *Amerikanische oder Kupferfarbige Race*, American or Copper-colored Race
V. *Malayische oder Olivenfarbige Race*, Malay or Olive-colored Race
F. 1 bis 4. Grundzüge (Typus) der Kaukasischen Race, Figures 1–4. Types of the Caucasian Race
Figur 5. Grundzüge der Mongolischen Race, Figure 5. Type of the Mongolian Race
Figur 6. Grundzüge der Æthiopischen Race, Figure 6 Type of the Ethiopian Race
F. 7, 8. Grundzüge der Kupferfarbigen Race, Figures 7, 8. Type of the Copper-colored Race
Figure 9. Grundzüge der Olivenfarbigen Race, Figure 9. Type of the Olive-colored Race

Afghanen, Afghans
Algonkiren, Algonkins
Araber, Arabs
Azteken, Azteks
Berbern, Berbers
Birmanen, Birmans
Bucharen, Bucharians
Caffern, Caffres
Californier, Californians
Canadier, Canadians
Caraiben, Caribbeans
Celten, Celts
Chaldäer, Chaldæans
Chinesen, Chinese
Cinbebassen, Cinbebasses
Colombier, Colombians
Eleuten, Aleutians
Eskimos, Esquimaux
Ethiopier, Ethiopians
Fellatas, Fellatah
Finnen, Finns
Germanen, Germans
Gothen, Goths
Hindus, Hindoos
Hottentotten, Hottentots
Iberier, Iberians
Jakuten, Yacoots
Japanesen, Japanese
Jukaghiren, Youkaghirs
Kalmücken, Calmucks
Kamtschadalen, Kamskadales
Kaukasier, Caucasians
Kirghisen, Kirghese
Koriälen, Koreans
Kosaken, Cossacks
Kriks, Creek Indians
Lappen, Laplanders
Letten, Lethonians
Madagassen, Madagassées
Mandschus, Manchoos
Mauren, Moors
Mongolen, Mongols
Neger, Negroes
Negritos, Negritoes
Neuseeländer, New Zealanders
Osagen, Osages
Osmanen, Osmanli
Ostiaken, Ostiaks
Patagonen, Patagonians
Pelasger, Pelasgians
Perser, Persians
Samojeden, Samoeids
Sius, Sioux Indians
Slaven, Slavonians
Soyten, Soyetes
Tibetaner, Thibetans
Tschucktschen, Tchoukches
Tungusen, Tungus
Wogulen, Voguls

PLATE 121.
Illustrating the Psychological Relations of the Brain (Phrenology)

Figures 1–21.

PLATE 122.
The Bones of the Head

Figures 1–19.

PLATE 123.
Anatomy of the Bones

Figures 1–31.

PLATE 124.
Anatomy of the Bones

Figures 1–50.

PLATE 125.
Anatomy of the Ligaments and Muscles

Figure
1–14. Anatomy of the ligaments
15–17. Anatomy of the muscles

PLATE 126.
Anatomy of the Ligaments and Muscles

Figure
1–18. Anatomy of the ligaments
19, 20. Anatomy of the muscles

PLATE 127.
Anatomy of the Ligaments and Muscles

Figure
1–19. Anatomy of the ligaments
20, 21. Anatomy of the muscles

PLATE 128.
Anatomy of the Muscles

Figures 1–15.

PLATE 129.
Anatomy of the Muscles

Figures 1–19.

PLATE 130.
Anatomy of the Fasciae, Integuments, and Organs of Mastication and Respiration

Figure
1–22. Anatomy of the fasciæ
23–26. Anatomy of the integuments
27–30. Organs of mastication and deglutition
31–38. Organs of respiration and voice

PLATE 131.
Anatomy of the Organs of Digestion

Figures 1–21.

PLATE 132.
Anatomy of the Eye

Figures 1–45.

PLATE 133.
Anatomy of the Ear and Nose

Figure
1–25. Anatomy of the ear
26–45. Anatomy of the nose

PLATE 134.
Anatomy of the Vascular System

Figures 1–13.

PLATE 135.
Anatomy of the Vascular System

Figures 1–13.

PLATE 136.
Anatomy of the Vascular System

Figures 1–17.

PLATE 137.
Anatomy of the Vascular System

Figures 1–16.

PLATE 138.
Anatomy of the Brain and Nerves

Figures 1–21.

PLATE 139.
Anatomy of the Nerves

Figures 1–14.

PLATE 140.
Various Surgical Operations

Figures 1–35.

PLATE 141.
Various Surgical Instruments

Figures 1–90.

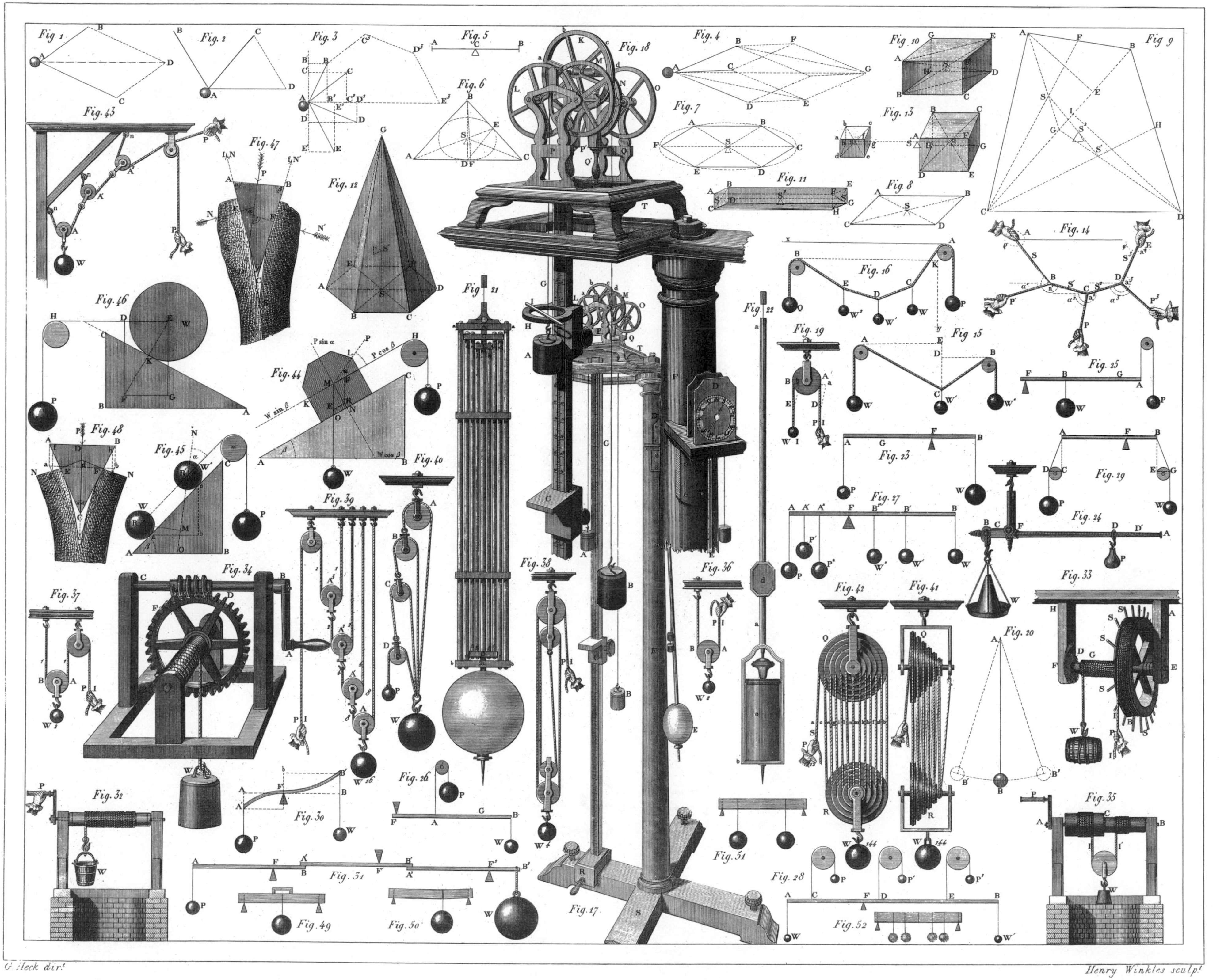

PLATE 16. THEORIES OF FORCE AND GRAVITY; DEMONSTRATIONS OF THESE AND OTHER PHYSICAL LAWS

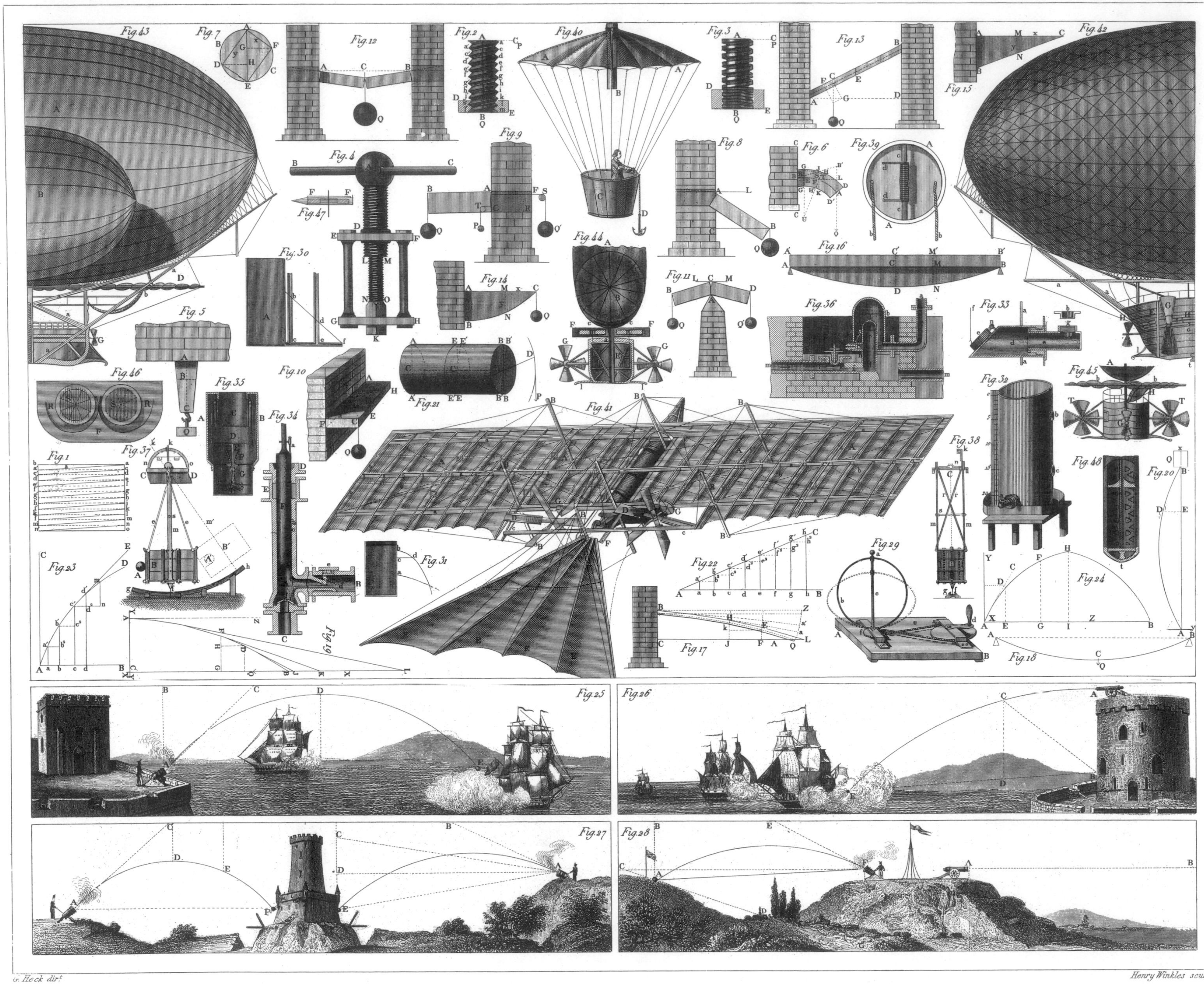

G. Heck dir.t Henry Winkles sculp.t

PLATE 17. ILLUSTRATING THEORIES OF DYNAMICS AND OTHER PHYSICAL LAWS

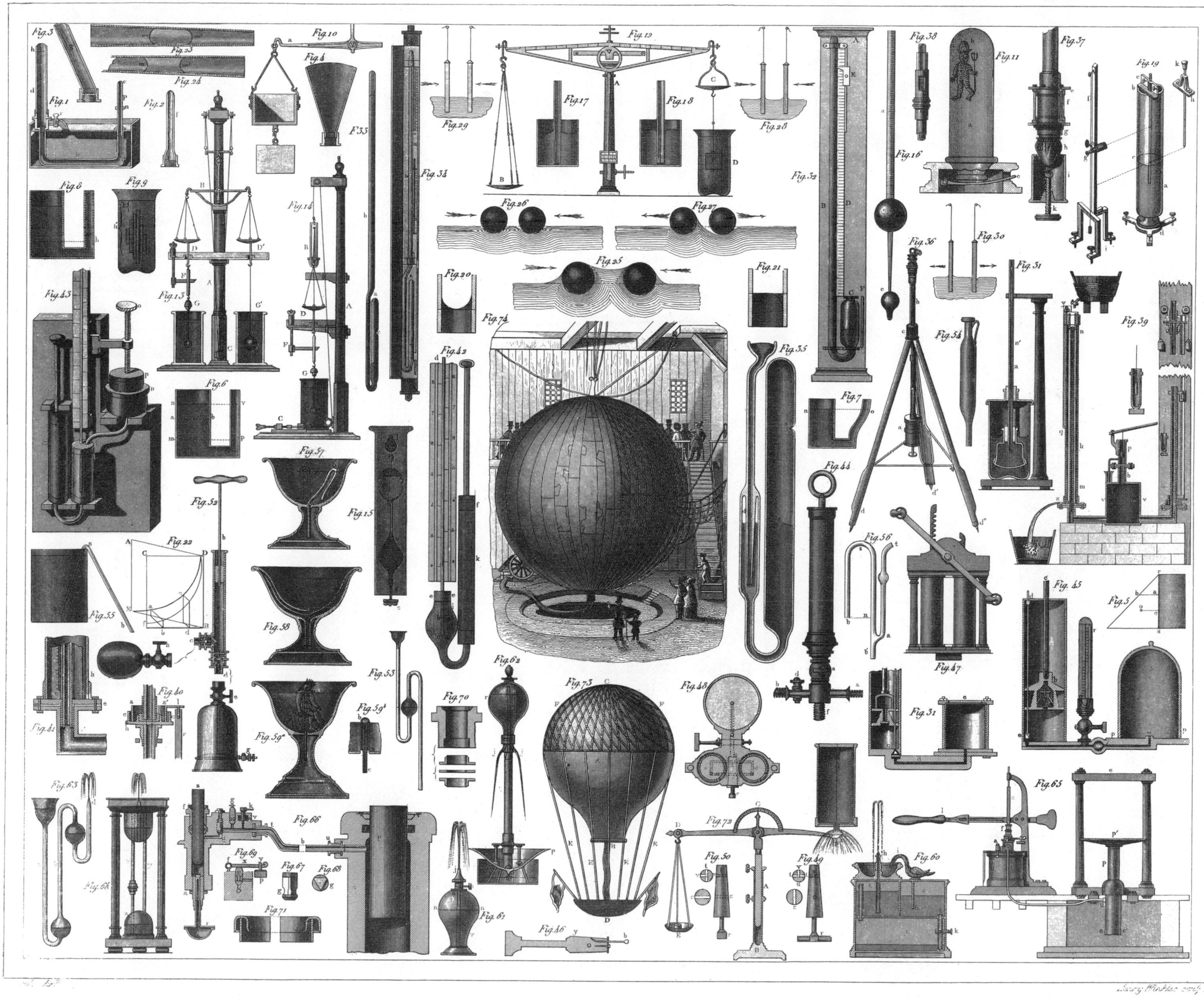

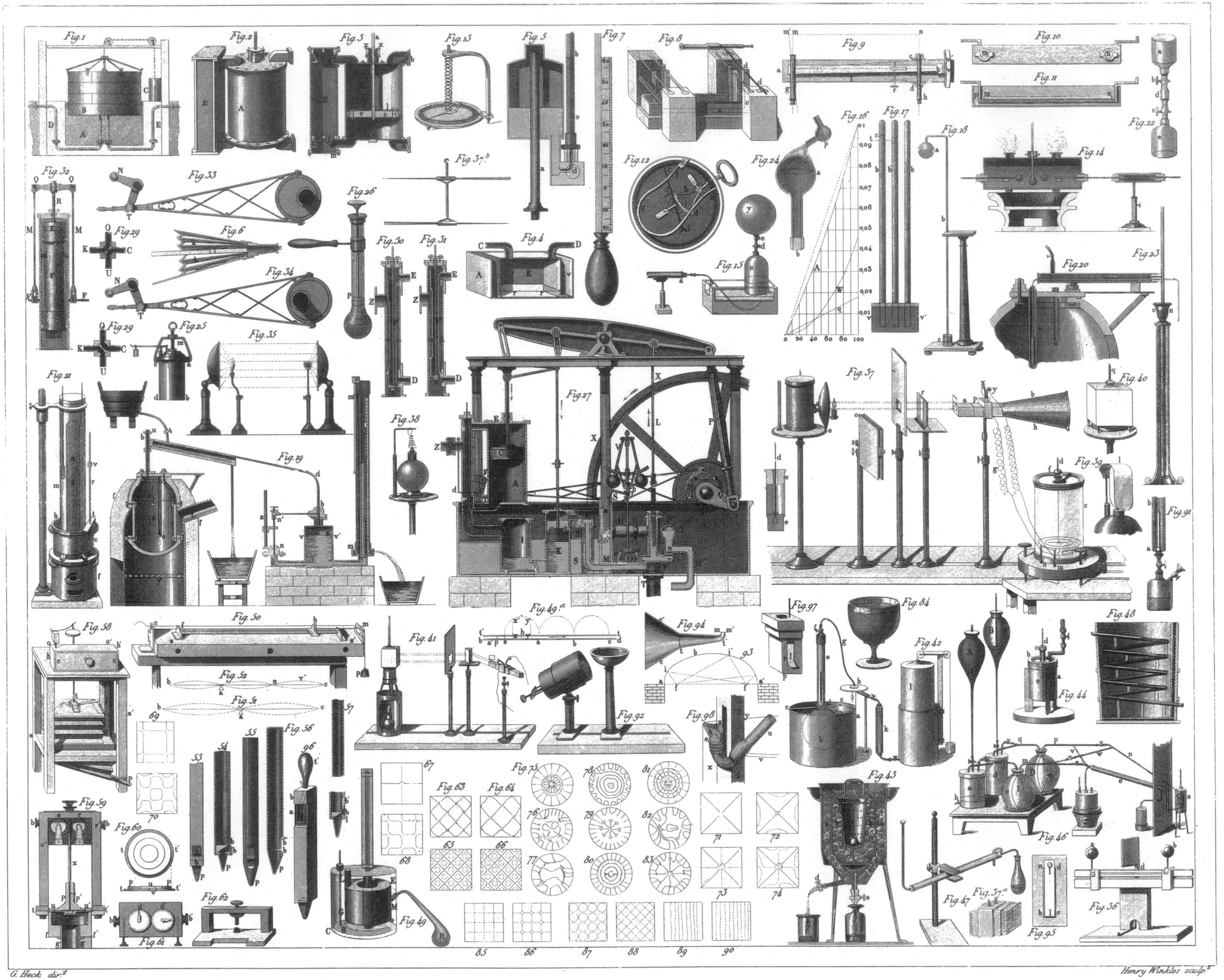

G. Heck dir.t

Henry Winkles sculp.t

PLATE 19. THEORIES AND INSTRUMENTS OF MECHANICS, THERMODYNAMICS, AND ACOUSTICS

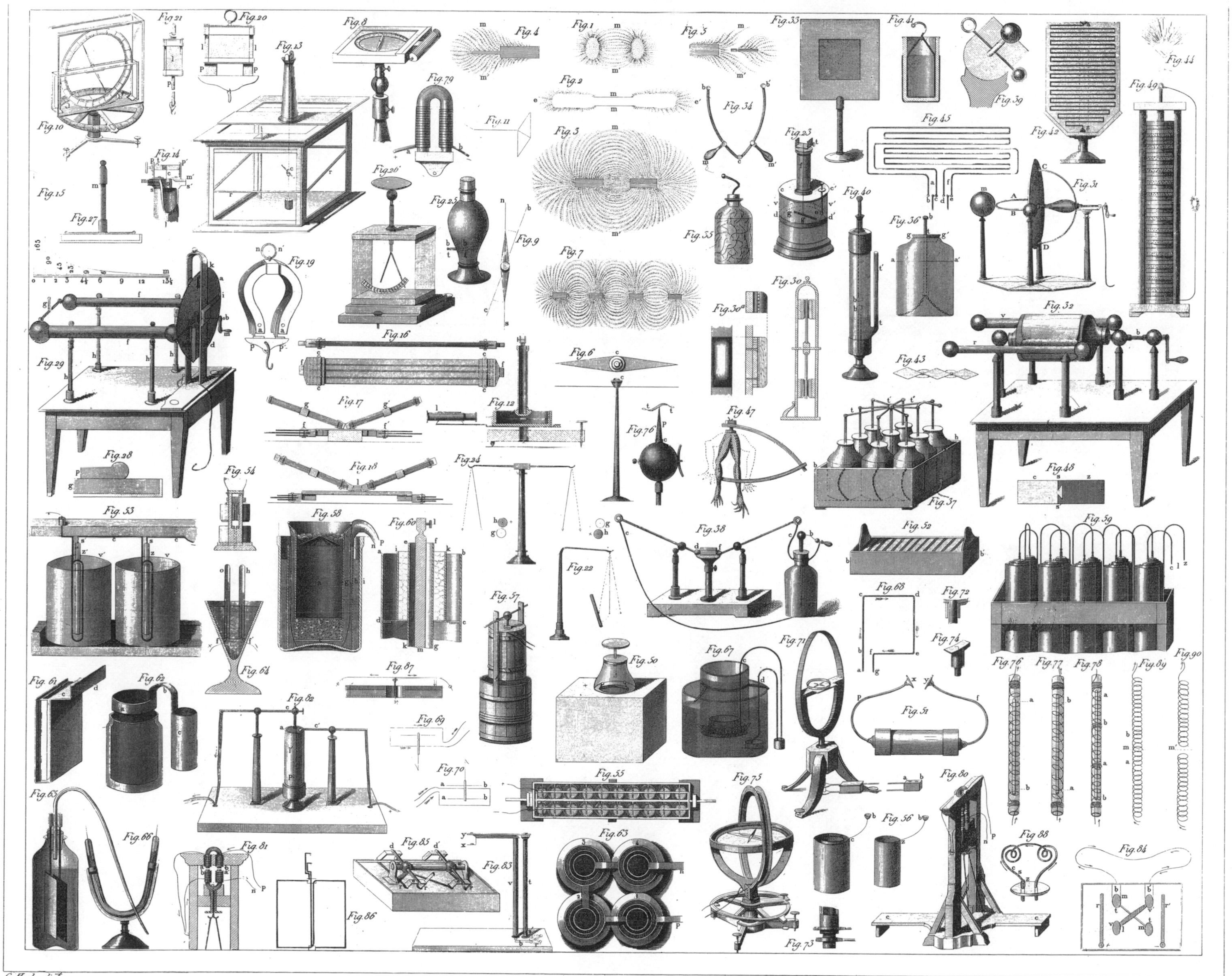

G. Heck dir.^t

Henry Winkles sculp.^t

PLATE 20. THEORIES AND INSTRUMENTS OF ELECTRICITY AND MAGNETICS

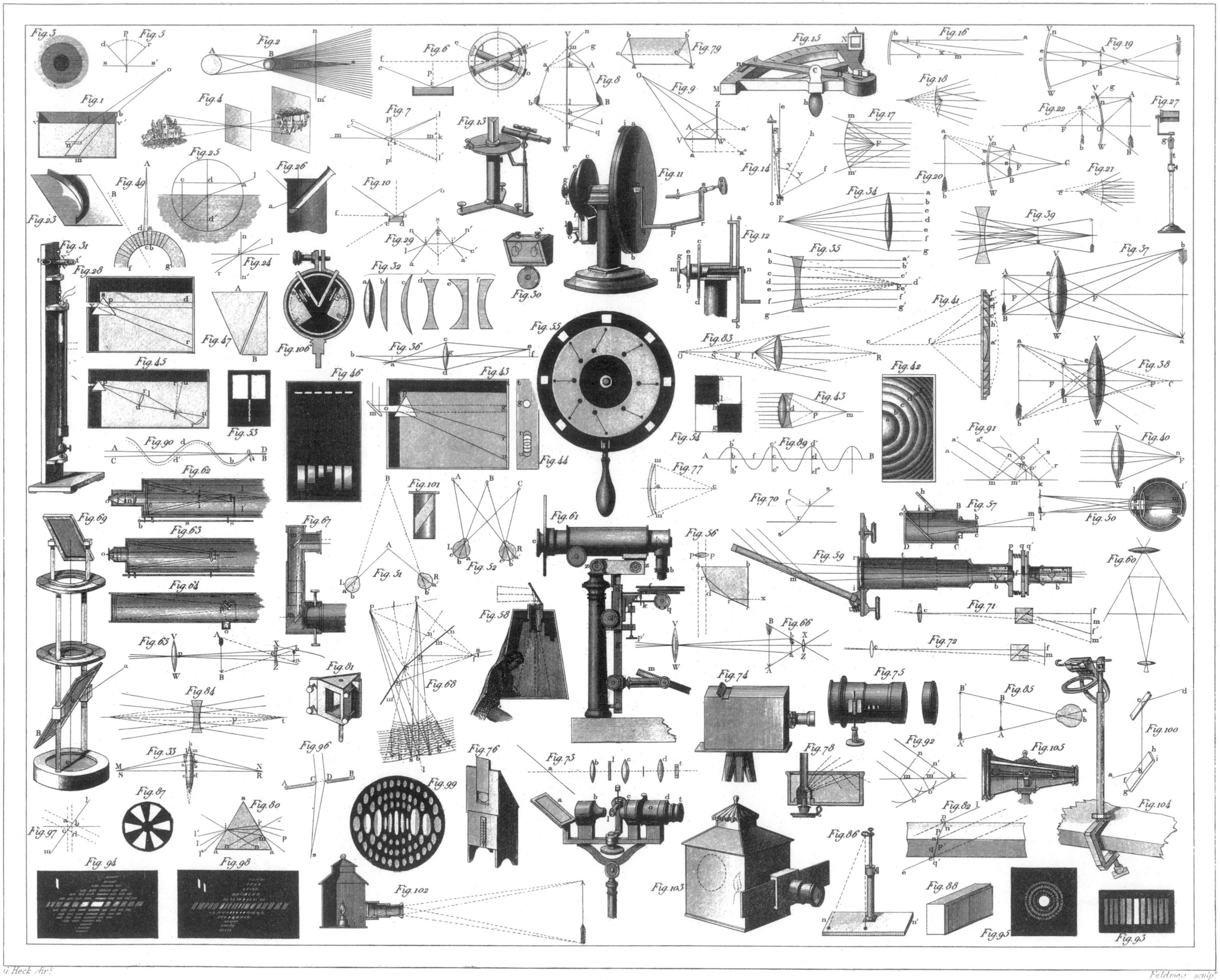

G. Heck dir.   Feldweg sculp.

 PLATE 21. THEORIES AND INSTRUMENTS OF OPTICS

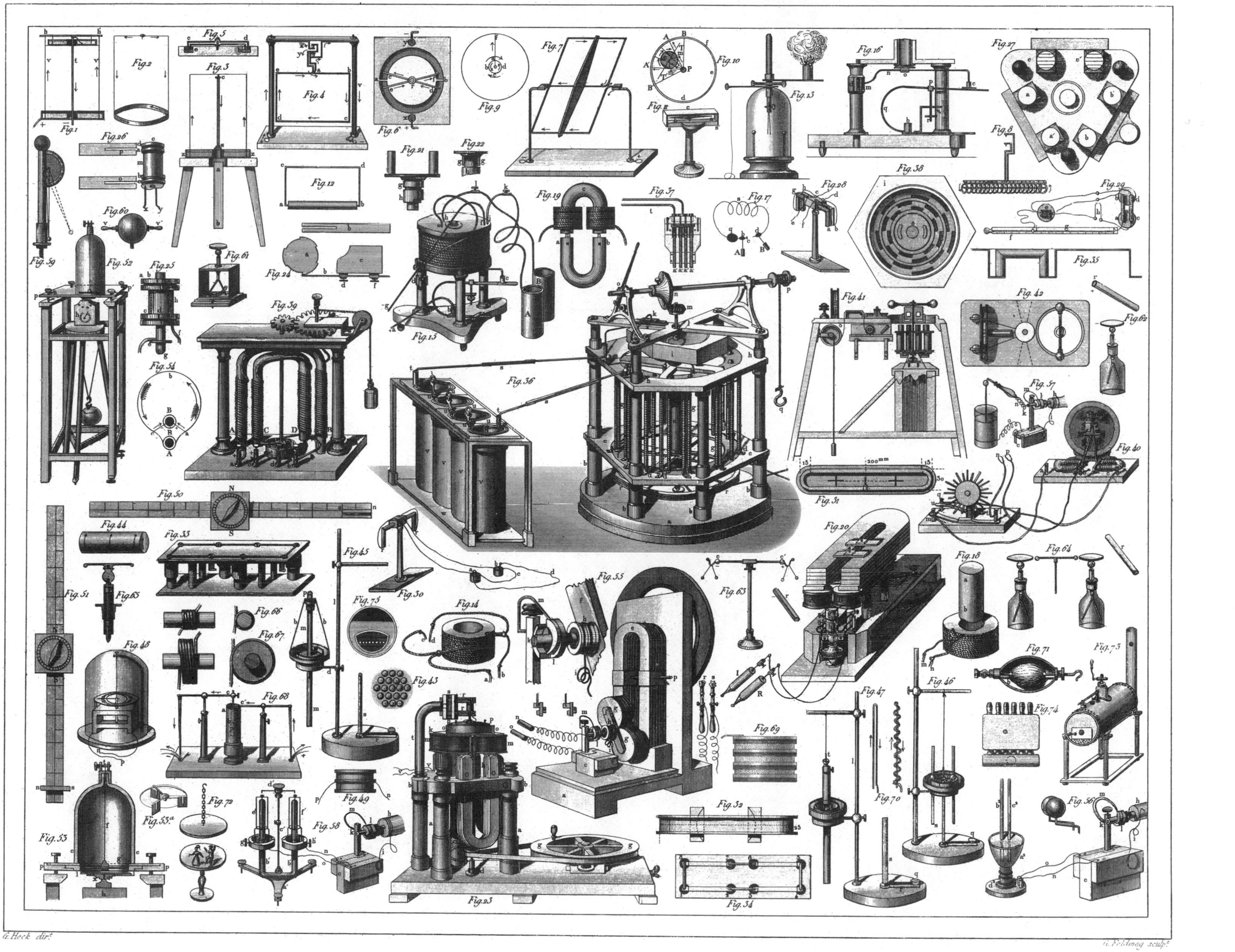

G.Heck dir.t G.Feldweg sculp.t

PLATE 22. PHENOMENA AND APPARATUS OF ELECTRICITY AND MAGNETICS

G. Heck dir.

Henry Winkles sculp.

PLATE 23. SUN RAYS, WINDS, PRECIPITATION, AND CONDENSATION PHENOMENA

G. Heck dir.t

Henry Winkles sculp.t

PLATE 24. PHENOMENA OF CONDENSATION AND AIR CURRENTS

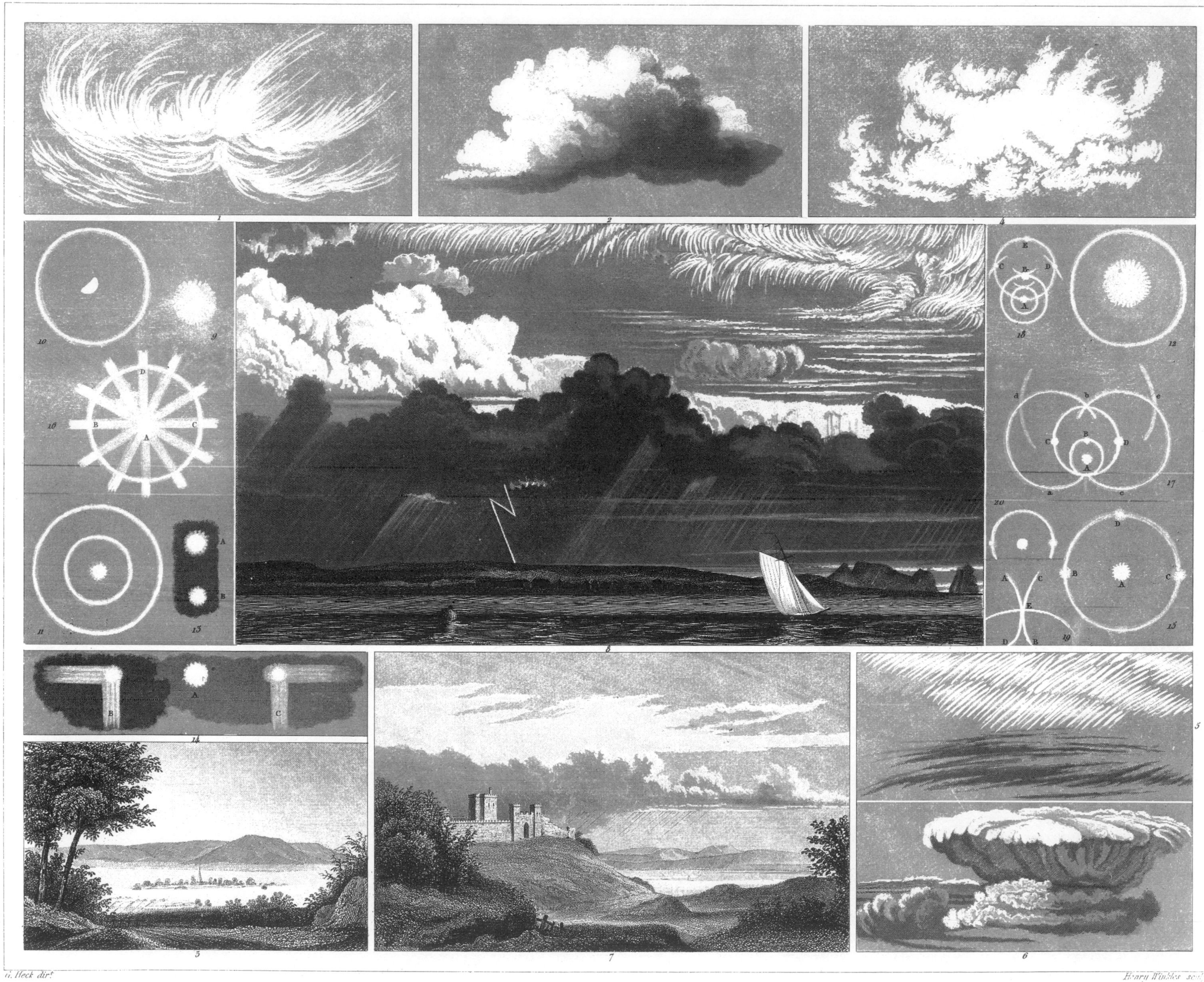

G. Heck dir.t

Henry Winkles sculp.

PLATE 25. CLOUD FORMATION AND LIGHT REFRACTION

PLATE 26. PHENOMENA OF CLOUDS AND LIGHT

 PLATE 27. METEOROLOGICAL ELEMENTS AND INSTRUMENTS

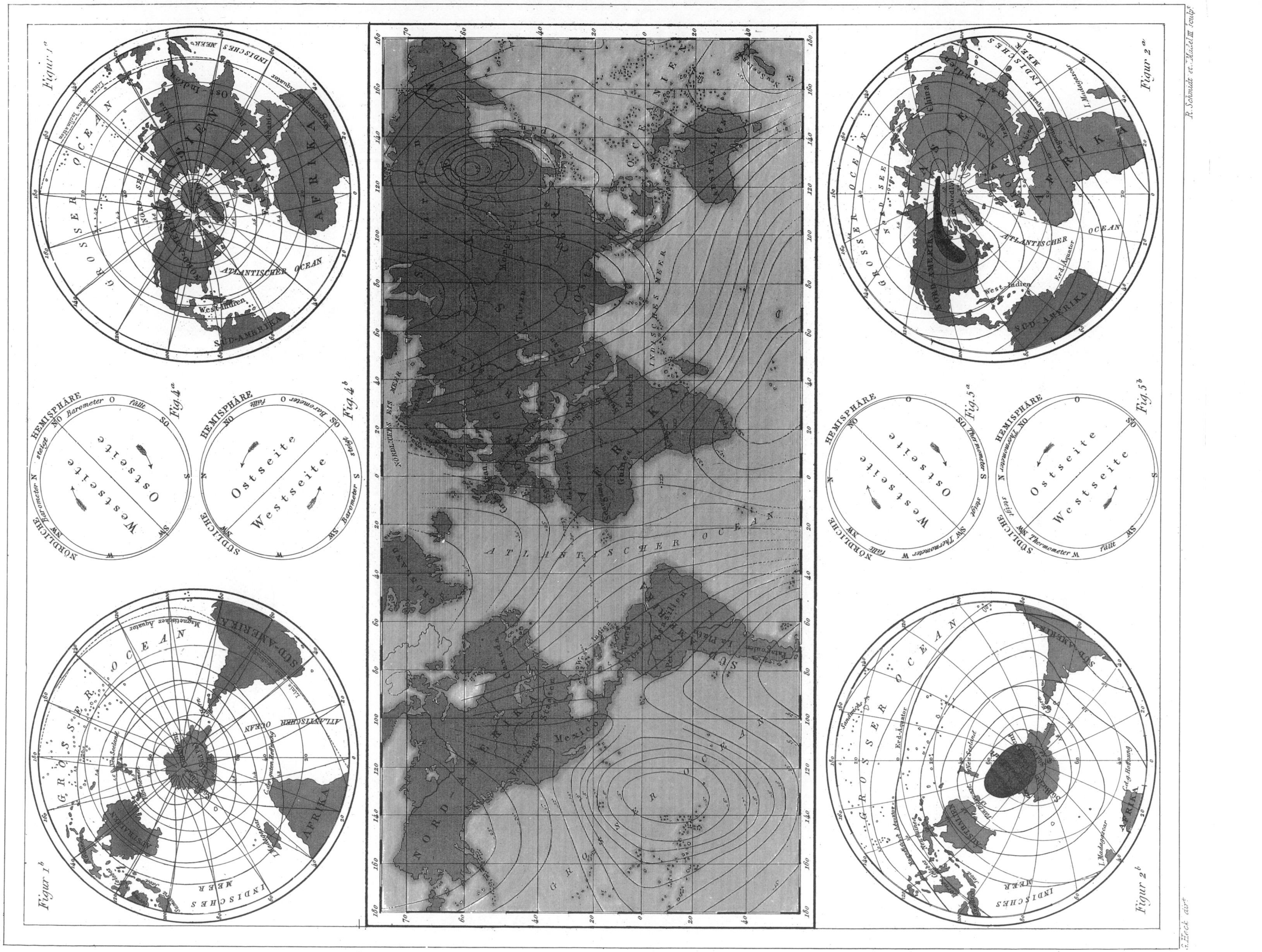
Figur 1a
Figur 2a
Figur 1b
Figur 2b
Fig. 4a
Fig. 4b
Fig. 5a
Fig. 5b
NÖRDLICHE HEMISPHÄRE
SÜDLICHE HEMISPHÄRE
Ostseite
Westseite
Barometer
Thermometer
steigt
fällt
ATLANTISCHER OCEAN
GROSSER OCEAN
INDISCHES MEER
AFRIKA
ASIEN
SÜD-AMERIKA
NORD-AMERIKA
AUSTRALIEN
West-Indien
Magnetischer Äquator
Erd-Äquator
Mexico
China
L. Madagascar

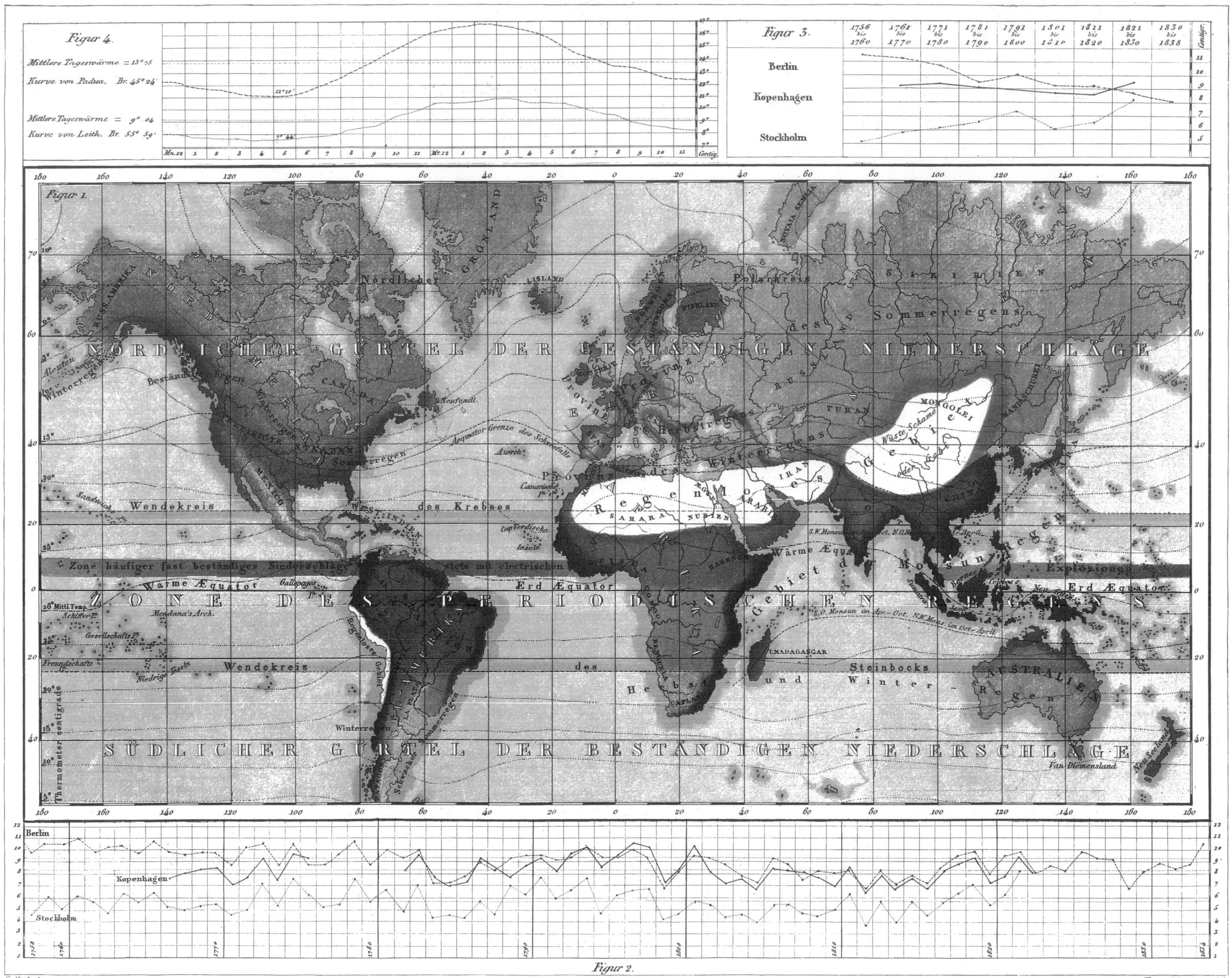

G. Heck del. Henry Winkles sculp.

PLATE 29. RAINFALL AND TEMPERATURE MAP; TEMPERATURE CHARTS

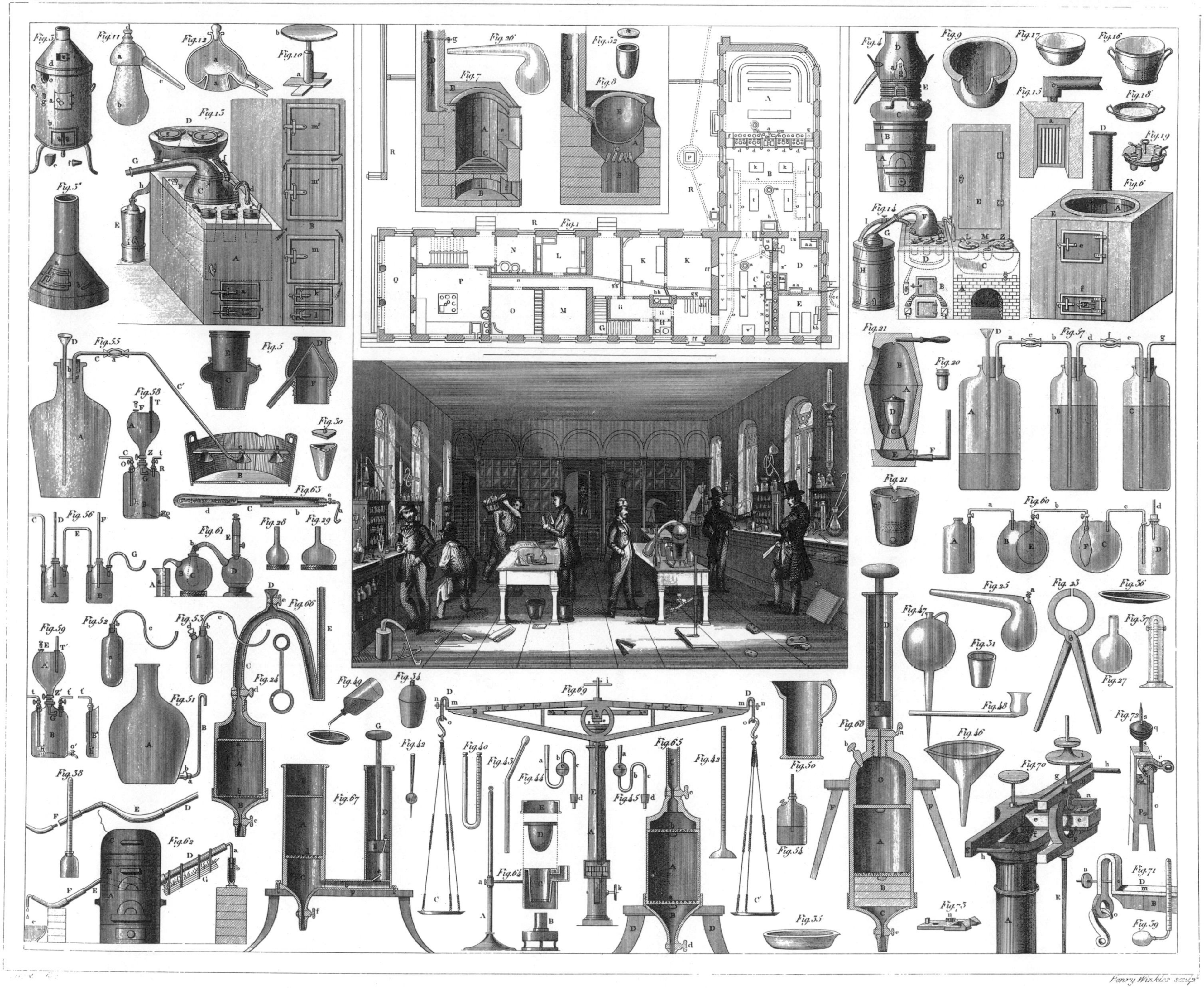

PLATE 30. CHEMICAL LABORATORY, APPARATUS, AND EQUIPMENT

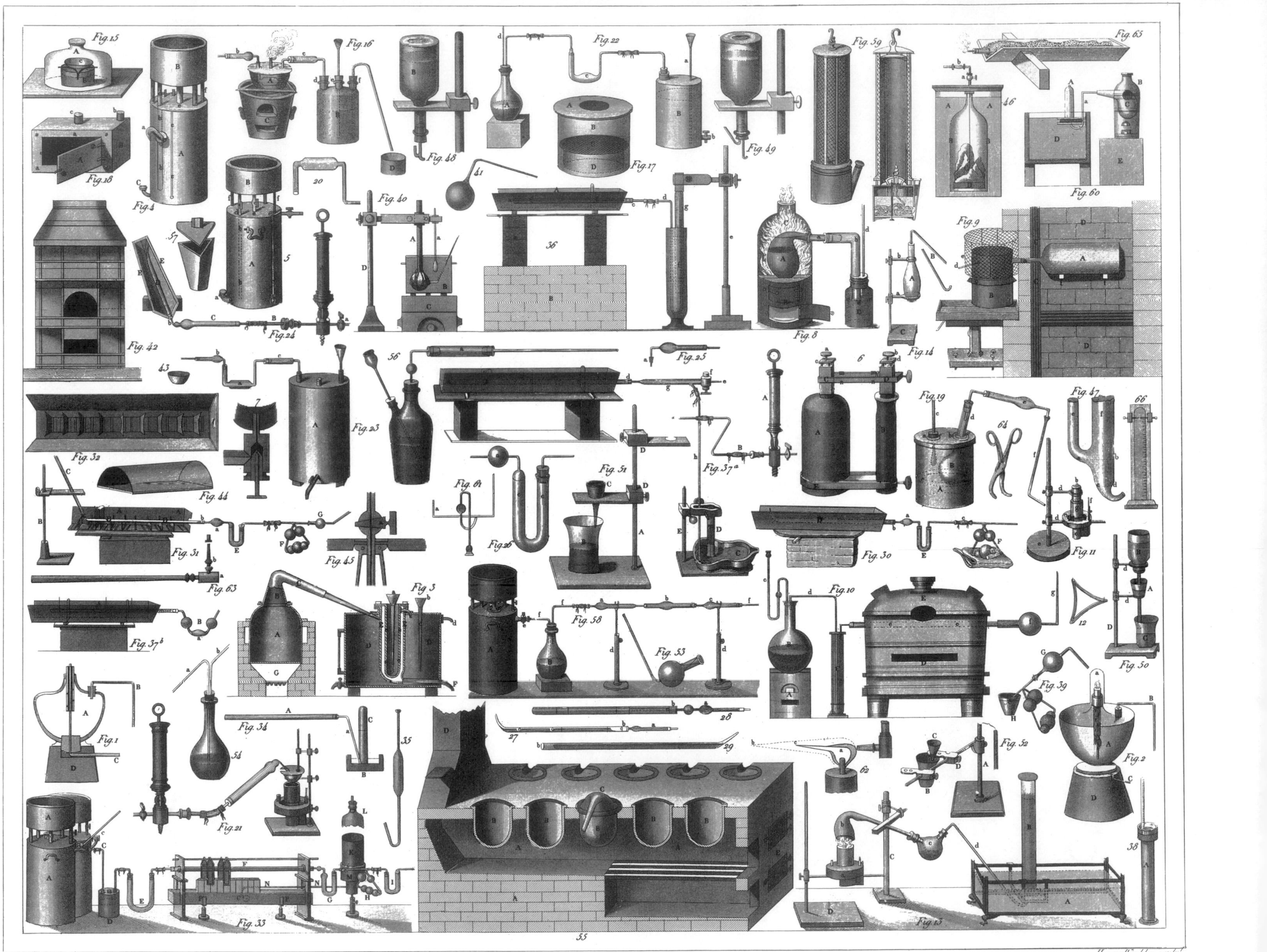

G. Heck dir.t

Henry Winkles sculp.t

 PLATE 31. CHEMICAL APPARATUS AND EQUIPMENT

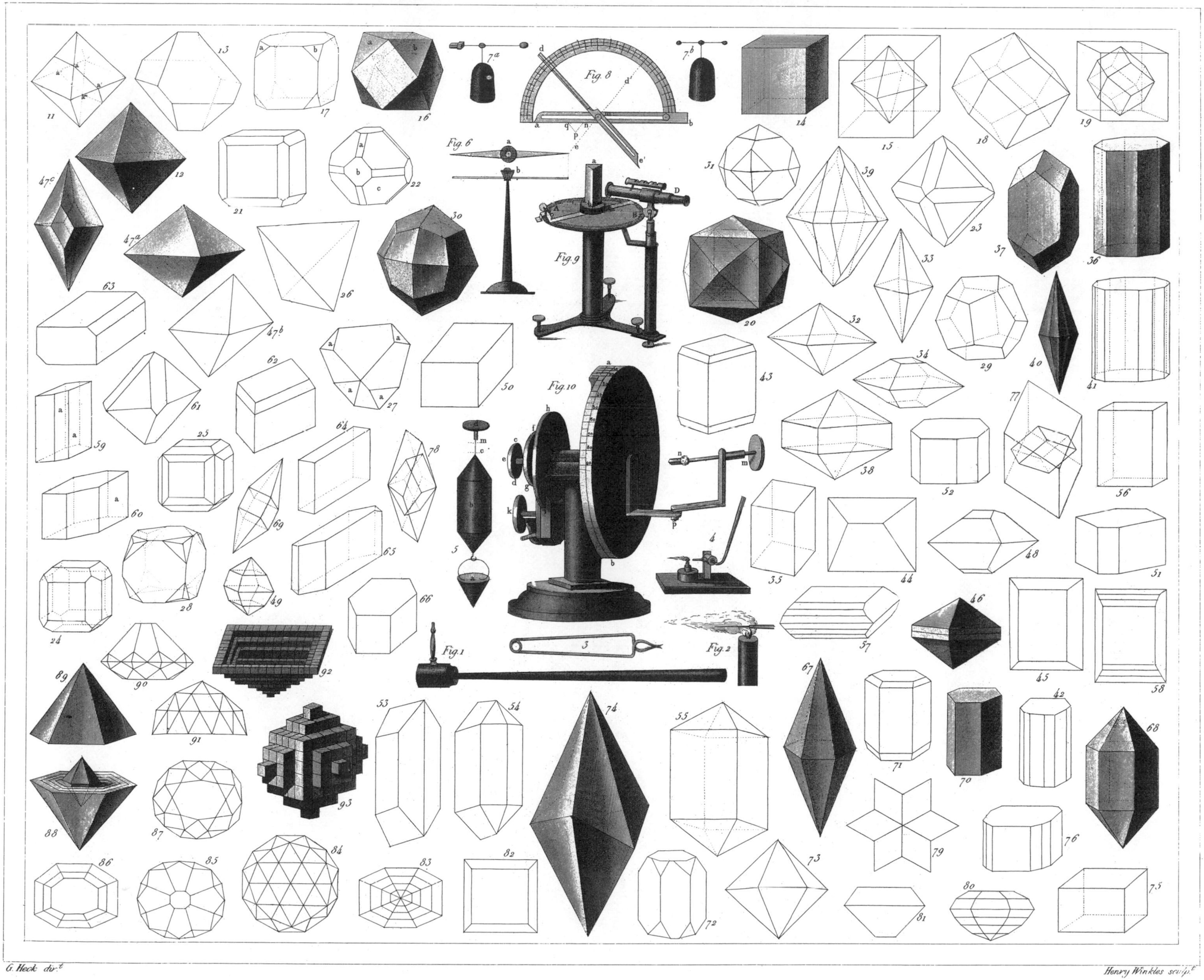

PLATE 32. FORMS OF CRYSTALLIZATION; VARIOUS INSTRUMENTS

G. Heck dir.t

Henry Winkles sculp.t

PLATE 33. MINERALS AND THEIR CRYSTALLINE FORMS

G. Heck dir.t *Henry Winkles sculp.t*

PLATE 34. MINERALS AND THEIR CRYSTALLINE FORMS

G. Heck dir.[t] *Henry Winkles sculp.*[t]

PLATE 35. MINERALS AND THEIR CRYSTALLINE FORMS

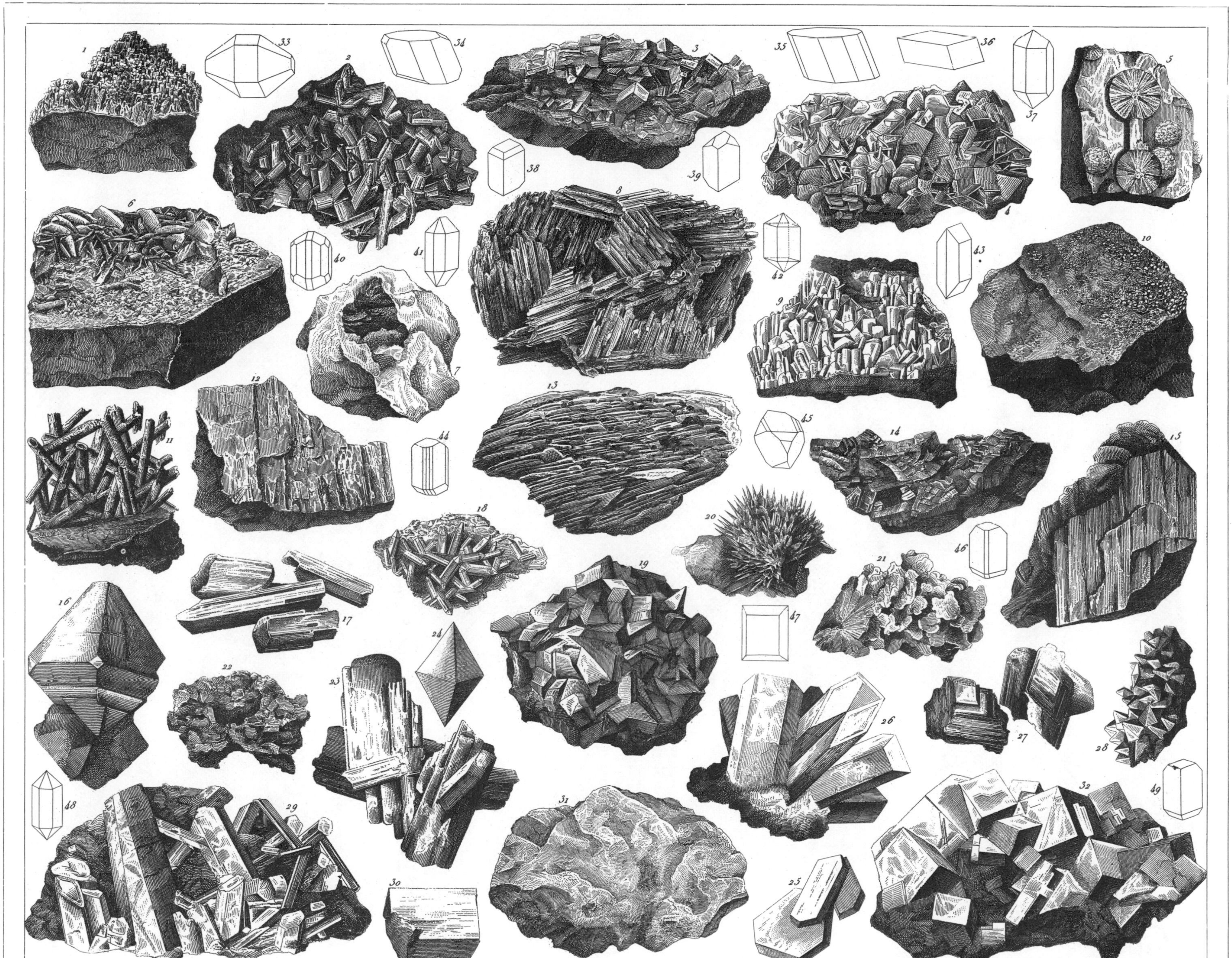

PLATE 36. MINERALS AND THEIR CRYSTALLINE FORMS

G. Heck dir.t

Henry Winkles sculp.t

PLATE 37. FOSSILS AND REPRESENTATION OF ANIMALS OF THE LIAS

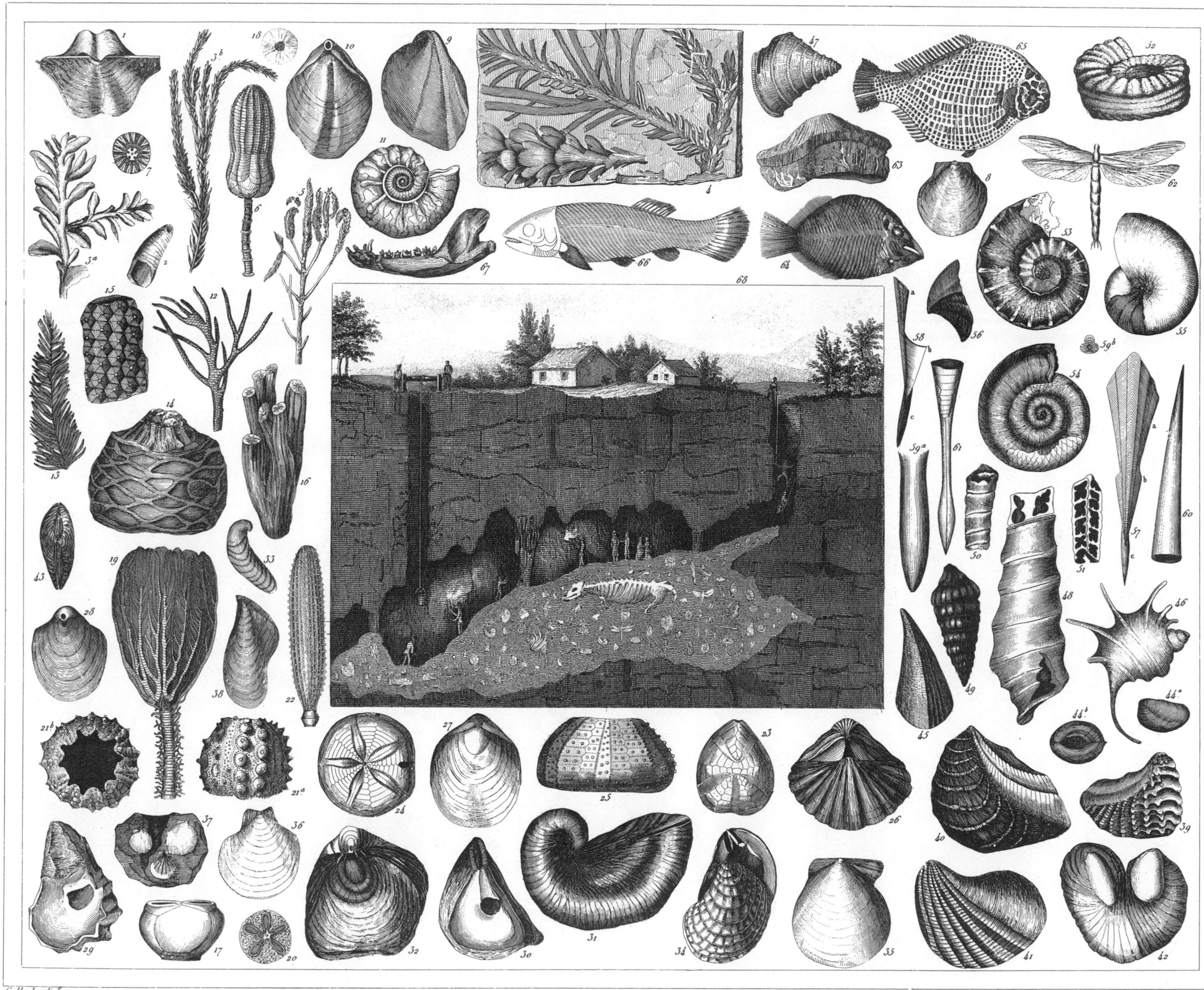

G. Heck dir.[t]

Henry Winkles sculp.[t]

PLATE 38. SECTION OF THE WIRKSWORTH CAVE AND FOSSILS

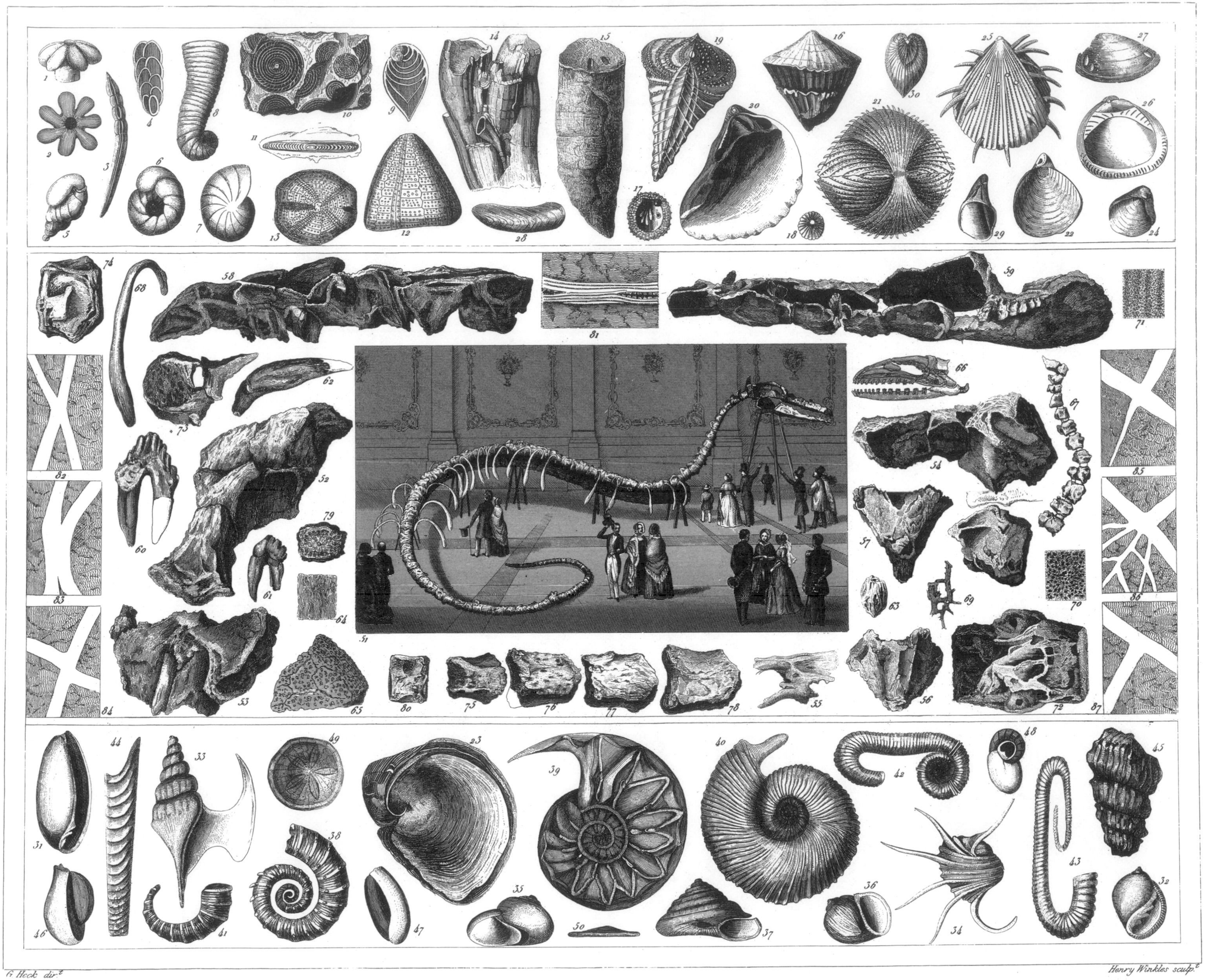

G. Heck dir.^t

Henry Winkles sculp.^t

PLATE 39. FOSSILS, A SKELETON, AND VEINS OF ORE

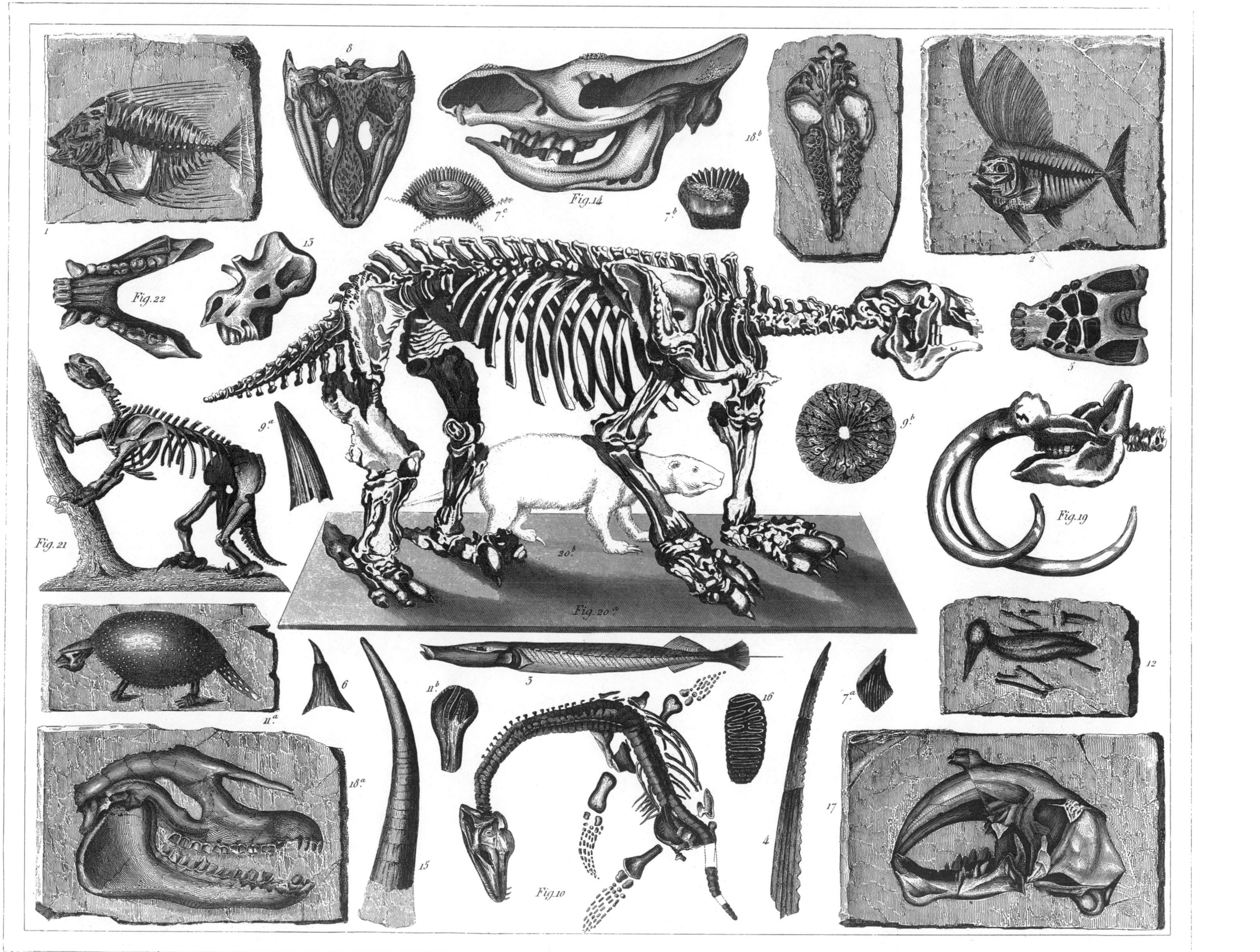

Fig.14
Fig.22
Fig.21
Fig.19
Fig.20
Fig.10

G. Heck dir.	Henry Winkles sculp.

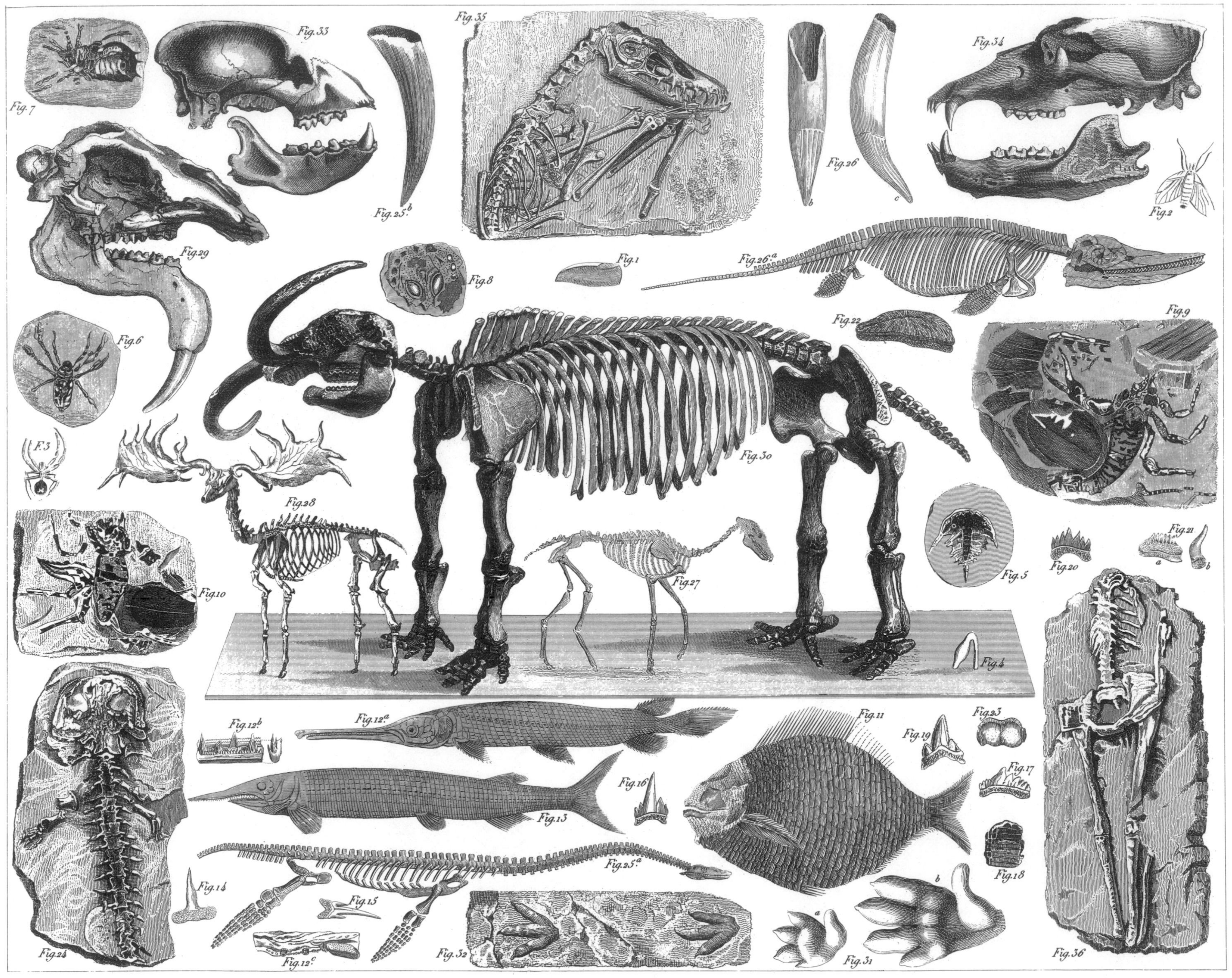

G. Heck dir.t

Henry Winkles sculp.t

PLATE 41. FOSSILS, SKELETONS, AND TRACKS

G. Heck dir.t Henry Winkles sculp.t

G. Heck dir.t Henry Winkles sculp.t

PLATE 43. ROCK AND VALLEY FORMATIONS AND STRATIFICATION

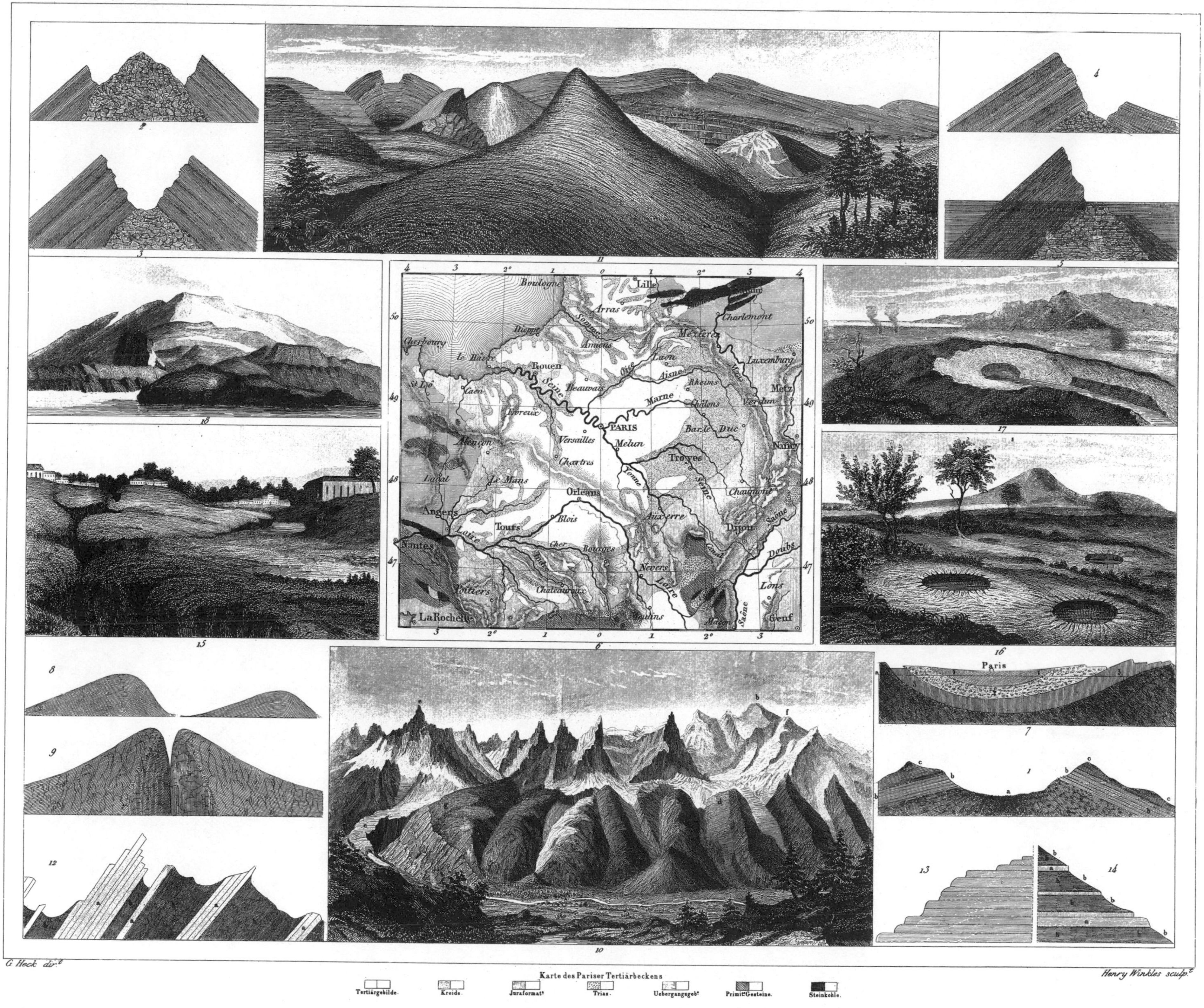

PLATE 44. STRATIFICATION IN MOUNTAINS AND BASINS; FISSURES AND CRATERS

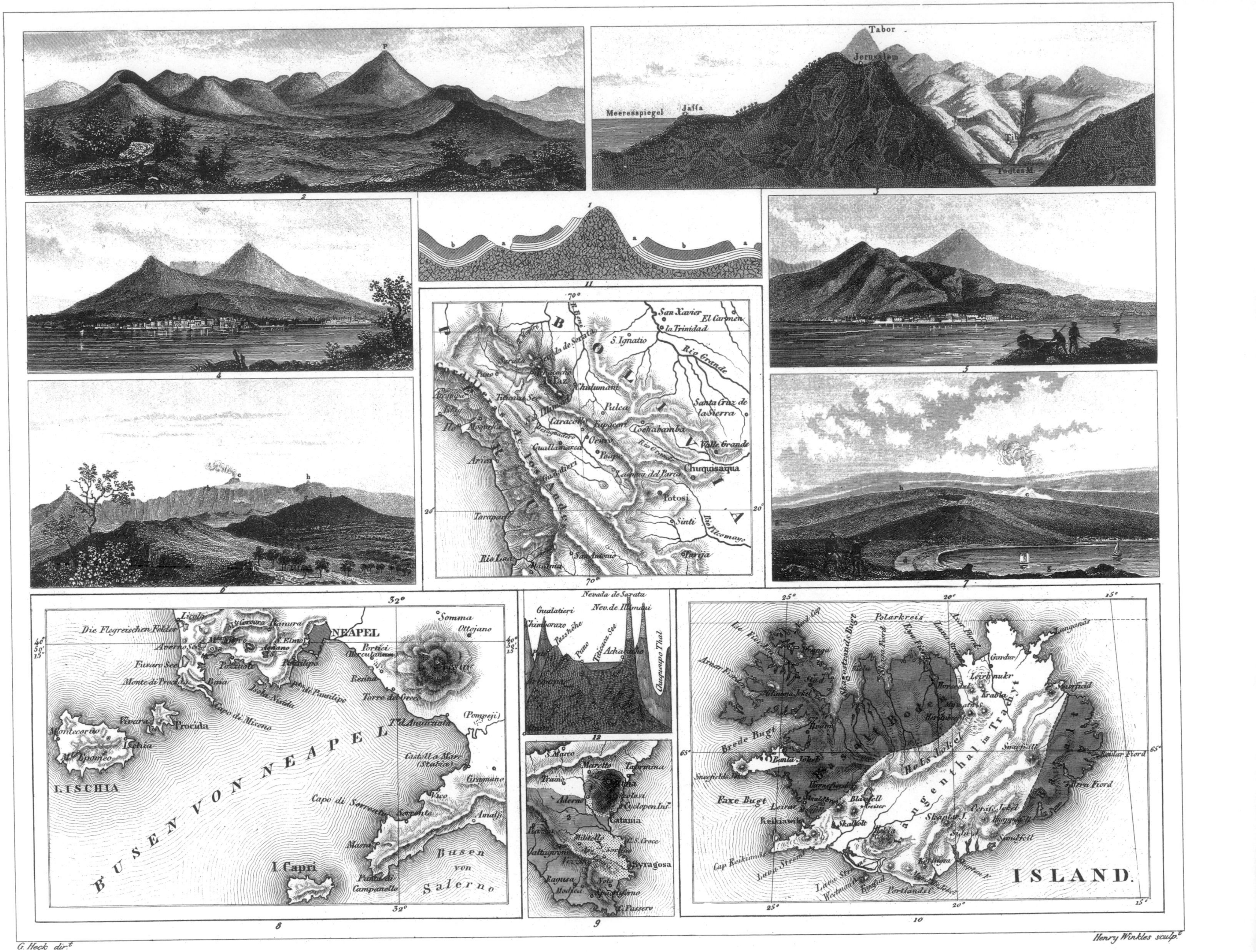

G. Heck dir.^t

Henry Winkles sculp.^t

PLATE 45. VOLCANOES AND VOLCANIC FORMATIONS

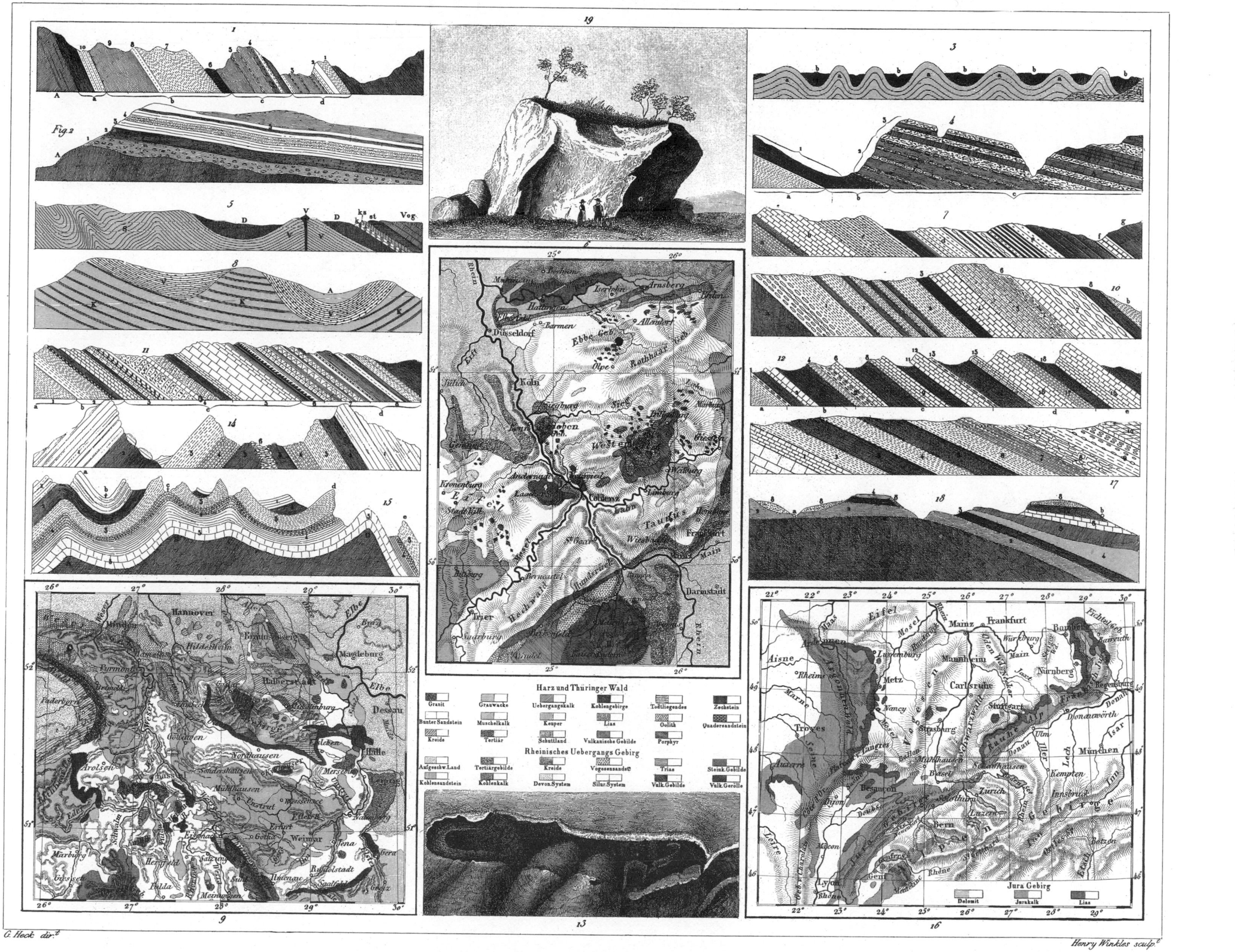
Harz und Thüringer Wald
Granit
Grauwacke
Uebergangskalk
Kohlengebirge
Todtliegendes
Zechstein
Bunter Sandstein
Muschelkalk
Keuper
Lias
Oolith
Quadersandstein
Kreide
Tertiär
Schuttland
Vulkanische Gebilde
Porphyr
Rheinisches Uebergangs Gebirg
Aufgeschw. Land
Tertiärgebilde
Kreide
Vogesensandst.
Trias
Steink. Gebilde
Kohlensandstein
Kohlenkalk
Devon. System
Silur. System
Vulk. Gebilde
Vulk. Gerölle
Jura Gebirg
Dolomit
Jurakalk
Lias

G. Heck dir.t

Henry Winkles sculp.t

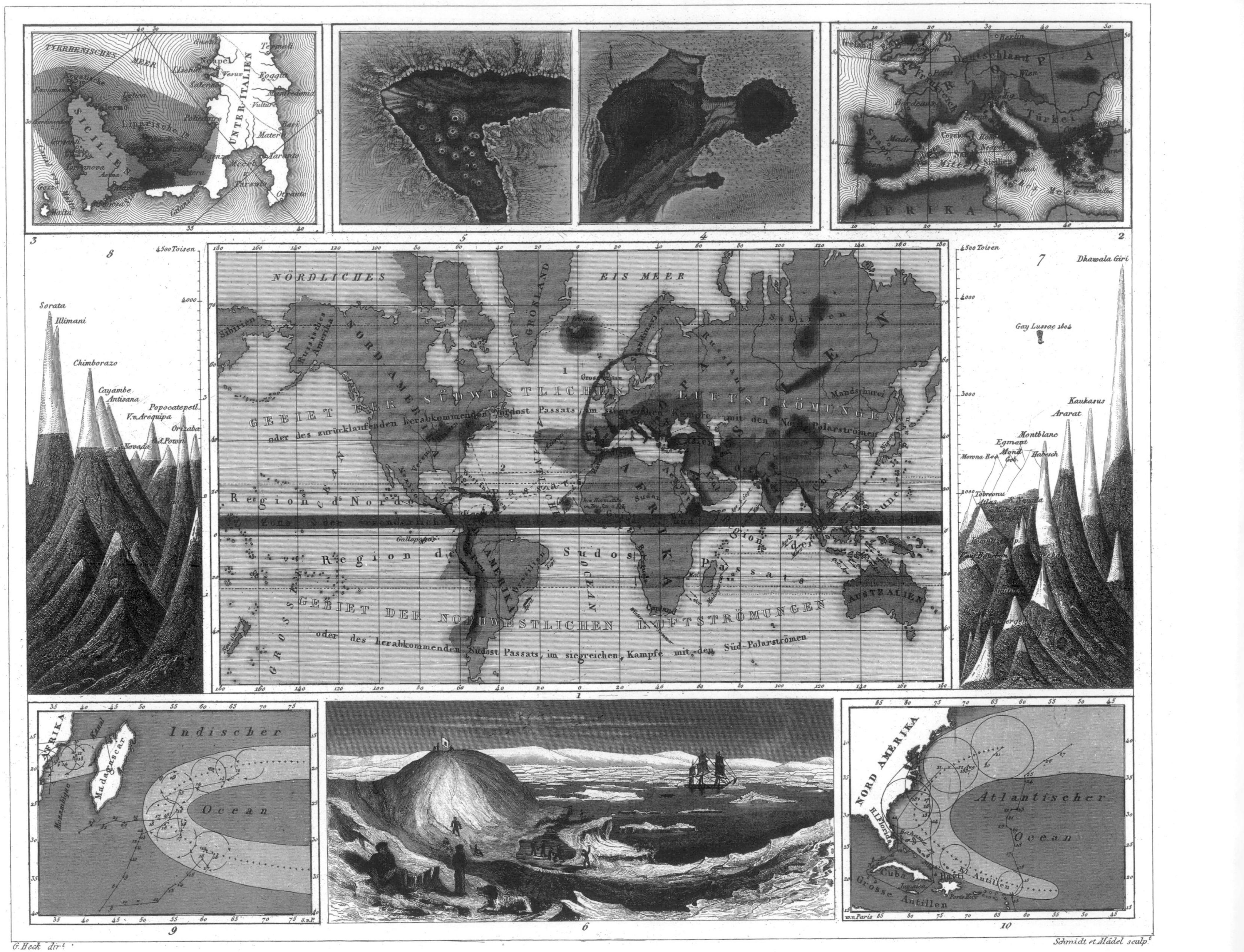

PLATE 47. VOLCANIC AND HURRICANE CHARTS; MOUNTAIN PROFILES; CRATERS; AND ANTARCTICA

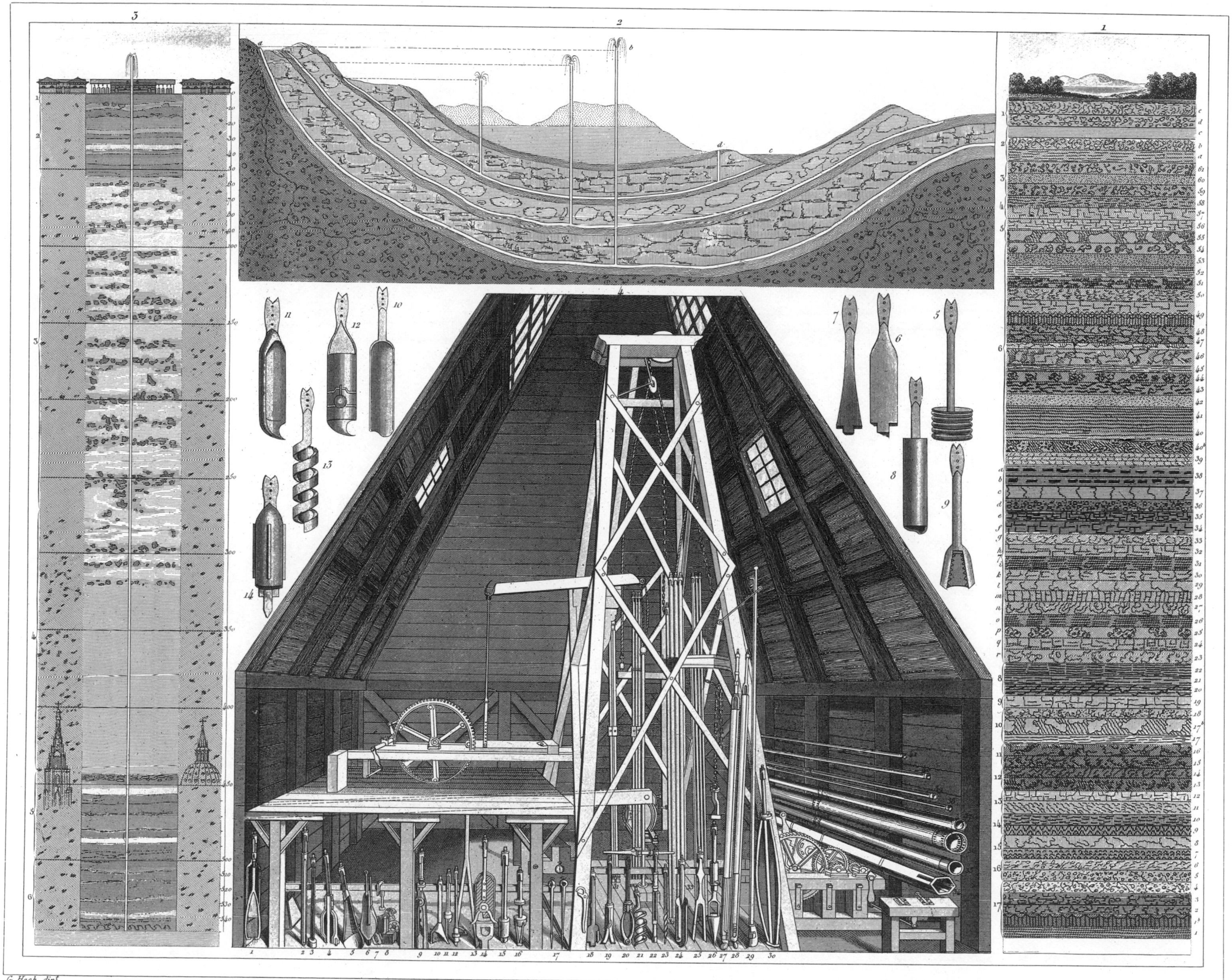

PLATE 48. BORING EQUIPMENT; STRATIFICATION AND ARTESIAN WELLS

G. Heck dir.

Henry Winkles sculp.

PLATE 49. NOTABLE GEOLOGICAL FORMATIONS

G. Heck dir.^t Henry Winkles sculp.^t

PLATE 50. VOLCANOES, GEYSERS, AND WATER FALLS

G. Heck dir.t Henry Winkles sculp.t

PLATE 51. FORESTS, LAKES, CAVES, AND UNUSUAL ROCK FORMATIONS

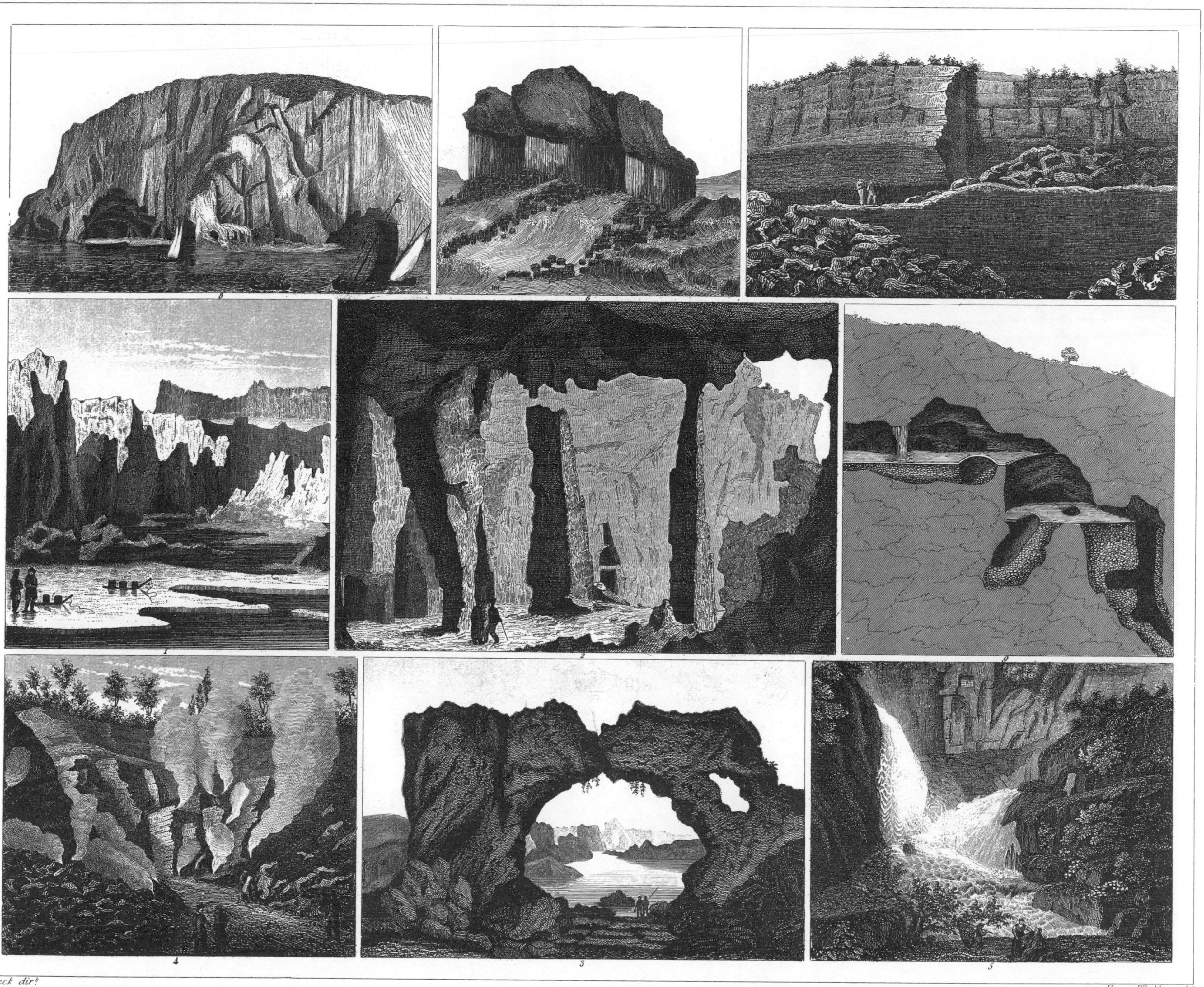

G. Heck dir.

Henry Winkler sculp.

PLATE 52. CAVES, ICEBERGS, LAVA, AND ROCK FORMATIONS

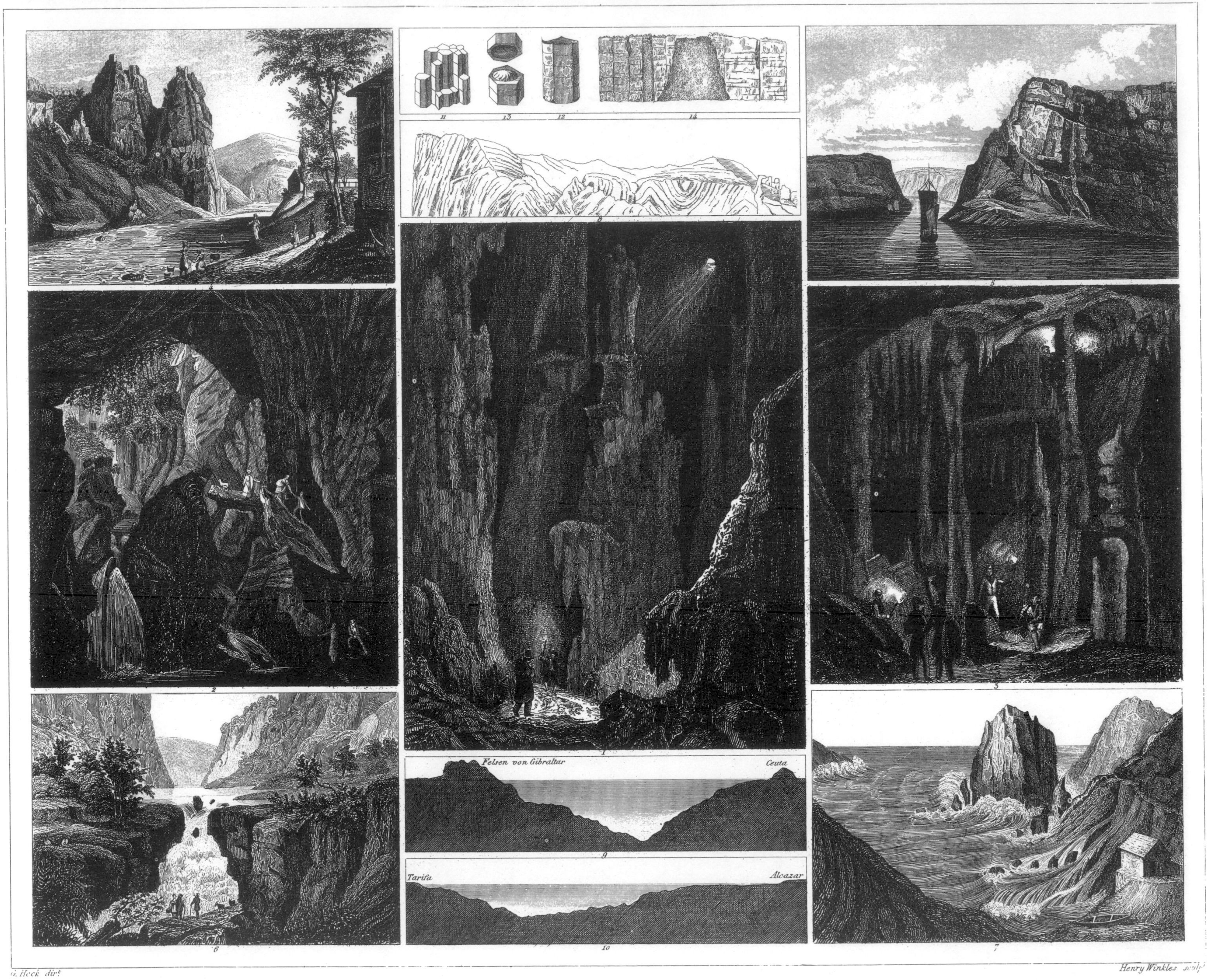
Felsen von Gibraltar
Ceuta
Tarifa
Alcazar
G. Heck dir.
Henry Winkles sculp.

PLATE 53. CAVES AND ROCK FORMATIONS

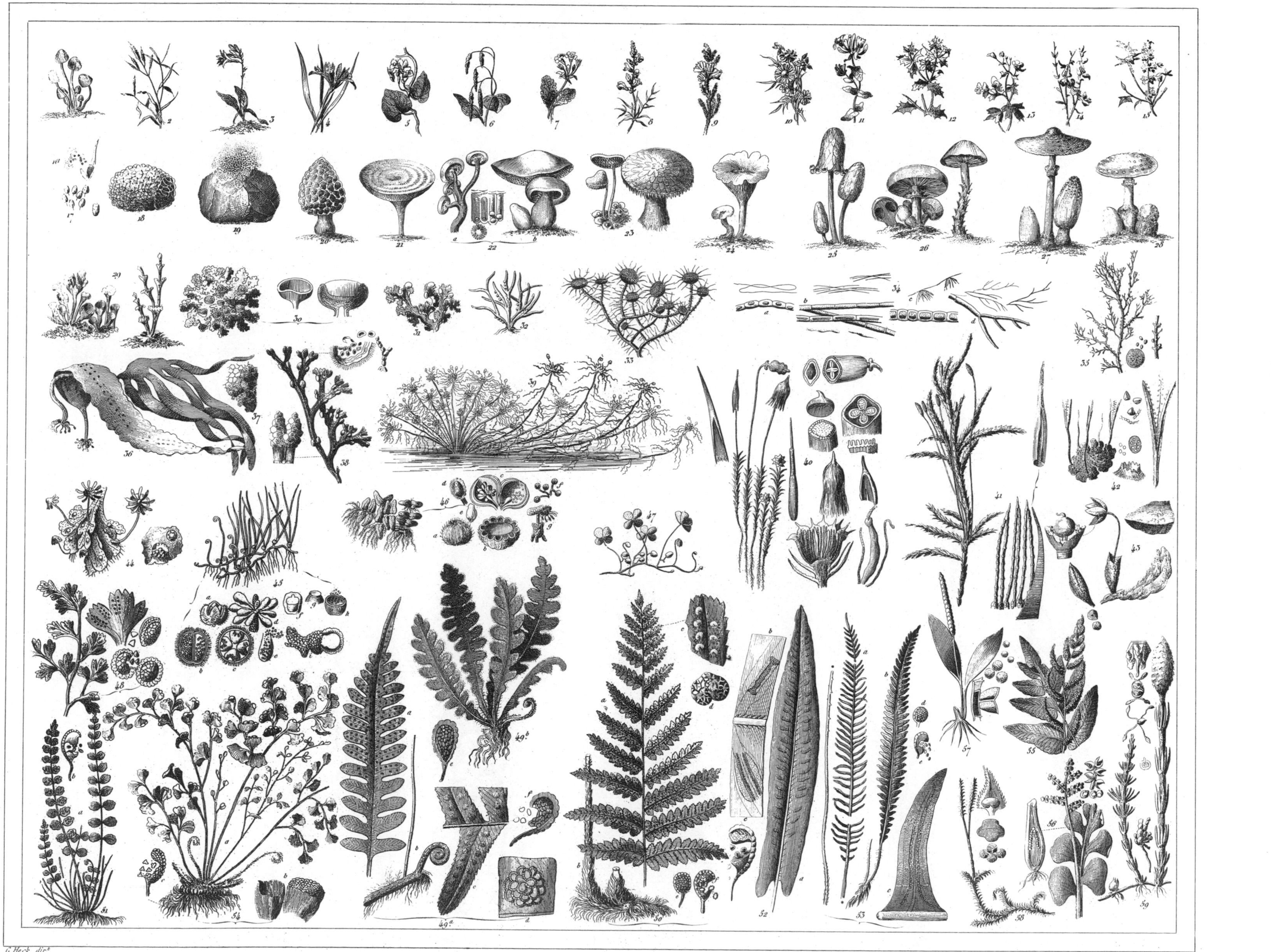

G. Heck dir.^t Henry Winkles sculp.^t

PLATE 54. REPRESENTATIVES OF THE ALGAE, FUNGI, BRYOPHYTA, POLYPODIOPHYTA AND OTHER NONFLOWERING PLANTS

G. Heck dir.t

Henry Winkles sculp.t

PLATE 55. FIG TREES, AQUATIC FLOWERING PLANTS, AND REPRESENTATIVES OF THE FAMILIES GRAMINEAE AND CYPERACEAE

Schmidt sculp Dresden

PLATE 56. HABITAT GROUPING AND REPRODUCTIVE PARTS OF VARIOUS WOODY MONOCOTS, ESPECIALLY PALMS AND CYCADS

G. Heck dir.t Henry Winkles sculp.t

PLATE 57. REPRESENTATIVES OF THE MONOCOT ORDER LILIALES

Fig. 9.
Fig. 16.
Fig. 2.
Fig. 3.
Fig. 1.
Fig. 8.
Fig. 11.
Fig. 17.
Fig. 13.
Fig. 5.
Fig. 4.
Fig. 14.
Fig. 15.
Fig. 10.
Fig. 6.
Fig. 7.
Fig. 12.

G. Heck dir.t Henry Winkles sculp.t

G. Heck dir.t Henry Winkles sculp.t

PLATES 60 AND 61. CULTIVATED PLANTS FROM DIVERSE FAMILIES: ORNAMENTAL, EDIBLE, OR MEDICINAL

G. Heck dir.ᵗ Wagenschieber sculp.ᵗ Berlin.

PLATE 62. MEMBERS OF THE ACANTHUS, OLIVE, VERBENA, MINT, FIGWORT AND MIGHTSHADE FAMILIES

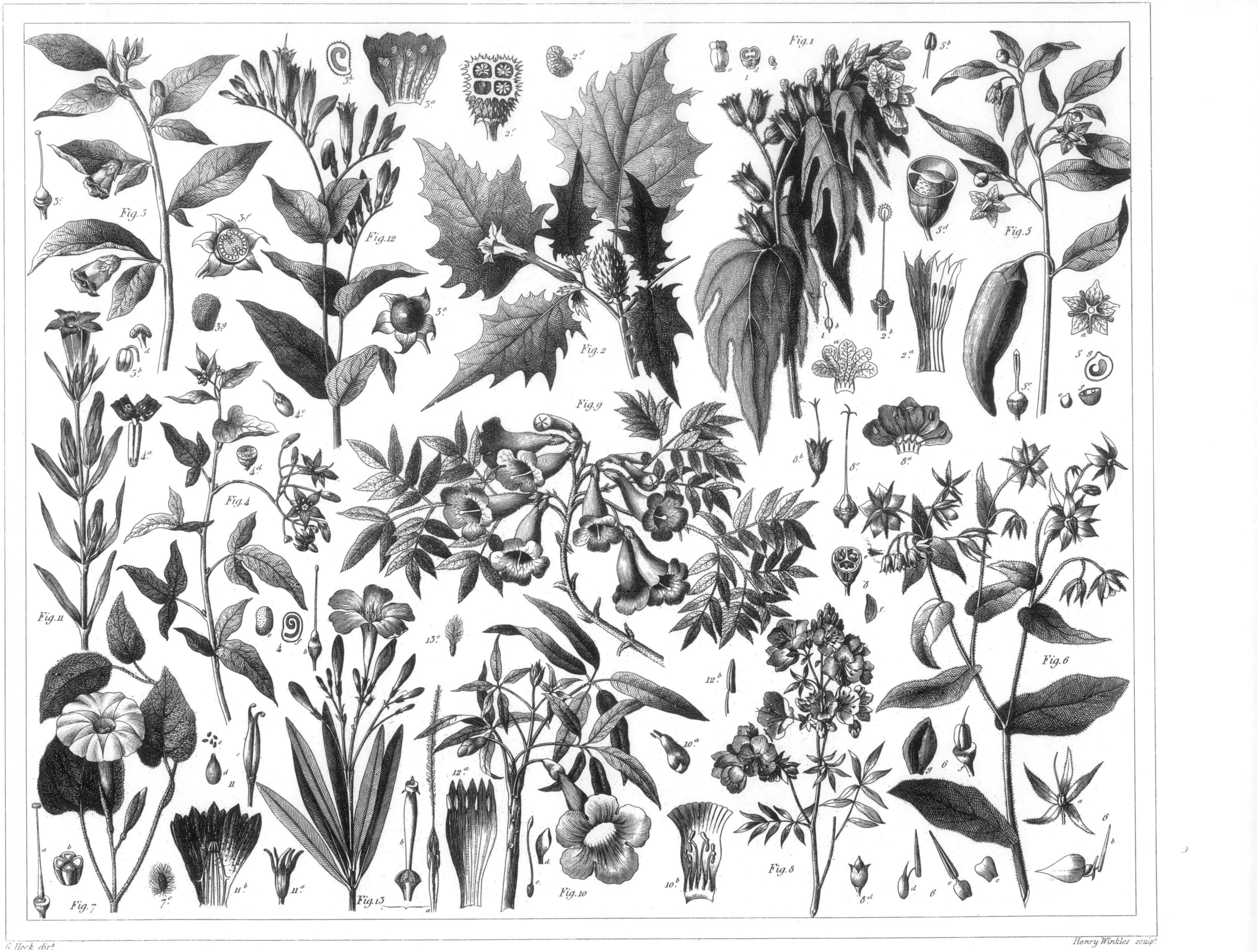

G. Heck dir.t Henry Winkles sculp.t

 PLATE 63. PLANTS OF SEVERAL FAMILIES WHICH CONTAIN TOXIC COMPOUNDS, ESPECIALLY OF THE ORDER POLEMONIALES

G. Heck dir.t

PLATE 64. PLANTS WITH A RESINOUS OR MILKY SAP

G. Heck dir.^t Henry Winkles sculp.^t

PLATE 65. PLANTS BREWED AS TEAS AND REPRESENTATIVES OF THE UMBELLIFERAE, SOME POISONOUS

G Heck dir.t

Wagenschieber sculp. Berlin

PLATE 66. CULTIVATED PLANTS OF THE RANUNCULACEAE AND OTHER FAMILIES

G. Heck dir.t

Wagenschieber sculp. Berlin.

PLATE 67. VARIOUS PLANTS OF ECONOMIC IMPORTANCE, INCLUDING TEA, WINE GRAPE, COTTON AND CACAO

G. Heck dir.t

Wagenschieber sculp.t Berlin.

PLATE 68. CULTIVATED PLANTS OF MANY FAMILIES, MOSTLY ORNAMENTAL

PLATE 69. PLANTS INDIGENOUS TO SANDY OR ROCKY SOIL, A SANDALWOOD, AND REPRESENTATIVES OF THE ORDER MYRTALES

G. Heck. dir.

Wagenschieber sculp. Berlin.

PLATE 70. LYTHRUM AND REPRESENTATIVES OF THE ORDER ROSALES

G. Heck dir. Henry Winkles sculps.

 PLATE 71. VARIOUS PLANTS, INCLUDING MEMBERS OF THE SUMAC, SPURGE AND GOURD FAMILIES

G. Heck dir.e

Henry Winkles sculp.t

PLATE 72. CONIFEROUS GYMNOSPERMS, AND ANGIOSPERMS OF THE MULBERRY, PEPPER, BEECH AND WITCH HAZEL FAMILIES

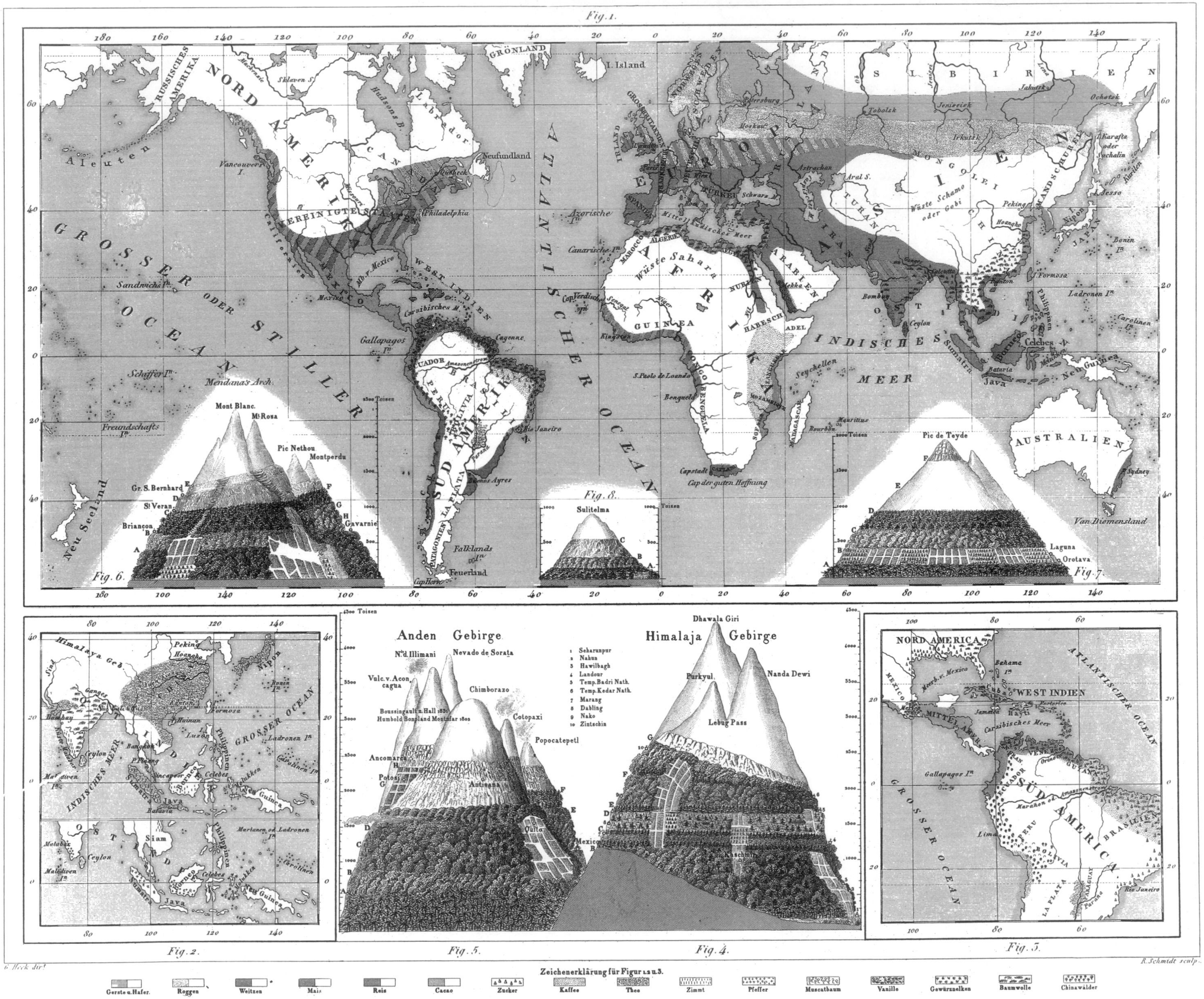
Fig. 1.
NORD AMERIKA
RUSSISCHES AMERIKA
GRÖNLAND
I. Island
Neufundland
Philadelphia
VEREINIGTE STAATEN
GROSSER ODER STILLER OCEAN
ATLANTISCHER OCEAN
EUROPA
ASIEN
SIBIRIEN
AFRIKA
Wüste Sahara
SÜD AMERIKA
INDISCHES MEER
AUSTRALIEN
Van Diemensland
Neu Seeland
Fig. 6.
Mont Blanc
Mt. Rosa
Pic Nethou
Montperdu
Gr. S. Bernhard
St. Veran
Briancon
Gavarnie
Fig. 8.
Sulitelma
Fig. 7.
Pic de Teyde
Laguna
Orotava
Fig. 2.
Fig. 5.
Anden Gebirge
Nd. Illimani
Nevado de Sorata
Vulc. v. Aconcagua
Chimborazo
Boussingault u. Hall 1831
Humbold Bonpland Montufar 1802
Cotopaxi
Popocatepetl
Ancomarca
Potosi
Antisana
Quito
Mexico
Fig. 4.
Himalaja Gebirge
Dhawala Giri
Purkyul
Nanda Dewi
Lebug Pass
Kaschmir
1 Seharunpur
2 Nahun
3 Hawilbagh
4 Landour
5 Temp. Badri Nath.
6 Temp. Kedar Nath.
7 Marang
8 Dabling
9 Nako
10 Zintschin
Fig. 3.
NORD AMERICA
WEST INDIEN
SÜD AMERICA
GROSSER OCEAN
ATLANTISCHER OCEAN
G. Heck dir.
R. Schmidt sculp.
Zeichenerklärung für Figur 1, 2 u. 3.
Gerste u. Hafer
Roggen
Weitzen
Mais
Reis
Cacao
Zucker
Kaffee
Thee
Zimmt
Pfeffer
Muscatbaum
Vanille
Gewürznelken
Baumwolle
Chinawälder

PLATE 73. MAPS AND CHARTS OF PLANT DISTRIBUTION

G. Heck dir. *Henry Winkles sculp.*

G. Heck dir.t Henry Winkles sculp.t

 PLATE 75. REPRESENTATIVES OF THE PHYLA PROTOZOA, PORIFERA, COELENTERATA, AND MOLLUSCA

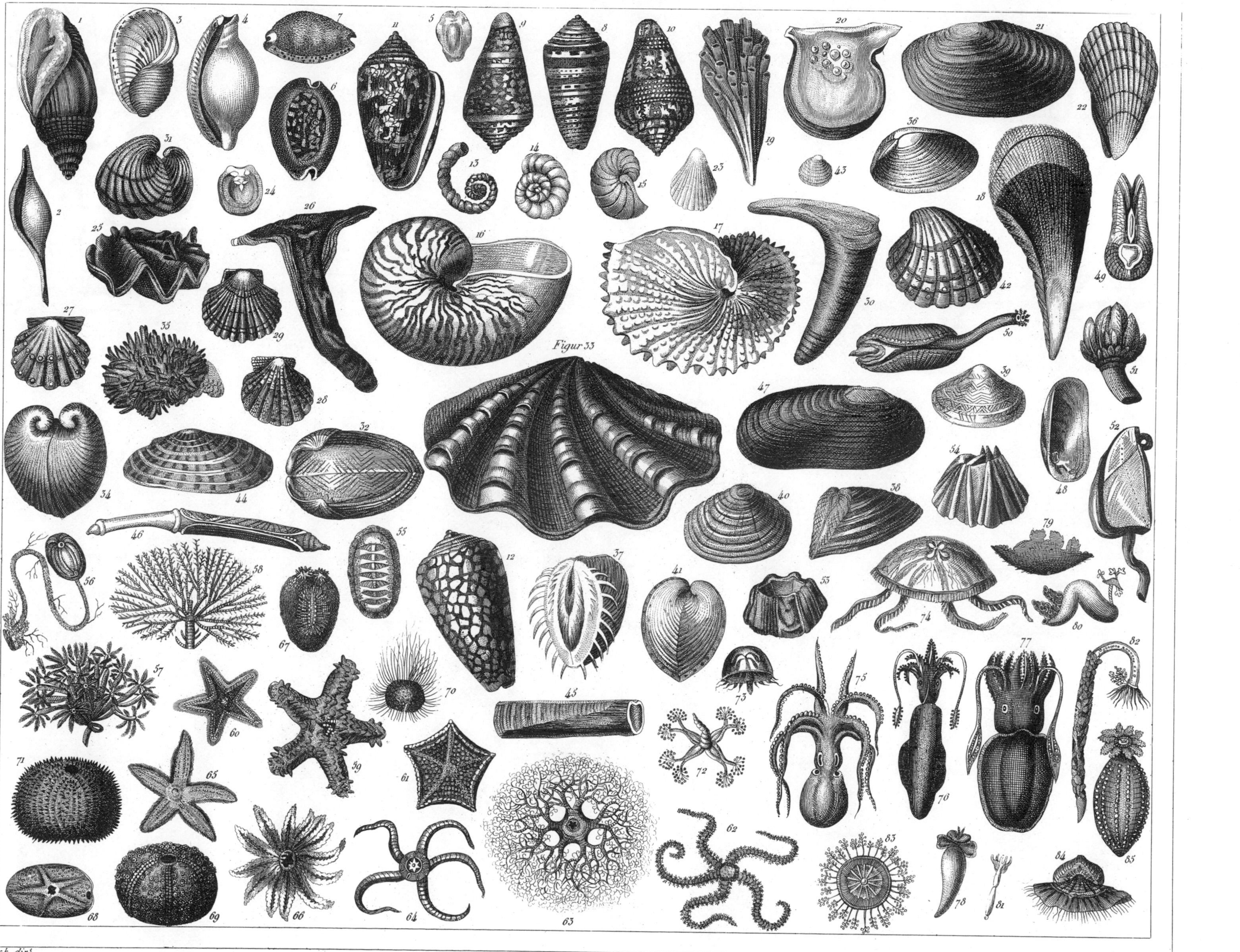

G. Heck dir.

Henry Winkles sculp.

PLATE 76. REPRESENTATIVES OF THE PHYLA MOLLUSCA, ECHINODERMATA, CTENOPHORA, AND ARTHROPODA

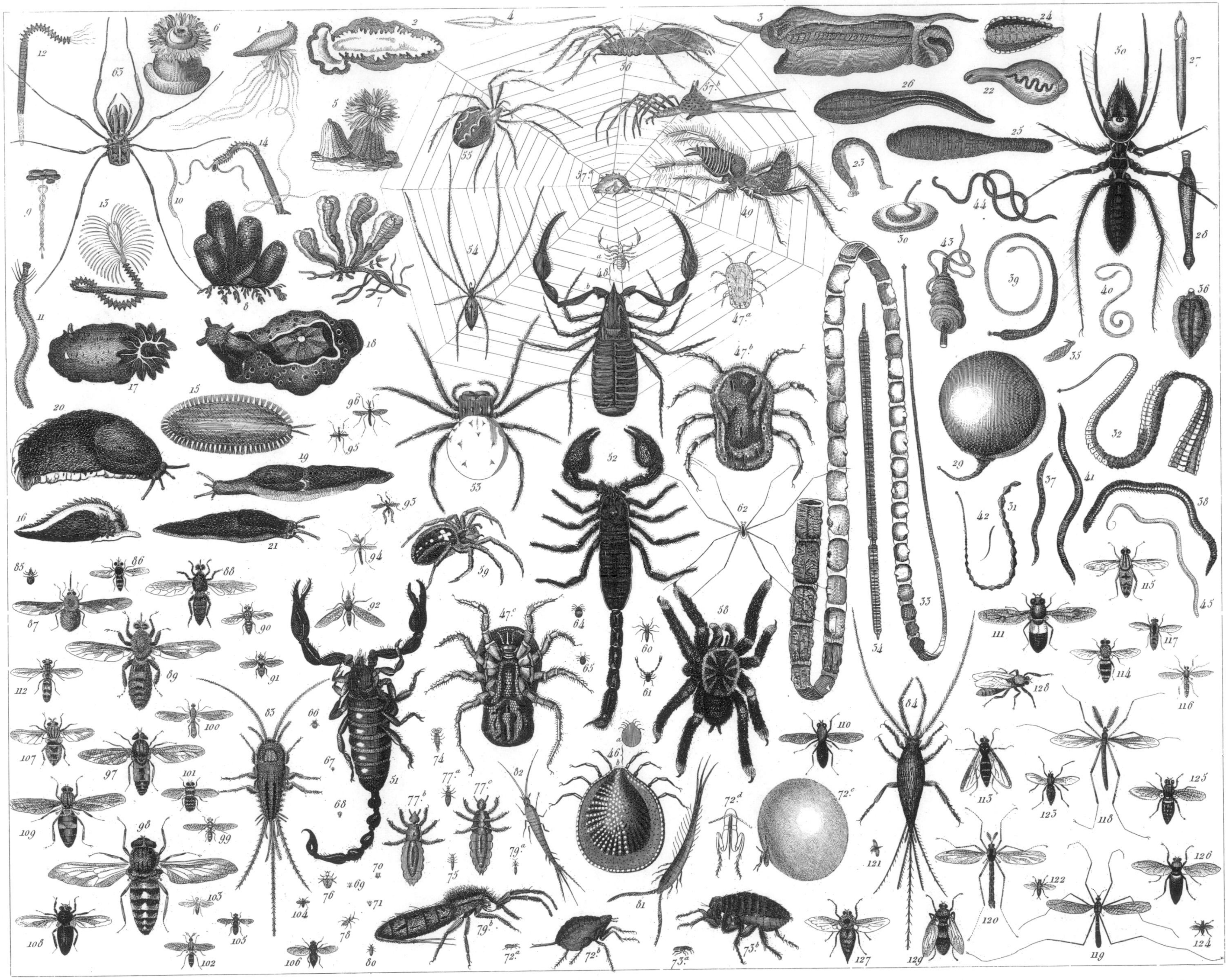

G. Heck dir.[t] Henry Winkles sculp.[t]

PLATE 77. REPRESENTATIVES OF THE PHYLA COELENTERATA, CHORDATA, MOLLUSCA, PLATYHELMINTHES, AND ARTHROPODA

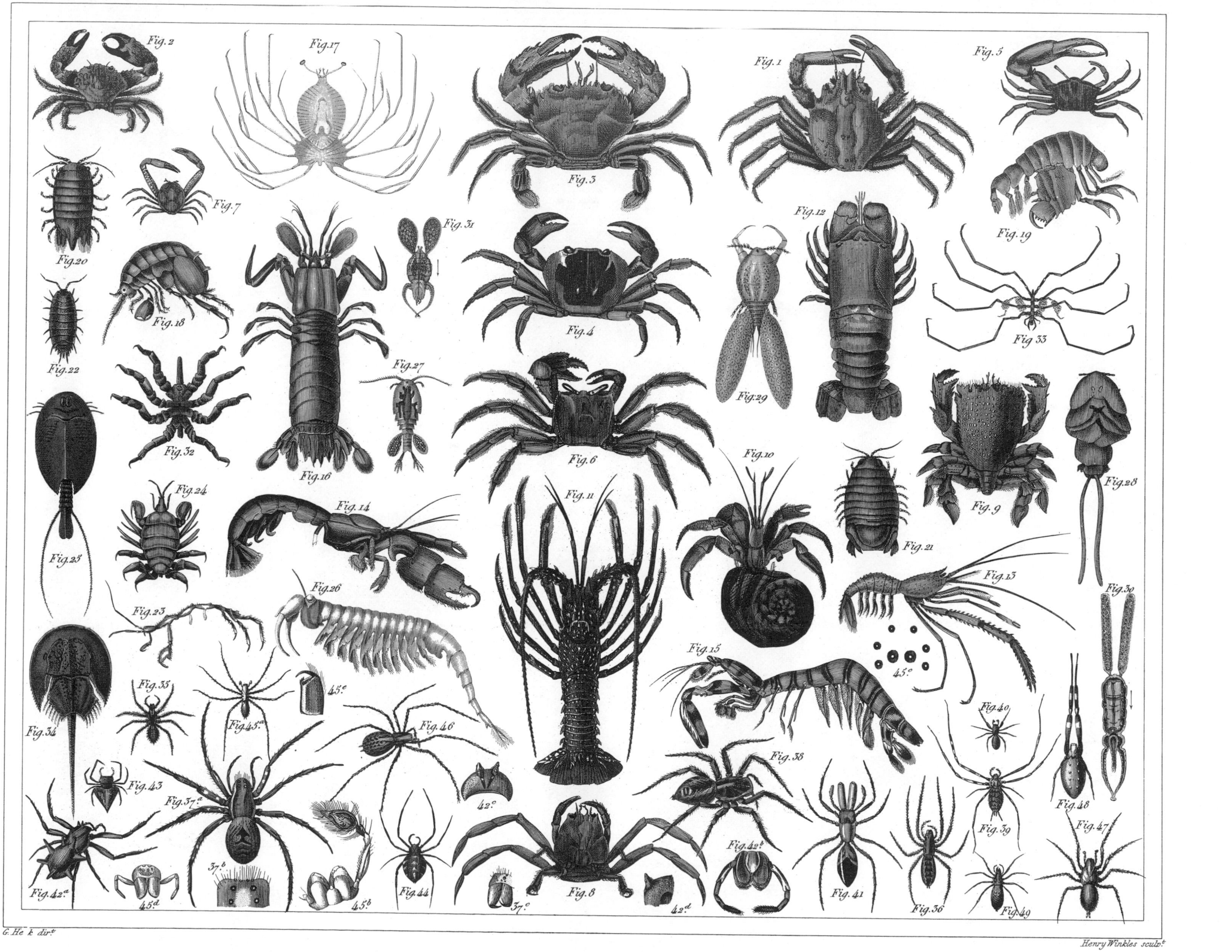

PLATE 78. REPRESENTATIVES OF THE PHYLUM ARTHROPODA: CLASSES CRUSTACEA AND ARACHNIDA

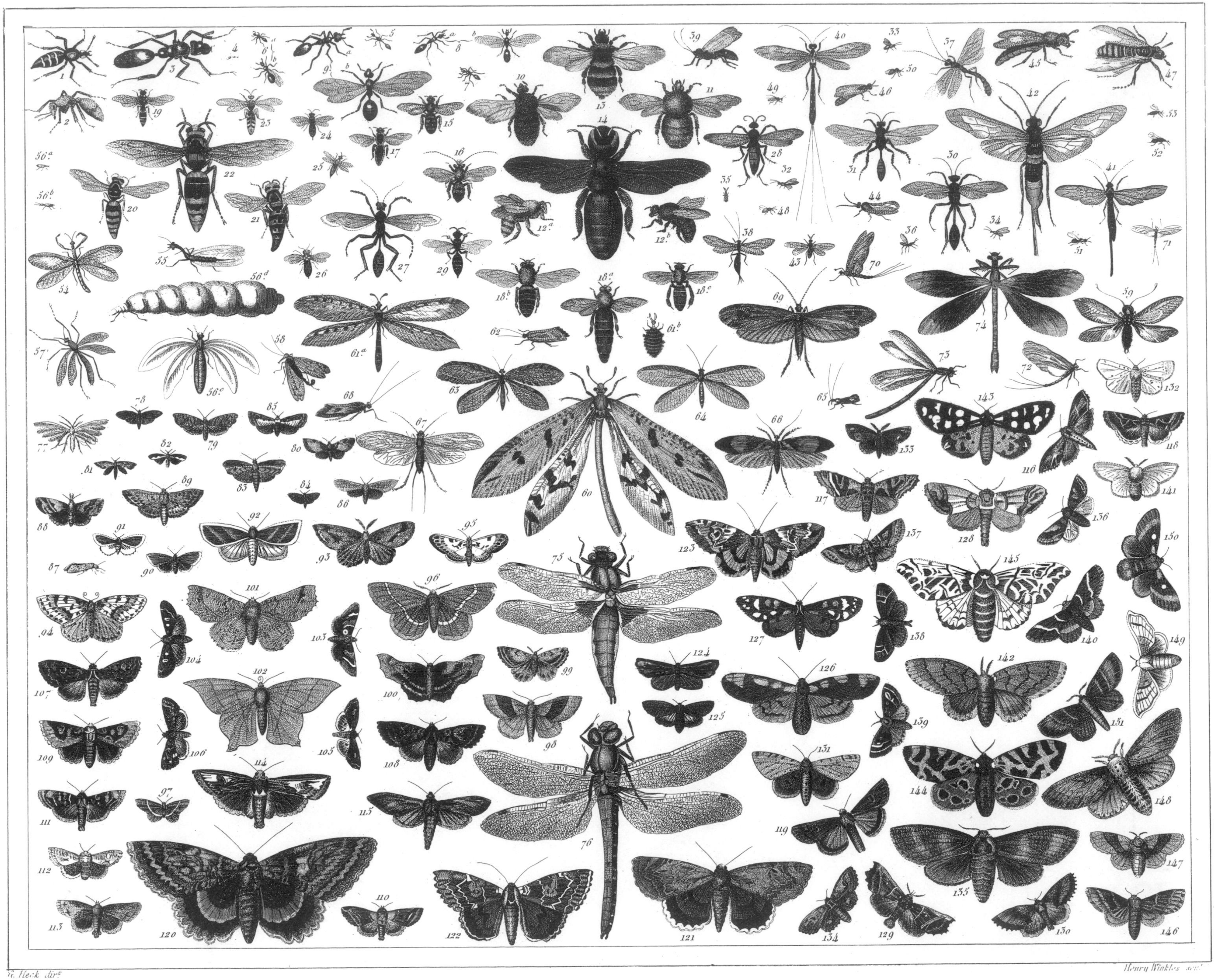

G. Heck dir.t Henry Winkles sculp.t

 PLATE 79. INSECTS OF THE ORDERS HYMENOPTERA, DIPTERA, LEPIDOPTERA, AND ODONATA

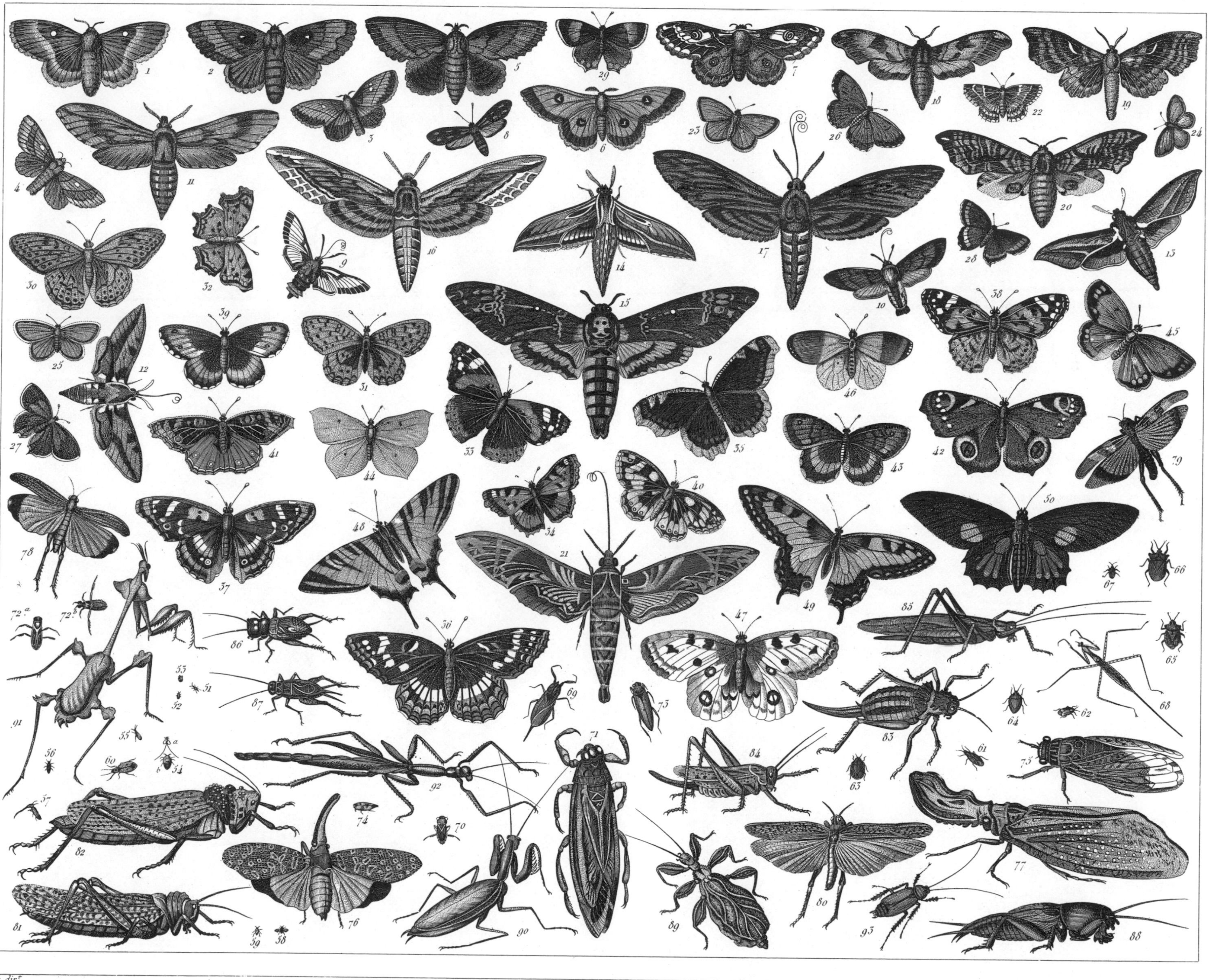

G. Heck dir.t

Henry Winkles sculp.

PLATE 80. INSECTS OF THE ORDERS LEPIDOPTERA, ORTHOPTERA, AND HEMIPTERA

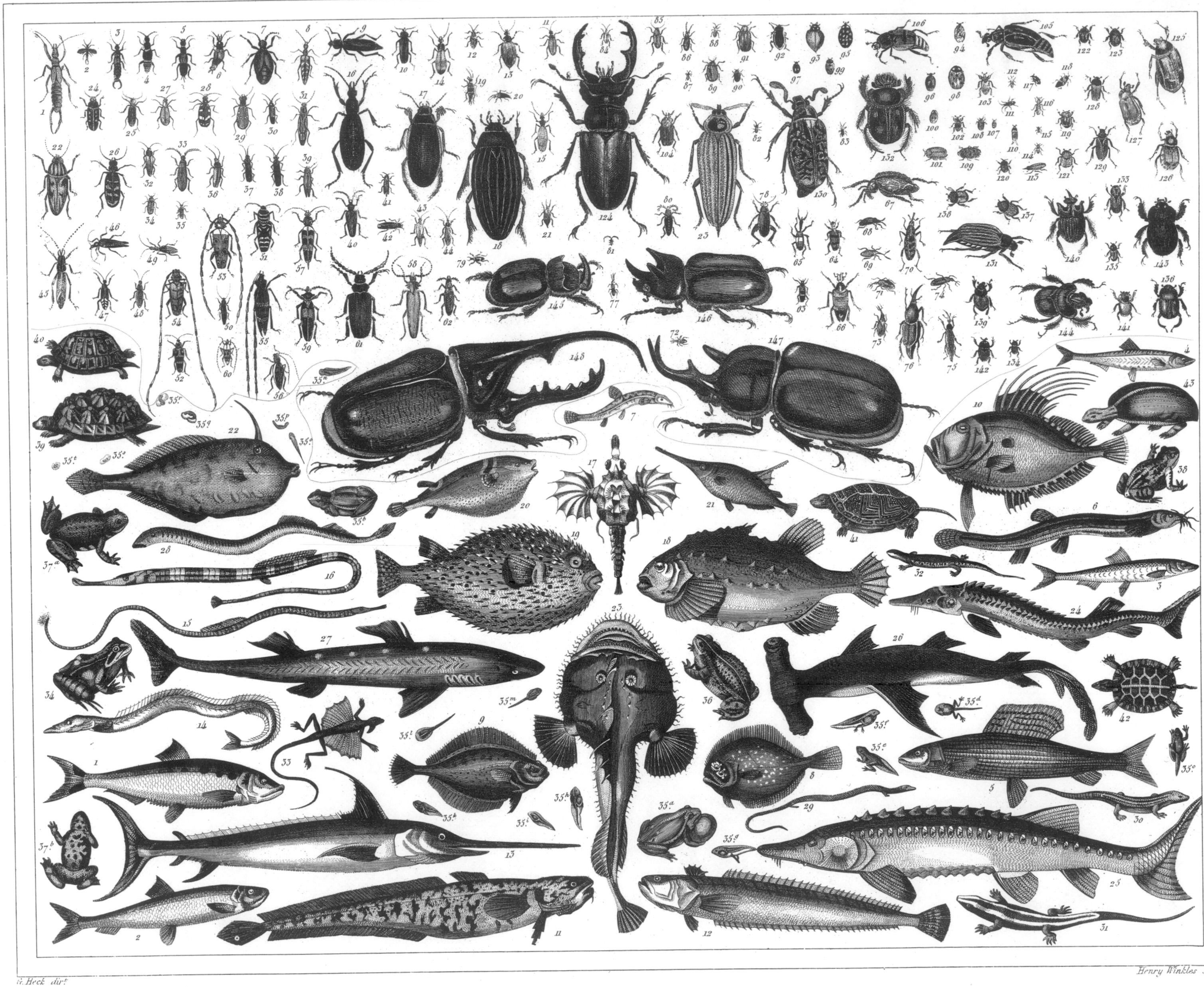

G. Heck dirt. Henry Winkles sculpt.

PLATE 81. INSECTS OF THE ORDER COLEOPTERA; AND MEMBERS OF VARIOUS CHORDATE CLASSES

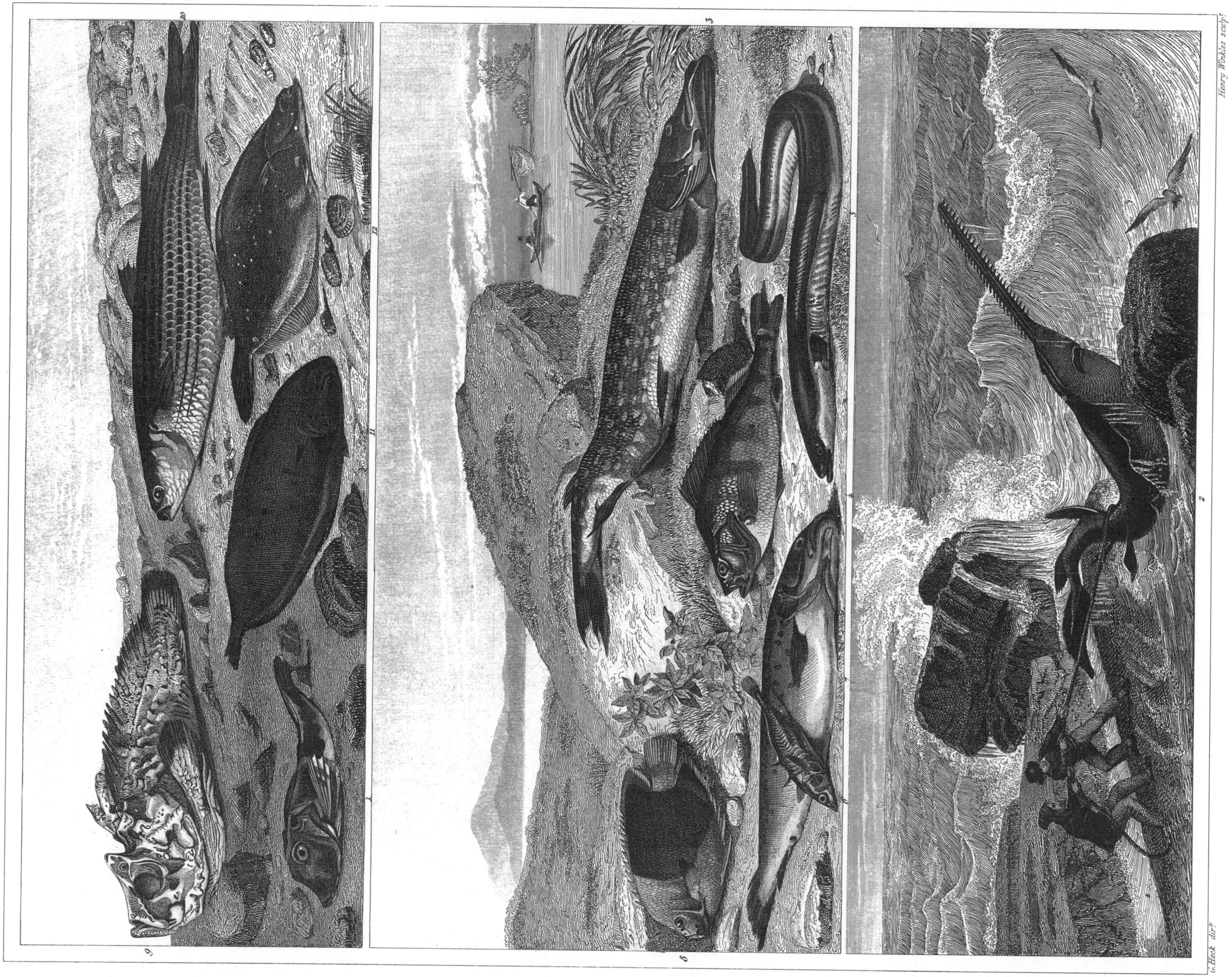

PLATE 82. CHORDATES OF THE CLASSES CHONDRICHTHYES AND OSTEICHTHYES

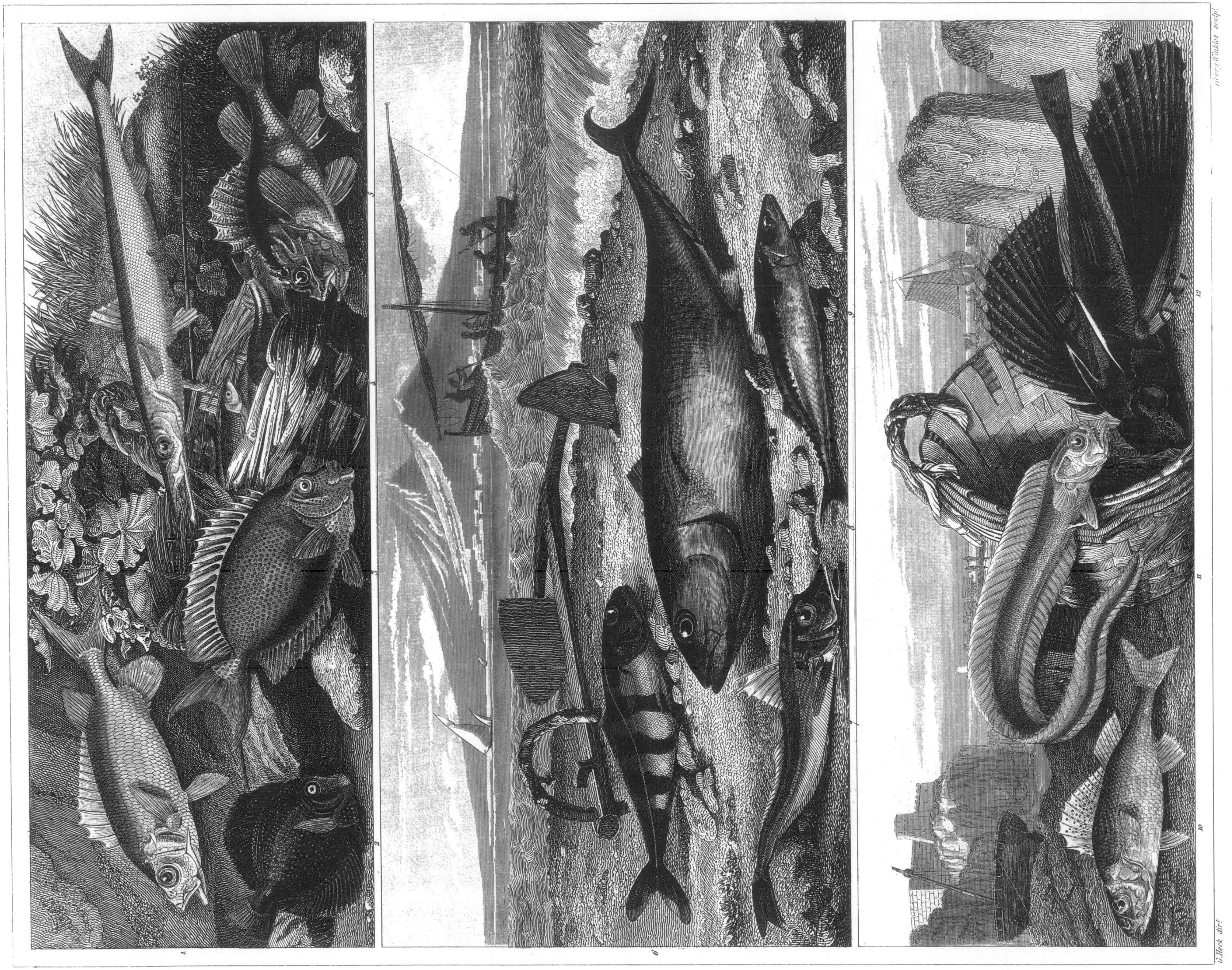

PLATE 83. OSTEICHTHYES OF THE ORDERS PERCIFORMES, SCORPAEINFORMES, BERYCIFORMES, AND DACTYLOPTERIFORMES

PLATE 84. MEMBERS OF THE CLASSES CHONDRICHTHYES, AND OSTEICHTHYES

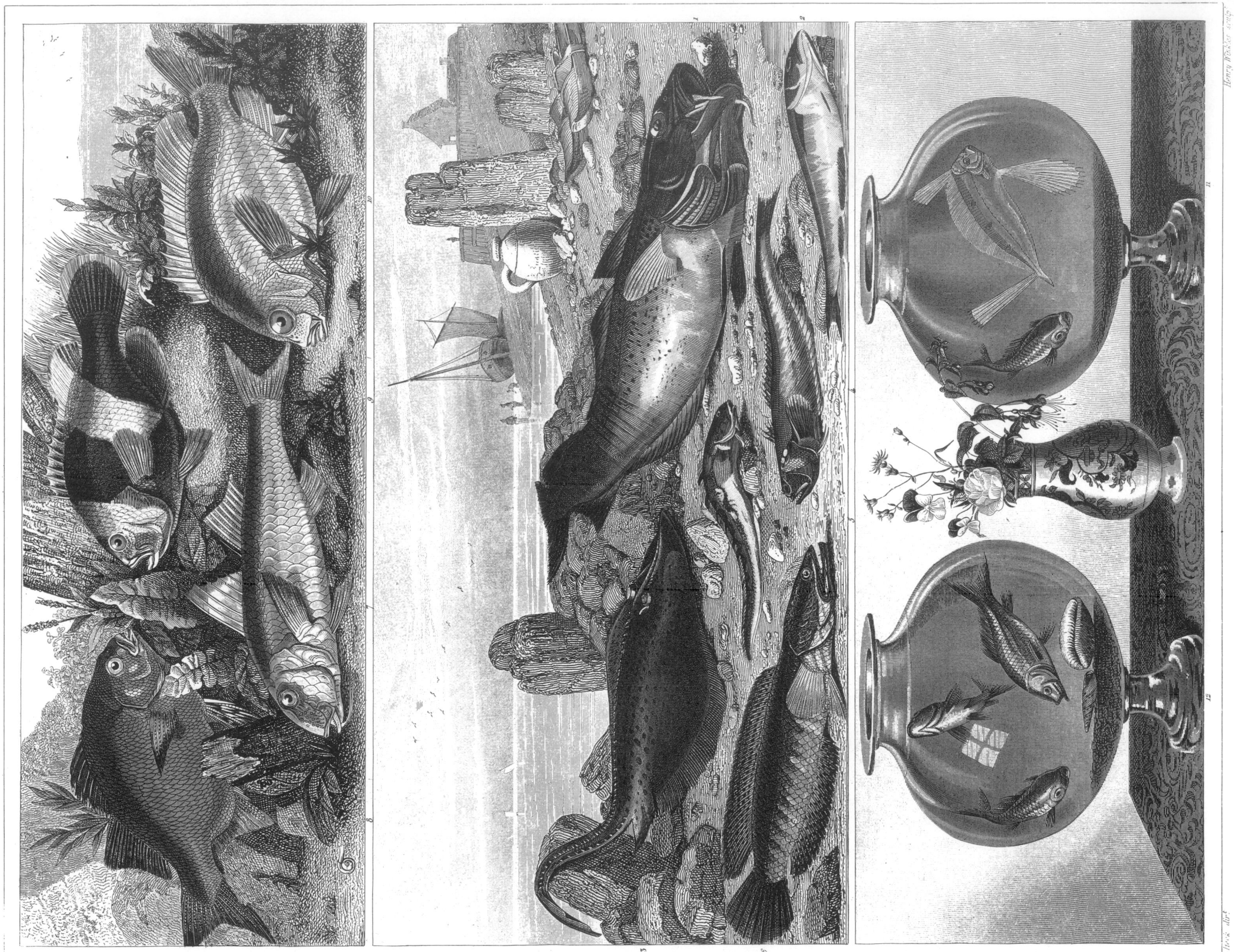

PLATE 85. REPRESENTATIVES OF THE CLASSES CHONDRICHTHYES AND OSTEICHTHYES

PLATE 86. REPTILES OF SUBORDERS SAURIA AND SERPENTES

PLATE 87. REPTILES OF THE SUBORDERS SAURIA AND SERPENTES

PLATE 88. AMPHIBIANS OF THE ORDER URODELA AND REPTILES OF THE ORDERS SQUAMATA AND CROCODYLIA

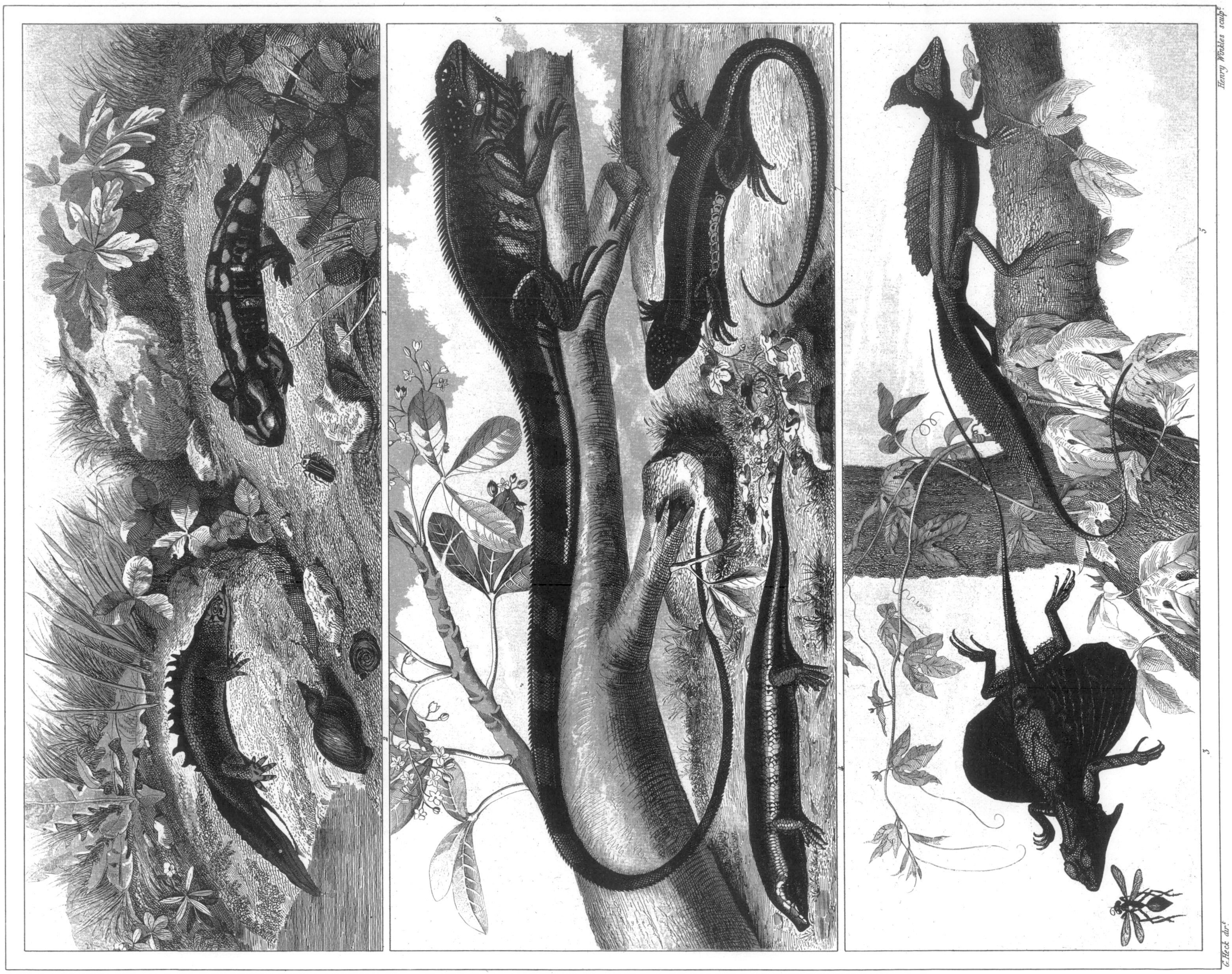

PLATE 89. AMPHIBIANS OF THE ORDER URODELA AND REPTILES OF THE SUBORDER SAURIA

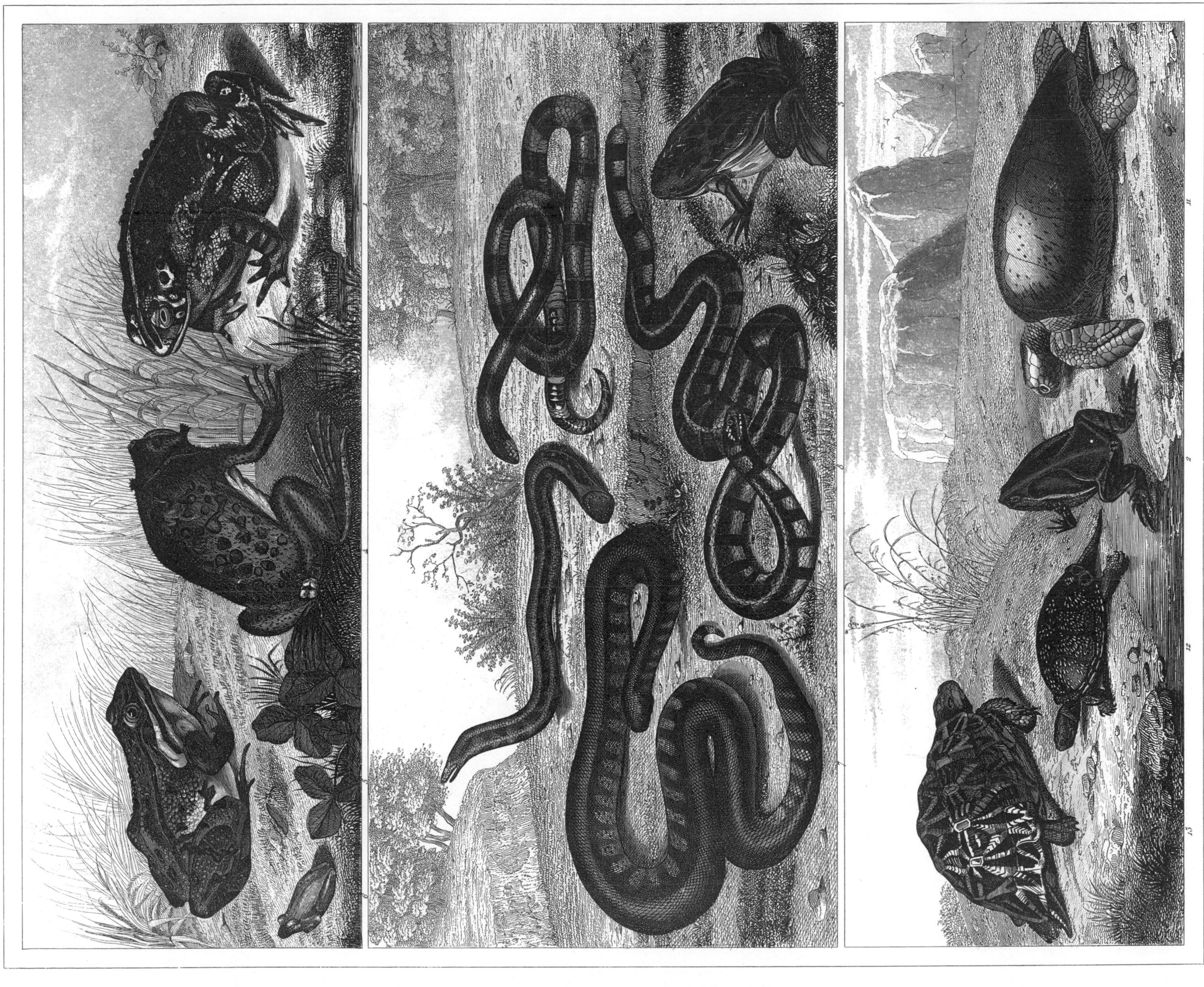

PLATE 90. MEMBERS OF THE CLASSES REPTILIA AND AMPHIBIA

 PLATE 91. AVES OF THE ORDERS PODICIPEDIFORMES, PELECANIFORMES, SPHENISCIFORMES AND GAVIIFORMES

PLATE 92. MEMBERS OF THE ORDERS ANSERIFORMES, PELECANIFORMES, CHARADRIIFORMES, AND SPHENISCIFORMES

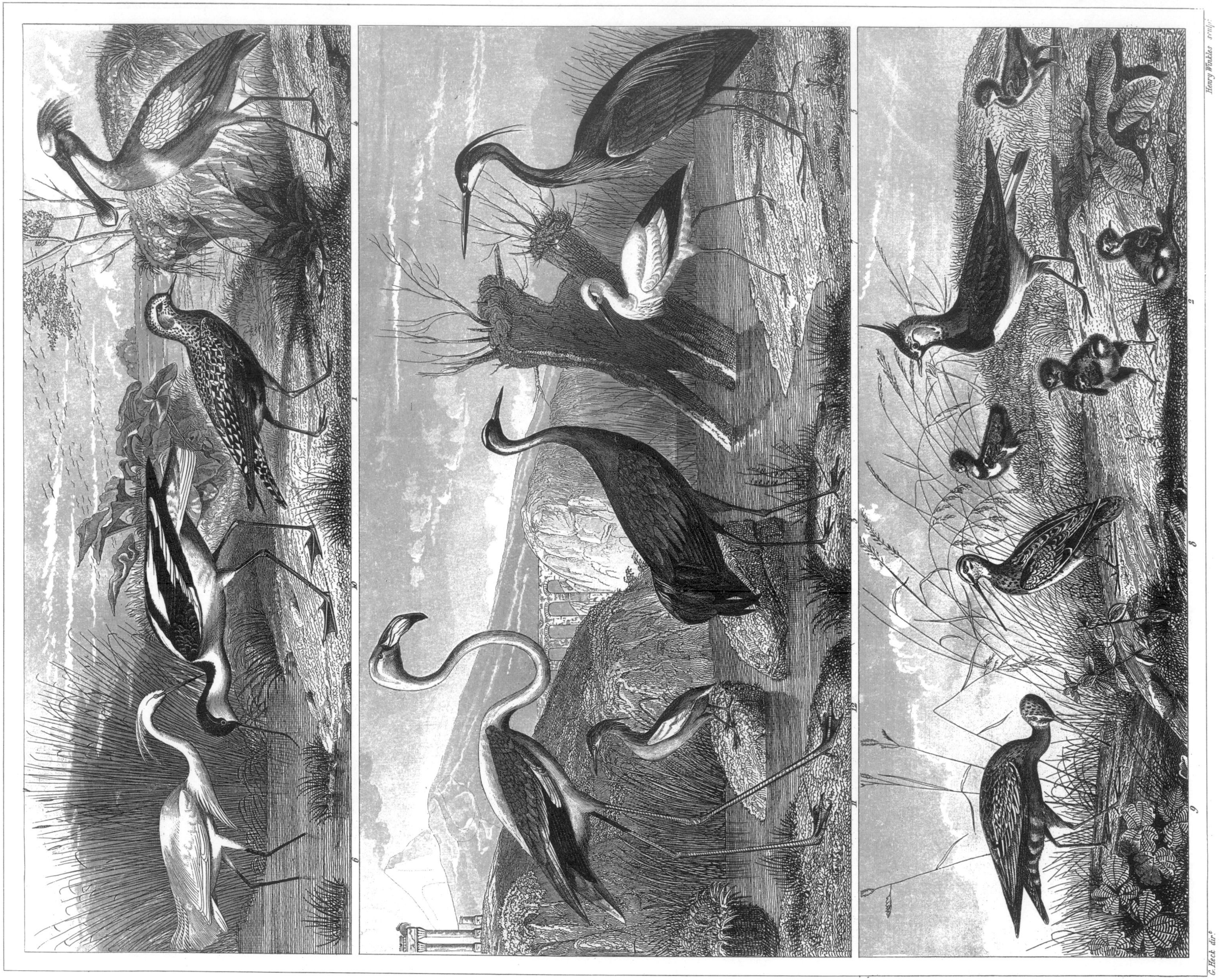

PLATE 93. MEMBERS OF THE ORDERS CICONIIFORMES, GRUIFORMES, AND CHARADRIIFORMES

PLATE 94. MEMBERS OF THE ORDERS STRUTHIONIFORMES, GRUIFORMES, CICONIIFORMES, AND CHARADRIIFORMES

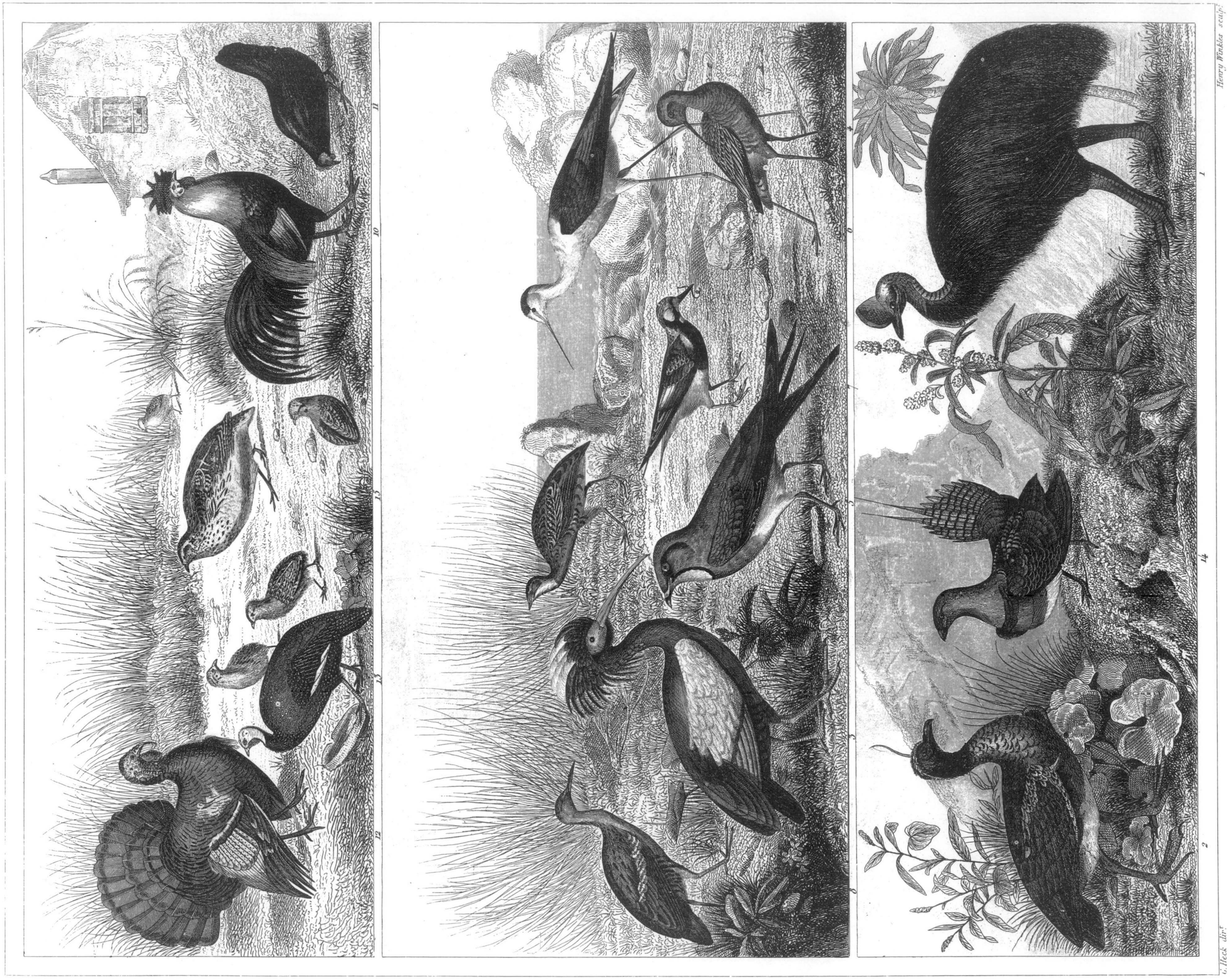

 PLATE 95. AVES OF THE ORDERS CASUARIIFORMES, ANSERIFORMES, CHARADRIIFORMES, GALLIFORMES, AND GRUIFORMES

PLATE 96. MEMBERS OF THE ORDERS GALLIFORMES AND COLUMBIFORMES

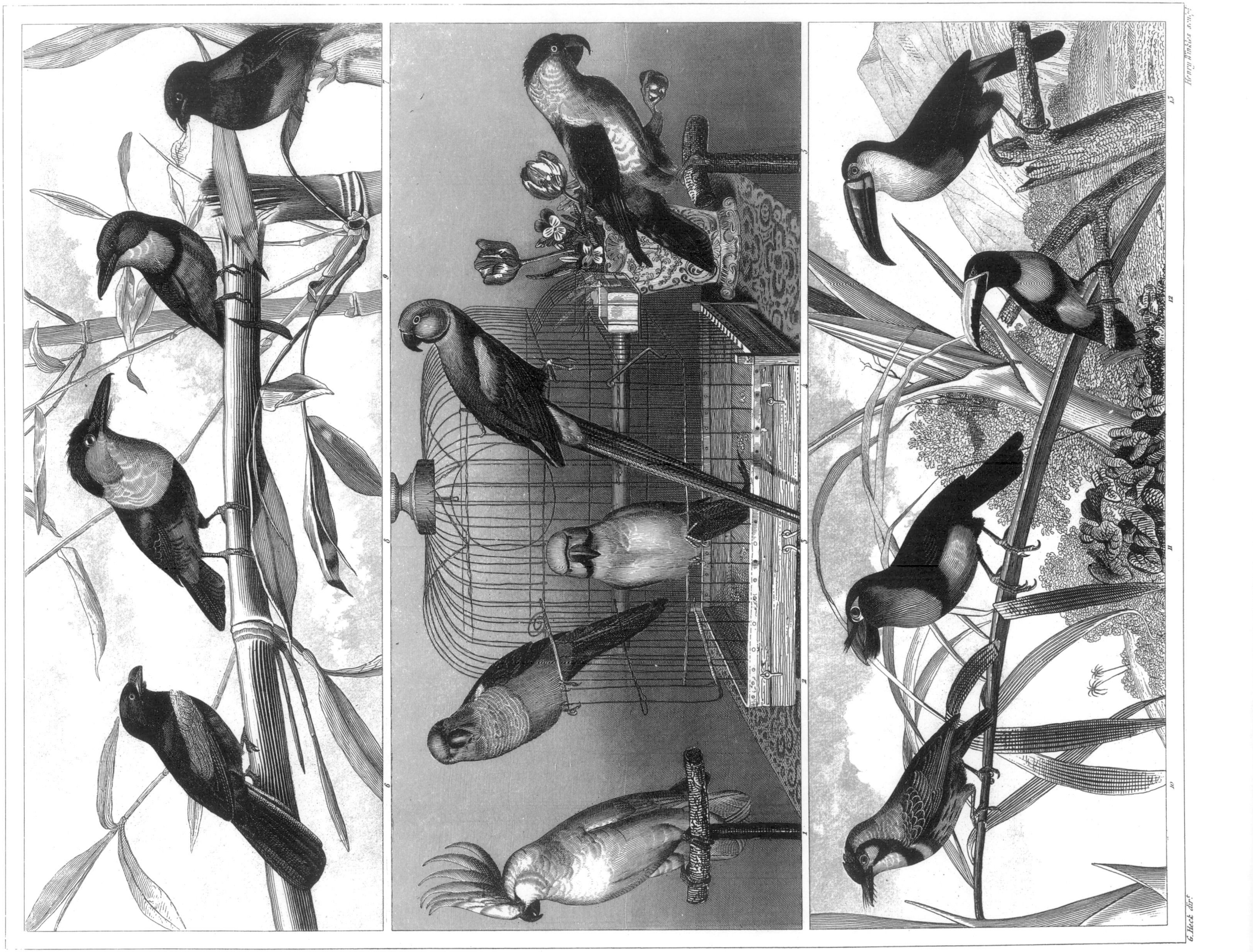

PLATE 97. REPRESENTATIVES OF THE ORDERS PSITTACIFORMES, PICIFORMES, AND TROGONIFORMES

PLATE 98. MEMBERS OF THE ORDERS PSITTACIFORMES, PICIFORMES, AND PASSERIFORMES

 PLATE 99. MEMBERS OF THE ORDERS APOPODIFORMES AND PASSERIFORMES

PLATE 100. REPRESENTATIVES OF THE ORDER PASSERIFORMES

 PLATE 101. MEMBERS OF THE ORDERS PASSERIFORMES, AND APOPODIFORMES

PLATE 102. REPRESENTATIVES OF THE ORDERS PASSERIFORMES AND APOPODIFORMES

 PLATE 103. MEMBERS OF THE ORDERS PASSERIFORMES, CORACIIFORMES, AND CAPRIMULGIFORMES

PLATE 104. MEMBERS OF THE ORDERS STRIGIFORMES AND FALCONIFORMES

PLATE 105. MEMBERS OF THE ORDER FALCONIFORMES

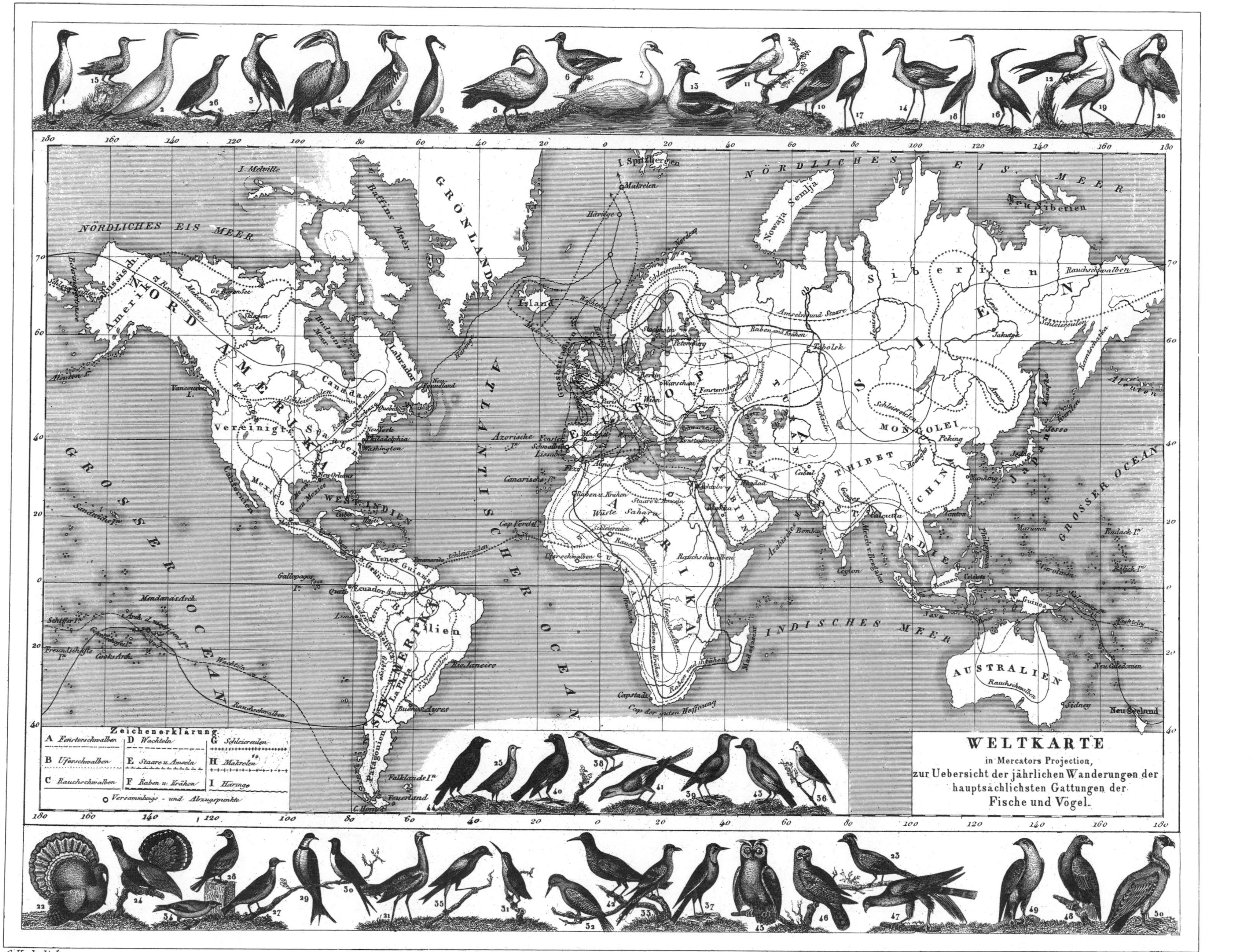

G. Heck dir.t

Henry Winkles sculp.

PLATE 106. CHART OF THE MIGRATIONS OF FISHES AND BIRDS

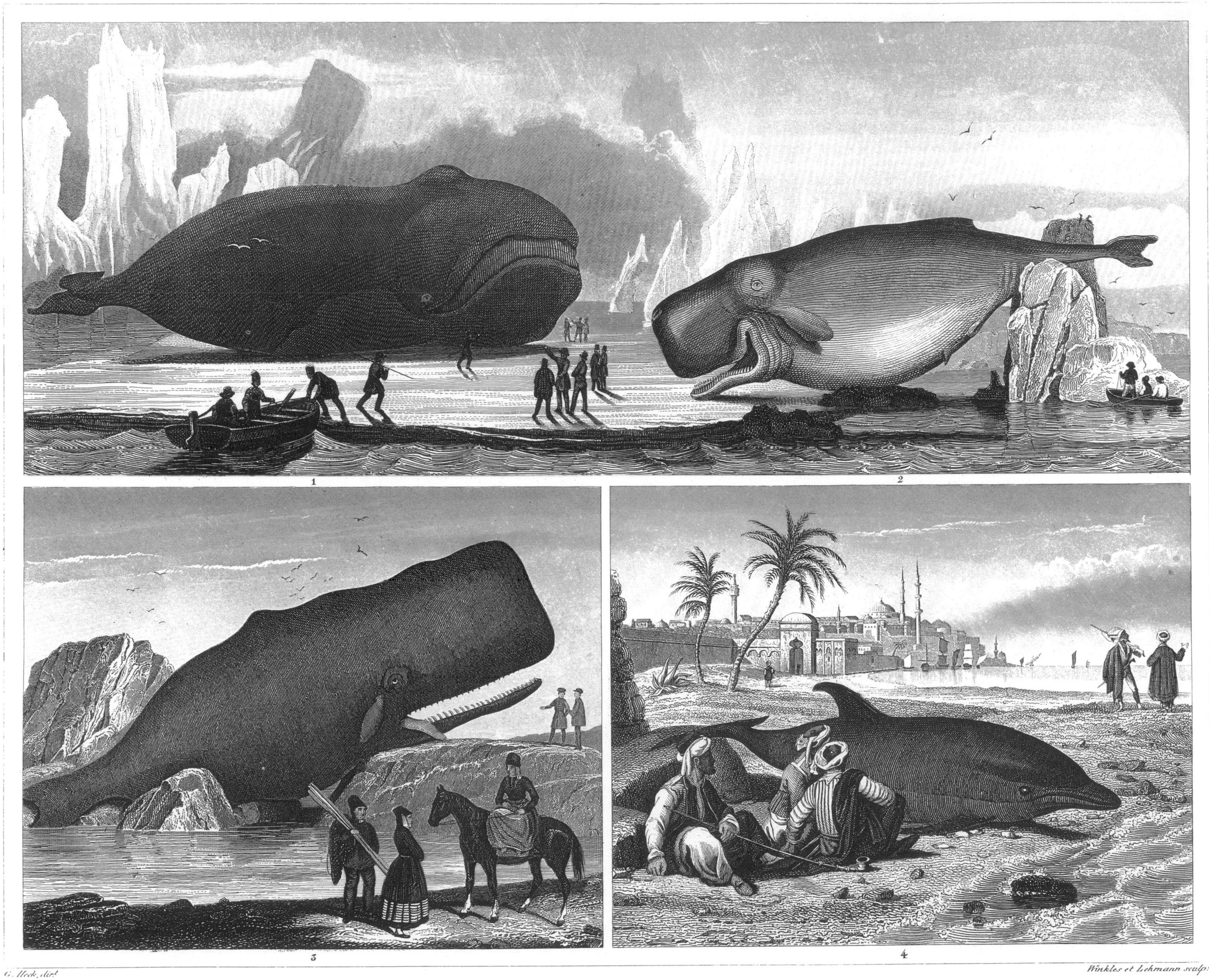

G. Heck, dir.t Winkles et Lehmann sculp.t

 PLATE 107. MAMMALS OF THE ORDER CETACEA: SUBORDERS ODONTOCETI AND MYSTECETI

PLATE 108. REPRESENTATIVES OF THE ORDERS ARTIODACTYLA, LAGOMORPHA, AND RODENTIA

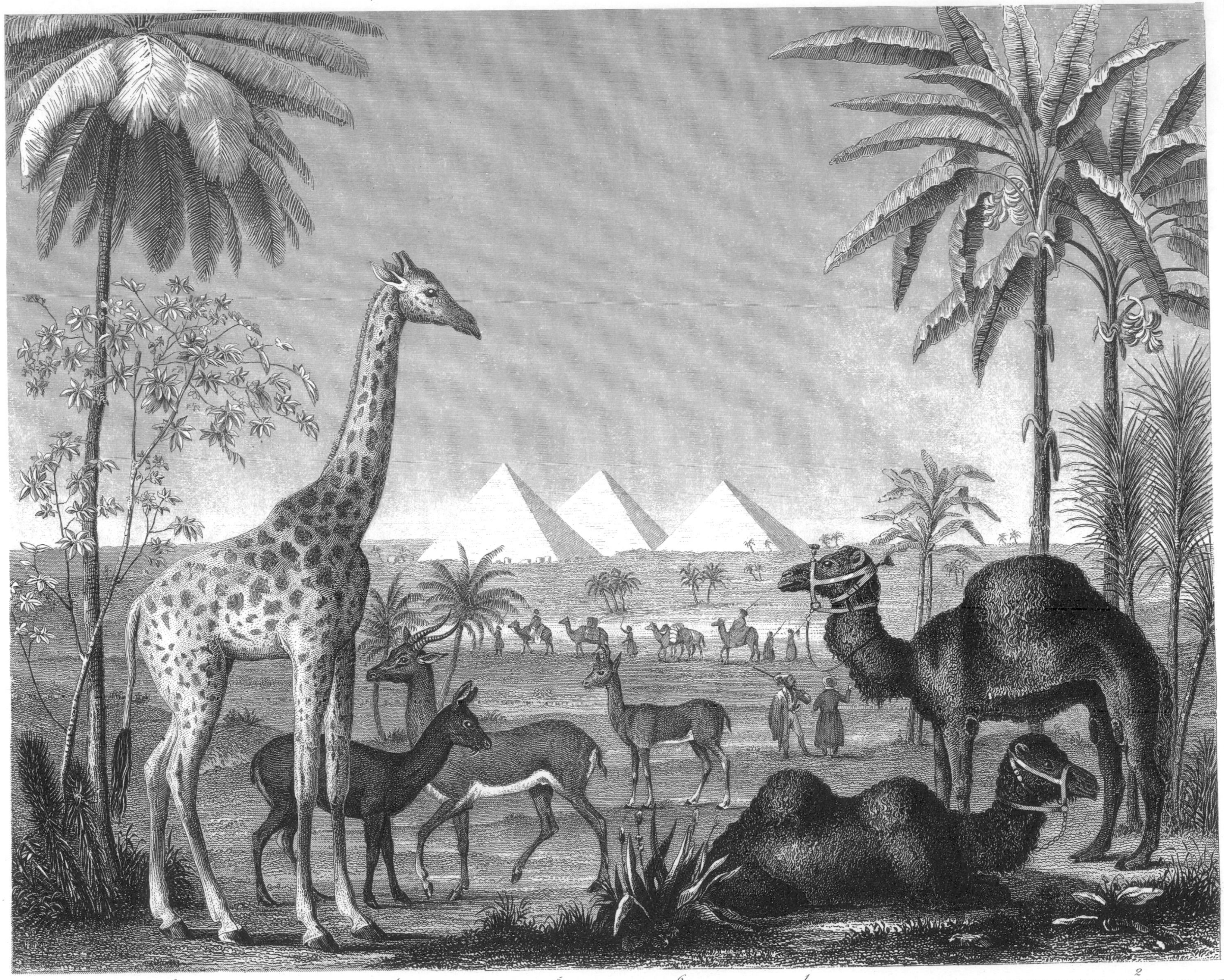

PLATE 109. REPRESENTATIVES OF THE ORDER ARTIODACTYLA: SUBORDERS TYLOPODA AND RUMINANTIA

PLATE 110. MEMBERS OF THE ORDERS ARTIODACTYLA AND PERISSODACTYLA

 PLATE 111. MEMBERS OF THE ORDER PERISSODACTYLA: FAMILY EQUIDAE

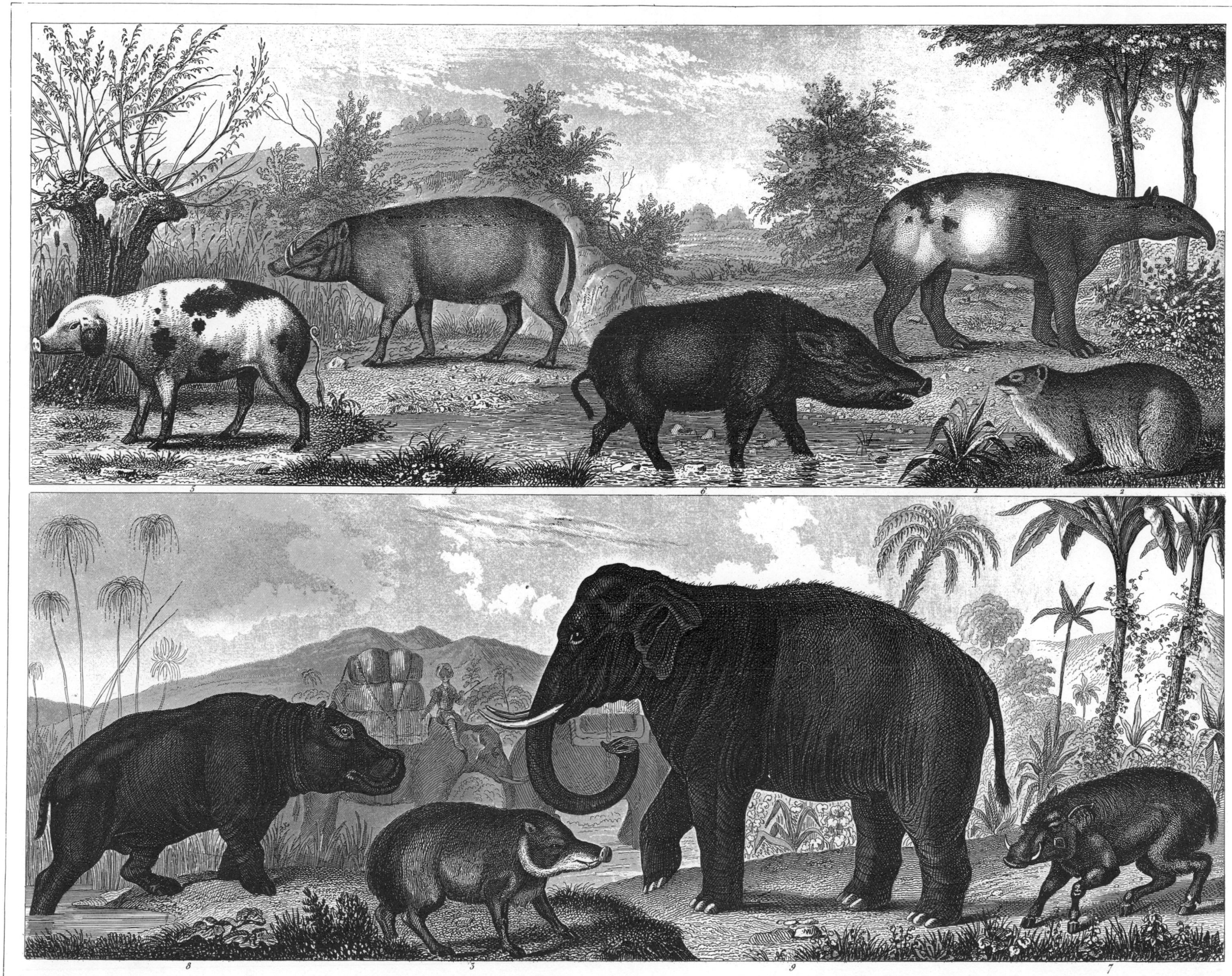

G. Heck dir.t Henry Winkles sculp.t

PLATE 112. REPRESENTATIVES OF THE ORDERS ARTIODACTYLA, PERISSODACTYLA, HYRACOIDEA, AND PROBOSCIDEA

PLATE 113. REPRESENTATIVES OF THE ORDERS EDENTATA, MARSUPIALIA, PHOLIDOTA, CARNIVORA, AND MONOTREMATA

PLATE 114. REPRESENTATIVES OF THE ORDERS INSECTIVORA CARNIVORA, RODENTIA, AND LAGOMORPHA

G. Heck dir.t

Henry Winkles sculp.t

PLATE 115. REPRESENTATIVES OF THE ORDERS RODENTIA AND CARNIVORA

PLATE 116. MEMBERS OF THE ORDER CARNIVORA: FAMILY FELIDAE

G. Heck dir.[t] Henry Winkles sculp.[t]

PLATE 117. REPRESENTATIVES OF THE ORDER CARNIVORA: FAMILIES CANIDAE, URSIDAE, AND MUSTELIDAE

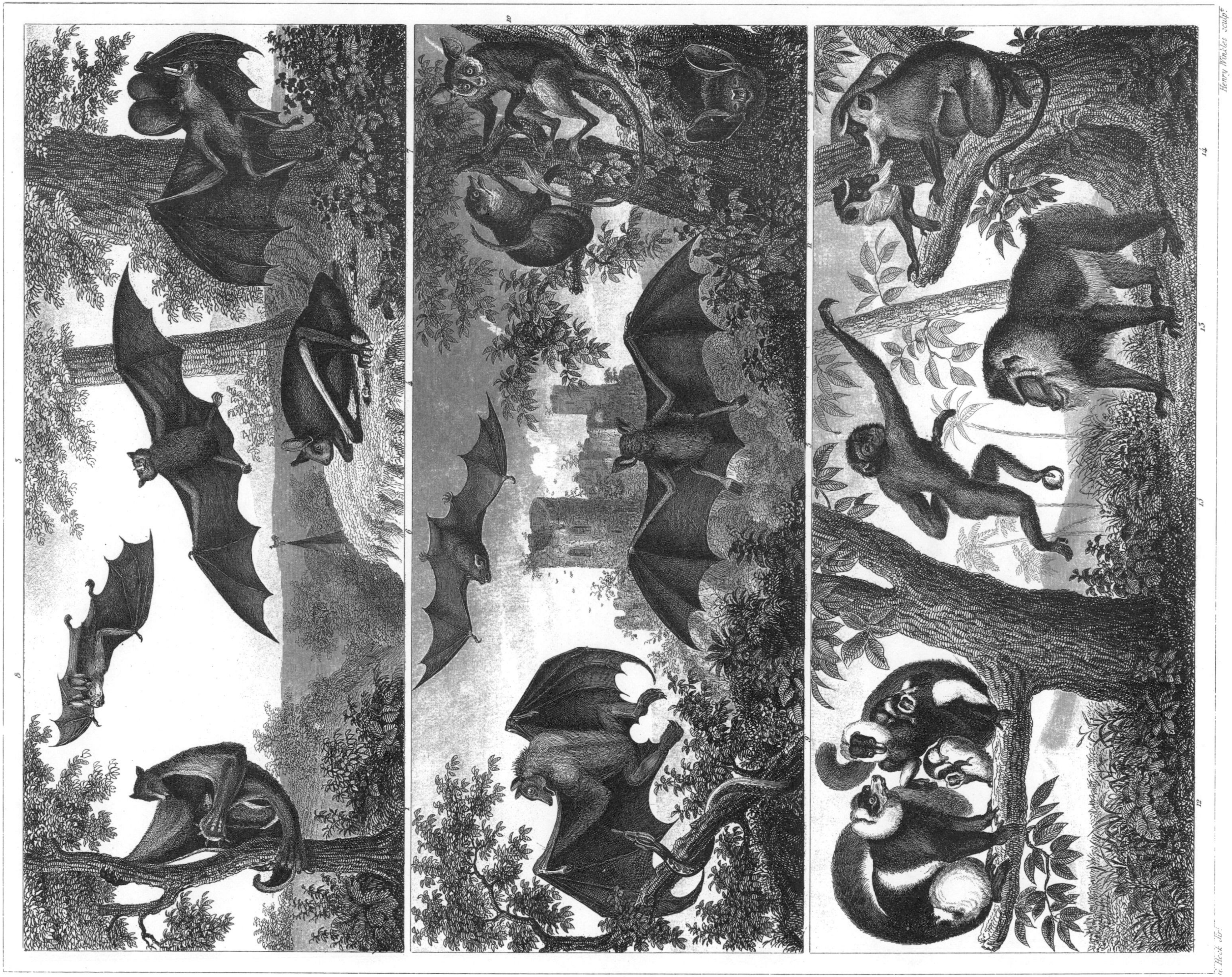

PLATE 118. REPRESENTATIVES OF THE ORDERS CHIROPTERA AND PRIMATES

PLATE 119. REPRESENTATIVES OF THE ORDERS PERISSODACTYLA AND PRIMATES

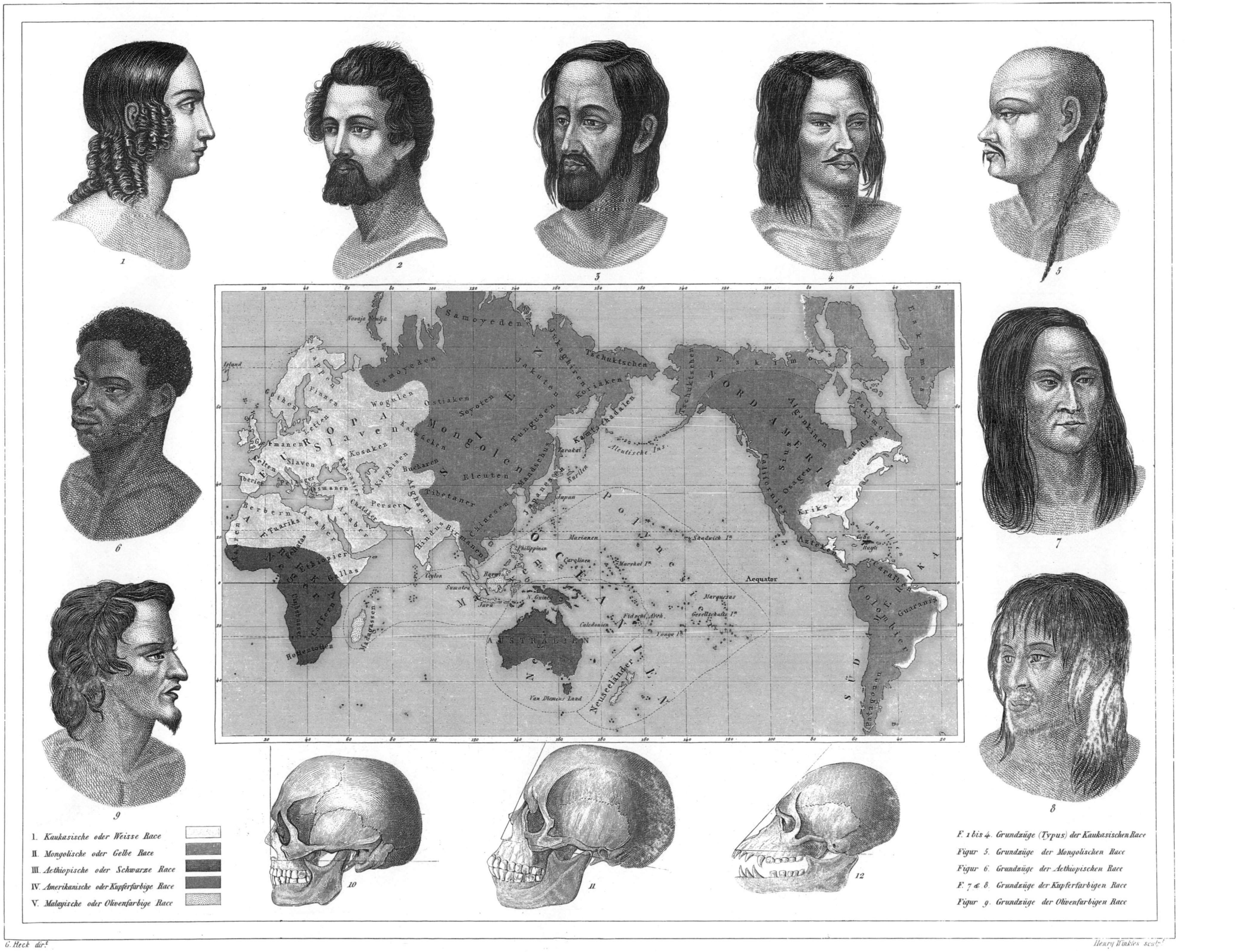
1
2
3
4
5
6
7
8
9
10
11
12
Samoyeden
Tschuktschen
Mongolen
Aequator
Australien
Neuseeländer
Van Diemens Land
Madagascar
Hottentotten
Philippinen
Sandwich I^n
Marquesas
Aleutische Ins.
Japan
Ceylon
Sumatra
Borneo
Java
I. Kaukasische oder Weisse Race
II. Mongolische oder Gelbe Race
III. Aethiopische oder Schwarze Race
IV. Amerikanische oder Kupferfarbige Race
V. Malayische oder Olivenfarbige Race
F. 1 bis 4. Grundzüge (Typus) der Kaukasischen Race
Figur 5. Grundzüge der Mongolischen Race
Figur 6. Grundzüge der Aethiopischen Race
F. 7 & 8. Grundzüge der Kupferfarbigen Race
Figur 9. Grundzüge der Olivenfarbigen Race
G. Heck dir.^t
Henry Winkles sculp.^t

PLATE 120. VARIETIES OF MANKIND

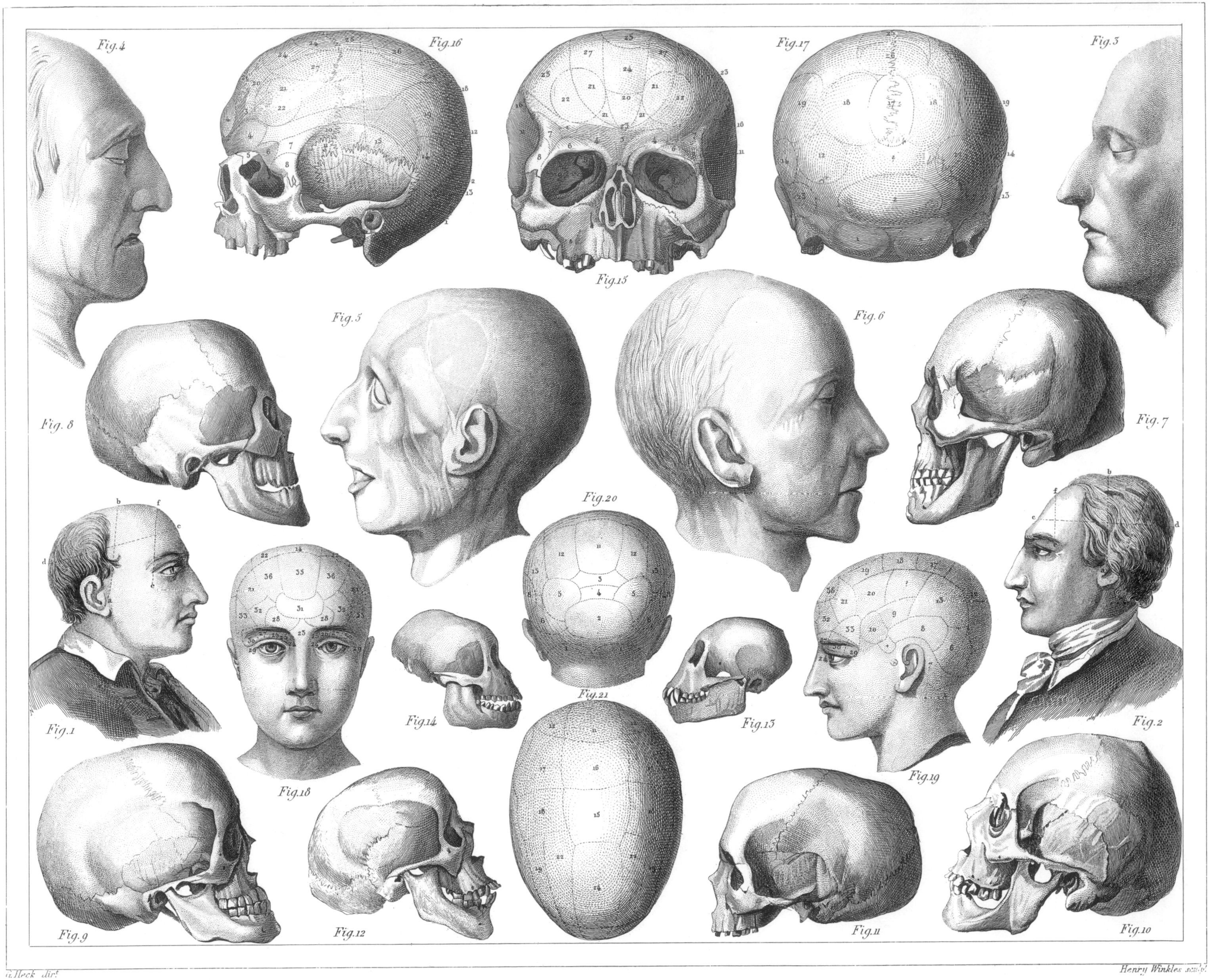

PLATE 121. ILLUSTRATING THE PSYCHOLOGICAL RELATIONS OF THE BRAIN (PHRENOLOGY)

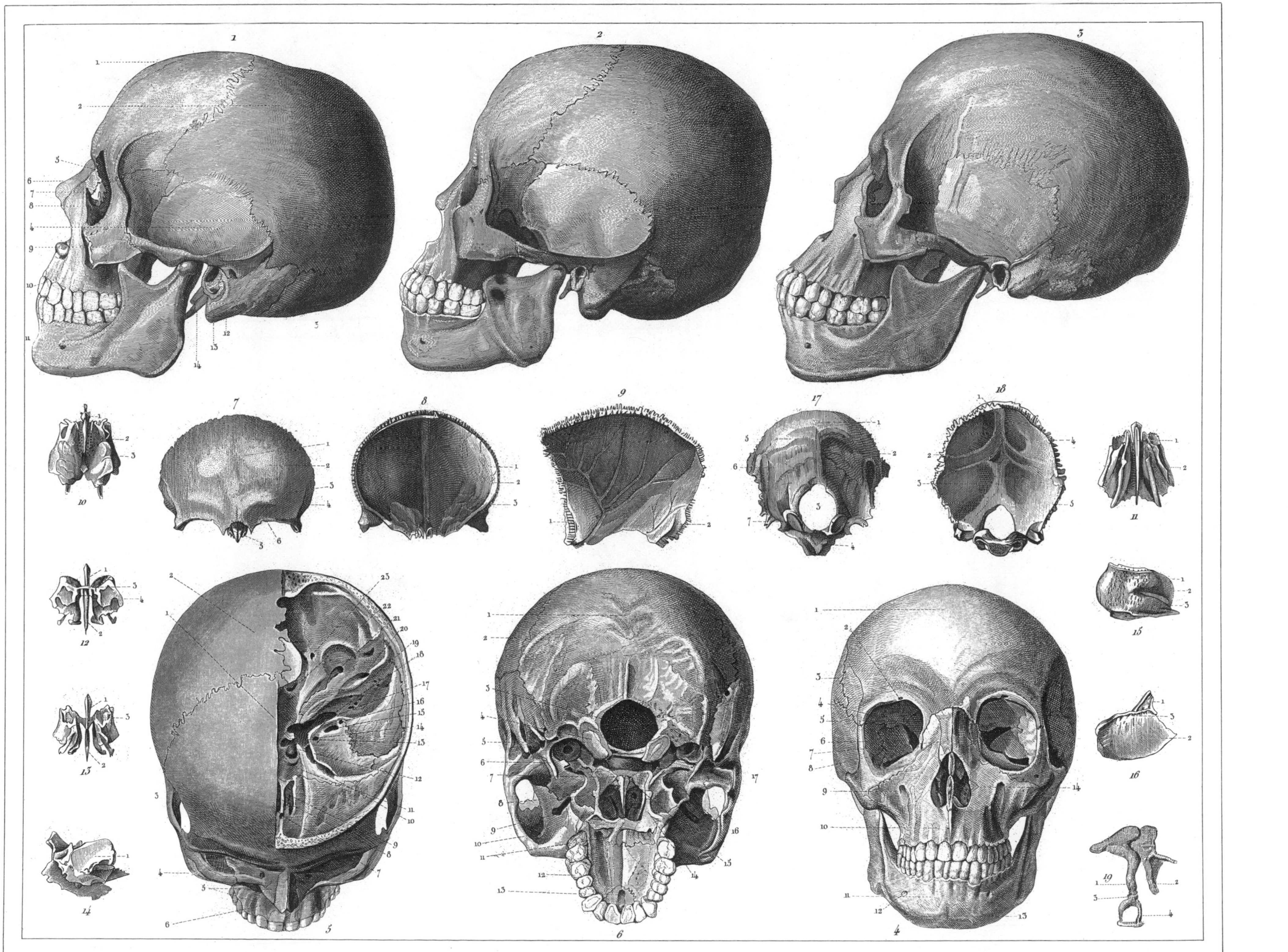

G. Heck dir.t Henry Winkles sculp.t

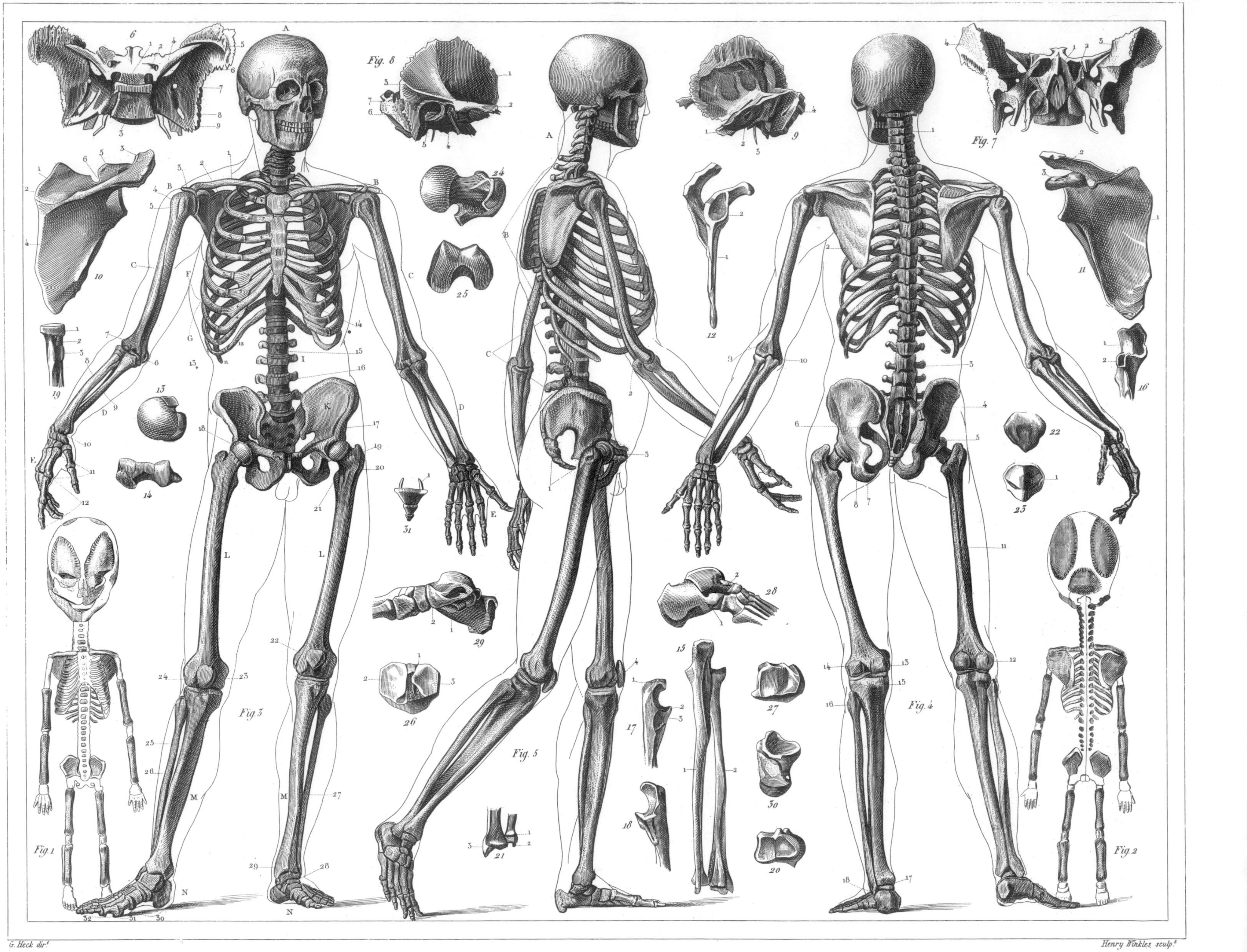

G. Heck dir.t Henry Winkles sculp.t

PLATE 123. ANATOMY OF THE BONES

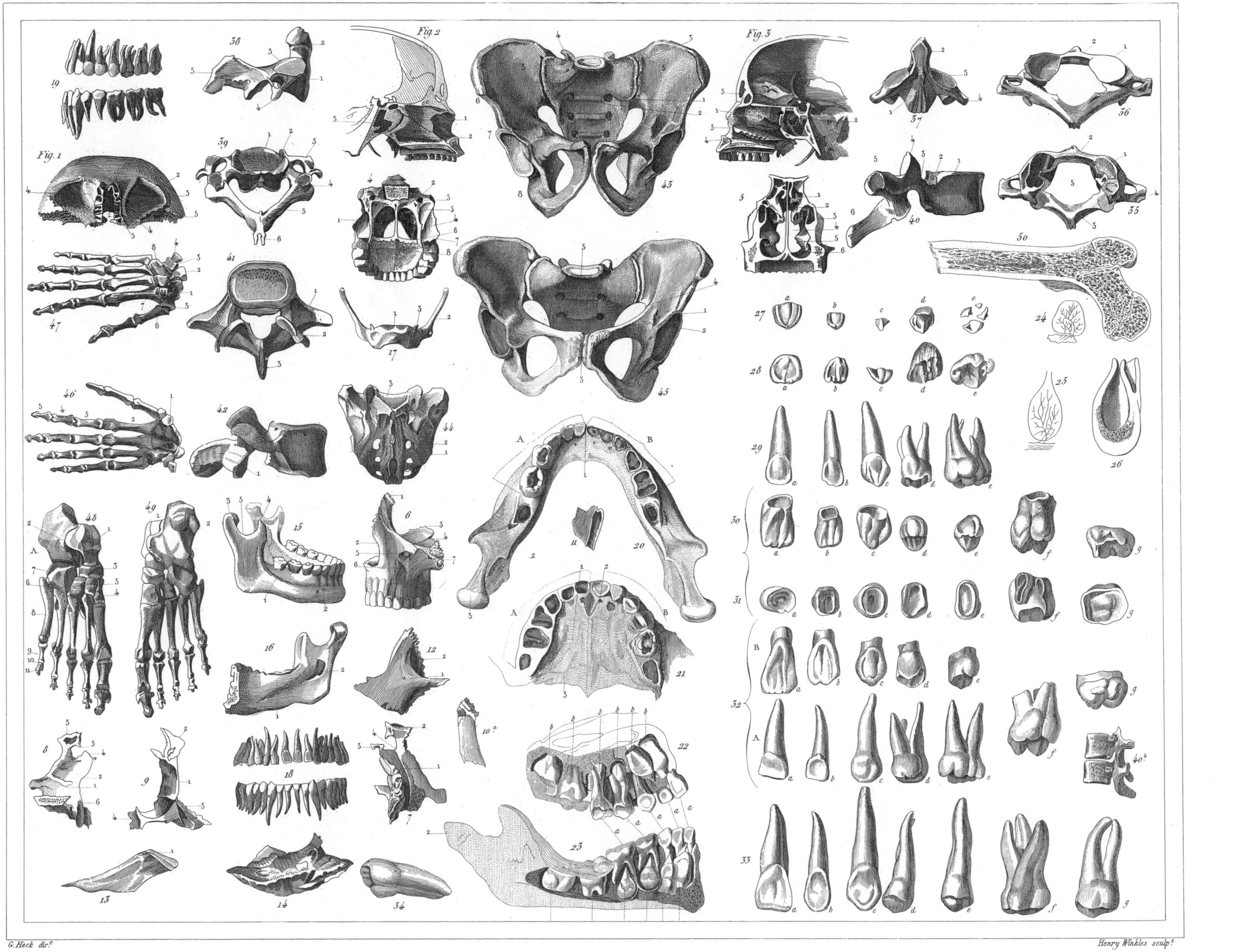

G. Heck dir.t Henry Winkles sculp.t

PLATE 124. ANATOMY OF THE BONES

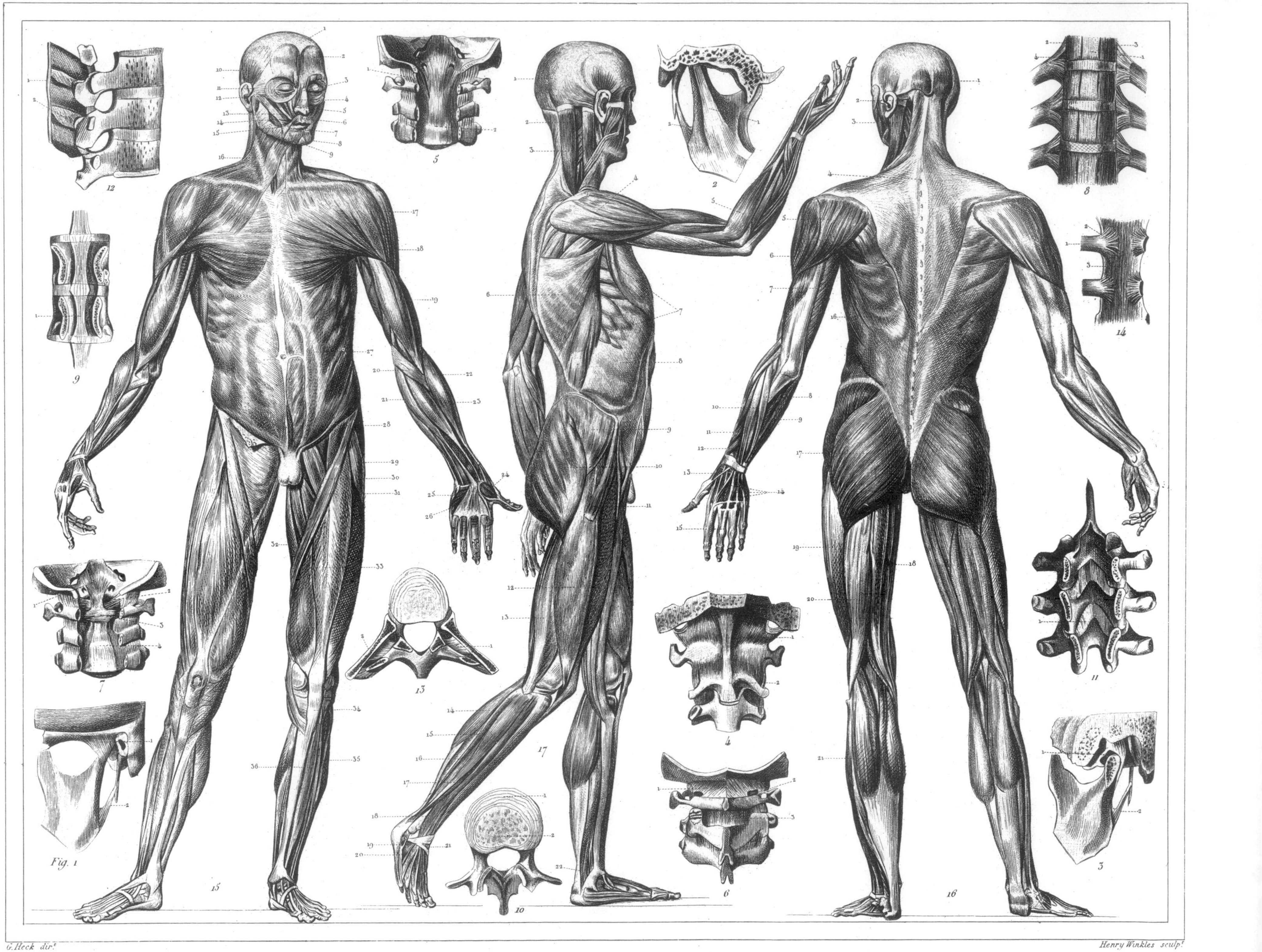

G. Heck dir.t Henry Winkles sculp.t

PLATE 125. ANATOMY OF THE LIGAMENTS AND MUSCLES

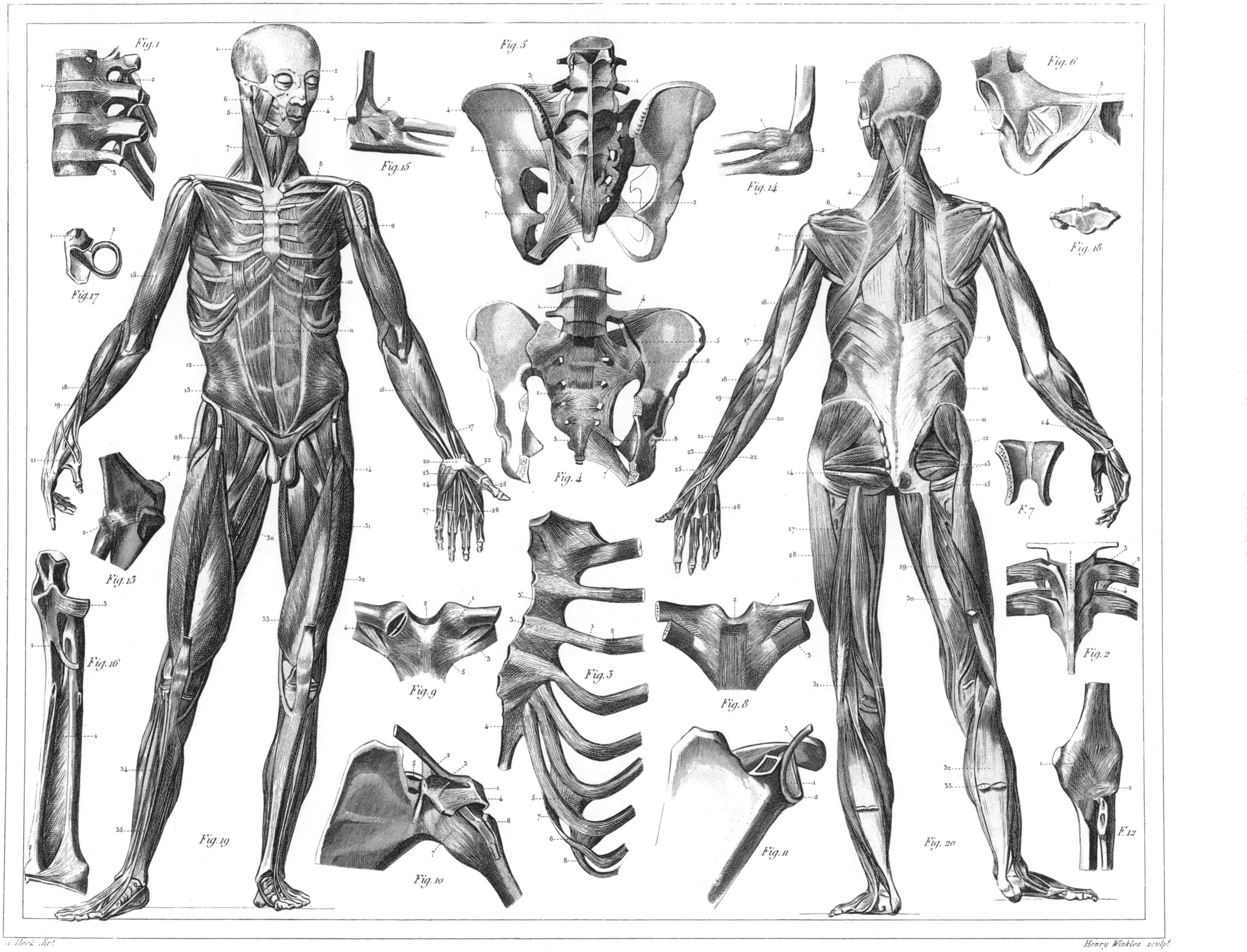
Fig. 1
Fig. 2
Fig. 3
Fig. 4
Fig. 5
Fig. 6
F. 7
Fig. 8
Fig. 9
Fig. 10
Fig. 11
F. 12
Fig. 13
Fig. 14
Fig. 15
Fig. 16
Fig. 17
Fig. 18
Fig. 19
Fig. 20

G. Heck dir.   Henry Winkles sculpt.

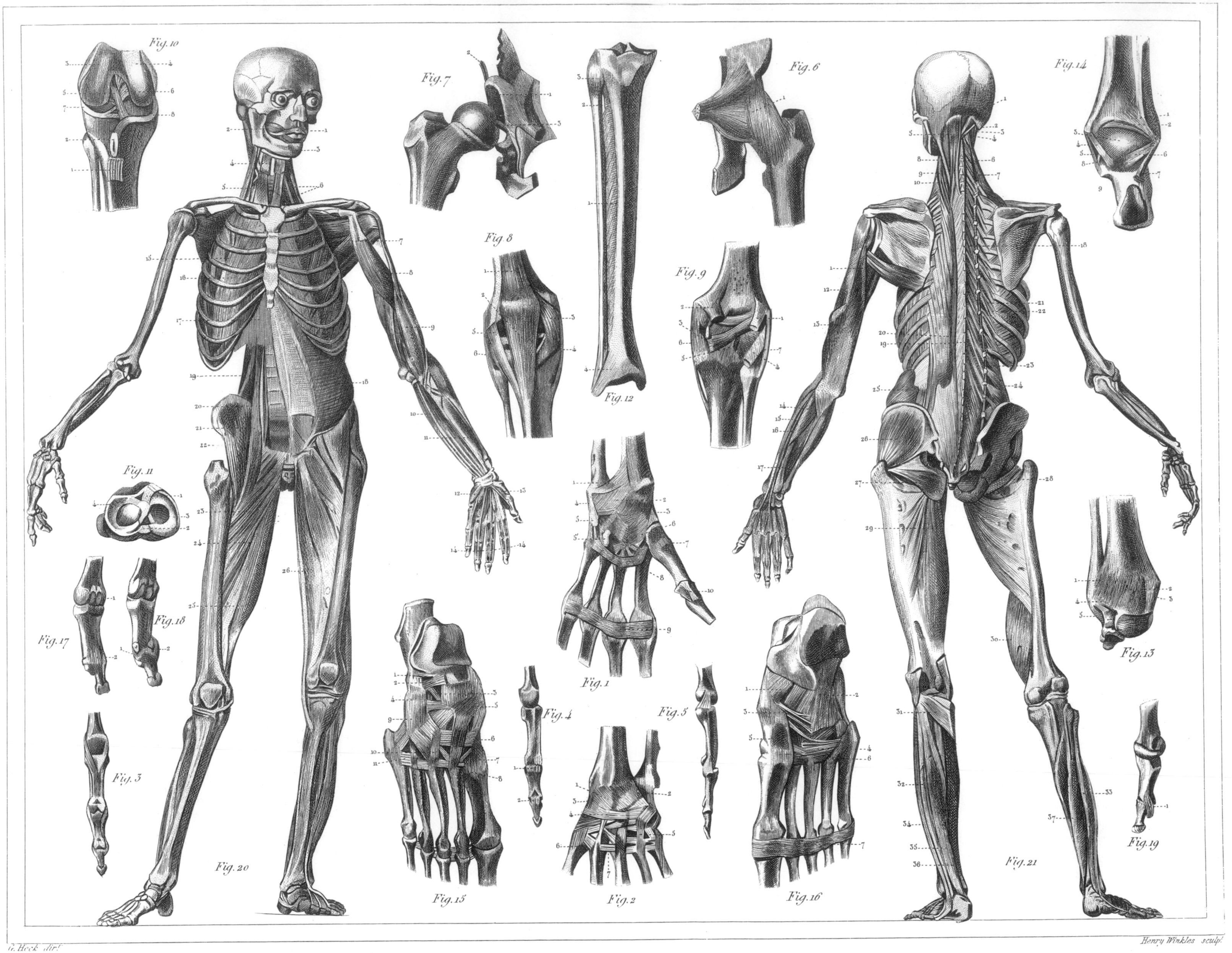

G. Heck dir.

Henry Winkles sculp.

PLATE 127. ANATOMY OF THE LIGAMENTS AND MUSCLES

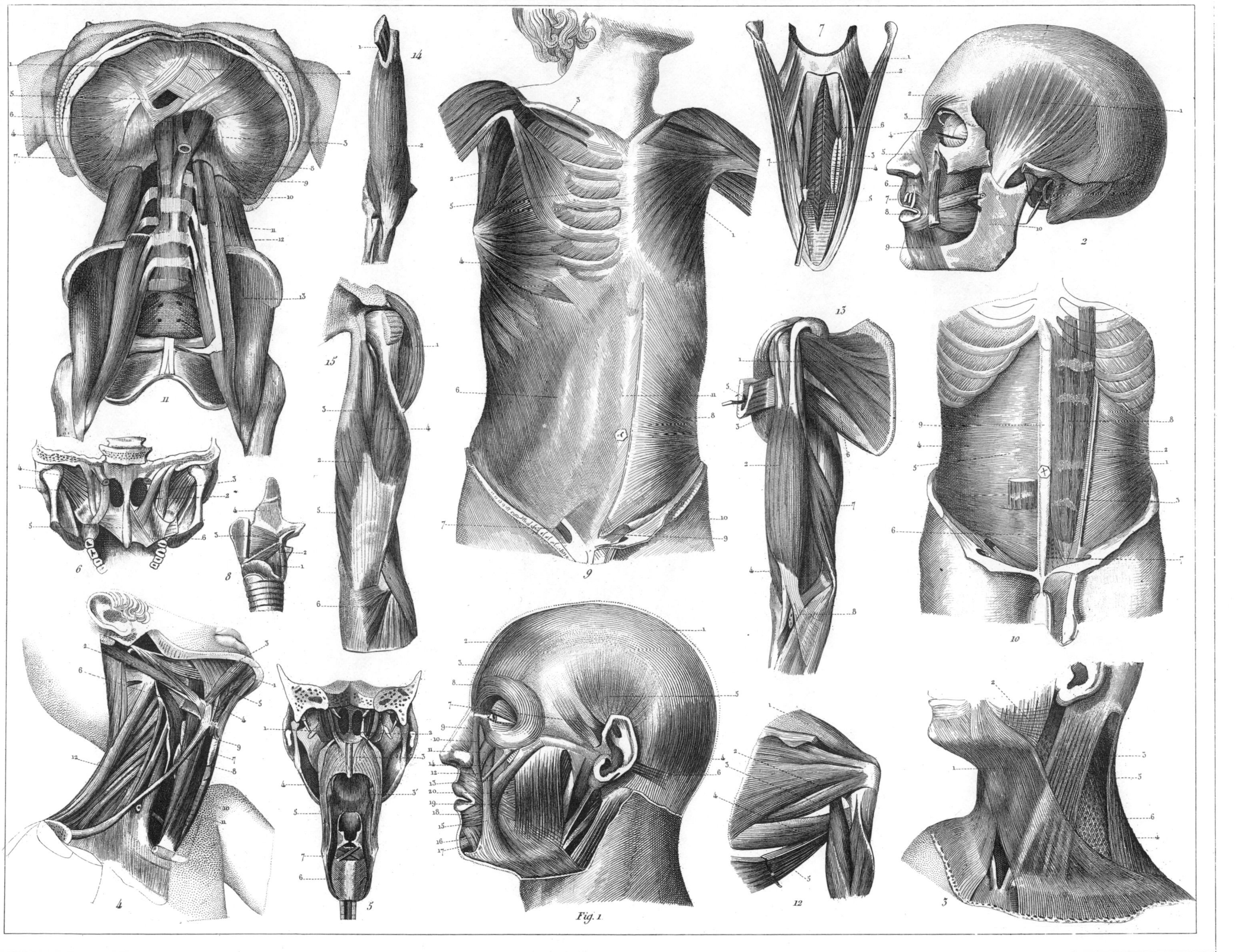

G. Heck dir.t Henry Winkles sculp.t

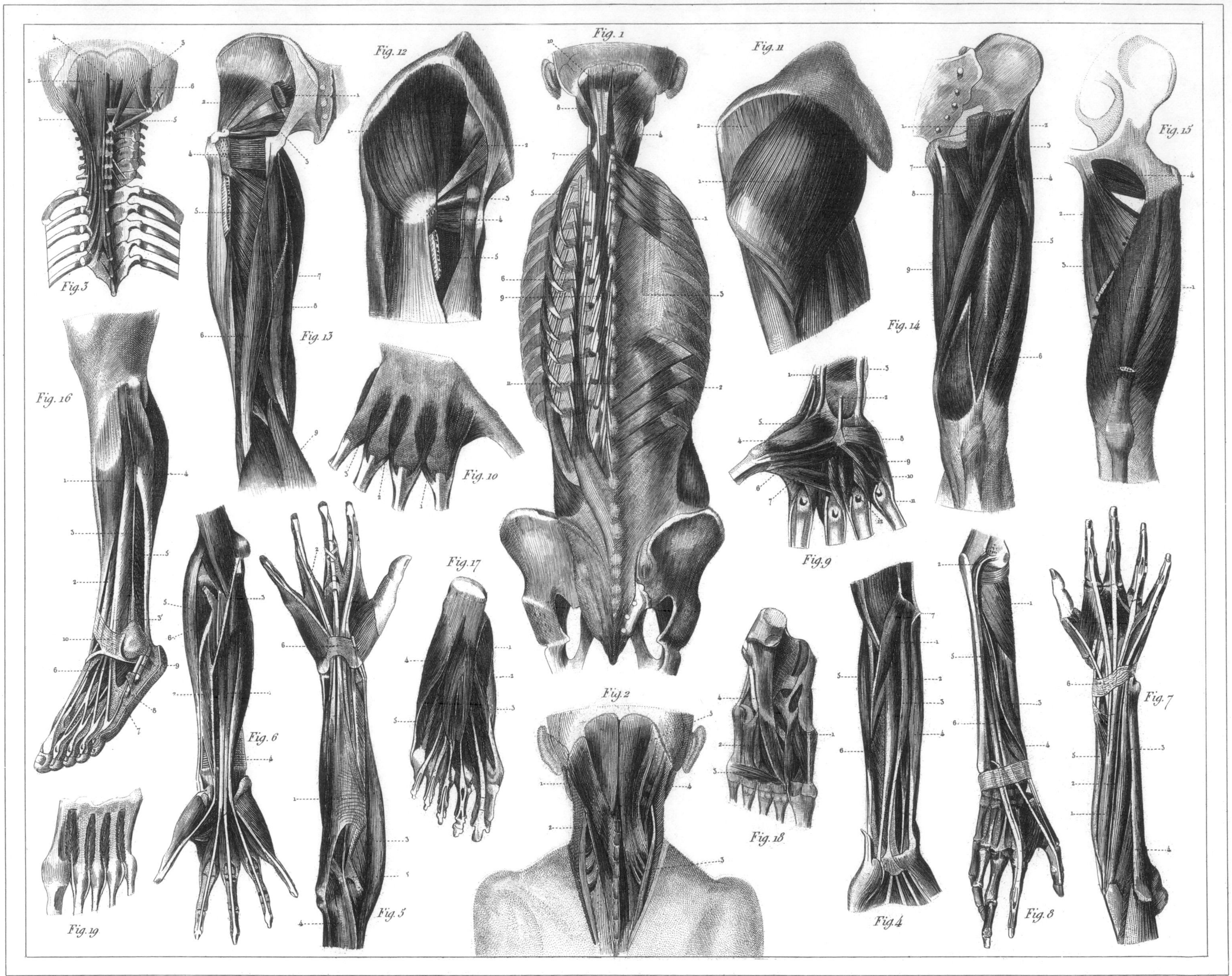

G. Heck dir.e Henry Winkles sculp.t

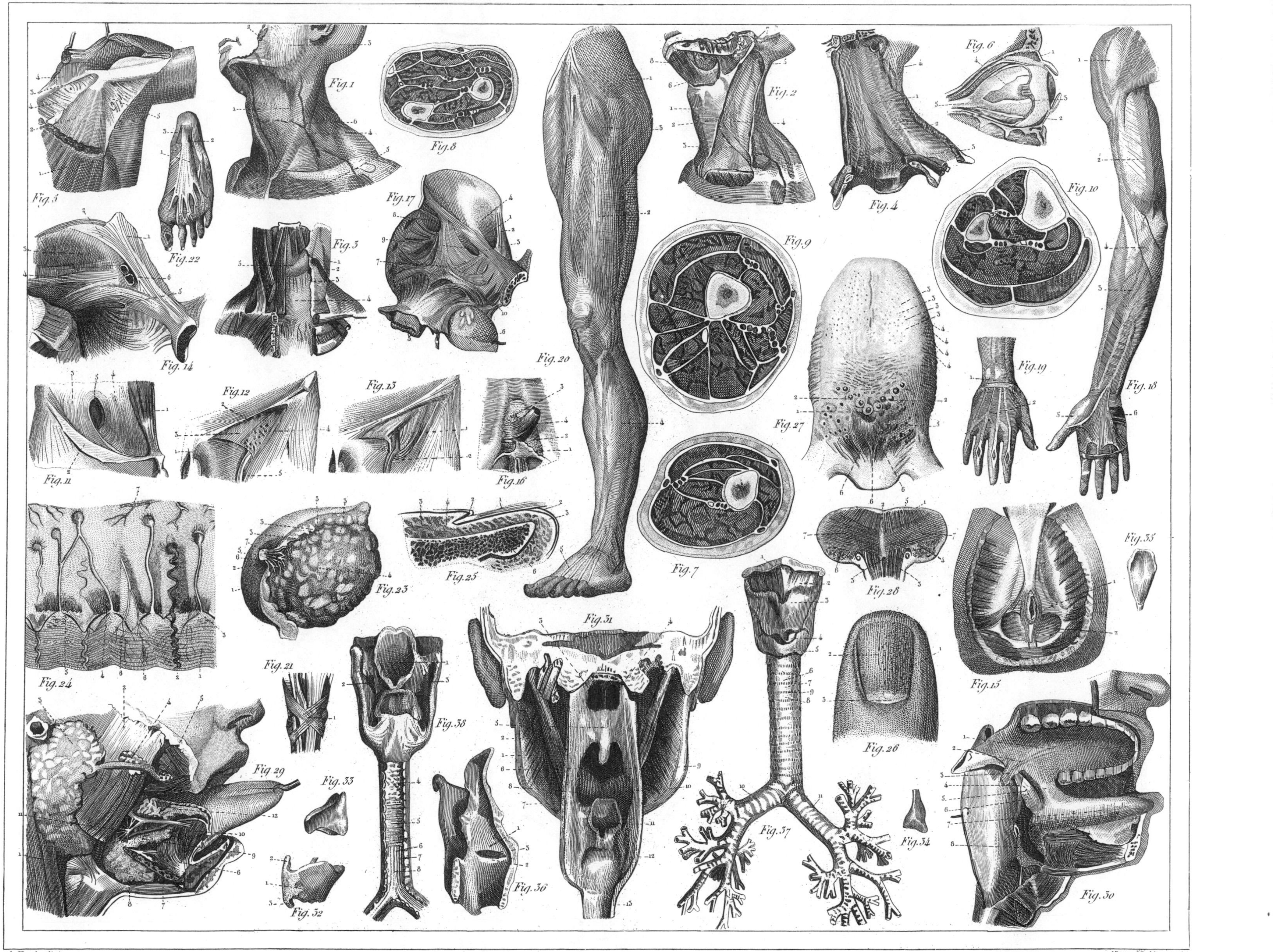

G. Heck dir.

Henry Winkles sculp.

PLATE 130. ANATOMY OF THE FASCIAE, INTEGUMENTS, AND ORGANS OF MASTICATION AND RESPIRATION

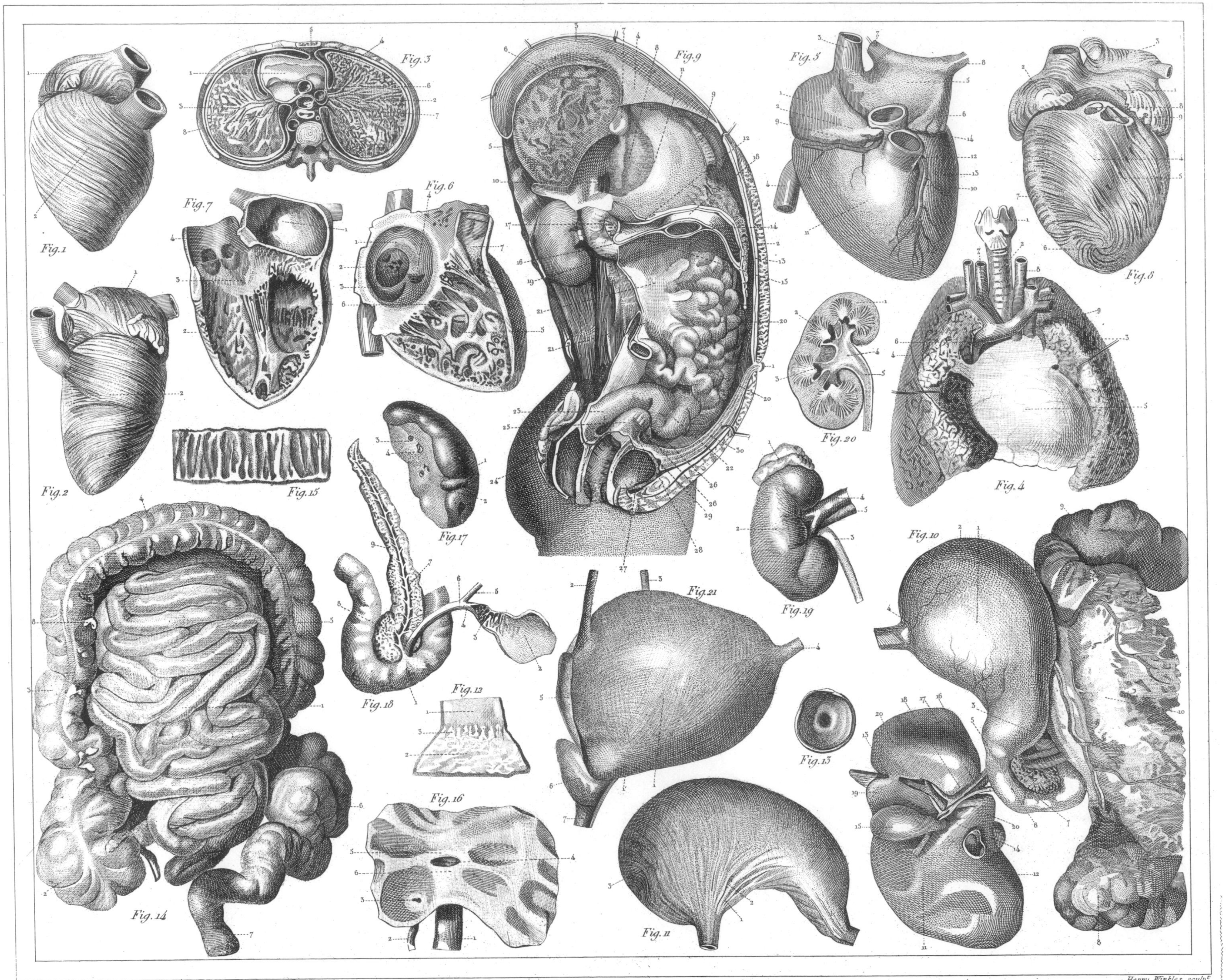

G. Heck dir.ᵗ Henry Winkles sculp.ᵗ

PLATE 131. ANATOMY OF THE ORGANS OF DIGESTION

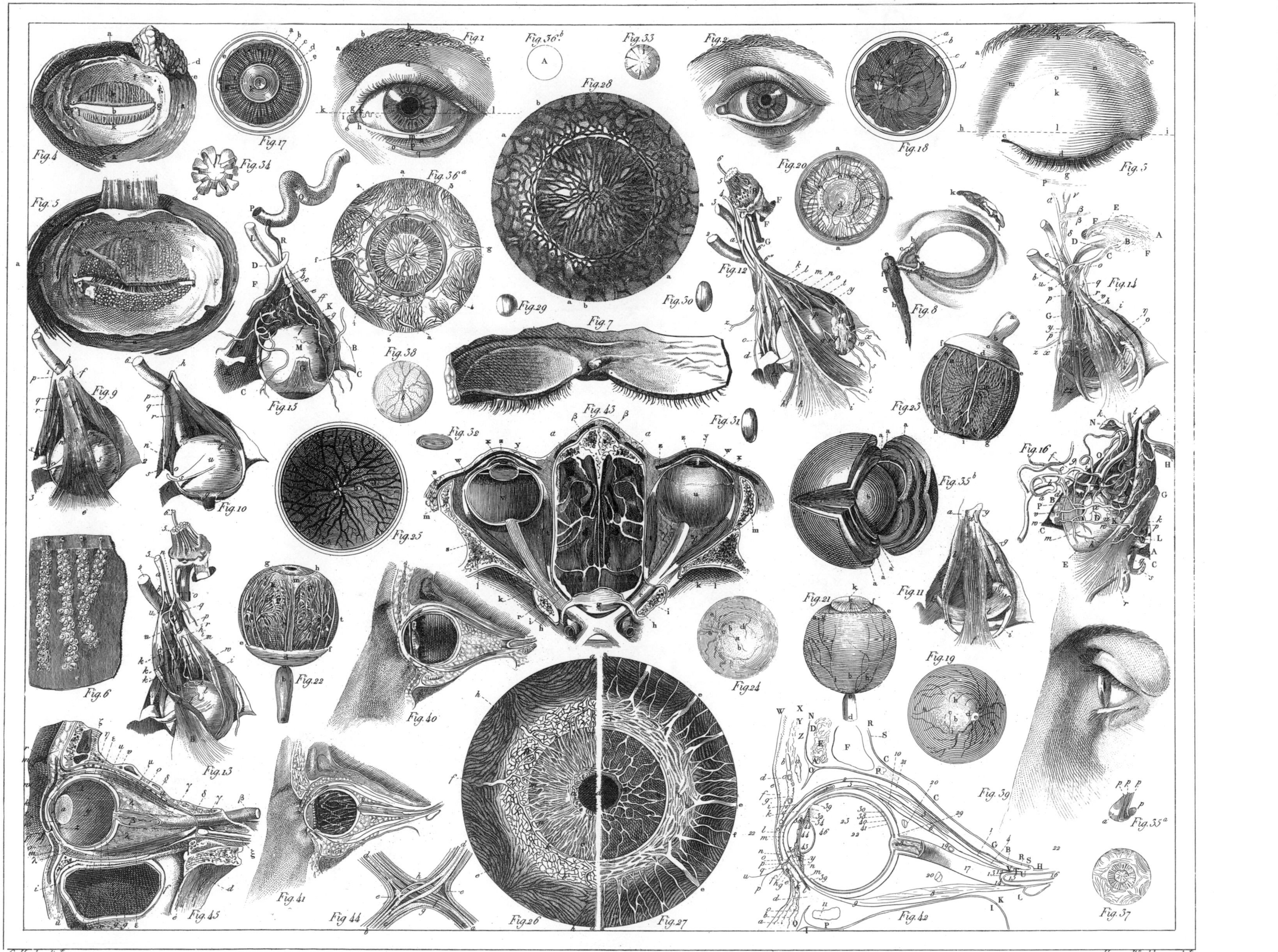

G. Heck dir.t Henry Winkles sculp.t

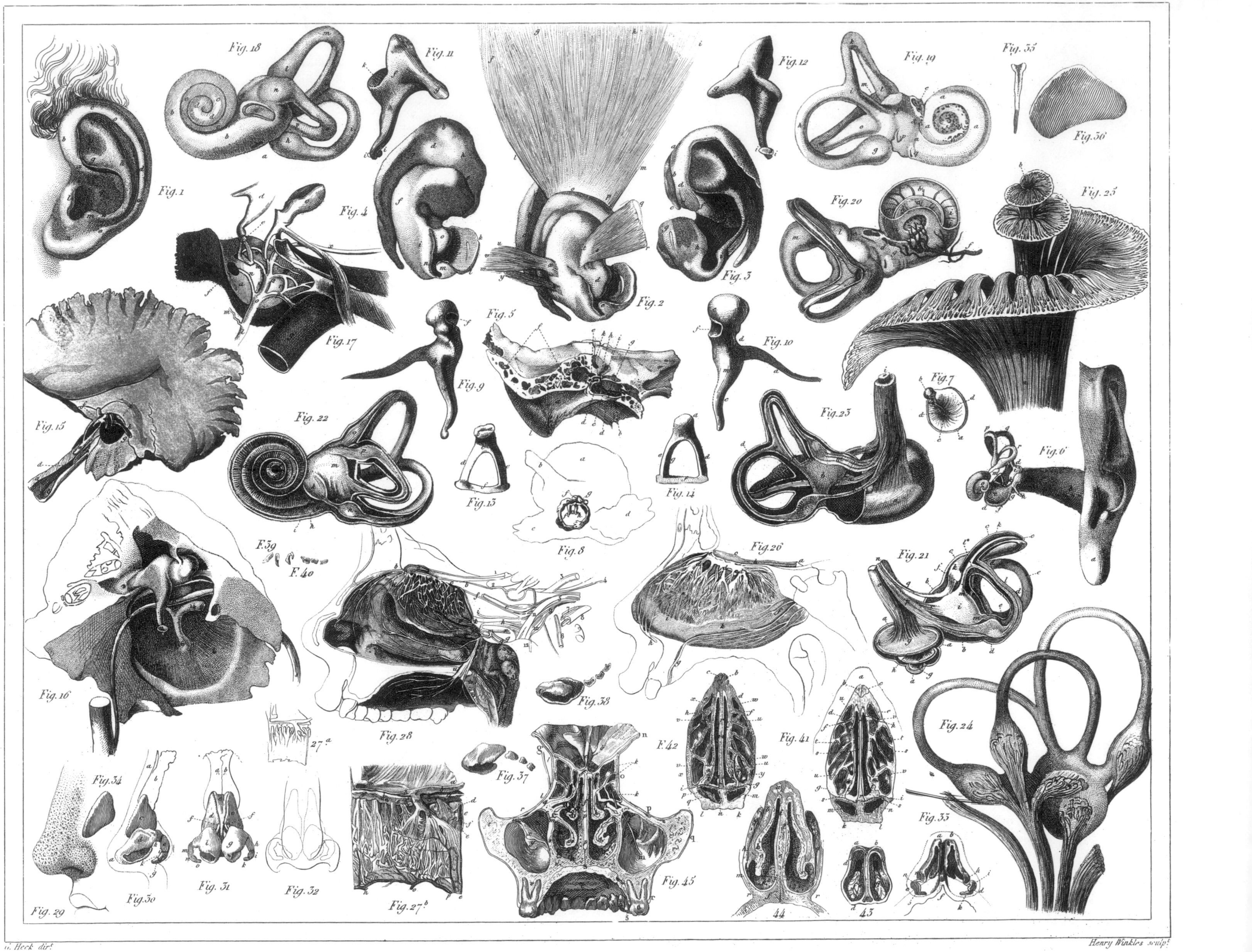

G. Heck dir.

Henry Winkles sculp.

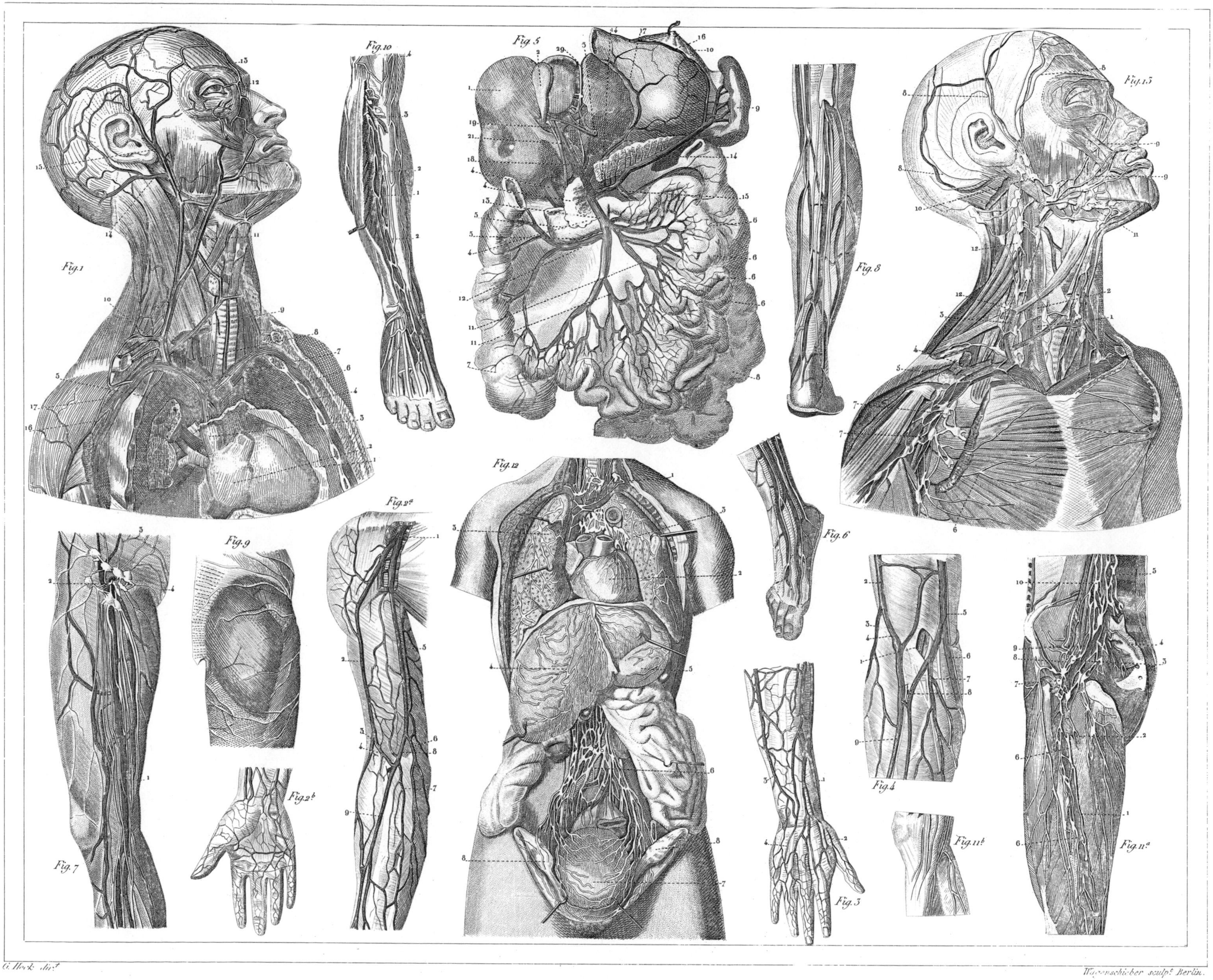
Fig. 1
Fig. 10
Fig. 5
Fig. 8
Fig. 13
Fig. 12
Fig. 6
Fig. 7
Fig. 9
Fig. 2a
Fig. 2b
Fig. 4
Fig. 3
Fig. 11b
Fig. 11a
G. Heck dir.
Wagenschieber sculp. Berlin.

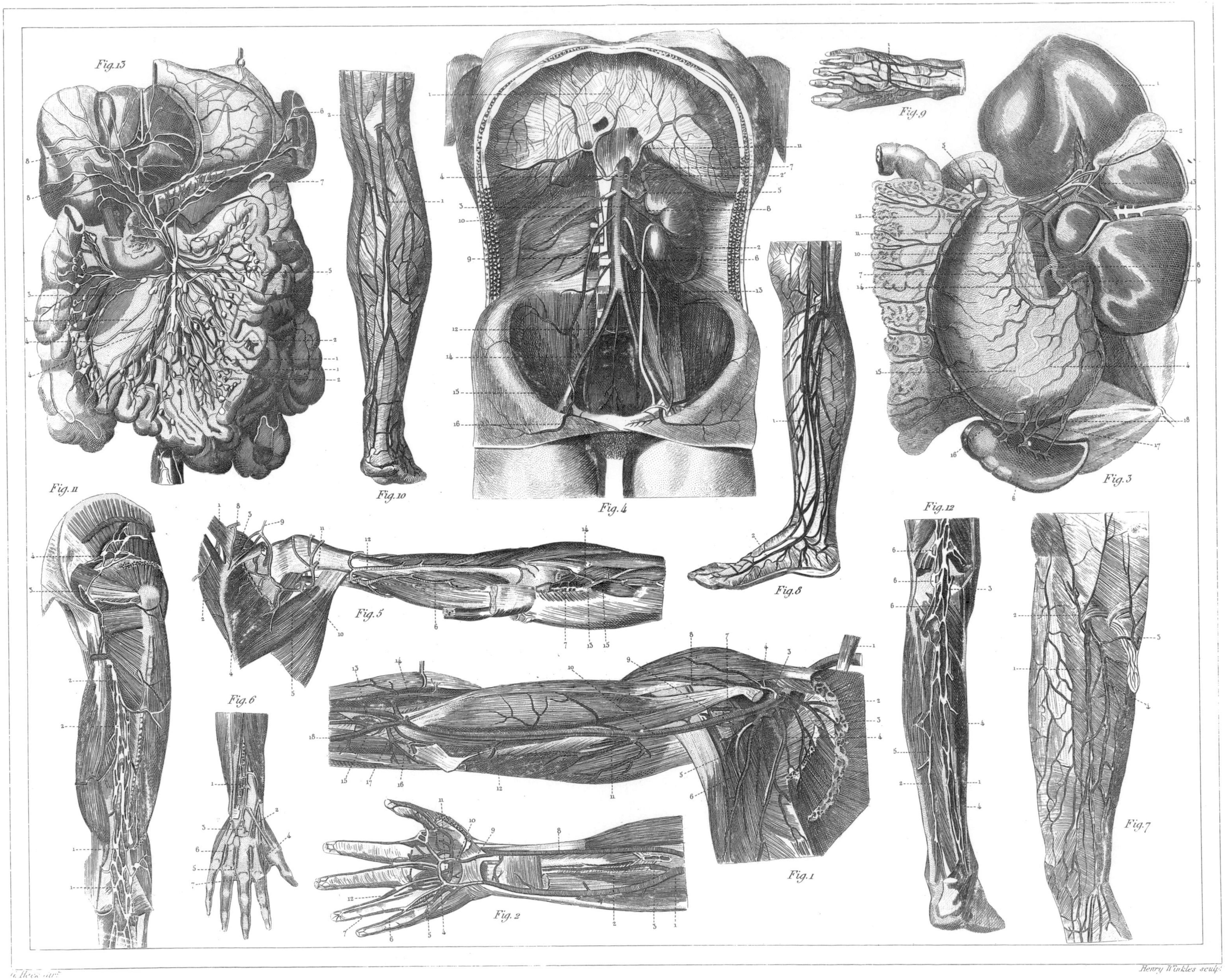

G. Heck dir.

Henry Winkles sculp.

PLATE 135. ANATOMY OF THE VASCULAR SYSTEM

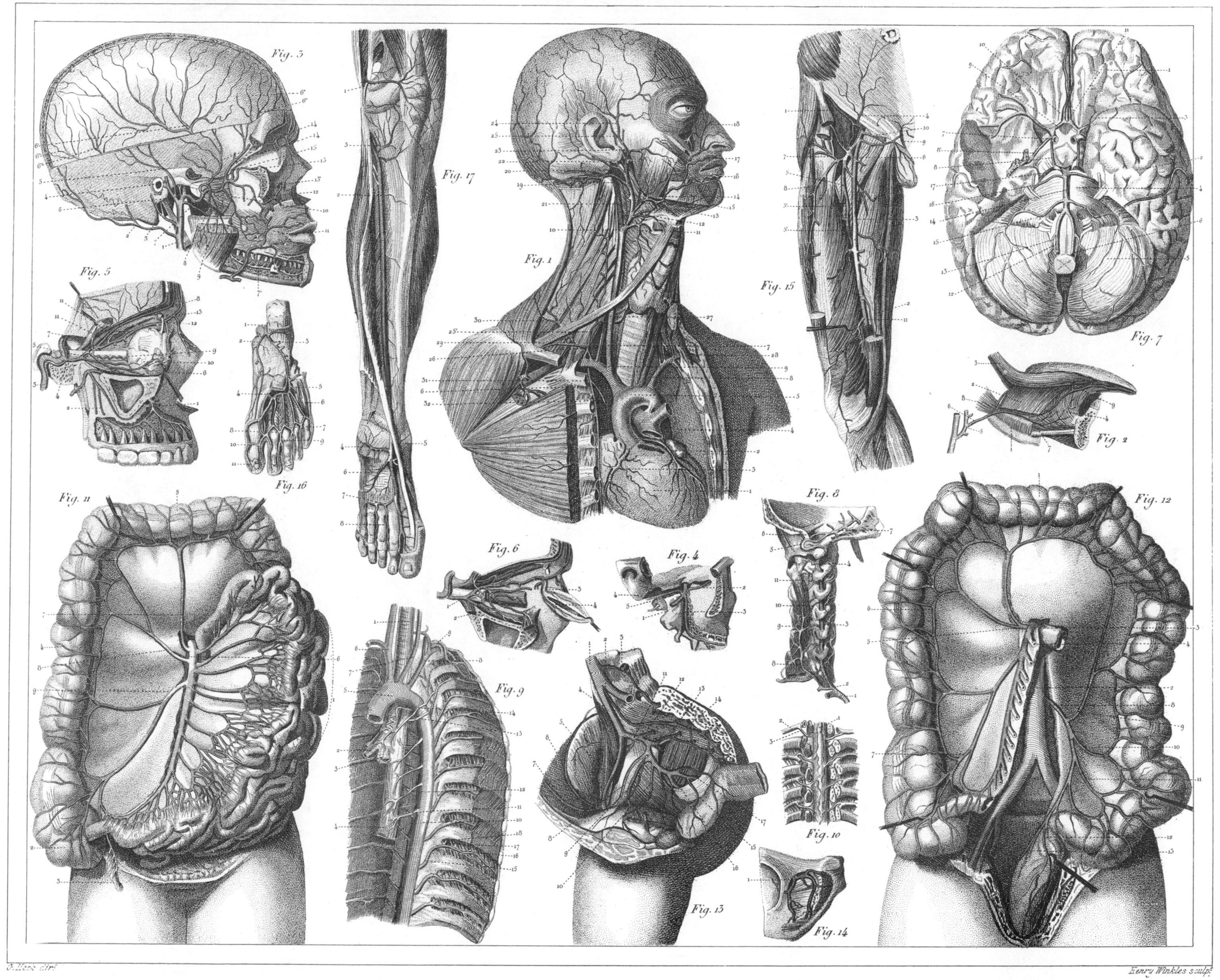
Fig. 3
Fig. 17
Fig. 1
Fig. 15
Fig. 7
Fig. 5
Fig. 16
Fig. 2
Fig. 11
Fig. 8
Fig. 12
Fig. 6
Fig. 4
Fig. 9
Fig. 10
Fig. 13
Fig. 14
Henry Winkles sculpt.

PLATE 136. ANATOMY OF THE VASCULAR SYSTEM

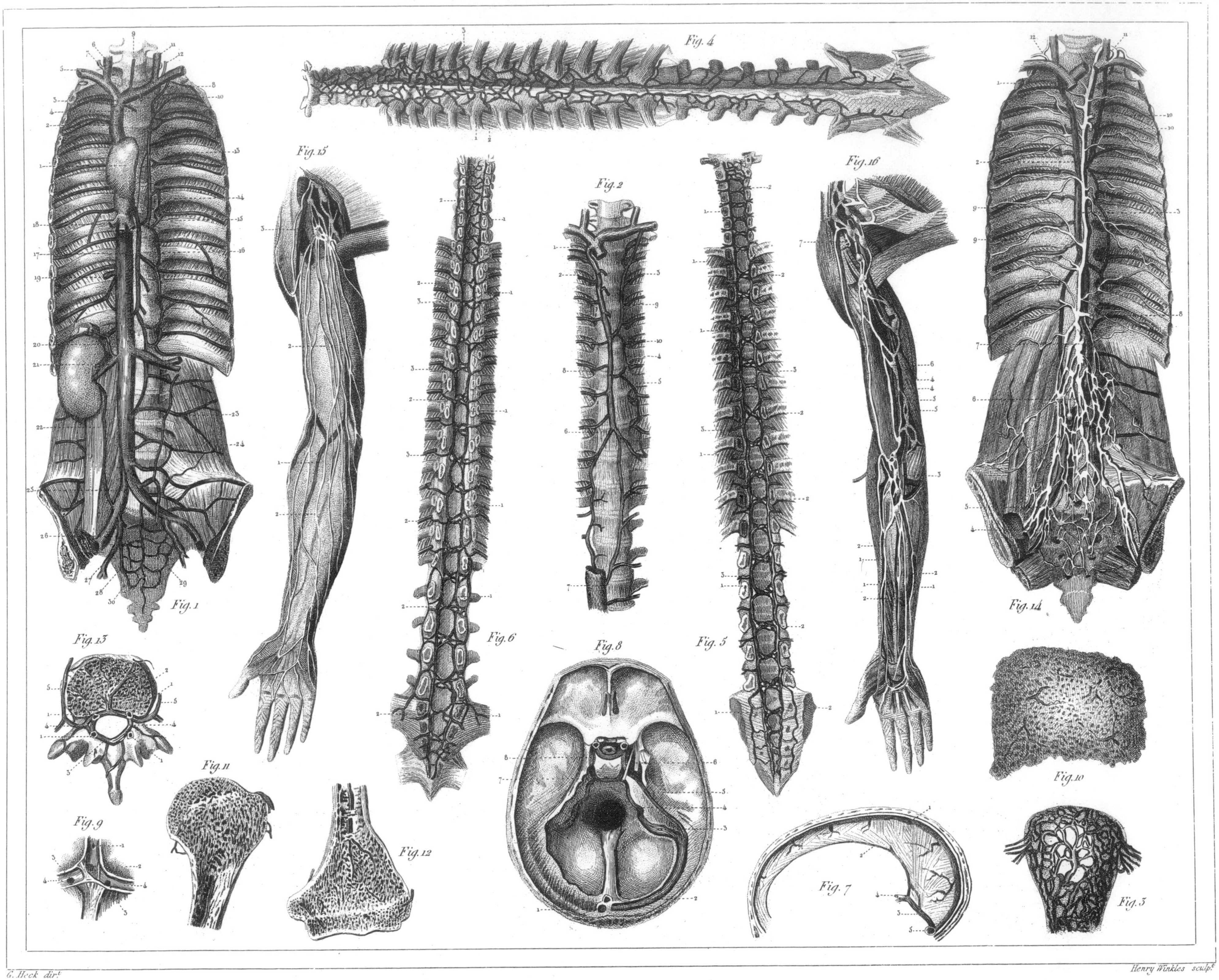

G. Heck dir.t Henry Winkles sculp.t

PLATE 137. ANATOMY OF THE VASCULAR SYSTEM

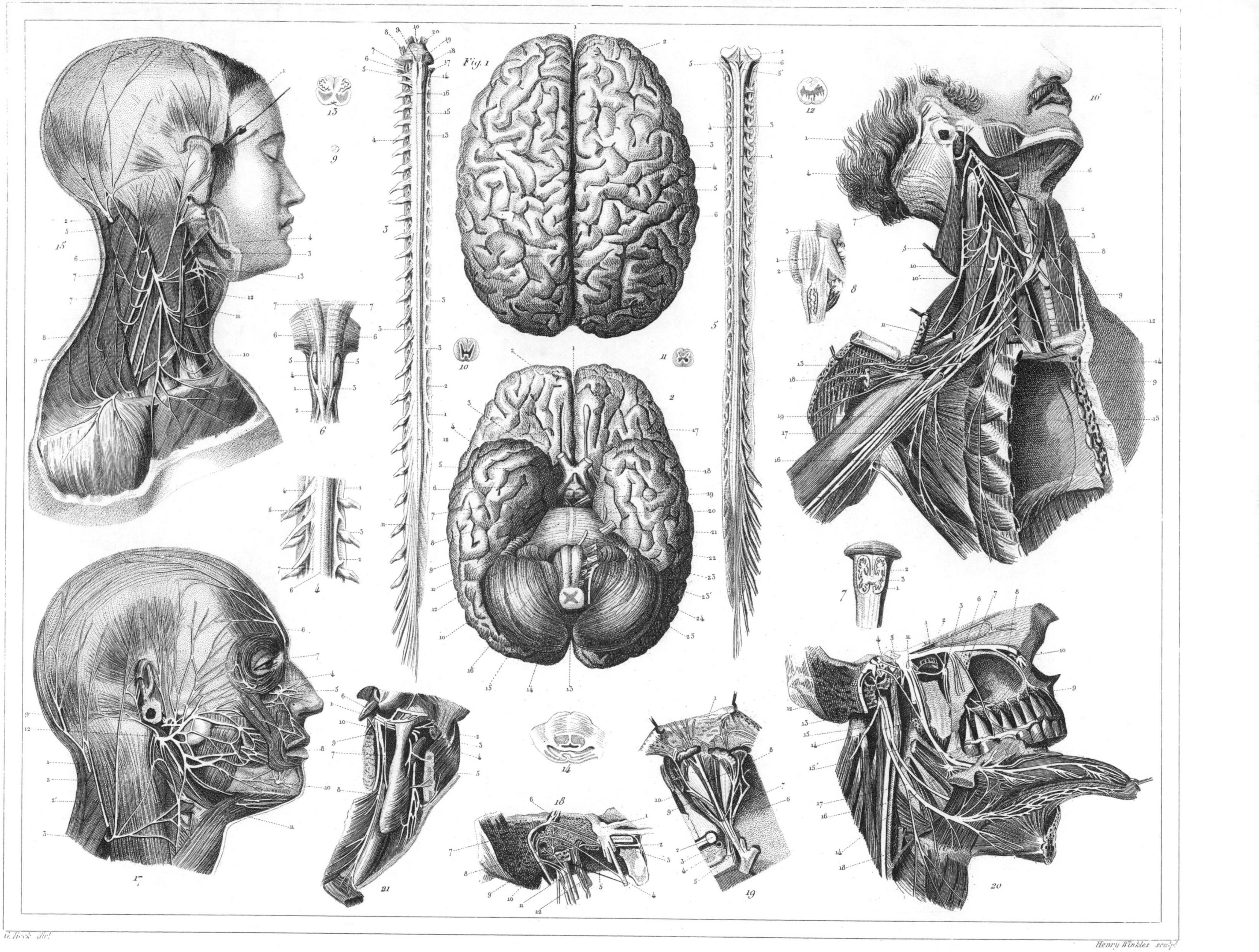

PLATE 138. ANATOMY OF THE BRAIN AND NERVES

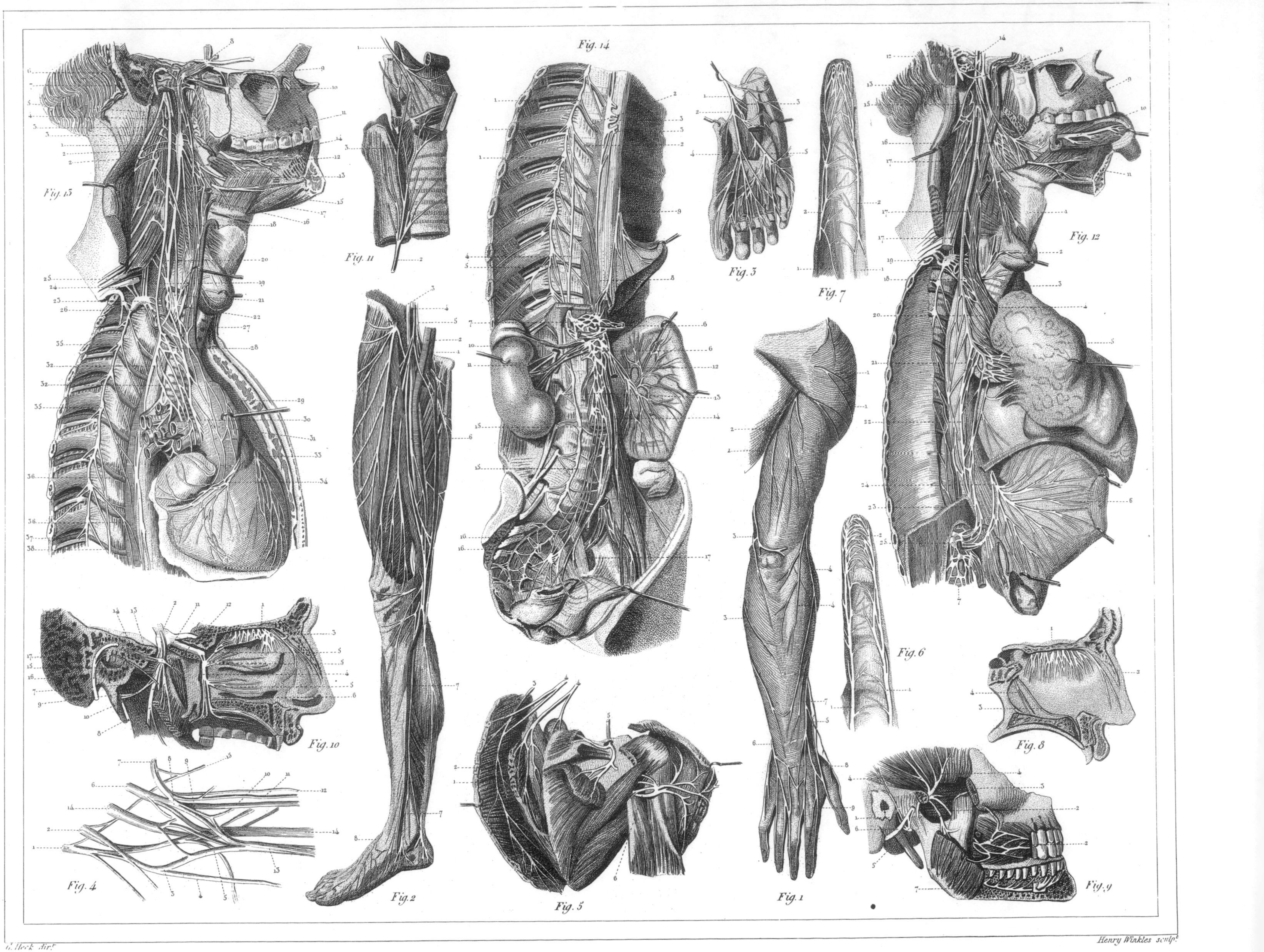
Fig. 14
Fig. 13
Fig. 11
Fig. 3
Fig. 7
Fig. 12
Fig. 6
Fig. 10
Fig. 8
Fig. 4
Fig. 2
Fig. 5
Fig. 1
Fig. 9

G. Heck dir.t Henry Winkles sculp.t

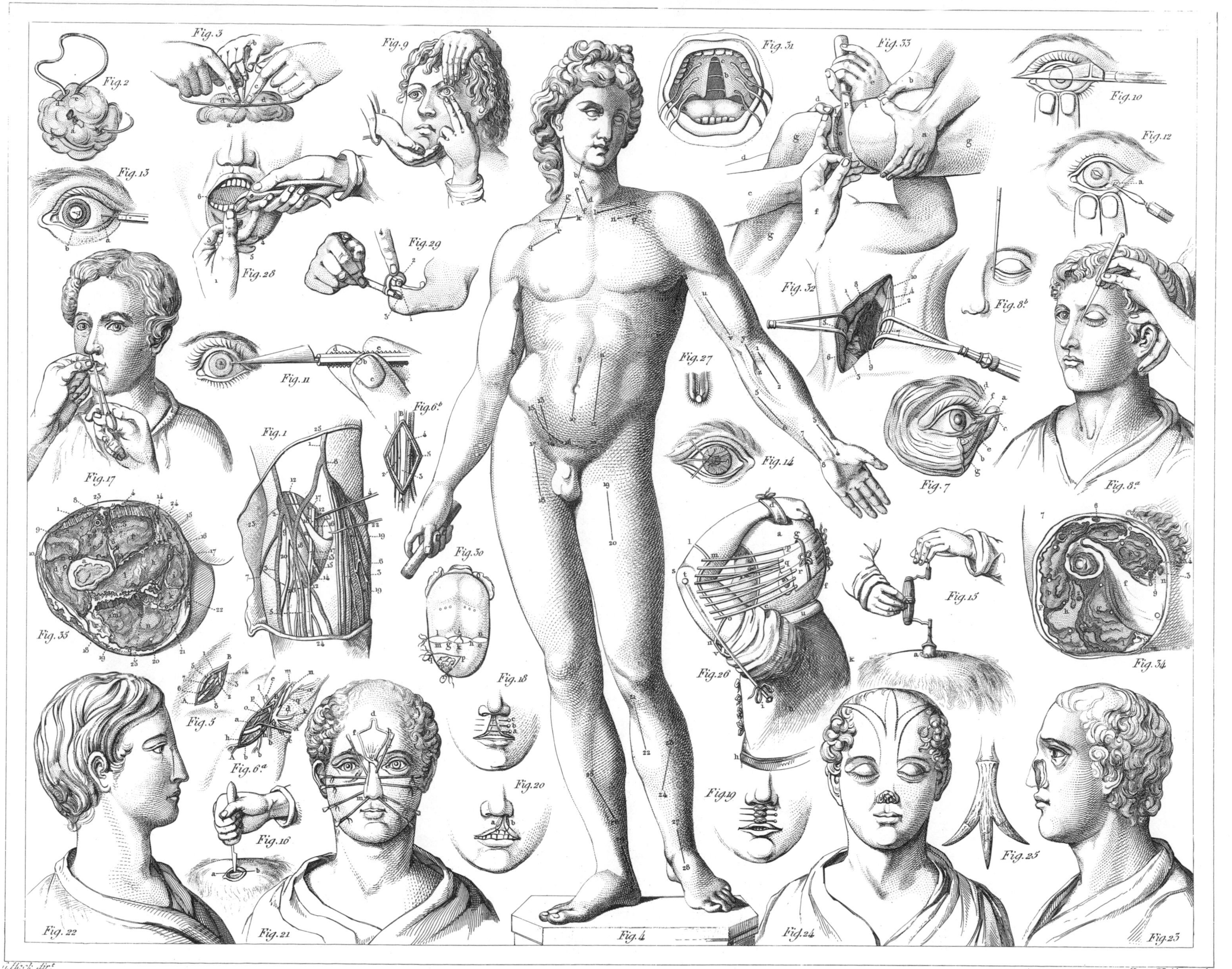

G. Heck dir.t Henry Winkles sculp.t

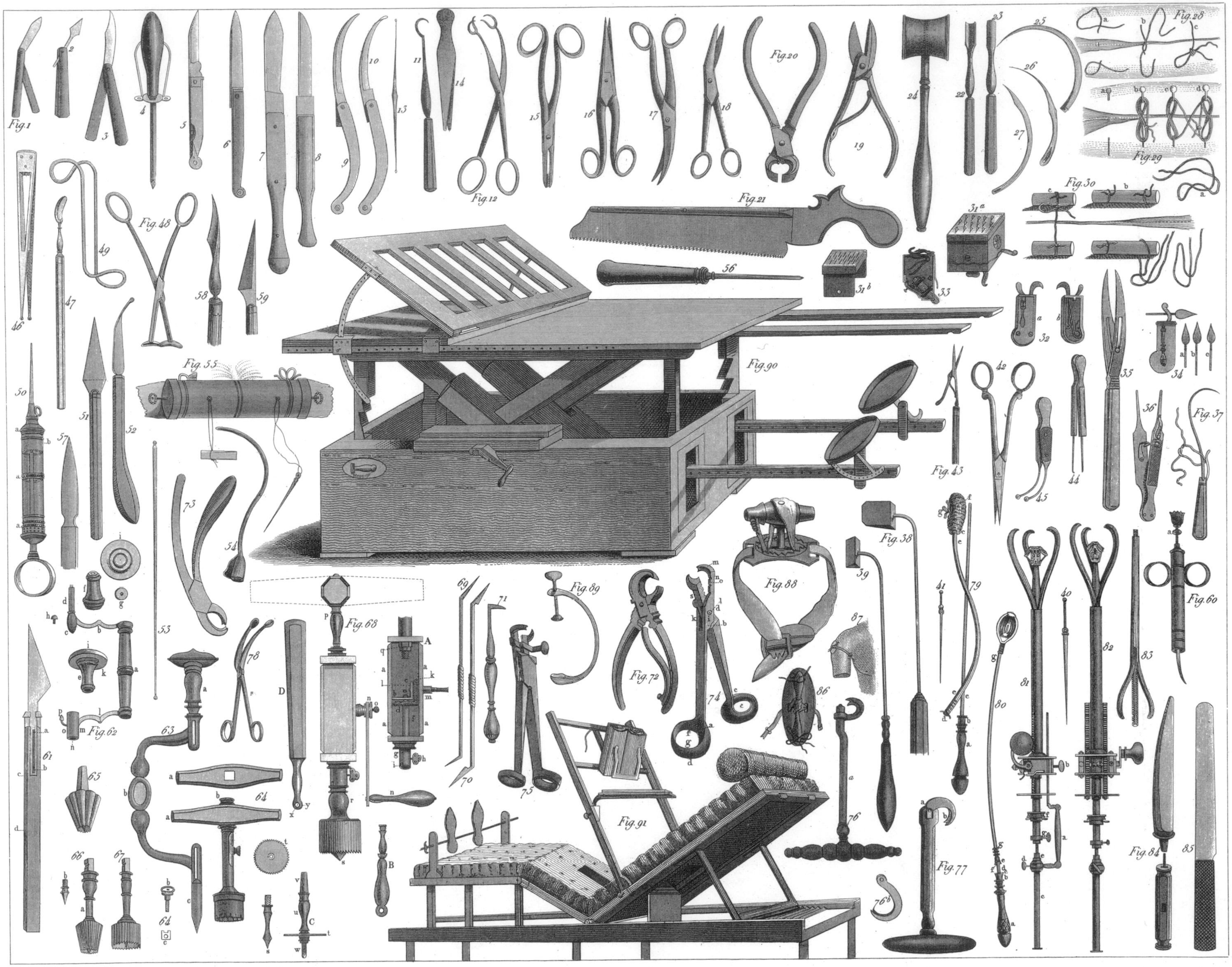

G. Heck dir.t Henry Winkles sculp.t

 PLATE 141. VARIOUS SURGICAL INSTRUMENTS

GEOGRAPHY AND PLANOGRAPHY

Glossary to the Geographical Maps, Plates 142–185

[The Longitude in the Maps is reckoned from the meridian of Ferro. To reduce it to the meridian of Greenwich, add 18° 10′ for W. long., and subtract the same for E. long.]

Abasgia, Abkhas
Abassien, Abassi (tribe in North Africa)
Abbitibes, Abbitibbe River
Abdera, Adra
Abrincate, Abrincafui
Abyssinien, Abyssinia
Acci, Gaudix
Achalziche, Akalzike
Achen, Aix la Chapelle
Acincum, Buda Pest
Adagk, Island Adack
Admiralitäts Is., Admiralty Islands
Adrianopel, Adrianople
Adriatisches Meer, Adriatic Sea
Adulis, St. Gothard
Ægadische In., the islands of Levanso, Favignana, and Maritimo (the ancient Ægades)
Ægäisches Meer, Archipelago
Aegypten, Egypt
Ægyptische Schöne wovon $18\frac{4}{5}$ *a.d. Gr.*, Egyptian miles $18\frac{4}{5}$ to a degree
Ælana, Akaba
Æmona, Laybach
Æquat. d. ewigen Schnees, Equator of perpetual snow
Æquatorgrenze d. Schneefalles, Equatorial boundary of snow
Æquatorialgrenze d. europ. tropn. Getreides, Equatorial boundary of European tropical grain
Æquatorialgr. des ewigen Schnees, Equatorial boundary of perpetual snow
Æthiopien, Ethiopia
Æthiopisches Meer, Ethiopian Sea
Agrigentum, Girgenti
Aguja Sp., Cape Aguya
Akjerman, Akerman
Alands In., Aland Islands
Alanen, Alani
Albanien, Albany
Albaracin, Albarracin
Albersche, Alberche River
Albis, Elbe River
Albufeira, Albufera
Albufera See, Lake Albufera
Alemannen, Alemanni
Aleschki, Aleshki
Aleuten Inseln, Aleutian Islands
Alexandrien, Alexandria
Algesiras, Al Gezira
Algier, Algiers
Alpen 1200 t. mittlere Höhe, Alps 1200 toises mean height
Alpen Gebirge, the Alps
Alpes Bastarnicæ, Lower Alps
Alpes Rhætiæ, Rhætian Alps
Alsen, Isle of Als
Alt Californien, Upper California
Alter Molo, Old pier
Amassera, Amasserah
Amboser Hochland, Ambose Highlands
Amenis, Ameni Island
Amiranten I., Amirante Islands
Amisia, Ems River
Ammonia, Hargiah
Ancyra, Angora
Andalusien, Andalusia
Andamanen, Andaman Islands
Andes von Peru, the Andes of Peru
Andes von Quito, the Andes of Quito
Andöe, Island of Andoen
Andros mit Hafen, Andros with port
Anemurium, Cape Anamour
Angeln, Angli
Anten, Antæ (Sarmatian tribe)
Antinoe, Enseneh
Antwerpen, Antwerp
Anurigrammum, Anurajapoera
Aornus, Ohund
Aosta Thal, Aosta Valley
Apeliotes (Ost), Southeast tradewind
Apenninen Geb, the Apennines
Apulien, Apulia
Aquæ Sextiæ, Aix
Aquitanien, Aquitania
Arabien, Arabia
Arabische Wüste, Arabian Desert
Arab. Mb., Arabian Gulf
Arabisches od. Persisches Meer, Arabian or Persian Sea
Arachosia, S. E. Cabul
Arachotus, Lora River
Aral See, Aral Sea
Aran, Karabagh
Araxes, Aras River
Arbela, Arbay
Archangelsk, Archangel
Archipel von Neu Britannia, Archipelago of New Britain
Archipel der Niedrigen Inseln, Low Islands
Archipelagus, Archipelago
Ardennen, Ardennes
Arelate, Arles
Argolische In., Archipelago of Nauplia
Argelis, Argellez
Argentoratum, Strasbourg
Argonnen Wald, the Argonne Forest
Aria, Khorasan
Aria See, Lake of Zarrah
Ariaspæ, Ariaspes (inhabitants of Aria, in ancient Drangiana, in Persia)
Ariminum, Rimini
Armenier, Armenians
Armoricum, ancient Aquitania (S. W. France)
Arnheim, Arnhem
Aroe, Patras
Arsanus, Murad River
Arsinoe, Suez
Art. Magazin, Artillery Arsenal
Aru In., Aroo Islands
Arvernum, Auvergne
Asiatisches Russland, Asiatic Russia
Asiatisches Sarmatn., Asiatic Sarmatia
Asow, Azov
Asowsches Meer, Sea of Azov
Assomtion, Asuncion
Assyrn., Assyria
Asta, Asti
Asturica, Astorga
Asturien, Asturias
Athabasca S., Lake Athapescow
Athen, Athens
Athenæ, Athens
Athribis, Tel Atrib
Atlantischer Ocean, Atlantic Ocean
Atschin, Acheen
Attalia, Adalia
Attici, Inhab. of Attica
Augila, Augela
Aug. Turinorum, Turin
Aug. Vindelicorum, Augsburg
Augustodunum, Autun
Aulona, Valona
Auster (Süd), South Wind
Australien, Australia
Austral. Busen, Gulf of Australia
Austrasien, Empire of Chlodwig
Avalites, Zeyla
Avalitischer G., Bay of Zeyla
Aventicum, Avenche
Avernum, Lake Averno
Azania, Ajan
Azorische Inseln, Portugiesisch, the Azores, Portuguese
Azowsches Meer, Sea of Azov

B. von Athen od. v. Ægina, Bay of Athens or of Ægina
B. von Nauplia od. v. Argos, Bay of Nauplia or of Argos
Babadagh, Baba Dag
Bagistanus, Beesitoon
Bagous Geb., Bagous Mountains
Bahama Inseln, Bahama Islands
Bai u. Dorf Catalan, Bay and village of Catalan
Baiern, Bavaria
Baikal S. u. Geb., Baikal Lake and Mountains
Baireuth, Bayreuth
Bairischer Wd., Bavarian Forest
Baktrien, Bactriana
Balearen, Balearic Islands
Baleares, Balearic Islands
Balearischer Canal, Balearic Channel
Balkan Geb., Balkan Mountains
Balkasch S., Lake Balkash
Baltica, Sweden
Banasa, Meheduma
Banater Geb., Banat Mountains
Banater Milit. Grenge, Military frontier of the Banat
Banks Land, Banks' Island
Barcelonnetti, Barceloneta
Barcino, Barcelona
Baschkiren, Bashkirs
Bass Strasse, Bass's Strait
Bassistis, Bashnia
Baumwolle, Cotton
Baumwolle u. Reis, Cotton and rice
Bayrische Alpen, Bavarian Alps
Bayrisches Hochland, Bavarian Highlands
Behrings Meer, Behring's Strait
Behrings Meer od. Meer von Kamtschatka, Behring's Strait or Kamtschatkian Sea

Belgien, Belgium
Belice, Belici River
Belochrobaten, Belochrobati (Slavonian tribe)
Belzoi See, Lake Belzoi
Berenike, Bengazi
Berg Andros, Mount Andros
Berkley Sund, Berkeley Sound
Bermudas od. Sommer I., Bermudas or Somers Islands
Berner Alpen, Bernese Alps
Bernstein Küste, Amber Coast
Bessarabien, Bessarabia
Bieler S., Lake of Biel
Bjelos See, Lake Biellos
Biled-ul-gerid, od. Dattelland, Biled-ul-gerid, or Land of Dates
Biscayscher Meerbusen, Bay of Biscay
Bithynien, Bithynium
Blaue Bge., Blue Mountains
Bodensee, Lake of Constance
Böhmische Höhe, Bohemian Highlands
Böhmischer Kessel, Bohemian Basin
Bogen Indianer, Strongbow Indians (tribe of the Chippeways)
Bolzoi, oder Grosser See, Bolzoi or Large Lake
Boreas (Nord), North Wind
Borysthenes, Pripet River
Borysthenes (Danapris), Dniepr River
Bosnien, Bosna
Bostra, Boszra
Bothnischer Busen, Gulf of Botnia
Bracara, Braga
Brasilien, Brazil
Brasilische Gebirge, Brazil Mountains
Brasilische Strömung, Brazil Current
Brasilisches Guyana, Brazil Guyana
Braunschweig, Brunswick
Brede Bugt, Bay of Brede
Brienzer S., Lake of Brienz
Brigantium, Briançon
Britannien, Gr. Britain
Britisches Guyana, British Guyana
Brivates Haf, Bay of Brest
Brüssel, Brussels
Brundisium, Brindisi
Brundusium, Brindisi
Bucephala, Ihylum
Bucharest, Bukarest
Bucharien, Bokhara
Buchweitzen, Buckwheat
Bucinarische In., Buccinarian Islands
Bulgaren, Bulgari (tribe on the lower Danube)
Burdigala, Bordeaux
Burgunder, Burgundians
Busen von Bengalien, Bay of Bengal
Busen von Cadix, Bay of Cadiz
Busen Carpentaria, Bay of Carpentaria
Busen v. Danzig, Bay of Dantzig
Busen von Lepanto oder von Korinth, Gulf of Lepanto or of Corinth
Busen v. Lion, Gulf of Lyons
Busen v. Lübeck, Bay of Lubeck
Busen von Panama, Bay of Panama
Busen von Taranto, Gulf of Taranto
Busen von Tehuantepec, Gulf of Tehuantepec
Busen von Triest, Gulf of Trieste
Busen von Venedig, Bay of Venice
Byblos, Djebail
Byzacium, Tunis
Byzant., Constantinople

C. d. guten Hoffnung, Cape of Good Hope
C. Horner Strömung, Cape Horn current
Cabillonus, Chalons
Cæsar Augusta, Saragossa
Cætobriga, Setobal
Cajeta, Gaeta
Caledonien, Caledonia
Caledonischer Canal, Caledonian Canal
Calvadosfelsen, Calvados Rocks
Canal oder La Manche, the British Channel
Canal u. Strömung v. Mozambique, Channel and current of Mozambique
Canal von Yucatan, Channel of Yucatan
Canarische Inseln, Canary Islands
Candriaces, Nugor River
Canopus, Aboukir
Cantabrisches Geb. 600 *t.*, Santillanos Mountains 600 toises
Cantal G., Cantal Mountains
Cap Strom, Cape current
Cap u. Ins. Breton, Cape and Island of Breton
Cappadocien, Cappadocia
Capsa, Wataras
Capstadt, Cape Town
Capverdische Inseln, Cape Verde Islands
Caraibisches Meer, Caribbean Sea
Caralis, Cagliari
Carenisches Gebirg, Sutherland Highlands
Carmania, Kerman
Carpathus, Scarpanto
Carteja, Ocana
Carthaginiensis Sinus, Gulf of Tunis
Carthago, Carthage
Carthago nova, Cartagena
Casp. Engpässe, Caspian or Caucasian passes
Caspisches Meer, Caspian Sea
Caspisch. See liegt 33 t. unter d. Niveau d. Oceans, Caspian Sea, lies 33 toises lower than the level of the ocean
Caspische See, Caspian Sea
Cassiterides Ins., Scilly Islands
Catalonien, Catalonia
Celænæ, Dingla
Cerasus, Keresoun
Cevennen, Cevennes Mountains
Chalifat der Abassiden, Caliphate of the Abassides
Charolais Geb., Charolles Mountains
Chemnis, Ekhmin
Cherson, Kherson
Chersonesus, Cape Razatin
Cheviot Gebirge, Cheviot Hills
Chile, Chili
China Wälder, Bathbark Forests
Chinesisches Meer, Chinese Sea
Chios, Scio
Choco Kette, Choco Mountain Chain
Chorasmia See, Lake Kharasm
Chorasmii, Kharasm
Churhessen, Electoral Hesse
Cibalis, Palanha
Cilicia, Itshili; *Die Cilicischen Thore*, the Passes of Itshili
Cimbrische Halb I., Cimbrian Peninsula (Jutland)
Clearwater See, Clearwater Lake
Cnossus, Macritichos
Colchis, Mingrelia
Colchischer G., Gulf of Mingrelia
Colonia, Cologne
Comana, Bostan
Comer S., Lake of Como
Comum, Como
Conimbriga, Coimbra
Constantinopel, Constantinople
Constantinopolis, Constantinople
Constanz, Constance
Cooks Strasse, Cook's Strait
Cophas, Guadel
Cophes, Ghizni River
Coptos, Ghouft
Corcyra, Corfu
Cordofan, Kordofan
Corduba, Cordova
Corps unter Hephæstion, Corps under Hephæstion
Croatien, Croatia
Croatische Militair Grenze, Croatian military frontier
Curene, Kuren
Curland, Courland
Cydonia, Canea
Cynopolis, Nesle Sheik Hassan
Cypern, Cyprus
Cyrene, West Barca
Cyropolis, Enzellee
Cyrus, Politica
Cythere, Citria
Cyzicus, Kyzik
Dacia, Hungary and Transylvania
Daenemark, Denmark
Dakien, Dacia (Hungary)
Dalmatien, Dalmatia
Dampfschiffe von Triest der Œstn. Lloyd Ges., Steamers of the Austrian Lloyd Company from Trieste
Dänen, Danes
Danubius, Danube River
Danzig, Dantzig
Daphne, Daia
Dardanellen Schlösser, Palaces at the Dardanelles
Dardanellen Str., Dardanelles
Darnis, Derna
Das Alpen Gebirge, the Alps
Das Po Thal, the Po Valley
Daurisches Alpenland, the Da Oural Alps (branch of the Oural Mountains)
Davis Strasse, Davis's Strait
Delphi, Castri
Dembo Hochland, Dembo Highlands
D'Entrecasteaux Spitze, Point d'Entrecasteaux
Der Normannen Reiche, the Norman Empires
Der Spiegel des todten Meeres liegt 220 t. tiefer als der Ocean, the surface of the Dead Sea lies 220 toises below the level of the ocean
Der Wash, the Wash
Dergh See, Lake Derg
Dertosa, Tortosa
Deutsche Meilen 15 *auf den Grad*, German miles 15 to the degree
Deutsche unter Kaiser Friedrich II., Germans under Emperor Frederick II
Deutsches Kaiserreich, German Empire
Deva, Ayas
Die Aleuten od. Catharinas Archipel, the Aleutian Islands or Catharine's Archipelago
Die Aleutischen Inseln, the Aleutian Islands

Die Azoren, the Azores
Die bekannte Welt des Alterthums, the world known to the Ancients
Die Carolinen, the Caroline Islands
Die 3 Oder Mündn., the three mouths of the Oder
Die Eols Grotten, the Grottoes of Æolus
Die grosse osteuropäische Ebene in welcher kein Punkt die Höhe von 180 t. erreicht, the large East-European plain, in which no point reaches the height of 180 toises
Die Nord See oder das deutsche Meer, the North Sea or the German Sea
Die Ostsee, oder das Baltische Meer, the Baltic
Die Philippinen, the Philippine Islands
Die Schweiz, Switzerland
Die sieben Kuhfirsten, the Seven Cowridges
Diemtiger Th., Diemtig Valley
Dinarisches Alpen Gebirg, Dinarian Alps (on the lower Danube)
Dio Adelphi (Die 2 Brüder), Dio Adelphi (The Two Brothers)
Dioscorides I., Island of Socotra
Dioscurias, Iskuria
District diesseits der Donau, District north of the Danube
District diesseits der Theiss, District west of the Theiss
District jenseits der Donau, District beyond the Danube
District jenseits der Theiss, District beyond (east of) the Theiss
Dobrudscher, Dobrodje
Donau, Danube
Donaumündungen, Mouths of the Danube
Donauwörth, Donauwerth
Donische Kosaken, Cossacks of the Don
Dora Baltea, Doria Baltea River
Drapsaea, Bamian
Drontheim, Trondheim
Dschebil el Kamar od. Mond Geb., Gebel Komri, or Mountains of the Moon
Düna, Dvina River
Dünkirchen, Dunkirk
Durius, Douro River
Durovernum, Canterbury

Eblana, Dublin
Eboracum, York
Ebro Mündung, Mouth of the Ebro
Ebusus, Iviza
Eisenbahnen, Railroads
Eisenbahnkarte von Mitteleuropa, Railroad chart of Central Europe
Eismeer, Arctic Ocean
Eisstarre Sand u. Morast Fläche, Frozen Sand and Swamp Plain
Elusa, Eauze
Emerita Aug., Merida
Emirat v. Cordova, Emirate of Cordova
Enara See, Lake Enara
Engländer unter Richard Löwenherz, the English under Richard Cœur de Lion
Engl. Colonien am Schwanflusse, K. Georg's Sund und N. S. Wales, English Colonies on Swan River, King George's Sound, and New South Wales
Englische Meilen 69 22/100 auf den Grad, English miles, 69 22/100 to the degree
Engpass v. Kaipha, *Pass of Kaipha*
Ephesus, Ayasaluk
Epidaurus, Ragusa Vecchia
Epirus, Albania
Eregli, Erekli
Erklärung der Zahlen, Explanation of the figures
Erne See, Erne Loch
Erymanthus, Mount Olonos
Eskimos, Esquimaux
Esthland, Esthonia
Euböa, Negropont
Euphrat, Euphrates
Europa vor der Französischen Revolution, Europe before the French Revolution
Europa zur Zeit der Kreussüge, Europe during the Crusades
Europa zur Zeit Karls des Grossen, Europe at the time of Charlemagne
Europäisch Sarmatien, European Sarmatia
Europäische Besitzungen in Nord Guinea, European possessions in North Guinea
Europäisches Russland, European Russia
Europäisches Scythien, European Scythia

Fadejewski, Fadevskoi
Fær Œer, Faro Islands
Falklands Ins., Falkland Islands
Falsche Bai, Bay of Falso
Faltschi, Faltsi
Fan Œ., Fano I.
Favonius (West), West Wind (Zephyr)
Feuerland, Terra del Fuego
Finnischer Busen, Gulf of Finland
Fischereien von Agoutinitza, Fisheries of Agoutinitza
Fittre See, Bahr Fittre
Flachs u. Hanf, Flax and Hemp
Flandern, Flanders
Flavia Cäsariensis, Central England
Flaviobriga, Bilbao
Flavionavia, Laviana
Flevus, Flevo, Zuyder Zee
Florentia, Florence
Florenz, Florence
Franken, Franconia
Frankfurt, Frankfort
Fränkisches Italien, Frankish Italy
Fränkisches Plateau, Franconian plateau
Frankreich, France
Französ. Guyana, French Guyana
Französische Lieues 25 auf den Grad, French leagues 25 to the degree
Franzosen unter Philipp August, The French under Philip Augustus
Franzosen unter Ludwig IX., The French under Louis IX
Freiburg, Freeburg
Freie Indianer, Free Indians
Freundschafts oder Tonga In., Friendly or Tonga Islands
Friedens Fl., Peace River
Frobischer Str., Frobisher's Strait
Fuchs Ins., Fox Islands
Fünen, Fyen
Fuglæ, Bird Island
Fürstm. Benevent, Principality of Benevento
Fürstenthum Neuenburg, Principality of Neuenburg

Gabæ, Chavos
Gades, Cadiz
Gaditanum, Gibraltar
Galætia, Anadolia
Galicien, Galicia
Galizien, Galicia
Gallien, Gallia (France)
Gallische Wegestunden wovon 50 auf den Grad, Gallic miles 50 to the degree
Gangischer oder Indischer Golf, Bay of Bengal
Garamantes, Fezzaneers and Tibboo (tribe)
Garda See, Lake of Garda
Gaugamela, Kamalis
Gaulos, Island of Goza
Geb. v. Granada, Granada Mountains
Gebirge von Auvergne, Mountains of Auvergne
Gedros, Mekran
Gelbes Meer, Yellow Sea
Genf, Geneva
Genfer See, Lake of Geneva
Gent, Ghent
Genua, Genoa
Geographen B., Geographer's Bay
Geogr. Meilen 15 auf den Grad, Geographical miles 15 to the degree
Gepiden, Gepidæ (tribe)
Germanen, Germans
Germanien, Germany
Germanische Meer, North Sea
Germanische Tiefebene, German Low Plain
Gerste, Barley
Gerste, Hafer, Roggen, Barley, Oats, Rye
Gerste, Roggen, Kartoffeln und Buchweitzen, Barley, rye, potatoes, and buckwheat
Gesellschafts In., Society Islands
Gesoriacum, Boulogne
Geten, Getæ (tribe)
Gletscher, Glacier
Glückliches Arabien, Arabia Felix
Gogana, Congoon
Göksschai See, Lake Gokshai
Goldener Chersonesus, Golden Khersonesus (Malaya)
Gordium, Sarilar
Gorsynia, Atchicola
Gothen, Goths
Gr. Bären See, Great Bear Lake
Gr. Minsh oder Caledonisches Meer, Great Minsh or Caledonian Sea
Gr. Scleven S., Great Slave Lake
Grampian Gebirge, Grampian Mountains
Graubündner Alpen, Grison Alps
Griechenland, Greece
Griechisches Italien, Greek Italy
Grönland, Greenland
Gross Britannien und Ireland, Great Britain and Ireland
Gross Phrygia, Phrygia Major
Gross Russland, Great Russia
Grosse Antillen, the larger Antilles (West India Islands)
Grosse Eskimos, Great Esquimaux
Grosser Atlas, Mount Atlas
Grosser oder Stiller Ocean, Pacific Ocean
Grossherz. Hessen, Grand Duchy of Hesse
Grüne Berge, Green Mountains
Grünes Vorgebirge, Cape Verde
Gürtel des Getreides, Zone of the grains

Gürtel ohne Cultur, Zone without cultivation
Guräus, Kamah River

H. l. or *Halbinsel* stands for "Peninsula" before the respective names
Haag, the Hague
Habesch, Habesh
Hadrianopolis, Adrianople
Hæmus, Balkan Mountains
Haf. v. or *Hafen von* stands for "Port of" before the respective names
Hafer, Oats
Hafer u. Gerste, Oats and barley
Hafer u. Weitzen, Oats and wheat
Halbinsel Methana, Peninsula of Dara (Methana)
Halicarnassus, Boodroom
Haliez oder Galizien, Galicia
Han Hai (Südl. Meer), South Sea
Harz Gb., Harz Mountains
Hasen Ind., Hare Indians
Haupt Æquatorial Strömung, Principal equatorial current
Haupstadt, Capital
Hebräische Stadien wovon 750 *a. d. Gr.*, Hebrew stadia 750 to the degree
Hebriden oder Western Inseln, Hebrides or Western Islands
Hecatompylos, Danghan
Hedschas, Hedjas
Heiliges Vgb., Promontorium Sacrum
Heliopolis, Baalbec
Hellas, Greece
Hellespontus, Dardanelles
Helsingör, Elsinore
Heniochi, Tribe in Armenia
Hermopolis, Eshmounein
Hermunduren, Hermunduri (tribe in central Germany)
Herodots Erdtafel, Herodotus's Map of the World
Heruler, Heruli (tribe in North Germany)
Herzogl. Sächsische Länder, Saxon Duchies
Herzogthum, Duchy
Hibernien, Hibernia
Hinter Rhein, Hind Rhine (one of the rivulets tributary to the Rhine)
Hippo Regius, Bona
Hispalis, Seville
Hispanien, Spain
Hoch Alp, High Alp
Hoch Sudan, Soudah Mountains
Hochland von Africa, Highlands of Africa
Hohe Tatarei, Tartar Highlands
Hoher Atlas, Mount Atlas
Hügelgruppe v. Sandomir, Group of Hills of Sandomir
Hunds Ribben Ind, Dogrib Indians
Hunigaren oder Ungrier, Hungarians
Hydraotes, Ravee River
Hypanis, Kuban River
Hyphasis, Beyah River
Hyrcania, Gyrgaun
Hyrkanisch. Meer, Caspian Sea

I., *Ia.*, *Ins.*, or *Insel* stands for "Island" before the respective names
I. Helgoland, Island of Heligoland
I. Kängurah, Kangaroo Island
I. u. Stadt Cayenne, Island and Town of Cayenne
Ibenes, Ebro River
Iberia, Georgia
Ichthyophagen, Fish-eaters
Iconium, Konia
Illyricum, Illyria
Illyrien, Illyria
Im Sommer 15°, In the summer 66 degrees F.
Im Winter 5°, In the winter 43 degrees F.
Imandra See, Lake Imandra
Imaus Geb., Altai Mountains
Indischer Ocean, Indian Ocean
Indsche Burun, Cape Indjeh
Indus Mündn., Mouths of the Indus
Ins. d. günen Vorgebirges, Cape Verde Islands
Ins. unter d. Winde, Caribbean Islands
Ipsus, Ipsilihissar
Irgis, Irghiz River
Irische See, Irish Sea
Irland, Ireland
Irtisch, Irtish River
Is, Hit
Isca, Exe River
Island, Iceland
Issedones, Mongolian tribe
Ister (Donau), Danube
Ister Mündn., Mouths of the Danube
Italien, Italy

Jacobs Thal, Jacob's Valley
Jadera, Zarah
Japanisches Meer, Sea of Japan
Jasygien, Jassygia
Jaxartes, Sihon River
Jazygen (Sarmaten), Sarmatians
Jenseits d. Ganges, Beyond the Ganges
Jenseits d. Imaus, Beyond the Altai
Jernis, Dunkerrin
Jomanes, Jumna River
Jonische Inseln, Ionian Islands
Joppe, Yaffa
Joux See, Lake Joux
Jülich, Juliers
Juliobriga, Reynosa
Julische Alpen, Carnic or Julian Alps
Jura Geb., Jura Mountains
Jura Sund, Jura Sound
Jüten, Jutlanders
Juvavia, Saltzburg

K. Charlotte S., Queen Charlotte's Sound
Kärnthen, Carinthia
Kaiser Canal, Emperor's Canal
Kaiserthum Œsterreich, Empire of Austria
Kalmüken, Calmucks
Kamische Bulgaren, Kama Bulgarians
Kanäle, Canals
Kanal von Bristol, Bristol Channel
Kaptschak, Cabjak (tribe in Bokhara)
Karafta oder Sachalin, Caraphta or Sachalin
Karazubazar, Kara Soo
Karchedon, Carthage
Karischer B., Bay of Caria
Karmanien, Kerman
Karolinen, Caroline Islands
Karpathen 2000 *t. mittl. Höhe*, Carpathian Mountains 2000 toises mean height
Karpathen Geb., Carpathian Mountains
Karpathisches Waldgebirge, Carpathian Forest
Kartagena, Cartagena
Karthago, Carthage
Kartoffeln u. Hafer, Potatoes and oats
Kartoffeln u. Buckweitzen, Potatoes and buckwheat
Kaspisches Meer, Caspian Sea
Kattegat, Cattegat
Kaukasien, Caucasia
Kaukasus Gebirge, Caucasian Mountains
Kaukasische Steppe, Caucasian Steppes
Keine Bäume ab. Graswuchs, No trees but grass
Kelten, Celts
Kemi See, Lake Kemin
Kgn. Charlotte I., Queen Charlotte's Island
Kimbrischer Cherson, Cimbrian Chersonesus (Jutland)
Kjölen Gebirge, Koelen Mountains
Kirchenstaat, Papal States
Kirgisen Horde, Kirghis Horde
Kirghisen Steppe, Kirghis Steppes
Kizil Ermak, Kizil Irmak River
Kl. Antillen, Little Antilles (Caribbean Islands)
Kl. Karpathen, Little Carpathians
Kl. Kumanien, Kis Kunsag
Klein Phrygia, Phrygia Minor
Klein Russland, Little Russia (Russian Province)
Kleinasien, Asia Minor
Kleine Kirgisen Horde, Little Kirghis Horde
Koblenz, Coblentz
Köln, Cologne
Kön. Georg Sund, King George's Sound
König. Georg's I., King George's Islands
Königin Charlotte Sund, Queen Charlotte's Sound
Königreich stands for "kingdom" before the respective names
Konäguen, Tribe of Esquimaux
Kong Gebirge, Mountains of Kong
Kopenhagen, Copenhagen
Kosaken, Cossacks
Krakau, Cracow
Krym, Crimea
Kuba, Cuba
Kupfer Ind., Copper Indians

L. I. Sund, Long Island Sound
Ladoga See, Lake Ladoga
Lakeneig, Lakeneigh
Laminium, Alambra
Lamose, Lamusa River
Lampsacus, Lamsaki
Lanai, Tribe in North Germany
Lancerote, Lancerota Island
Land der Finnen, Land of the Finns
Land der kleinen Eskimos, Land of the dwarf Esquimaux
Larice, Lack
Lauriacum, Lorch
Lausitzer Gebirg, Lusatian Mountains
Leba See, Lake Leba
Leman S., Lake Leman
Leptis, Lebida
Lerdalsöer, Lerdals Islands
Lesbos, Mytilene
Lessöewerk, Lessoe forge
Leucas, Amaxiki
Leuce, Island of Adasi
Ljæchen, Bohemians
Libyen, Africa
Libysche Wüste, Libyan Desert
Lieukieu In., Loo Choo Islands
Ligeris, Loire River
Liguria, Genoa
Ligurisches Meer, Gulf of Genoa

Likeio In., Loo Choo Islands
Lilybæum, Boe
Lindum, Lincoln
Liptauer Alp, Liptau Alps
Lissus, Allessio
Lithauer, Lithuania
Litus Saxonum, Coast of Sussex
Litwanen, Lithuania
Livadien, Livadia
Liviner Thal, Livin Valley
Livland, Livonia
Livorno, Leghorn
Lixus, Luccos River
Loja, Loxa
Lombardei, Lombardy
Lomond S., Lake Lomond
Londinum, London
Longobarden, Longobardi (Lombards)
Lucentum, Alicante
Luceria, Lucera
Lüneburger Heide, Luneburg Heath
Lüttich, Liège
Lugdunensis, North West France
Lugdunum, Leyden
Lugovallum, Carlisle
Lugumkloster, Lugum Convent
Lulea See, Lake Lulea
Lumnitz B., Mount Lomnitz
Lusitania, Portugal
Lutitschen, Luititsi or Wilzi (Tribe in North Germany)
Luzern, Lucerne
Lycaonia, N. W. Karamania
Lyon, Lyons
Lystra, Illisera

Maas, Meuse River
Maasstäbe, Scales
Macedonien, Macedonia
Mackenzie In., Mackenzie's Islands
Macquarie In., Macquarie's Island
Madgyaren, Magyars
Mähren, Moravia
Mährische Höhe, Moravian Highlands
Mælar See, Lake Mælar
Maeotis See, Sea of Azov
Magelhaens Strasse, Straits of Magellan
Mahadia, Mahedia
Mahrah, Mahran
Mailand, Milan
Mainz, Mayence, Maynz
Mais und Weitzen, Indian corn and wheat
Makarjew, Makariv
Mal Ström, Malstrom
Malaca, Malacca
Malmö, Malmo
Malmysch, Malmish
Malouinen, Falkland Islands
Mandeln, Almonds
Mandschurei, Manchooria
Manytsch, Manich River
Maraniten, Maranites, tribe in Arabia Felix
Marcomannen, Marcomanni, tribe in S. E. Germany
Mare Adriaticum, Adriatic Sea
Mare Caspium, Caspian Sea
Mare Erythræum (Indisches Meer), Indian Ocean
Mare Hyrcanum oder Caspium, Caspian Sea
Mare Internum (Mittelländisches Meer), Mediterranean Sea
Marea, El Khreit
Margaret In., Margaret's Island
Margus, Murghab River
Marianen od. Ladronen, Marian Islands
Marinestunden 25 auf den Grad, Marine leagues 25 to the degree
Marisus, Maros River
Marmara Meer, Sea of Marmora
Marschall Inseln, Mulgrave Islands
Marseille, Marseilles
Martyropolis, Meia Farekin
Mascarenen Inseln, Mascarenhas Islands (Mauritius, Bourbon, etc.)
Massaga, Massa
Massilia, Marseilles
Mater, Matter
Mauritania, Algiers
Mauritanien, Algiers
Maxima Cæsariensis, Northern England
Mb. v. Issus (Sinus Issilicus), Bay of Iskenderoon
Meder, Medes (nation)
Mediolanum, Milan
Medus, Abkuren River
Meer Alpen, Maritime Alps
Meer von Ochotsh, Sea of Okotsk
Meer von Turrakai, Gulf of Tartary
Meerb. v. Californien, Gulf of California
Meerb. v. Sues, Gulf of Suez
Meerbusen von Mexico, Gulf of Mexico
Meiningen, Meinungen
Melgig Sumpf, Melgig Swamp
Melitene, Malatia
Memel od. Niemen, Meman River
Memel Niederung, Tilsit Lowlands
Memnis, Korkor Baba
Memphis, Mangel Mousa, or Mit Raheni
Meninx, Jerba Island
Mergui In., Mergue Archipelago
Meroe, Gibbainy
Mesagna, Mesagne
Mesembria, Missivri
Mesopotamia, Al Gezira
Messana, Messina
Mettis, Metz
Mexicanische Küstenströmung, Mexican Coast current
Miletus, Palatia
Militär Colonien, Military colonies
Militair Grenze, Military boundary
Minius, Minho River
Mië See, Lake Miœ
Mioritz See, Lake Mioritz
Mississippi Mündüngen, Mouths of the Mississippi
Mittelländisches Meer, Mediterranean Sea
Mittlere Kirgisen Horde, Middle Kirghis Horde
Mittlere Temperatur nach Celsius, Mean temperature according to Celsius
Mittlere Temperatur nach Reaumur, Mean temperature according to Reaumur
Mogontiacum, Maynitz
Molukken, Molucca Islands
Molukken Str., Molucca Passage
Mond Gebirg, Mountains of the Moon
Mongolei, Mongolia
Monreale, Monreal
Montagnes Noires, Black Mountains (Black Forest)
Mordwinen, Mordwines (tribe in Asiatic Russia)
Moreton C. u. B., Moreton Cape and Bay
Moscha, Morebat
Mosel, Moselle River
Moskenasö, Mosken Island
Moskau, Moscow
Moskwa, Moskow
Mosyneoci (tribe on the Black Sea)
Mozyr, Mozir
Mühlhausen, Mulhouse
München, Munich
Mündung des Amazonen Stroms, Mouth of the Amazon River
Mündung der Elbe, Mouth of the Elbe
Mündung des Tajo, Mouth of the Tagus
Murray Busen, Murray Firth
Muthmassliche Grenze der den Alten bekannten Binnenländer von Afrika nach den Geographen Walkenuer und Gosselin, Probable boundary of the African inland known to the Ancients according to the geographers Walkenaer and Gosselin
Mutina, Modena

N. Schottl., North Scotland
N. W. Ausflüsse des Æquatorial Stroms, Northwest termination of the equatorial current
Nabathæer, Nabathæi (nation in Arabia)
Nadel Banck, Cape Agulhas
Naissus, Nissa
Namadus, Nerbuddah River
Napeta, Mograt
Narbona, Narbonne
Narbonensis, Narbonne
Nasamonen, Nasamones (tribe in West Barca)
Natal Küste, Natal Coast
Navusa mit Hafer, Nausa, with port
Nazareth Bank und Ins., Nazaret Bank and Island
Neagh S., Lake Neagh
Neapel (Neapolis), Naples
Nelson Canal, Nelson Channel
Nemausus, Nismes
Nerbudda, Nerbuddah River
Neu stands for "New" before the respective names
Neu Californien, New California
Neu Georgien, New Georgia
Neu Helvetien, New Helvetia
Neu Karthago, New Carthage
Neu Scotia, Nova Scotia
Neu Sibirien, New Siberia
Neue Hebriden, New Hebrides
Neue Saline, New Saltwork
Neuenburg, Neufchatel
Neuenburger S., Lake of Neufchatel
Neustrien, Neustria (the part of France lying between the Meuse, Loire, and the Atlantic Ocean)
Nicasia, Island of Karos
Nicobaren, Nicobar Islands
Nicomedia, Izmid
Nieder Canada, Lower Canada
Nieder Ungarische Ebene, Lower Hungarian Plain
Niederl. Guyana, Dutch Guyana
Niederlande, Netherlands
Niger, Niger River
Nil, Nile River
Nil Mündungen, Mouths of the Nile
Nilus, Nile River
Nîmes, Nismes
Niphates Geb., Sepan Mountains
Nizza, Nice
Norba Cæsaria, Alcantara
Nördlicher Oceanus, Arctic Ocean
Nördlicher Polarkreis, Arctic Circle

Nördlicher Wolga Rücken, Northern Volga Ridge
Nördliches Eismeer, Arctic Ocean
Nord stands for "North" before the respective names
Nord Afrikanische Strömung, North African current
Nord Albinger, North Albingians (tribe in Holstein)
Nord Georgien, North Georgia
Nord Georgien I., North Georgia Island
Nord See, North Sea
Noricum, Styria, Salzburg, etc.
Norische Alpen, Noric Alps
Normanische Inseln, Normandy Islands (Guernsey, Jersey, Alderney, Sark)
Northlined S., Northlined Lake
Norwegen, Norway
Notium Vgb., Mizen Head
Nuba See, Nuba Lake
Nuba Sumpf, Nuba Swamp
Nubier, Nubians (tribe)
Nubische Wüste, Nubian Desert
Numidien, Numidia (East Algiers)
Nursa, Norcia
Nymegen, Nimegue

Obdorisches Gebirge, Obdorsk Mountains (Northern extremity of the Oural Mountains)
Ober See, Lake Superior
Obi, Oby Island
Obotriten, Obotrites (Vandal tribe in North Germany)
Oceanus Atlanticus, Atlantic Ocean
Oceanus Germanicus, North Sea
Ochus See, mit dem Kaspisches Meere früher wahrscheinlich zusammenhängend, Ochus Sea (Aral Sea), probably formerly connected with the Caspian Sea
Odessus, Odessa
Odyssus, Odessa
Œ. L. v. Ferro, East longitude from the Island of Ferro
Œ. L. v. Paris, East longitude from Paris
Œca, Tripoli
Œlbäume, Olive trees
Œsterreich, Austria
Œsterreichische Alpen, Austrian Alps
Œsterreichische Landestheile, Austrian dependencies
Œstl. Gats, Eastern Ghauts
Œstliche Länge von Ferro, East longitude from the Island of Ferro
Œstliche Länge von Paris, East longitude from Paris
Offene B., Open Bay
Olisibon (Olisipo), Lisbon
Olite, Olitte
Olivenza, Olivenca
Olympia, Miracca
Olympische Stadien wovon 600 *a. d. Grad*, Olympic stadia, 600 to the degree
Onega See, Onega Lake
Ophiusa, Island of Formentera
Orange od. Gariep, Orange or Gariep River
Orangen, Oranges
Orbelus, Mt. Gliubotin
Orchoe, Bassora
Oregon oder Felsen Gebirge, Rocky Mountains
Oregon od. Columbia, Columbia River
Orinoco Münd., Mouth of the Orinoco
Orkaden, Orkney Islands
Orscha, Orsha
Orsowa, Orsoya
Ortles Sp., Ortler Spitz
Ortospanum, Kandahar
Osca, Huesca
Osmanisches Asien, Ottoman Asia
Osmanisches Reich, Ottoman Empire
Ossa, Mount Kissovo
Ossadiæ (tribe in India)
Ost stands for "East" before the respective names
Ost Küste von Brasilien, East Coast of Brazil
Ost Preussen, East Prussia
Ost Pyrenäen, East Pyrenees
Ost See, Baltic
Ost Römisches Kaiserreich, East Roman Empire
Ostphalen, Eastphalians (tribe of the Saxon nation)
Ostracine, Ras Straki
Ostrogothen, Ostrogoths
Othrys Gebirg, Othrys (Hellovo) Mountains
Ottomaken, Ottomak Indians
Oxus, Amoo River
Oxyrynchus, Behenese
Oxydraces, Oxydracæ (tribe in Moultan)
Ozark Gebirg, Ozark Mountains

P. Gr. d. Getreides u. d. Zone d. Regens, Polar boundary of grain and of the zone of rain
P. Gr. d. Weines u. d. europäisch. tropen. Getreides, Polar boundary of the grape vine and of European tropical grain
Padua, Padova
Padus, Po River
Pæstum, Pesto
Palästina, Palestine
Palibothra (Palimbothra), Patna
Palks Strasse, Palk's Straits
Palmyra oder Tadmor, Palmyra or Tadmor
Palus Mæotis, Sea of Azov
Pamphylia, S. E. Anadolia
Pandosia, Mendicino
Pannonia, Hungary
Pannonien, Hungary
Panormus, Raphti
Panticapæum, Kertch
Paphlagonia, N. E. Anadolia
Paphos, Baffa
Parætonium, Al Bareton
Parisii, nation in North France
Paropanusus Geb., Hindoo Koosh
Parthia, Province in Khorasan and N. E. Irak
Parthiscus (Tibiscus), Theiss River
Pasargadæ (Persepolis), Istakar
Pastona, Pasten
Patagonien, Patagonia
Patagonische Kette, Patagonian Cordilleras
Pax Julia, Beja
Pella, Allahkilissia
Pelopones, Morea
Pelusium, Tineh
Penninische Alpen, Pennine Alps
Pentapolis, Chittagong
Pentland Strasse, Pentland Firth
Pergamus, Pergamo
Pers. Golf, Gulf of Persia
Persien, Persia
Persische Parasangen, wov. 25 *a. d. Gr.*, Persian parasangs, 25 to the degree
Persischer M. B., Gulf of Persia
Peruanische Strömung, Peruvian current
Petschenegen, Petshenegs (Tartar tribe)
Peucetia, Terra di Bari
Peuciner, Peucini (tribe in Galicia, etc.)
Phanagoria, Tmutarakan
Pharsalus, Pharsala
Pharselis, Tekrova
Phazania, Fezzan
Philippi, Filibah
Philippinen, Philippine Islands
Philippopel, Philippopolis
Phocæa, Fokies
Phryger, Phrygians (nation in Anadolia)
Physikalische Karte von Europa (—Afrika, —Asien, —Nord America, —Süd Amerika), Physical map of Europe (—Africa, —Asia, —North America, —South America)
Pictavi (nation in Gallia Aquitania)
Picten, Picts (nation in Scotland)
Pielis See, Lake of Pielis
Pindus Mn., Agrafa and Smocovo Mountains
Pisidia, S. E. Anadolia
Pithyusen (Pityusæ), Islands of Iviza, Formentera, etc.
Pityus, Soukoum
Pitkarainen, Pitcairn's Island
Plateau v. (or *von*) stands for "Plateau of" before the respective names
Plateau von Ost Galizien, Plateau of East Galicia
Plattkopf Indr., Flathead Indians
Podolien, Podolia
Polænen, Polænæ (Slavonic tribe)
Polargr. d. Bäume, Polar boundary of trees
Polargr. d. Moose u. Beeren, Polar boundary of mosses and berries
Polargr. d. Obstbaumes, Polar boundary of fruit trees
Polargr. d. Œlbaumes, Polar boundary of the olive tree
Polargr. d. Weinstocks, Polar boundary of the grape vine
Polargrenze, Polar boundary
Polargrenze d. Banane u. d. tropischen Getreides, Polar boundary of the banana and of the tropical grain
Polargrenze des Getreides, Polar boundary of grain
Polargrenze d. Palmen, Polar boundary of palm trees
Polargrenze d. Weinstocks u. d. europäisch. trop. Getreides, Polar boundary of the grape vine and of the European tropical grain
Polar Kreis, Arctic (or Antarctic) Circle
Polen, Poland
Polesiens Urwälder u. Sümpfe, Primitive forests and swamps of Polesia (now Minsk in Russia)
Pommern, Pomerania
Pompelo, Pampeluna
Pont. Eux. (Pontus Euxinus), Black Sea
Pontinische In., Ponza Islands
Pontus, N. E. Bulgaria
Pontus Euxinus (Schwarzes Meer), Black Sea
Porata, Pruth River
Portland Sp., Portland Point
Prag, Prague
Prairien, Prairies
Premnis, Cas. of Ibrim

Pr. Holland, Prussian Holland (district in East Prussia)
Preussen, Prussia
Preussische Landestheile, Prussian districts
Preussische Höhe, Prussian Plateau
Prophtasia (Prophthasia), Dookshak
Propontis, Sea of Marmora
Pskow, Pskov
Psyllen, Psylli (tribe in N. Africa)
Ptolemäische Erdtafel, Map of the world according to Ptolemy
Ptolemäische Stadien wovon 700 *auf den Grad*, Ptolemæan stadia 700 to the degree
Pudosh, Pudog
Pura, Pureg
Purpur Ins., Purpureæ Insulæ (probably Salvage Islands)
Putea, Fuentes
Putziger Wiek, Bay of Putzig
Pyrenæi, Pyrenees
Pyrenäen, Pyrenees
Pyreneos Geb., Pyrenees

Quaden, Quadi (nation in Hungary)
Quadra u. Vancouvers I., Vancouver's Island
Querimbe, Querimba

Rathenow, Rathenau
Ratiaria, Arcer Palanka
Rauhe Alp, Rauhe Alpe
Rauraci, Tribe in Alsace
Rch. d. Picten, Kingdom of the Picts
Ree See, Lake Ree
Regen Fluss, Rain River
Regen S., Rain Lake
Regenloses Gebiet, Rainless territory
Regensburg, Ratisbon
Reich der Aglabiten, Kingdom of the Aglabites (dynasty of Ibrahim ben Aglab)
Reich Alexanders des Grossen, Empire of Alexander the Great
Reich der Bulgaren, Empire of the Bulgarians
Reich der Chazaren, Empire of the Chazares (nation in East Russia)
Reich Karls d. Gr., Empire of Charlemagne
Reich des Porus, Kingdom of Porus (in India)
Reich der Seleuciden, Kingdom of the Seleucidæ (dynasty of Seleucus)
Reich der Slaven, Empire of the Slavonians
Reiche d. Angelsaxen, Anglo-Saxon possessions
Reiche d. Briten, Possessions of the Britons
Reiche d. Dänen, Possessions of the Danes
Reiche d. Scoten, Possessions of the Scots
Reis und Kaffee, Rice and coffee
Reis und Mais, Rice and Indian corn
Republik Genua, Republic of Genoa
Republik Venedig, Republic of Venice
Reus, Reuss
Reval, Revel
Rha (Wolga), Rha (Volga)
Rhätische Alpen, Rhætian Alps
Rhagæ, Rha
Rhein, Rhine River
Rhein Bayern, Rhenish Bavaria
Rhegium, Reggio
Rheims, Reims
Rhenus, Rhine
Rhoda, Rosas
Rhodanus, Rhone River
Rhodus, Rhodes
Rhön Gb., Hohe Rhœne Mountains
Rhoxolanen, Rhoxolani (Sarmatian tribe)
Römisch Deutsches. Kaiserreich, Romano-Germanic Empire
Römische Meilen wovon 75 auf den Grad, Roman miles 75 to the degree
Römisches Reich, Roman Empire
Römisches Reich zur Zeit Constantins des Grossen, Roman Empire in the time of Constantine the Great
Roggen, Gerste, Weitzen, Rye, barley, wheat
Roggen u. Gerste, Rye and barley
Roggen und Weitzen, Rye and wheat
Rom, Rome
Roma, Rome
Rothes od Erythräisches Meer, Red Sea
Rothes Meer od. Arabischer Meerb, Red Sea
Rotomagus, Rouen
Roxolanen, Roxolani (Sarmatian tribe)
Rückkehr der Flotte unter Nearch, Return of the fleet under Nearchus
Rücklaufende Strömung, Counter current
Ruinen v. Babylon, Ruins of Babylon
Ruinen von Carthago, Ruins of Carthage
Ruinen v. Palmyra, Ruins of Palmyra
Ruinen v. Susa, Ruins of Susa
Rumanier, Rumini (tribe in Bulgaria, Moldavia, and Moravia)
Rusadir, Melilla
Rusicada, Stora
Ruspæ, Sbea
Russische Werste 104.3 *auf den Grad*, Russian Wersts 104.3 to the degree
Russisches America, Russian America
Russlands beste Kornfelder, Russia's best grainfields
Rusucurrum, Koleah

Saas Thal, Saas Valley
Sabier, Sabians (St. John the Baptist's disciples; sect in Persia)
Sachalites Golf, Bay of Seger
Sachsen, Saxony
Sächsische Schweiz, Saxonian Switzerland
Saguntum, Murviedro
Saima S., Lake Saim
Saker, Sakr
Salamis, Coulouri
Salmantica, Salamanca
Salomons Ins., Solomon Islands
Saloniki, Salonica
Salz Seen, Salt Lakes
Salz Wüste, Salt Desert
Sambus, Chumbul River
Samojeden, Samoyedes
Samoa oder Schiffer In., Navigators' Islands
Samosate, Samisat
Samsun, Samsoun
Sandw. Cobi od. Hanhai, Desert of Cobi
Sand Wüste, Sandy Desert
Sangarius, Sakariah River
Sarazenen, Saracens or Moors
Sardes, Sart
Sardica, Sophia
Sardinien, Sardinia
Sariphi Geb., Shar Mountains
Sarmatæ, Sarmatians
Sarmatien, Sarmatia
Sarmatische Tiefebene, Sarmation Lowland (East Prussia, Poland, and part of Russia)
Sarmatisches Meer, Sarmatian Sea (part of the Baltic)
Sarnia, Island of Guernsey
Satala, Shaygran
Sauromaten, Sarmatians
Saxen, Saxony (Saxonians, Saxons)
Scandinavisches Meer, Scandinavian Sea
Schetland In., Shetland Islands
Schlangen Indr., Snake Indians
Schlesien, Silesia
Schloss v. Romelli, Romelli Castle
Schnee Alp, Snowy Alps
Schotland, Scotland
Schwäbische Alp, Suabian Mountains
Schwarzes Meer 52 t. tief, Black Sea 52 toises deep
Schwarzw. (ald), Black Forest
Schweden, Sweden
Schweden, Norwegen und Dänemark, Sweden, Norway, and Denmark
Schwedische Landestheile, Swedish districts
Schweiz, Switzerland
Sclaven K. (üste), Slave Coast
Scodra, Scutari
Scordisci, tribe in Slavonia
Scythopolis, Bysan
Scupi, Uskup
Scylacium, Squillace
See, Sea or Lake
See Alpen, Maritime Alps
See Alpen von Californien, Maritime Alps of California
See Alpen der Nord West Küste, Maritime Alps of the N. W. Coast
See Arsissa, Lake Van
See Küsten Kette v. Venezuela, Sea coast mountain chain of Venezuela
See Likari, Lake Likaris
Seehunds B., Seal's or Shark's Bay
Seeland, Zealand
Seemeilen 20 *auf den Grad*, Sea miles 20 to the degree
Segobriga, Segorbe
Seliger S., Lake Seligero
Selinus, Vostizza River
Senegambien, Senegambia
Senogallia (Lugdunensis quarta), Isle of France and Champagne
Senus, Shannon River
Septentrio (Nord), North
Septimanen, Septimani (tribe in Languedoc)
Serbien, Servia
Sesamus, Amasserah
Setuval, Setubal
Sevennen, Cevennes Mountains
Seyschellen Ins., Seychelle Islands
Shetland Inseln, Shetland Islands
Shin See, Shin Lake
Sicilia, Sicily
Sidodona, Shenaas
Sidon, Sayda
Siebenbürgen, Transylvania
Siebenbürgisches Plateau, Plateau

of Transylvania
Siena, Sienna
Siga, Takumbreet
Signia, Segni
Sil, Sile River
Simferopol, Taurida
Simmen Thal, Simm Valley
Singaglia, Sinigaglia
Singara, Sinjar
Singidunum, Belgrade
Siniope, Sinub
Sinus Arabicus, Red Sea
Sirmium, Alt Schabacz
Siscia, Sziszek
Sitacus, Sita Rhegian River
Sitife, Seteef
Skagerak, Skager Rack
Skagestrandsbugt u. Handelsted, Skager Beach Bay and commercial town
Skandien (Scandia), Sweden
Skythen, Scythians (nation)
Skythini (Scythini), probably Saracens in Armenia
Slaven, Slavonians
Slavonische Militair Grenze, Slavonian military frontier
Slowenen, Wends (Slavonic nation)
Sogdiana, Great Bukaria
Sogdianien (Sogdiana), Great Bukaria
Solanus (Ost), East
Soledad od. Ost I., Soledad or Eastern Island (Falkland Islands)
Soli, Mezetlu
Soraben, Sorbi (Slavonic tribe)
Span. Mark, Spanish mark (modern Catalonia, Navarre, and part of Arragonia)
Spanien, Spain
Speier, Speyer
Spoletum, Spoleto
St. Georgs Kanal, St. George's Channel
St. Johann, St. John
Staaten der Mexicanischen Union, States of the Mexican Union
Staaten der Nordamerikanischen Union, States of the North American Union
Stattenland, Staten Island (S. A.)
Stadt der Getæ, City of the Getæ
Stalaktiden Grotte, Stalactite grotto
Steyermark, Styria
Str. v. (Strasse von) stands for "Straits of" before the respective names
Strabo's Erdtafel, Map of the World according to Strabo
Strasse v. Calais, the British Channel
Strom und Gebirgs-System von Mitteleuropa, River and Mountain System of Central Europe
Südamerika, South America
Süd Atlantische Strömung, South Atlantic current
Süd Cap, South Cape
Süd Georgien, South Georgia
Südl. Continent, Southern Continent
Südl. Grenze des Weinstocks, Southern boundary of the grape vine
Südliche Verbindungs Strömung, Southern Connecting current
Südlicher Polarkreis, Antarctic Circle
Süd oder Neu Georgien, South or New Georgia
Süd Schetland, New South Shetland
Süd West, South West
Sümpfe in gleicher Höhe m. d. Ocean, Swamps on a level with the ocean
Sumpf, Swamp
Sund, Sound
Sunda See, Sea of Sunda
Sunda Strasse, Straits of Sunda
Susiana, Khuzistan and Louristan
Swilly See, Lake Swilly
Sybaris, Cochyle River
Syracusa, Syracuse
Syrdaria, Sir River
Syrien, Syria
Syrisch Arabische Wüste, Syro-Arabian Desert
Syrische Wüste, Syrian Desert
Syrtes, Gulf of Sidra
Syrtika (Seli or Psylli), in Tripolis

Tabor, Mt. Tor
Tabraca, Tabarca
Tacape, Cabes
Tafelland von Armenien 250 *t.*, Armenian Plateau 250 toises
Tafelland von Iran 650 *t. üb. d. Meere*, Plateau of Iran 650 toises above the level of the sea
Tafelland v. Mexico od. Anahuac, Plateau of Mexico or Anahuac
Taifalen, Taifalæ (tribe on the Danube)
Tajo, Tagus River
Tambow, Tambov
Tamesis, Thames River
Tanais (Danaber), Don River
Tape, Bostam
Tapes Ind., Tappe Indians
Taprobana, Ceylon
Tarnowitzer Höhe, Plateau of Tarnowitz
Tarsus, Tersoos
Tarum, Tarem
Tatra Gebirg, Tatra Mountains (part of the Carpathian Mountains)
Taurica, Crimea
Taurien, Tauria
Taurischer Cherson, Crimea
Taxila, Attock
Tay Mündung, Firth of Tay
Teate, Chieti
Telmissus, Macry
Tenerifa, Teneriffe
Termessus, Schenet
Teufels Inseln, Devil's Islands
Thapsacus, Der
Thebais, Upper Egypt
Theben, Thebes
Thebunte, Melhafa
Themse, Thames River
Therwinger, Thervingi (Gothic tribe)
Thessalonica, Salonica
Thracia, Rumilia
Thrakien (Thracia), Rumilia
Thuner See, Lake of Thun
Tiberis, Tevere River
Tief Sudan, Low Soudan
Tiefland von Afrika, Lowlands of Africa
Tingis, Tangiers
Tischit, Tisheet
Titianus, Tezzano
Titicaca See, Lake Titicaca
Todtes Meer, Dead Sea
Toletum, Toledo
Tomi, Tomisvar
Torneo See u. Elf, Tornea Lake and River
Torres Strasse, Torres' Strait
Toscana, Tuscany
Toskanisches Hochland, Tuscan Highlands
Transylvanische Alpen, Transylvanian Alps
Trapezunt, Trebisonde
Trapezus, Trebisonde
Tremitische In., Tremiti Islands
Tridentum, Trento
Trier, Treves
Triest, Trieste
Trileucum, Ortegal
Troglodyten, Troglodytes (tribe on the Red Sea)
Tschad See, Lake Tchad
Tscheremissen, Tchermisses (Finnish tribe in Russian Asia)
Tscherkessien, Circassia
Tschernomorische Kosaken, Cirnomorian Cossacks
Tschuktschen, Tchookches (tribe in N. E. Asia)
Türkei, Turkey
Türkisch Croatien, Turkish Croatia
Tunes, Tunis
Tungusen, Tungouski (nation in Asia)
Turini, Turin
Turkmanen, Turcoman (Tartar tribe)
Tusculum, Frascati
Tyana, Kiliss Hissar
Tyras, Dniestr River
Tyras Donaster, Dniestr River
Tyroler Alpen, Tyrol Alps
Tyrrhenen, Tyrrheni (Pelasgian tribe)
Tyrrhenisches Meer, Tyrrhenian Sea (part of the Mediterranean)
Tyrus, Soor

Umgebung von Neu York, Vicinity of New York
Unerforschte Alpengebirge, Unexplored mountain region
Ungarisches Erzgebirge, Hungarian Erzgebirge
Ungarn, Hungary
Unterirdische Wasserleitung, Subterranean Aqueduct
Unzugängliche Felsenküste, Inaccessible rocky coast
Ural Gebirge, Oural Mountains
Uralische Kosaken, Oural Cossacks
Urumija See, Lake Uromija
Usa, Ouse River
Ursprung der Peruanischen Küsten Ström. kalten Wassers, Origin of the Peruvian cold water current
Uzen, Cumanen oder Polowzer, Utses Camanes or Polovzi (Mongolian tribe)

Vandalen, Vandals (Gothic tribe)
Vanille u. Cacao, Vanilla and Cacao
Vaterland des Kaffeebaumes, Country of the coffee tree
Veldidena, Wilden
Venedicus Sinus, Gulf of Venice
Venedig, Venice
Venetæ, Venetes (tribe in Britany)
Veneten, Venetes (tribe in Britany)
Venetia, Venice
Vereingte Staaten, United States
Verschiedene Ind. Stämme, Various Indian tribes
Vesuv, Vesuvius
Vgb. Comaria, Cape Comorin
Vgb. Maceta, Cape Musseldom
Vgb. Prionotus, Point Comol
Vgb. Syagros, Cape Ras Vire

Viadrus, Oder River
Viennensis, Dauphiny
Vierwaldstädter See, Lake of Lucerne
Vindhy Kette, Vindhya Mountains
Vindobona, Vienna
Virunum, Waren
Visurgis, Weser River
Vogesen, Vosges Mountains
Volhynien, Volhynia
Volubilis, Pharaoh's Castle
Vorder Rhein, Fore Rhine (one of the rivulets tributary to the Rhine)
Vorgeb Aromata, Cape Guardafui
Vorgeb Simylla, Cape Simylla
Votiaken, Wotyaks (Finnish tribe)

Wälder S., Lake of the Woods
Wahabiten, Wahabites (Mahomedan sect)
Walachei, Walachia
Waldai Geb., Waldai Mountains
Walfisch B., Whale Bay
Wallachisches Tiefland, Wallachian Lowlands
Wallenstädter See, Lake of Wallenstadt
Wan See, Lake Van
Wanger Oge, Wanger Oog
Warasdiner Geb., Warasdin Mountains
Warschau, Warsaw
Weichsel, Vistula River
Weichsel Niederung, Vistula Lowlands
Weisse Bai, White Bay
Weisse Berge, White Mountains
Weisse Bulgaren, White Bulgarians
Weisses Meer, White Sea
Weisses Vorgeb., Cape Blanc
Weitzen, Gerste u. Hafer, Wheat, barley and oats
Weitzen, Mais und Baumwolle, Wheat, Indian corn and cotton
Weitzen u. Baumwolle, Wheat and cotton
Weitzen u. Reis, Wheat and rice
Wendekreis des Krebses, Tropic of Cancer
Wendekreis des Steinbocks, Tropic of Capricorn
Wenden, Wends (Slavonic tribe)
Wenern See, Lake Wenern
Wesegothen, Visigoths (nation)
Weser Gb., Weser Mountains
West Gats, West Ghauts
West Indien, West Indies
West Preussen, West Prussia
West Pyrenäen, West Pyrenees
West Russland, West Russia
Wester W., Wester Wald
Westliche Länge von Paris, W. Longitude from Paris
Westphalen, Westphalia
Wettern See, Lake Wettern
Wien, Vienna
Wilde Völker, Savage nations
Windtafel der Griechen nach Aristoteles, Windchart of the Greeks according to Aristotle
Windtafel der Römer nach Vitruvius, Windchart of the Romans according to Vitruvius
Winipeg S., Winnipeg Lake
Winipigoos S., Lake Winnipigoos
Wogulen, Woguls or Uranfi (Finnish tribe)
Wolga, Volga River
Wüste al Ahkaf, Desert Al Ahkaf
Wüste Hochebene, Sandy Plateau
Wüste Kharasm, Desert of Kharasm
Wüste Sahara, Desert of Sahara
Wüste Sahel, Desert of Sahel
Wüstes Arabien, Arabia Deserta

Zacynthus, Zante
Zadracasta, Goorgaun
Zagrus Geb., Aiagha Mountains
Zahn u. Elfenbein K., Ivory Coast
Zalissa, Tiflis
Zana See, Lake Zana
Zembre S., Lake Zembe
Zariaspa später Baetra (Zariaspa, later Baetra), Balkh
Zeiton, Zeitoun
Zenobia, Zelebi
Zephyros (West), West wind
Zerstückelung des Reiches, Dismembering of the Empire
Zimmt, Muskatnuss u. Gewürznelke, Cinnamon, nutmeg, and clove
Zoromba, Dustee River
Zucker, Sugar
Zucker, Kaffee, Thee, Sugar, coffee, tea
Zucker u. Kaffee, Sugar and coffee
Züricher See, Lake of Zurich
Zug unter Gottfried von Bouillon, Crusade under Godfrey of Bouillon
Zug unter Conrad III. u. Ludwig VII., Crusade under Conrad III and Louis VII
Zug unter Ludwig IX. v. Frankr., Crusade under Louis IX of France
Zug unter Friedrich Barbarossa, Crusade under Frederick Barbarossa
Zug unter Kaiser Friedrich II., Crusade under Emperor Frederick II
Zug unter Richard I u. Phil. August, Crusade under Richard I and Philip Augustus
Zuyder See, Zuyder Zee
Zwarte Bge., Black Mountains
Zweibrücken, Bipont
Zwischen 0° *und* 10°, Between 0° and 10°

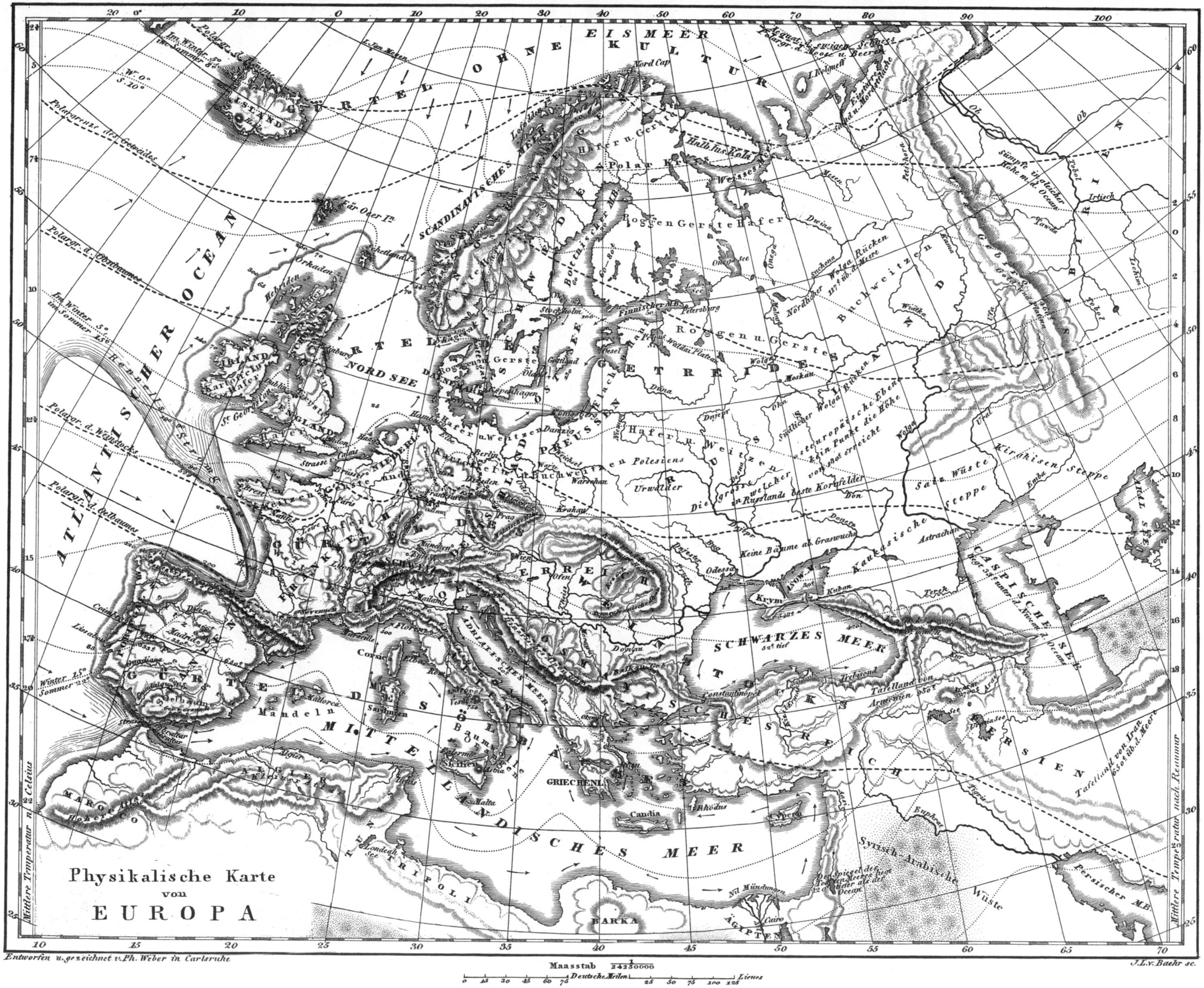

Physikalische Karte
von
EUROPA
EISMEER
GÜRTEL OHNE KULTUR
ATLANTISCHER OCEAN
NORD SEE
OST SEE
SCANDINAVISCHES
SCHWARZES MEER
CASPISCHE SEE
MITTELLÄNDISCHES MEER
ADRIATISCHES MEER
Nord Cap
Polar Kr.
Halbins. Kola
Weisses M.
Orkaden
Hebriden
IRLAND
ENGLAND
Roggen Gerste Hafer
Roggen u. Gerste
Hafer u. Weitzen
Buchweitzen
Salz Wüste
Kirghisen Steppe
Kaukasische
Keine Bäume ab. Graswuchs
Odessa
Krym
Constantinopel
Corsica
Sardinien
Malta
Candia
Rhodus
Cypern
GRIECHENL.
Mandeln
BARKA
ÄGYPTEN
Nil Mündungen
Cairo
TRIPOLI
Syrisch-Arabische Wüste
Persischer M.B.
Euphrat
Tigris
PERSIEN
Tafelland von Iran
Mittlere Temperatur n. Celsius
Mittlere Temperatur nach Reaumur
Entworfen u. gezeichnet v. Ph. Weber in Carlsruhe
J.L.v. Baehr sc.
Maasstab 1/24250000
Deutsche Meilen
Lieues

PLATE 142. PHYSICAL MAP OF EUROPE

 PLATES 143 AND 144. MOUNTAIN AND RIVER SYSTEMS OF CENTRAL EUROPE

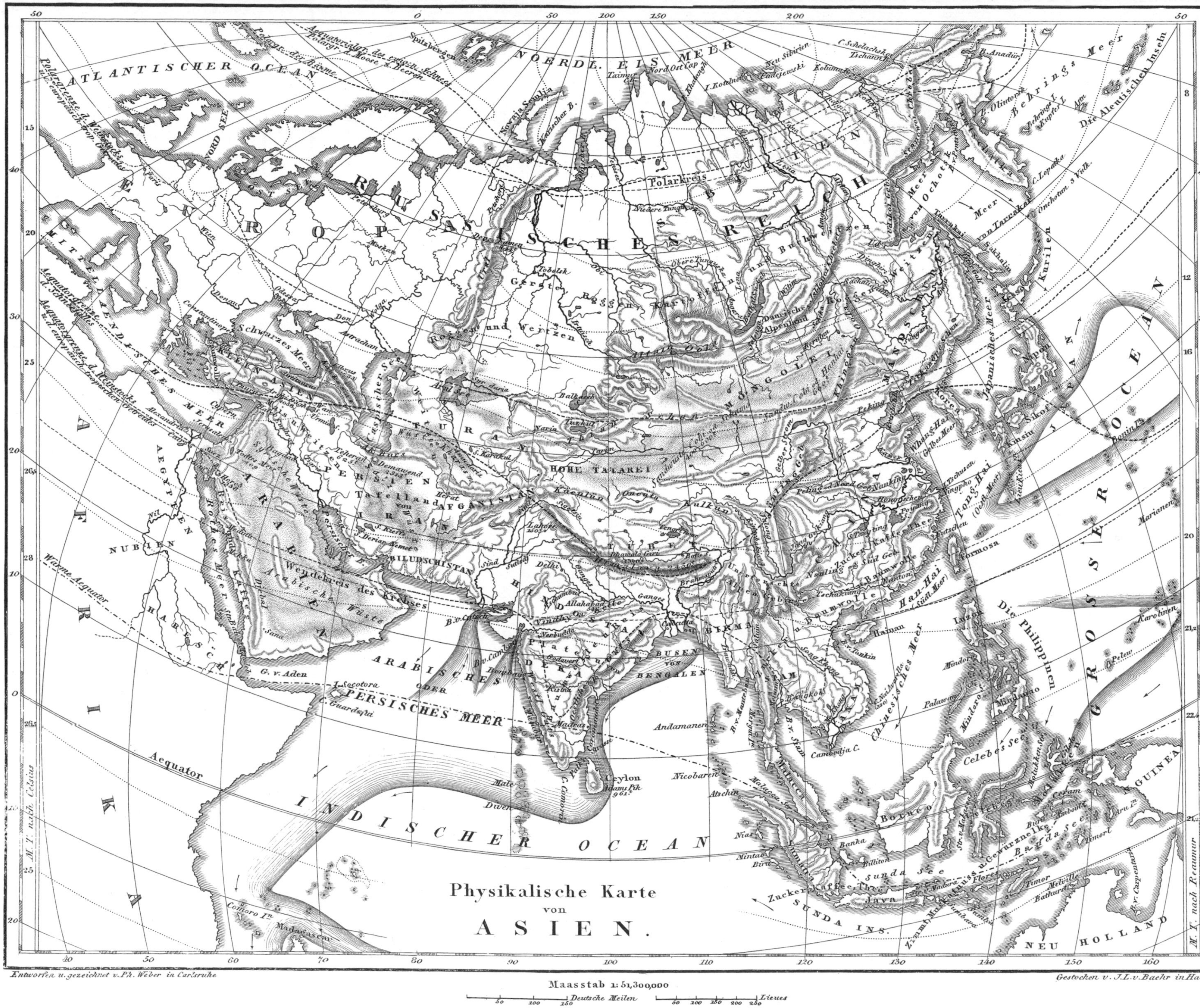
Physikalische Karte
von
ASIEN.
Entworfen u. gezeichnet v. Ph. Weber in Carlsruhe
Gestochen v. J. L. v. Baehr in Halle
Maasstab 1: 51,300,000
Deutsche Meilen
Lieues
NOERDL. EIS MEER
ATLANTISCHER OCEAN
EUROPA
RUSSISCHES REICH
SIBIRIEN
Polarkreis
MONGOLEI
HOHE TATAREI
PERSIEN
AFGANISTAN
BILUDSCHISTAN
ARABIEN
Wendekreis des Krebses
ARABISCHES ODER PERSISCHES MEER
BUSEN VON BENGALEN
INDISCHER OCEAN
Aequator
AFRIKA
NUBIEN
AEGYPTEN
Schwarzes Meer
Caspischer See
Chinesisches Meer
Japanisches Meer
GROSSER OCEAN
Die Philippinen
Celebes See
Sunda See
SUNDA INS.
NEU HOLLAND
Borneo
Java
Ceylon
Madagascar
Nipon
Formosa
Marianen
Karolinen
Die Aleutischen Inseln
Behrings Meer
Meer von Ochotsk
Kurilen
M. T. nach Celsius
M. T. nach Reaumur

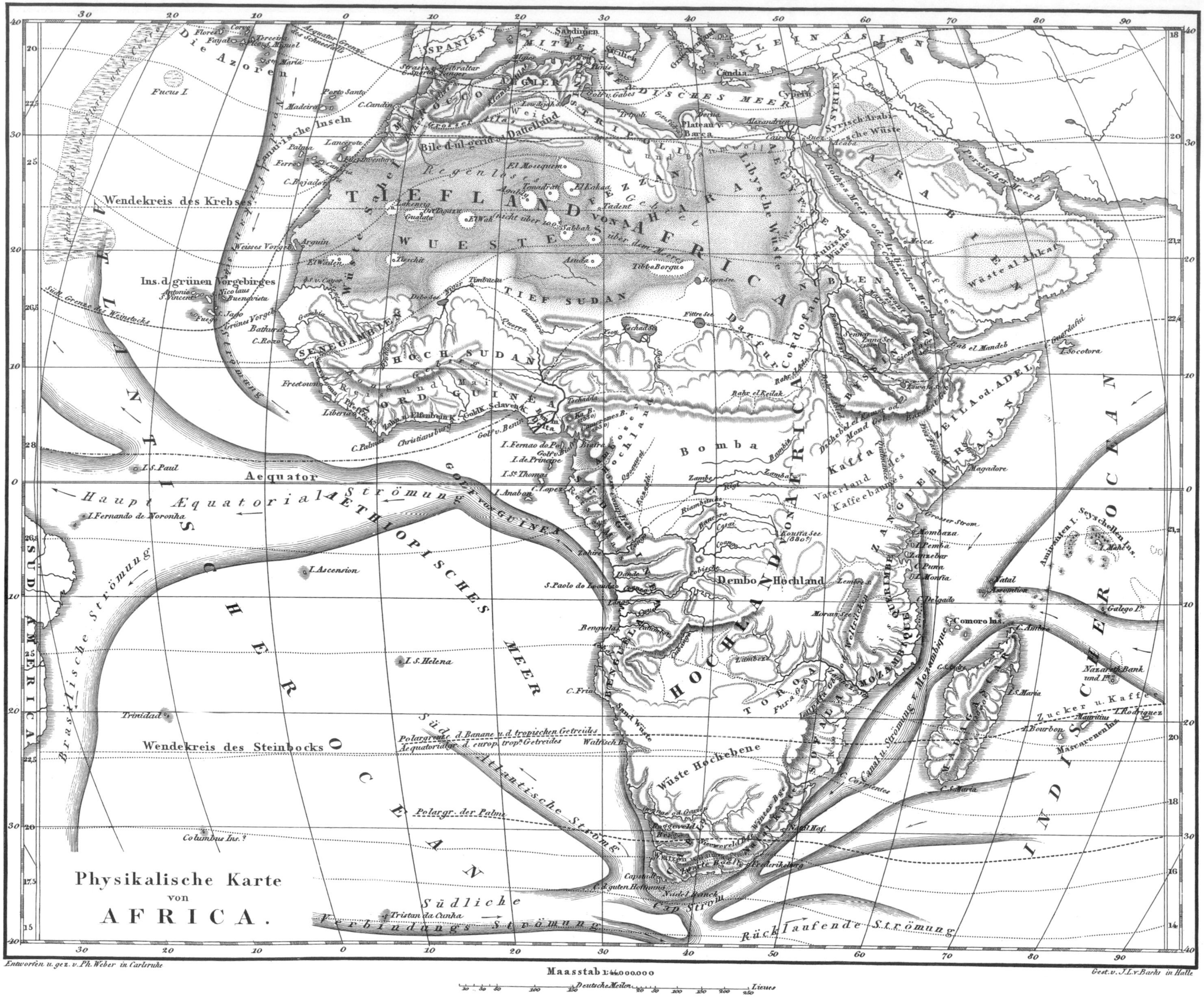
Physikalische Karte
von
AFRICA.
Entworfen u. gez. v. Ph. Weber in Carlsruhe
Gest. v. J.L.v.Bachs in Halle
Maasstab 1:44,000000
Deutsche Meilen
Lieues
Die Azoren
Fucus I.
Madeira
Porto Santo
Canarische Inseln
Wendekreis des Krebses
Ins. d. grünen Vorgebirges
Aequator
Haupt Æquatorial Strömung
I. S. Paul
I. Fernando de Noronha
I. Ascension
I. S. Helena
Trinidad
Wendekreis des Steinbocks
Columbus Ins.?
Tristan da Cunha
Südliche Verbindungs Strömung
Brasilische Strömung
SÜD AMERICA
ÆTHIOPISCHES MEER
Südl. Atlantische Strömung
Golf von GUINEA
SPANIEN
KLEIN ASIEN
MITTELLÄNDISCHES MEER
ARABIEN
TIEFLAND V. SAHARA
WUESTE
TIEF SUDAN
HOCH SUDAN
SENEGAMBIEN
NORD GUINEA
Bomba
Dembo Hochland
HOCHLAND
Libysche Wüste
Nubische Wüste
Wüste Hochebene
Polargrenze d. Banane u. d. tropischen Getreides
Æquatorialgr. d. europ. trop. Getreides
Polargr. der Palme
Cap Strom
Rücklaufende Strömung
Canal u. Strömung v. Mozambique
Comoro Ins.
Seychellen Ins.
Mascarenen Ins.
Zucker u. Kaffee
INDISCHER OCEAN
Timbuctu
Tschad See
Kaffa
Vaterland des Kaffeebaumes
Capstadt
C. d. guten Hoffnung
Nadel Bank
Bab el Mandeb
I. Socotora
Persischer Meerb.
Rothes Meer od. Arabischer Meerb.
Wüste al Ahkaf
Mecca
Candia
Cypern
Alexandrien
Tripoli
Sardinien
Sicilien

PLATE 146. PHYSICAL MAP OF AFRICA

Entworfen u. gezeichnet v. Ph. Weber in Carlsruhe — *Gest. v. J. L. v. Baehr in Halle*

Maasstab 1:39,300.000

Deutsche Meilen — Lieues

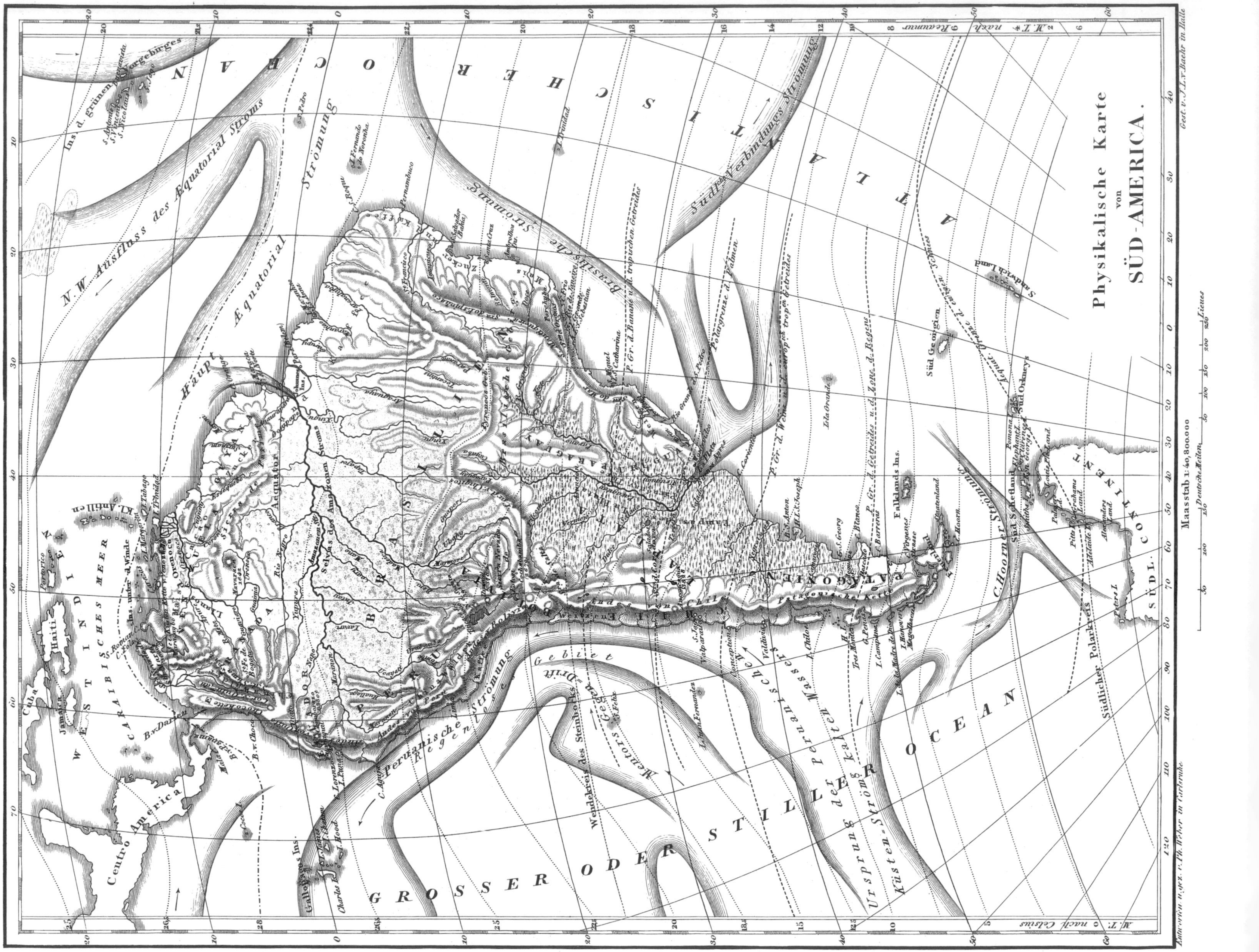
Physikalische Karte
von
SÜD-AMERICA.
Maasstab 1:40,800,000
GROSSER ODER STILLER OCEAN
Peruanische Strömung
Brasilische Strömung
Südl. Verbindungs Strömung
N.W. Ausfluss des Æquatorial Stroms
Haupt Æquatorial Strömung
Westindisches Meer
Caraibisches Meer
Centro America
Südlicher Polarkreis
Wendekreis des Steinbocks
Falklands Ins.
Süd Georgien
Süd Orkneys
Sandwich Land
Galloppagos Ins.

PLATE 148. PHYSICAL MAP OF SOUTH AMERICA

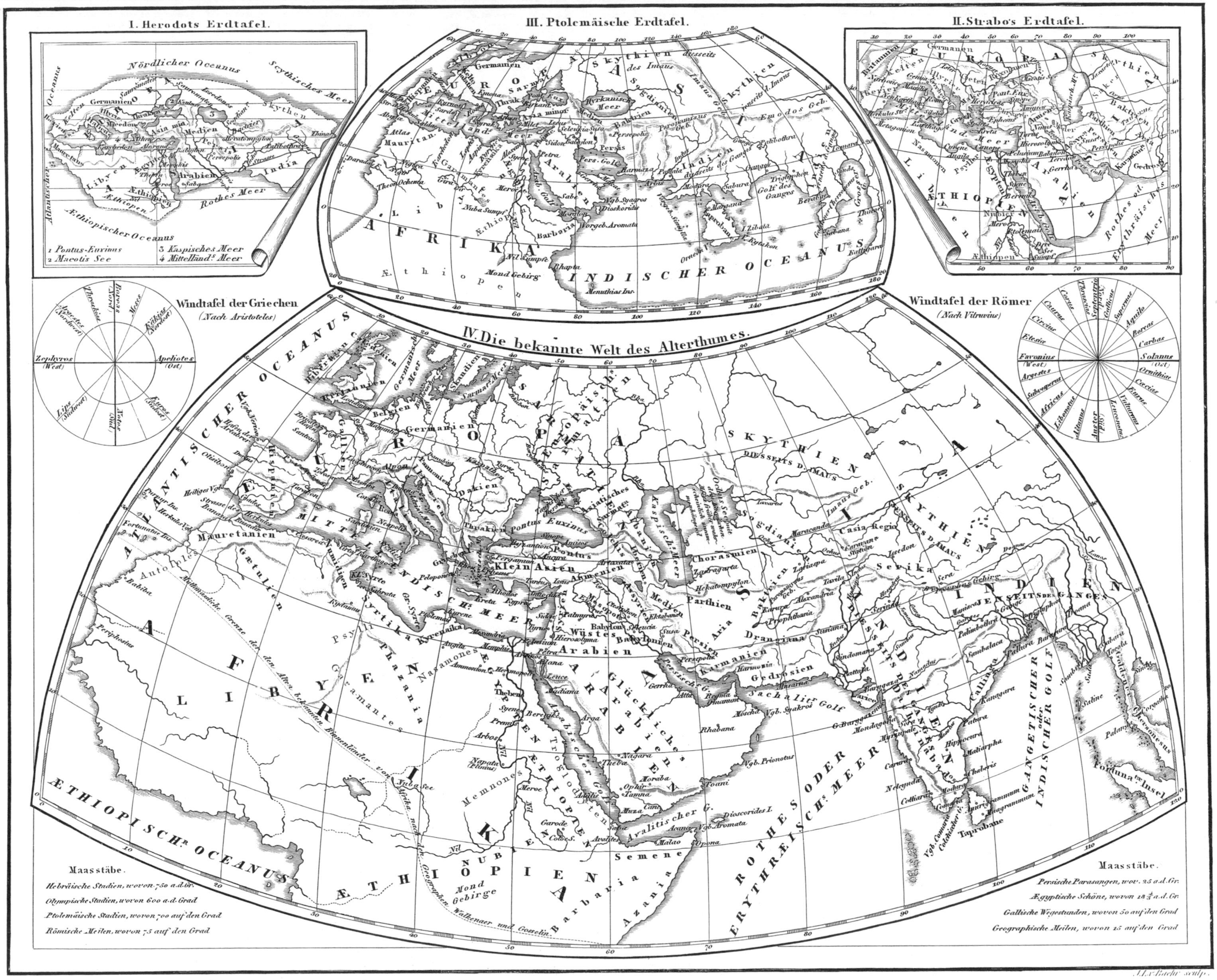

PLATE 149. MAPS OF THE WORLD ACCORDING TO: HERODOTUS(I), STRABO(II), PTOLEMY(III), THE ANCIENTS(IV)

REICH ALEXANDER'S
DES GROSSEN
Olympische Stadien, 600 auf den Grad.
Deutsche Meilen, 15 auf den Grad.
Alexander's Heerzüge.
Zerstückelung des Reiches
REICH DER SELEUCIDEN
1 Pergamus
2 Bithynien
3 Pontus
4 Cappadocien
5 Judaea
1 Termessus
2 Aspendus
EUROPA
ASIA
EUROPÆISCHES SKYTHIEN
ASIATISCHES SKYTHIEN
PONTUS EUXINUS
(SCHWARZES MEER)
MARE CASPIUM
MARE HYRCANUM ODER
MARE INTERNUM
(MITTELLÄNDISCHES MEER)
MARE ERYTHRÆUM
(INDISCHES MEER)
ARABIA
LIBYA
AEGYPTEN
INDIA
BACTRIA
SOGDIANA
MARGIANA
PARTHIA
MEDIA
ARMENIA
PERSIS
CARMANIA
GEDROSIA
ARACHOSIA
DRANGIANA
PAROPAMISADAE
Babylon
Susa
Persepolis
Ecbatana
Alexandria
Memphis
Thebae
Wendekreis
Persischer Meerbusen
Arabischer Meerbusen
Rückkehr der Flotte unter Nearch.
G. Heck dir.
R. Schmidt sculp.

PLATE 150. THE KINGDOM OF ALEXANDER THE GREAT

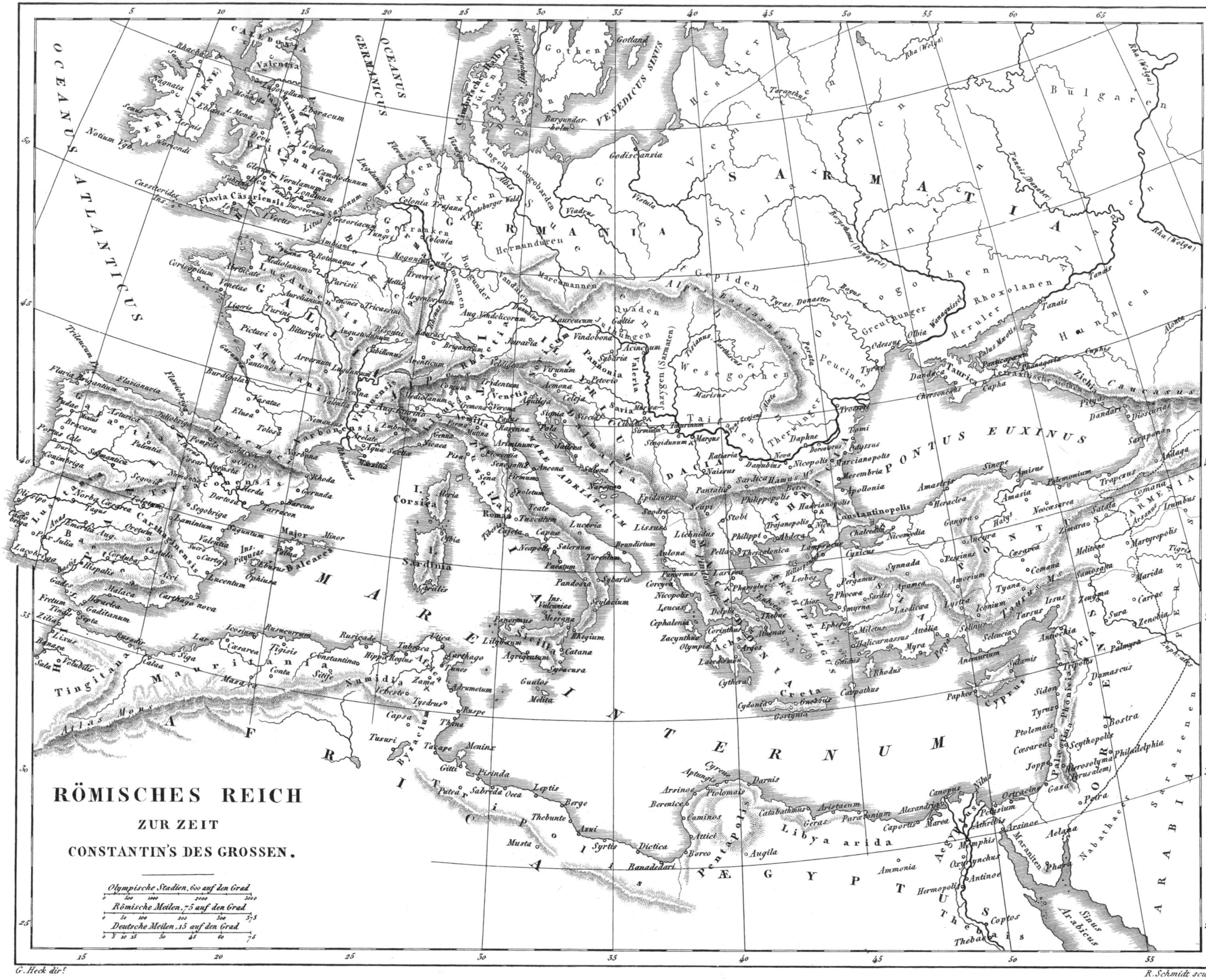

PLATE 151. ROMAN EMPIRE UNDER CONSTANTINE THE GREAT

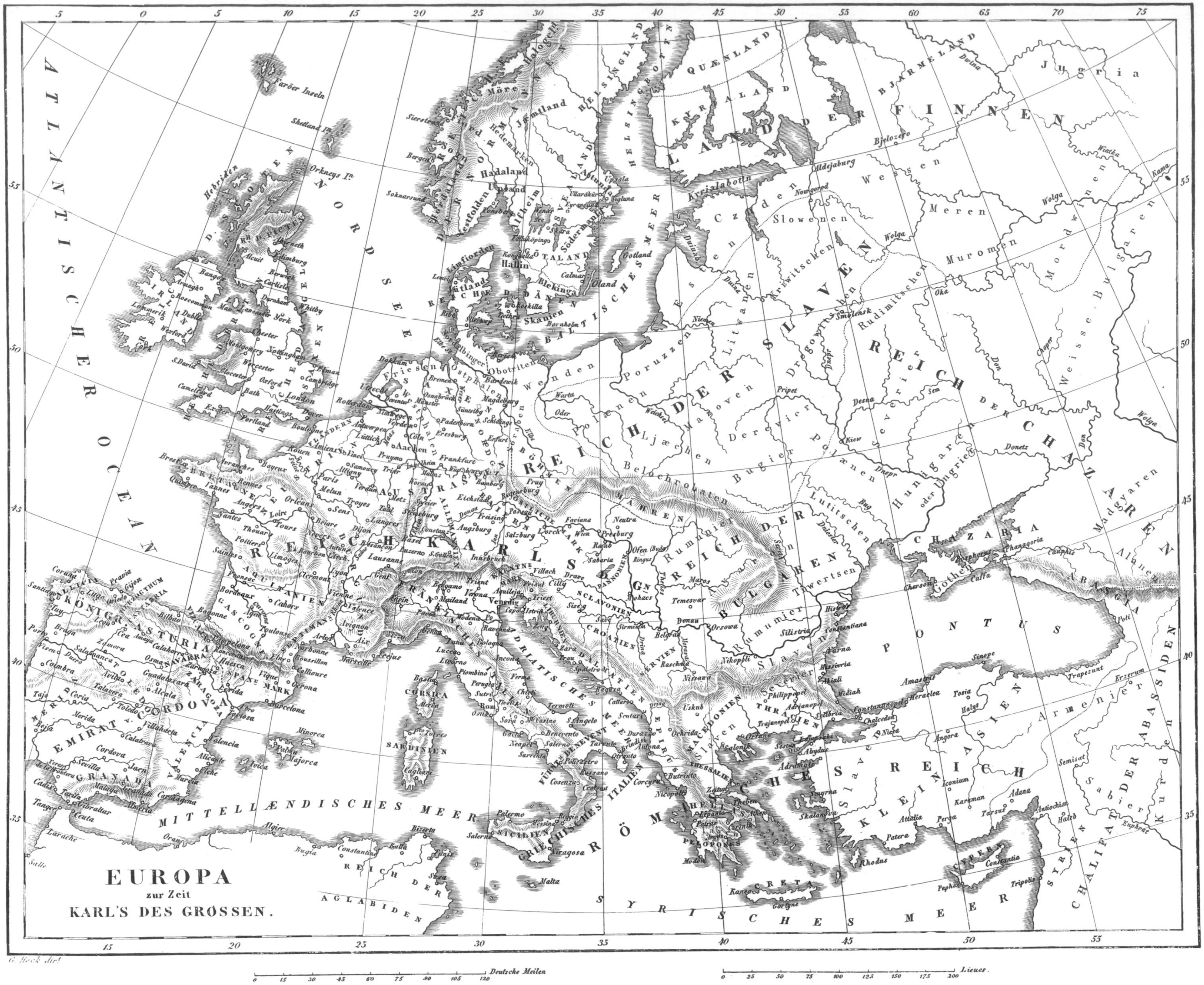
EUROPA
zur Zeit
KARL'S DES GRØSSEN.
ATLANTISCHER OCEAN
NORDSEE
BALTISCHES MEER
MITTELLÆNDISCHES MEER
SYRISCHES MEER
PONTUS
REICH KARLS D. GR.
REICH DER SLAVEN
REICH DER CHAZAREN
REICH DER BULGAREN
RÖMISCHES REICH
LAND DER FINNEN
KÖNIGR. ASTURIA
EMIRAT V. CORDOVA
CHALIFAT DER ABASSIDEN
REICH DER AGLABIDEN
Deutsche Meilen
Lieues
G. Heck dir.

 PLATE 152. EUROPE IN THE TIME OF CHARLEMAGNE

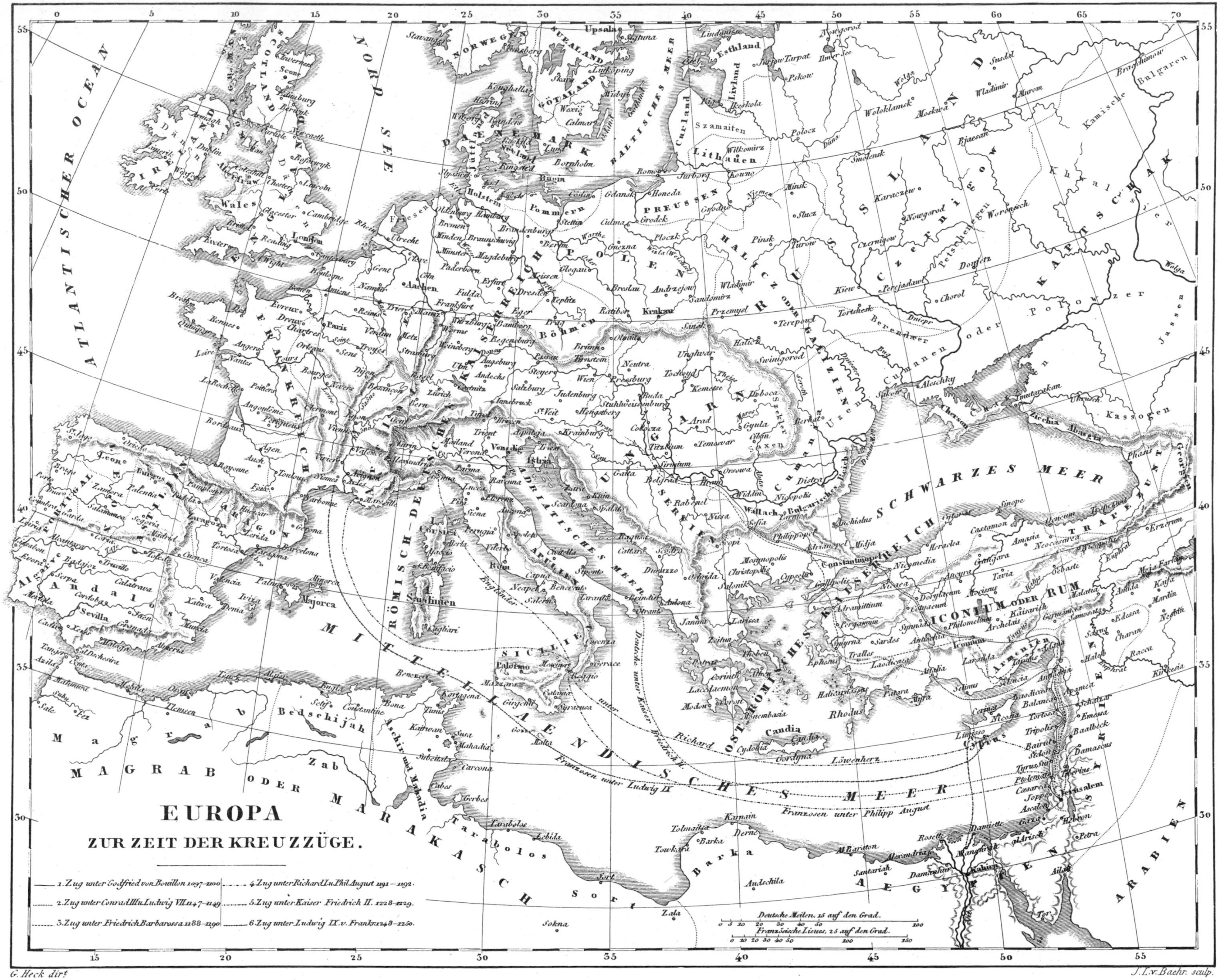
EUROPA
ZUR ZEIT DER KREUZZÜGE.
1. Zug unter Godfried von Boüillon 1097–1100
2. Zug unter Conrad III u. Ludwig VII. 1147–1149
3. Zug unter Friedrich Barbarossa 1188–1190
4. Zug unter Richard I. u. Phil. August 1191–1192.
5. Zug unter Kaiser Friedrich II. 1228–1229.
6. Zug unter Ludwig IX. v. Frankr. 1248–1250.
ATLANTISCHER OCEAN
NORD SEE
BALTISCHES MEER
SCHWARZES MEER
MITTELLAENDISCHES MEER
ADRIATISCHES MEER
RÖMISCH-DEUTSCHES REICH
FRANKREICH
POLEN
UNGARN
RUSSLAND
DÄNEMARK
ENGLAND
SCOTLAND
IRLAND
NORWEGEN
PREUSSEN
LITHAUEN
SICILIEN
ICONIUM ODER RUM
OSTRÖMISCHES KAISERREICH
MAGRAB ODER MARAKASCH
AEGYPTEN
ARABIEN
Deutsche Meilen, 15 auf den Grad.
Französische Lieues, 25 auf den Grad.
G. Heck dir.t
J. L. v. Baehr. sculp.

G. Heck dir.t J.I.v.Baehr sculp.

PLATE 154. EUROPE BEFORE THE FRENCH REVOLUTION OF 1789

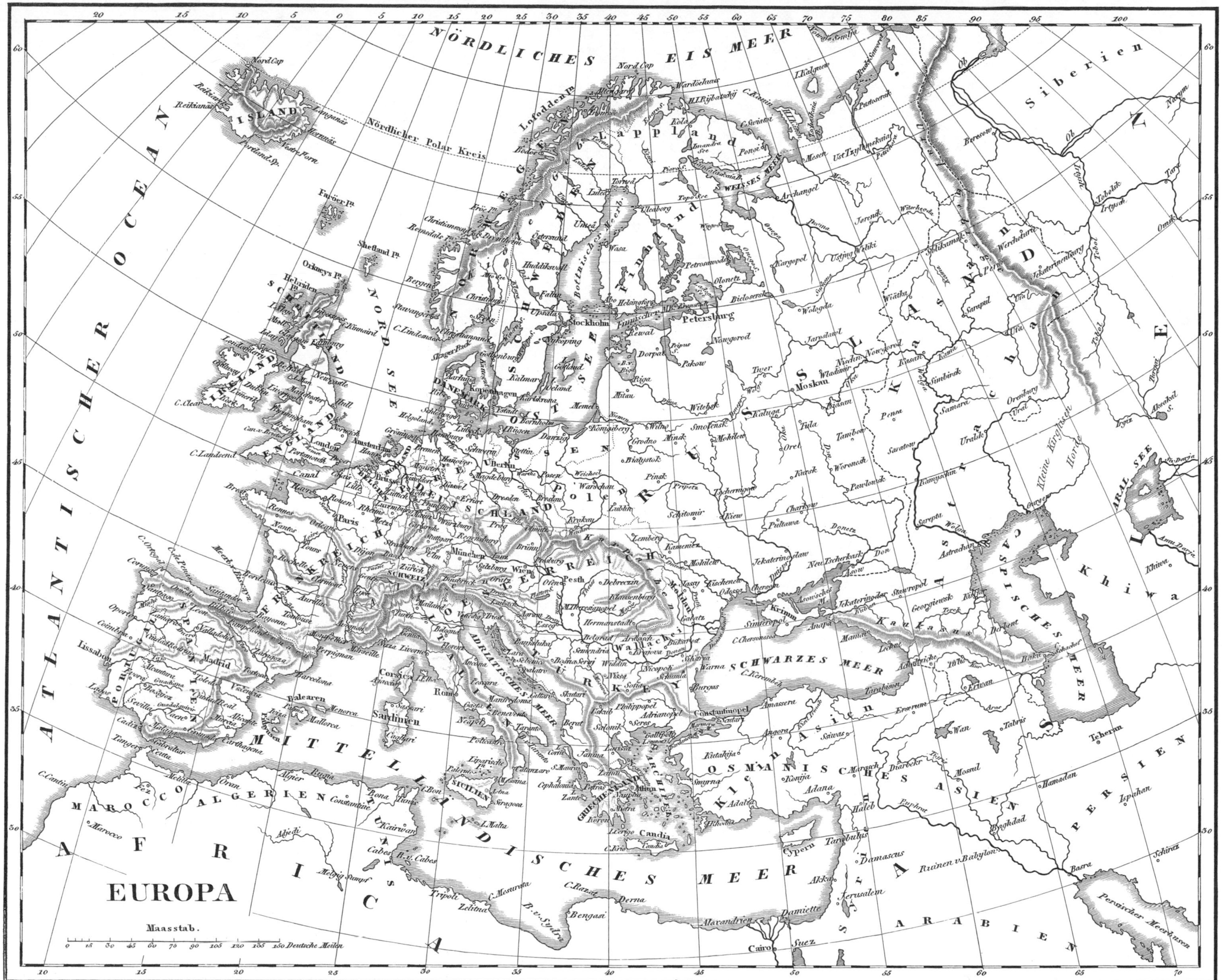

G.Heck dir.

J.L.v.Baehr sculp.

PLATE 155. EUROPE IN THE NINETEENTH CENTURY

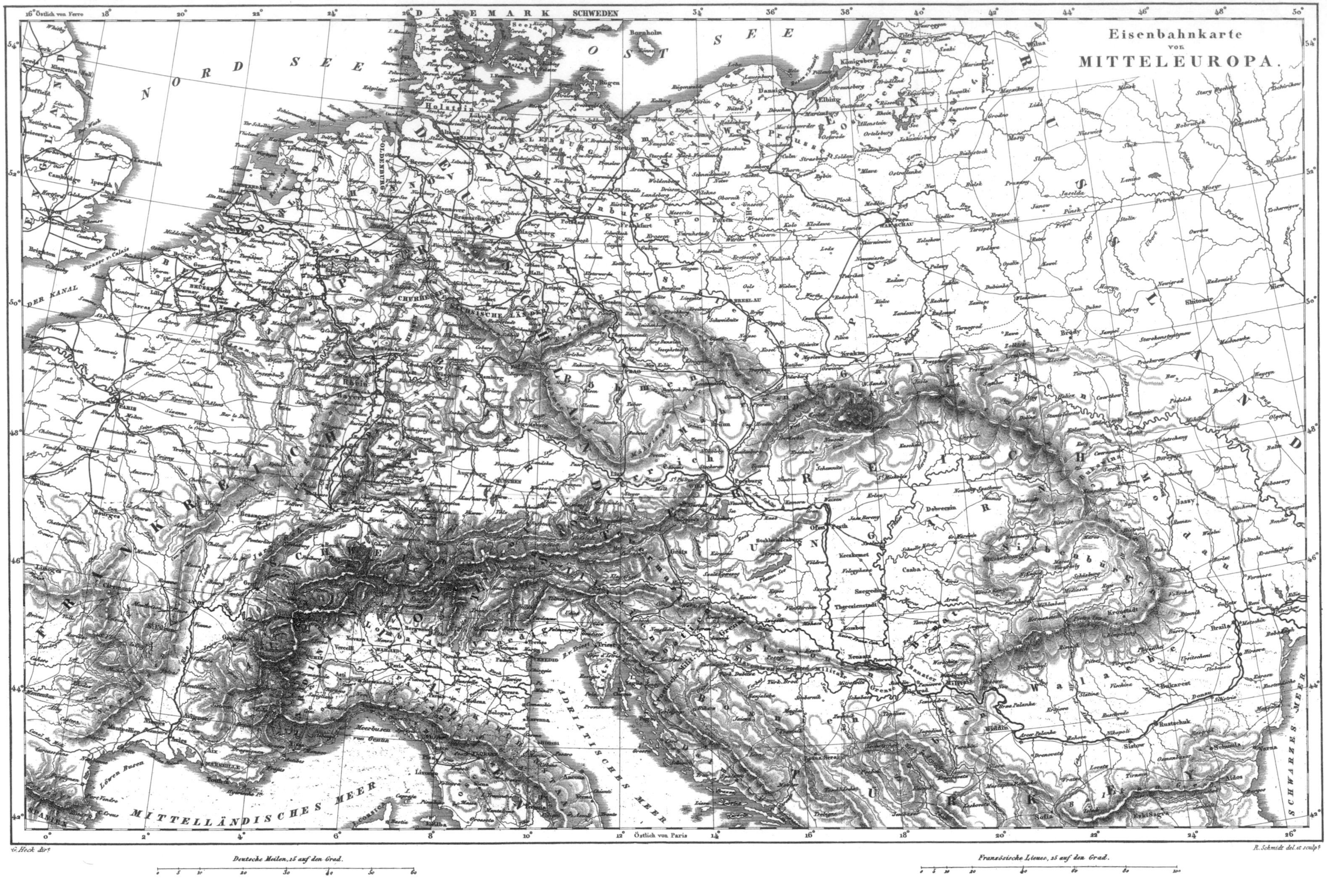

 PLATES 156 AND 157. THE RAILROADS OF CENTRAL EUROPE

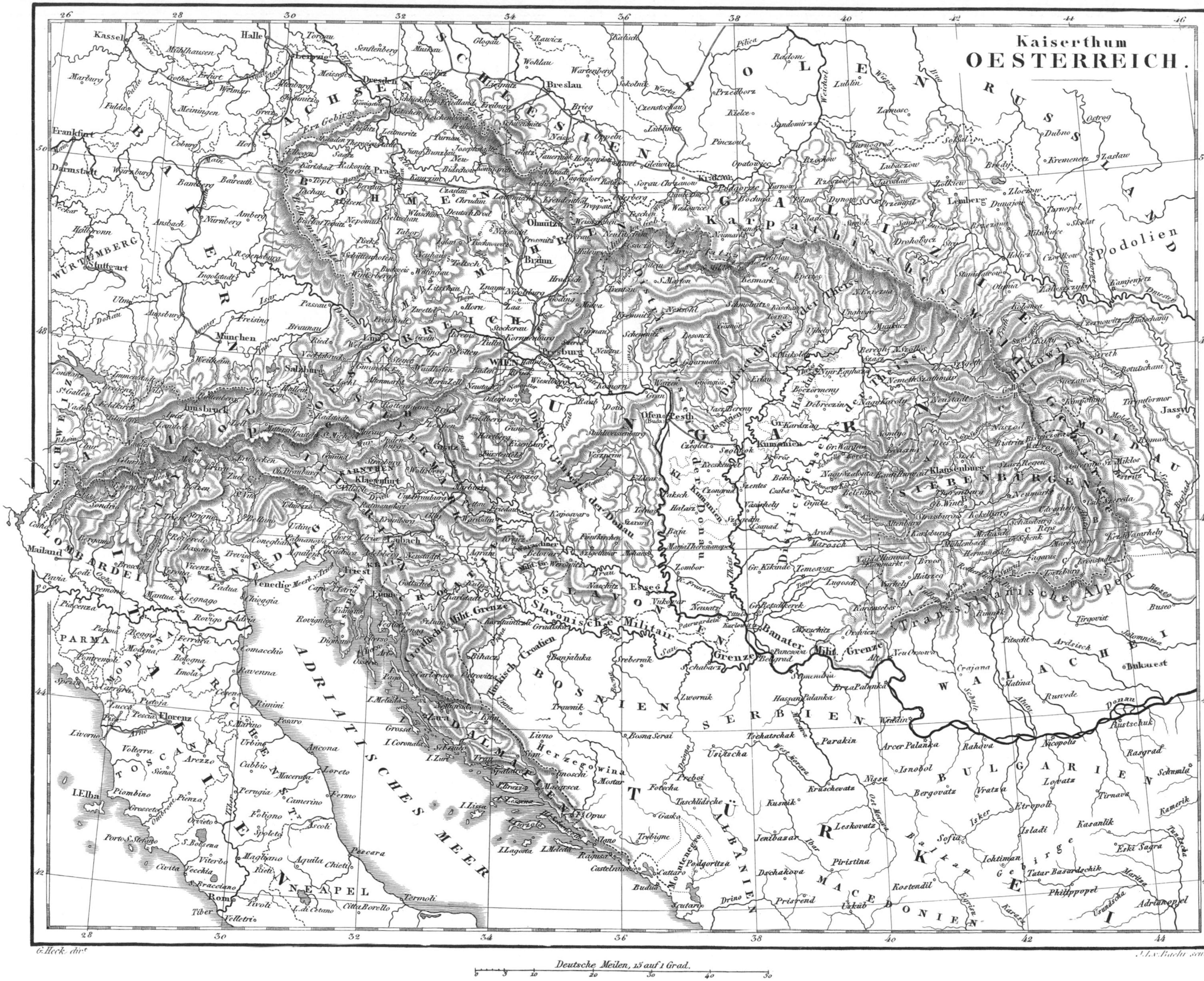
Kaiserthum
OESTERREICH.
G. Heck. dir.
J. A. v. Bach. sculp.
Deutsche Meilen, 15 auf 1 Grad.
0 5 10 20 30 40 50
SACHSEN
SCHLESIEN
POLEN
RUSSLAND
Podolien
GALIZIEN
BÖHMEN
MÄHREN
BAIERN
WÜRTEMBERG
OESTERREICH
UNGARN
SIEBENBÜRGEN
Bukowina
MOLDAU
WALACHEI
LOMBARDEI
VENEDIG
PARMA
MODENA
TOSCANA
KIRCHENSTAAT
NEAPEL
ADRIATISCHES MEER
CROATIEN
Croatische Milit. Grenze
Slavonische Militair Grenze
Banater Milit. Grenze
SLAVONIEN
BOSNIEN
Herzegowina
DALMATIEN
SERBIEN
BULGARIEN
ALBANIEN
MACEDONIEN
TÜRKEI
Transsylvanische Alpen
Karpathisches Gebirge
Balkan Gebirge
Donau
WIEN
Prag
Pesth
Ofen
Triest
Venedig
Mailand
Florenz
Rom
Breslau
München
Dresden
Lemberg
Jassy
Bukurest
Belgrad

Königreich
PREUSSEN
FÜRSTENTHUM NEUENBURG
Deutsche Meilen, 15 auf den Grad.
KATTEGAT
DIE NORD SEE ODER DAS DEUTSCHE MEER
DIE OST SEE ODER DAS BALTISCHE MEER
SCHWEDEN
OESTERREICH
KOENIGR. BOEHMEN
KOENIGREICH BAIERN
KOENIGR. SACHSEN
Bornholm
I. Rügen
Danzig
Königsberg
Stettin
BERLIN
Potsdam
Frankfurt
Posen
WARSCHAU
Hamburg
Lübeck
Bremen
Hannover
Magdeburg
Leipzig
Dresden
Breslau
Prag
Olmütz
Brünn
Nürnberg
Regensburg
Augsburg
Stuttgart
Mannheim
Darmstadt
Frankfurt
Mainz
Kassel
Düsseldorf
Köln
Coblenz
Trier
Erfurt
Halle
Stralsund
Tilsit
Memel
Elbing
Thorn
Kalisz
Krakau
Karpathen Geb.
Tatra Geb.
Gez. v. Ph. Weber in Carlsruhe
Deutsche Meilen, 15 auf den Grad.
Französische Lieues, 25 auf den Grad.

 PLATE 159. PRUSSIA

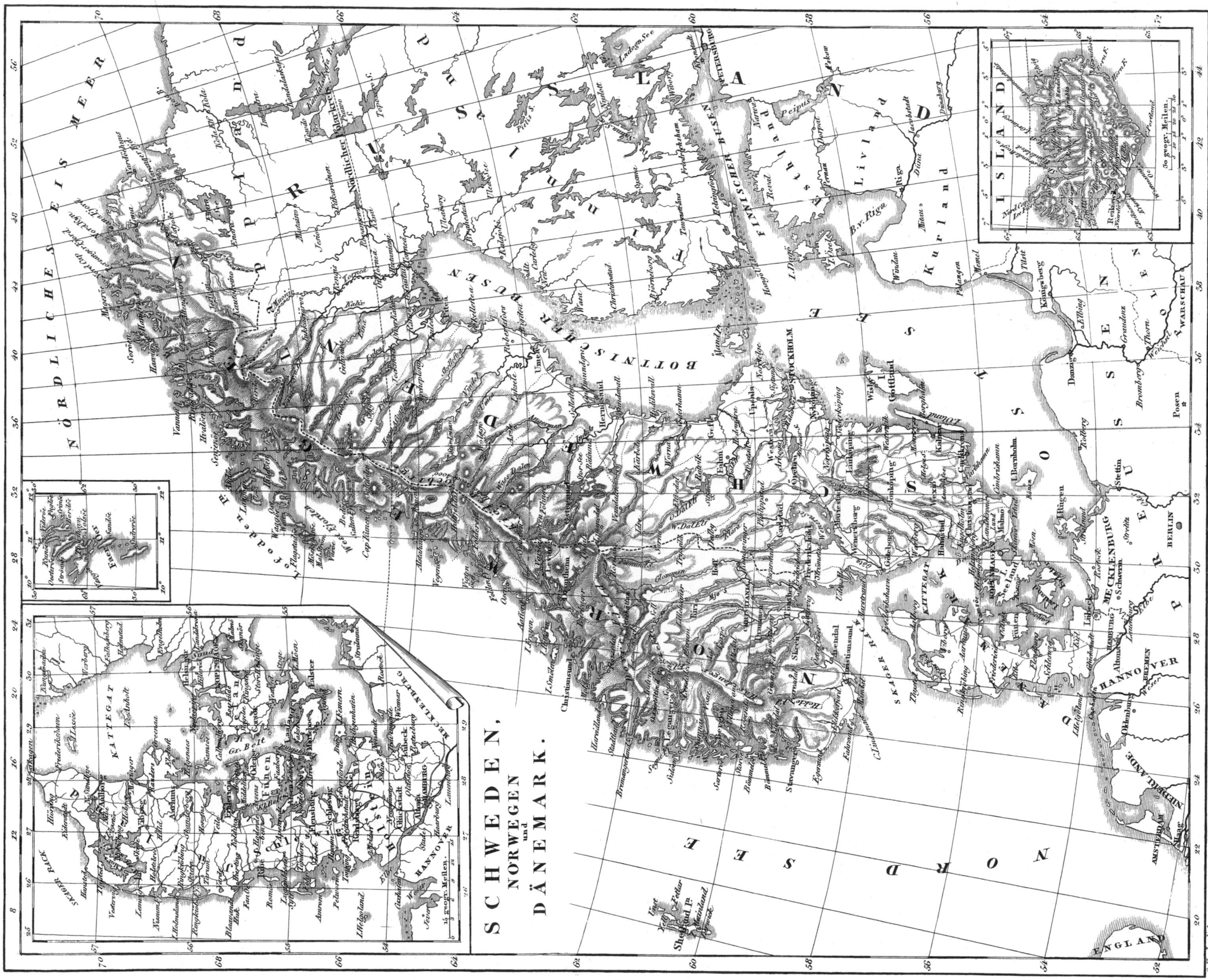

PLATE 160. SWEDEN, NORWAY, AND DENMARK

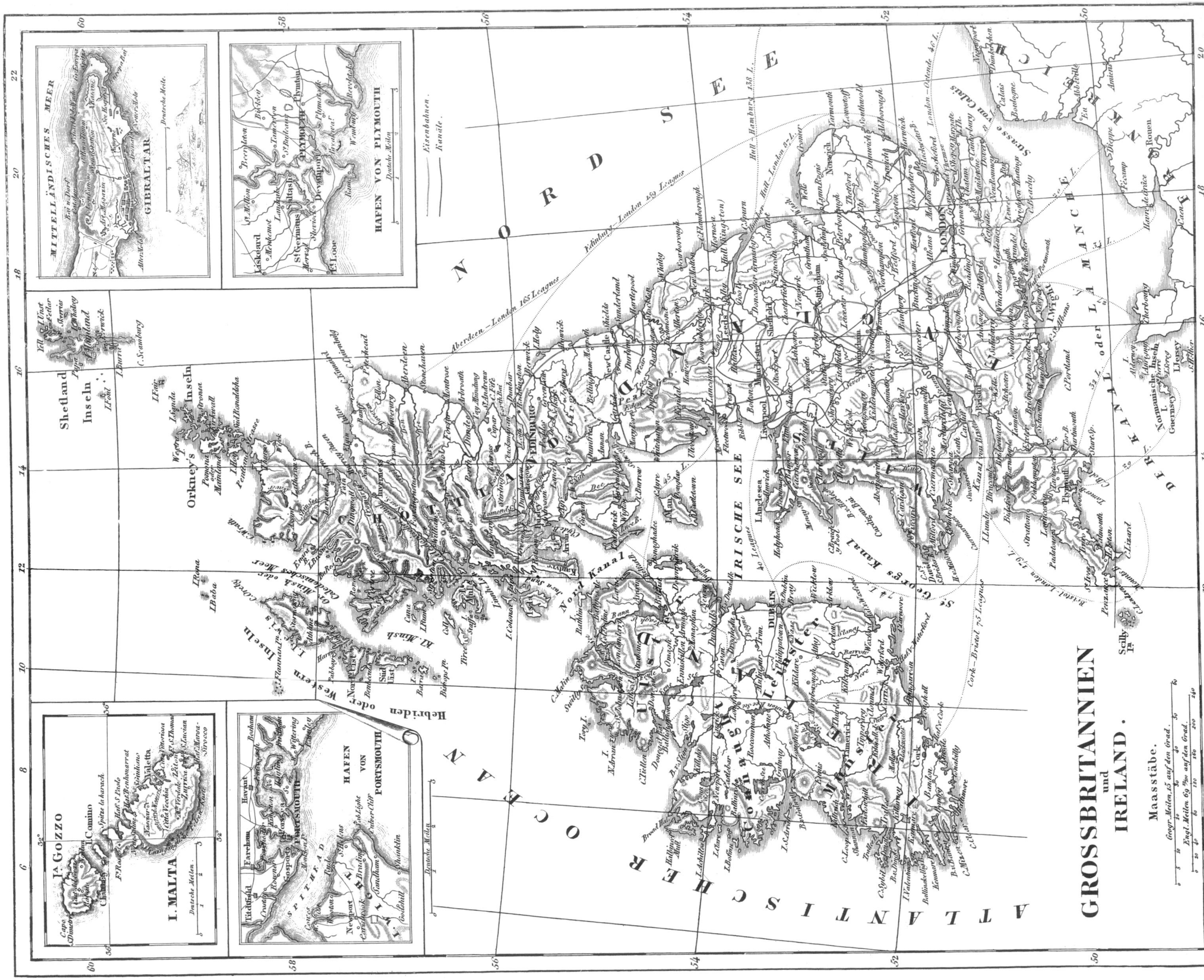
GROSSBRITANNIEN
und
IRELAND.
Maasstäbe.
NORD SEE
ATLANTISCHER OCEAN
IRISCHE SEE
St. Georges Kanal
Nord Kanal
DER KANAL oder LA MANCHE
Shetland Inseln
Orkney's Inseln
Hebriden oder Western Inseln
GIBRALTAR
MITTELLÄNDISCHES MEER
HAFEN VON PLYMOUTH
HAFEN VON PORTSMOUTH
I. MALTA
I. GOZZO
LONDON
DUBLIN
EDINBURG
Eisenbahnen.
Kanäle.
Deutsche Meilen
Ph. Weber del. Carlsruhe

 PLATE 161. GREAT BRITAIN AND IRELAND

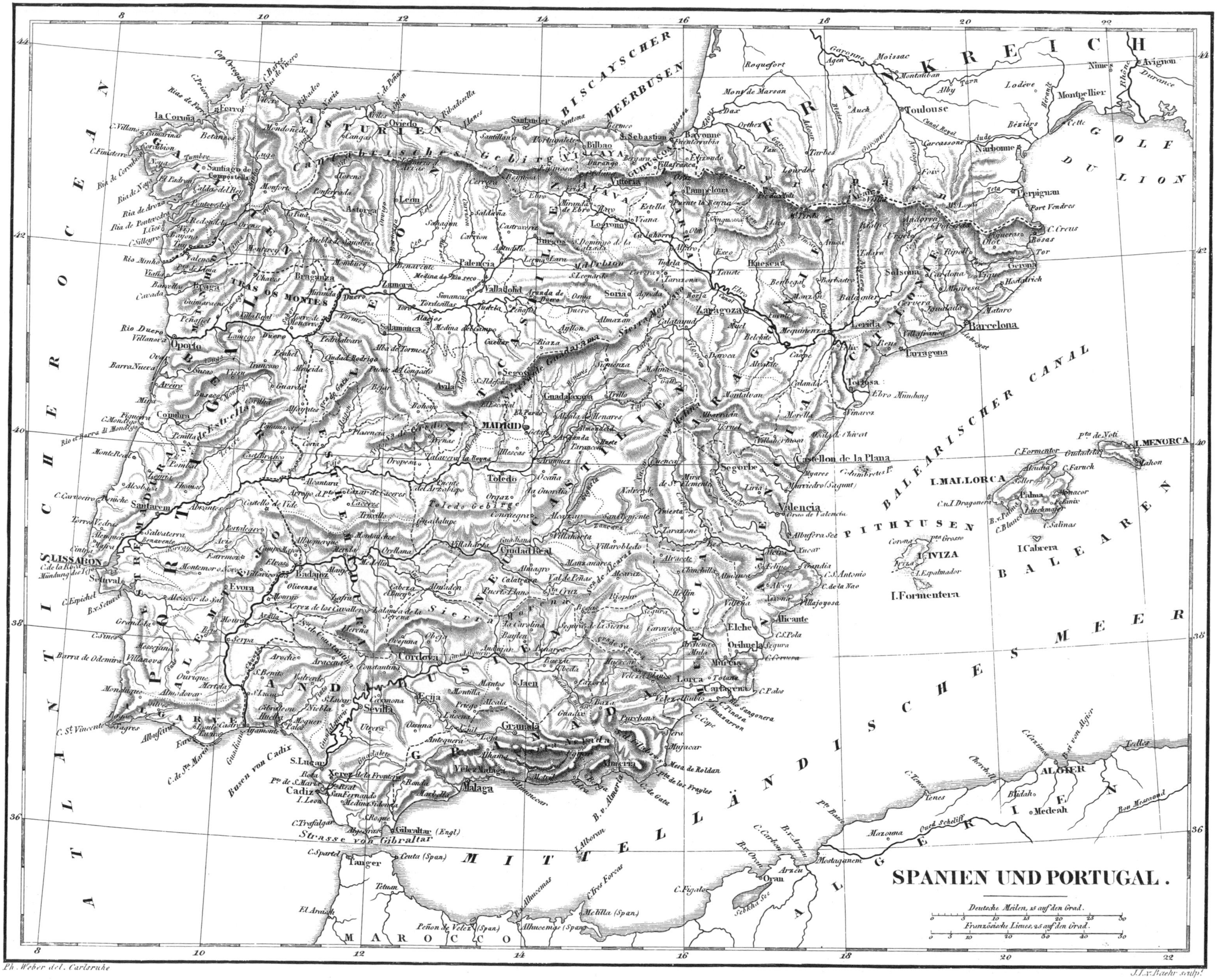

Ph. Weber del. Carlsruhe

J. L. v. Baehr sculp.

PLATE 162. SPAIN AND PORTUGAL

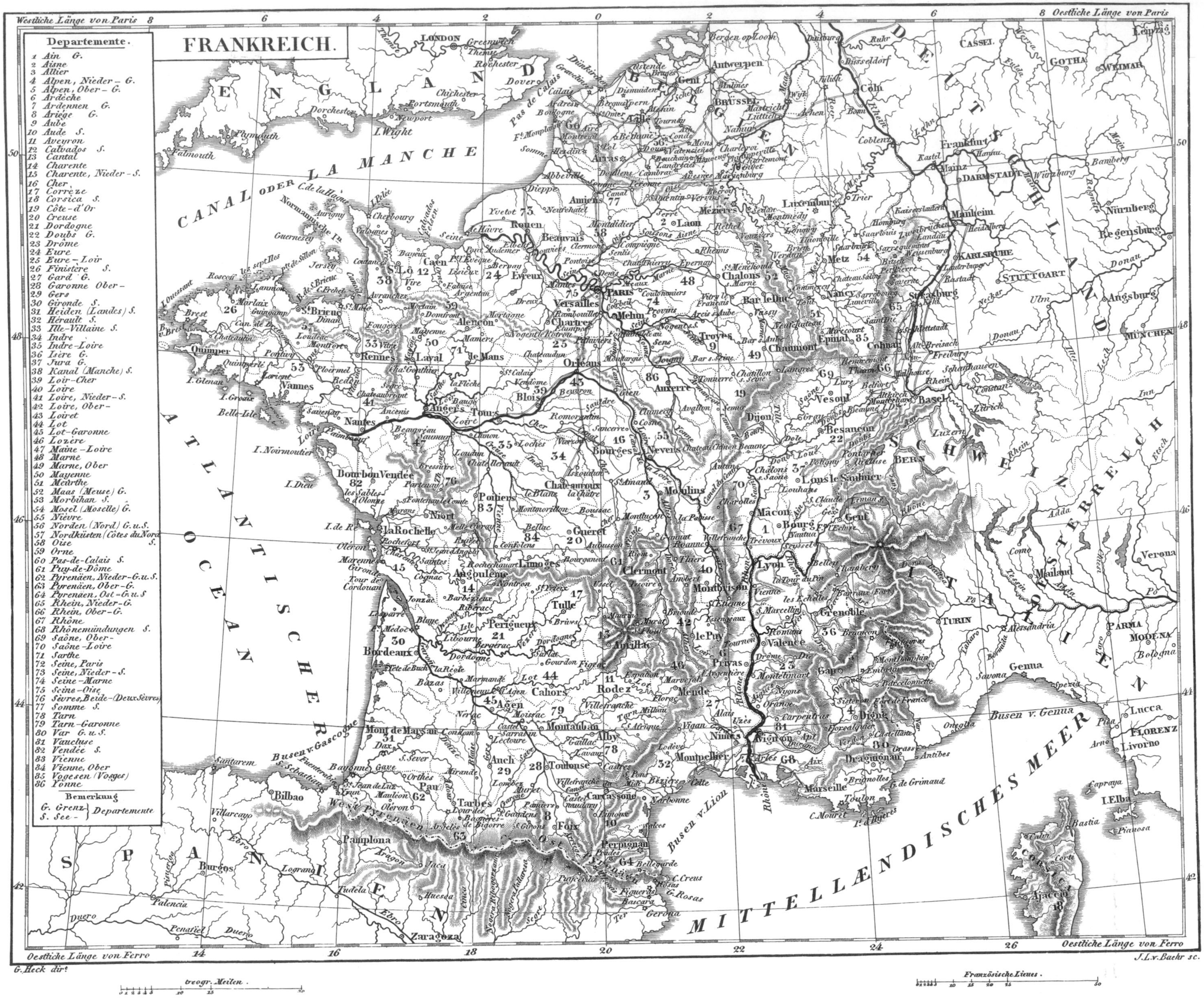

FRANKREICH.
Westliche Länge von Paris
Oestliche Länge von Paris
Oestliche Länge von Ferro
Departemente.
1 Ain G.
2 Aisne
3 Allier
4 Alpen, Nieder - G.
5 Alpen, Ober - G.
6 Ardèche
7 Ardennen G.
8 Ariège G.
9 Aube
10 Aude S.
11 Aveyron
12 Calvados S.
13 Cantal
14 Charente
15 Charente, Nieder - S.
16 Cher
17 Corrèze
18 Corsica S.
19 Côte-d'Or
20 Creuse
21 Dordogne
22 Doubs G.
23 Drôme
24 Eure
25 Eure-Loir
26 Finistère S.
27 Gard G.
28 Garonne Ober-
29 Gers
30 Gironde S.
31 Heiden (Landes) S.
32 Hérault S.
33 Ille-Villaine S.
34 Indre
35 Indre-Loire
36 Isère G.
37 Jura G.
38 Kanal (Manche) S.
39 Loir-Cher
40 Loire
41 Loire, Nieder - S.
42 Loire, Ober -
43 Loiret
44 Lot
45 Lot-Garonne
46 Lozère
47 Maine-Loire
48 Marne
49 Marne, Ober
50 Mayenne
51 Meurthe
52 Maas (Meuse) G.
53 Morbihan S.
54 Mosel (Moselle) G.
55 Nièvre
56 Norden (Nord) G.u.S.
57 Nordküsten (Côtes du Nord) S.
58 Oise
59 Orne
60 Pas-de-Calais S.
61 Puy-de-Dôme
62 Pyrenäen, Nieder-G.u.S.
63 Pyrenäen, Ober-G.
64 Pyrenäen, Ost-G.u.S.
65 Rhein, Nieder-G.
66 Rhein, Ober-G.
67 Rhône
68 Rhônemündungen S.
69 Saône, Ober-
70 Saône-Loire
71 Sarthe
72 Seine, Paris
73 Seine, Nieder - S.
74 Seine-Marne
75 Seine-Oise
76 Sèvres, Beide-(Deux Sèvres)
77 Somme S.
78 Tarn
79 Tarn-Garonne
80 Var G.u.S.
81 Vaucluse
82 Vendée S.
83 Vienne
84 Vienne, Ober
85 Vogesen (Vosges)
86 Yonne
Bemerkung
G. Grenz-
S. See- Departemente
ENGLAND
DEUTSCHLAND
BELGIEN
SCHWEIZ
OESTERREICH
ITALIEN
SPANIEN
CANAL ODER LA MANCHE
ATLANTISCHER OCEAN
MITTELLÆNDISCHES MEER
Busen v. Gascogne
Busen v. Lion
Busen v. Genua
LONDON
PARIS
BRÜSSEL
Antwerpen
Cöln
Frankfurt
Mainz
Manheim
Karlsruhe
STUTTGART
Strassburg
Metz
Nancy
Rheims
Amiens
Rouen
Caen
Cherbourg
Brest
Rennes
Nantes
Angers
Tours
Orleans
Versailles
Bourges
Dijon
Besançon
Lyon
Genf
BERN
TURIN
Genua
Grenoble
Valence
Avignon
Nîmes
Montpellier
Marseille
Toulon
Bordeaux
Toulouse
Bayonne
Pau
Tarbes
Perpignan
Limoges
Poitiers
Clermont
Rodez
Cahors
Agen
La Rochelle
Bilbao
Pamplona
Burgos
Zaragoza
Corsica
Ajaccio
Bastia
I.Elba
Livorno
FLORENZ
Pisa
Lucca
PARMA
MODENA
Bologna
Mailand
Verona
Zürich
Basel
München
Nürnberg
Regensburg
Würzburg
GOTHA
WEIMAR
CASSEL
Leipzig
G. Heck dir.
J.L.v. Baehr sc.
Geogr. Meilen.
Französische Lieues.

PLATE 163. FRANCE

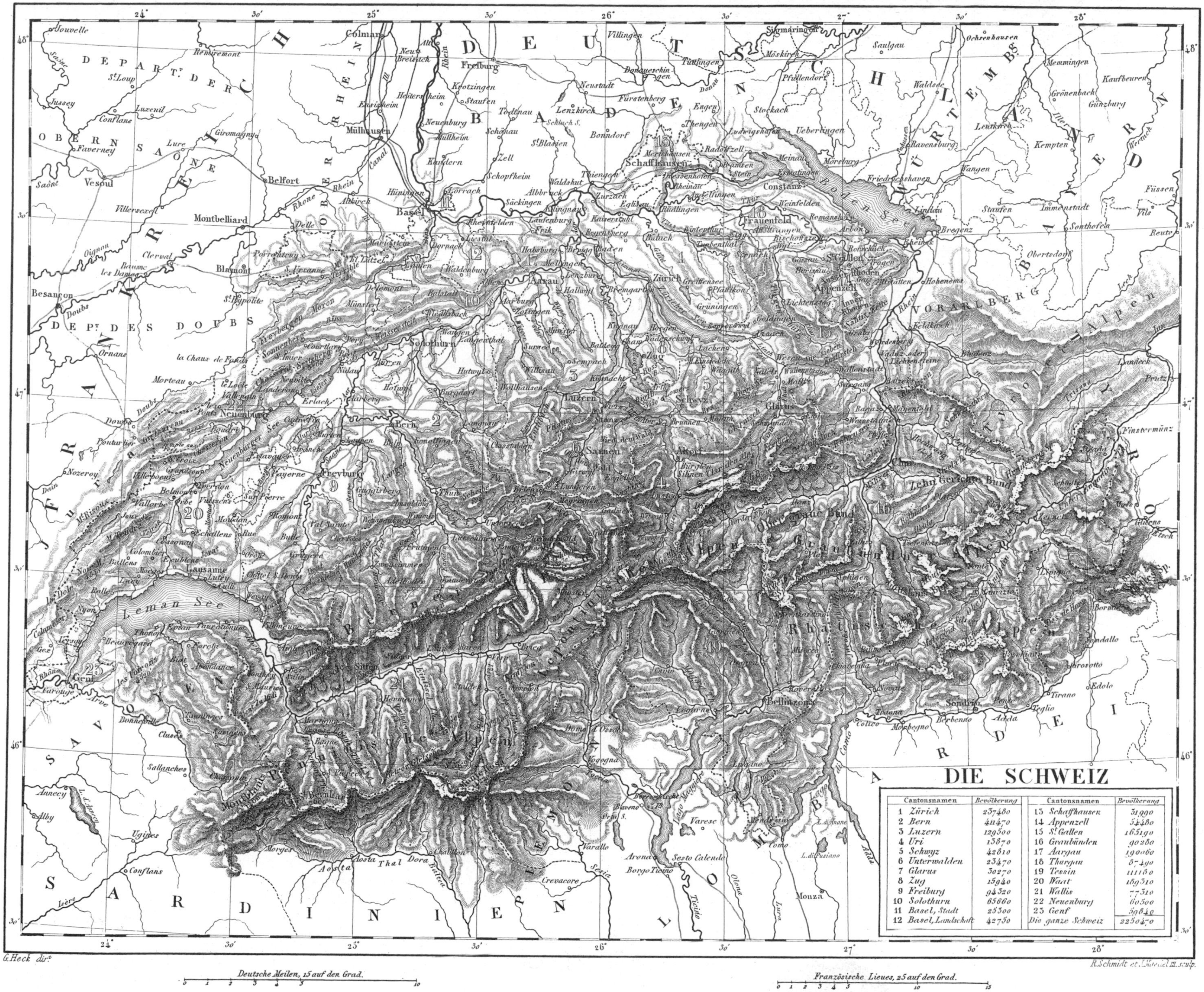
DIE SCHWEIZ
Cantonsnamen | Bevölkerung
1 Zürich 237480
2 Bern 411470
3 Luzern 129500
4 Uri 13870
5 Schwyz 42810
6 Unterwalden 23470
7 Glarus 30270
8 Zug 15940
9 Freiburg 94320
10 Solothurn 65660
11 Basel, Stadt 25300
12 Basel, Landschaft 42750
13 Schaffhausen 31990
14 Appenzell 54480
15 St. Gallen 165190
16 Graubünden 90280
17 Aargau 190060
18 Thurgau 87490
19 Tessin 111180
20 Waat 189310
21 Wallis 77310
22 Neuenburg 60500
23 Genf 59840
Die ganze Schweiz 2250470
G. Heck dir.
R. Schmidt et
Deutsche Meilen, 15 auf den Grad.
Französische Lieues, 25 auf den Grad.
DEUTSCHLAND
BADEN
WÜRTEMBERG
BAYERN
FRANKREICH
SARDINIEN
LOMBARDEI
TYROL
VORARLBERG
SAVOYEN
PIEMONT
Leman See
Boden See
Zürich
Bern
Luzern
Basel
Genf
Lausanne
Freyburg
Solothurn
Schaffhausen
Constanz
Chur
Bellinzona
Sitten
Altorf
Glarus
Zug
Aarau
Neuenburg

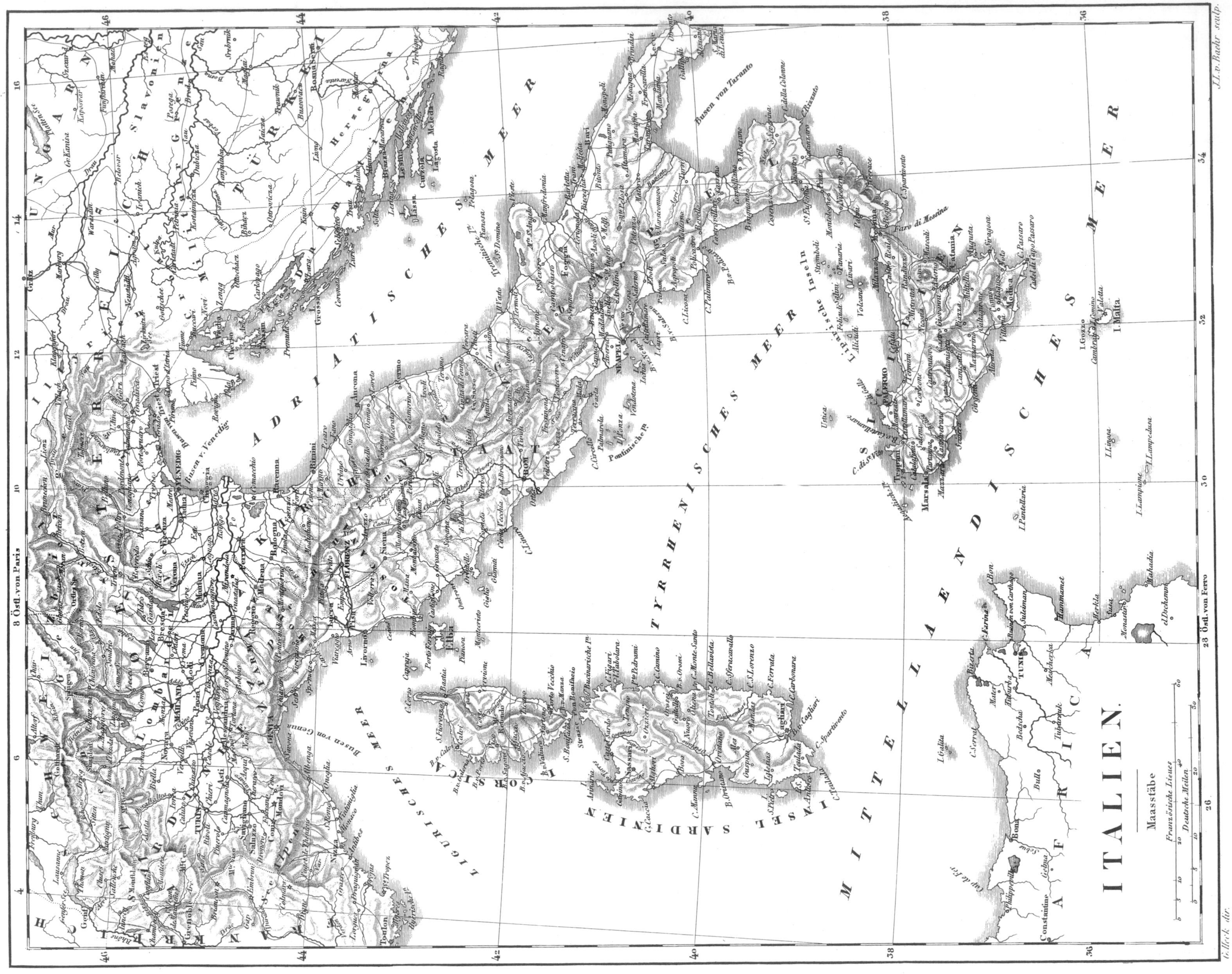
ITALIEN.
Maasstäbe
Französische Lieues
Deutsche Meilen
ADRIATISCHES MEER
TYRRHENISCHES MEER
MITTELLAENDISCHES MEER
LIGURISCHES MEER
INSEL SARDINIEN
CORSICA
AFRICA
Liparische Inseln
Busen von Taranto
Busen von Genua
8 Östl. von Paris
28 Östl. von Ferro
G. Heck dir.
J.J.v. Baehr sculp.

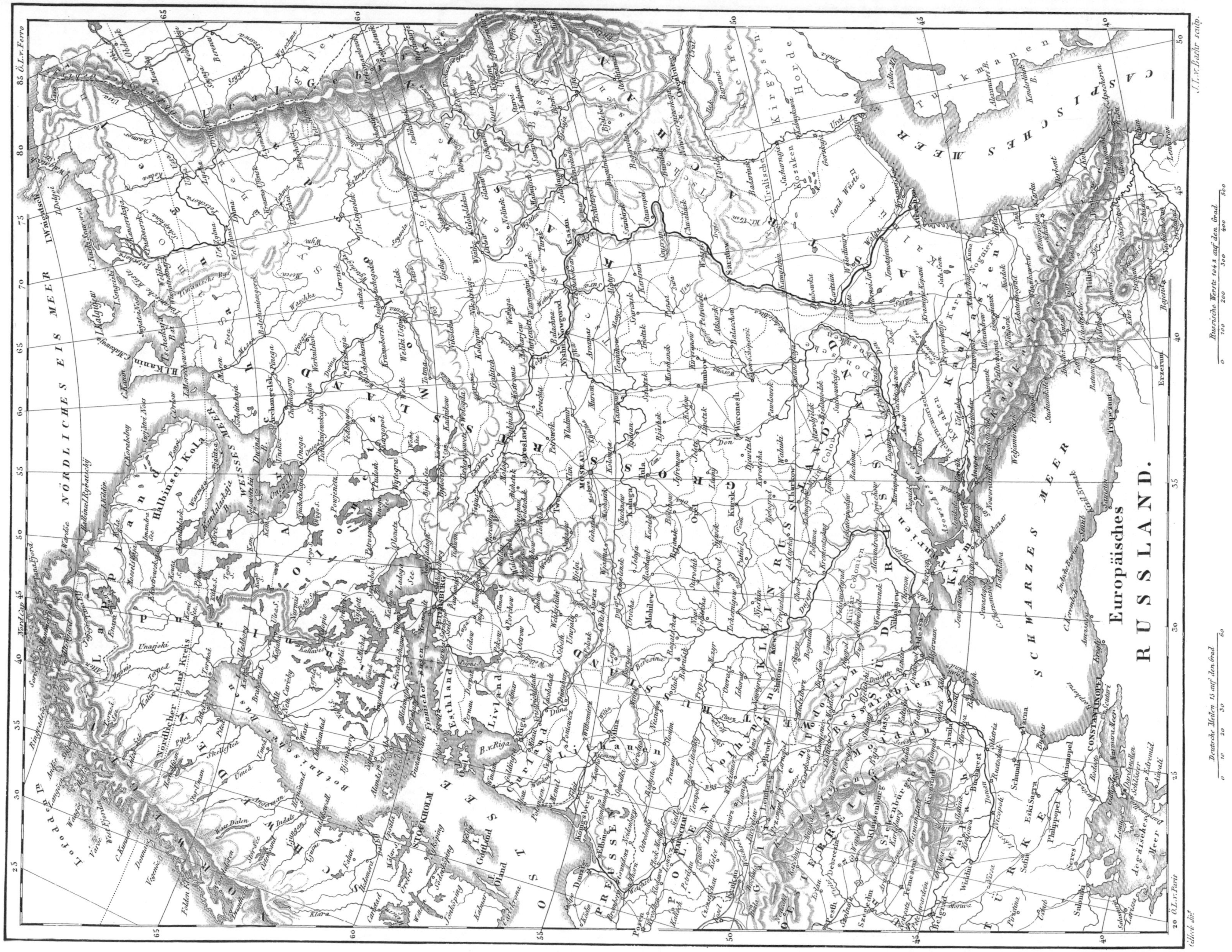
Europäisches
RUSSLAND.
SCHWARZES MEER
CASPISCHES MEER
NÖRDLICHES EIS MEER
WEISSES MEER
OST SEE
Russische Werste 104½ auf den Grad
Deutsche Meilen 15 auf den Grad
J. L. v. Bähr sculp.

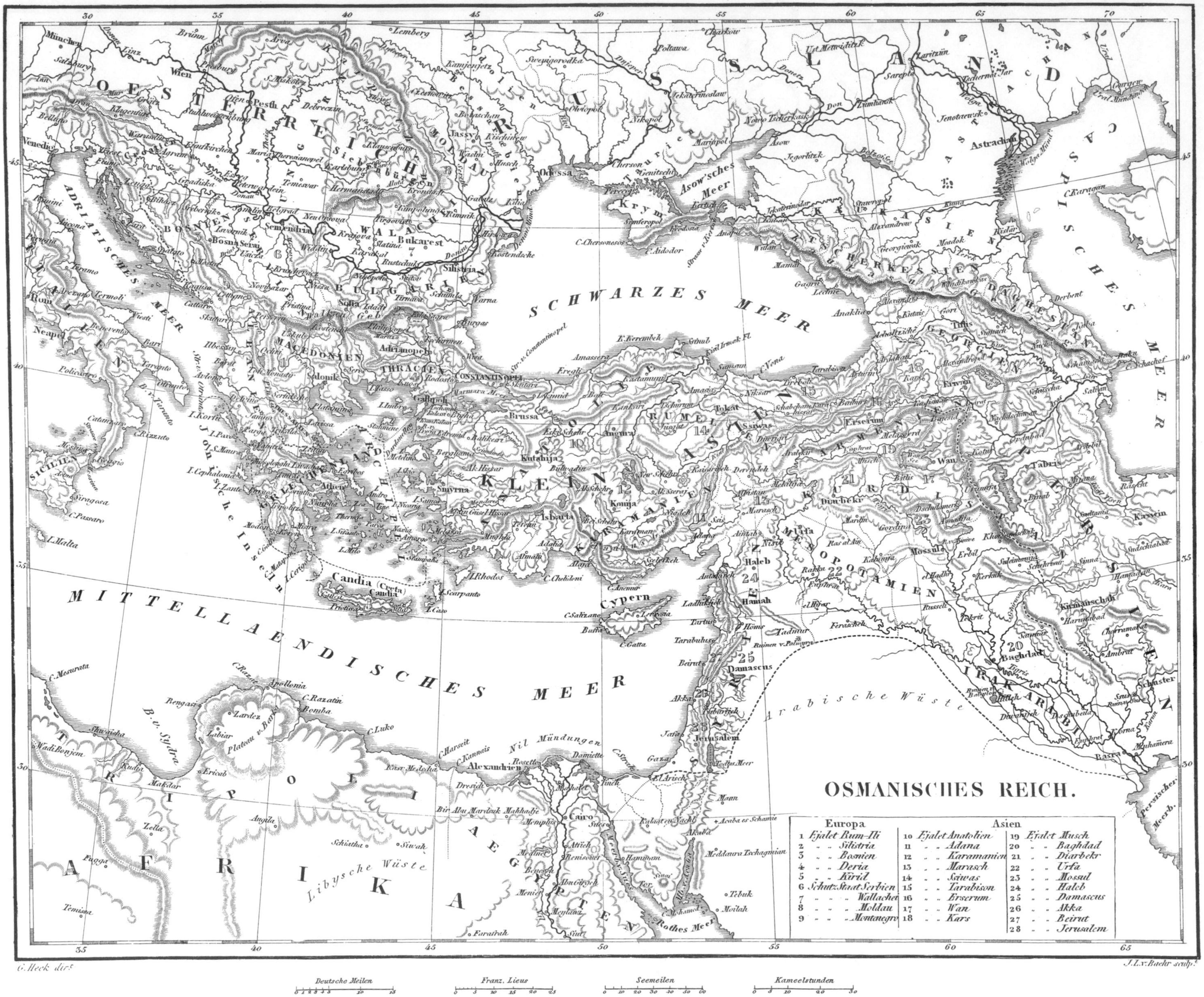
OSMANISCHES REICH.
Europa
1 Ejalet Rum-Ili
2 .. .. Silistria
3 .. .. Bosnien
4 .. .. Deria
5 .. .. Kirid
6 Schutz Staat Serbien
7 .. .. .. Wallachei
8 .. .. .. Moldau
9 .. .. .. Montenegro
Asien
10 Ejalet Anatolien
11 .. .. Adana
12 .. .. Karamanien
13 .. .. Marasch
14 .. .. Ssiwas
15 .. .. Tarabison
16 .. .. Erserum
17 .. .. Wan
18 .. .. Kars
19 Ejalet Musch
20 .. .. Baghdad
21 .. .. Diarbekr
22 .. .. Urfa
23 .. .. Mossul
24 .. .. Haleb
25 .. .. Damascus
26 .. .. Akka
27 .. .. Beirut
28 .. .. Jerusalem
SCHWARZES MEER
MITTELLAENDISCHES MEER
ADRIATISCHES MEER
CASPISCHES MEER
Asow'sches Meer
KLEIN ASIEN
MESOPOTAMIEN
Arabische Wüste
Libysche Wüste
AFRIKA
AEGYPTEN
TRIPOLI
OESTERREICH
RUSSLAND
Constantinopel
Cypern
Candia (Creta)
Jerusalem
Damascus
Baghdad
Alexandrien
Cairo
G. Heck dir.
J. L. v. Baehr sculp.
Deutsche Meilen
Franz. Lieus
Seemeilen
Kameelstunden

 PLATE 167. THE TURKISH EMPIRE

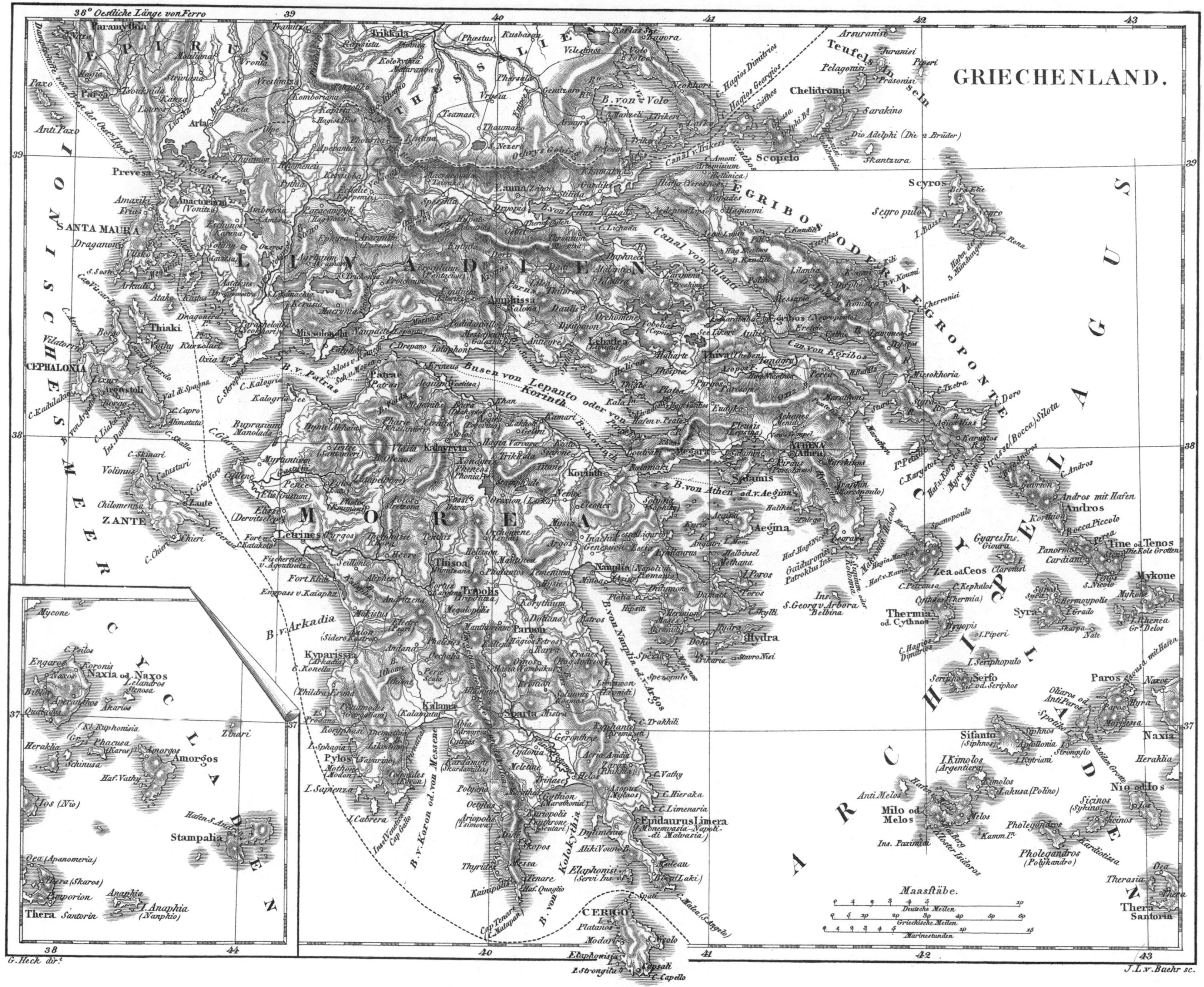

GRIECHENLAND.
38° Oestliche Länge von Ferro
39
40
41
42
43
EPIRUS
THESSALIEN
LIVADIEN
MOREA
EGRIBOS ODER NEGROPONTE
ARCHIPELAGUS
CYCLADEN
IONISCHES MEER
SANTA MAURA
CEPHALONIA
ZANTE
CERIGO
Arta
Prevesa
Missolonghi
Patrae
Lamia
Amphissa
Lebadea
Thiva (Theben)
ATHINA (Athen)
Megara
Korinth
Argos
Nauplia
Tripolis
Kalamata
Sparta
Mistra
Pylos
Kyparissia
Salamis
Aegina
Hydra
Andros
Tine od. Tenos
Mykone
Syra
Zea od. Ceos
Thermia od. Cythnos
Serfo
Sifanto
Paros
Naxia
Milo od Melos
Scopelo
Scyros
Chelidromia
Busen von Lepanto oder von Korinth
B. von Athen od. v. Aegina
Canal von Talanti
Epidaurus Limera
Stampalia
Amorgos
Thera Santorin
Maasstäbe.
Deutsche Meilen
Griechische Meilen
Marinestunden
G. Heck dir.
J.L.v.Baehr sc.

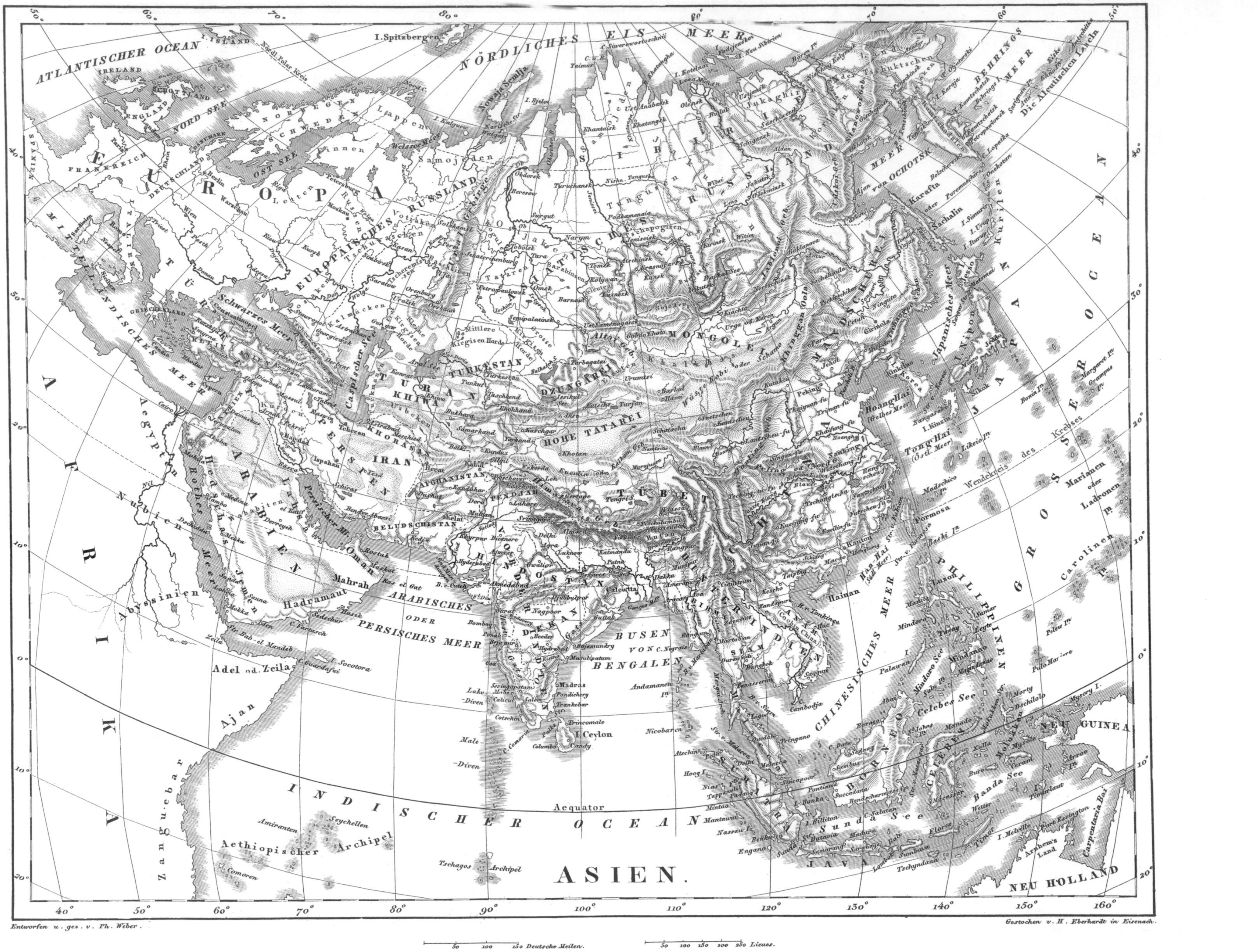
ASIEN.
NÖRDLICHES EIS MEER
ATLANTISCHER OCEAN
EUROPA
EUROPÄISCHES RUSSLAND
ASIATISCHES RUSSLAND
MITTELLÄNDISCHES MEER
Schwarzes Meer
Caspischer See
TURAN
TURKESTAN
DZUNGAREI
MONGOLEI
HOHE TATAREI
TÜBET
PERSIEN
IRAN
AFGHANISTAN
BELUDSCHISTAN
ARABIEN
Hadramaut
Mahrah
Oman
Persischer M.
Rothes Meer
HINDOSTAN
ARABISCHES ODER PERSISCHES MEER
BUSEN VON BENGALEN
I. Ceylon
INDISCHER OCEAN
Aequator
Aethiopischer Archipel
Seychellen
Amiranten
Comoren
Tschagos Archipel
Zanguebar
Ajan
Adel od. Zeila
I. Socotora
Abyssinien
Nubien
Aegypten
AFRIKA
CHINESISCHES MEER
Hainan
Formosa
PHILIPPINEN
Luzon
Mindanao
Palawan
BORNEO
Celebes See
Banda See
NEU GUINEA
NEU HOLLAND
Carpentaria Bai
Arnhem's Land
JAVA
Sunda See
Sumatra
GROSSER OCEAN
JAPANISCHES MEER
Japanisches Meer
MEER von OCHOTSK
BEHRINGS MEER
Die Aleutischen Inseln
Sachalin
Karafta
Hoang Hai (Gelbes Meer)
Tong Hai (Östl. Meer)
Wendekreis des Krebses
Marianen oder Ladronen
Carolinen In.
Bonin In.
Entworfen u. gez. v. Ph. Weber.
Gestochen v. H. Eberhardt in Eisenach.
50 100 150 Deutsche Meilen.
50 100 150 200 250 Lieues.

 PLATE 169. ASIA

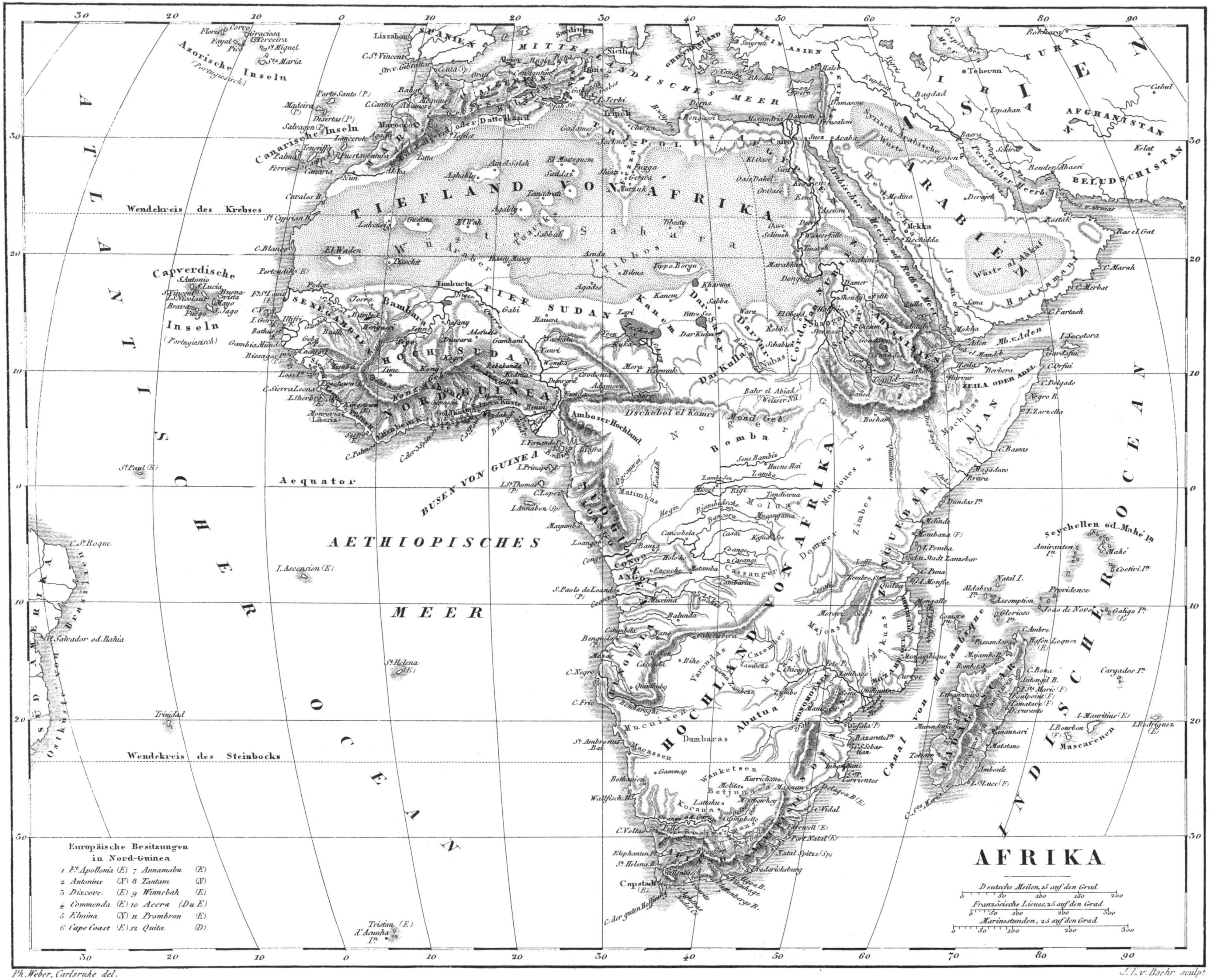
AFRIKA
Deutsche Meilen, 15 auf den Grad
Französische Lieues, 25 auf den Grad
Marinestunden, 25 auf den Grad
Europäische Besitzungen in Nord-Guinea
1 F.t Apollonia (E) 7 Annamabu (E)
2 Antonius (N) 8 Tantam (N)
3 Dixcove (E) 9 Winnebah (E)
4 Commenda (E) 10 Accra (Du E)
5 Elmina (N) 11 Prombron (E)
6 Cape Coast (E) 12 Quita (D)
ATLANTISCHER OCEAN
AETHIOPISCHES MEER
INDISCHER OCEAN
MITTELLÄNDISCHES MEER
TIEFLAND VON AFRIKA
Wüste Sahara
TIEF SUDAN
HOCH SUDAN
NORD GUINEA
HOCHLAND VON AFRIKA
ARABIEN
ASIEN
KLEIN ASIEN
TURAN
AFGHANISTAN
BELUDSCHISTAN
SÜD AMERIKA
Wendekreis des Krebses
Wendekreis des Steinbocks
Aequator
Azorische Inseln (Portugiesisch)
Canarische Inseln
Capverdische Inseln (Portugiesisch)
BUSEN VON GUINEA
Canal von Mozambique
MADAGASCAR
Seychellen od. Mahé I.n
Persischer Meerb.
Rothes Meer
Dschebel el Komri (Mond Geb.)
Ambosei-Hochland
St. Helena (E)
I. Ascension (E)
Tristan d'Acunha I.n
Trinidad
Capstadt (E)
C. der guten Hoffnung

Ph. Weber, Carlsruhe del.

J. L. v. Baehr sculp.t

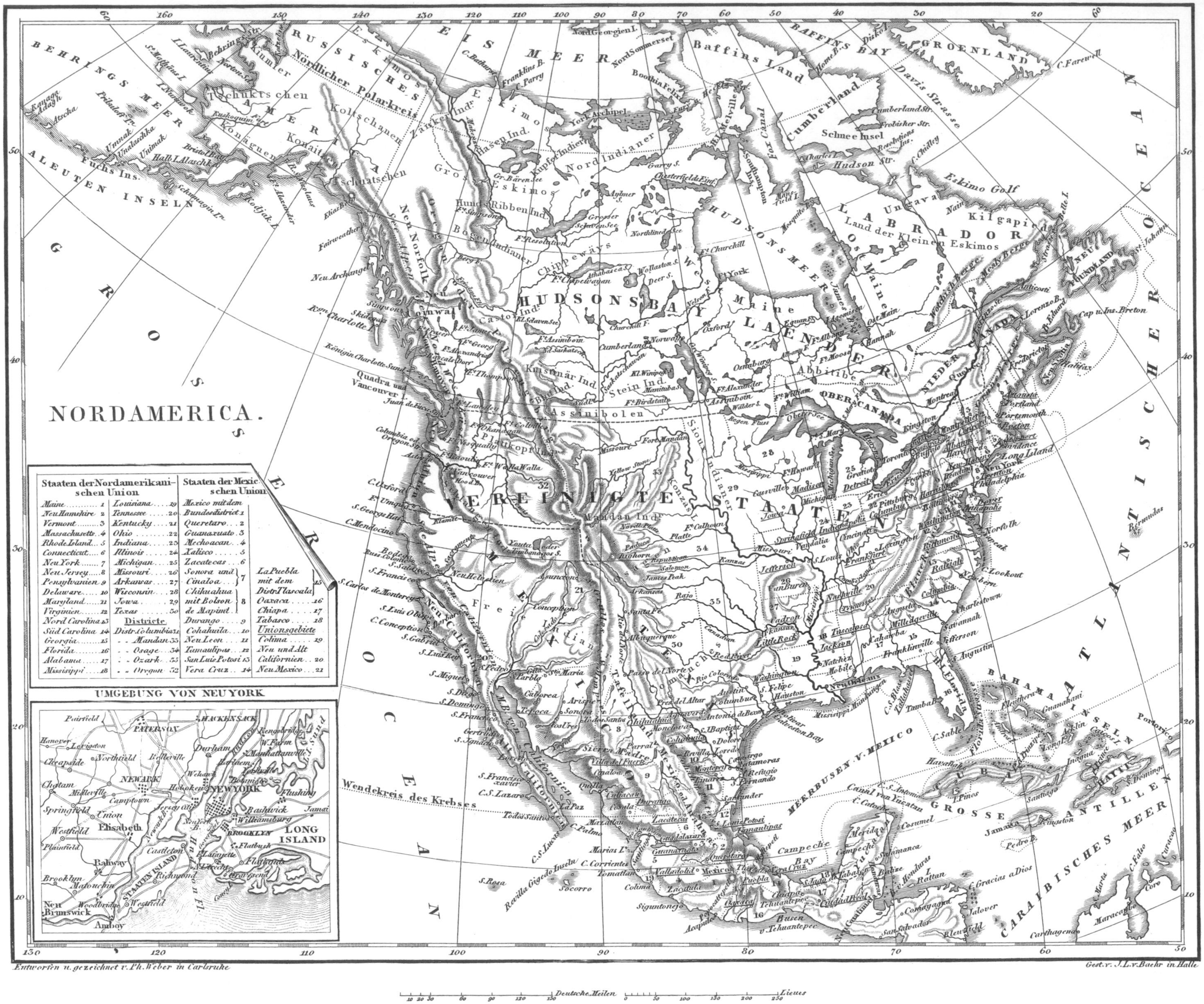
NORDAMERICA.
Staaten der Nordamerikanischen Union
Maine 1
Neu Hamshire 2
Vermont 3
Massachusetts 4
Rhode Island 5
Connecticut 6
Neu York 7
Neu Jersey 8
Pensylvanien 9
Delaware 10
Maryland 11
Virginien 12
Nord Carolina 13
Süd Carolina 14
Georgia 15
Florida 16
Alabama 17
Mississippi 18
Louisiana 19
Tennessee 20
Kentucky 21
Ohio 22
Indiana 23
Illinois 24
Michigan 25
Missouri 26
Arkansas 27
Wisconsin 28
Jowa 29
Texas 30
Districte
Distr. Columbia 31
" " Mandan 33
" " Osage 34
" " Ozark 35
" " Oregon 32
Staaten der Mexicschen Union
Mexico mit dem Bundesdistrict 1
Queretaro 2
Guanaxuato 3
Mechoacan 4
Xalisco 5
Zacatecas 6
Sonora und Cinaloa 7
Chihuahua mit Bolson de Mapiml 8
Durango 9
Cohahuila 10
Neu Leon 11
Tamaulipas 12
San Luis Potosi 13
Vera Cruz 14
La Puebla mit dem Distr. Tlascala 15
Oaxaca 16
Chiapa 17
Tabasco 18
Unionsgebiete
Colima 19
Neu und Alt Californien 20
Neu Mexico 21
UMGEBUNG VON NEUYORK
EIS MEER
BEHRINGS MEER
ALEUTEN INSELN
RUSSISCHES AMERICA
Nördlicher Polarkreis
GROENLAND
BAFFINS BAY
Baffins Land
Davis Strasse
HUDSONS MEER
LABRADOR
HUDSONS BAY LAENDER
VEREINIGTE STAATEN
CANADA
MEXICO
MEERBUSEN V. MEXICO
Wendekreis des Krebses
GROSSE ANTILLEN
CARAIBISCHES MEER
GROSSER OCEAN
ATLANTISCHER OCEAN
Entworfen u. gezeichnet v. Ph. Weber in Carlsruhe
Gest. v. J. L. v. Baehr in Halle
Deutsche Meilen
Lieues

 PLATE 171. NORTH AMERICA

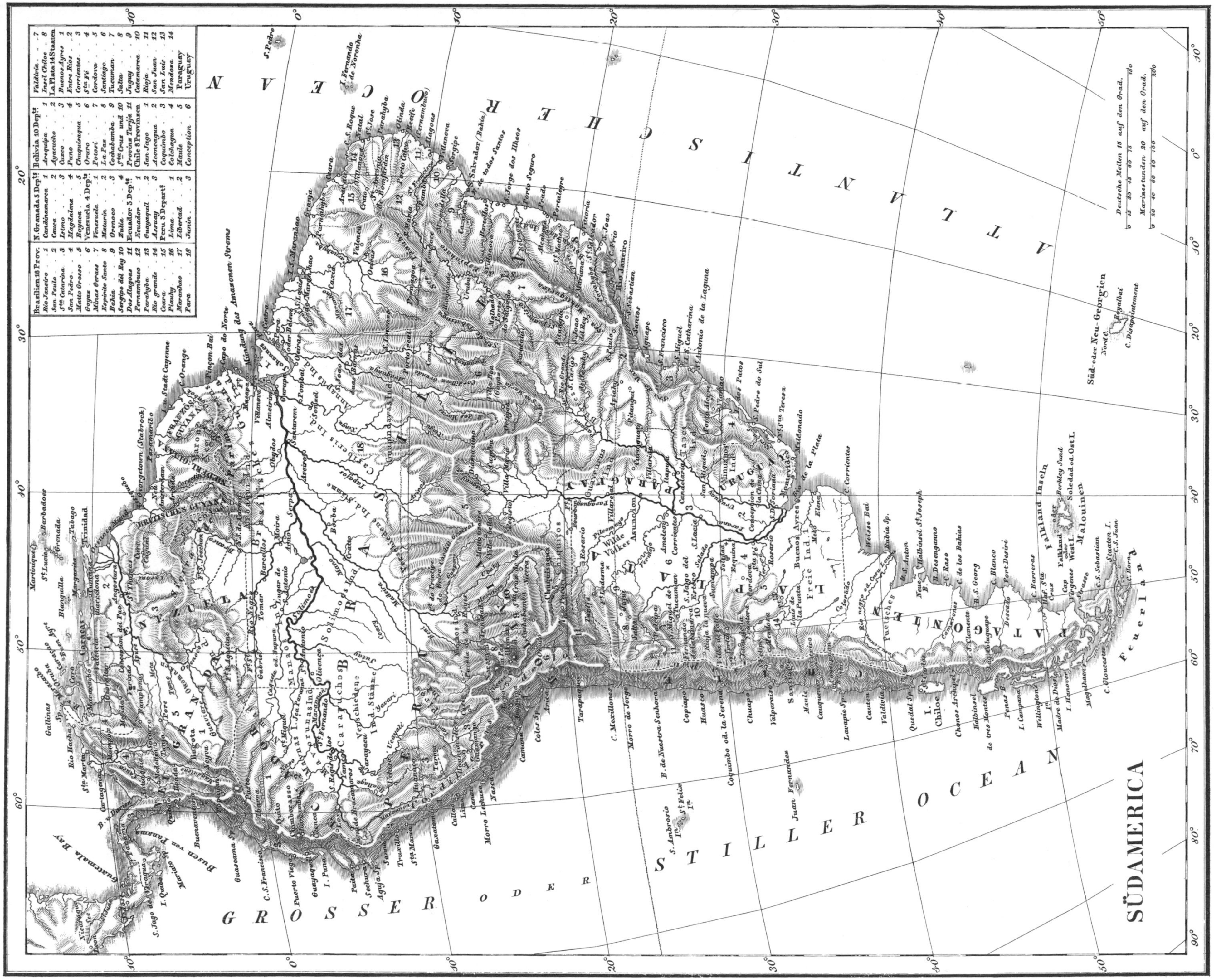
SÜDAMERICA
ATLANTISCHER OCEAN
GROSSER ODER STILLER OCEAN
Gestochen von H. Eberhardt in Eisenach.

PLATE 172. SOUTH AMERICA

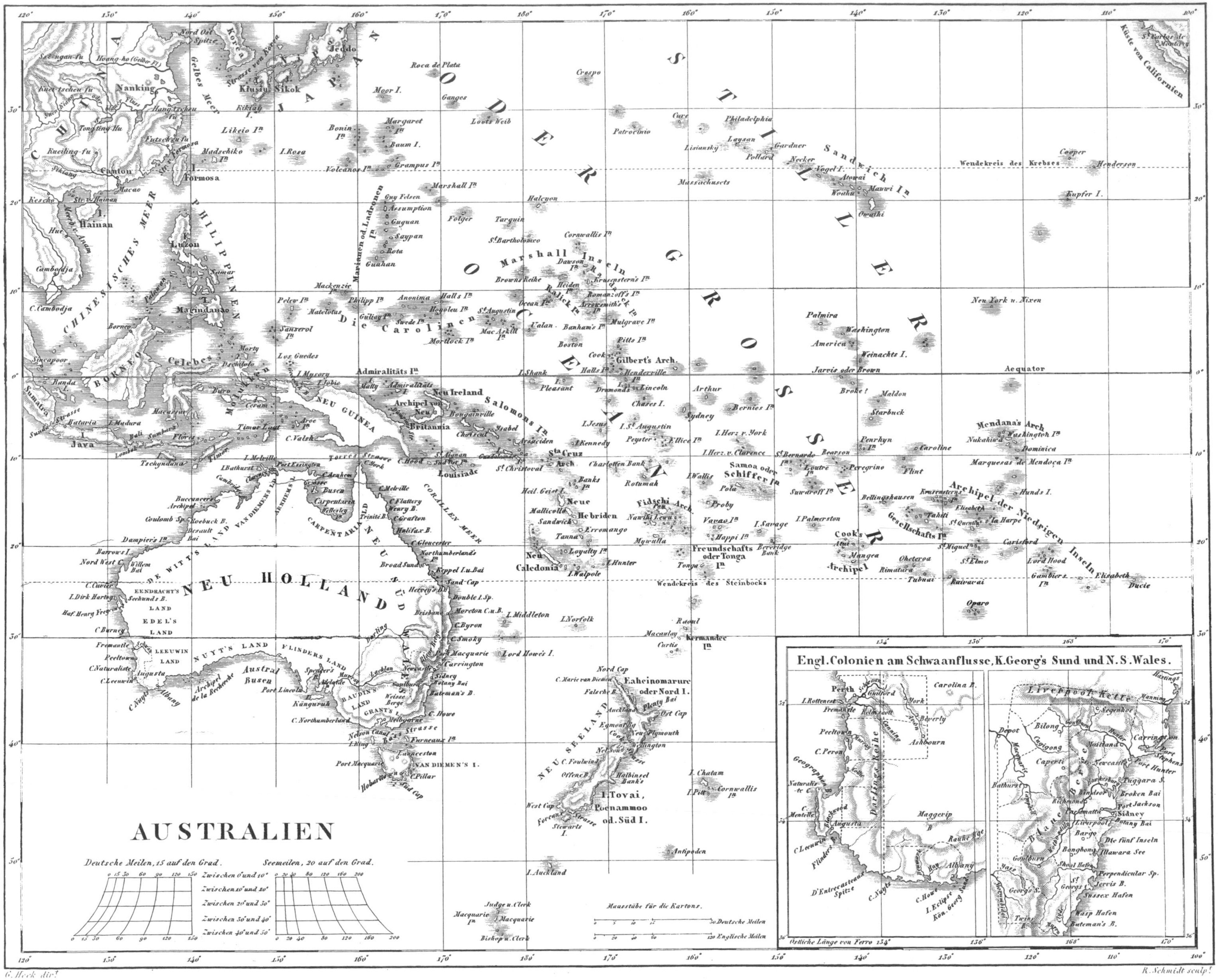
AUSTRALIEN
Deutsche Meilen, 15 auf den Grad.
Seemeilen, 20 auf den Grad.
Zwischen 0° und 10°
Zwischen 10° und 20°
Zwischen 20° und 30°
Zwischen 30° und 40°
Zwischen 40° und 50°
Maasstäbe für die Kartons.
Deutsche Meilen
Englische Meilen
Engl. Colonien am Schwaanflusse, K. Georg's Sund und N. S. Wales.
Östliche Länge von Ferro
GROSSER ODER STILLER OCEAN
NEU HOLLAND
NEU SÜD WALES
NEU GUINEA
NEU SEELAND
CHINA
JAPAN
PHILIPPINEN
BORNEO
CHINESISCHES MEER
CORALLEN MEER
Die Carolinen
Marshall Inseln
Salomons Iⁿ
Sandwich Iⁿ
Gilbert's Arch.
Samoa oder Schiffer Iⁿ
Fidschi Arch.
Freundschafts oder Tonga Iⁿ
Gesellschafts Iⁿ
Archipel der Niedrigen Inseln
Cook's Archipel
Mendana's Arch.
Marquesas de Mendoça Iⁿ
Neu Caledonia
Neue Hebriden
Neu Ireland
Archipel von Neu Britannia
Admiralitäts Iⁿ
Marianen od. Ladronen Iⁿ
Eaheinomaurue oder Nord I.
I. Tovai, Poenammoo od. Süd I.
VAN DIEMEN'S I.
Bass Strasse
Austral Busen
Carpentaria Busen
Torres Strasse
Wendekreis des Krebses
Wendekreis des Steinbocks
Aequator
Küste von Californien
Celebes
Sumatra
Java
Timor
Luzon
Formosa
Hainan
Canton
Nanking
Sidney
Port Jackson
Botany Bai
Perth
Albany
Liverpool Kette
Blaue Berge
G. Heck dir.
R. Schmidt sculp.

G. Heck dir.

R. Schmidt et Mädel III. sc.

Engl. Meile
Deutsche Meile
Kilomètres

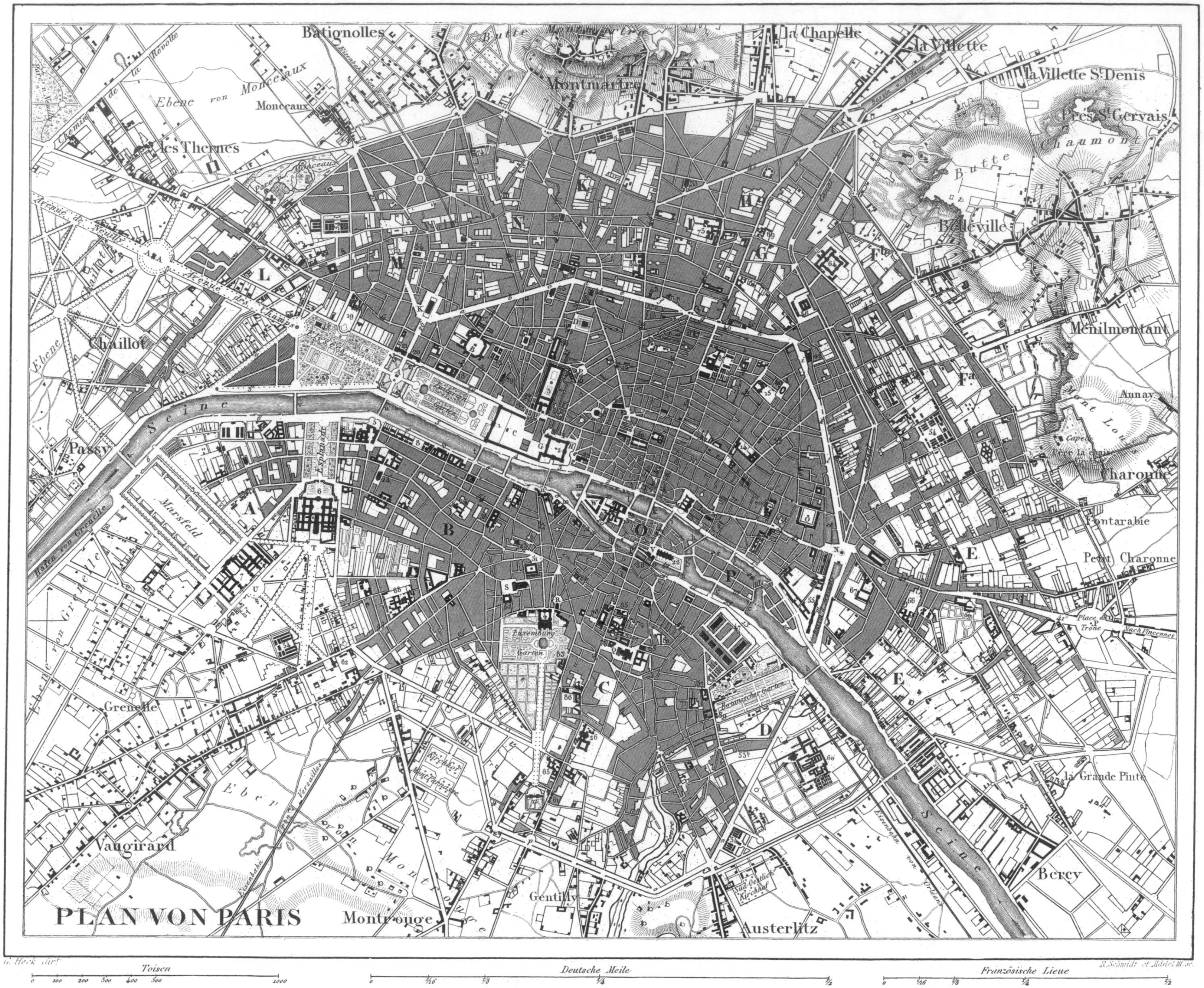
PLAN VON PARIS
Batignolles
la Chapelle
la Villette
la Villette St. Denis
Montmartre
Monceaux
Ebene von Monceaux
les Thernes
Pres St. Gervais
Belleville
Ménilmontant
Aunay
Charonne
Fontarabie
Petit Charonne
Place du Trône
Chaillot
Passy
Marsfeld
Seine
Luxemburg Garten
Botanische Garten
Grenelle
Vaugirard
Montrouge
Gentilly
Austerlitz
Bercy
la Grande Pinte
Toisen
Deutsche Meile
Französische Lieue

 PLATE 175. PARIS AND ENVIRONS

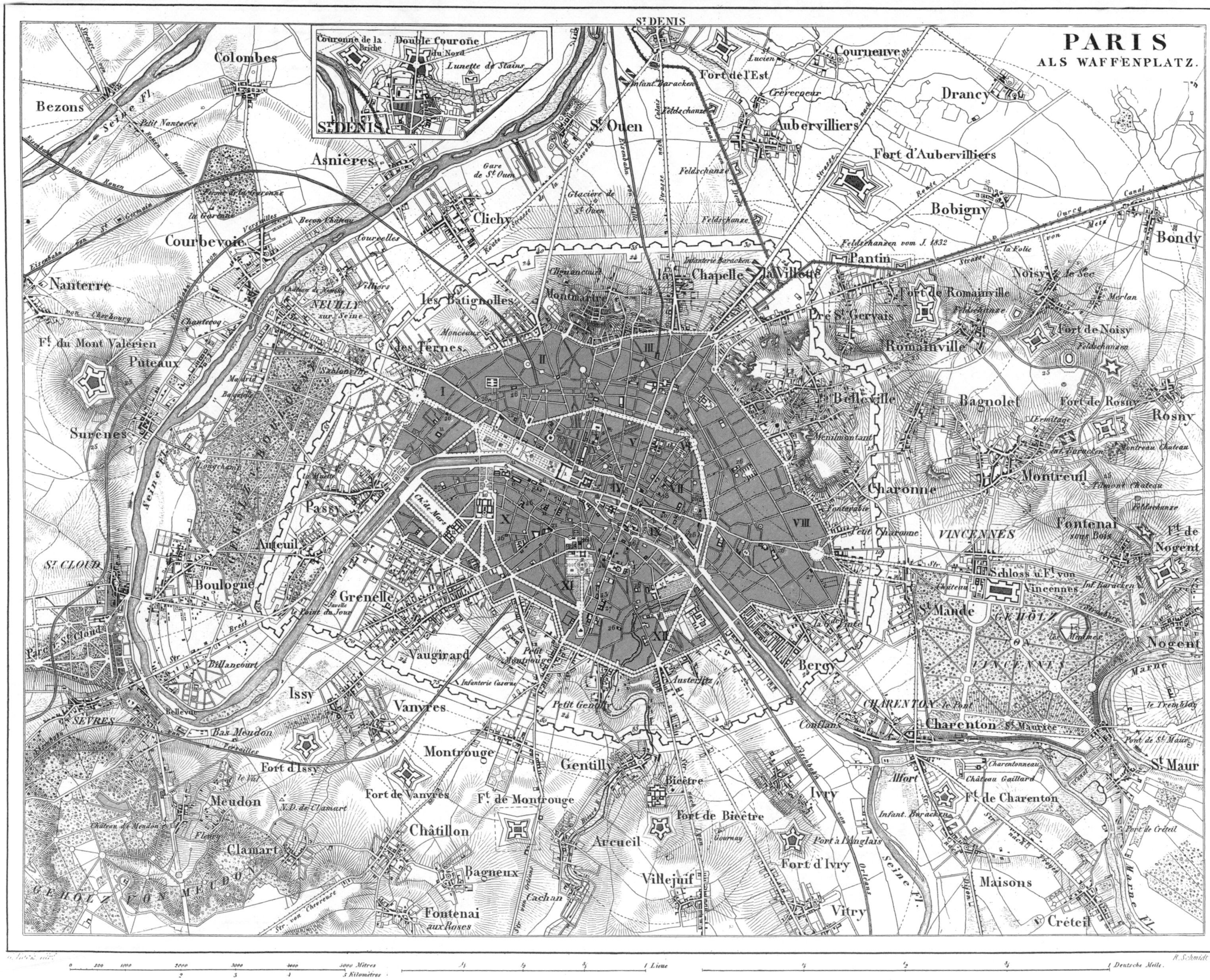
PARIS
ALS WAFFENPLATZ.
St DENIS
Couronne de la Briche
Double Couroñe du Nord
Lunette de Stains
St DENIS
Colombes
Bezons
Seine Fl.
Petit Nanterre
Asnières
Gare de St Ouen
St Ouen
Clichy
Glacière de St Ouen
Courbevoie
Nanterre
Neuilly sur Seine
les Batignolles
Montmartre
la Chapelle
la Villette
Fort de l'Est
Cornneuve
Crèvecoeur
Aubervilliers
Fort d'Aubervilliers
Drancy
Bobigny
Bondy
Pantin
Feldschanzen vom J. 1832
Noisy le Sec
Fort de Romainville
Pré St Gervais
Romainville
Fort de Noisy
Belleville
Bagnolet
Fort de Rosny
Rosny
Ft du Mont Valérien
Puteaux
Suresnes
les Ternes
Menilmontant
Charonne
Montreuil
Passy
Auteuil
Boulogne
St CLOUD
Grenelle
Billancourt
Vaugirard
Petit Montrouge
Issy
Vanvres
Petit Gentilly
Austerlitz
Bercy
Petit Charonne
VINCENNES
Schloss u. Ft von Vincennes
St Mandé
Fontenai sous Bois
Ft de Nogent
Nogent
Marne
CHARENTON le Pont
Charenton St Maurice
Conflans
St Maur
SEVRES
Bellevue
Bas Meudon
Fort d'Issy
Meudon
Fort de Vanvres
Ft de Montrouge
Montrouge
Gentilly
Bicêtre
Fort de Bicêtre
Ivry
Alfort
Ft de Charenton
Châtillon
Clamart
Arcueil
Fort d'Ivry
Port à l'Anglais
Bagneux
Villejuif
Cachan
Maisons
Vitry
Fontenai aux Roses
Créteil
GEHÖLZ VON MEUDON
GEHÖLZ VON VINCENNES
Parc de St Cloud
Ch de Mars
I
II
III
IV
V
VI
VII
VIII
IX
X
XI
XII
0 500 1000 2000 3000 4000 5000 Mètres
2 3 4 5 Kilomètres
1 Lieue
1 Deutsche Meile
R. Schmidt sc.

PLATE 176. FORTIFICATIONS OF PARIS

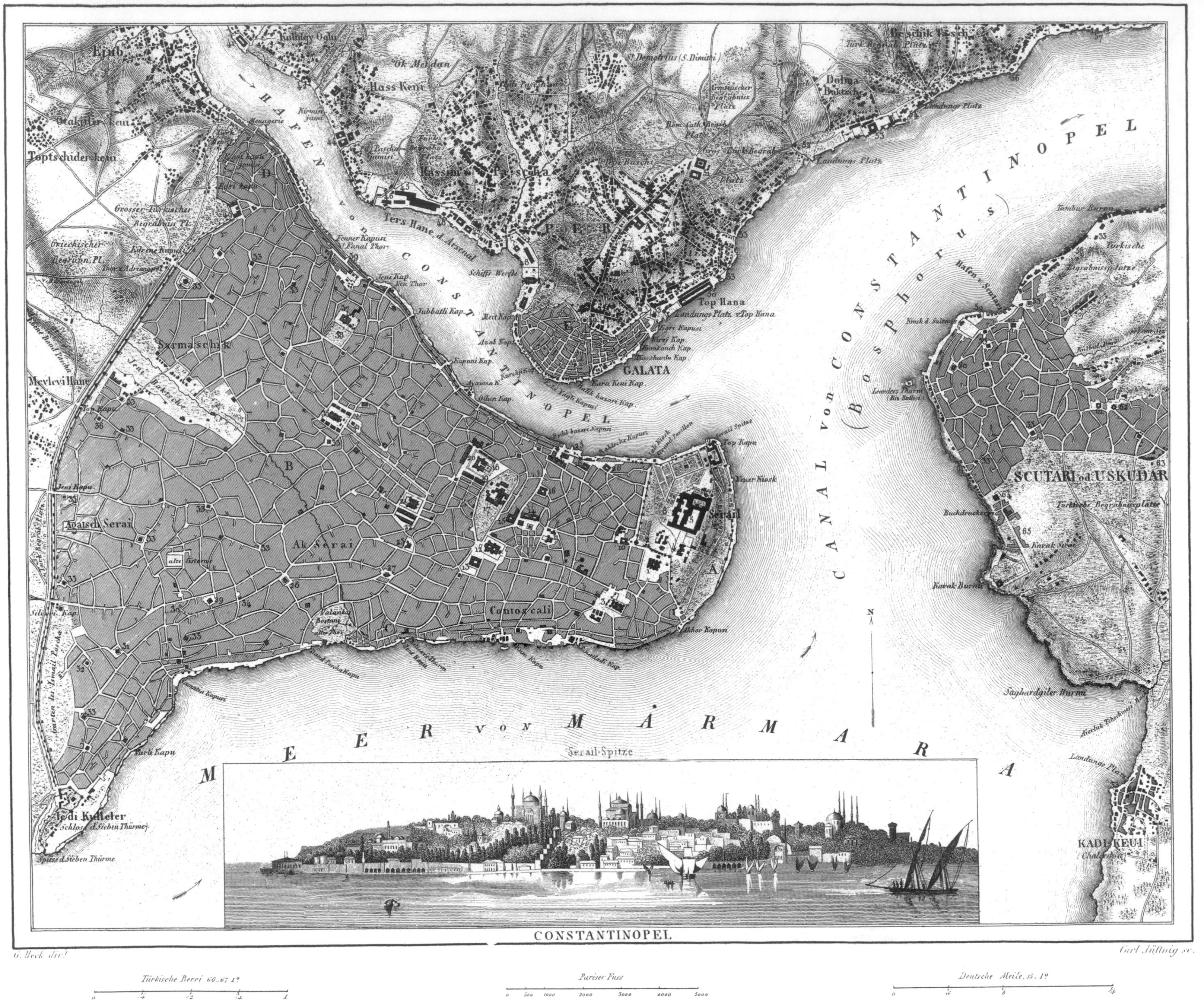

CONSTANTINOPEL
MEER VON MARMARA
CANAL von CONSTANTINOPEL (Bosphorus)
HAFEN von CONSTANTINOPEL
GALATA
PERA
Top Hana
SCUTARI od. USKUDAR
KADI-KEUI
(Chalcedon)
Serai
Serai-Spitze
Ak Serai
Contoscali
Agatsch Serai
Sarmaschik
Mevlevi Hane
Topschider-keui
Hass Kent
Ok Meidan
Ters Hane d. Arsenal
Jedi Kulleler
Schloss d. Sieben Thürme
Spitze d. Sieben Thürme
Leanders Thurm
Kavak Burnu
Türkische Berri 66. 67 1°
Pariser Fuss
Deutsche Meile. 15. 1°

PLATE 177. CONSTANTINOPLE

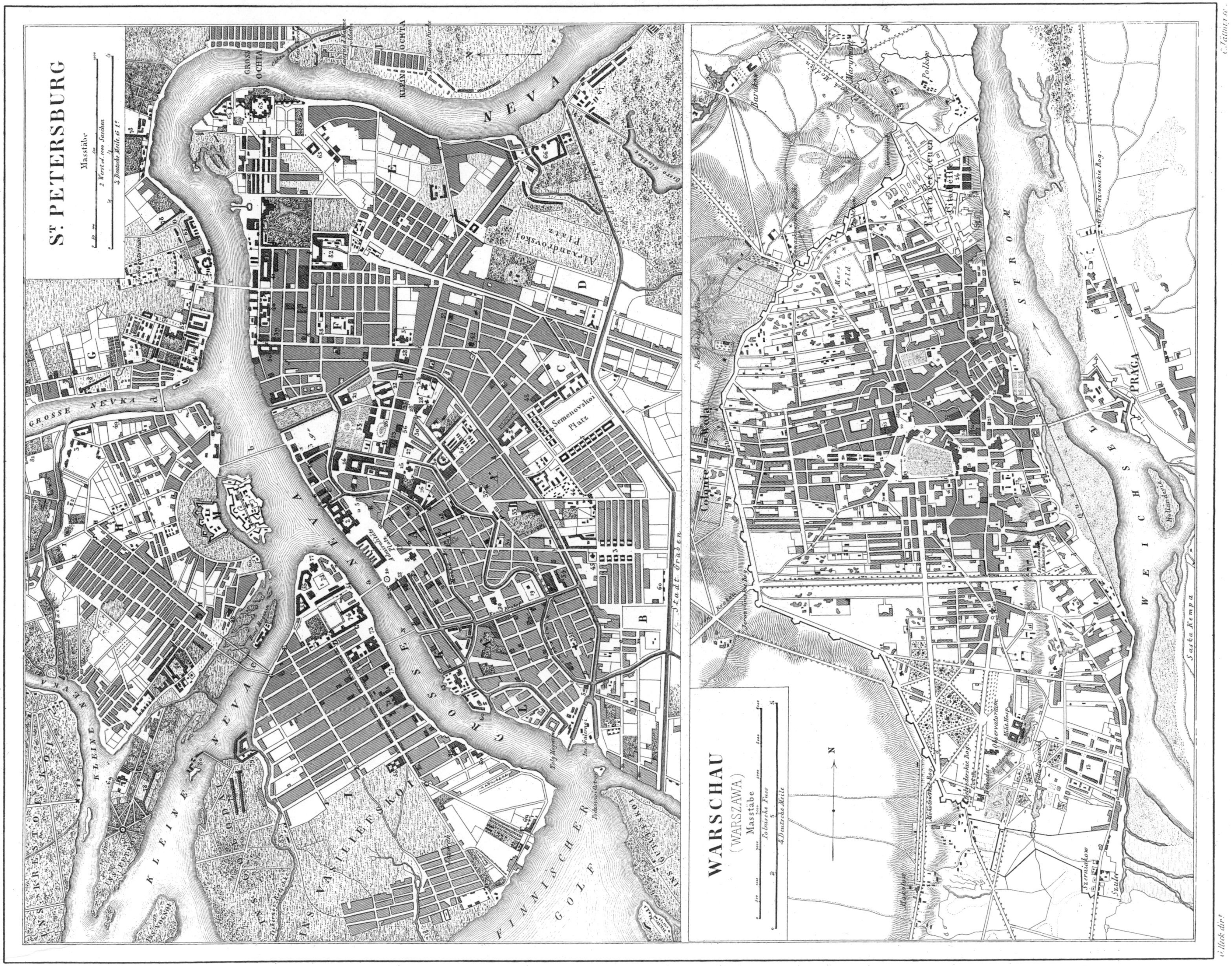
St. PETERSBURG
Masstäbe
NEVA
GROSSE NEVKA
Semenovskoi Platz
Alexandrovskoi Platz
FINNISCHER GOLF
WARSCHAU
(WARSZAWA)
Masstäbe
Polnische Fuss
Deutsche Meile
PRAGA
WEICHSEL STROM
Mars Feld
Saska Kempa

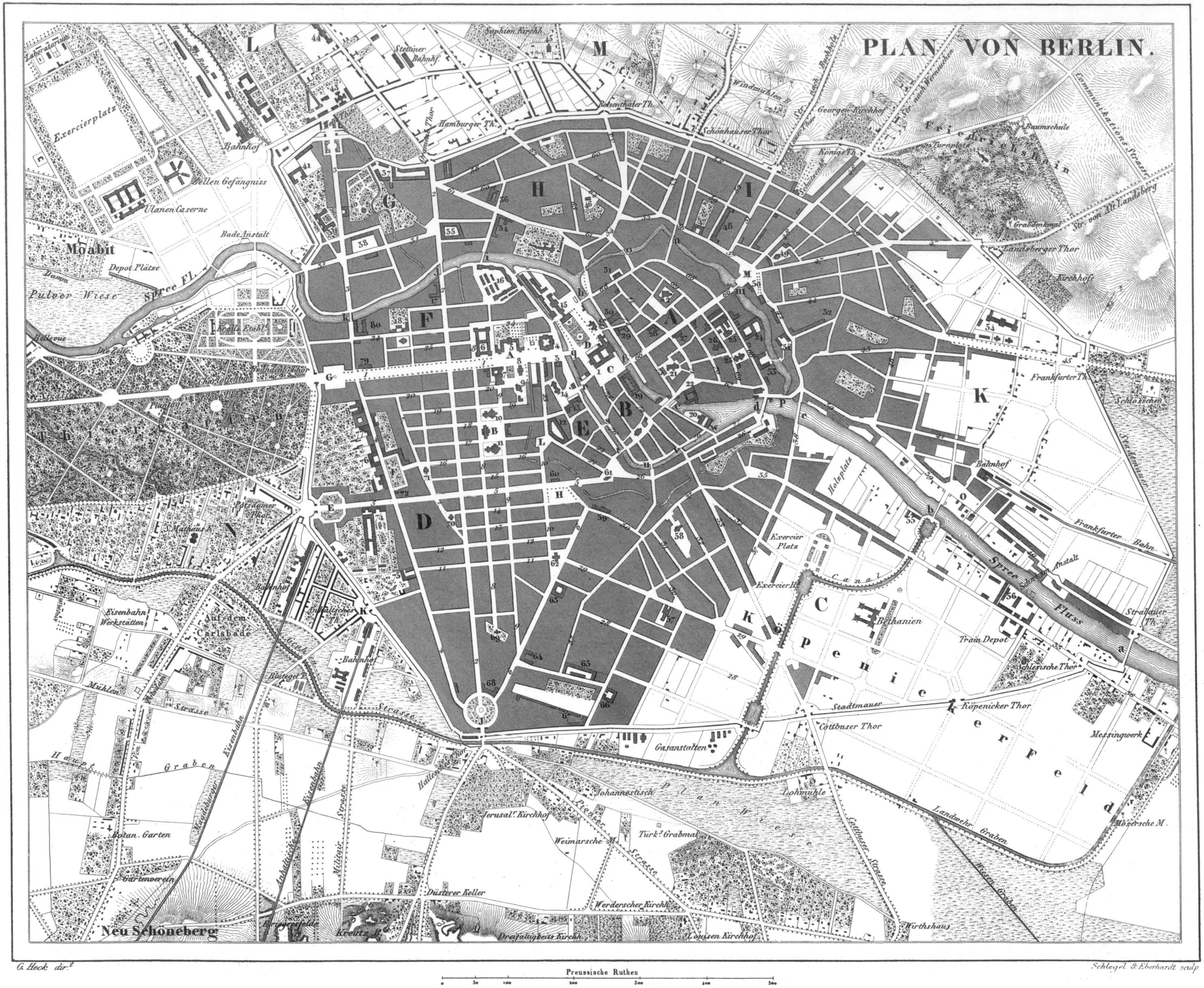
PLAN VON BERLIN.
Exercierplatz
Zellen Gefängniss
Ulanen Caserne
Bade Anstalt
Moabit
Depot Plätze
Pulver Wiese
Spree Fl.
Bahnhof
Stettiner Bahnhf.
Hamburger Th.
Rosenthaler Th.
Schönhauser Thor
Windmühlen
Georgen Kirchhof
Königs Th.
Friedrichshain
Baumschule
Turnplatz
Grabdenkmal
Landsberger Thor
Kirchhof
Frankfurter Th.
Schlösschen
Holzplatz
Bahnhof
Frankfurter Bahn
Exercier Platz
Canal
Exercier H.
Bethanien
Train Depot
Schlesische Thor
Stralauer Th.
Spree Fluss
Potsdamer Thor
Eisenbahn Werkstätten
Auf dem Carlsbade
Mühlen
Strasse
Graben
Eisenbahn
Botan. Garten
Gartenverein
Neu Schöneberg
Halle'sches Thor
Gasanstalten
Stadtmauer
Cottbuser Thor
Köpenicker Thor
Messingwerk
Köpenicker Feld
Johannestisch
Jerusal. Kirchhof
Weimarsche M.
Türk. Grabmal
Lohmühle
Plan Wiese
Landwehr Graben
Mösersche M.
Cottbuser Strasse
Düsterer Keller
Werderscher Kirchh.
Dreifaltigkeits Kirchh.
Louisen Kirchhof
Wirthshaus
Kreutz B.
G. Heck dir.
Preussische Ruthen
0 50 100 200 300 400 500
Schlegel & Eberhardt sculp

PLATE 179. BERLIN

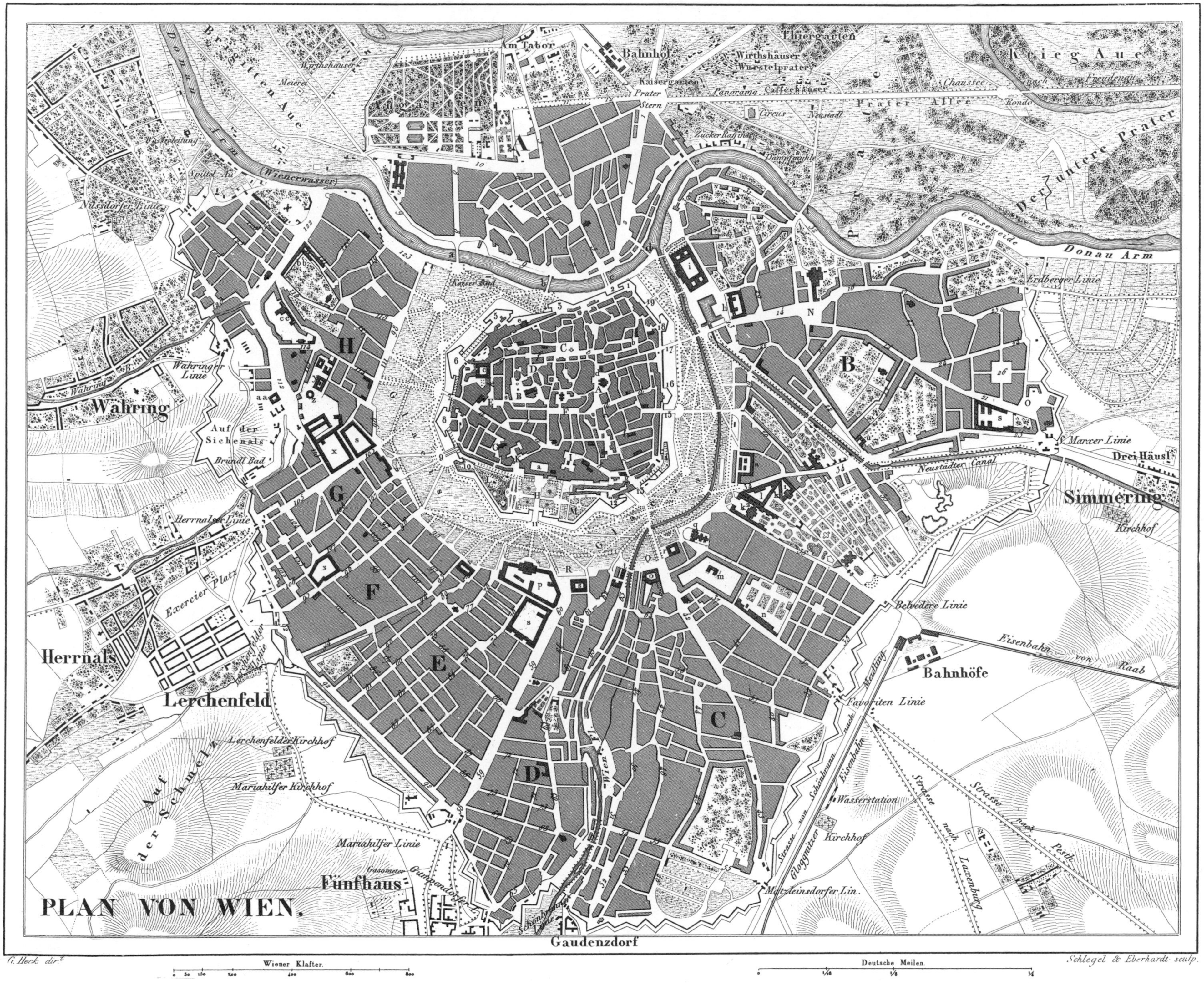
PLAN VON WIEN.
Währing
Herrnals
Lerchenfeld
Fünfhaus
Gaudenzdorf
Simmering
Bahnhöfe
Prater Allee
Der untere Prater
Donau Arm
Brigitten Aue
Am Tabor
Bahnhof
Thiergarten
Wirthshäuser
Wurstelprater
Kaisergarten
Panorama
Caffeehäuser
Circus
Neustadt
Zuckerraffinerie
Dampfmühle
Gänseweide
Erdberger Linie
S. Marxer Linie
Drei Häusl
Neustädter Canal
Kirchhof
Belvedere Linie
Eisenbahn von Raab
Favoriten Linie
Wasserstation
Kirchhof
Strasse nach Laxenburg
Strasse nach Pesth
Matzleinsdorfer Lin.
Mariahülfer Linie
Gasometer
Gumpendorfer Linie
Mariahülfer Kirchhof
Lerchenfelder Kirchhof
Auf der Schmelz
Exercier Platz
Herrnalser Linie
Brundl Bad
Auf der Sichenals
Währinger Linie
Nussdorfer Linie
Spittel Au
Wienerwasser
Meierei
Kaiser Bad
Wien Fl.
Chaussee
Rondo
Prater Stern
A
B
C
D
E
F
G
H
G. Heck dir.
Wiener Klafter.
Deutsche Meilen.
Schlegel & Eberhardt sculp.

PLATE 180. VIENNA

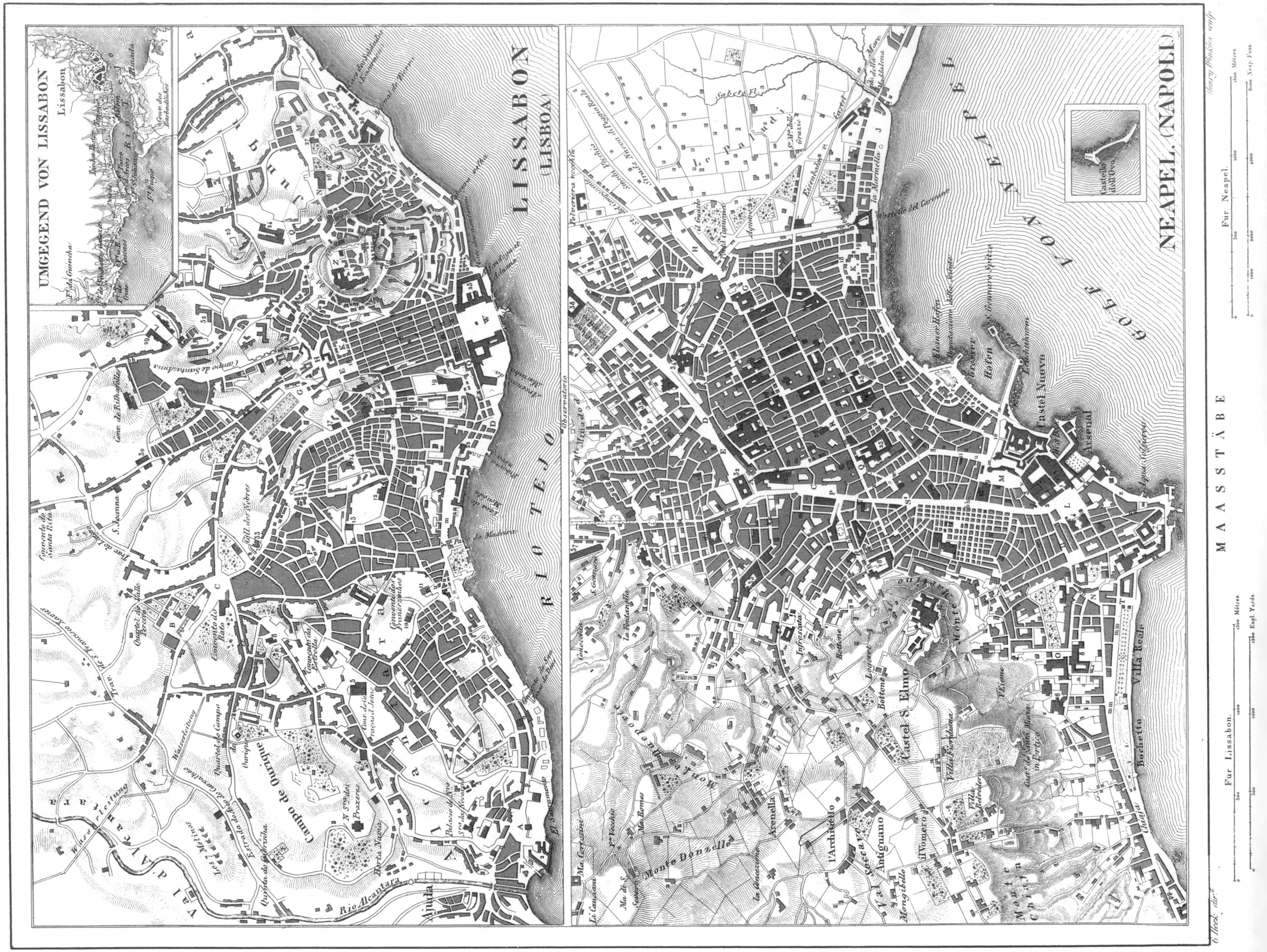
UMGEGEND VON LISSABON
LISSABON (LISBOA)
RIO TEJO
NEAPEL (NAPOLI)
GOLF VON NEAPEL
MAASSTÄBE
Für Lissabon.
Für Neapel.

PLATE 181. LISBON AND NAPLES

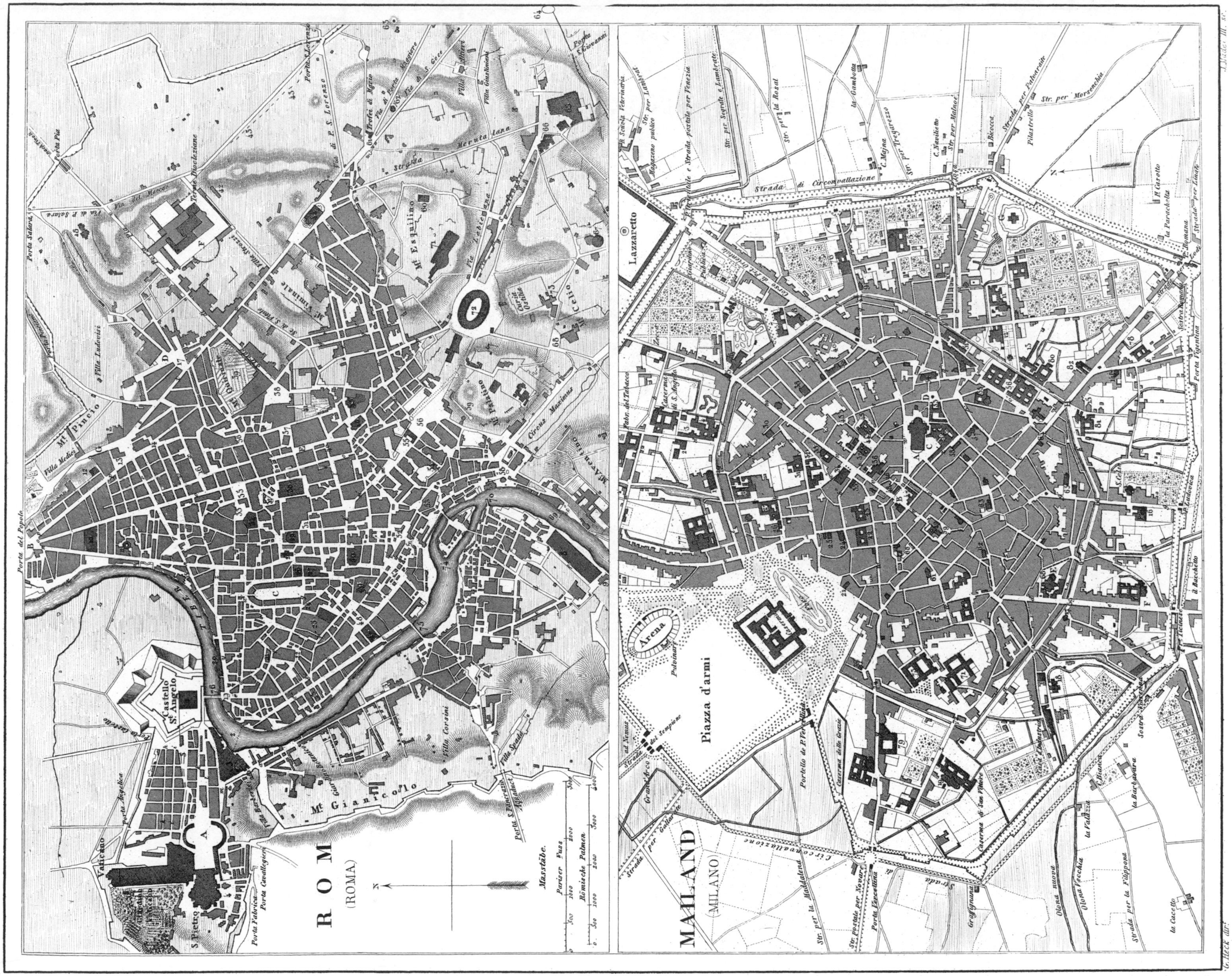
ROM
(ROMA)
Mt Pincio
Villa Medici
Villa Ludovisi
Porta del Popolo
Porta Pia
Mt Esquilino
Mt Viminale
Mt Palatino
Circus Maximus
Mt Aventino
Celio
TIBER
Castello St Angelo
Mt Gianicolo
Villa Corsini
Villa Spada
Porta S. Pancrazio
Vaticano
S. Pietro
Porta Fabrica
Porta Cavalleggieri
Porta S. Lorenzo
Porta S. Giovanni
Terme Diocleziane
Mastäbe.
Pariser Fuss
Römische Palmen
MAILAND
(MILANO)
Lazzaretto
Arena
Piazza d'armi
Strada di Circonvallazione
Circonvallazione
Porta Vercellina
Porta Romana
Porta Tosa
Parizer Fuss
Mailander Fuss

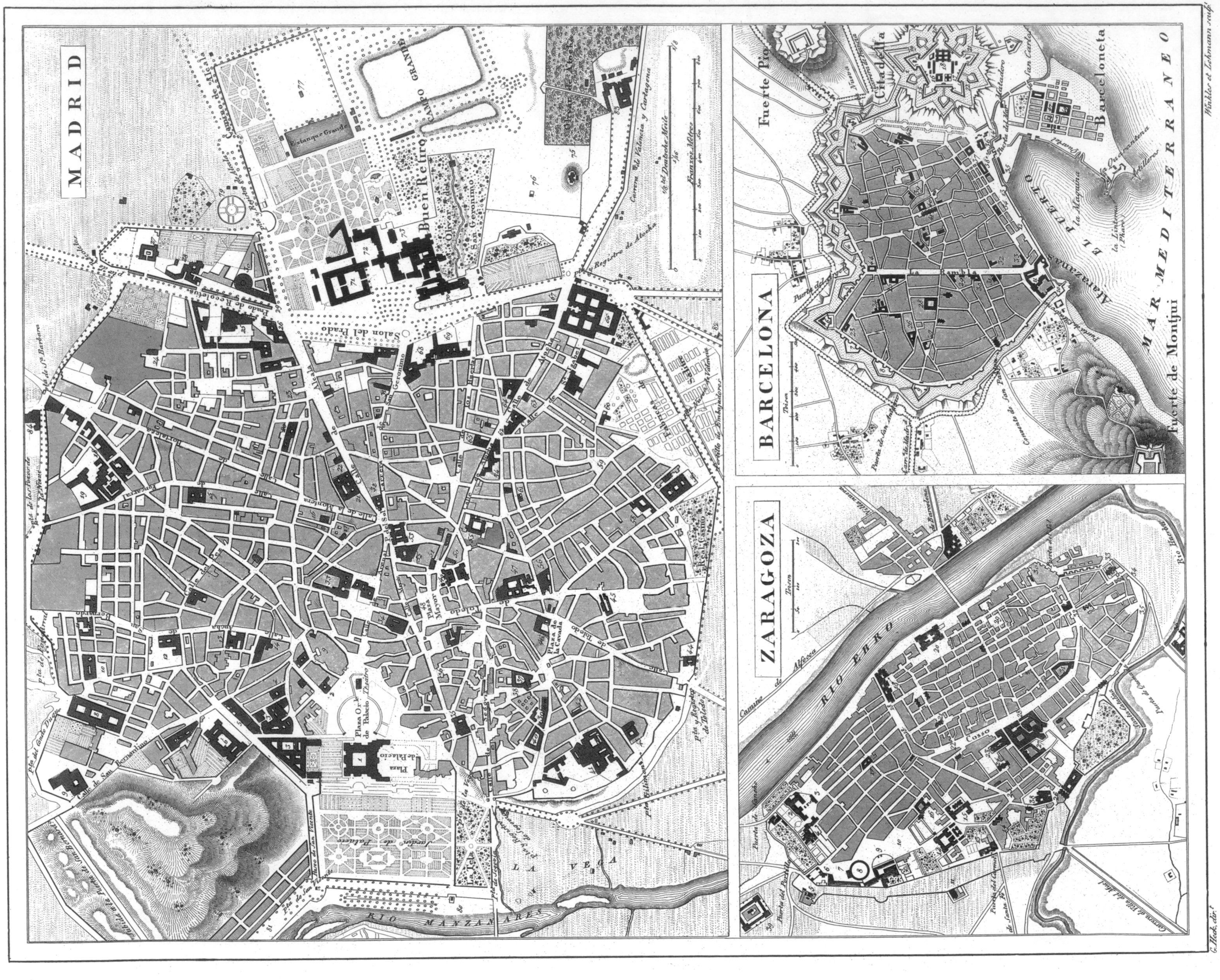
MADRID
BARCELONA
ZARAGOZA
Buen Retiro
Salon del Prado
Plaza Mayor
Plaza de Palacio
RIO MANZANARES
LA VEGA
Citadella
Barceloneta
Fuerte Pio
Fuerte de Montjui
MAR MEDITERRANEO
EL PUERTO
RIO EBRO
Cosso
Winkler et Lehmann sculp.

PLATE 183. MADRID, SARAGOSSA, AND BARCELONA

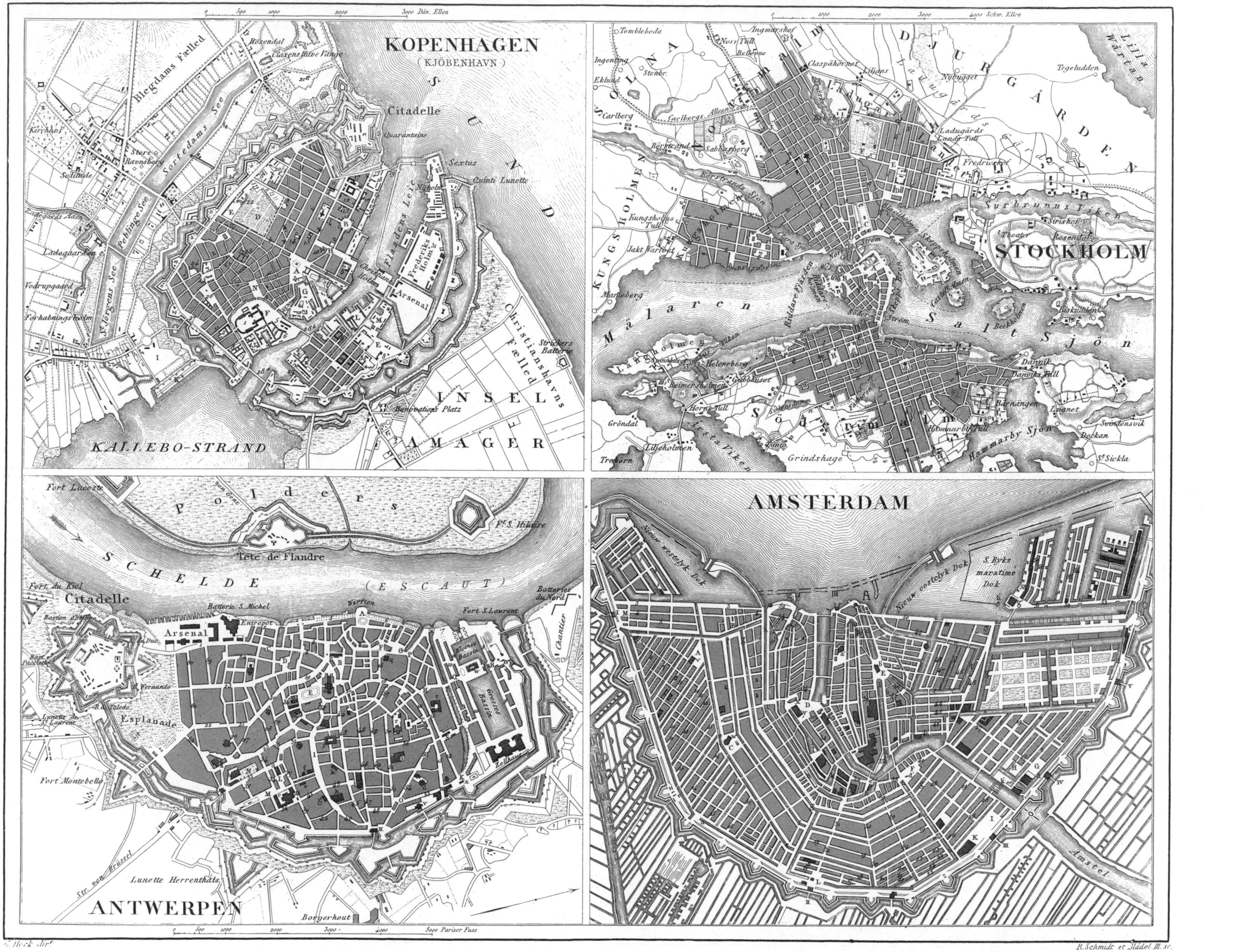
KOPENHAGEN
(KJÖBENHAVN)
500 1000 2000 3000 Dän. Ellen
Citadelle
Quarantaine
Blegdams Fælled
Sortedams See
Peblinge See
S. Jörgens See
Store Ravnsborg
Solitude
Kirchhof
Rosendal
Ladegaarden
Vodrupgaard
Forhabnings Holm
Sextus
Quinti Lunette
Nyholm
Flådens Leie
Frederiks Holm
Arsenal
Christianshavns Fælled
Strickers Batterie
INSEL AMAGER
Renovations Platz
KALLEBO-STRAND
STOCKHOLM
1000 2000 3000 4000 Schw. Ellen
Tombleboda
Ingmarshof
Norr Tull
Bellevue
Ingenting
Eklund
Carlberg
Carlbergs Alleen
Claspähörnet
Liljans
Tegeludden
Lilla Wärtan
SOLNA
NORRMALM
DJURGÅRDEN
Ladugårds Lands Tull
Sabbatsberg
Rörstrands Sjön
KUNGSHOLMEN
Kungsholms Tull
Jakt Warfvet
Mariaberg
Surbrunns Viken
Rosendal
Theater
Biskudden
Beckholmen
Castelholmen
Skeppsholmen
Mälaren
Salt Sjön
Söder Ström
Norr Ström
Långholmen
Helenebergs
Gubbhuset
Horns Tull
Dannik
Danviks Tull
Lugnet
Barnängen
Hammarby Sjön
Hammarby Tull
Sundensvik
Dockan
St. Sickla
SÖDERMALM
Liljeholmen
Gröndal
Trekorn
Grindshage
Årsta Viken
ANTWERPEN
500 1000 2000 3000 4000 5000 Pariser Fuss
Fort Lacoste
Polders
Tête de Flandre
Ft. S. Hilaire
SCHELDE (ESCAUT)
Fort du Kiel
Citadelle
Batterie S. Michel
Werften
Entrepot
Arsenal
Fort S. Laurent
Batterie du Nord
Chantier
Kleines Bassin
Grosses Bassin
Zollhaus
Esplanade
Fort Montebello
Lunette Herrenthals
Str. von Brüssel
Borgerhout
AMSTERDAM
Nieuw westelyk Dok
Nieuw oostelyk Dok
S. Ryks maratime Dok
Amstel
G. Heck dir.
R. Schmidt et Hädel M. sc.

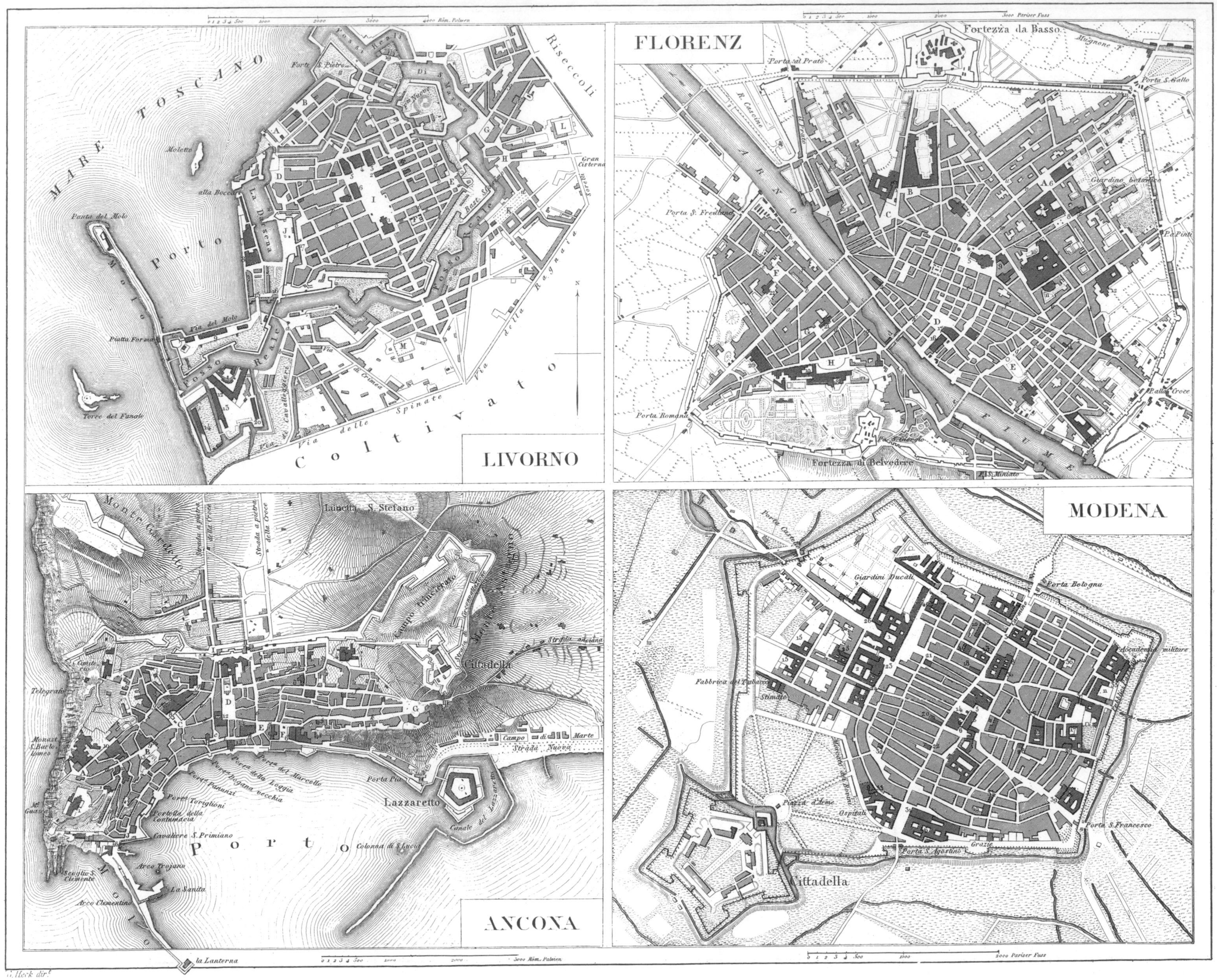
FLORENZ
Fortezza da Basso
Porta al Prato
Porta S. Gallo
Giardino botanico
Porta S. Frediano
Porta Romana
Fortezza di Belvedere
ARNO
FIUME
LIVORNO
MARE TOSCANO
Porto
Coltivato
Fosso Reale
Riseccoli
Gran Cisterna
Torre del Fanale
Via del Molo
ANCONA
Porto
Cittadella
Campo trincerato
Lazzaretto
Porta Pia
Strada Nuova
Campo di Marte
Lunetta S. Stefano
Telegrafo
Colonna di S. Lucia
Arco Trajano
Arco Clementino
la Lanterna
MODENA
Porta Bologna
Giardini Ducali
Accademia militare
Fabbrica del Tabacco
Piazza d'Arme
Porta S. Francesco
Porta S. Agostino
Cittadella
G. Heck dir.

PLATE 185. LEGHORN, FLORENCE, ANCONA, AND MODENA

HISTORY AND ETHNOLOGY

Captions to the History and Ethnology Plates 186–266

ANCIENT TIMES AND MIDDLE AGES

PLATE 186.
Egypt

Figure
1. The court of the dead
2–4. Different trades
5. Agriculture
6, 7. Hunting and fishing
8. Vintage
9. King in his chariot
10. King on his throne, receiving presents

PLATE 187.
Ancient Middle East and the Orient

Figure
1–3. Egyptian costumes
4. Lybian costume
5. Chinese
6–14. Assyrians
15, 16. Medes
16–20. Persians

PLATE 188.
Tombs and Funerary Objects

Figure
1–4. Egyptian features and headdresses, from monuments
5*ab*. Heads of male mummies
6*ab*. Heads of female mummies
7. Mummy with the inner fillets
8. Mummy with the exterior cover
9–11. Mummies with the coffins
12. Coffin with its cover
13, 14. Embalmed animals
15, 16. Vases
17–19. Large stone vases
20*ab*. Pitchers
21, 22. Altars
23, 24. Chairs
25. Folding chair
26, 27. Thrones
28, 29. Lounge and footstool
30. Knife
31. Royal sceptre
32, 33. Sphinxes
34, 35. Obelisks
36. Entrance to the Egyptian labyrinth
37–39. Indian pyramids, ground plan, elevation, and section
40. Rock-tombs near Persepolis

PLATE 189.
Various Peoples of Antiquity

Figure
1. Carthaginian king
2. Mauritanian
3. Persian woman
4–6. Armenians
7. Arab
8. Phrygian
9, 10. Dacians
11, 12. Dacian women
13. Syrian
14. Parthian
15. Celtiberian
16. Iberian woman
17. British woman
18–23. Germans

PLATE 190.
Scenes of Germans and Gauls

Figure
1. German dwelling
2. German infant plunged in the river
3. German wedding
4–8. Gauls

PLATE 191.
Tombs and Funerary Objects

Figure
1, 2. Egyptian sphinxes
3–6. Altars
7. Table
8–14*ab*. Pitchers and vases
15–19. Cups and other drinking vessels
20. Bowl
21. Dipper (*Simpulum*)
22*ab*. Royal necklace and sceptre
23, 24. Ethiopian royal headgear
25. Numidian royal headgear
26. Armenian royal headgear (*Kidaris*)
27. Dacian headgear
28. Sarmatian headgear
29. Scythian royal tiara
30, 31. Persian royal tiara
32. Assyrian tiara
33–37. Indian caps
38. Assyrian helmet
39. Phrygian cap
40*ab*. Assyrian headgear
41, 45*b*. Indian necklace and girdle
42. Chinese imperial cap
43–45. Fans and fly-brushes
46. Persian covering for the feet
47. Persian fan
48–50. Persian drinking vessels
51. The rock-tomb of Midas in Asia Minor
52. Rock-tombs at Persepolis
53. Monument near Tortosa in Syria
54. Absalom's tomb in the valley of Josaphat, near Jerusalem
55–75*ab*. Carthaginian coins and medals

PLATE 192.
Grecian Costumes

Figure
1, 2*ab*. Maidens
3. Youth
4. Spinner
5. Singer
6. Amazon
7–13. Women
14. Phrygian
15, 16. Greeks from Mount Ida
17. Philosopher
18. Poet
19. Prefect
20. War-leader

PLATE 193.
Greek and Roman Scenes

Figure
1. Ceremony at a Greek wedding
2. Greek dancer
3. Roman funeral ceremony
4. Interior of a Greek dwelling
5. The Areopagus

PLATE 194.
Grecian Games

Figure
1–6. Games of Greek youth
7–24. Olympian games

PLATE 195.
Grecian Garden and Artifacts

Figure
1. The philosophers' garden at Athens
2–34. Various Grecian articles of furniture
35–39. Various Grecian tools
40–54. Various Grecian articles of toilet

PLATE 196.
Tombs, Urns, and Coins

Figure
1. The rock-tombs of Tarquinii
2. Those of Assus
3, 4. Those of Ceræa, and their ground plan
5, 6. Tombs of Orela; elevation
7, 8. The same; the ground plan
9, 10. Tombs in Telmessus; elevation and ground plan
11, 12. Tomb in Falerii; ground plan and section
13, 14. Tomb in Agrigentum; elevation and section
15. Tomb from an antique vase
16–20. Urns and vases
21–23. Tripods
24–34*ab*. Greek coins

PLATE 197.
Rome

Figure
1–3. Emperors
4, 5. Empresses
6, 7. Senators
8. Philosopher
9. Lictor
10. Citizen and his wife
11, 12. Youths
13–16. Women
17–29. Female headgear
30–32. Male headgear

PLATE 198.
Rome

Figure
1. Exhibition of captives in the forum
2. Gladiators in the theatre
3. Gladiators at funerals
4. Funeral of emperors

PLATE 199.
Details from the Circensian Games

Figures 1–16.

PLATE 200.
Scene in Roman Coliseum and Roman Coins

Figure
1. Combat with wild beasts in the Coliseum at Rome, under Domitian
2–19. Roman consular coins
20–25. Roman imperial coins

PLATE 201.
Roman Furniture and Tools

Figures 1–66.

PLATE 202.
Roman Tombs, Sarcophagi, and Artifacts

Figure
1. The street of tombs in Pompeii

2–4. Monuments
5–7. Sarcophagi
8–59. Roman furniture and tools

PLATE 203.
Scenes and Artifacts from Gaul and Various Monuments

Figure
1. Gallic women of the Roman time
2–6. Bas-reliefs from Gaul
7, 8*ab*. Gallic coins
9, 10. Gallic sepulchral urns
11–39. Various Gallic trinkets and utensils
40–42. German sepulchral urns
43–56. Coins, medals, and matrices
57, 58. Carthaginian monuments
59, 60. Gallic monuments
61. The Roman column at Cussy

PLATE 204.
Catacombs, Churches and Chapels

Figure
1. The Apostles' grotto near Jerusalem
2. The catacombs of Syracuse
3–6. The catacombs of Naples; ground plan; vertical section of a part; horizontal section of another part; the chapel
7–10. The catacombs of San Marcellino near Rome; ground plan, perspective view, and details
11. Plan of Platonia, near St. Sebastian, before the walls of Rome
12, 13. Tombs of Christian martyrs
14. Christian sarcophagus from the catacombs
15. Chapel of St. Hermes
16. Chapel of St. Agnes
17. Plan of the subterranean church of St. Hermes
18. External elevation of the subterranean church of St. Prisca
19. Tabernacle of the church of St. Nereus and St. Achilleus, near the baths of Antoninus at Rome

PLATE 205.
The Tribes of the Migration

Figure
1. Goth
2. Sueve
3. Gepide
4. Vandal
5. Marcoman
6. Quade
7. Herulian
8. Briton
9. Frank
10. Hun
11–14. Picts
15. Anglo-Saxon chieftain
16–18. Anglo-Saxons
19. Danish king
20. Danish warrior
21–23. Danes

PLATE 206.
Costumes of Central Europe

Figure
1. Queen Clotilda (6th century)
2. Maid of honor
3. Frankish leader
4*ab*. Frankish warriors
5. King Clovis
6. Charlemagne
7, 8. Prince and princess of his house
9, 10. Noble and his wife
11. Leader under Charlemagne
12*ab*. Warriors
13. Bishop
14. Common people
15–18. Frankish king, queen, prince, and princess
19, 20. Prebendary and nun
21. Citizen
22, 23. Norman king and queen
24–26. Norman nobles
27, 28. Norman citizen and peasant

PLATE 207.
Scenes and Artifacts from the Time of Charlemagne and the Franks

Figure
1, 2. Clovis, king of the Franks, and his queen Clotilda
3. Fredegonda, from her tomb
4. Childebert, king of the Franks
5, 6. Statues of females from the 8th century
7. Charlemagne
8. Charlemagne receiving the submission of Wittekind
9–37. Arms, utensils, and furniture of Charlemagne's time
38. Statue of Wittekind
39–63. Utensils and furniture of Charlemagne's time

PLATE 208.
Scenes of French Medieval Life

Figure
1. Travelling of Frankish kings in the 8th century
2. Manner of transporting wounded or sick princes in the 13th century
3. St. Louis administering justice in the open field
4. Clerical punishment of French princes in the 13th century
5. Vassals paying homage to their liege lord

PLATE 209.
German and English Armor and Tournaments

Figure
1. Full armor of Emperor Maximilian
2. Full armor of King Henry VIII
3. English knight
4. German knights
5. Squires
6. English knights in tournament
7. German knights before a tournament
8. Judge of the tournament

PLATE 210.
Different Modes of Combat

Figure
1. Joust with lances in Germany
2. Judicial combat
3. Combat with maces in France
4. Judicial combat with shields
5. Combat with swords
6. Combat with lance points
7. Carrying the ring in the carrousel
8. Squire taking the oath of knighthood on the sword

PLATE 211.
Becoming a Knight

Figure
1. Young knight taking the solemn oath on the altar
2. The ceremony of dubbing a knight

PLATE 212.
Crowns and Shields

Figure
1–13. Forms of shields
14–32. Colors and figures of shields
33–63. Divisions of shields
64–86. Different crowns
87–92. Crests of shields

PLATE 213.
Coats of Arms

Figures 1–21.

PLATE 214.
Coats of Arms

Figures 1–31.

PLATE 215.
The Inquisition

Figure
1. Session of the tribunal
2. The punishment of the scourge
3. Nailing the hand to the post
4. The punishment of strangling
5. The fire-torture on the wheel
6. Auto-da-fé at Seville

PLATE 216.
The Inquisition

Figure
1. The torture of the rope and pulley
2. The water-torture
3. The fire-torture
4. Auto-da-fé in Spain

PLATE 217.
Founders and Representatives of Various Monastic Institutions

Figure
1. St. Augustin
2. St. Antony
3, 4. Maronite patriarch and monk
5, 6. Armenian patriarch and monk
7. St. Basil
8. Greek monk in Poland
9. Jacobite monk
10, 11. Benedictine monk and nun
12. Nun of Fontevrault
13, 14. Augustine monk and nun
15. Prebendary of the Congregation of the Lateran
16. Barefoot Carmelite monk
17. Carmelite nun
18. Carthusian nun
19. Calmalduensian monk
20. Valombrose monk
21. Bernardine nun
22, 23. Capuchin monks
24. Nun of St. Clarissa
25. Sylvestrine monk
26, 27. Dominican monk and nun

PLATE 218.
Representatives of Religious Communities

Figure
1. Monk of the Holy Sepulchre
2. Cœlestine monk
3. Franciscan monk
4. Ursuline nun
5. Theatine nun
6. Beguine
7. Hospitaller of *St. Jacques du haut pas*
8. Alexian monk
9. Ambrosian monk
10. Religious of the order of Jesus
11. Annunciate nun
12. Nun of "the Immaculate Conception"
13. Nun of "the Visitation of St. Mary"
14. Nun of "the Word become Flesh"
15. Franciscan nun
16. Hospital nun of Hotel-Dieu in Paris

17. Jesuit
18. Jesuit missionary in China
19. Sister of Charity
20. Bethlehemite monk
21. Priest of the Oratory in France
22. Doctrinary
23. Barnabite monk
24. Priest of the pious schools of France and Belgium
25, 26. Feuillantine monk and nun
27. Monk of St. Maurus

PLATE 219.
Members of Various Religious and Military Orders

Figure
1. Visitantine nun in Flanders
2. Nun of *"Notre-Dame"*
3. Nun of *"Notre Dame de la Miséricorde"*
4. Priest of the Congregation of Missions
5. Sister of Charity of St. Vincent de Paula
6. Hospital nun of La Flèche
7a. Trappist monk
7b. Poor volunteer monk of Flanders
8. Grand master of the Order of Malta
9. Grand cross of the same
10. Knight of Malta
11. Lady of the Order of St. John of Jerusalem
12. Templar in house dress
13. Templar in war costume
14. Templar in full armor mounted
15. Grand master of the German Knights
16. Knight of St. James of the Sword
17. Knight of the Order of Calatrava
18. Knight of the Order of Alcantara
19. Knight of St. Avis in Portugal
20. Knight of St. Stephen
21. Knight of the Holy Ghost
22. Hospitaller of the Holy Ghost
23. Religious of the Order d'Aubrac

PLATE 220.
Freemasonry

Figure
1. Initiation of apprentice
2. Initiation of master
3. Initiation of the 33d degree of the Scottish lodge
4. Funeral of a companion

PLATE 221.
Hawking and Crusaders

Figure
1. Hawking in France
2. Departure of crusaders for Palestine

PLATE 222.
Crusaders

Figure
1. Combat between crusaders and Saracens
2. Harangue to crusaders before the walls of Jerusalem

PLATE 223.
Knights Returning from Crusade and at Tournament

Figure
1. Return of crusaders from Palestine
2. Tournament in Germany

PLATE 224.
Church of the Holy Sepulchre and Church of St. Mary of the Manger

Figure
1. Ground plan of the church of St. Mary of the Manger at Bethlehem
2. Interior of the church of St. Mary of the Manger in Bethlehem, with the entrance to the chapel of the Holy Grotto
3. Interior of the chapel with the Holy Grotto
4. Ground plan of the church of the Holy Sepulchre in Jerusalem
5. Portico and entrance to the same
6. Interior of the same, with the Holy Chapel

ETHNOLOGY OF THE NINETEENTH CENTURY

PLATE 225.
The Five Principal Races

1. Caucasian Race

Figure
1. Inhabitants of Central Europe
2. Greek
3. Turk
4. Cossack
5. Persian
6. Hindoo
7. Bedouin
8, 9. Cabyles

2. Mongolian Race

10. Kalmuck
11. Chinese
12. Samoyede
13. Esquimaux

3. Ethiopian Race

14. Guinea Negro
15. Boussa Negro
16. Hottentot
23, 24. Papuas (Australia)

4. American Race

17–21. Indians

5. Malay Race

22. Native of New Zealand

PLATE 226.
Germanic Peoples

Figure
1. Peasant girl from Baden
2. Peasant from the Baden highlands
3, 4. Inhabitants of the Black Forest
5–9. Wirtembergers
10–15. Bavarians
16, 17. Hessians
18, 19. Inhabitants of Rhenish Prussia
20. Inhabitants of Brunswick
21, 22. Inhabitants of the District of Coblentz (Rhine)
23, 24. Inhabitants of Altenburg (Saxony)

PLATE 227.
Germanic and Austrian Peoples

Figure
1. Inhabitants of the District of Erfurt (Thuringia)
2. Inhabitants of Holstein
3. Inhabitants of the District of Lüneburg (Hanover)
4, 5. Inhabitants of the District of Hamburg
6–8. Inhabitants of East Friesland (Hanover)
9–11. Inhabitants of Silesia
12–15. Inhabitants of Tyrol
16–19. Inhabitants of Austria
20–22. Inhabitants of Styria
23. Inhabitants of Bohemia
24. Inhabitants of Illyria

PLATE 228.
Gymnasium and Acrobatics

Upper Division

Figure
1–12. The German gymnasium

Lower Division

Figure
1–8. Acrobatic feats

PLATE 229.
Equestrian Feats

Figures 1–3.

PLATE 230.
Races and a Ball

Figure
1, 2. Horse races
3. Masked ball at Paris

PLATE 231.
Scenes of Public Events

Figure
1. Grand promenade in the Elysian Fields (Paris)
2. Festival at St. Petersburg
3. Public meeting in England

PLATE 232.
Outdoor Celebrations

Figure
1. Naumachy on the Seine in Paris
2. Rural ball
3. Illumination in Rome

PLATE 233.
Spanish and Sardinian Scenes

Figure
1. Spanish barn
2. Sardinian barn
3. Sardinian wedding
4. The Bolero (Spanish dance)
5. Spanish bull-fight

PLATE 234.
Russian and Caucasian Tribes

Russian Tribes

Figure
1, 2. Strielzi
3. Russo-Polish guard
4–7. Inhabitants of Little Russia
8–10. Fishermen from the Volga
11. Inhabitants of Novgorod
12, 13. Inhabitants of the district of Twer
14. Inhabitants of the Ukraine
15. Cossack of the Don
16. Inhabitants of the district of Moscow

Caucasian Tribes

17–22. Circassians
23. Turkoman
24. Abasian
25. Mingrelian
26. Imeritian
27. Georgian

PLATE 235.
Scenes of Russian Life

Figure
1, 2. Russian rural games
3. Russian public bath
4, 5. Russian large and small knout

PLATE 236.
Scenes of Russian Life

Figure
1. Russian sleighing and gliding hill
2. Russian serfs on the Don
3. Russian national dance
4. Festivity at Pergola (Russia)

5. Lapland winter cabins

PLATE 237.
Eastern Peoples and Costumes

Figure
1 *a–s*. Oriental headgear
2. Syrians
3, 4. Smyrnese
5–8. Maronites
9. Girl of Nablous
10. Nazarenes
11–15. Arabs
16, 17. Armenians
18. Turk of Mardin

PLATE 238.
Scenes from Middle Eastern Life

Figure
1. Public baths for women in Turkey
2. Interior of a harem
3. Supper at the grand vizier's
4. Ceremony in the sultan's presence chamber
5. Dance of the dervises
6. Prayer and ablution of the Mahomedans
7. Penitent dervise

PLATE 239.
Persians and Other Eastern Peoples

Figure
1–9. Persians
10. Beludshis
11. Usbek
12. Afghan
13. Kurd
14. Kirghis
15. Imeritian
16. Georgian
17. Mingrelian
18. Caucasian mountaineer

PLATE 240.
Scenes of Eastern Life

Figure
1–3. Bashkirs and Kirghis in camp
4–6. Tartars
7, 8. Kurds
9. Persian nobleman

PLATE 241.
Scenes of Persian Life

Figure
1. Wedding in Persia
2. Persian women travelling
3. Persian music
4. Persian meal
5. Persian game
6, 7. Persian punishments

PLATE 242.
Scenes of the English East Indies

Figure
1. Rajah of Cutch and his vassals (English East Indies)
2. Caravan in Kattiavar (English East Indies)

PLATE 243.
East Indian and Arabian Scenes

Figure
1. Arabian nomades
2. Bedouin camp
3, 4. Arabian music and dance
5, 6. Travelling in Lahore

PLATE 244.
Scenes from Indian, Arabian, and Persian Life

Figure
1–3. Indian women and girls
4. Slave of a harem
5. Indian harem
6. Car festival in India
7. Salutation of the Arabians
8. Persian funeral

PLATE 245.
Hindoo Scenes

Figure
1. Penitent Hindoo fanatic
2. Burning of a Hindoo widow with the remains of her husband
3. Wedding ceremony of the Tzingaris (Indian gipsies)
4. Nuptial procession of wealthy Hindoos

PLATE 246.
Oriental Peoples

Figure
1–6. Chinese
7. Corean
8. Loo-Choo islander
9–14. Japanese

PLATE 247.
Scenes from Chinese Life

Figure
1. Tea culture in China
2. Silk culture in China
3. Chinese rice-dealer

PLATE 248.
Chinese Entertainment and Punishment

Figure
1. Chinese jugglers
2. Chinese theatre
3. Chinese punishment

PLATE 249.
Chinese Street Scenes

Figure
1. Chinese puppet-show
2. Chinese mandarin visiting
3. Chinese quack

PLATE 250.
African Scenes and Peoples

Figure
1. Moorish baths in Algiers
2, 3. Moorish noble and merchant
4. Arabian chief in Algiers
5. Jewess of Algiers
6. Slave
7. Lady of Cairo
8. Girl of Bornou (Senegal)
9. Negro king of Boussa
10, 11. Girls of Timbuktoo and Sokna (Fez)
12. Idolatry in Central Africa

PLATE 251.
Arabian and Egyptian Scenes

Figure
1. Egyptian Fellahs
2. Arabian dames and tents
3. Bedouins
4, 5. Arabian caravan
6. Nuptial procession in Cairo

PLATE 252.
Peoples of African Tribes

Figure
1. Abyssinian costumes
2. Abyssinian travelling
3. Elephant hunting
4. Negro chief and suite
5. Negro funeral south of the Coango River
6. Christian negro-women of Benguela
7. Negro soldier (Portuguese Africa)
8. Molua negroes guarding their king's dwelling
9. Human sacrifices of the Cassange negroes

PLATE 253.
Sports of Indian Tribes

Figures 1–7.

PLATE 254.
Peoples and Costumes of Mexico and South America

Figure
1. Mexican
2, 3. Inhabitants of La Puebla
4. Woman of Jalapa
5, 6. Costumes of Guatemala
7. Rich mulatto woman
8. Brazilian Mestizo
9, 10. Costumes of Bolivia
11. Girl of Bogota
12. Girl of Lima
13. Squaw of the district of Quito
14. Muleteers of the Cordilleras
15, 16. Costumes of La Conception
17. Costumes of Chili
18. Gaucho of Buenos Ayres

PLATE 255.
Brazilian Scenes

Figure
1. Travelling farmer from the Rio Grande in Brazil
2. Traveller from the province of Minas
3. Brazilian planter's family driving to mass
4. Townsmen from the Brazilian Rio Grande travelling
5. Caravan of Brazilian merchants
6. Convoy of diamonds

PLATE 256.
Various South American Peoples

Figure
1. Brazil Camacans in the forest
2. Festivity of the Camacans
3. Negroes from Bahia
4. Free negro bringing up a fugitive slave
5. Inhabitants of San Paulo
6, 7. Civilized Paraguay Indians

PLATE 257.
Life in Brazil and Patagonia

Figure
1. Brazilian plantation
2, 3. Diamond washing
4, 5. Brazilian sports
6. Brazilian planter's family walking to mass
7. Patagonian camp

PLATE 258.
Brazilian Slave Trade

Figures 1–6.

PLATE 259.
Scenes from Greenland, Brazil, and Patagonia

Figure
1. Greenland seal-hunting
2. Brazilian Indians bird-shooting
3. Attack by Guaycouros horsemen (Brazil)
4. Cattle-hunting on the Pampas (Brazil)
5. Negro dances at San Paulo
6. South Patagonian huts and graves

PLATE 260.
Sports and Duels of Various South American Indians

Figure
1–4. Sports of Brazilian Indians
5*ab*. Duels and combats among the Botocudos
6. Duel among the Purvis

PLATE 261.
Rites and Ceremonies of Mexican and South American Indians

Figure
1. Human sacrifice of the

ancient Mexicans
2. Cannibals of the Paraguay forests
3. Cannibals preparing a peculiar beverage
4–6. War-dance, execution of captives, and funeral with the Tupinambas

PLATE 262.
Scenes of the Pacific

Figure
1, 2. Funeral of a chief (Sandwich Islands)
3. Funeral in New Zealand
4. Tahitian girl, carrying presents
5. Dance of the Tahitians
6. Dance of the aborigines of the Caroline Islands

PLATE 263.
Scenes of Australian and Polynesian Natives

Figure
1. Chief from the Tonga islands
2. Combat of Tonga women
3–5. Girlish sports on the Tonga islands
6. Dance of Australian aborigines
7–9. Wedding ceremony, funeral, and ball of Australian aborigines
10. Ceremony of the Gna-Lung

PLATE 264.
Natives of the South Pacific

Figure
1. War dance of the Booro islanders
2. Cock-fight on the Philippine islands
3. Making brandy on the Marian islands
4. Caroline islander
5, 6. Aborigines of New Zealand
7. Dance of the same

PLATE 265.
Rites and Ceremonies of the Pacific

Figure
1. Ceremonial salutation among the aborigines of New Zealand
2. Tattooing of the same
3. Indian and his squaw from the Caroline islands
4. Dance of the Indians of this tribe
5–7. Indians of the island of Hawaï
8. Dance of Australian savages

PLATE 266.
Scenes from the Lives of Various Indian Tribes

Figure
1. Dance in Samoa
2. Dwelling of the Chinooks
3. Meeting on Drummond's island

G. Heck dirt. Henry Winkles sculpt.

 PLATE 187. ANCIENT MIDDLE EAST AND THE ORIENT

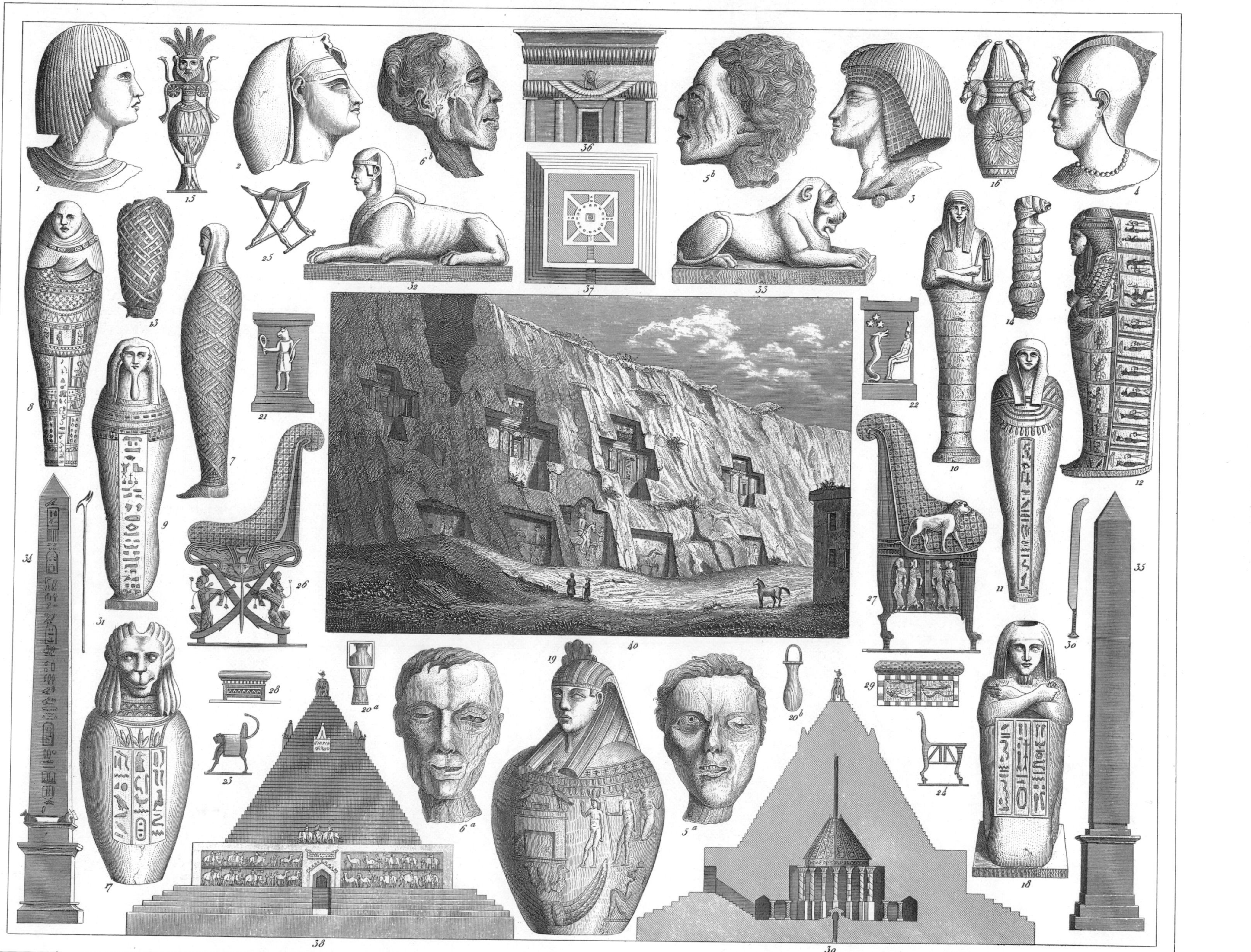

G. Heck dir.t

Henry Winkles sculp.t

PLATE 188. TOMBS AND FUNERARY OBJECTS

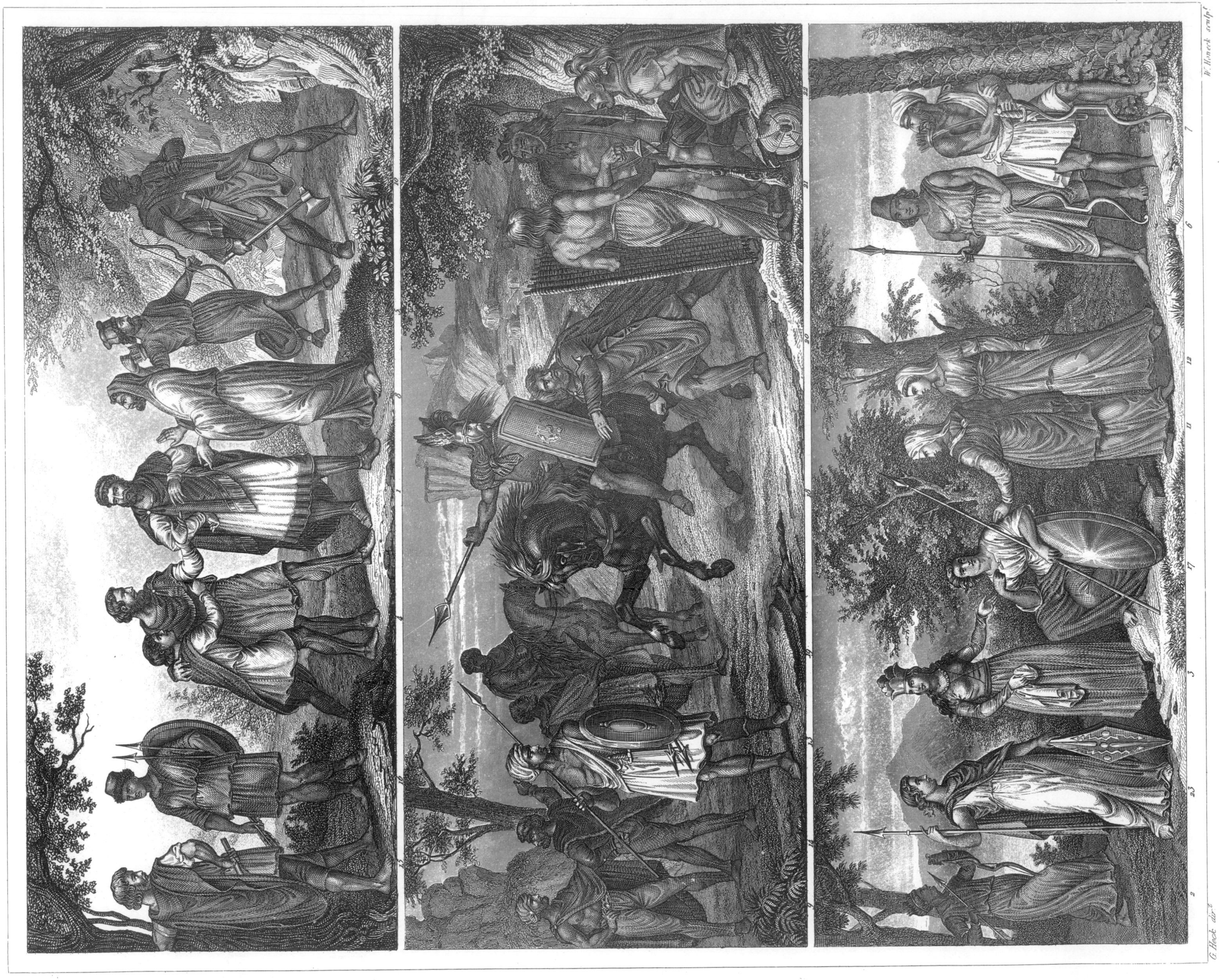

 PLATE 189. VARIOUS PEOPLES OF ANTIQUITY

G. Heck dir.

Henry Winkles sculp.

PLATE 190. SCENES OF GERMANS AND GAULS

G. Heck dir.^t A. Krausse sen. sculp.

PLATE 191. TOMBS AND FUNERARY OBJECTS

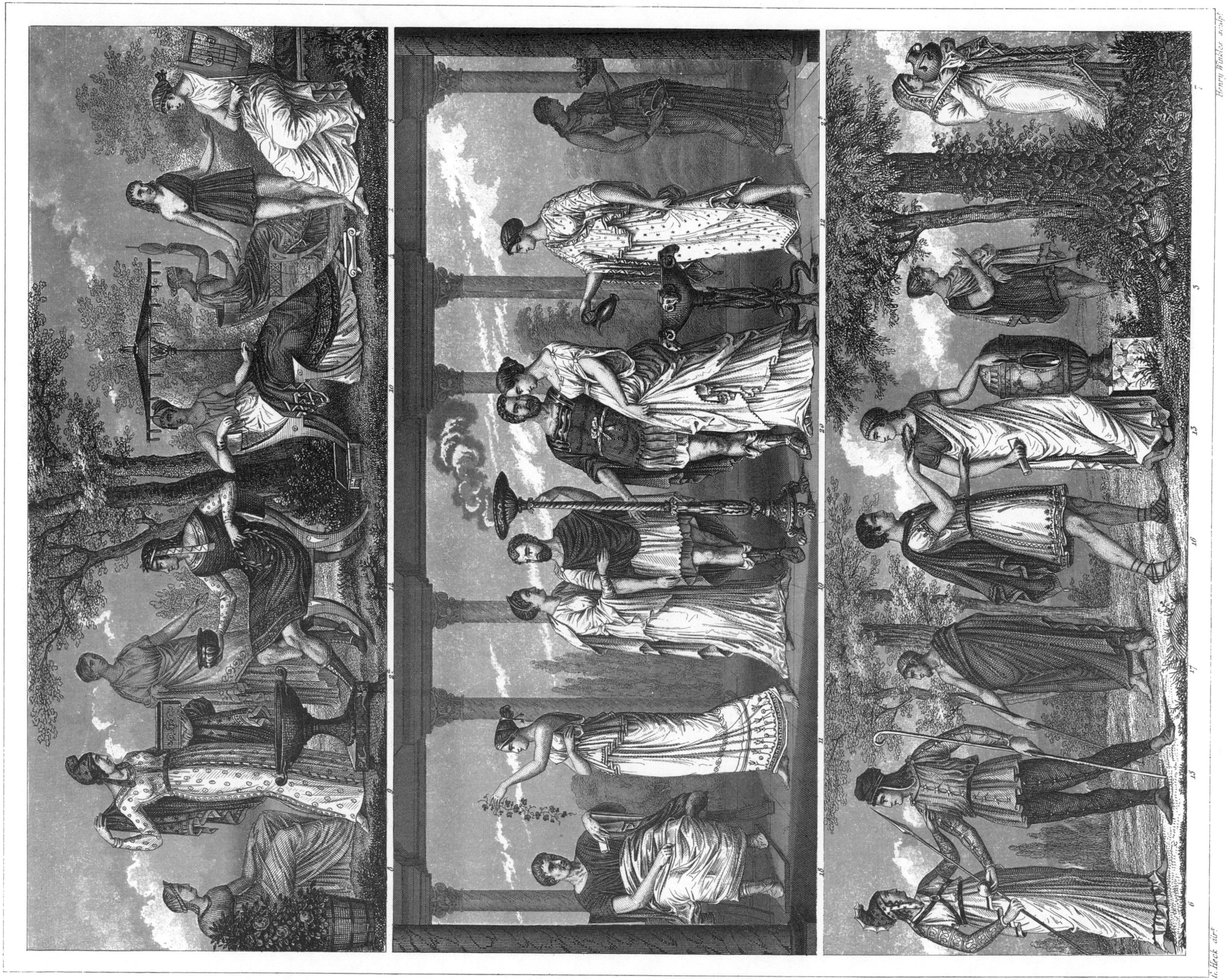

PLATE 192. GRECIAN COSTUMES

1 2

3

4

5

G. Heck dir.t Henry Winkles sculp.t

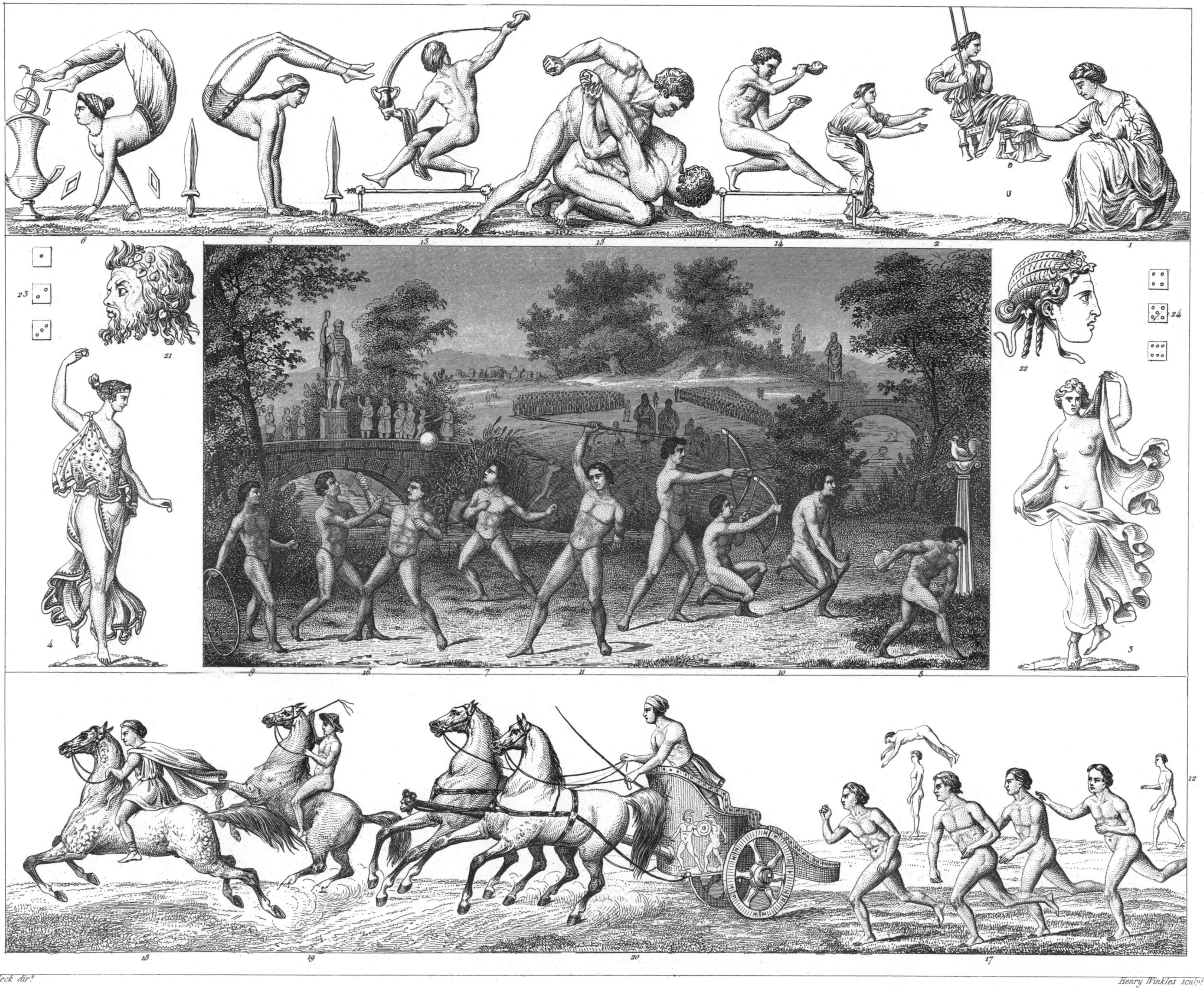

G. Heck dir.^t Henry Winkles sculp.^t

PLATE 194. GRECIAN GAMES

G. Heck dir.ᵗ Henry Winkles sculp.ᵗ

 PLATE 195. GRECIAN GARDEN AND ARTIFACTS

G. Heck dir.t Henry Winkles sculp.t

Maasstäbe in Metres.

zu Figur 4. — zu Figur 5 8. — zu Figur 11. — zu Figur 9 10. — zu Figur 13 14.

PLATE 196. TOMBS, URNS, AND COINS

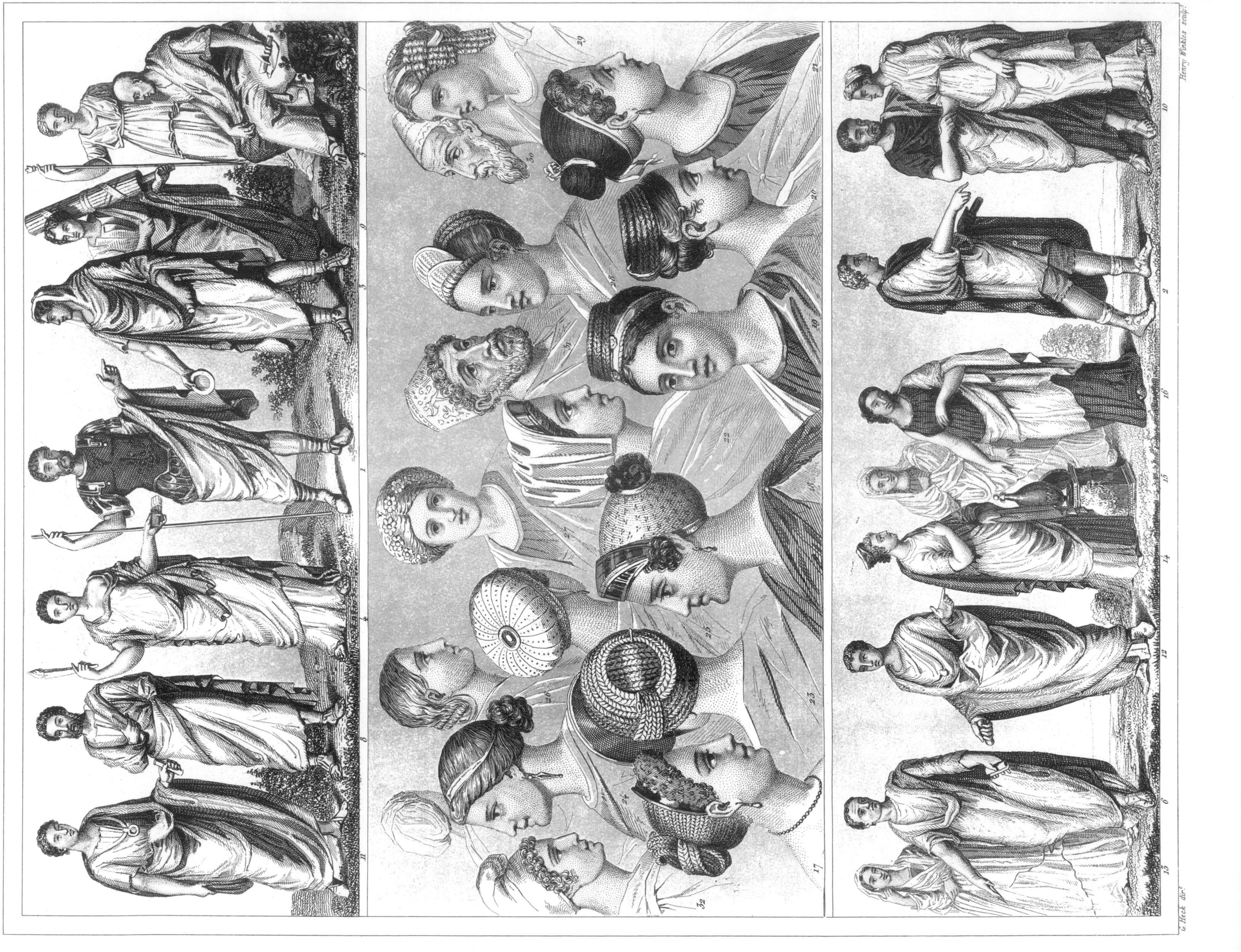
G. Heck dir.
Henry Winkles sculp.

G. Heck dir.t

Henry Winkles sculp.t

G. Heck dir.t Maschinenschrift von E. Kretschmar Leipz. *Henry Winkles sculp.t*

PLATE 199. DETAILS FROM THE CIRCENSIAN GAMES

Fig. 2
Figur 1.
ROMA
PIETAS AVGG
HADRIANVS AVGVSTVS P P
HILARITAS P R
S C
COS III
PLAVTILLA AVGVSTA
VENVS FELIX
AVGVSTO
S P Q R
COS IIII

G. Heck dir.t Henry Winkles sculp.t

G. Heck dir.t

Henry Winkles sculp.t

 PLATE 201. ROMAN FURNITURE AND TOOLS

G. Heck dir.t

Henry Winkles sculp.t

G. Heck dir.[t] Henry Winkles sculp.[t]

 PLATE 203. SCENES AND ARTIFACTS FROM GAUL AND VARIOUS MONUMENTS

J. Heck dir.^t Henry Winkles sculp.^t

PLATE 204. CATACOMBS, CHURCHES, AND CHAPELS

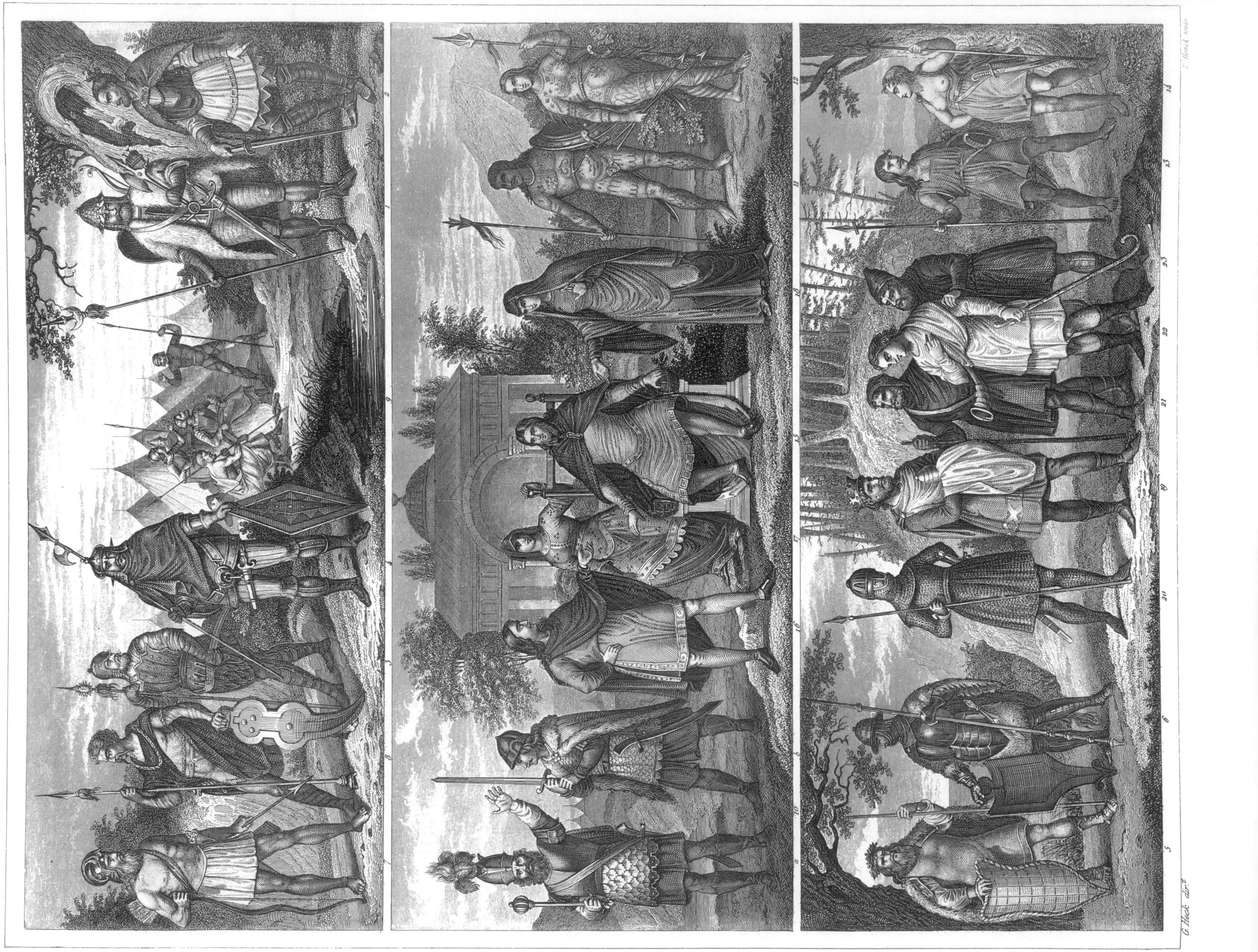

 PLATE 205. THE TRIBES OF THE MIGRATION

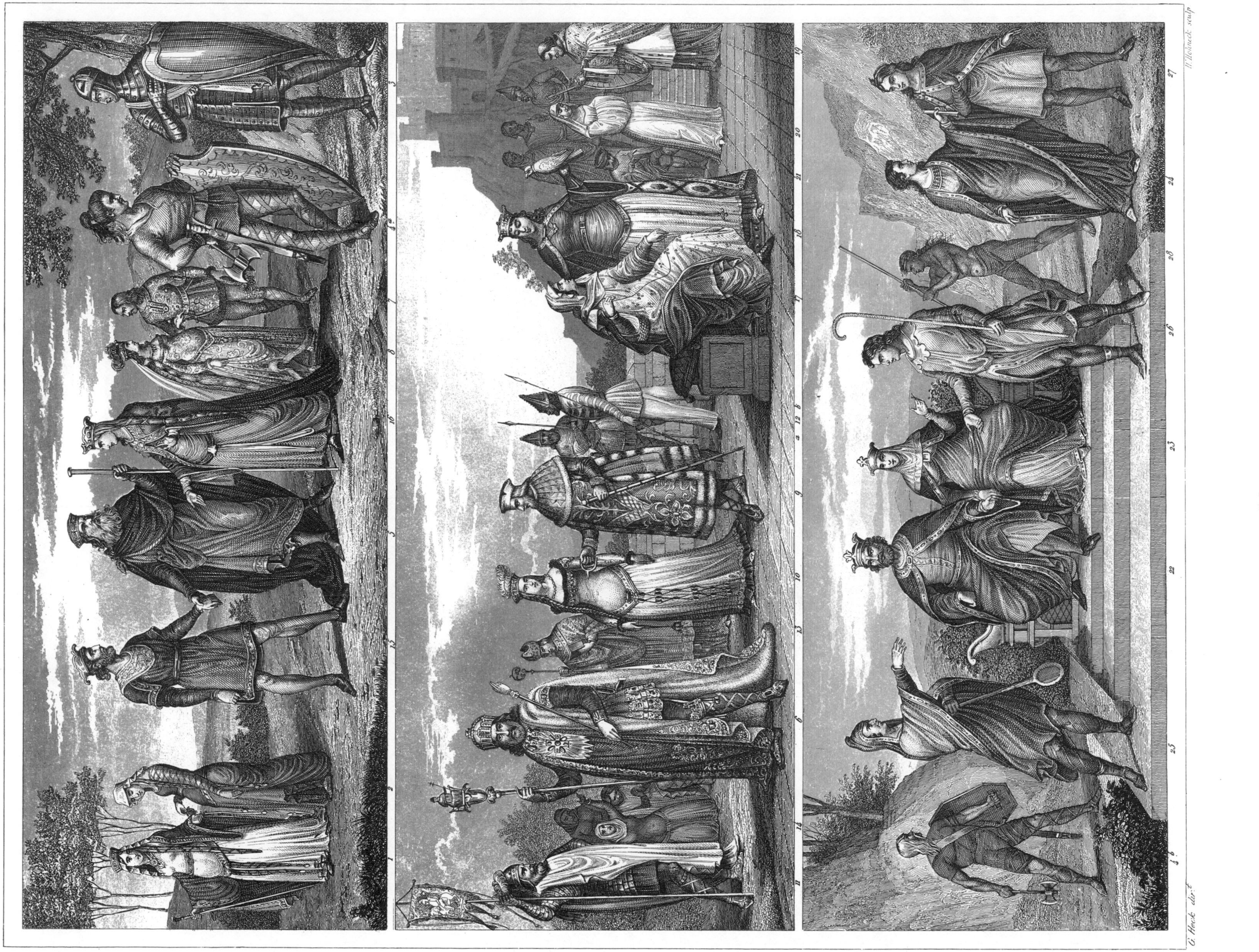

PLATE 206. COSTUMES OF CENTRAL EUROPE

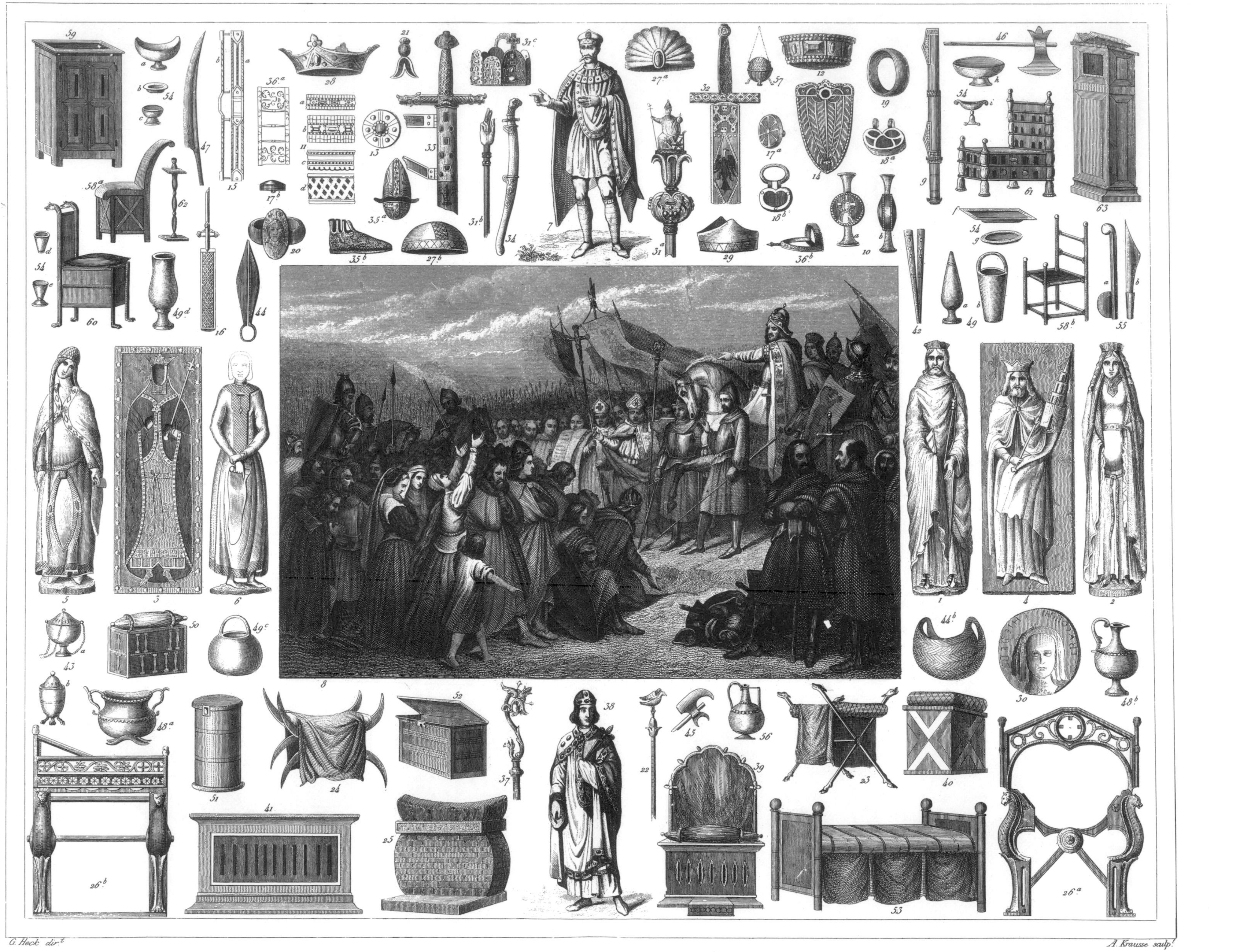

PLATE 207. SCENES AND ARTIFACTS FROM THE TIME OF CHARLEMAGNE AND THE FRANKS

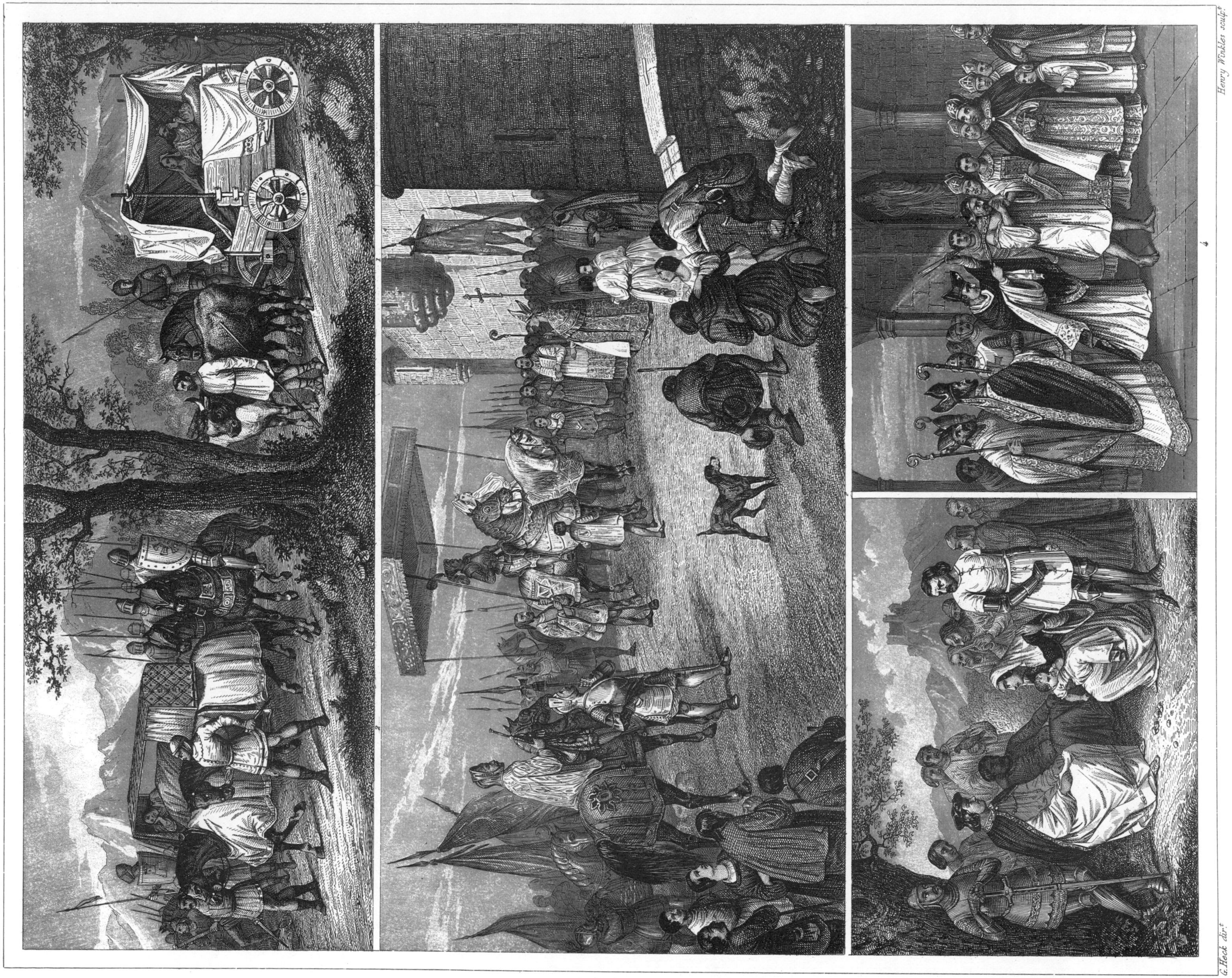

PLATE 208. SCENES OF FRENCH MEDIEVAL LIFE

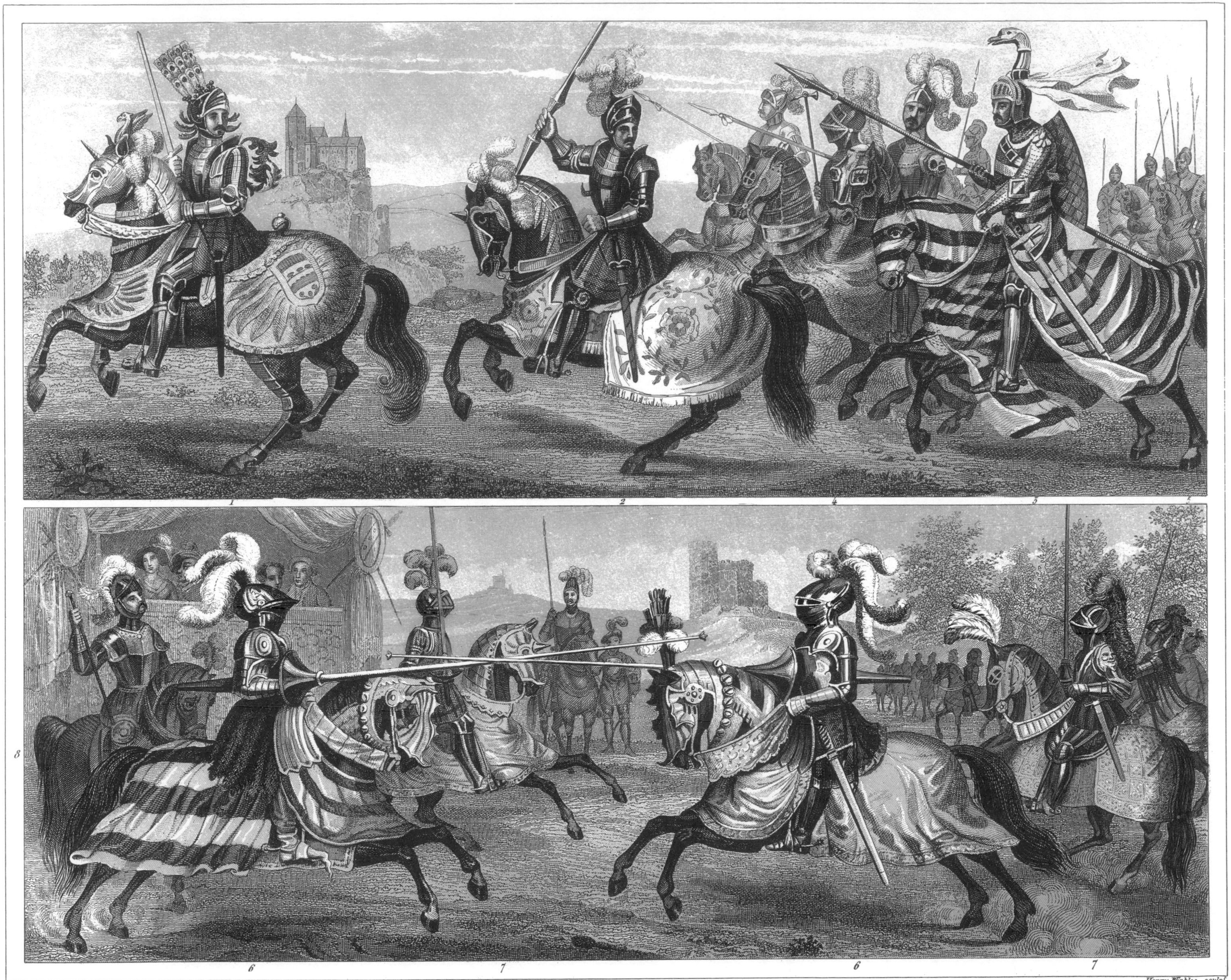

G. Heck dir.t Henry Winkles sculp.t

PLATE 209. GERMAN AND ENGLISH ARMOR AND TOURNAMENTS

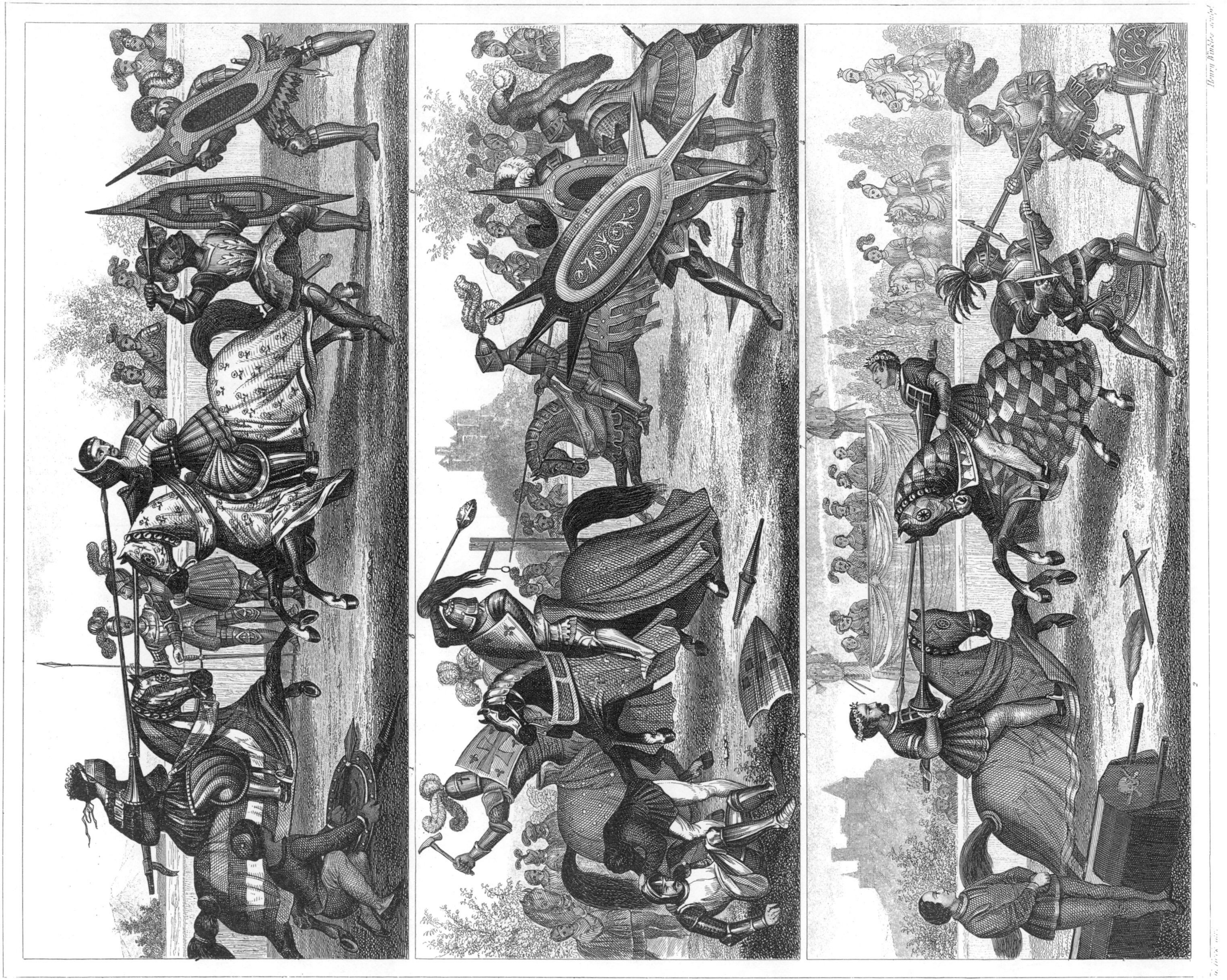

PLATE 210. DIFFERENT MODES OF COMBAT

1
2
Henry Winkles sculp.
G. Heck dir.

PLATE 211. BECOMING A KNIGHT

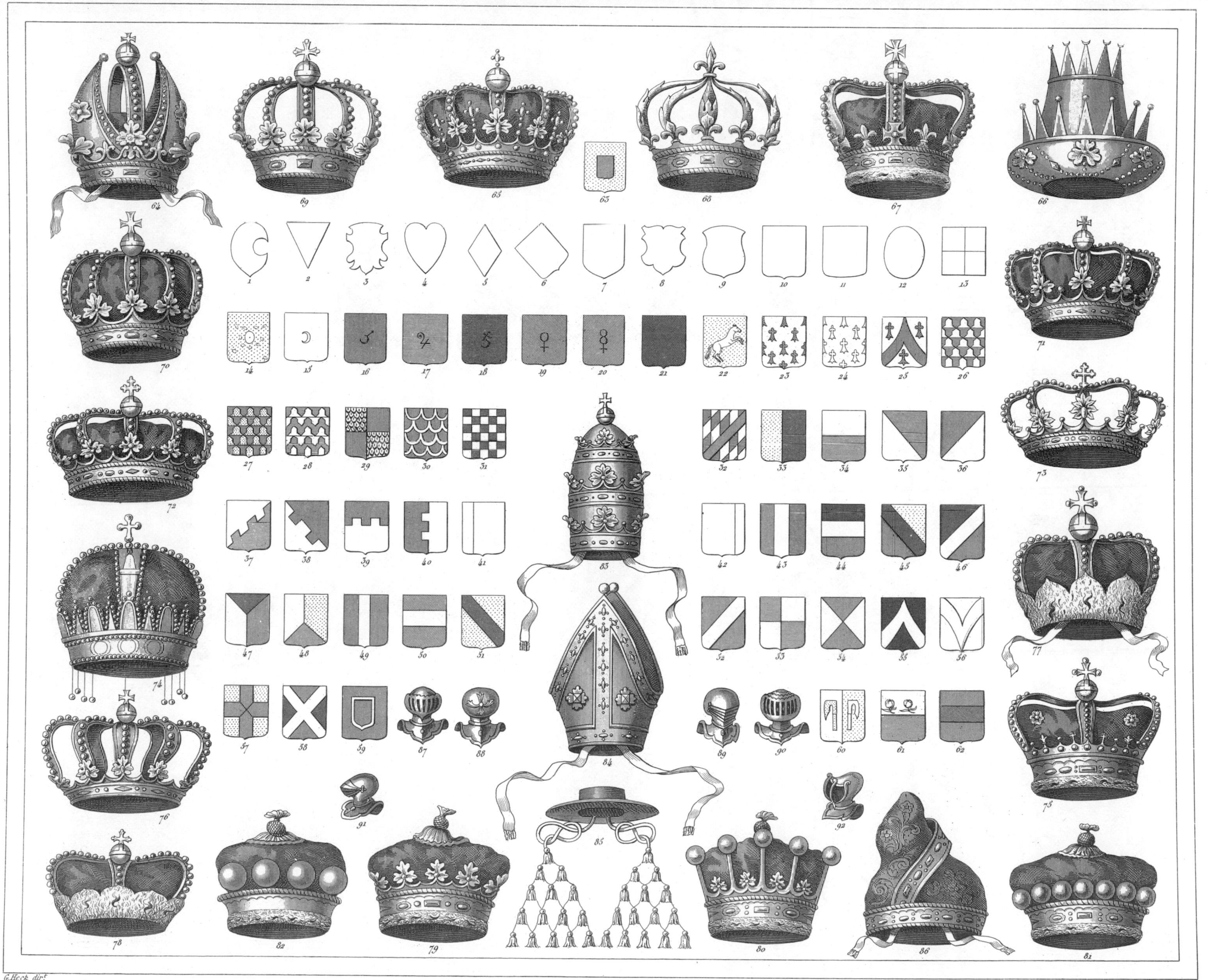

G. Heck dir.^t Henry Winkles sculp.^t

PLATE 212. CROWNS AND SHIELDS

G. Heck dir.t A. Krausse sen sculp

 PLATE 213. COATS OF ARMS

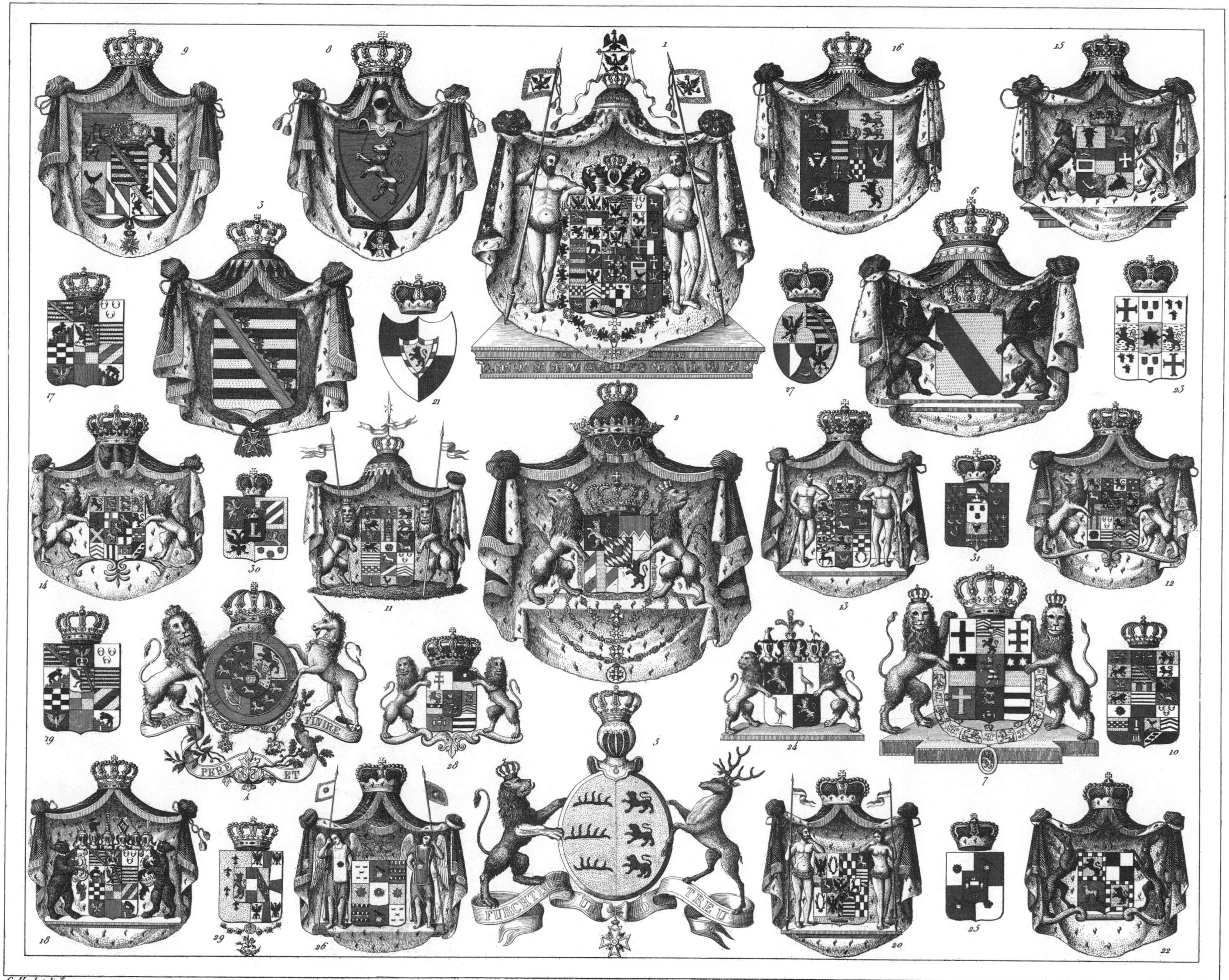

G. Heck dir.t

Schweissinger sculp.

PLATE 215. THE INQUISITION

PLATE 216. THE INQUISITION

 PLATE 217. FOUNDERS AND REPRESENTATIVES OF VARIOUS MONASTIC INSTITUTIONS

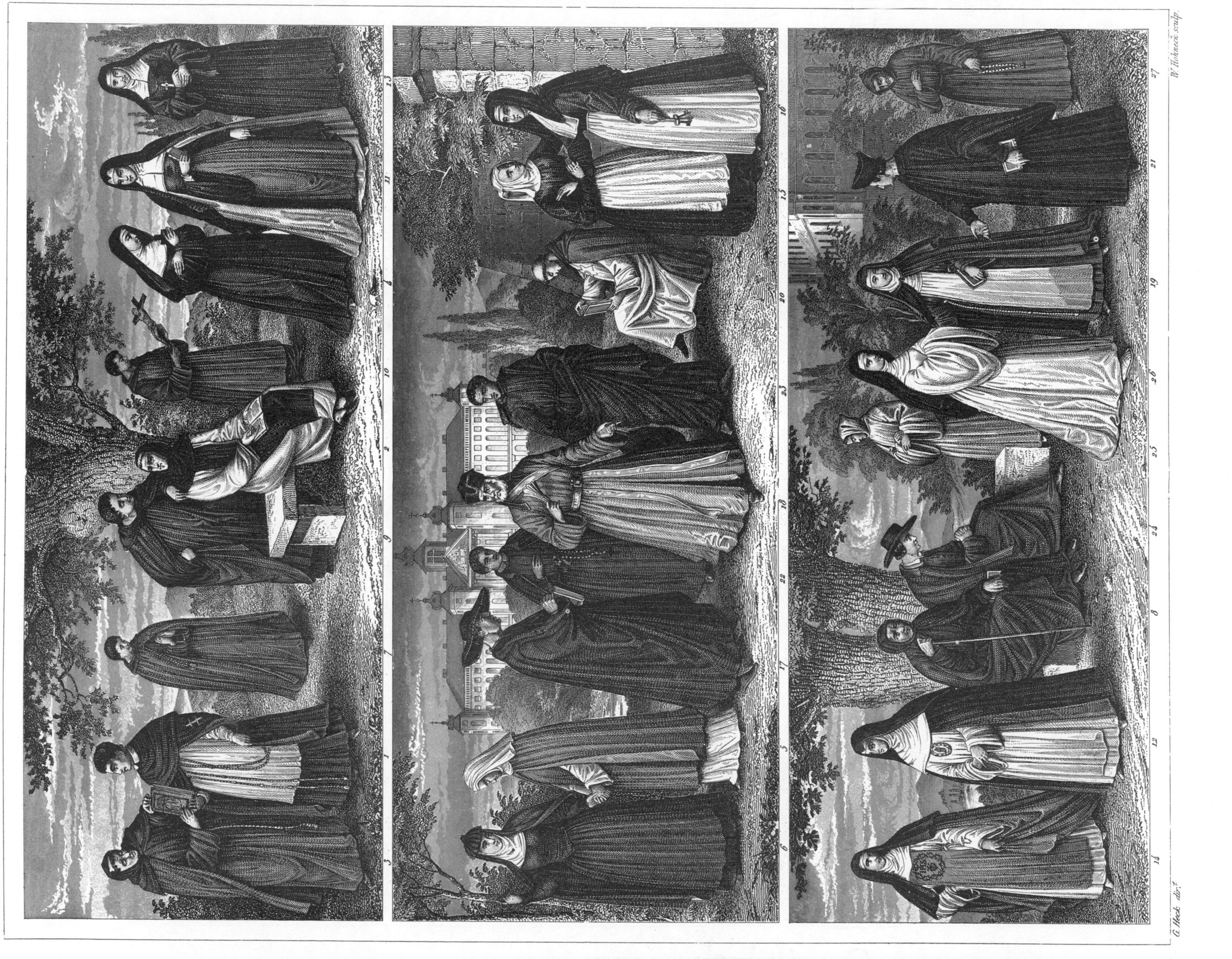

PLATE 218. REPRESENTATIVES OF RELIGIOUS COMMUNITIES

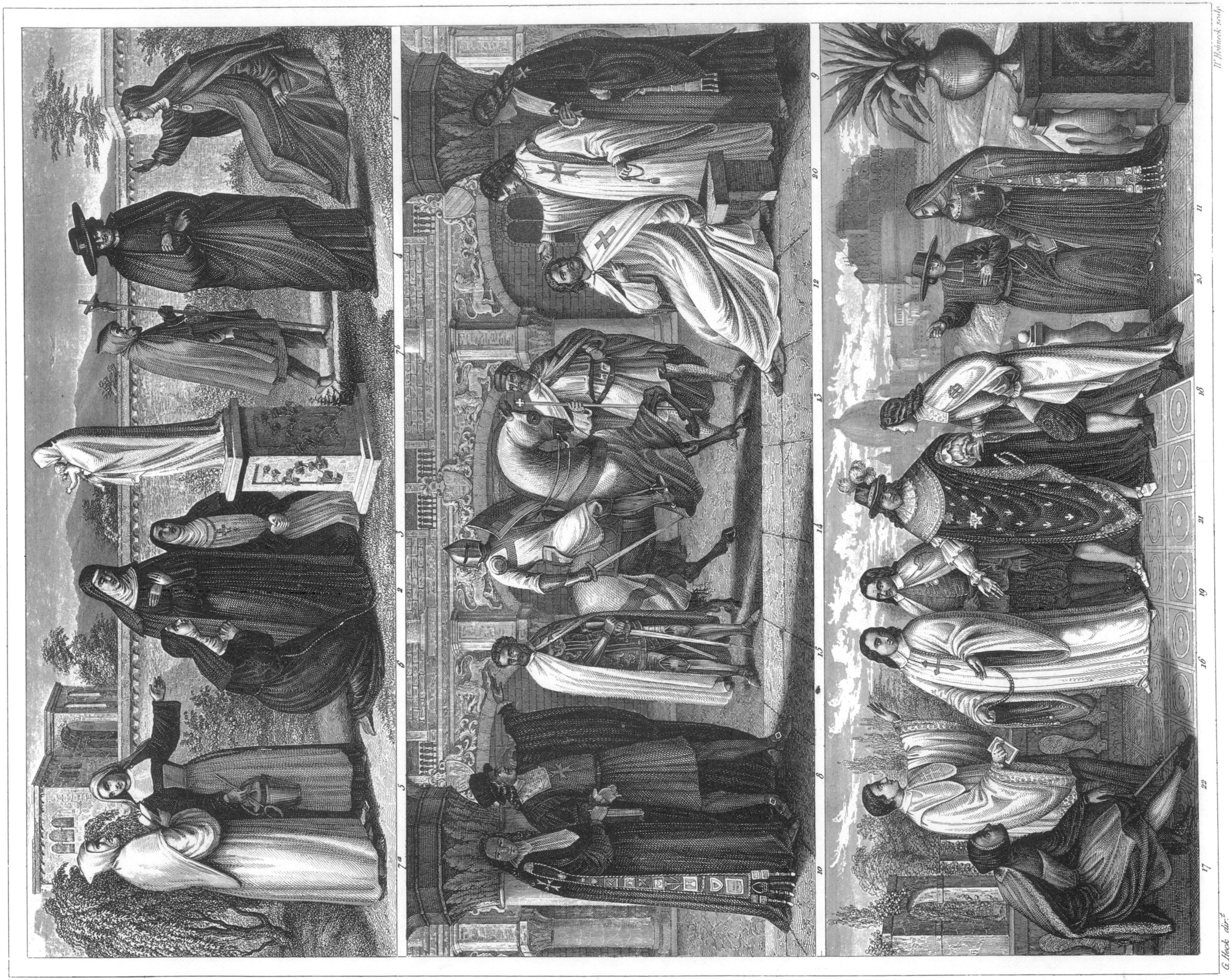

 PLATE 219. MEMBERS OF VARIOUS RELIGIOUS AND MILITARY ORDERS

G. Heck dir.ᵗ Henry Winkles sculpᵗ

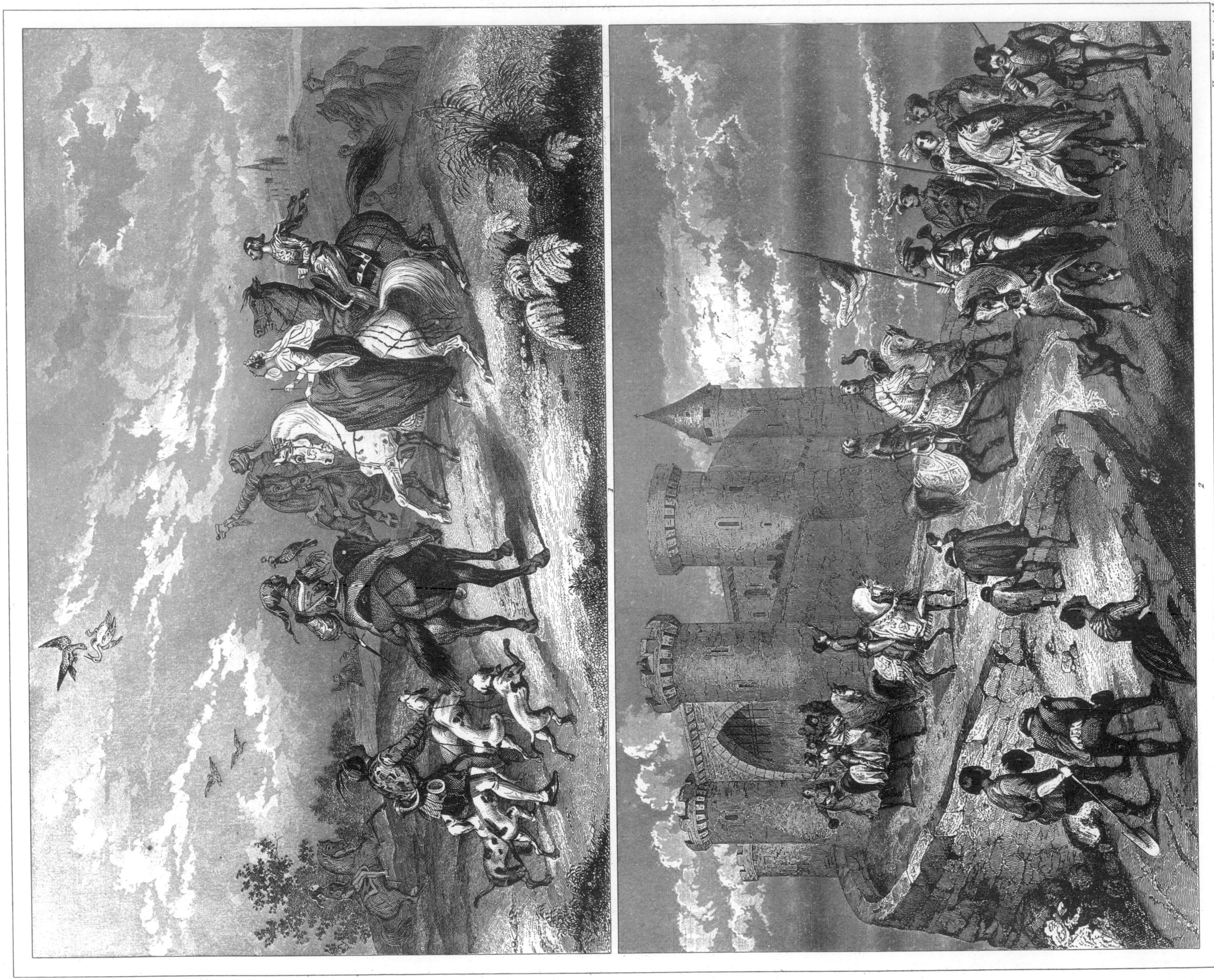

 PLATE 221. HAWKING AND CRUSADERS

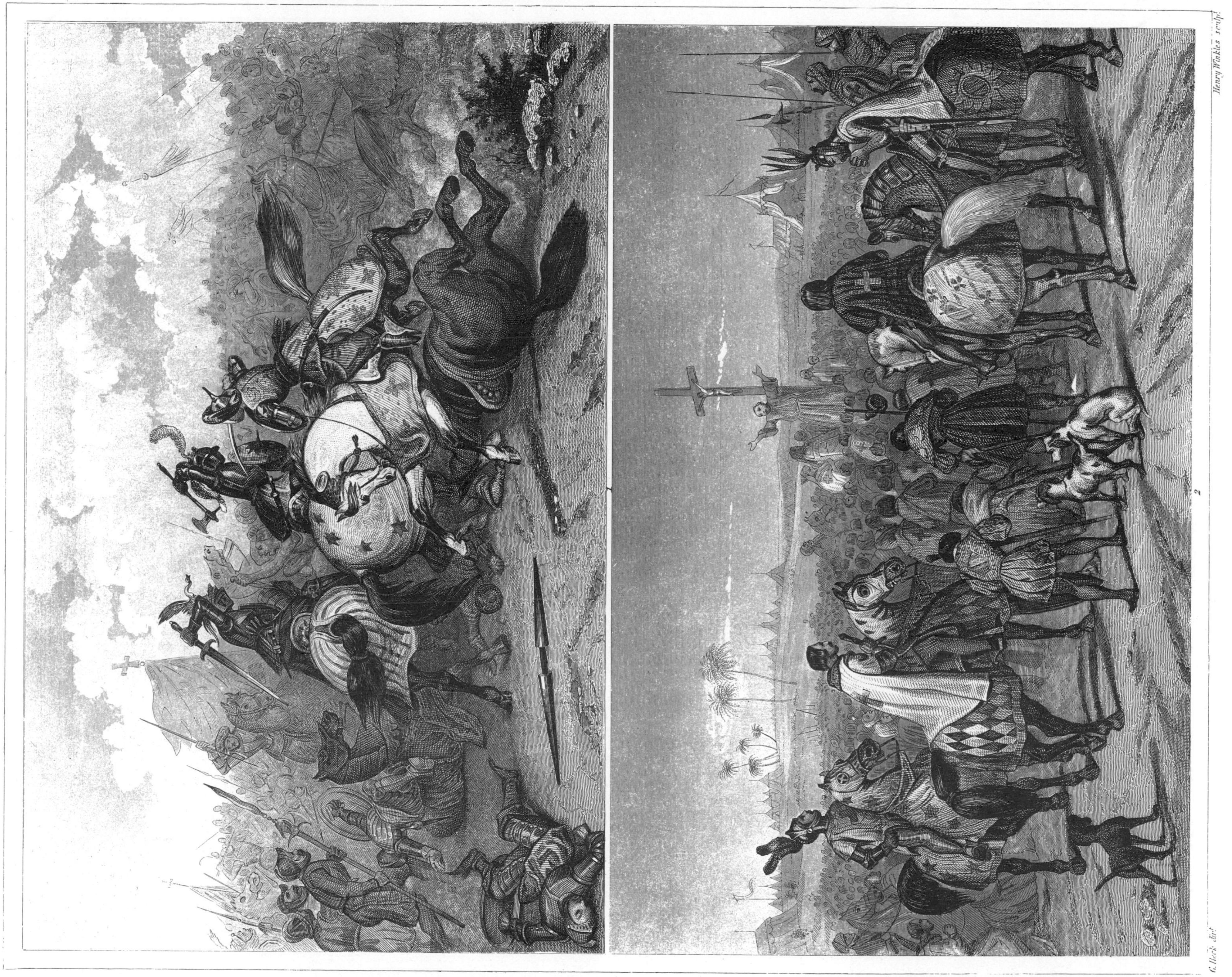

PLATE 222. CRUSADERS

 PLATE 223. KNIGHTS RETURNING FROM CRUSADE AND AT TOURNAMENT

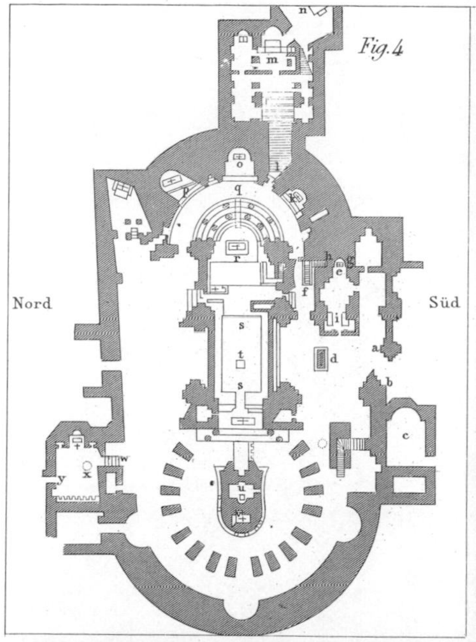

2

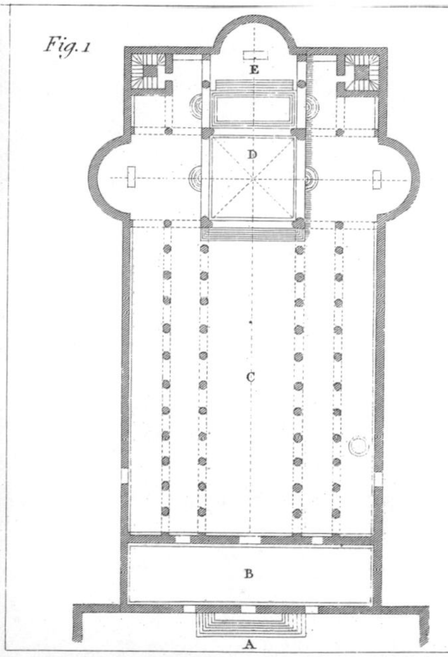

5

3

6

G. Heck dir.ᵗ

Henry Winkles sculp.ᵗ

PLATE 224. CHURCH OF THE HOLY SEPULCHRE AND CHURCH OF ST. MARY OF THE MANGER

 PLATE 225. THE FIVE PRINCIPAL RACES

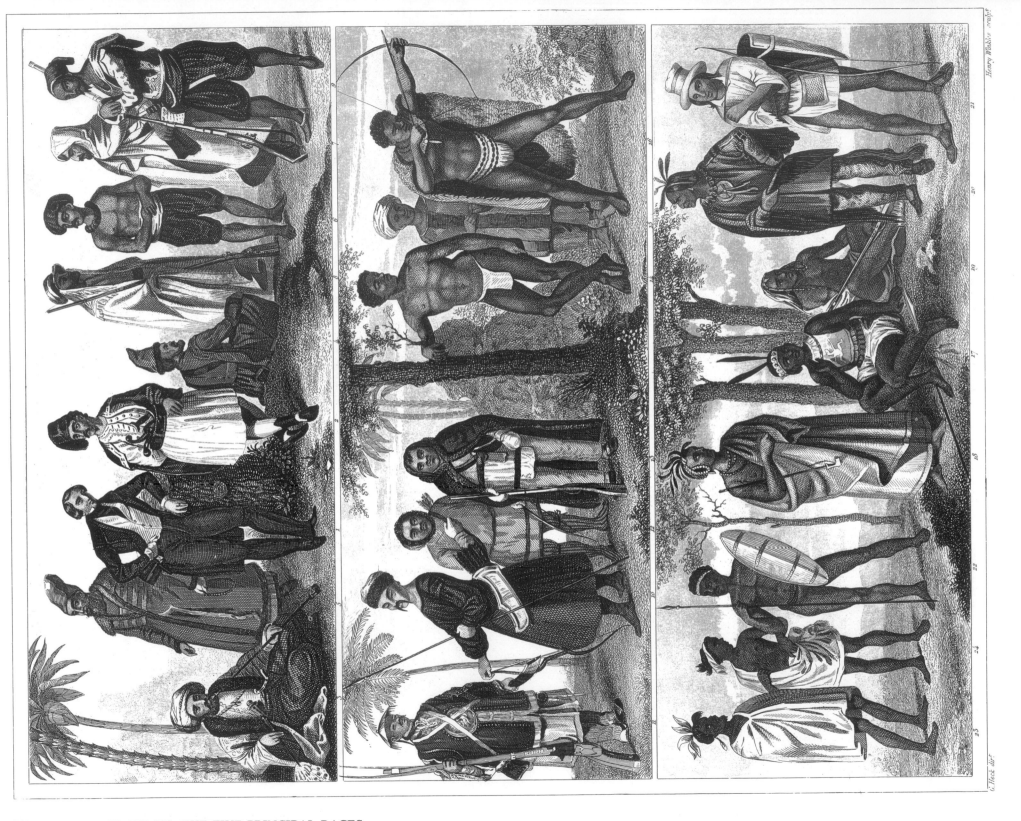

PLATE 226. GERMANIC PEOPLES

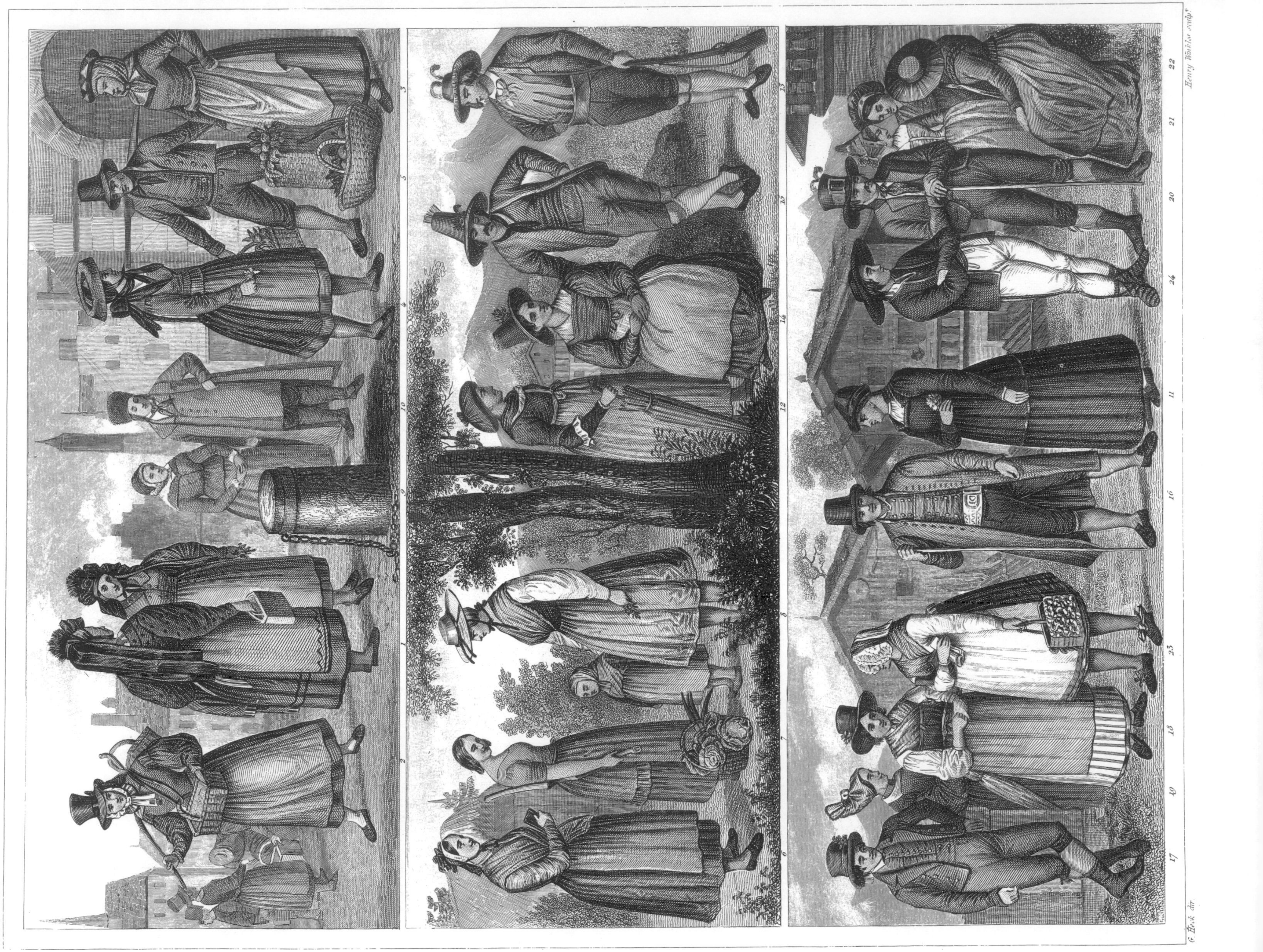

 PLATE 227. GERMANIC AND AUSTRIAN PEOPLES

PLATE 228. GYMNASIUM AND ACROBATICS

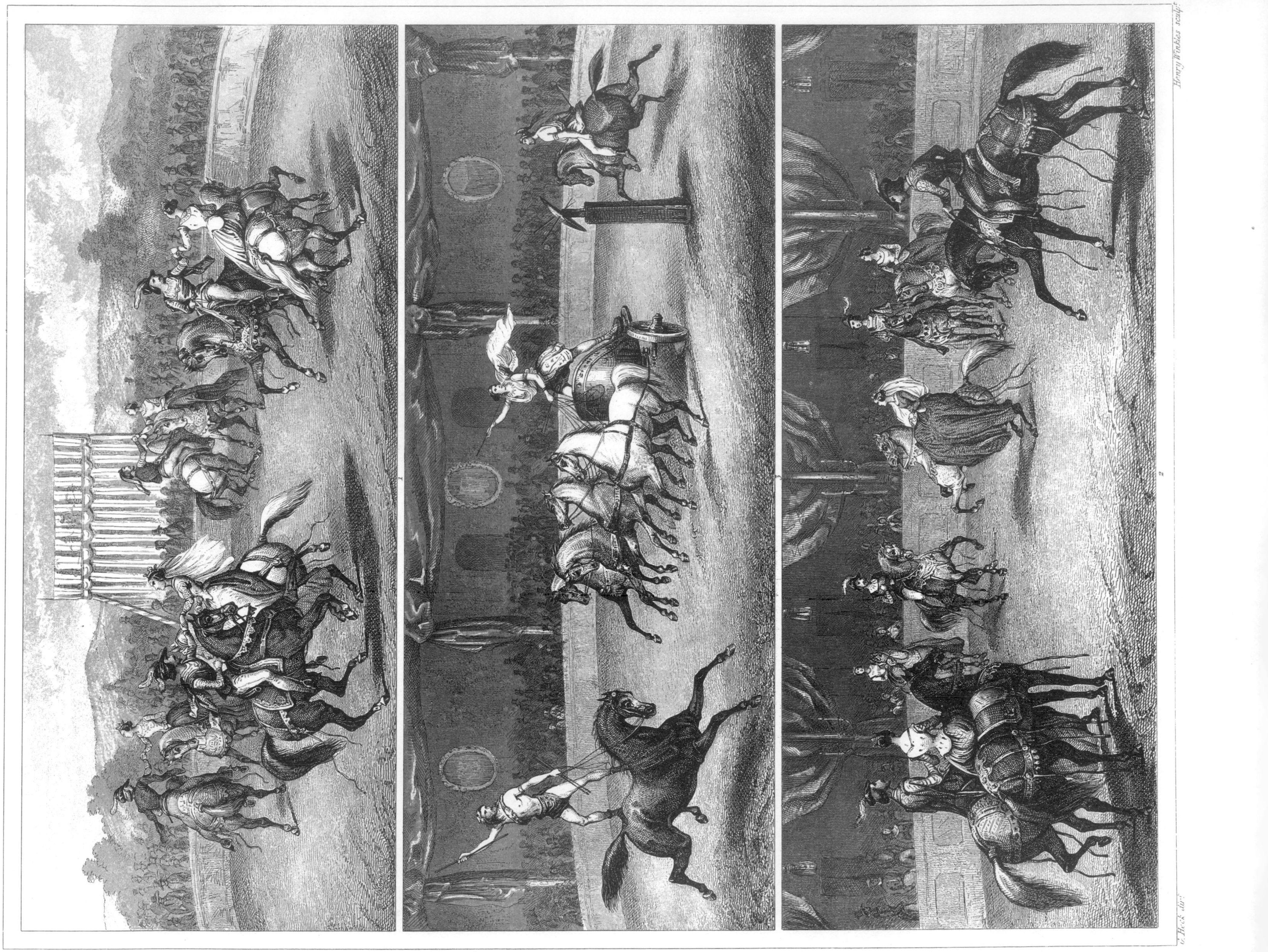

PLATE 229. EQUESTRIAN FEATS

PLATE 230. RACES AND A BALL

 PLATE 231. SCENES OF PUBLIC EVENTS

PLATE 232. OUTDOOR CELEBRATIONS

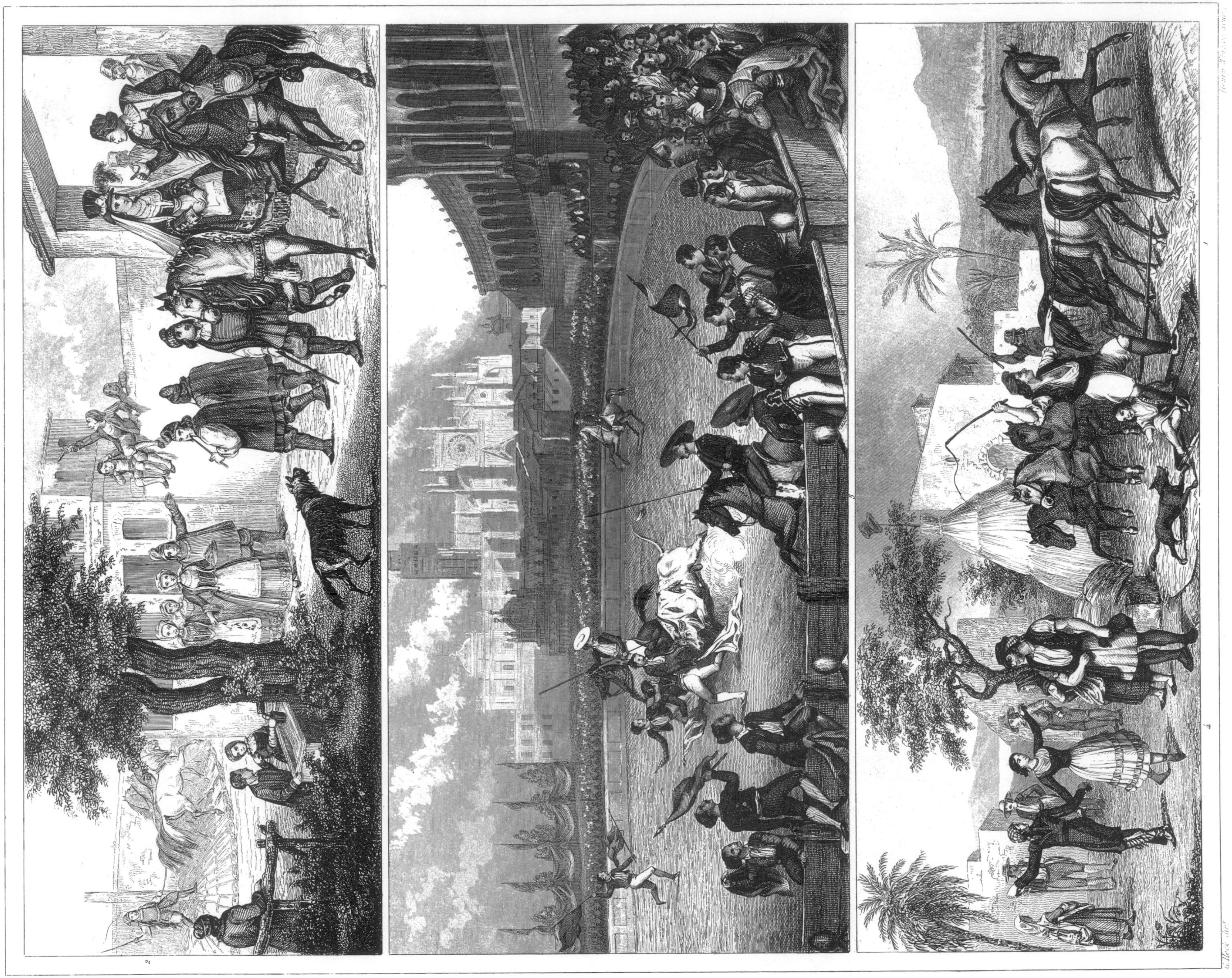

 PLATE 233. SPANISH AND SARDINIAN SCENES

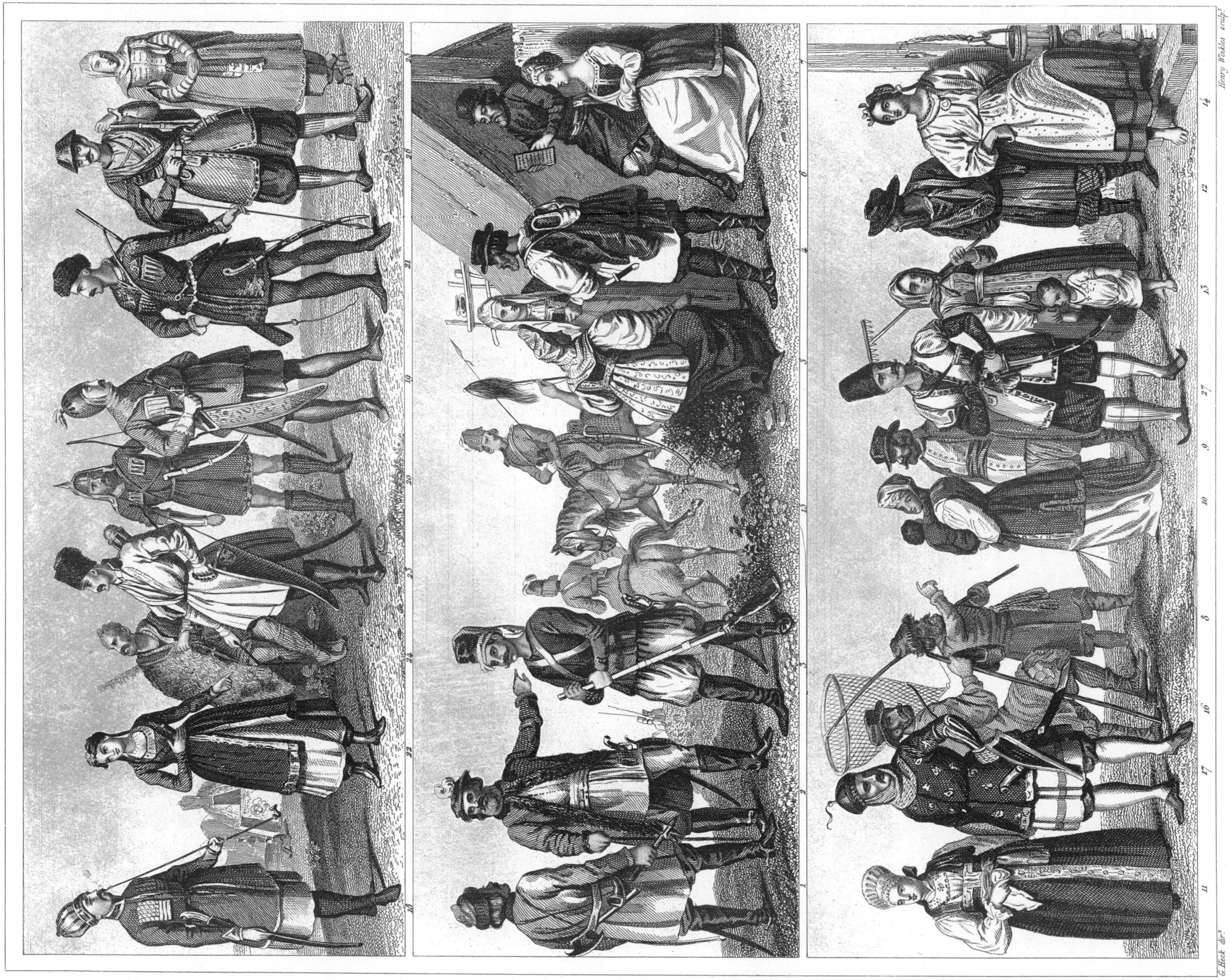

PLATE 234. RUSSIAN AND CAUCASIAN TRIBES

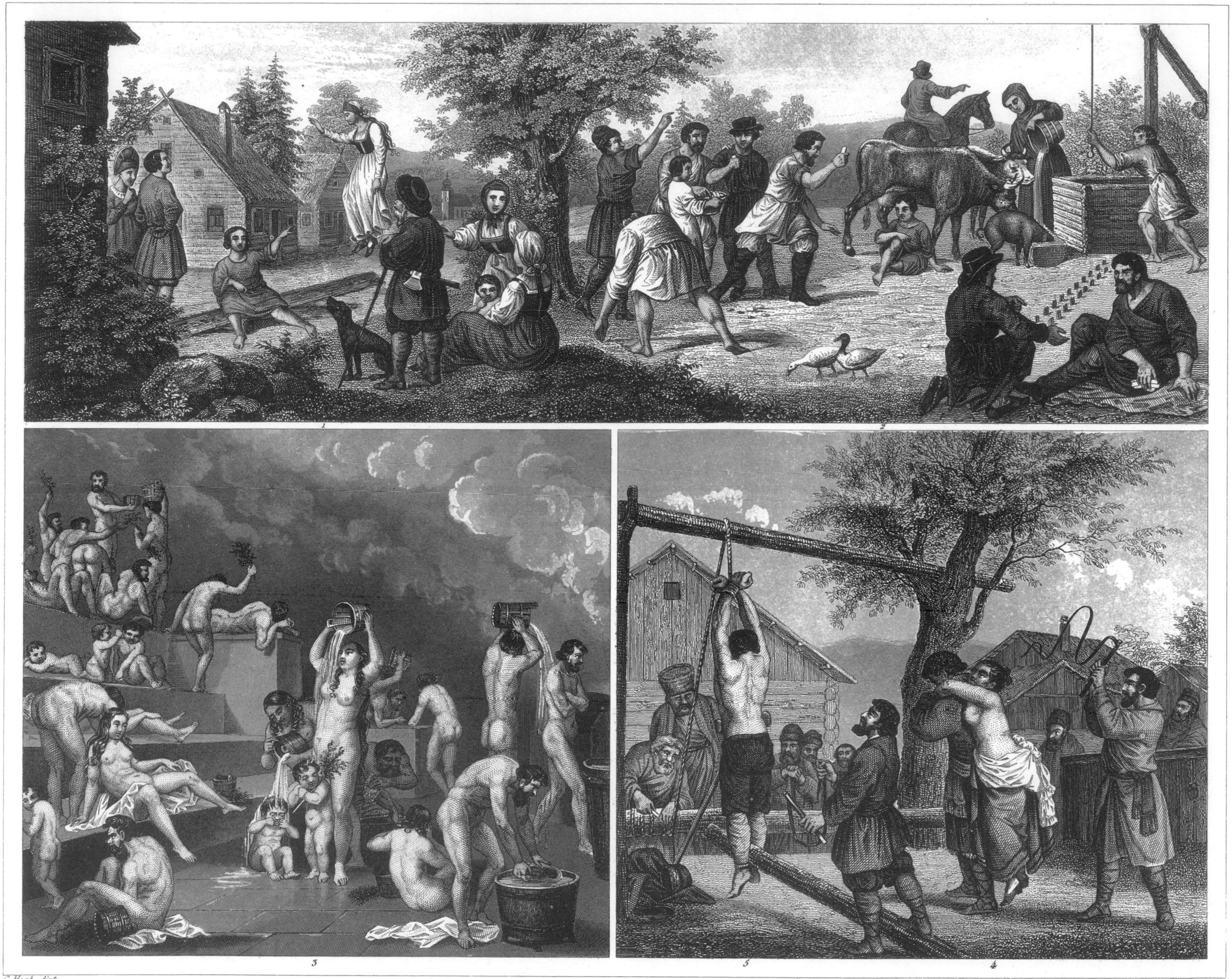

G. Heck dir.t Henry Winkles sculp.t

 PLATE 235. SCENES OF RUSSIAN LIFE

G. Heck dir.t Henry Winkles sculp.t

PLATE 236. SCENES OF RUSSIAN LIFE

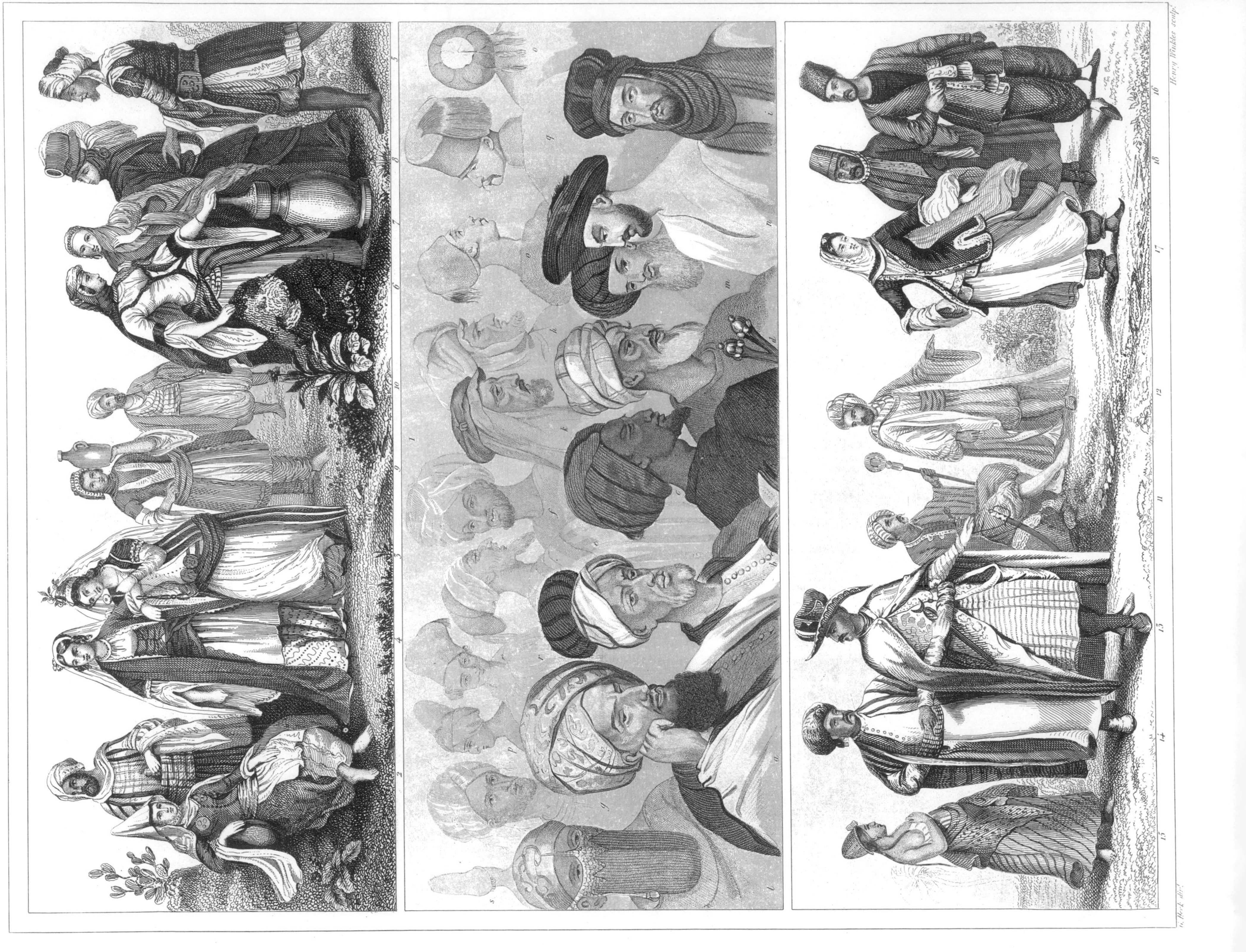

 PLATE 237. EASTERN PEOPLES AND COSTUMES

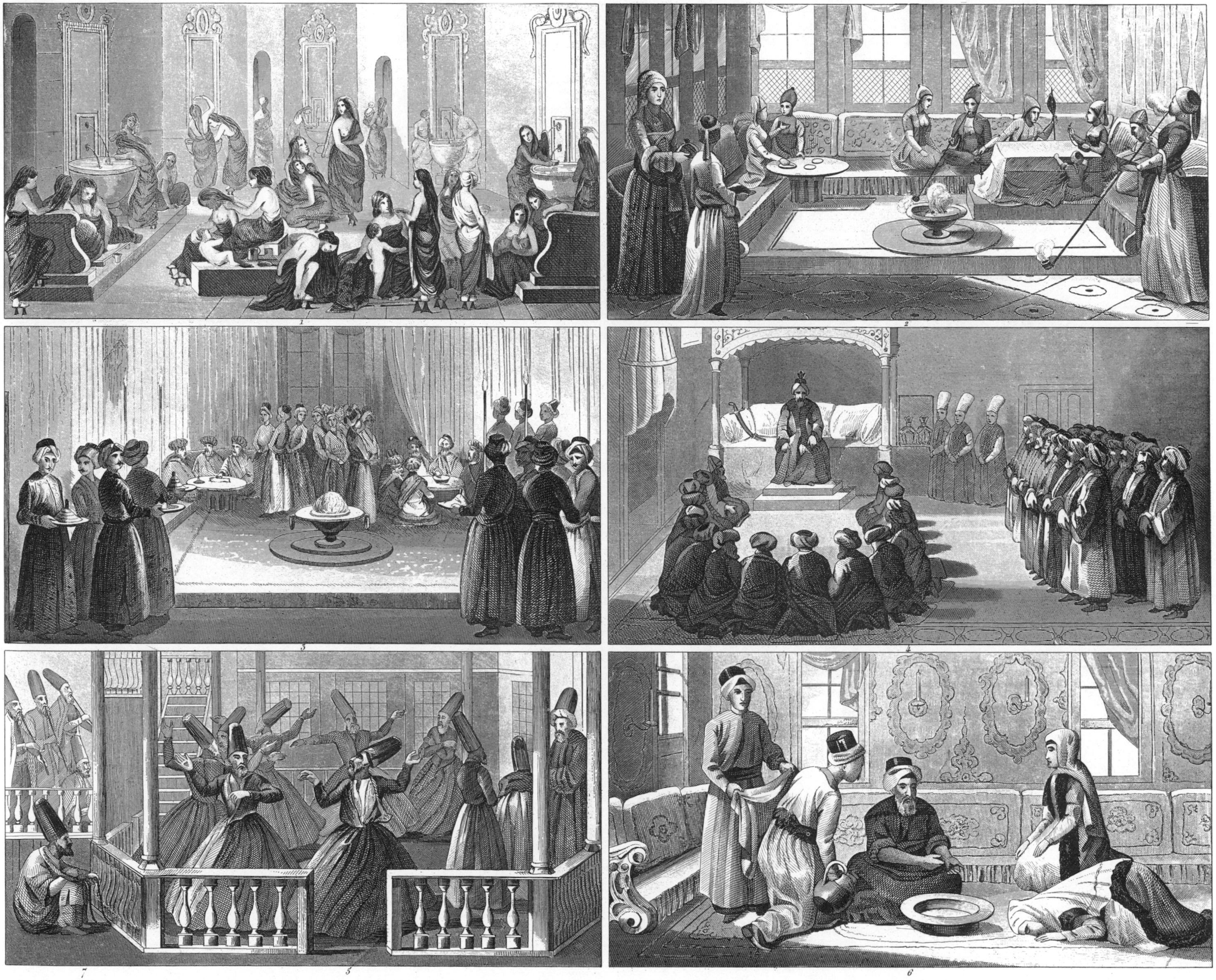

G. Heck dir.t Henry Winkles sculp.t

PLATE 238. SCENES FROM MIDDLE EASTERN LIFE

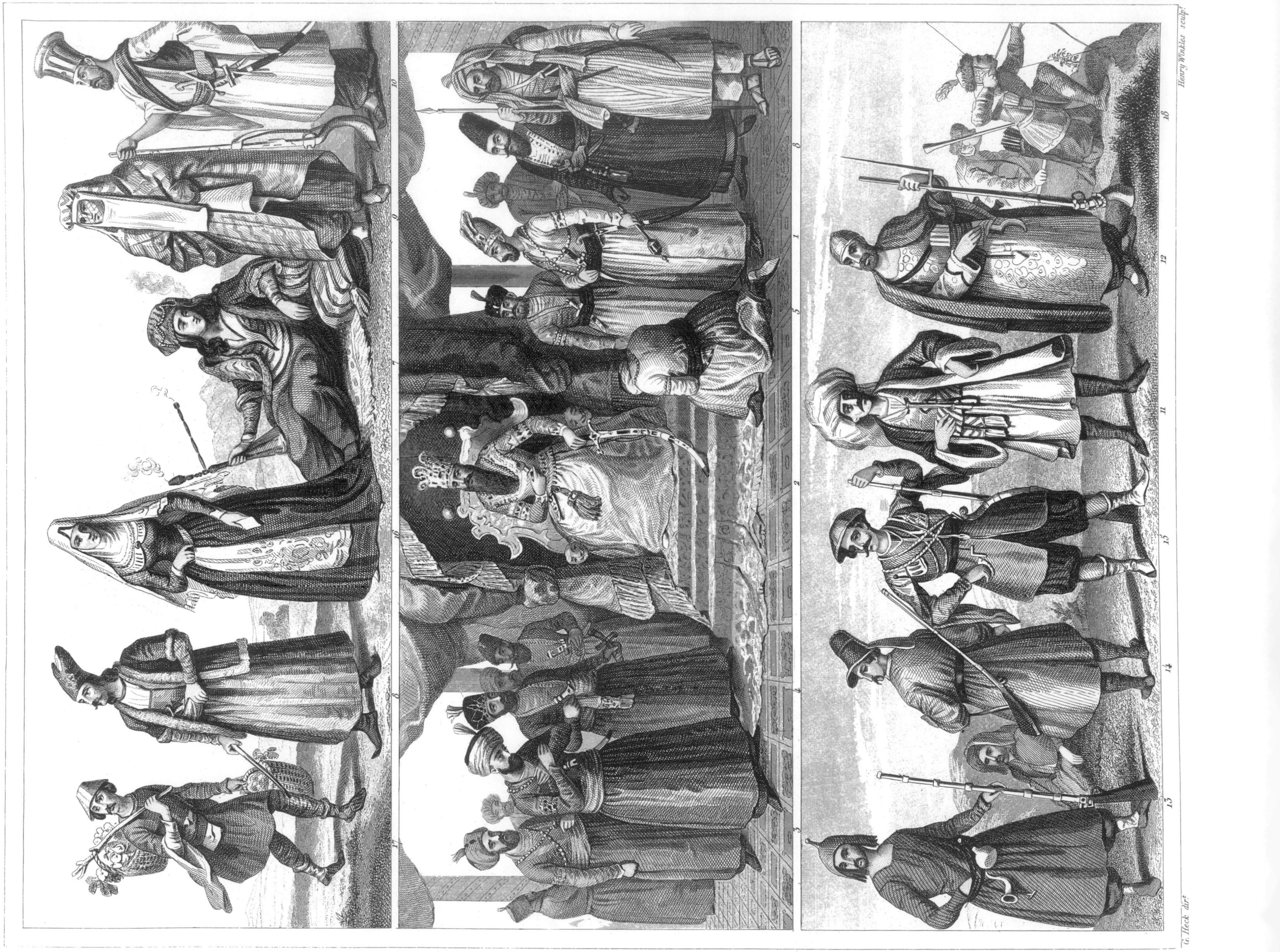

 PLATE 239. PERSIANS AND OTHER EASTERN PEOPLES

PLATE 240. SCENES OF EASTERN LIFE

G. Heck dir.^t Henry Winkles sculp.^t

PLATE 241. SCENES OF PERSIAN LIFE

1

2

G. Heck dir.^t

Winkles et Lehmann sculp.^t

 PLATE 243. EAST INDIAN AND ARABIAN SCENES

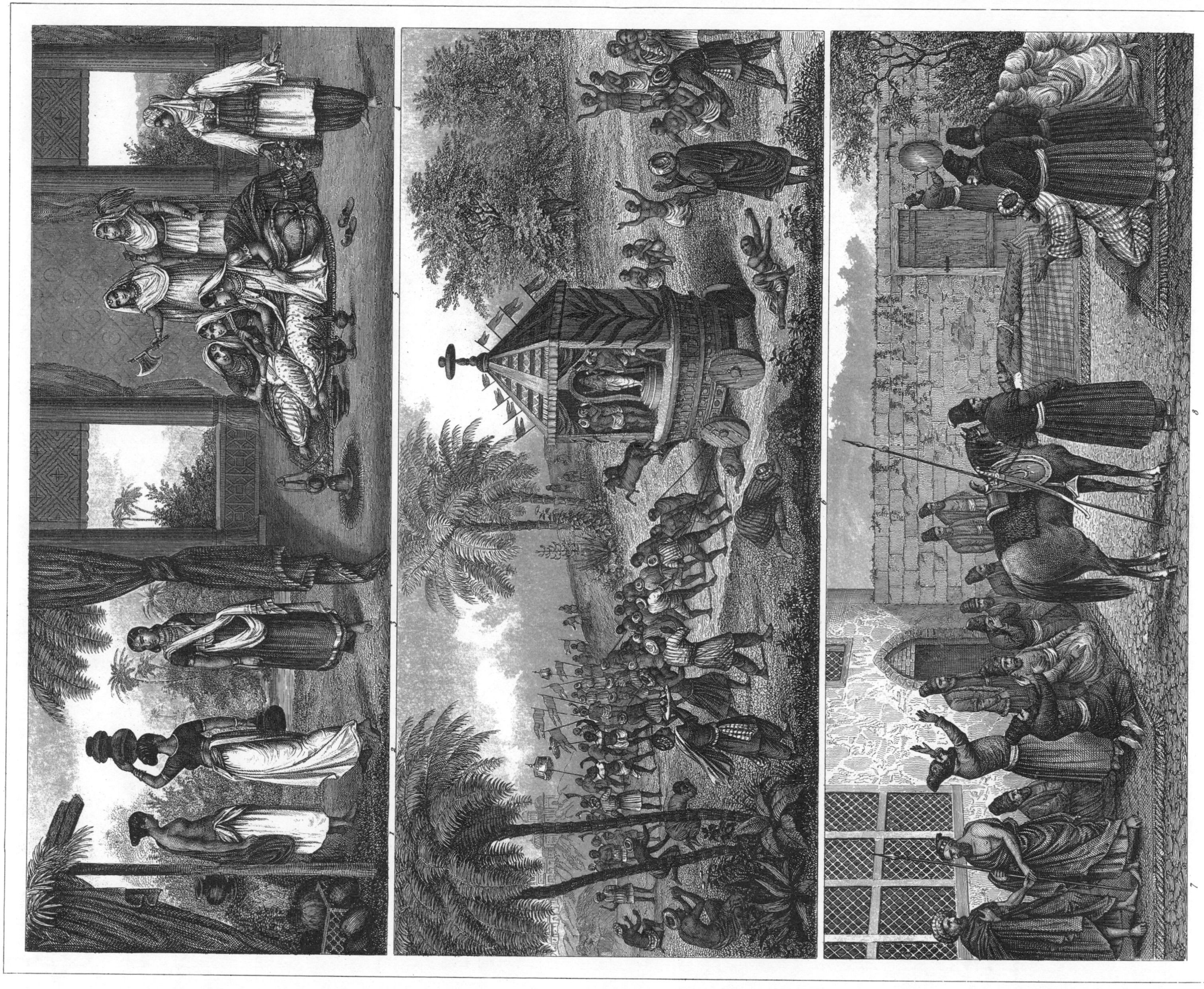

PLATE 244. SCENES FROM INDIAN, ARABIAN, AND PERSIAN LIFE

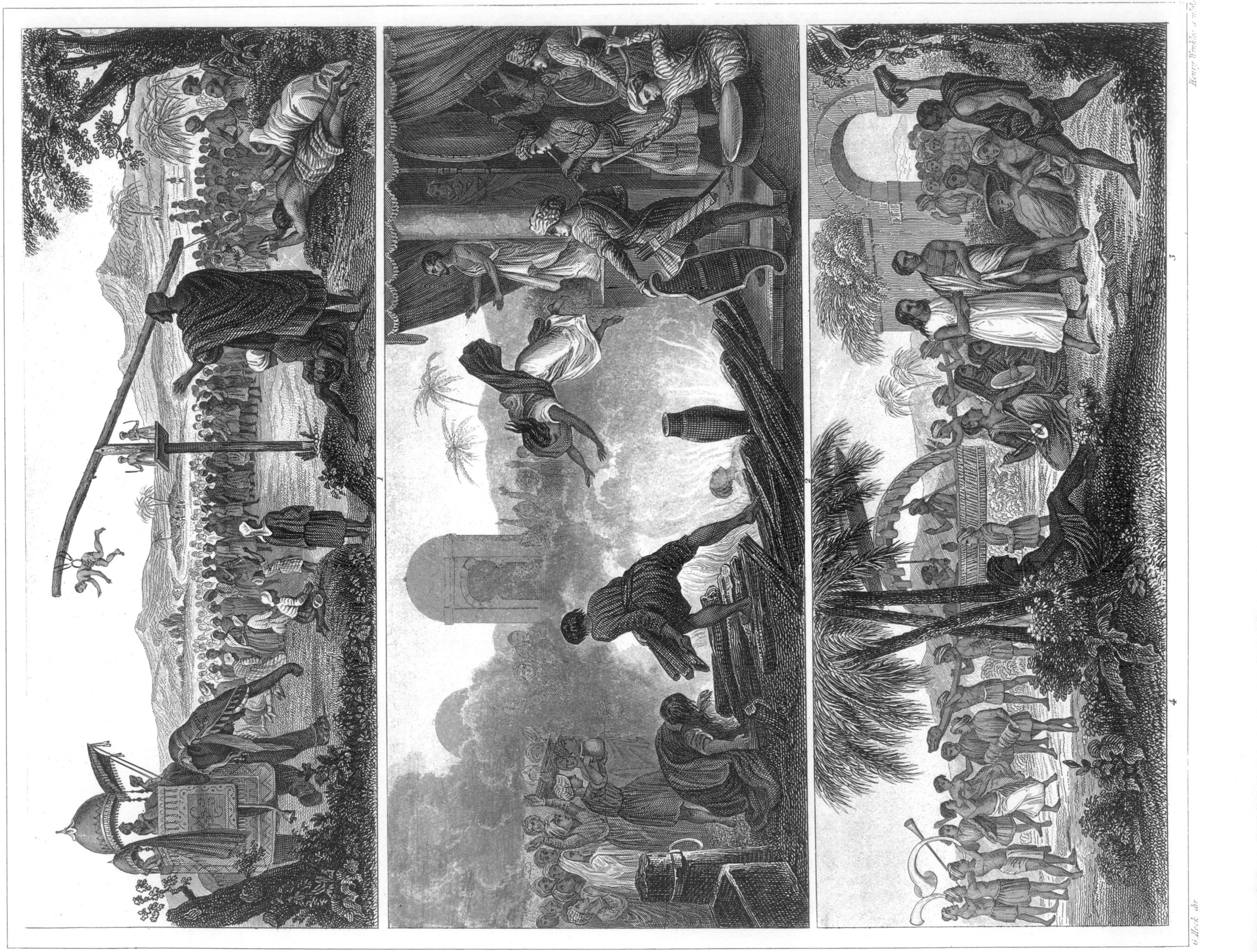

PLATE 245. HINDOO SCENES

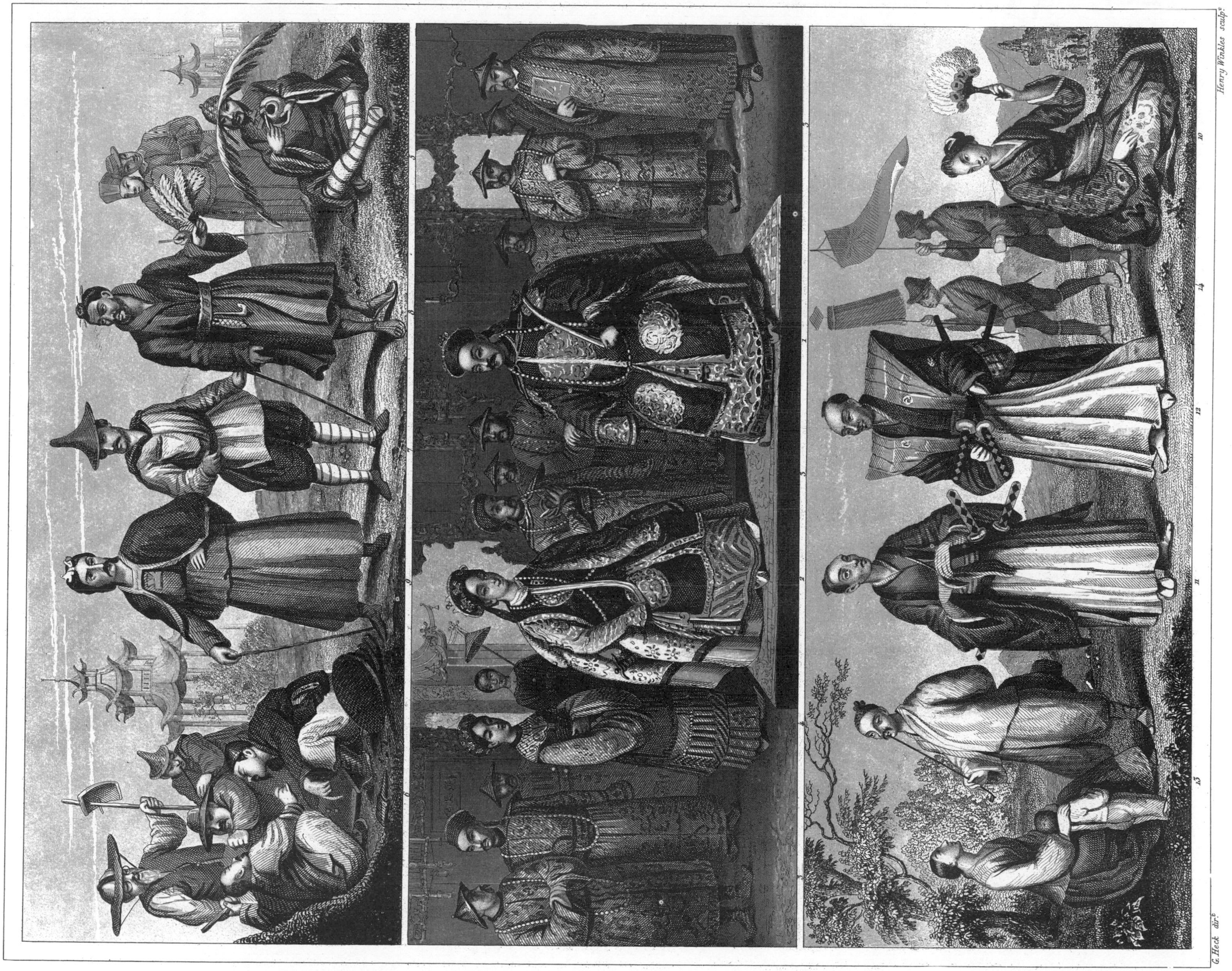

PLATE 246. ORIENTAL PEOPLES

 PLATE 247. SCENES FROM CHINESE LIFE

PLATE 248. CHINESE ENTERTAINMENT AND PUNISHMENT

PLATE 249. CHINESE STREET SCENES

PLATE 250. AFRICAN SCENES AND PEOPLES

 PLATE 251. ARABIAN AND EGYPTIAN SCENES

PLATE 252. PEOPLES OF AFRICAN TRIBES

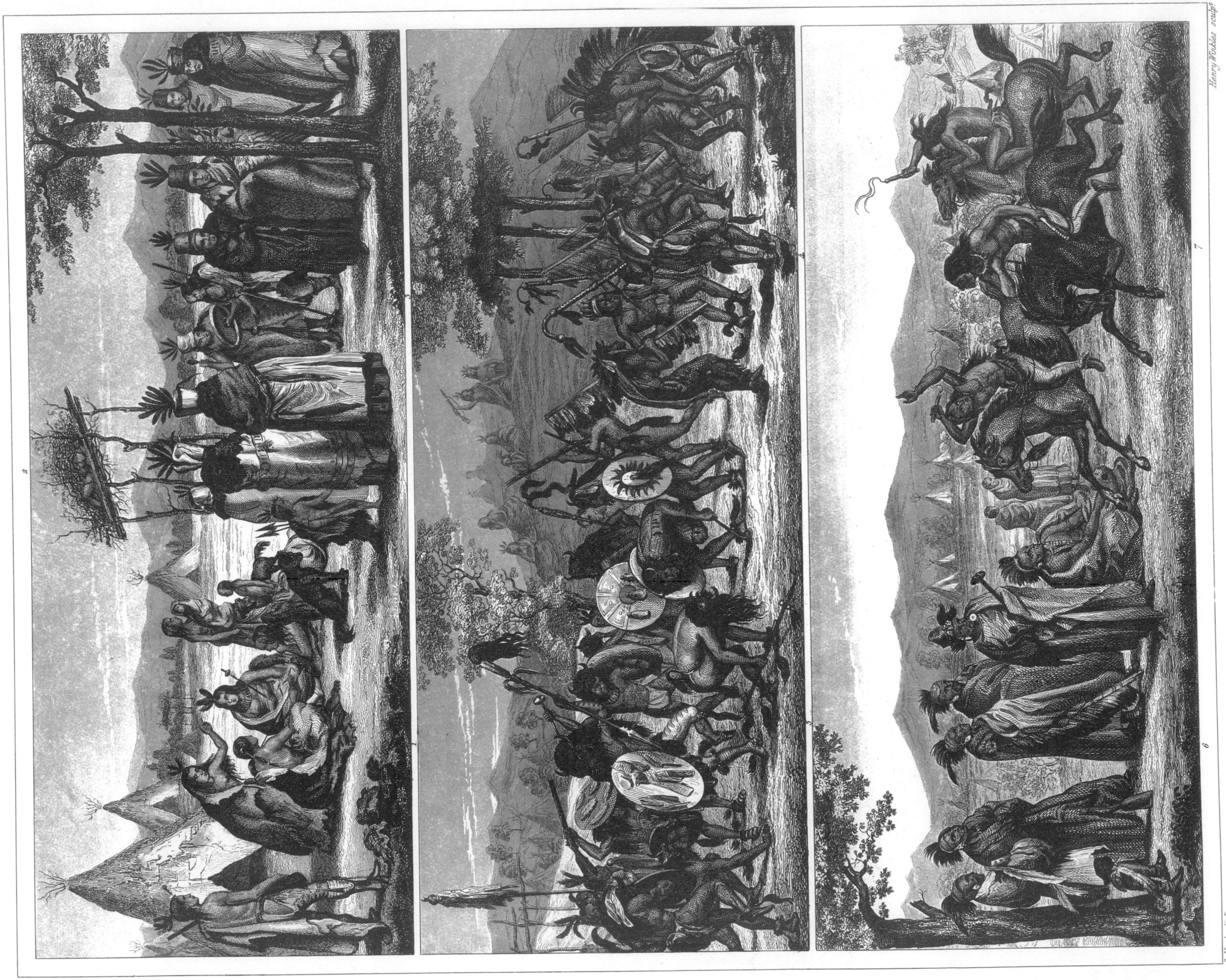

 PLATE 253. SPORTS OF INDIAN TRIBES

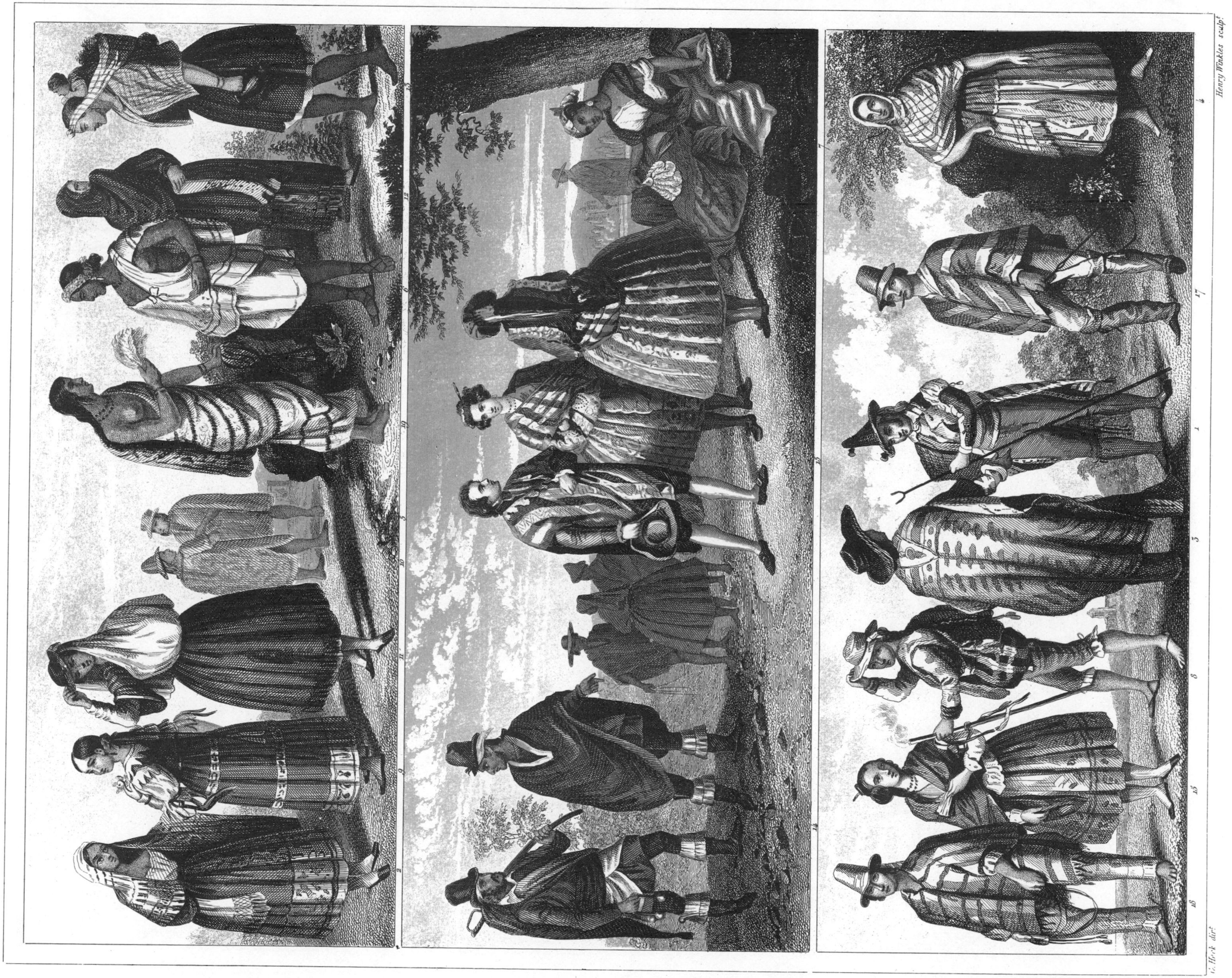

PLATE 254. PEOPLES AND COSTUMES OF MEXICO AND SOUTH AMERICA

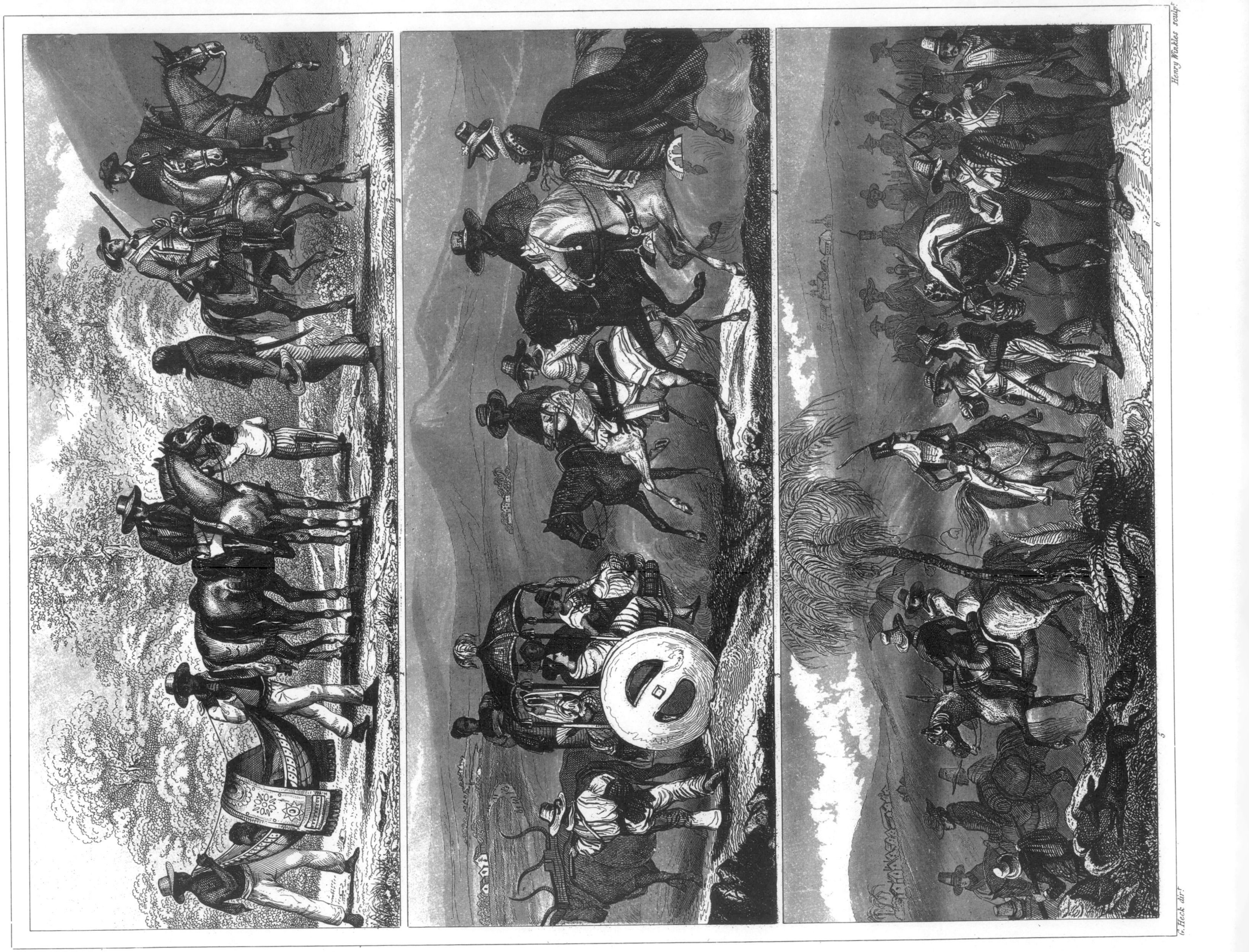

 PLATE 255. BRAZILIAN SCENES

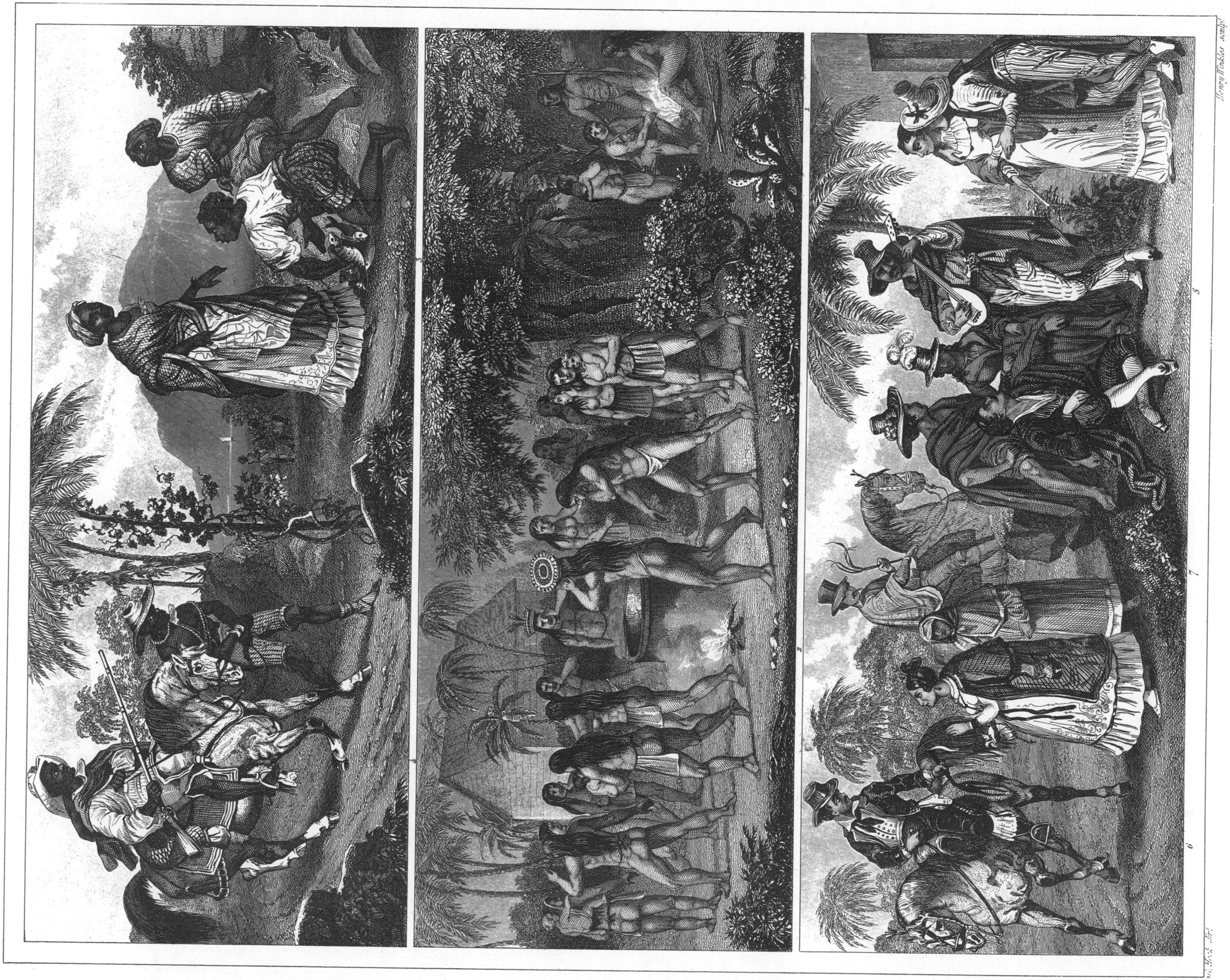

PLATE 256. VARIOUS SOUTH AMERICAN PEOPLES

 PLATE 257. LIFE IN BRAZIL AND PATAGONIA

PLATE 258. BRAZILIAN SLAVE TRADE

G. Heck dir.

Henry Winkles sculp.

 PLATE 259. SCENES FROM GREENLAND, BRAZIL, AND PATAGONIA

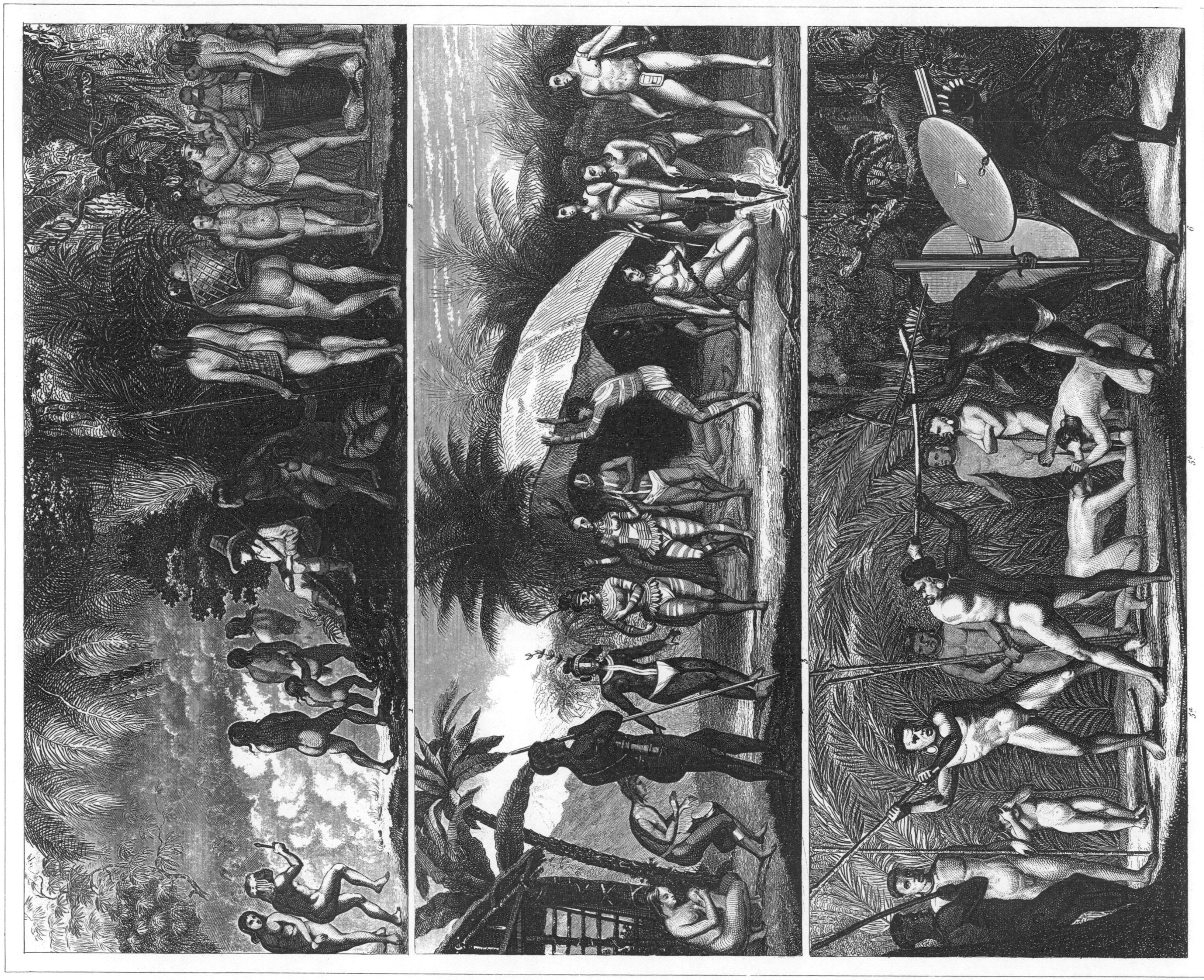

PLATE 260. SPORTS AND DUELS OF VARIOUS SOUTH AMERICAN INDIANS

G. Heck dir.^t Henry Winkles sculp.^t

PLATE 261. RITES AND CEREMONIES OF MEXICAN AND SOUTH AMERICAN INDIANS

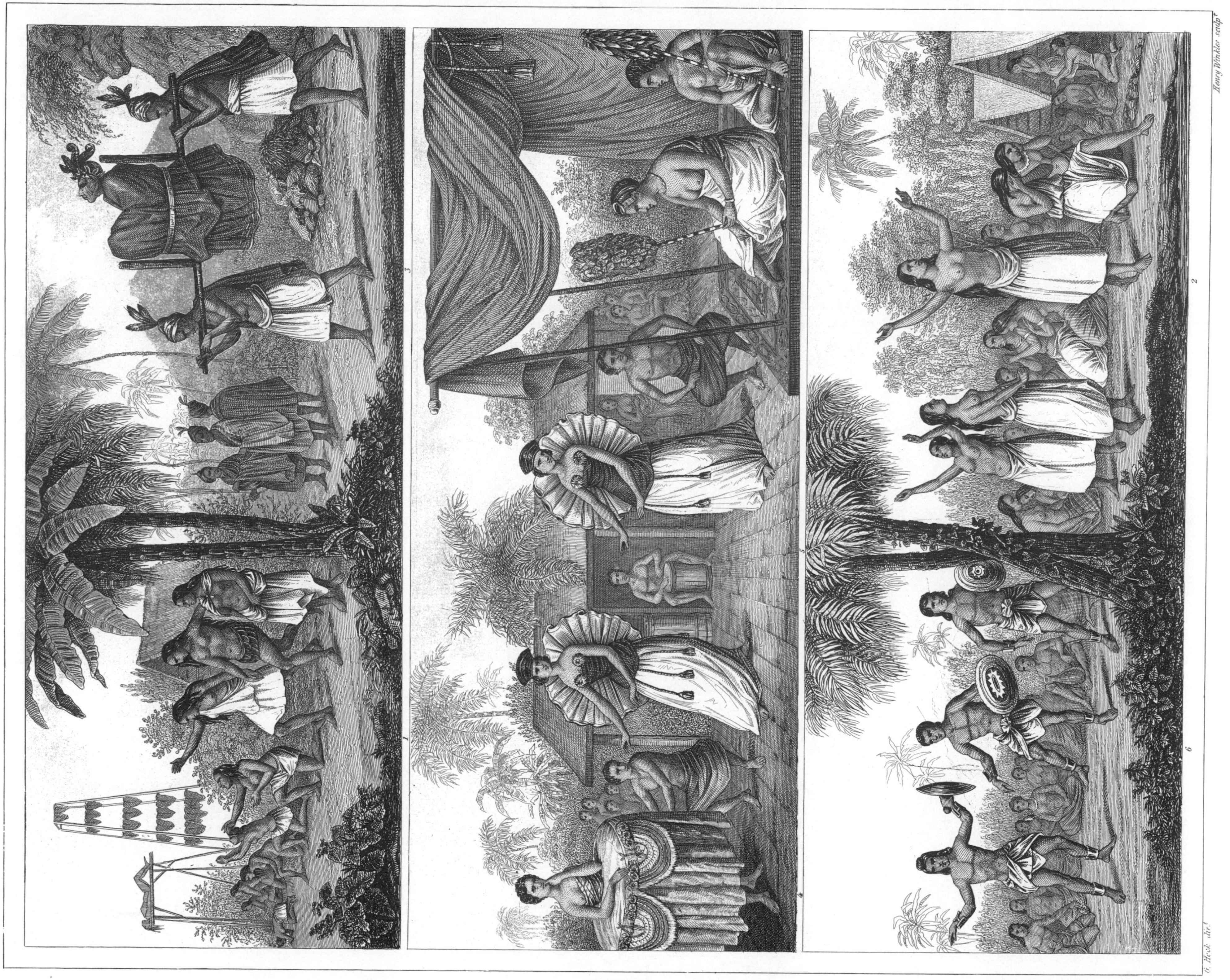

PLATE 262. SCENES OF THE PACIFIC

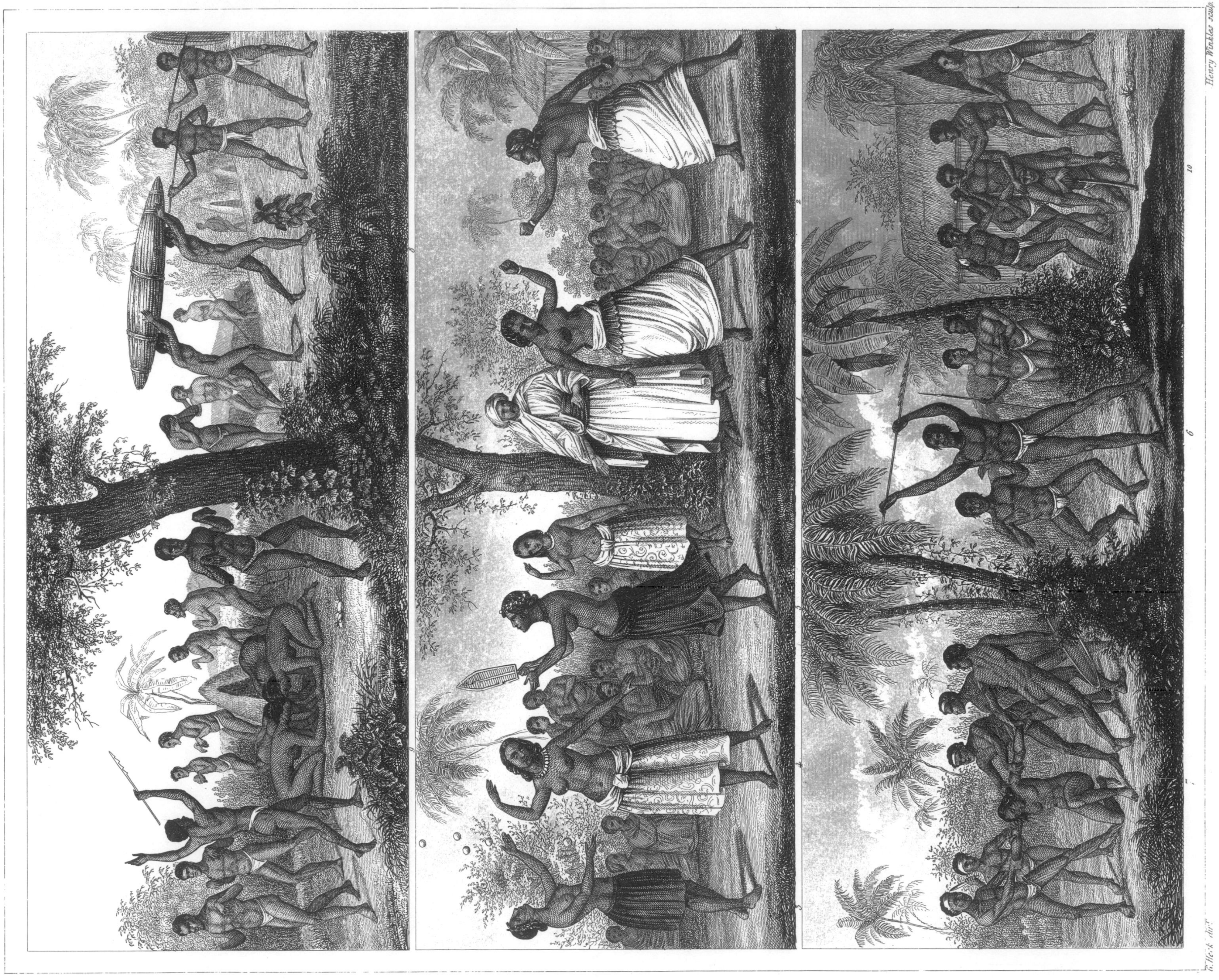

 PLATE 263. SCENES OF AUSTRALIAN AND POLYNESIAN NATIVES

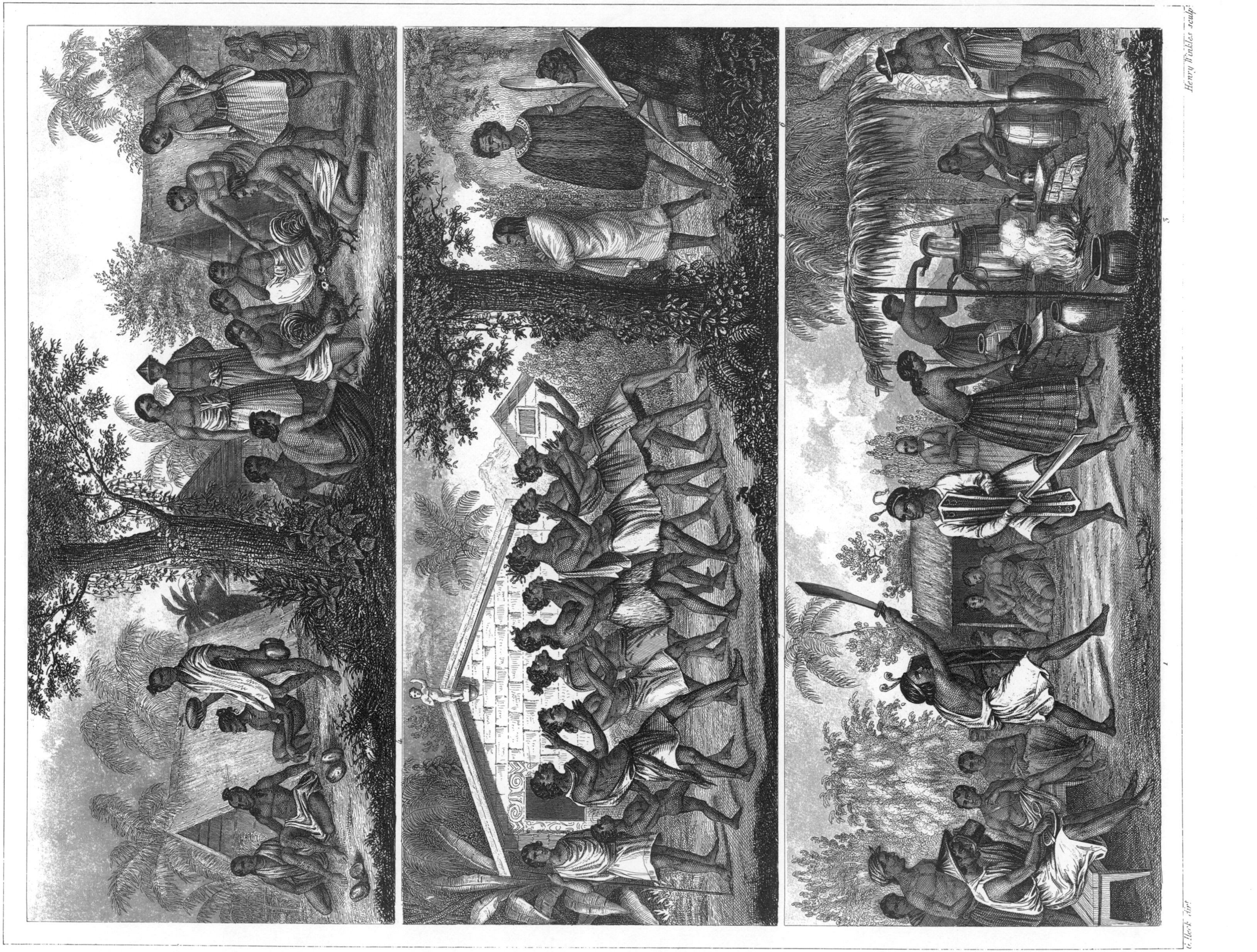

PLATE 264. NATIVES OF THE SOUTH PACIFIC

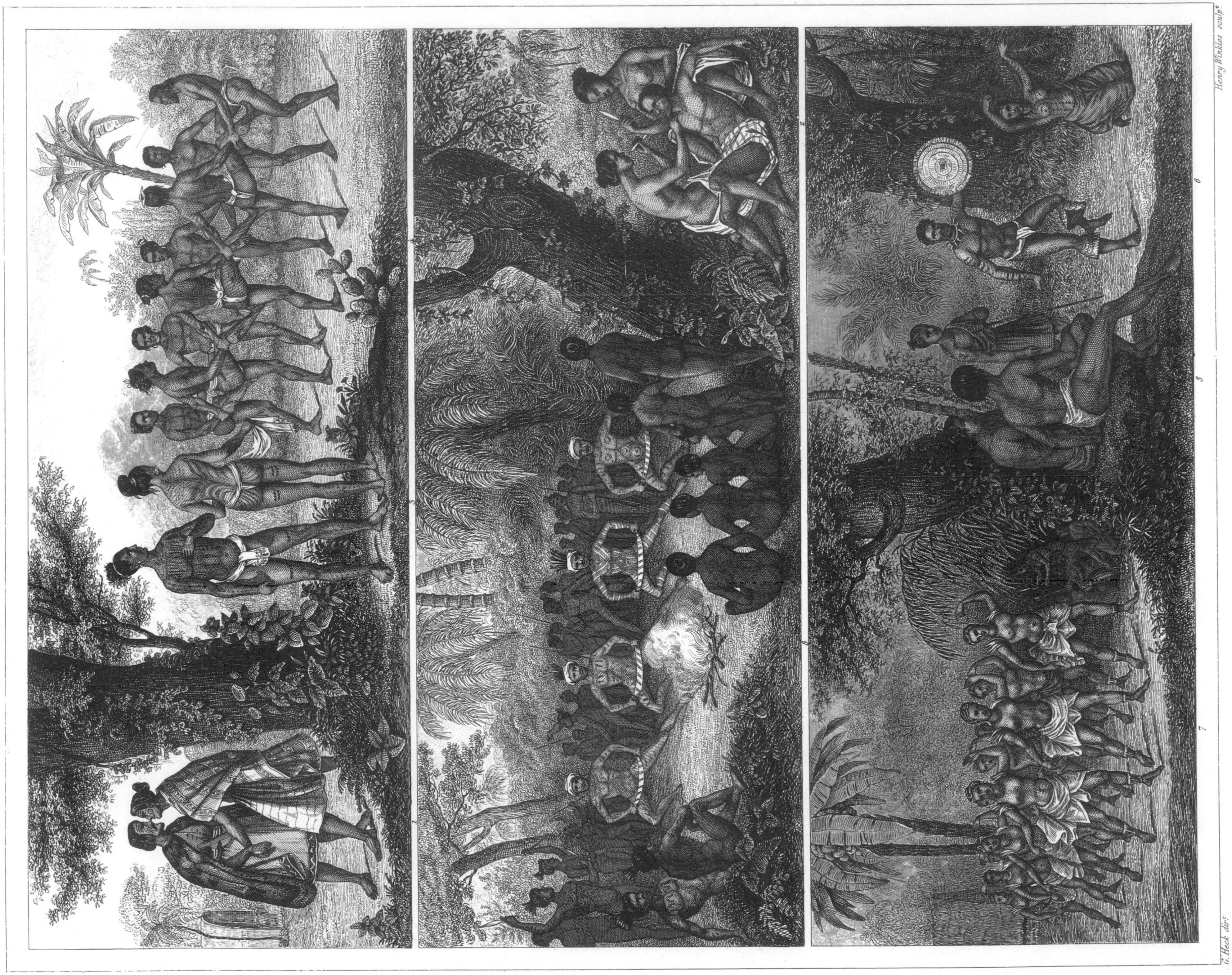

 PLATE 265. RITES AND CEREMONIES OF THE PACIFIC

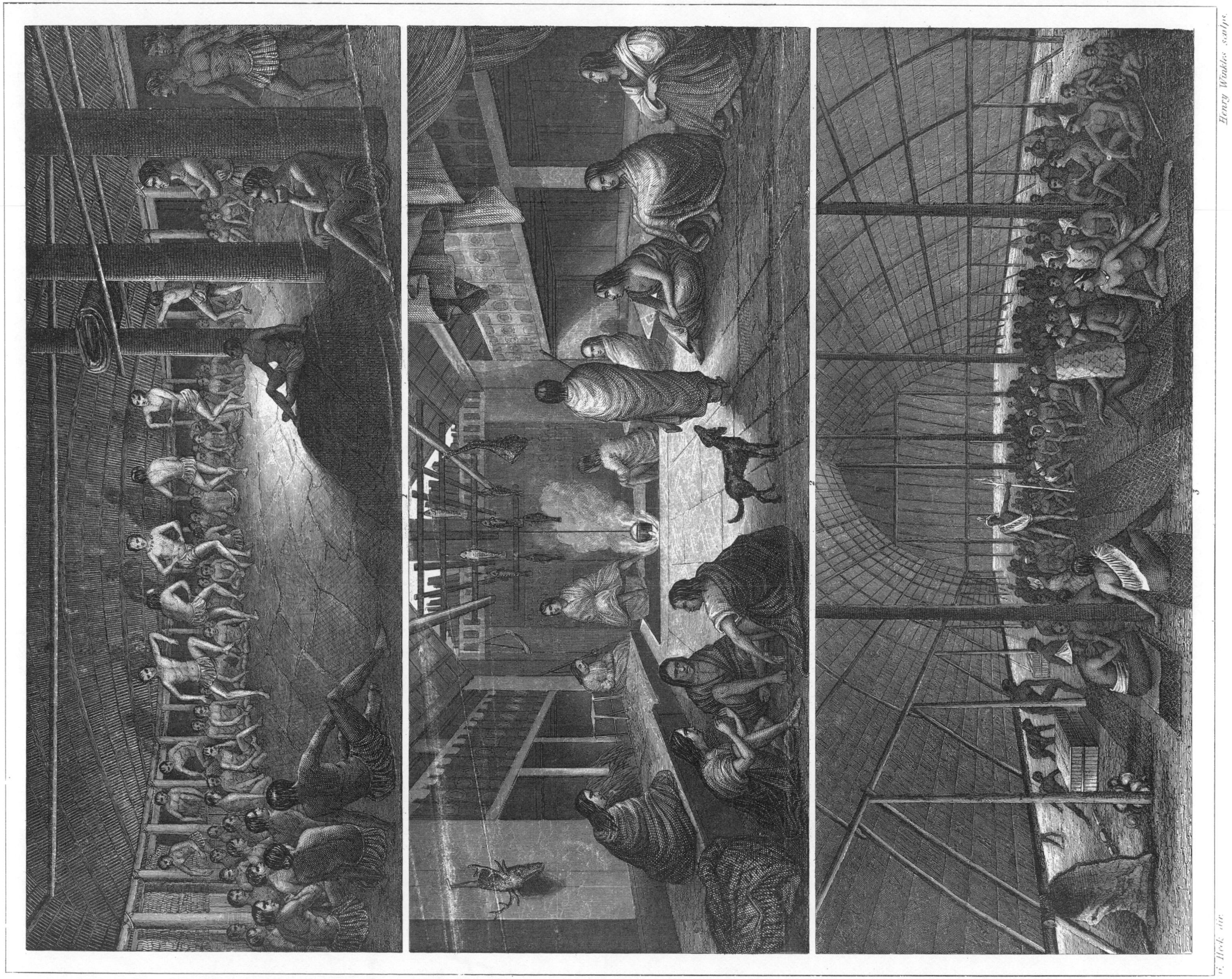

PLATE 266. SCENES FROM THE LIVES OF VARIOUS INDIAN TRIBES

MILITARY SCIENCES

Captions to the Military Sciences Plates, 267–317

PLATE 267.
Weapons of the Egyptians, Medes, and Persians

Figure
1–22. Weapons of the Egyptians
23–56. Weapons of the Medes and Persians

PLATE 268.
Greek and Etruscan Warriors

Figure
1. Grecian hero
2. Amazon from the Black Sea
3–8. Grecian warriors on foot
9. Grecian trumpeter
10. Grecian combat
11. Grecian herald
12, 13. Grecian horsemen
14. Etruscan archer
15. Etruscan hornblower
16–18. Etruscan soldiers

PLATE 269.
Weapons of the Greeks, Etruscans, and Romans

Figure
1–21. Weapons of the Greeks
22–35. Weapons of the Etruscans
36–43. Weapons of the Romans

PLATE 270.
Greek and Roman Troop Movements

Figure
1–30. Illustrating the movements of Grecian troops
31–51. Illustrating the movements of Roman troops

PLATE 271.
Scenes of Ancient Warriors

Figure
1. Grecian funeral and death feast
2. Roman imperator and suite
3. The war-elephant in combat
4. Armed chariot

PLATE 272.
Ceremonial Processions

Figure
1. Funeral procession of Alexander the Great
2. Triumphal procession of a Roman general

PLATE 273.
Ranks and Allies of the Roman Army

Figure
1–5. Roman Italian allies
6, 7. German allies
8. Roman trumpeter
9. Roman hornblower
10. Roman slinger
11. Roman lancers
12. Velites
13–19. Various ranks in the Roman army

PLATE 274.
Soldiers and Officers of Roman Times

Figure
1. Roman imperator
2. Roman general
3. Roman lictor
4. The Imperator's body-guard
5. Sarmatian mailed horseman
6. Roman legate
7. Roman standard-bearers
8. Roman decurion of cavalry
9. Roman cavalry soldier

PLATE 275.
Ancient and Medieval Weapons and Armaments

Figure
1–46. Weapons of the Gauls, Franks, Germans, Britons, Anglo-Saxons, and Anglo-Danes
47. Roman saddle
48. Anglo-Saxon saddle
49–62. Various saddles of the middle ages
63, 64. Spurs of the fourteenth century

PLATE 276.
Military Trappings of Ancient Rome

Figure
1, 2. Roman legion eagles
3, 4. Standards
5–15. Field badges
16–23. Honorary crowns
24, 25. Honorary medals
26, 27. Trophies
28. Trajan's column

PLATE 277.
Military Ceremonies and Processions of Rome

Figure
1. Roman prisoners passing under the yoke
2. Roman victor thanking the army
3–5. Triumphal processions

PLATE 278.
Military Life of the Germanic Tribes

Figure
1. The war dance of German youths
2. Ceremony of bestowing the right to bear arms
3. Ceremony of soothsaying before battle
4. Germans in combat

PLATE 279.
Roman and Carthaginian Military Formations

Figure
1. Roman camp
2. Roman order of battle
3. The solid wedge
4. The boar's head
5. The tortoise
6. Carthaginian order of battle with elephants

PLATE 280.
Medieval War Scenes

Figure
1. Decimation of prisoners
2. Election of commander
3. Combat of infantry against cavalry

PLATE 281.
Weapons of the Germans, Normans, Anglo-Saxons, and Danes

Figures 1–77.

PLATE 282.
Armor of the Middle Ages

Figures 1–23.

PLATE 283.
Medieval Armor and Tournaments

Figure
1. Emperor's suit of armor
2. Elector's suit of armor
3, 4. Knights' armor
5, 6. Footsoldiers
7–10. Tourney equipments
11. Awarding the prize at a tourney

PLATE 284.
Military Dignitaries and War Camps

Figure
1–10. Different dignitaries of the war-ban
11. The marching forth of an army from its camp

PLATE 285.
Prussian and French Infantry

Upper Division

Figure
1–14. Prussian infantry

Lower Division

Figure
1–12. French infantry

PLATE 286.
Prussian and French Cavalry

Upper Division

Figure
1–10. Prussian cavalry

Lower Division

Figure
11–19. French cavalry

PLATE 287.
Austrian and British Infantry

Upper Division

Figure
1–8. Austrian infantry

Lower Division

Figure
1–11. British infantry

PLATE 288.
British and Belgian Cavalry

Figure
1–9. British cavalry
10–20. Belgian cavalry, artillery, and engineers

PLATE 289.
Turkish Troops

Figure
1–10. Troops of the older Turkish military system
11–17. Modern Turkish army

PLATE 290.
Scenes from Turkish Military Life

Figure
1. Turkish pasha and suite
2. Encampment of a pasha of three tails

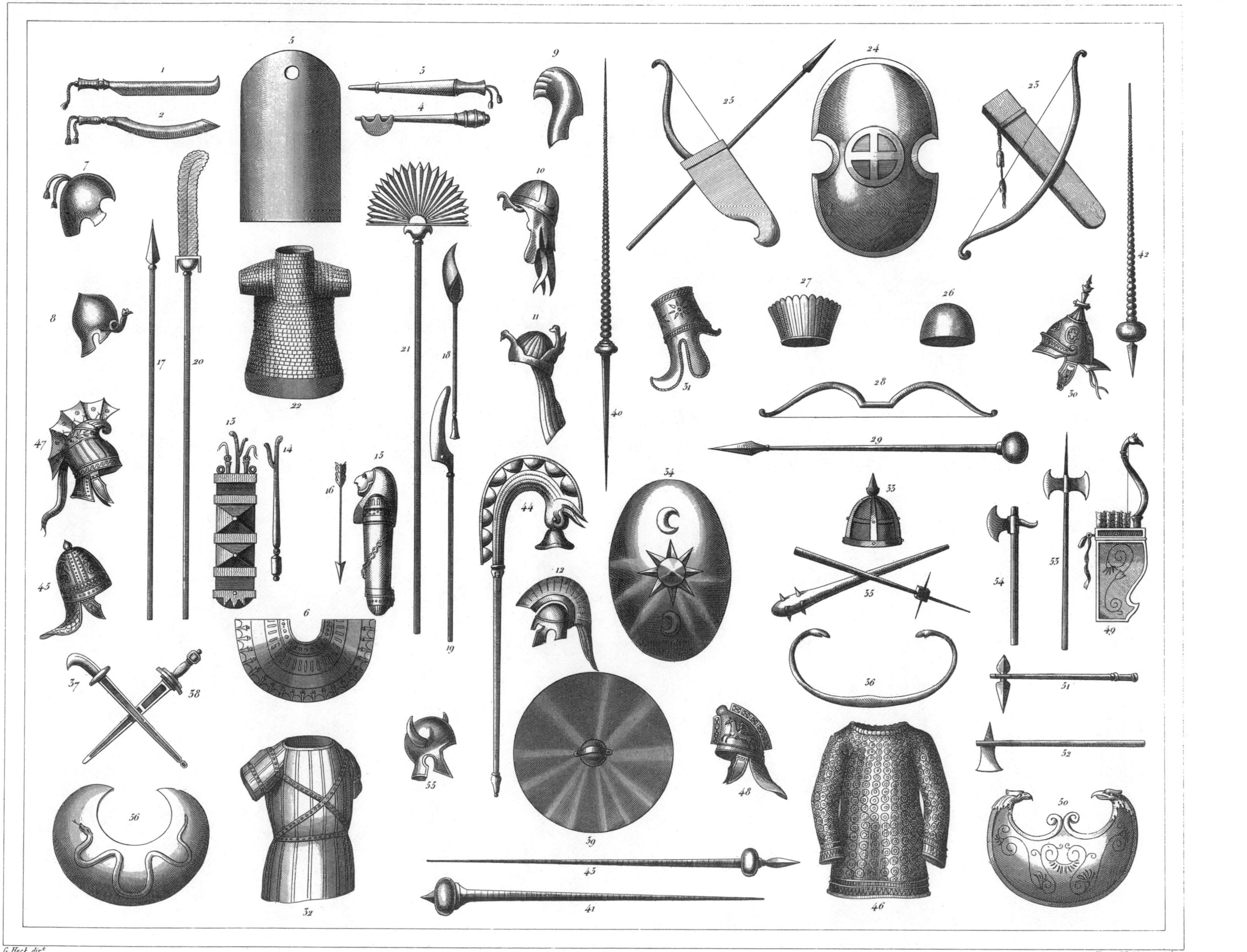

PLATE 267. WEAPONS OF THE EGYPTIANS, MEDES, AND PERSIANS

PLATE 268. GREEK AND ETRUSCAN WARRIORS

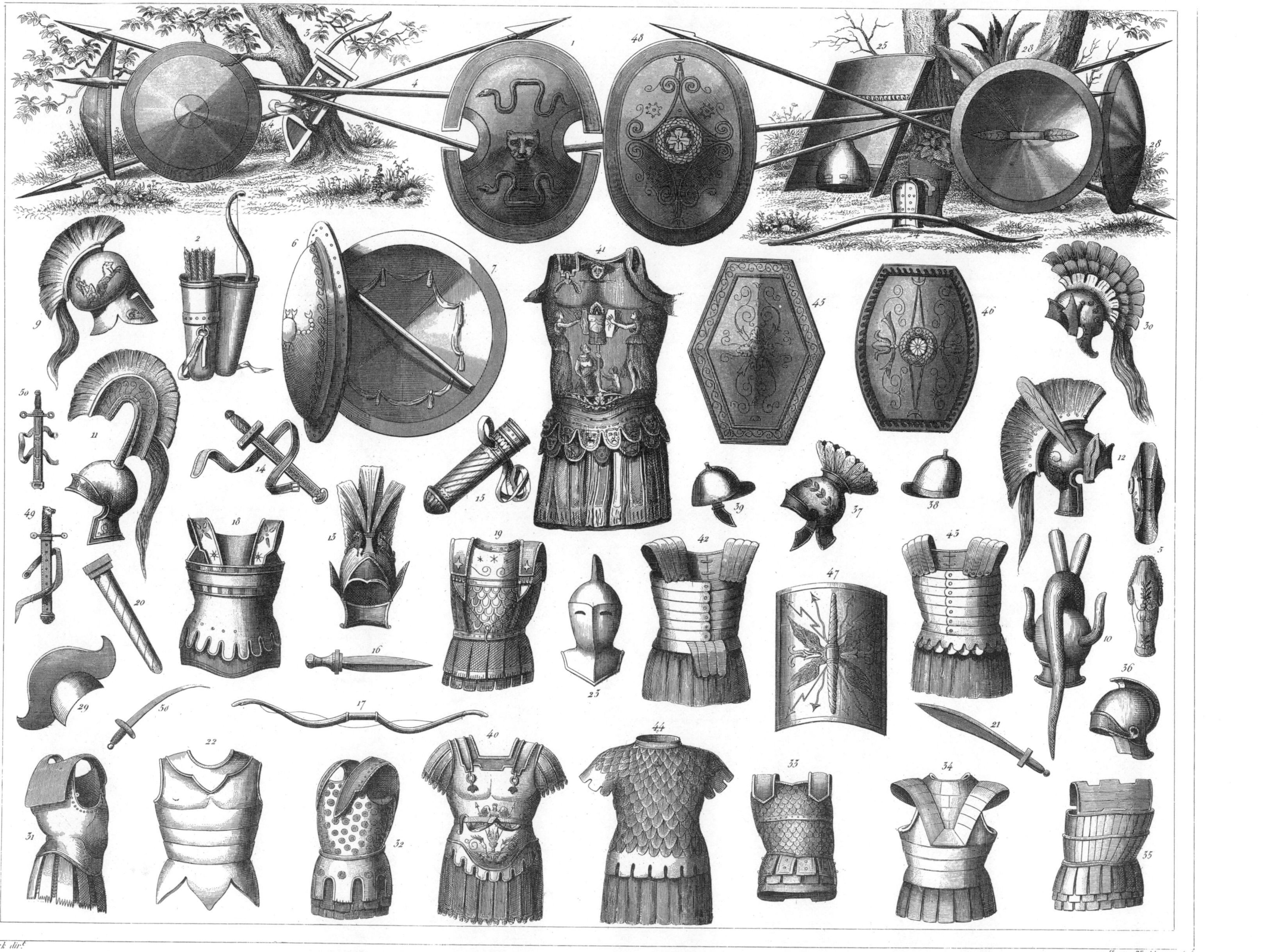

G. Heck dir.t Henry Winkles sculp.t

PLATE 269. WEAPONS OF THE GREEKS, ETRUSCANS, AND ROMANS

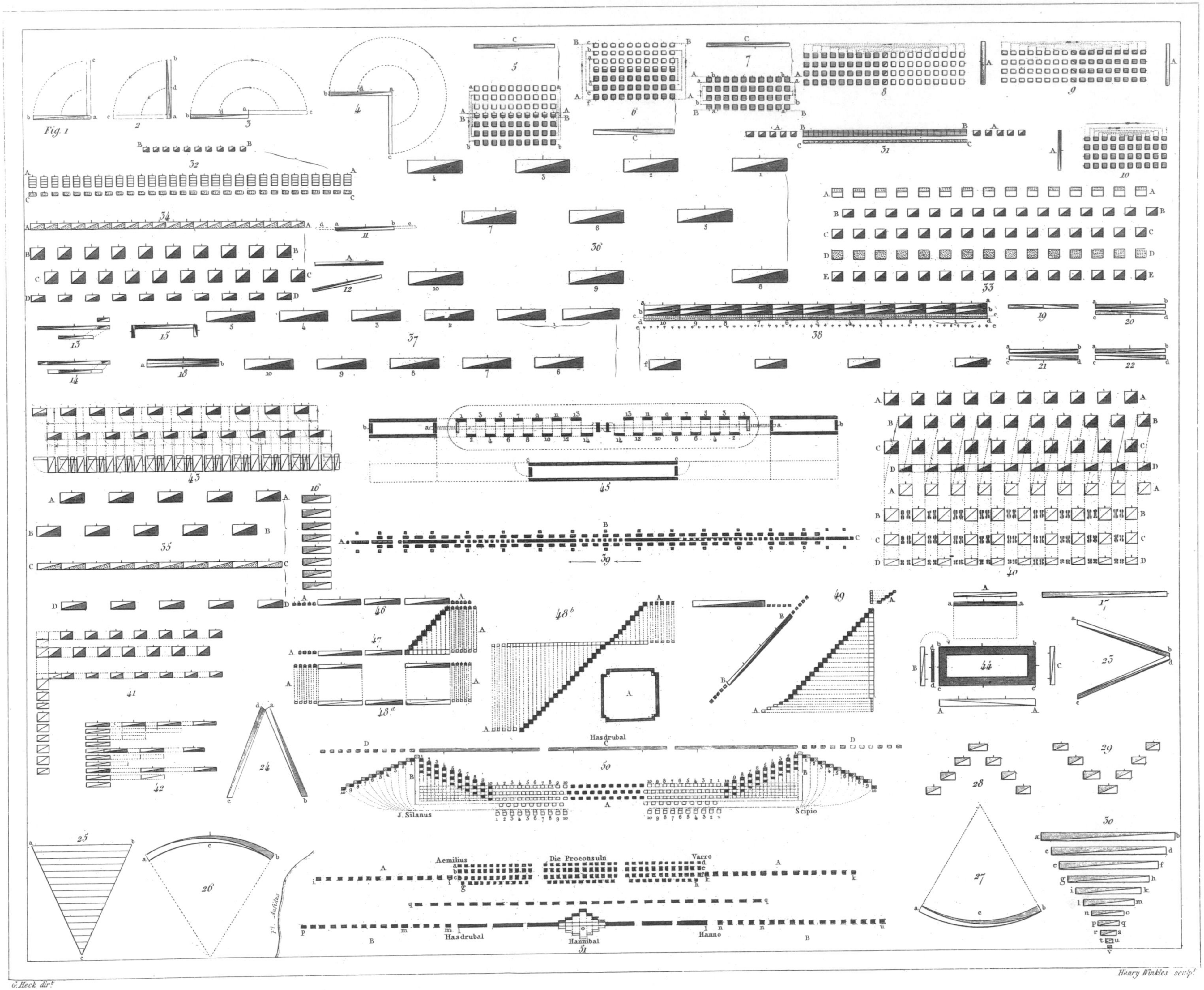

G. Heck dir.t Henry Winkles sculp.t

 PLATE 270. GREEK AND ROMAN TROOP MOVEMENTS

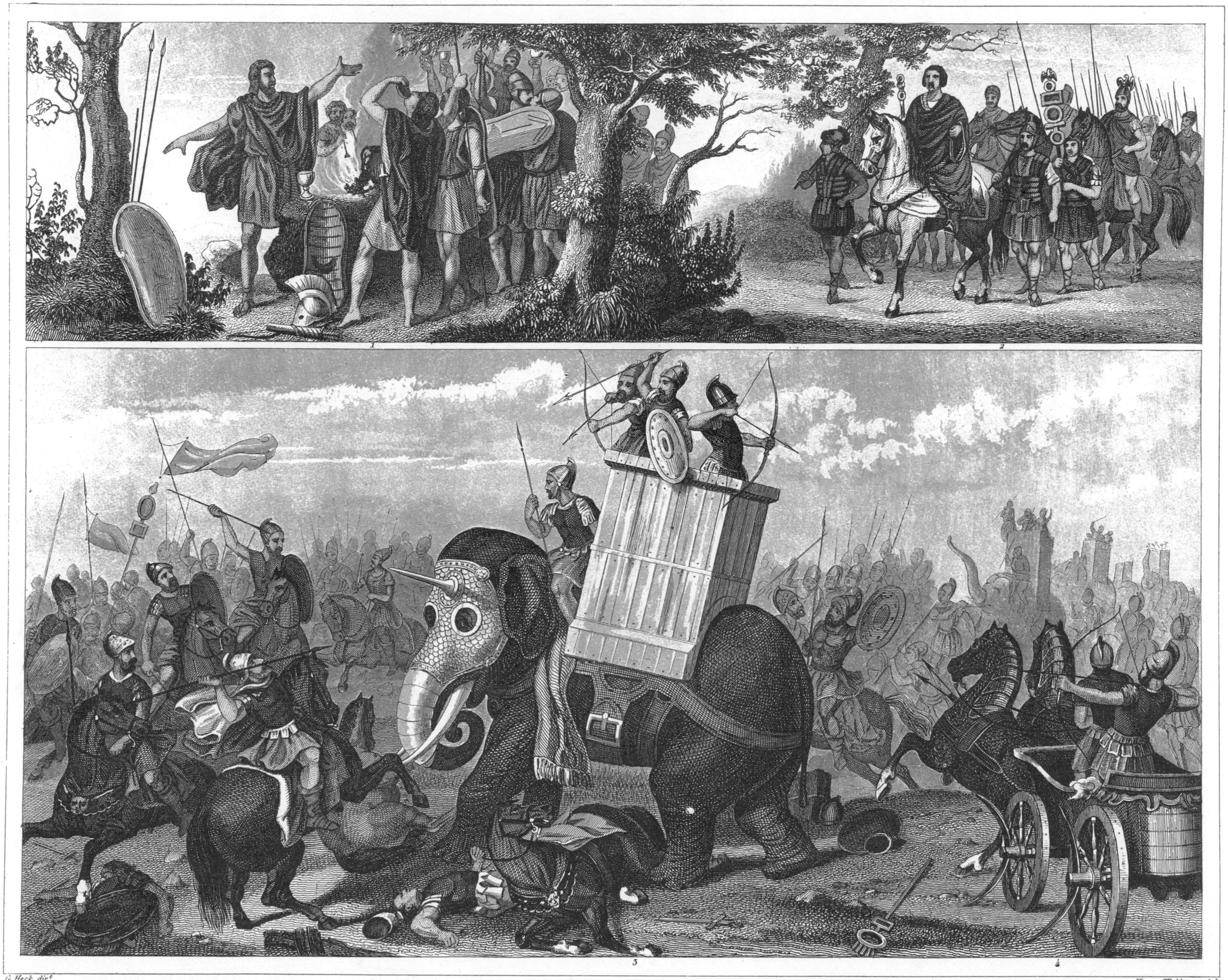

G. Heck dir.ᵗ Henry Winkles sculp.ᵗ

PLATE 271. SCENES OF ANCIENT WARRIORS

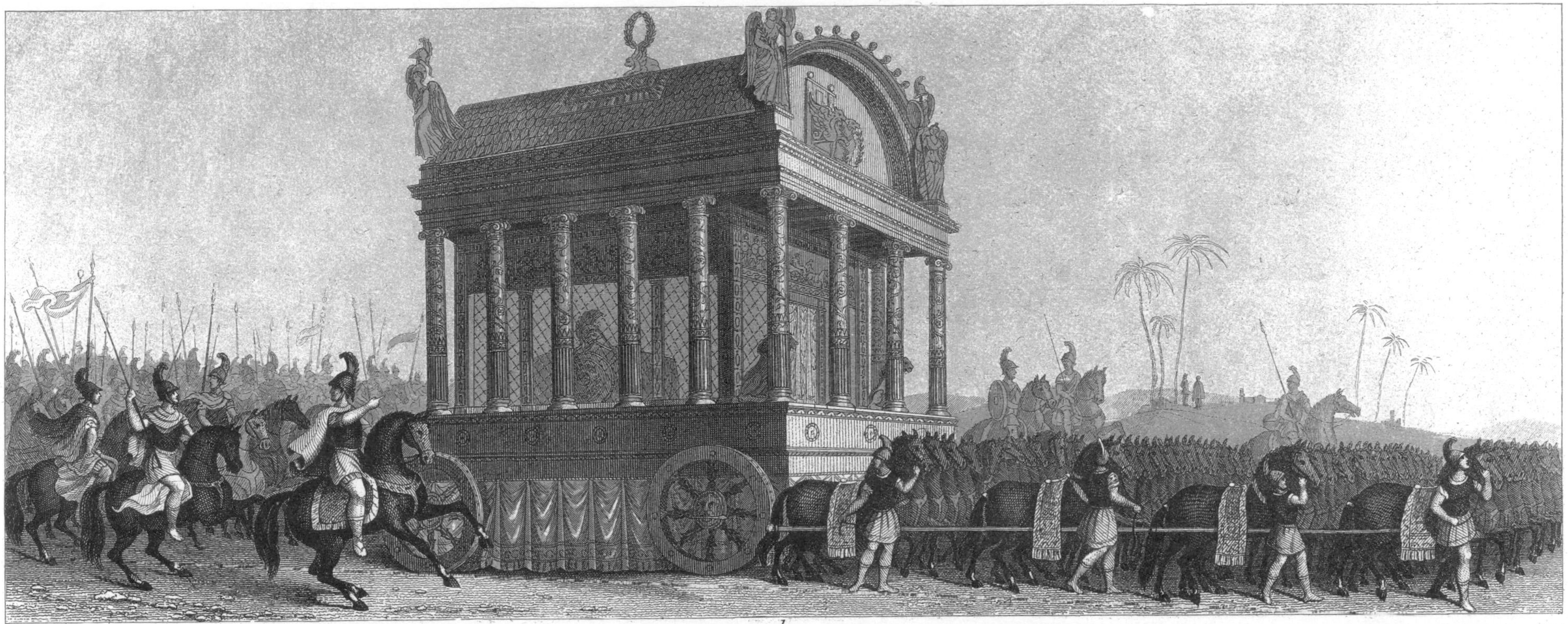

1

2

G. Heck dir.t Henry Winkles sculp.t

G. Heck dir.

Henry Winkles sculp.

PLATE 273. RANKS AND ALLIES OF THE ROMAN ARMY

G. Heck dir.ᵗ Henry Winkles sculp.ᵗ

PLATE 274. SOLDIERS AND OFFICERS OF ROMAN TIMES

G. Heck dir.^t — Henry Winkles sculp.^t

PLATE 275. ANCIENT AND MEDIEVAL WEAPONS AND ARMAMENTS

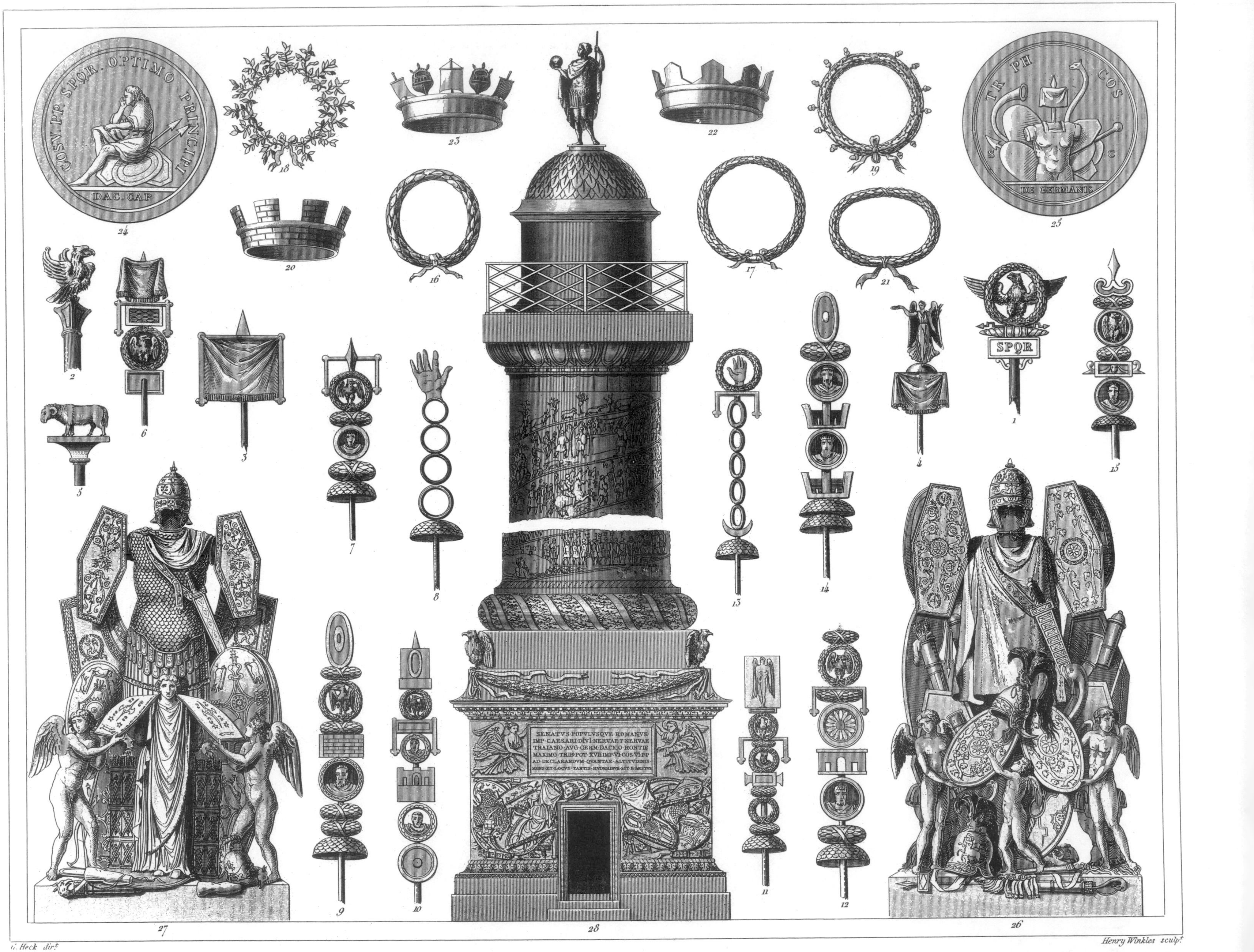

G. Heck dir.t Henry Winkles sculp.t

 PLATE 276. MILITARY TRAPPINGS OF ANCIENT ROME

G. Heck dir.t Henry Winkles sculp.t

PLATE 277. MILITARY CEREMONIES AND PROCESSIONS OF ROME

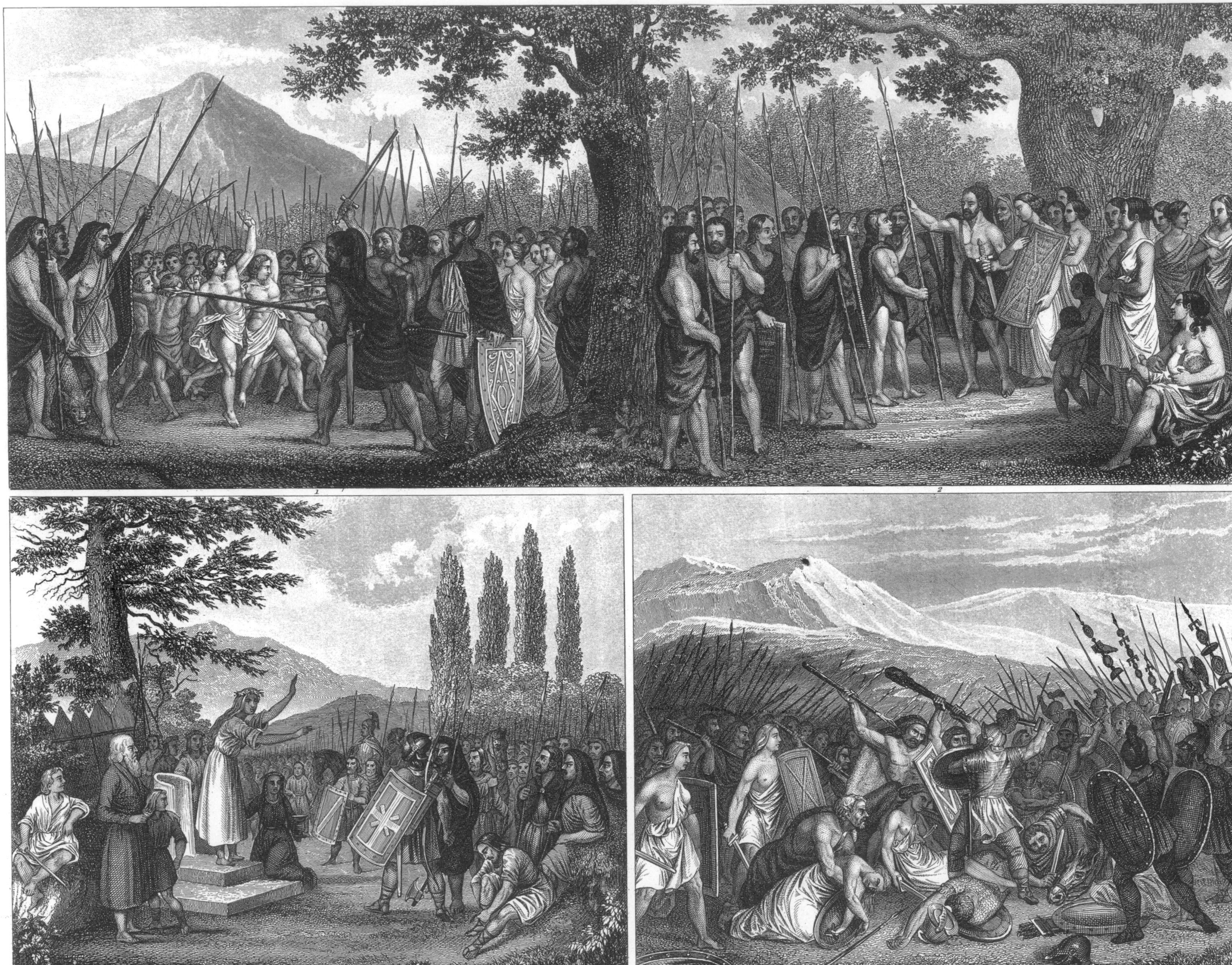

*G. Heck dir*t. *Henry Winkles sculp*t.

PLATE 278. MILITARY LIFE OF THE GERMANIC TRIBES

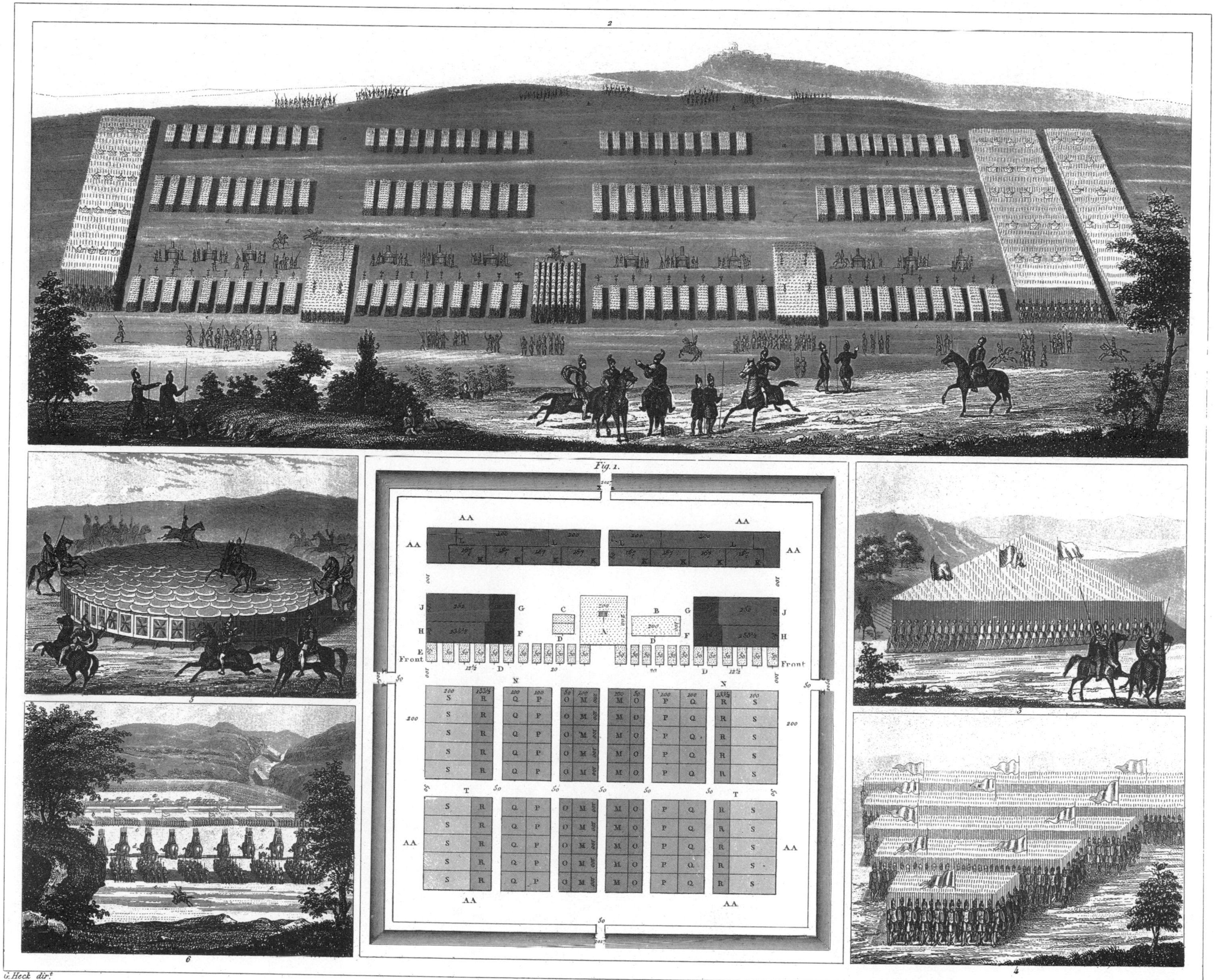

G. Heck dir.^t

Henry Winkles sculp.^t

PLATE 279. ROMAN AND CARTHAGINIAN MILITARY FORMATIONS

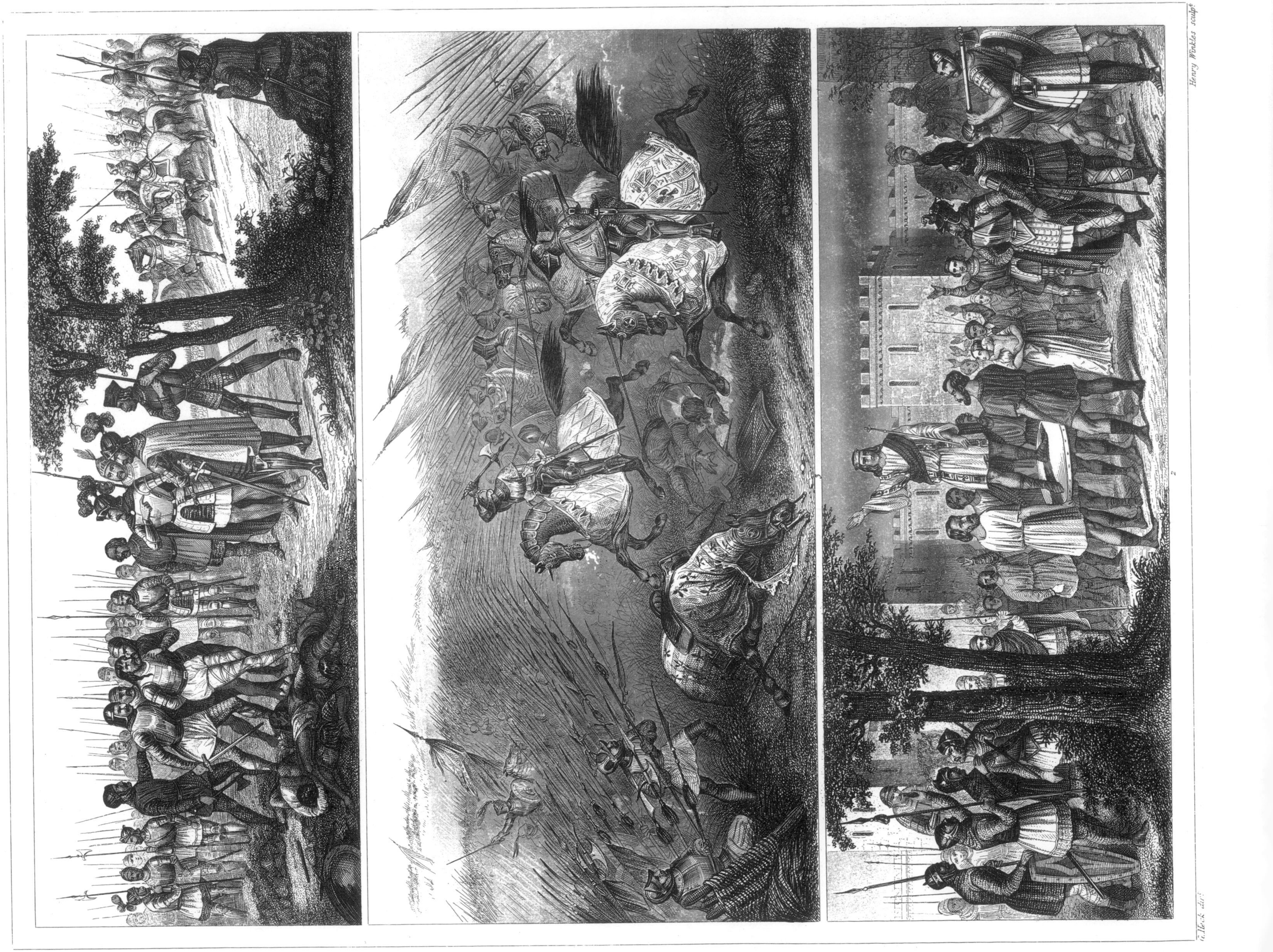

 PLATE 280. MEDIEVAL WAR SCENES

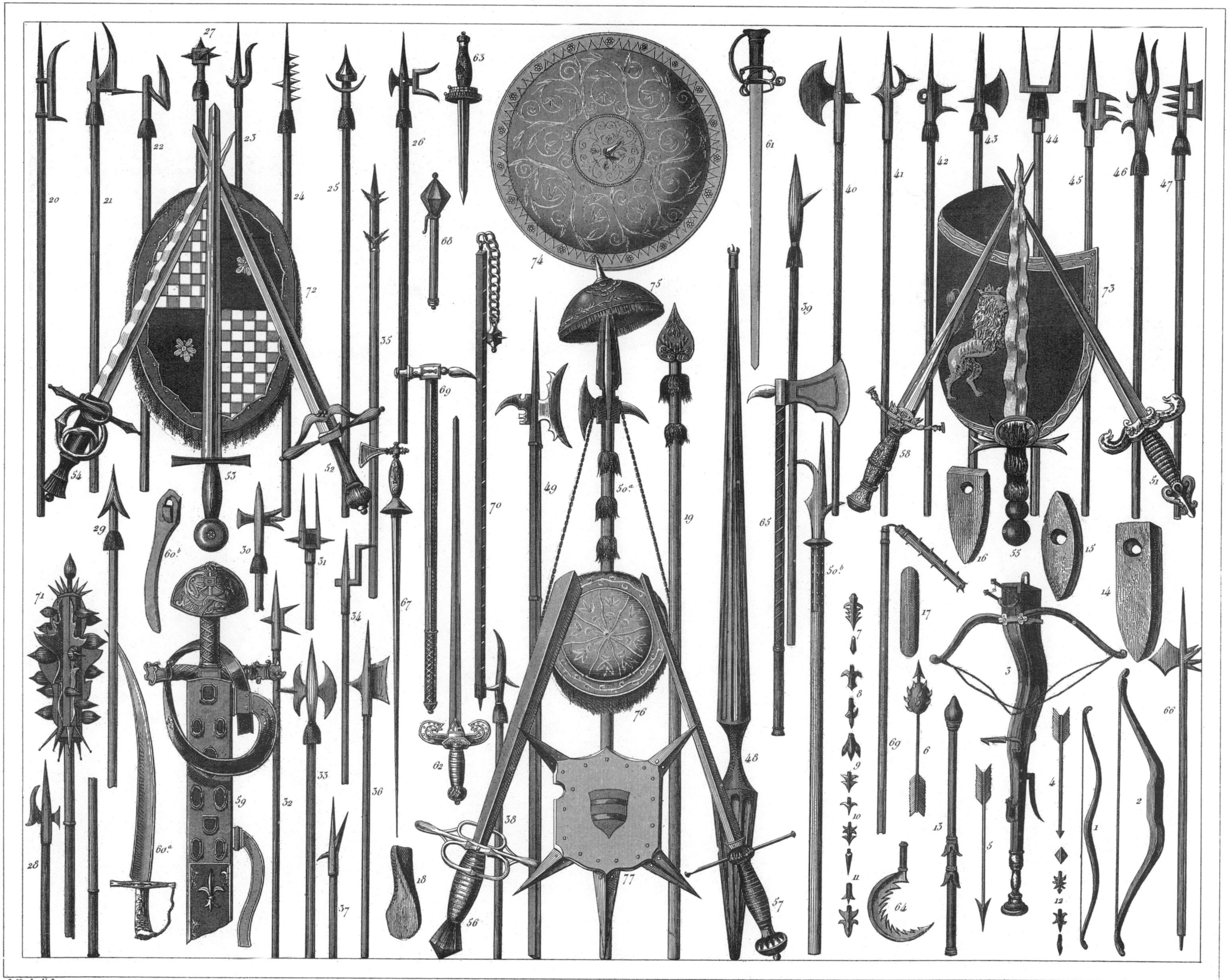

G. Heck dir.^t Henry Winkles sculp.^t

PLATE 281. WEAPONS OF THE GERMANS, NORMANS, ANGLO-SAXONS, AND DANES

G. Heck dir.^t Henry Winkles sculp.^t

 PLATE 282. ARMOR OF THE MIDDLE AGES

PLATE 283. MEDIEVAL ARMOR AND TOURNAMENTS

Henry Winkles sculp.
S.P.Q.R
Saulgew
Kirchberg
Stirie

 PLATE 284. MILITARY DIGNITARIES AND WAR CAMPS

G. Heck dir.t

Henry Winkles' sculp.t

PLATE 285. PRUSSIAN AND FRENCH INFANTRY

PLATE 286. PRUSSIAN AND FRENCH CAVALRY

PLATE 287. AUSTRIAN AND BRITISH INFANTRY

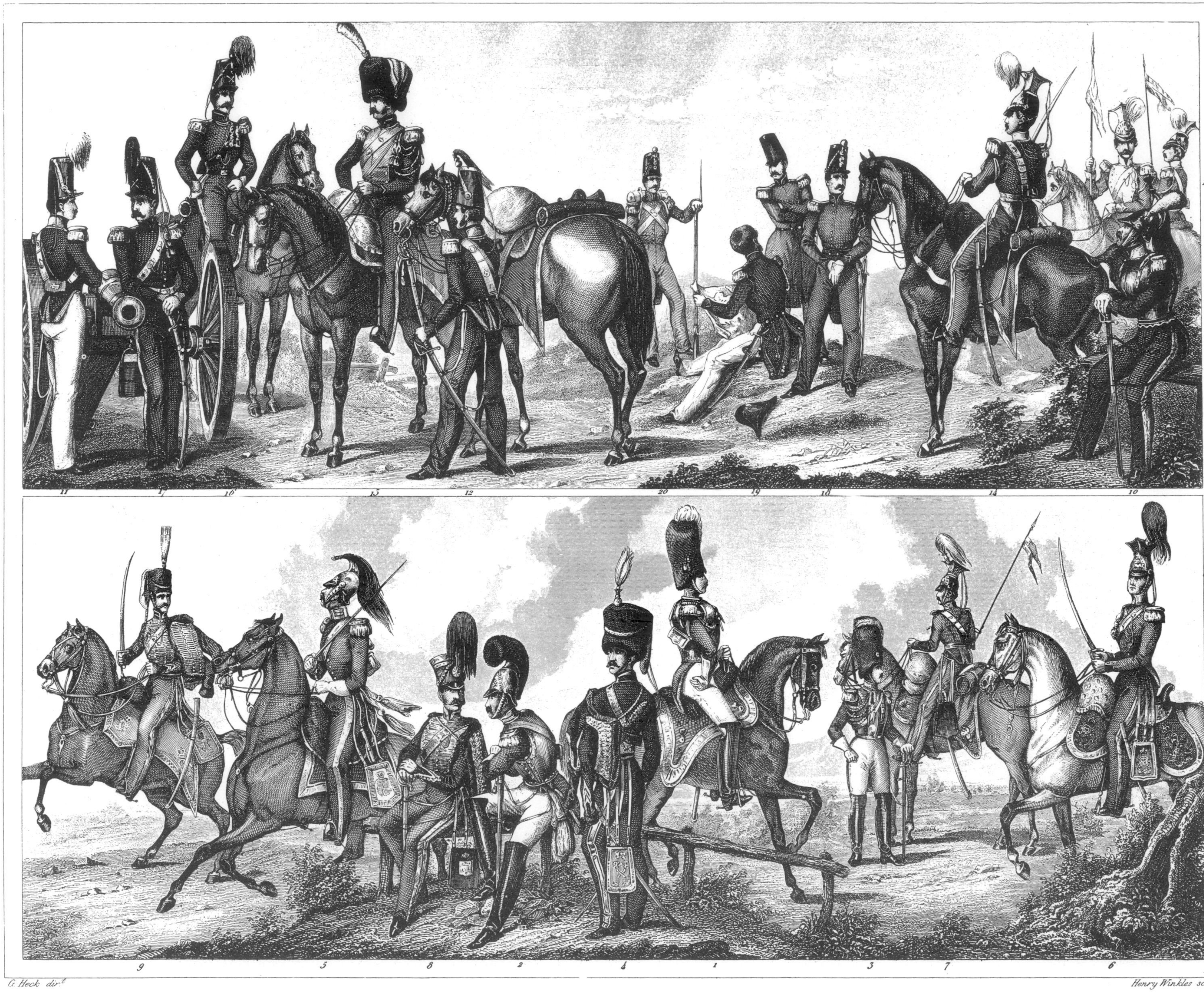

PLATE 288. BRITISH AND BELGIAN CAVALRY

G. Heck dir.^t Henry Winkles sculp.^t

G. Heck dir.^b Henry Winkles sculp.^t

PLATE 290. SCENES FROM TURKISH MILITARY LIFE

PLATE 291. ILLUSTRATING THE VARIOUS KINDS OF ARMS OF THE MID-NINETEENTH CENTURY

G. Heck dir[t] Henry Winkles sculp[t]

 PLATE 292. ILLUSTRATING MILITARY GYMNASTICS

Fig. 5
Fig. 7
Fig. 6a
Fig. 6b
Fig. 14
Fig. 15
Fig. 16
Fig. 12
Fig. 10
Fig. 11
Fig. 13
Fig. 8
Fig. 9
Fig. 17
Fig. 18
Fig. 19
Fig. 20
Fig. 30
Fig. 32
Fig. 21
Fig. 22
Fig. 23
Fig. 24
Fig. 25
Fig. 33
Fig. 31
Fig. 27
Fig. 28
Fig. 34
Fig. 35
Fig. 36
Fig. 37
Fig. 38
Fig. 29
26
Fig. 39
Fig. 40
Fig. 41
Fig. 42
Fig. 43
Fig. 44
Fig. 45
Fig. 46
Fig. 47
Fig. 48
Fig. 1
Fig. 2
Fig. 3

G. Heck dir.^t Henry Winkles sculp.^t

G. Heck dir.   Henry Winkles sculp.

PLATE 294. PRACTICAL EXERCISES IN FENCING

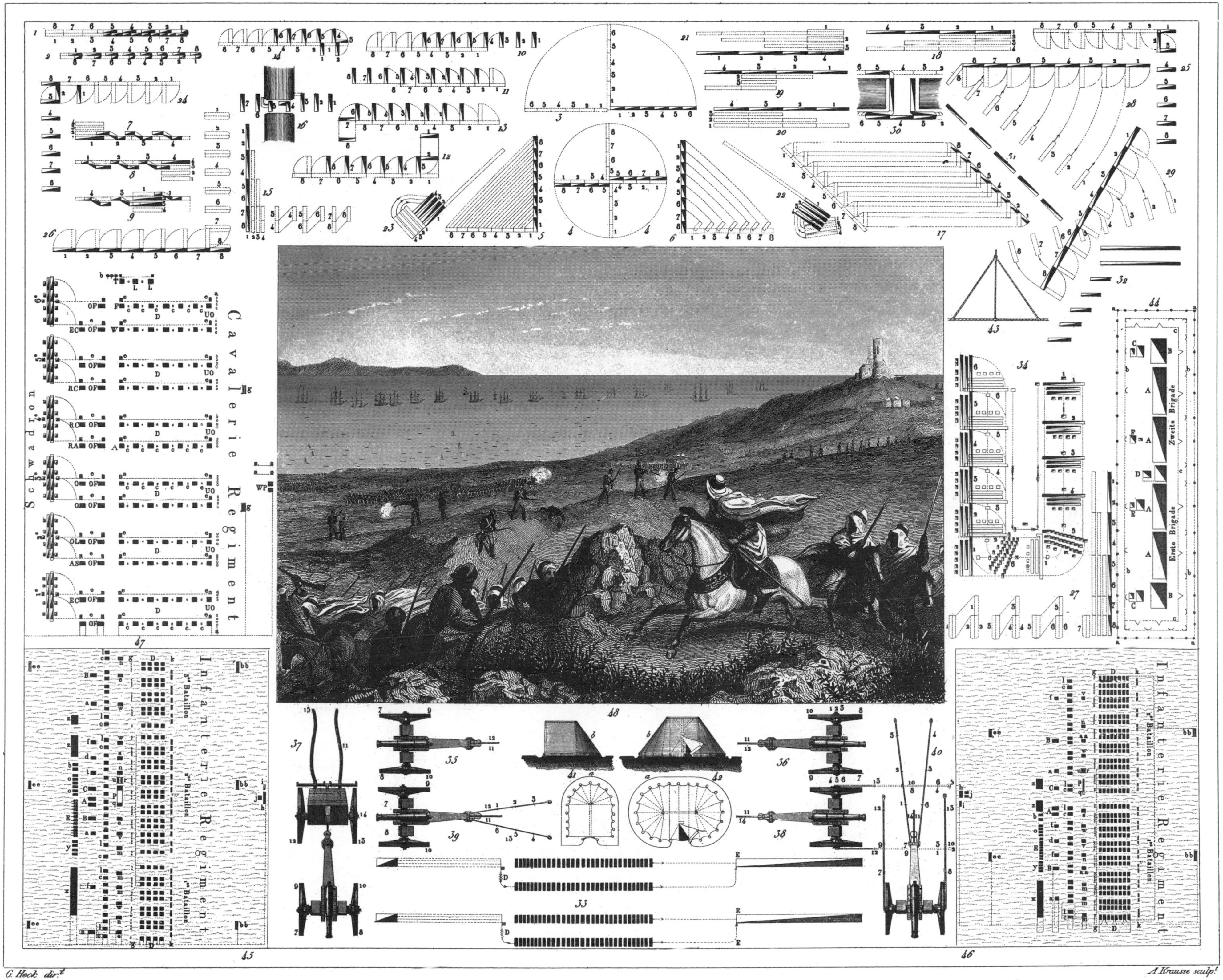

G. Heck dir.t A. Krausse sculp.t

PLATE 295. MILITARY TACTICS AND FRENCH TROOPS IN ALGIERS

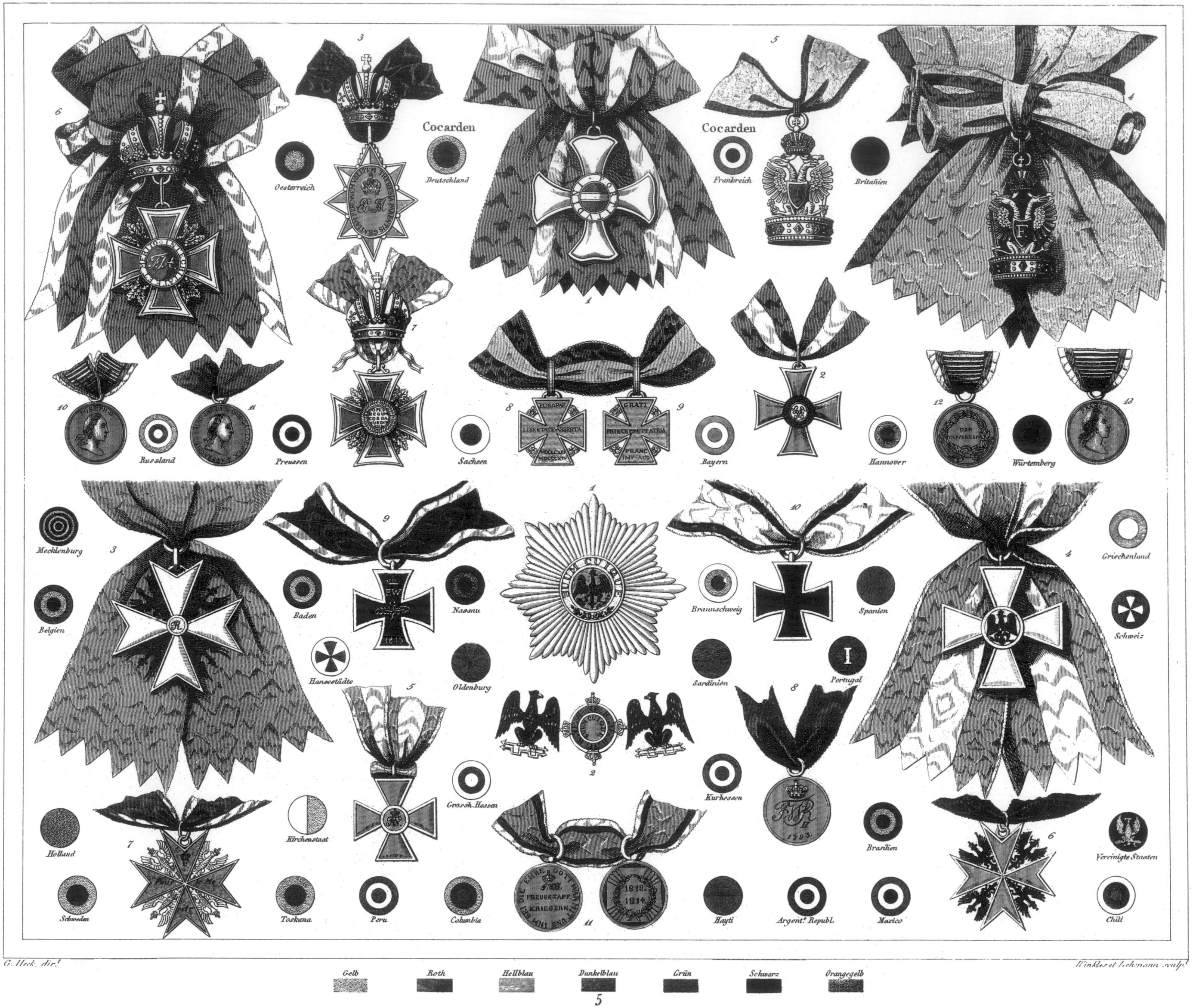
Cocarden
Oesterreich
Deutschland
Cocarden
Frankreich
Britanien
Russland
Preussen
Sachsen
Bayern
Hannover
Würtemberg
Mecklenburg
Belgien
Baden
Nassau
Hansestädte
Oldenburg
Braunschweig
Spanien
Sardinien
Portugal
Griechenland
Schweiz
Holland
Kirchenstaat
Grossh. Hessen
Kurhessen
Brasilien
Vereinigte Staaten
Schweden
Toskana
Peru
Columbia
Hayti
Argentᵉ Republ.
Mexico
Chili
SUUM CUIQUE
GRATI PRINCEPS ET PATRIA
1813. 1814.
G. Heck, dir.
Winkles et Lehmann sculp.
Gelb
Roth
Hellblau
Dunkelblau
Grün
Schwarz
Orangegelb
5

PLATE 296. AUSTRIAN AND PRUSSIAN ORDERS

G. Heck dir.t Henry Winkles sculp.t

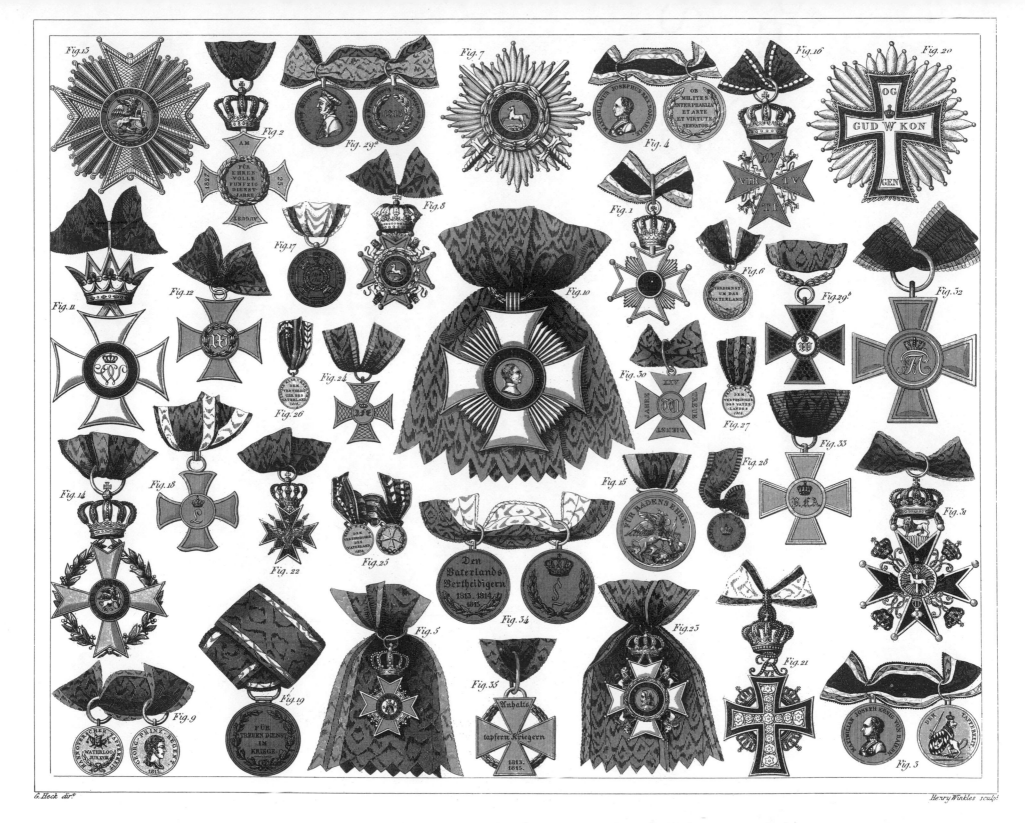

PLATE 297. GERMAN AND DANISH MEDALS AND MILITARY ORDERS

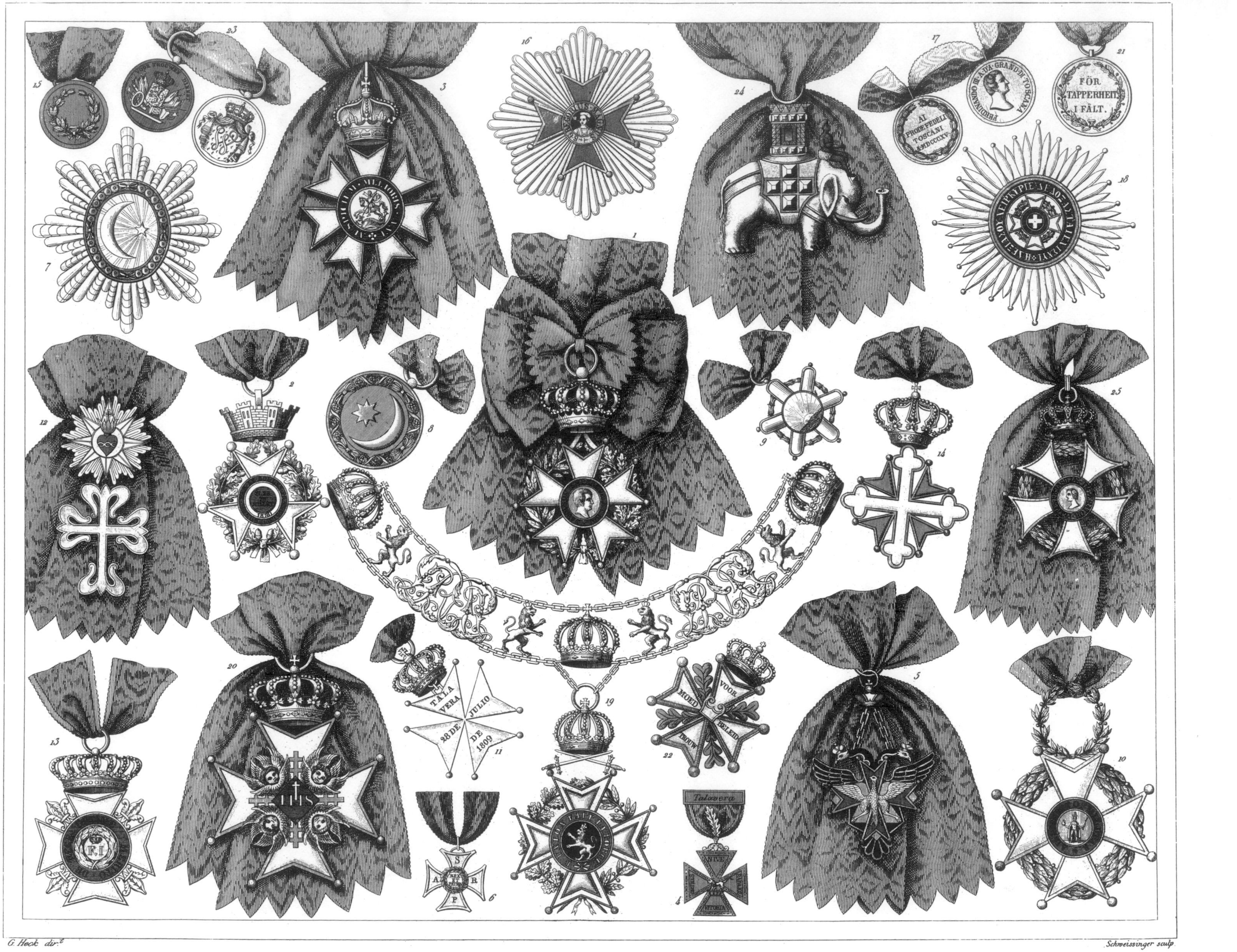

PLATE 298. MILITARY ORDERS OF MANY LANDS

Fig.10
Fig.12
Fig.13
Fig.11
Fig.9
Fig.14
Fig.8
Fig.18
Fig.19
Fig.23
Fig.20
Fig.16
Fig.6d
Fig.22
Fig.17
Fig.6a
Fig.6
Fig.15

PLATE 300. MILITARY ENGINES OF THE MIDDLE AGES

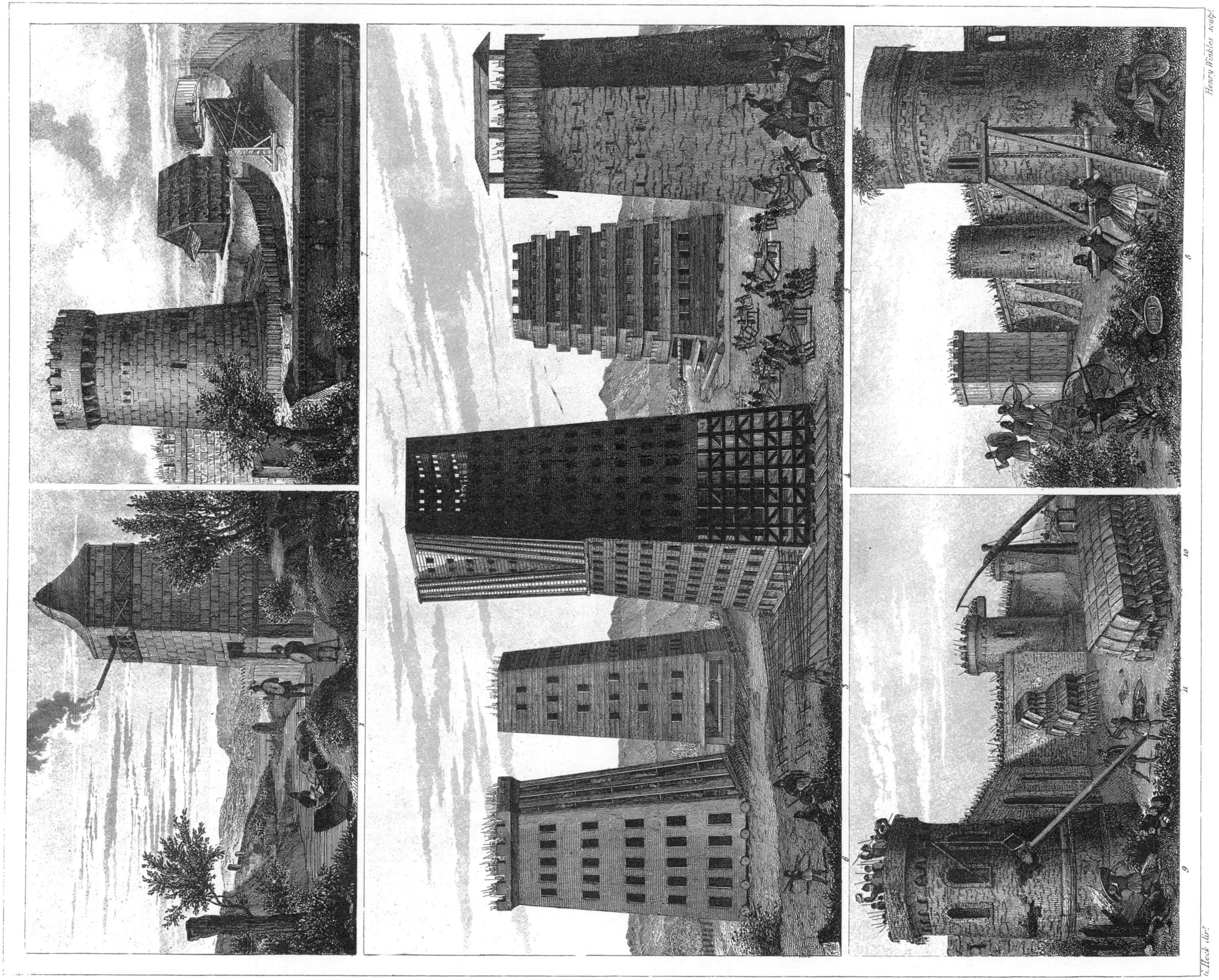

PLATE 301. MILITARY STRUCTURES, ENGINES, AND FORMATIONS OF ANCIENT AND MEDIEVAL TIMES

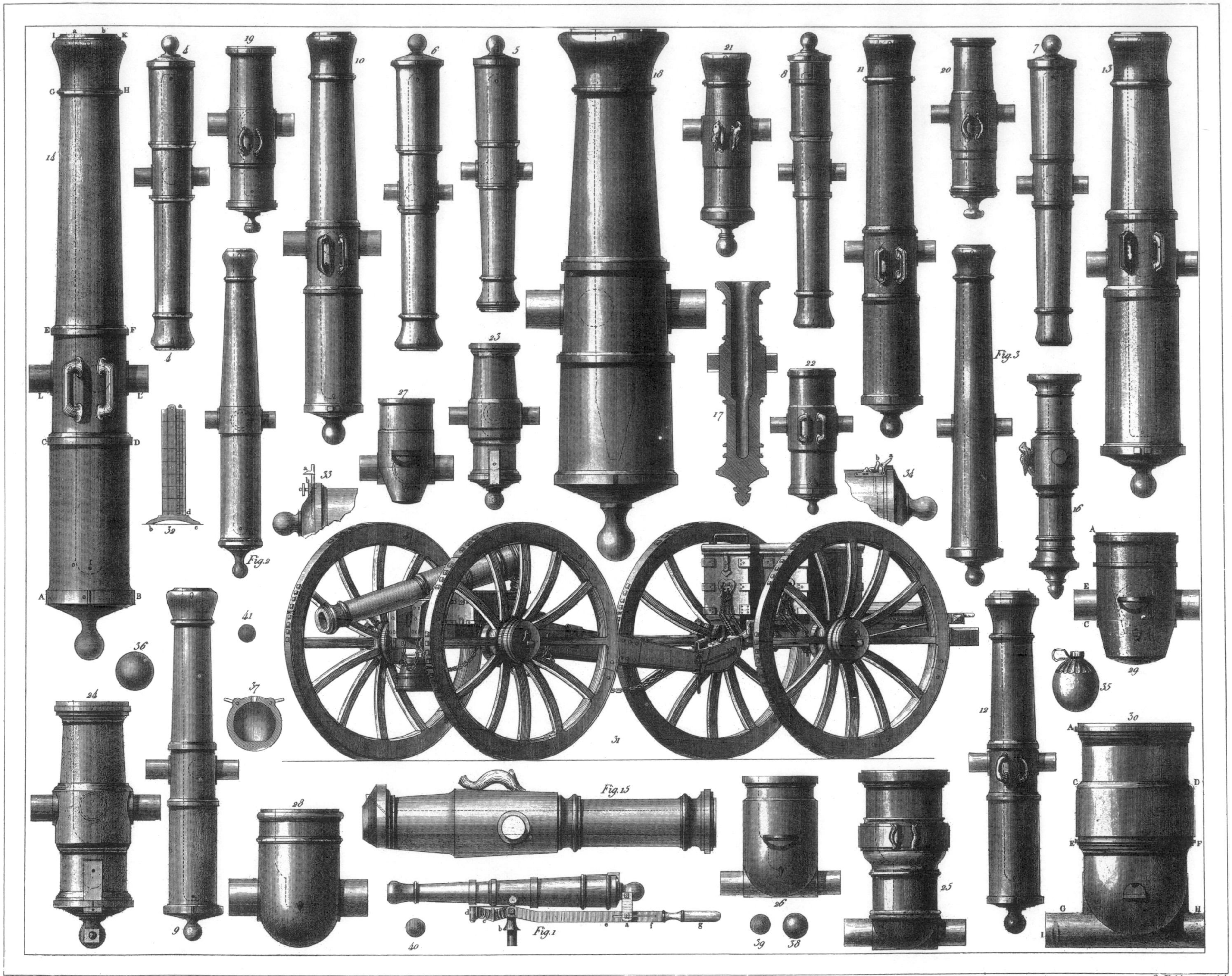

G. Heck dir.

G. Feldweg sculp.

Maasstab für Fig. 1. Maasstab für Fig. 2–29. Maasstab für Fig. 30.

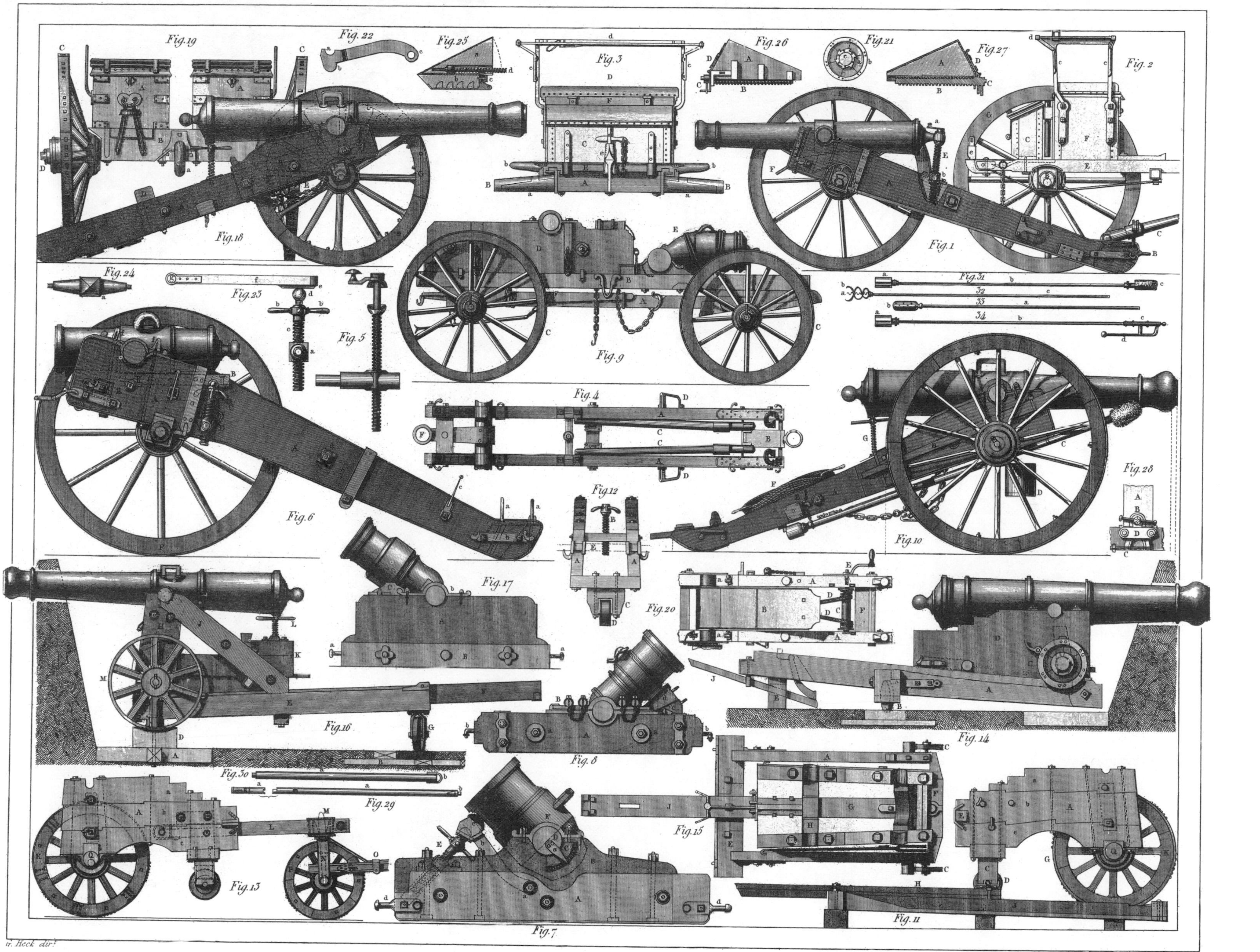

PLATE 303. ILLUSTRATING ARTILLERY CARRIAGES

PLATE 304. ILLUSTRATING ARTILLERY AND PONTOON CARRIAGES

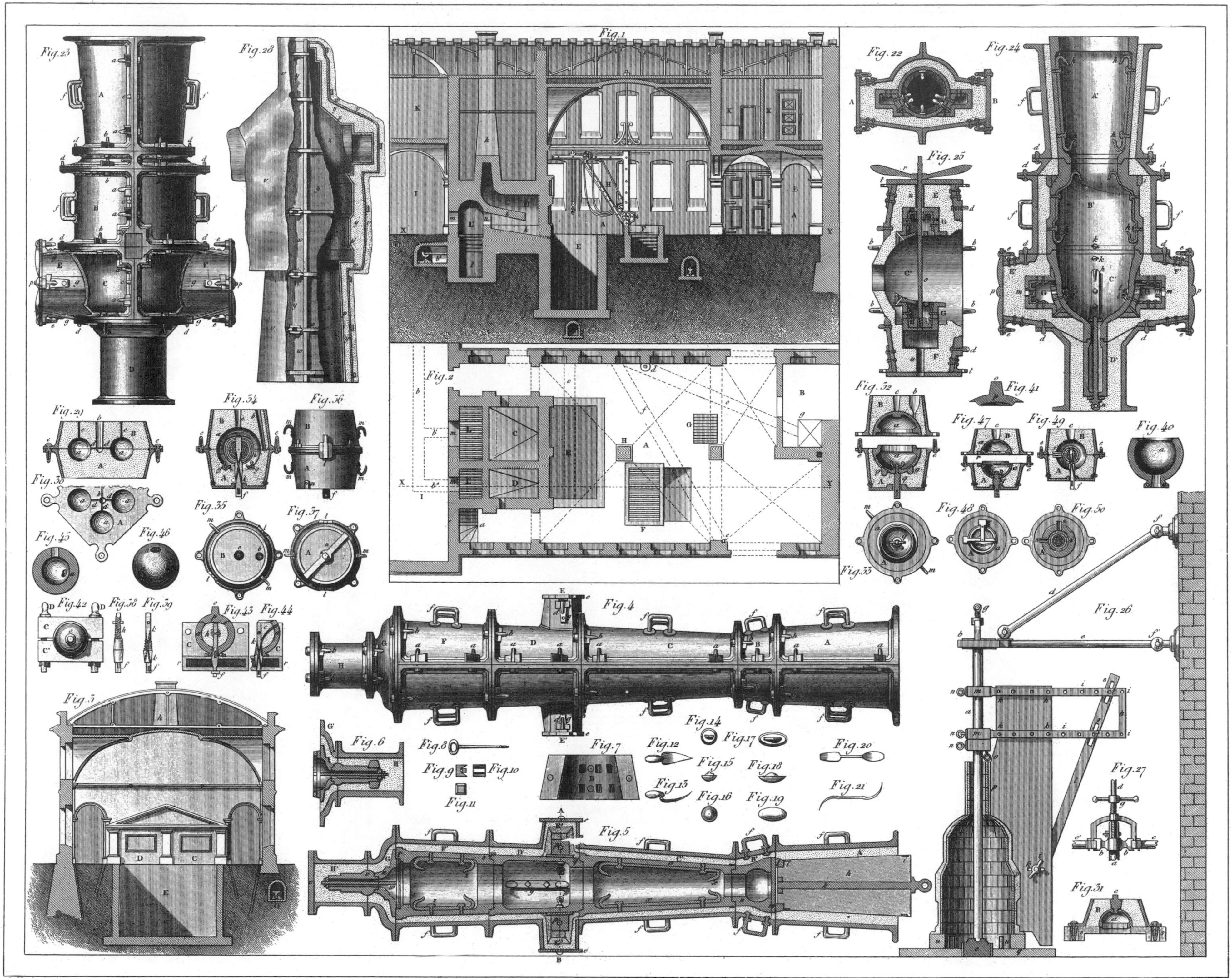

J. Heck dir.

Henry Winkles sculp.

PLATE 305. ILLUSTRATING THE FABRICATION OF ARTILLERY AND PROJECTILES, BALLS AND BOMBS

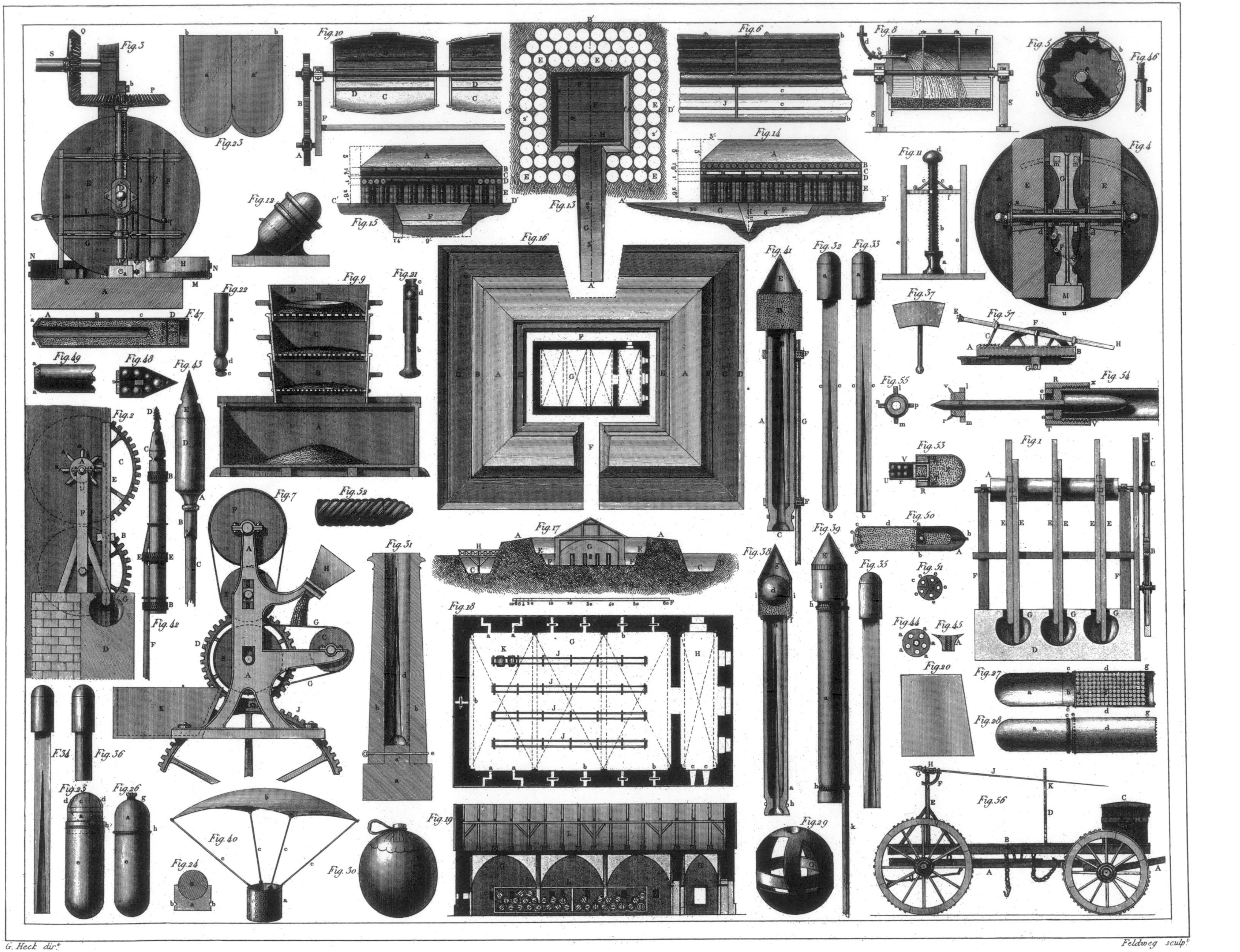

G. Heck dir.ᵗ

Feldweg sculp.ᵗ

PLATE 306. ILLUSTRATING MILITARY PYROTECHNY

PLATE 307. ROMAN MILITARY STRUCTURES AND TECHNIQUES

Henry Winkles sculpt.

 PLATE 308. GATES AND WALLS OF ANCIENT TIMES

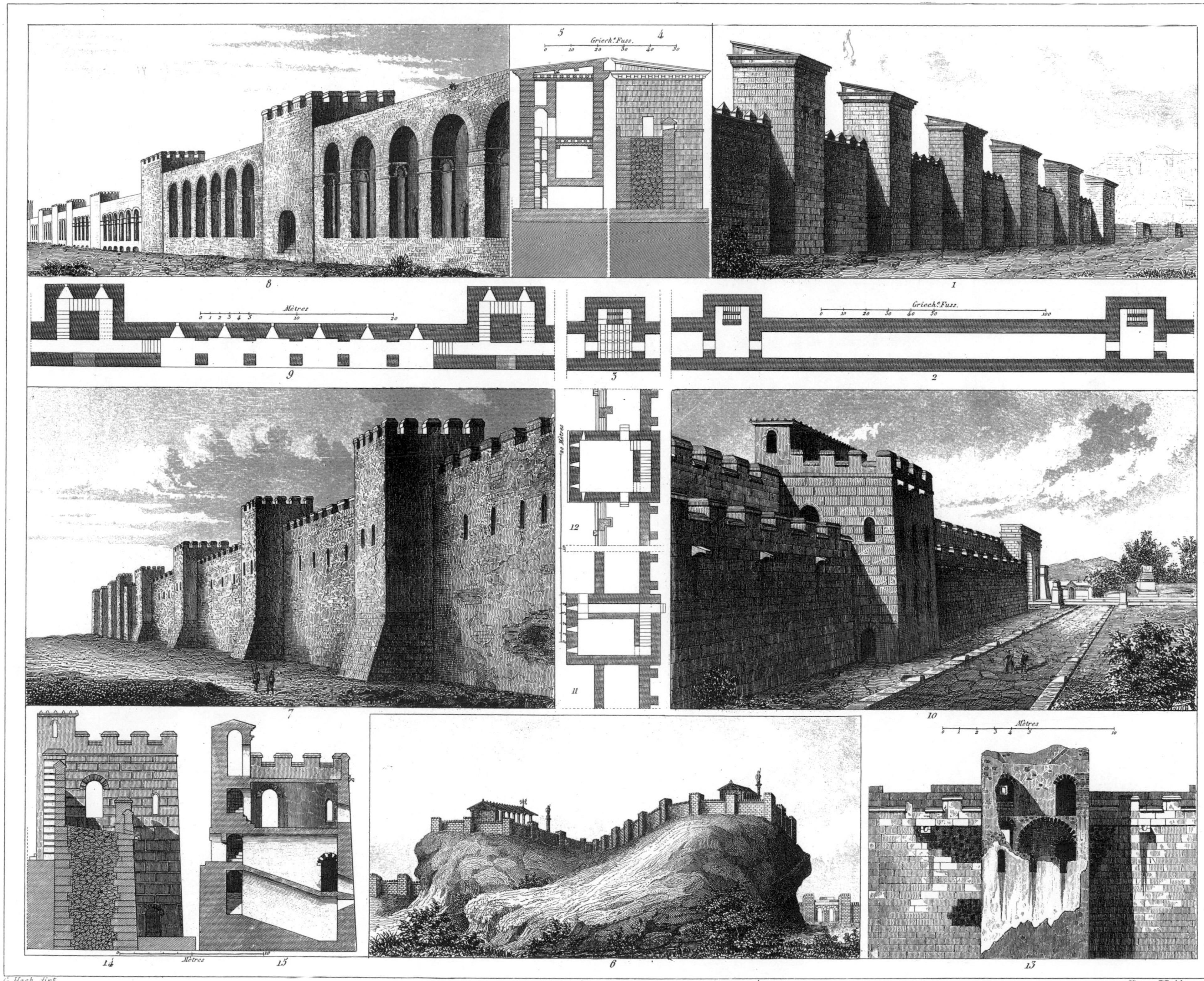

G. Heck dirᵗ. Henry Winkles sculpᵗ.

PLATE 309. WALLS OF GREECE AND ROME

Fig. 4
Fig. 1.a
Fig. 1.b
Fig. 7
15
12
16
13
Fig. 9
Fig. 2
A
B
C
8
10
11
14
3
5
6
G. Heck dir.
Henry Winkles sculp.

 PLATE 310. CASTLES OF THE MIDDLE AGES

PLATE 311. THE GREAT WALL OF CHINA; VARIOUS TOWERS AND BATTLEMENTS

PLATE 312. VARIOUS FORTIFIED STRUCTURES

Blockhaus
Reduit
Hauptwerk
Redoute
Landstrasse
Horsdorf
Blockhaus zur Vertheidigung des Grabens
Fig. 44
Blockhaus
Pulvermagaz.n
G. Heck dir.
Feldweg sculpt

PLATE 313. ILLUSTRATING FIELD FORTIFICATION

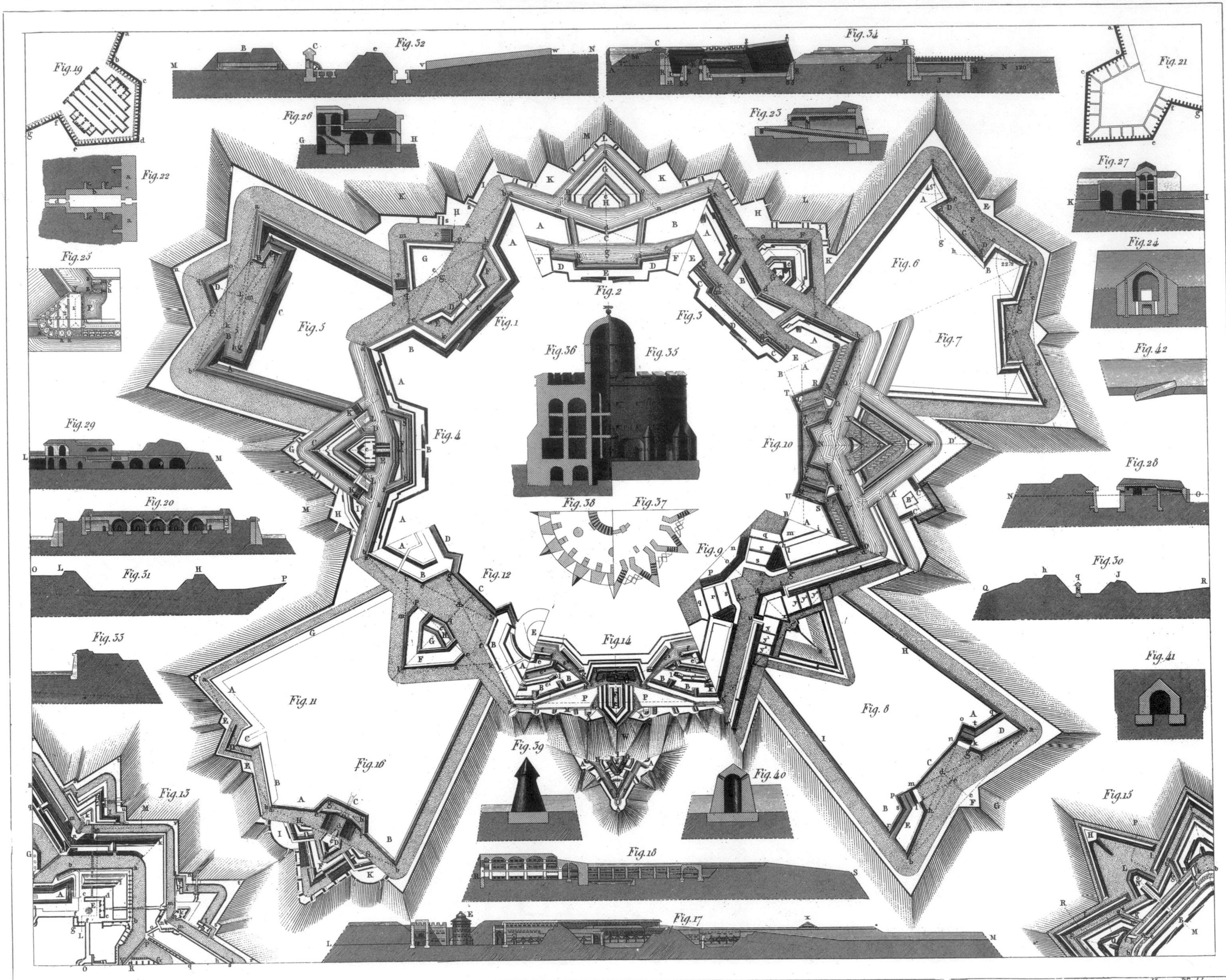

G. Heck dir.^t Henry Winkles sculp.^t

PLATE 314. ILLUSTRATING PERMANENT FORTIFICATIONS

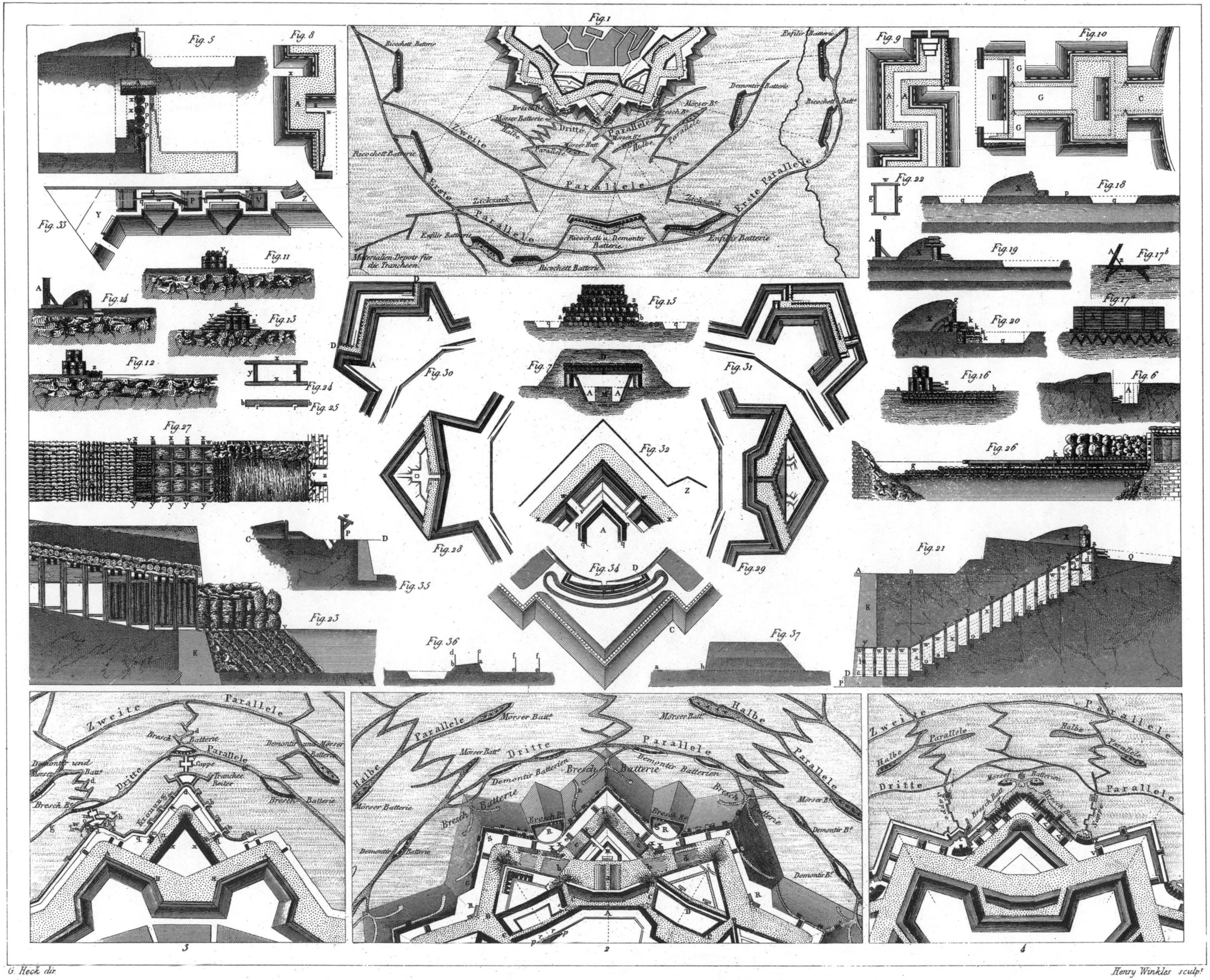

G. Heck dir.

Henry Winkles sculp.

PLATE 315. ILLUSTRATING ATTACK AND DEFENCE OF FORTIFIED PLACES

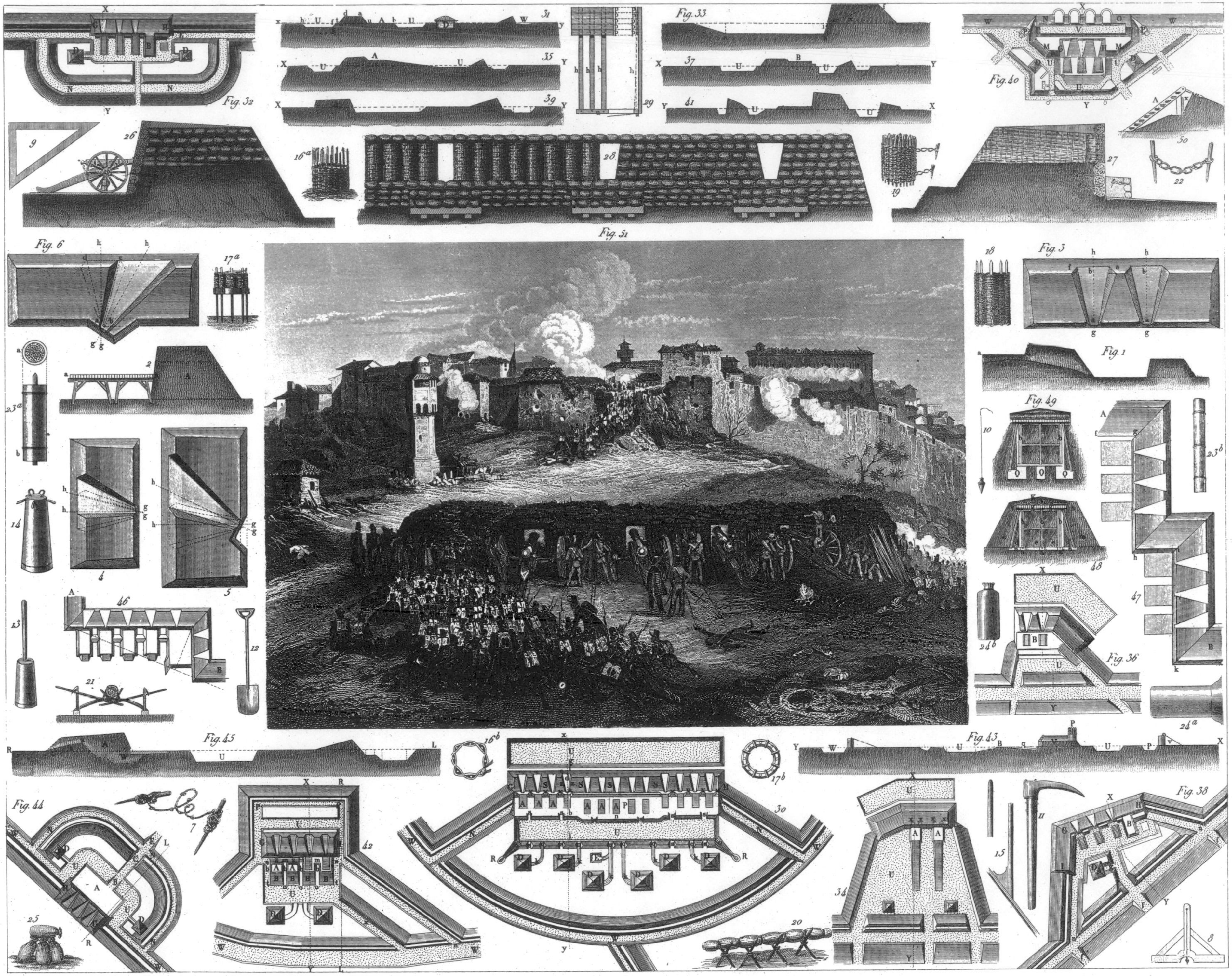

G. Heck dir.t

Henry Winkles sculp.t

PLATE 316. ILLUSTRATING ATTACK AND DEFENCE OF FORTIFIED PLACES

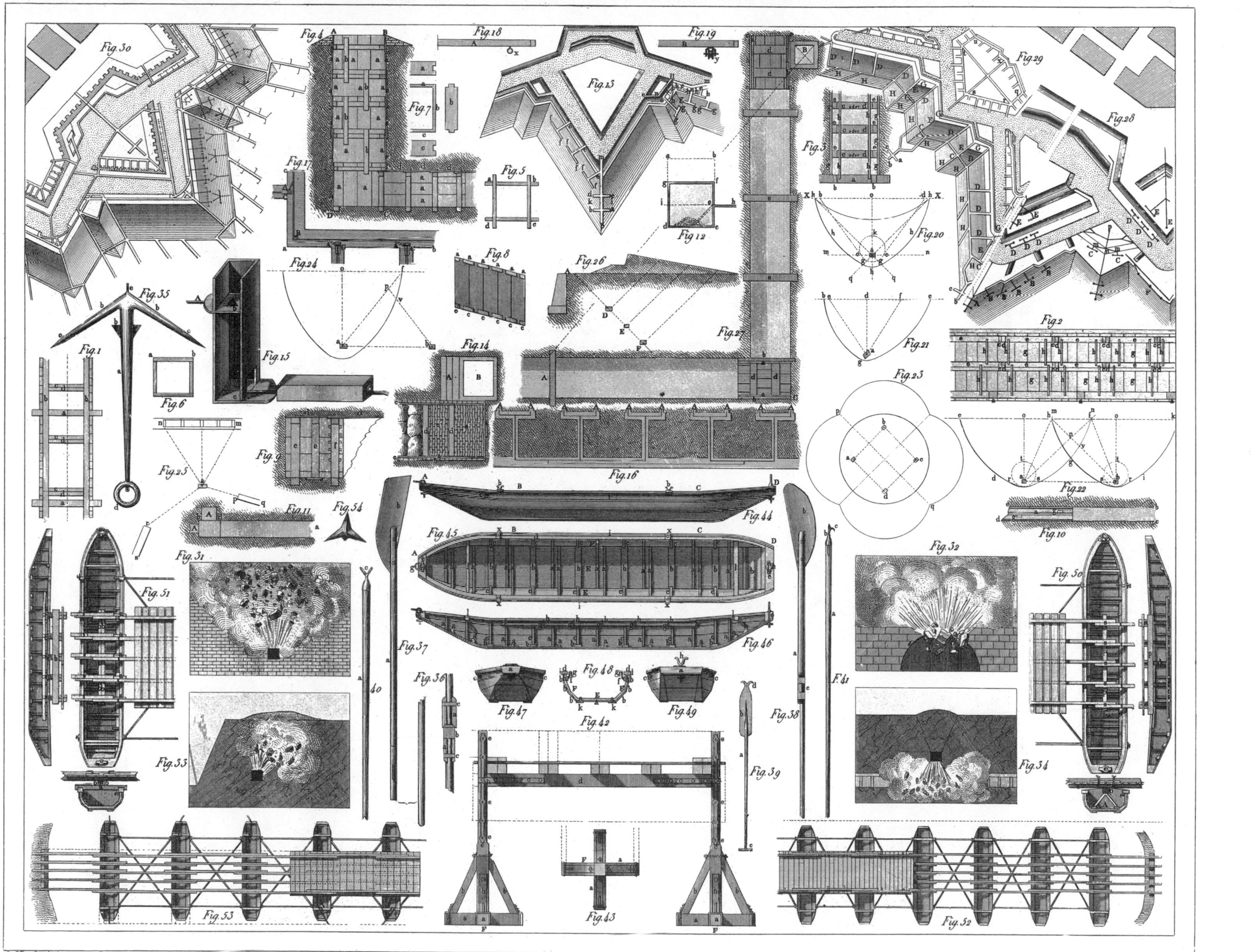

G. Heck dir.t Feldweg sculp.t

PLATE 317. ILLUSTRATING THE PIONEER AND PONTOON SERVICE

NAVAL SCIENCES

Captions to the Naval Sciences Plates, 318–349

PLATE 318.
Sea Vessels of Ancient Times and the Dark Ages

Figure
1, 2. Phœnician vessels
3, 4. Prows
5. Stern-figure (*aplustre*)
6, 7. Prow-figures
8. Hiero's show-ship
9. Vessel used in the Roman Naumachia
10. Ship with a tower
11–14. Roman vessels of war
15. Norman vessel of war
16. Roman sea-fight

PLATE 319.
Ancient Vessels and Naval Trappings; A Roman Naval Spectacle

Figure
1. Egyptian boat
2. Phœnician vessel
3, 4. Greek vessels
5, 6. Greek vessels
7. Roman vessel
8. Greek prow
9. Egyptian vessel
10. Cleopatra's show-ship
11. Ptolemy's show-ship
12. Roman Naumachia
13, 14. Anchors
15. Rudder
16. Oar
17. Oar-holes
18. Prow
19. Lighthouse
19 *a–d*. Ground-plans of the lighthouse
20–24. Coins showing lighthouses
25. Naval column

PLATE 320.
Ships of Several Nations

Figure
1. French vessel of the 16th century
2. Genoese prow
3. Spanish ship of war
4. The Sovereign of the Seas
5. Soleil royal
6. Venetian galley
7. The ship Ocean

PLATE 321.
Ships of Europe

Figure
1. Portuguese carac
2. The Great Harry
3. Stern of a ship
4. French galley
5. Observatory
6. Lighthouse
7, 8. French cutters
9. English cutter
10. Bomb ketch
11. Felucca

PLATE 322.
Ships of the Orient

Figure
1. European factory at Canton
2. Chinese war penish
3. The same under sail
4, 5. Chinese coasters
6, 7. Chinese gondolas
8. Chinese junk
9. Coaster of the Maldives
10. Malay coaster
11. Malay anchor
12, 13. Malacca vessels
14. Java vessel

PLATE 323.
Ships of the Far East and the Pacific

Figure
1. Macao vessel
2. Chinese coaster
3. Malacca vessel
4, 5. Vessels of the Moluccas
6. Java coaster
7, 8. Vessels of the Coromandel coast
9, 10. Manilla coasters
11, 12. Coasters of the Philippine islands
13, 14. Coasters of Celebes

PLATE 324.
Illustrating the Theory of Shipbuilding

Figures 1–33.

PLATE 325.
Construction and Maintenance of a Ship

Figure
1. Ship of the line on the stocks
2. Launch of a ship of the line
3. Caulking of a vessel
4. Graving of a vessel
5. Rope-walk
6. Sail bench

PLATE 326.
Basic Structure of a Ship

Figure
1. Longitudinal section of a ship of the line
2. Transverse section of the same
3. Iron knee
4. Construction of a ship's stern
5. Construction of deck
6–25. Illustrating Seppings's system of ship-building
26. A capstan
27. Longitudinal section of a ship of the line, showing its interior arrangement

PLATE 327.
Various Views and Equipment of a Ship

Figure
1. View from above of the lower gun deck
2. View from above of the upper deck
3. French frigate
4. Topsail-yard and topgallant sail
5, 6. Fore-and-aft sails
7. A vane
8, 9. Pennants
10. A ship's pump
11. A windlass
12, 13. Details of the same
14–29. Anchors
30. Splicing cables
31, 32. Anchor-buoys
33. Mushroom anchor

PLATE 328.
French Ship of the Line and Equipment

Figure
1. French ship of the line, showing the outfit of a ship
2. Normandy fishing-smack
3. Mainyard with its jeers
4. Upper part of a mainmast
5, 6. Caps
7. Dead-eyes
8. Tackle with runner
9. Winding tackle in threefold blocks
10–16. Various blocks and dead-eyes
17, 18. Pitch ladles
19. Axe
20. Pole-axe
21. Scraper
22. Double scraper
23. Horse-bait
24. Adze
25. Hatchet
26, 27. Caulking tools
28, 29. Trucks
30. Knobbed rope
31, 32*ab*. Caulking mallets
33. Tar brush
34. Callipers
35–40. Implements for serving guns
41–49. Various kinds of shot

PLATE 329.
Various Views of French Ships

Figure
1. Main forward deck of a French ship of the line
2. The after-deck
3. Lengthwise view of a French two-decker, with a portion of the planking removed

PLATE 330.
Flags of Various Nations

(The colors of the flags are indicated by the different lines and dots marked at the foot of the plate: *Gelb* meaning yellow; *Roth*, red; *Hellblau*, light blue; *Dunkelblau*, dark blue; *Schwarz*, black; *Hellgrün*, light green; *Dunkelgrün*, dark green; *Purpur*, purple; *Braun*, brown.)

Figure
1. Kingdom of Great Britain
2. Kingdom of France under L. Philippe
3. Empire of Russia
4. Empire of Austria
5. Kingdom of Spain
6. Kingdom of Portugal
7. Kingdom of Holland
8. Kingdom of Sweden and Norway
9. Kingdom of Prussia
10. Kingdom of Denmark
11. Kingdom of Naples
12. Kingdom of Hanover
13. British red flag
14. British white flag
15. British blue flag
16. British admiralty's flag
17. British admiral's flag
18. East India Company's flag
19. Republic of the Ionian islands
20. Maltese flag
21. French commercial flag
22. Franco-Algerine flag
23. Russian naval flag
24. Russo-American flag
25. Russian commercial flag
26. Austrian naval and commercial flag

27. Austro-Venetian flag
28. Spanish naval flag
29. Spanish commercial flag
30. Spanish-Philippine commercial flag
31. Portuguese naval and commercial flag
32. Dutch commercial flag
33. Dutch Batavian flag
34. Norwegian national flag
35. Swedish naval flag
36. Swedish commercial flag
37. Prussian naval flag
38. Prussian commercial flag
39. Danish naval flag
40. Danish commercial flag
41. Schleswig-Holstein flag
42. Hamburg admiralty flag
43. Hamburg commercial flag
44. Old Lubec naval flag
45. Lubec commercial flag
46. Bremen commercial flag
47. Hanoverian commercial flag
48. Oldenburg commercial flag
49. Mecklenburg commercial flag
50. Belgian naval and commercial flag
51. Flag of the Saxon river cities
52. Flag of the Bavarian river cities
53. Flag of the Wirtemberg river cities
54. Flag of the Baden river cities
55. Swiss flag
56. Flag of Frankfort on the Main
57. Hungarian flag
58. Servian flag
59. Moldavian flag
60. Wallachian flag
61. Neapolitan naval and commercial flag
62. Papal flag
63. Tuscan naval and commercial flag
64. Leghorn flag
65. Flag of Lucca
66. Flag of Massa-Carrara
67. Flag of Modena
68. Flag of Monaco
69. Royal Sardinian flag
70. Sardinian naval and commercial flag
71. Old Genoese flag
72. Old Savoy flag
73. Flag of the island of Sardinia
74. Greek naval flag
75. Greek commercial flag
76. Greek pirate's flag
77. Turkish imperial flag
78. Turkish naval flag
79. Turkish commercial flag
80. Flag of the grand vizier
81. Flag of Capudan Pasha
82. Comm. flag of Tunis, Tripoli, Morocco
83. Flag of Tunis
84. Flag of Morocco
85. Flag of the viceroy of Egypt
86. Egyptian commercial flag
87. Flag of Tripoli
88. Old Algerine flag
89. Algerine pirate's flag
90. Arabian flag
91. Abyssinian flag
92. The flag of the Shah of Persia
93. Persian commercial flag
94. Flag of Afghanistan
95. Flag of Beloochistan
96. Flag of the Great Mogul
97. Flag of Bengal
98. Flag of Scind
99. Flag of the Birmans
100. Flag of Pegu
101. Flag of Siam
102. Flag of Sumatra
103. Chinese imperial flag
104, 105. Chinese commercial flags
106. Flag of Cochin-China
107. Japanese imperial flag
108. Commercial flag of Japan
109. Flag of the United States, N. A.
110. Flag of Texas
111. Flag of Mexico
112. Flag of Guatemala
113. Flag of Hayti
114. Flag of Columbia
115. Flag of Venezuela
116. Flag of Bolivia
117. Flag of Peru
118. Flag of Chili
119. Flag of Brazil
120. Flag of La Plata
121. Flag of Equador
122. Flag of Otaheite
123. Flag of the Sandwich Islands
124. Flag of New Zealand

PLATE 331.
European Ships of Various Functions

Figure
1. A galliot
2. An English lugger
3. A sloop of war
4. French frigate
5. French ship of the line
6. Prison ship

PLATE 332.
Trading and Fishing Ships

Figure
1. Newfoundland fisherman
2. Havre de Grace fishing-smack
3. Coaster of the Mediterranean
4. French coaster
5. Mediterranean xebec
6. Mediterranean pink
7. Danish coaster
8. A galliot
9. Dutch brig galliot
10. A barque
11. Slave ship
12. After part of a French merchantman

PLATE 333.
Steamships and Sailing Ships of Various Rigs

Figure
1. A cutter
2. Hermaphrodite brig
3. Barque taking in freight
4. Whale ship
5. Emigrant ship
6. The Bremen steamboat Gutenburg
7. The American steamship Washington

PLATE 334.
French Steam-Propelled Sailing Ships; European Sailing Ships of War

Figure
1. Spanish gun-boat
2. French iron steam propeller
3. English war cutter
4. Swedish brig of war
5. English brig of war
6. French steam frigate

PLATE 335.
Illustrating the Construction of Steamships

Figures 1–22.

PLATE 336.
Illustrating the Construction of Steamships

Figures 1–31.

PLATE 337.
Naval Officers and Sailors

Figure
1–5. French naval officers
6–10. Russian naval officers
11–13. English naval officers
14. Naval cadet (midshipman)
15–19. Sailors, boatswains, etc.

PLATE 338.
Scenes from Shipboard Life

Figure
1. Officer on watch
2. The wheel
3. Middle deck
4. Starboard battery at night
5. Starboard battery in daytime
6. Midshipmen's cabin

PLATE 339.
Scene on a French Frigate

Figure
1. Forward part of a French frigate
2. After part of a French frigate
3. Carronade with its carriage
4. Gun with its carriage
5. Port-guard
6. Davits with lifting tackle

PLATE 340.
Sailors on Deck Duty

Figure
1. Caulking shot holes
2. Look-out from the topsail yard
3. Taking in sail and reefing
4. Throwing the lead
5. Hoisting out a boat
6. Heaving the log
7. Cleaning the deck

PLATE 341.
Incidents Aboard Ship

Figure
1. Court-martial
2. Keel-hauling
3. Hoisting the flag
4. Ship on fire

PLATE 342.
Ships on Parade and Shipboard Life

Figure
1. English ship of the line firing a salute
2. French ship of the line in flag parade
3. Hoisting flag in running into port
4. Striking flag in surrendering
5. Night signals
6. Top-men
7. Sailors playing cards
8. Confinement in irons

PLATE 343.
Ship Manoeuvers

Figure
1. Ship signalizing with flags
2. Ship drying sail
3. Ship inclosed with ice
4. Ship with all sails set
5. Ship setting sail
6. Ship getting under weigh
7. Ship bracing round
8*ab*. Ships sailing on a half wind
9*ab*. Ships going about
10. Ships bearing to windward
11. Ships shortening sail
12. Ship of the line under short sail

PLATE 344.
Ships at Sea

Figure
1. Ships getting under weigh
2. Ships pitching
3. Barque rolling
4. Barque under close-reefed topsails
5. Barque thrown on one side
6. Shipwreck

PLATE 345.
Illustrating Manœuvers of Fleets

Figures 1–35.

PLATE 346.
Ships at War

Figure
1. Manœuvers by schooners
2. Steamer of war carrying despatches
3. Line of battle
4. Naval battle

PLATE 347.
Ships in Drydock and in Port

Figure
1. Drydock in Toulon
2. Towing a vessel into port
3. Ship-ways dry at ebb tide
4. Graving-dock

5–7. Diving-bells

8, 9. Steam dredgers

PLATE 348.
Roadsteads and Harbor Equipment

Figure

1, 2. Roadsteads

3. Crane for setting masts
4. Pile-driving machine
5. Naval arsenal
6. Common dredging machine

PLATE 349.
Lighthouses and Docks

Figure
1. Ground plan of the West India docks in London
2. Ground plan of the harbor of Toulon

3–6. Prince's docks at Liverpool

7. Profile of the wall of the London docks
8. Profile of the Mersey quay at Liverpool

9–12. Dundee dry dock

13–17. The lighthouse of Trieste

18. Lighthouse of Bell rock (vertical section)

19–23. Iron lighthouse at Bermuda

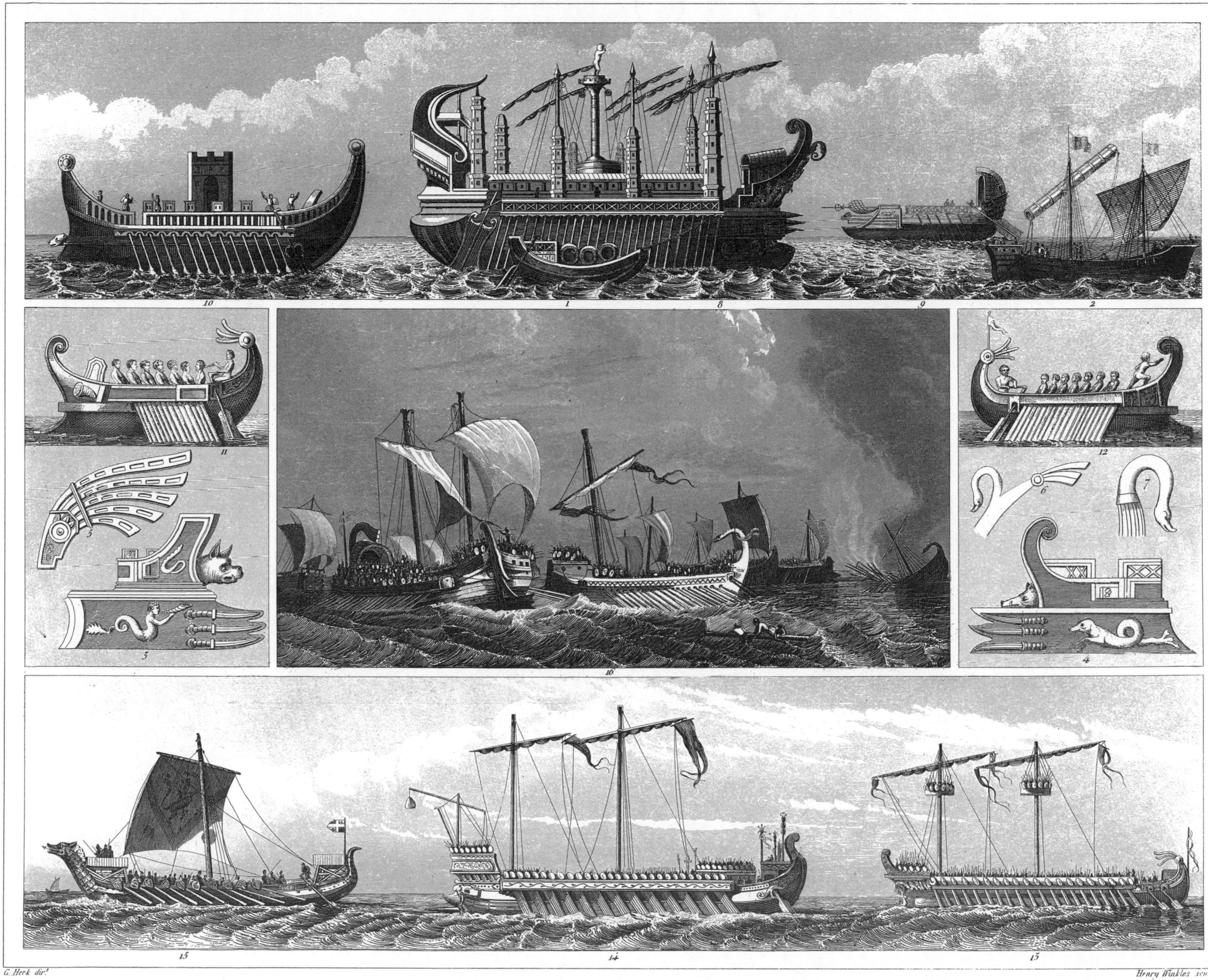

G. Heck dir.

Henry Winkles sculp.

PLATE 318. SEA VESSELS OF ANCIENT TIMES AND THE DARK AGES

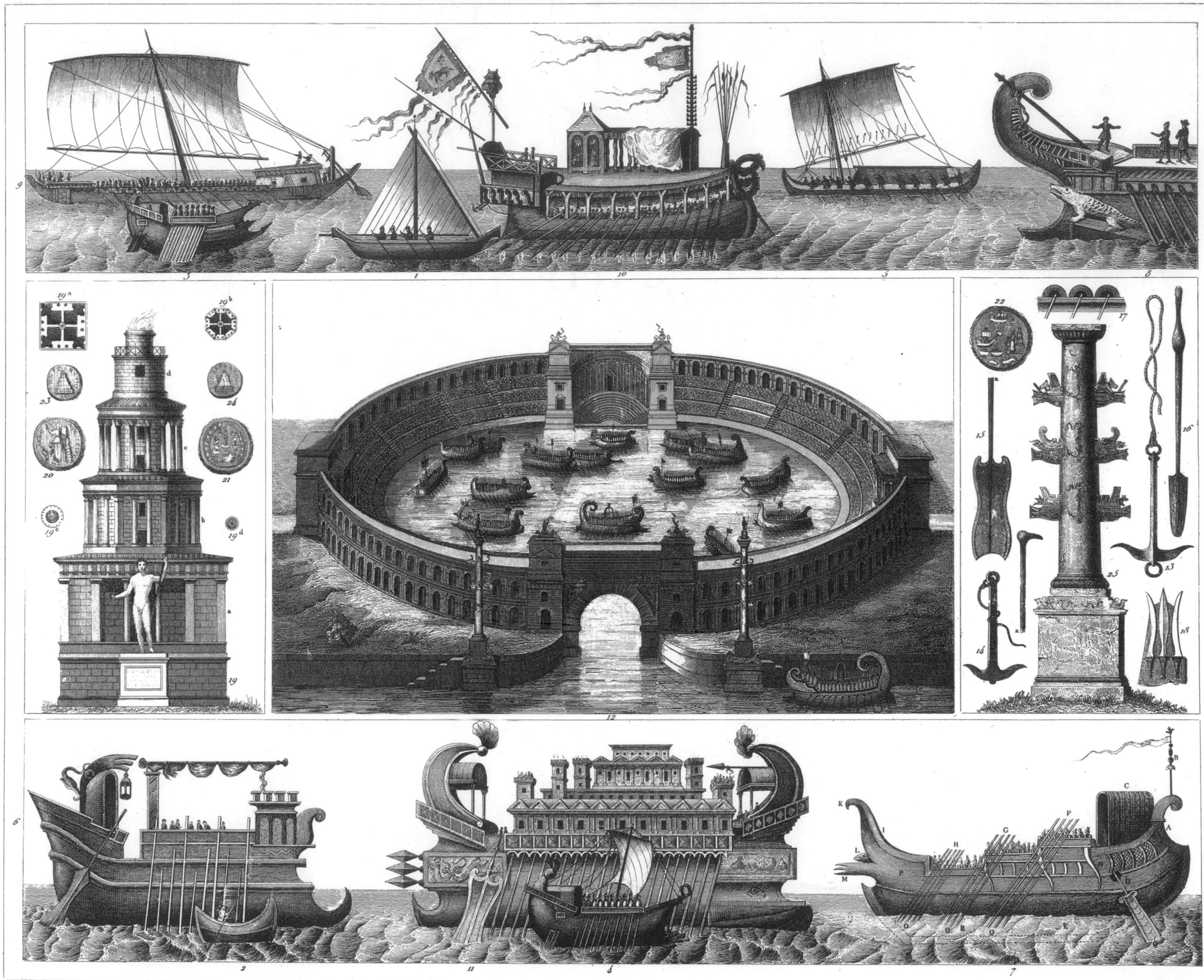

G. Heck dir.t

Henry Winkles sculp.t

 PLATE 319. ANCIENT VESSELS AND NAVAL TRAPPINGS; A ROMAN NAVAL SPECTACLE

4
6
7
2
1
5
3
G. Heck dir.
Henry Winkles sculp.

G. Heck dir.t Henry Winkles sculp.t

PLATE 321. SHIPS OF EUROPE

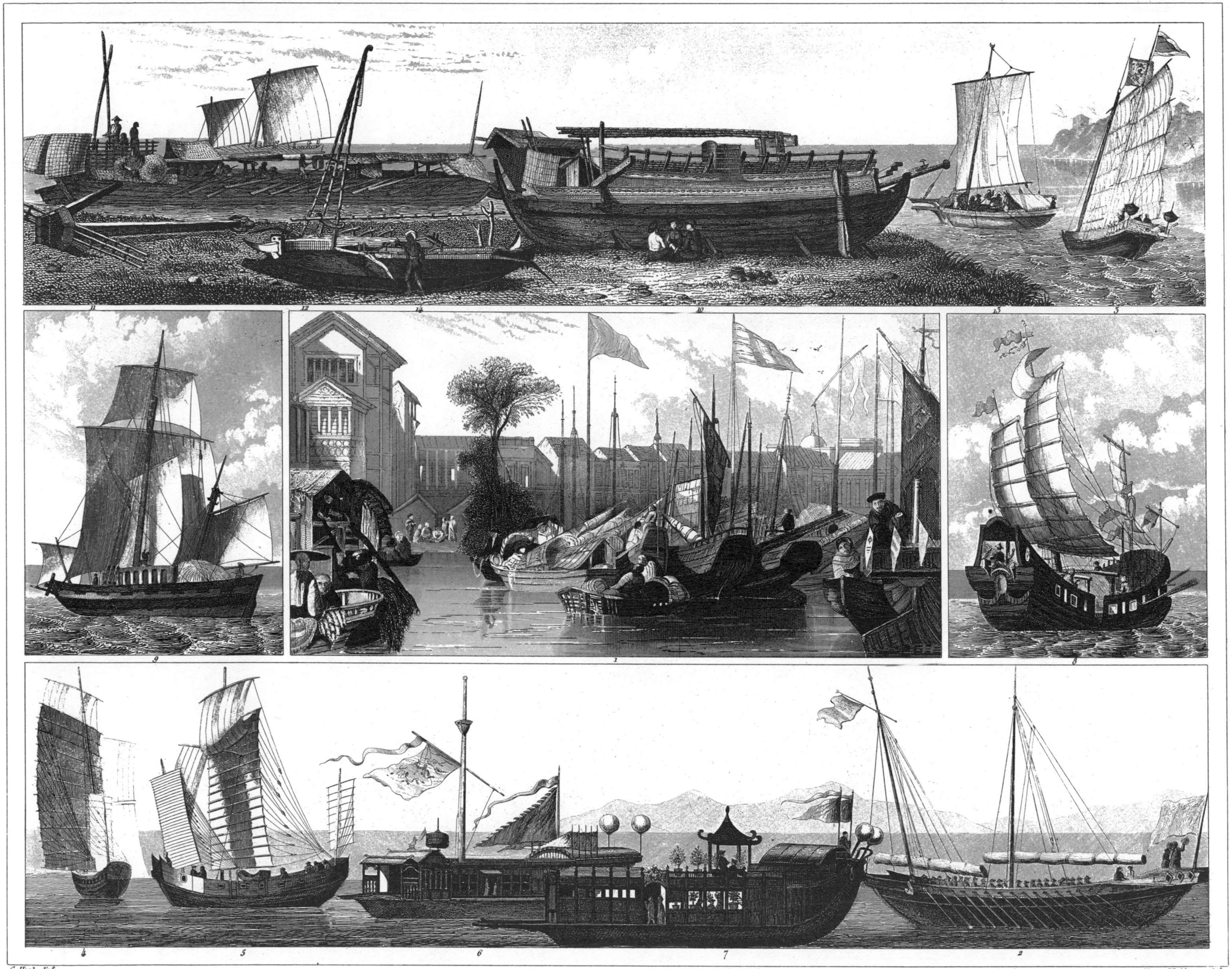

G. Heck dir^t. Henry Winkles sculp^t.

PLATE 322. SHIPS OF THE ORIENT

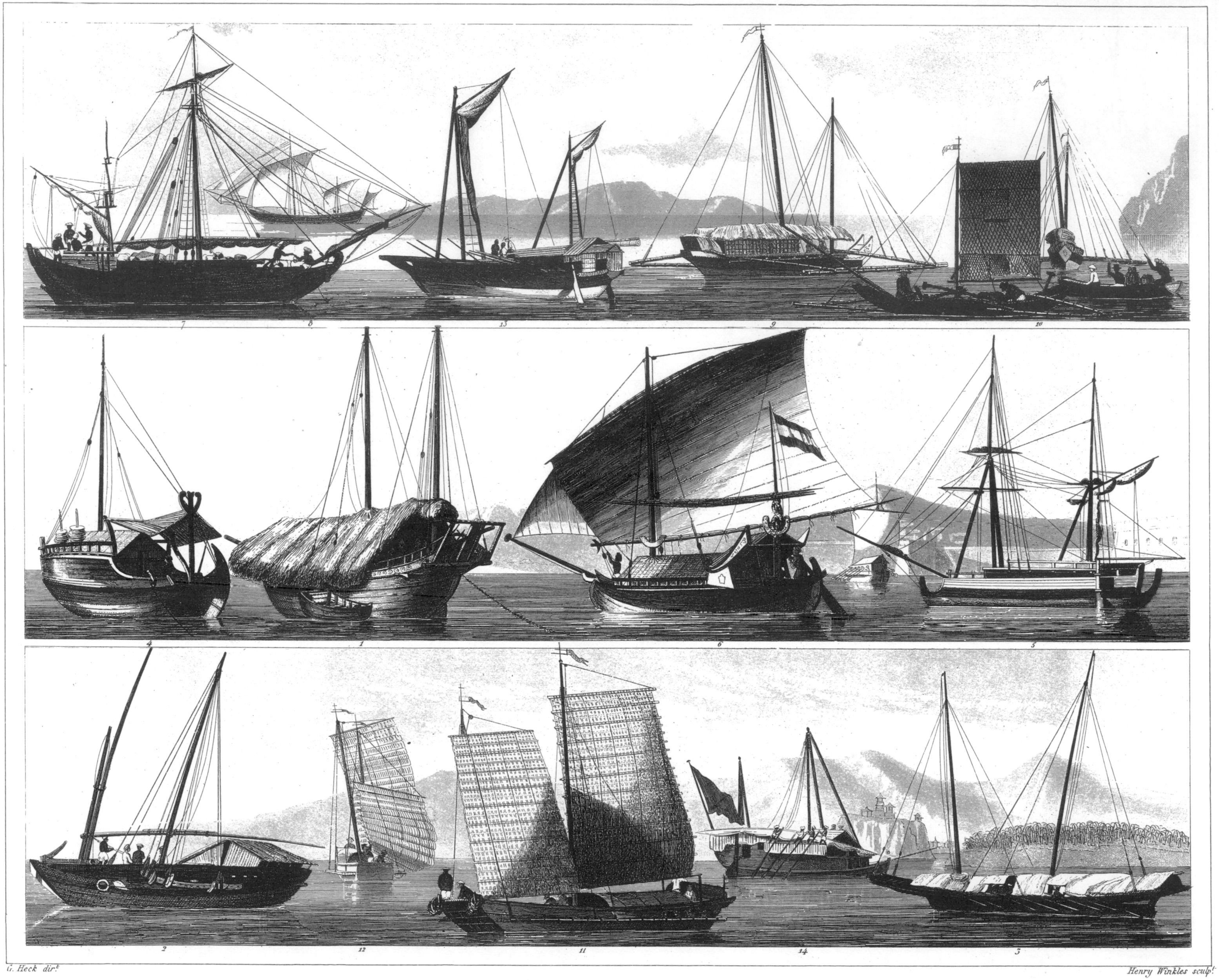

G. Heck dir.t Henry Winkles sculp.t

PLATE 323. SHIPS OF THE FAR EAST AND THE PACIFIC

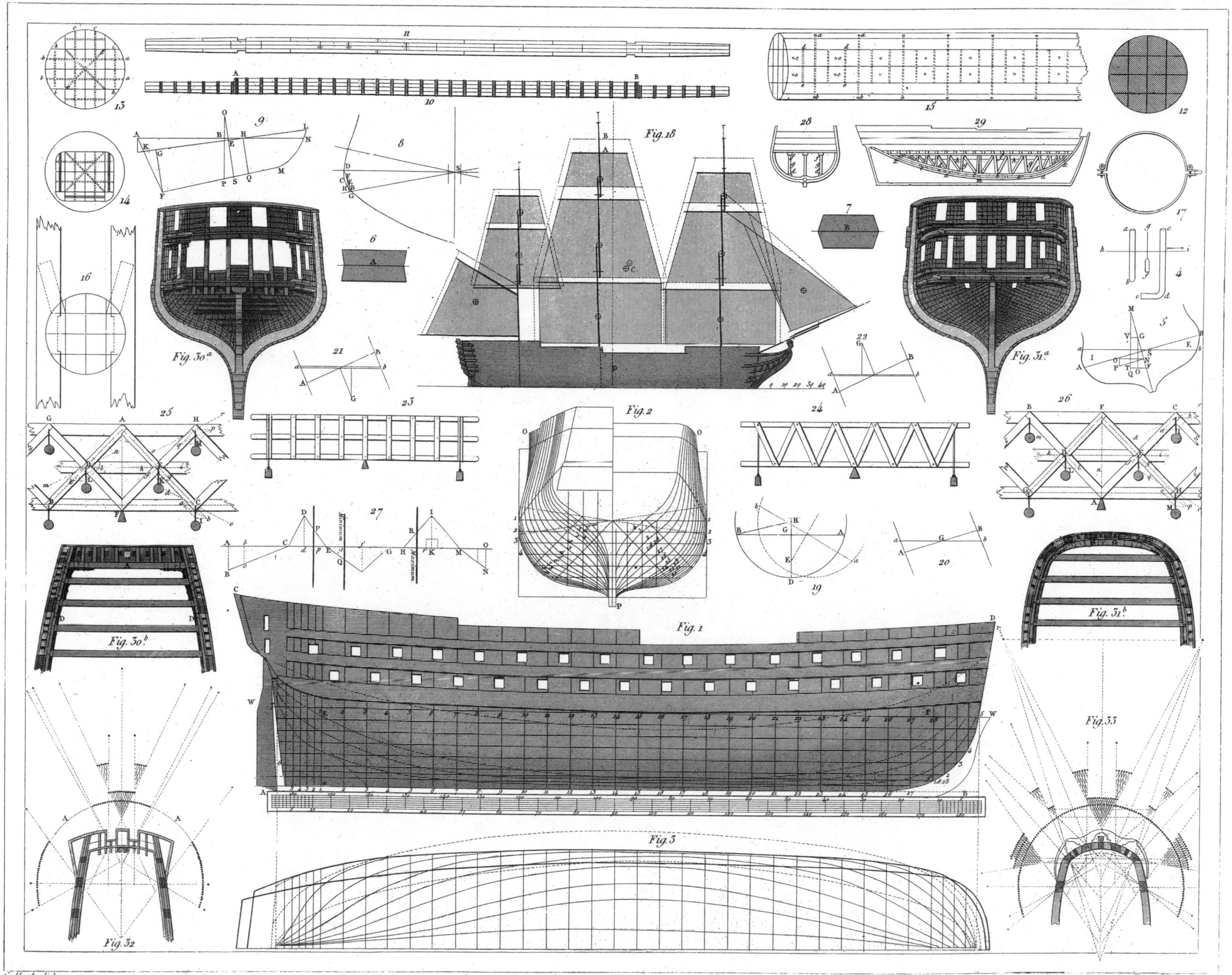

G. Heck dir.t Henry Winkles sculp.t

PLATE 324. ILLUSTRATING THE THEORY OF SHIPBUILDING

G. Heck dir^t. Henry Winkles sculp^t.

PLATE 325. CONSTRUCTION AND MAINTENANCE OF A SHIP

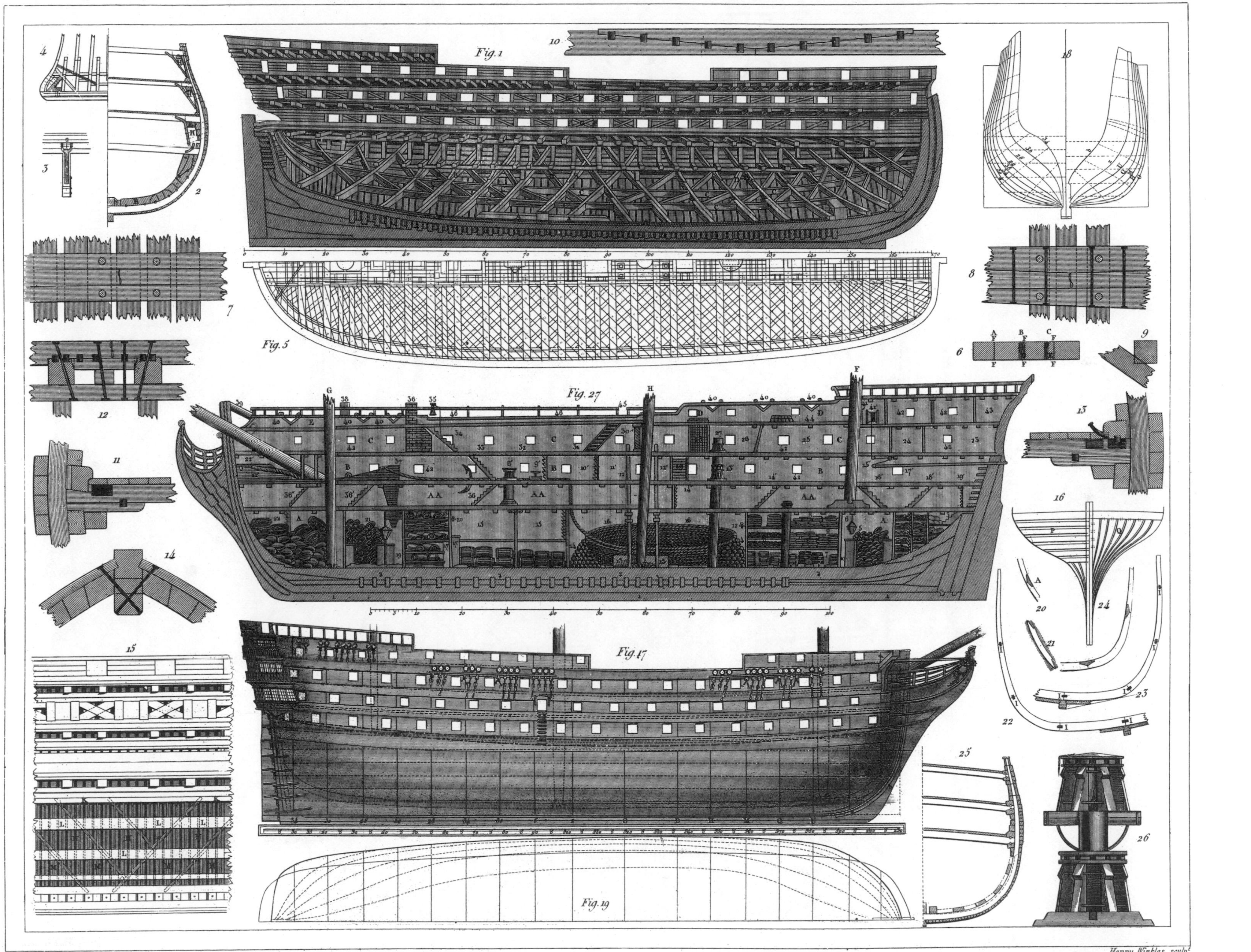

G. Heck dir.t Henry Winkles sculp.t

PLATE 326. BASIC STRUCTURE OF A SHIP

G. Heck dir. *Henry Winkles sculp.*

PLATE 327. VARIOUS VIEWS AND EQUIPMENT OF A SHIP

G. Heck dir.[t] Henry Winkles sculp.[t]

PLATE 328. FRENCH SHIP OF THE LINE AND EQUIPMENT

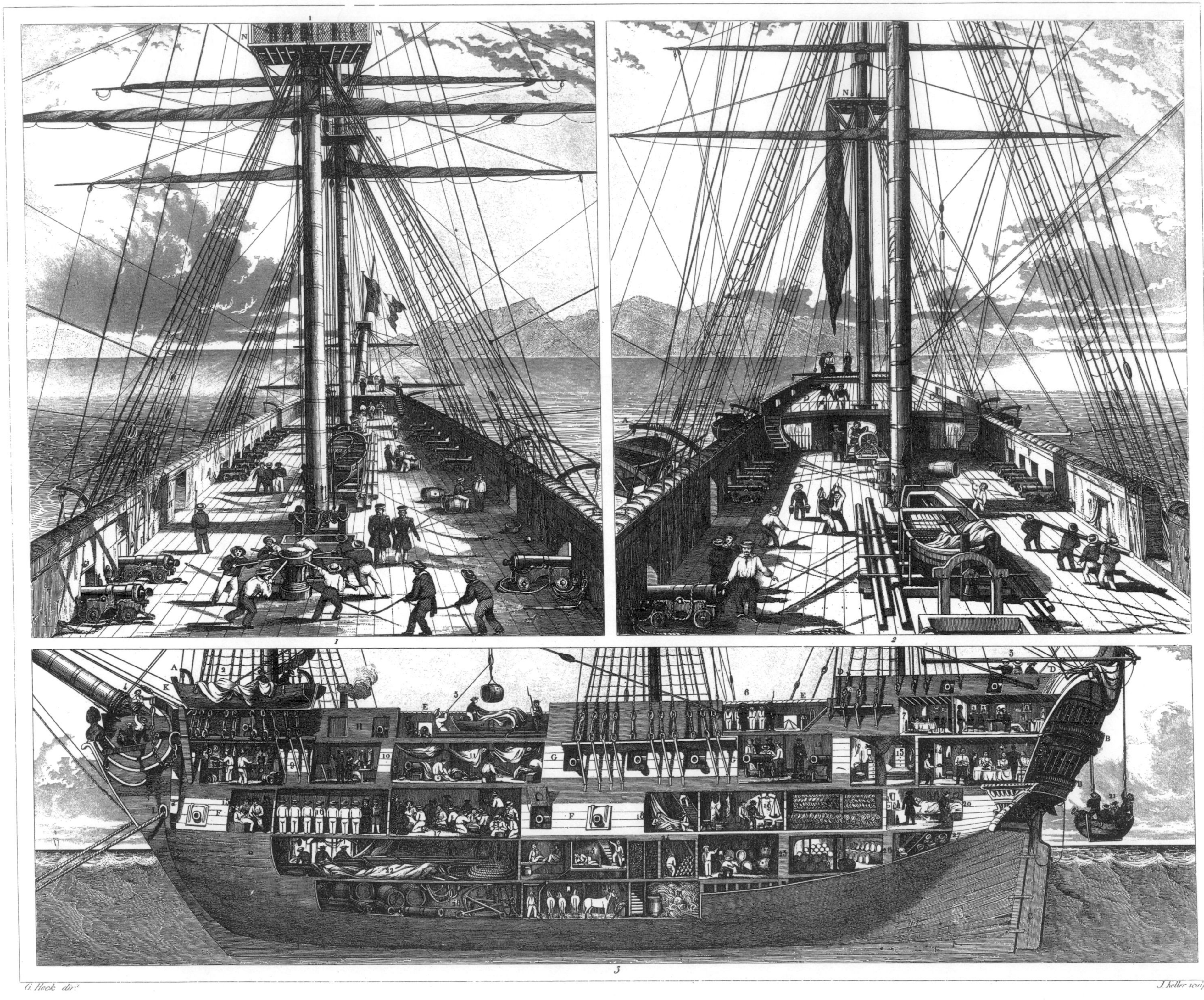

G. Heck dir. J. Keller sculp.

PLATE 329. VARIOUS VIEWS OF FRENCH SHIPS

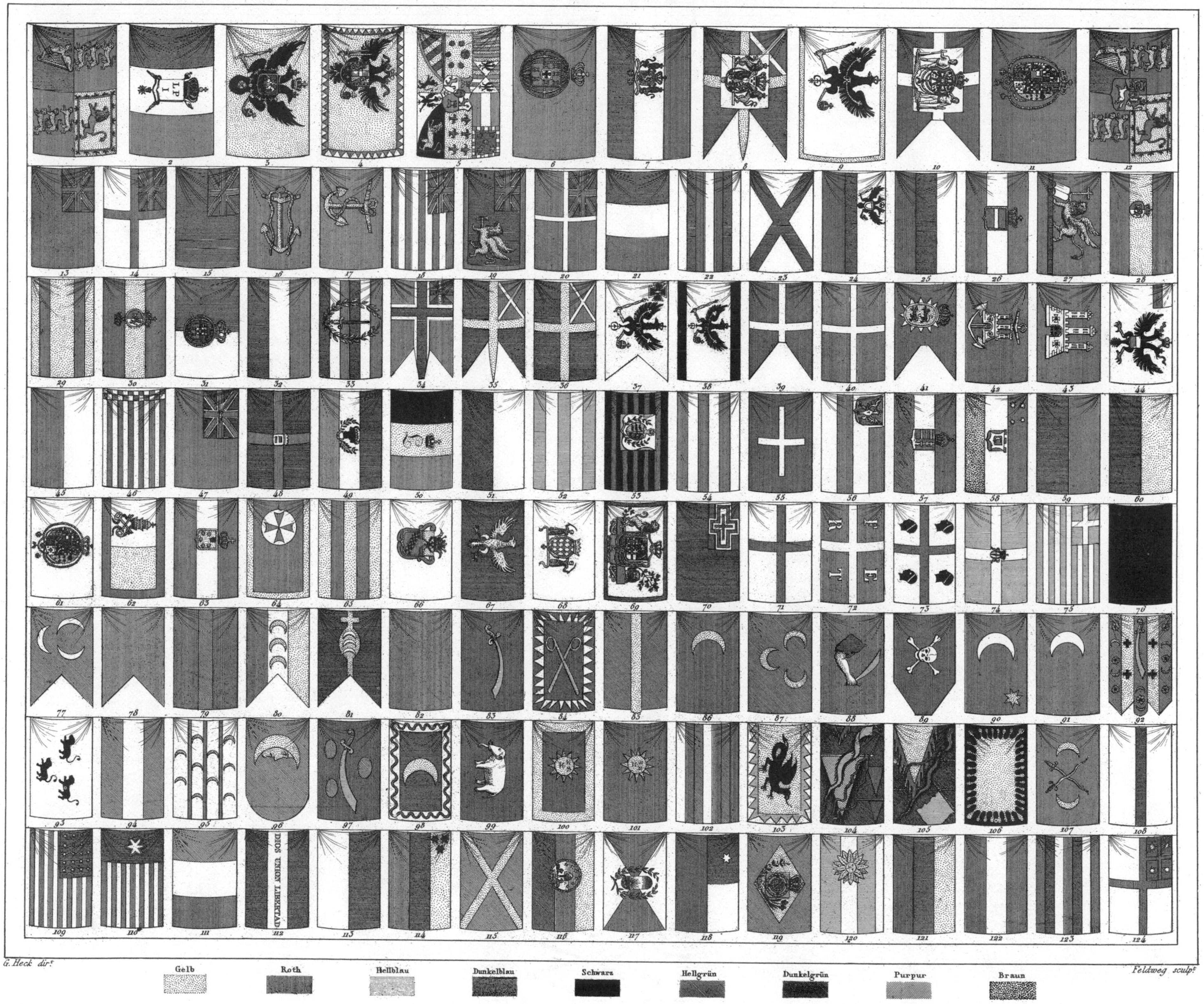
LP
I
DIOS UNION LIBERTAD
G. Heck dir.t
Feldweg sculp.t
Gelb
Roth
Hellblau
Dunkelblau
Schwarz
Hellgrün
Dunkelgrün
Purpur
Braun

PLATE 330. FLAGS OF VARIOUS NATIONS

G. Heck dir.

Henry Winkles sculp.

PLATE 331. EUROPEAN SHIPS OF VARIOUS FUNCTIONS

PLATE 332. TRADING AND FISHING SHIPS

G. Heck dir.t — *Henry Winkles sculp.t*

PLATE 333. STEAMSHIPS AND SAILING SHIPS OF VARIOUS RIGS

G. Heck dir.t

[H]enry Winkles sculp.t

PLATE 334. FRENCH STEAM-PROPELLED SAILING SHIPS; EUROPEAN SAILING SHIPS OF WAR

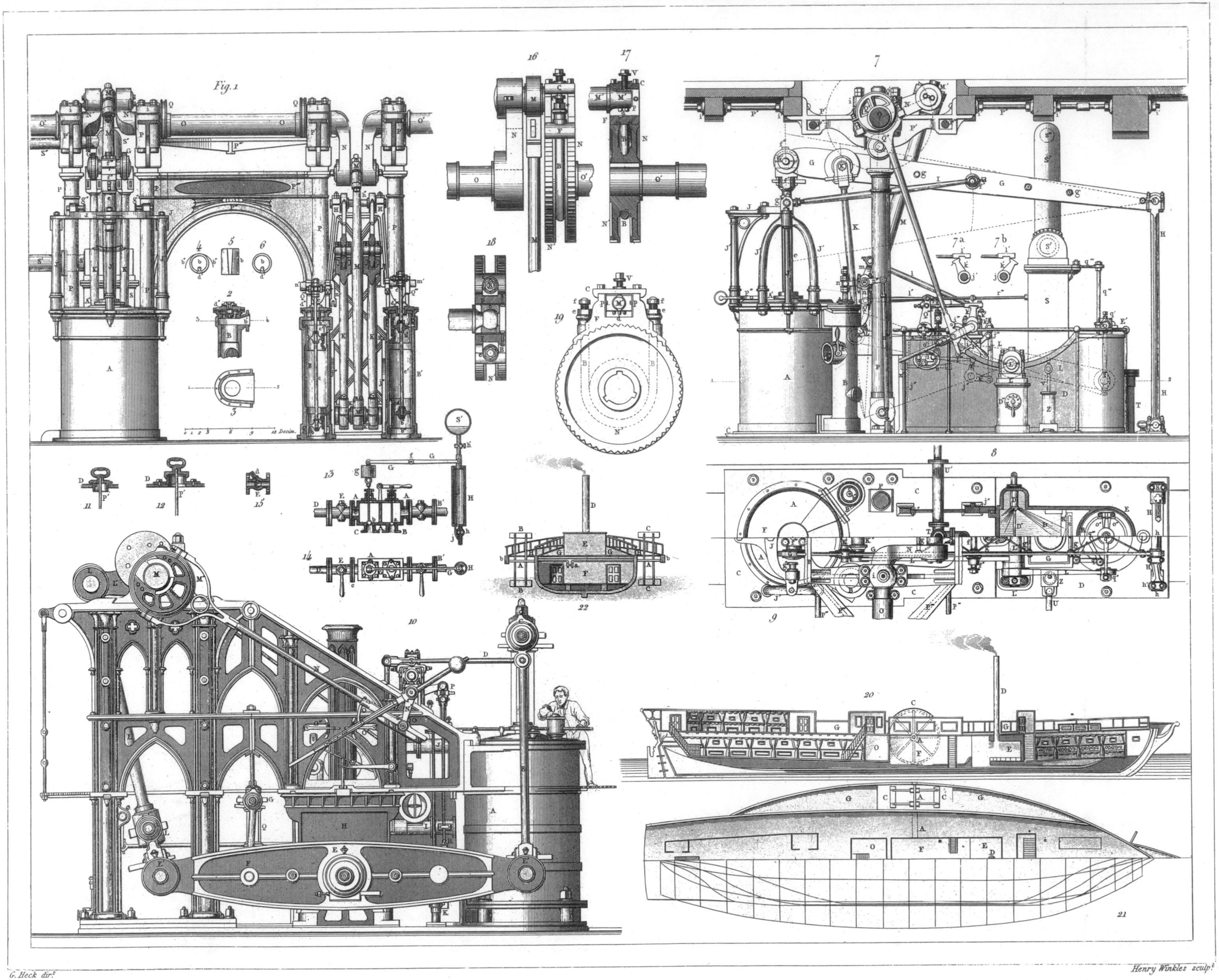

G. Heck dir.t Henry Winkles sculp.t

 PLATE 335. ILLUSTRATING THE CONSTRUCTION OF STEAMSHIPS

G. Heck dir.

Henry Winkles sculp.

PLATE 336. ILLUSTRATING THE CONSTRUCTION OF STEAMSHIPS

PLATE 337. NAVAL OFFICERS AND SAILORS

G. Heck dir.

Henry Winkles sculp.

PLATE 338. SCENES FROM SHIPBOARD LIFE

G. Heck dir.ᵗ Henry Winkles sculp.ᵗ

PLATE 339. SCENE ON A FRENCH FRIGATE

G. Heck dir.^t Henry Winkles sculp.^t

PLATE 340. SAILORS ON DECK DUTY

2

4

1

3

G. Heck, dir.t

Winkles et Lehmann sculp.t

PLATE 341. INCIDENTS ABOARD SHIP

G. Heck dir.^t Henry Winkles sculp.^t

PLATE 342. SHIPS ON PARADE AND SHIPBOARD LIFE

G. Heck dir.

Henry Winkles sculp.

PLATE 343. SHIP MANOEUVERS

G. Heck dir.t

Henry Winkles sculp.t

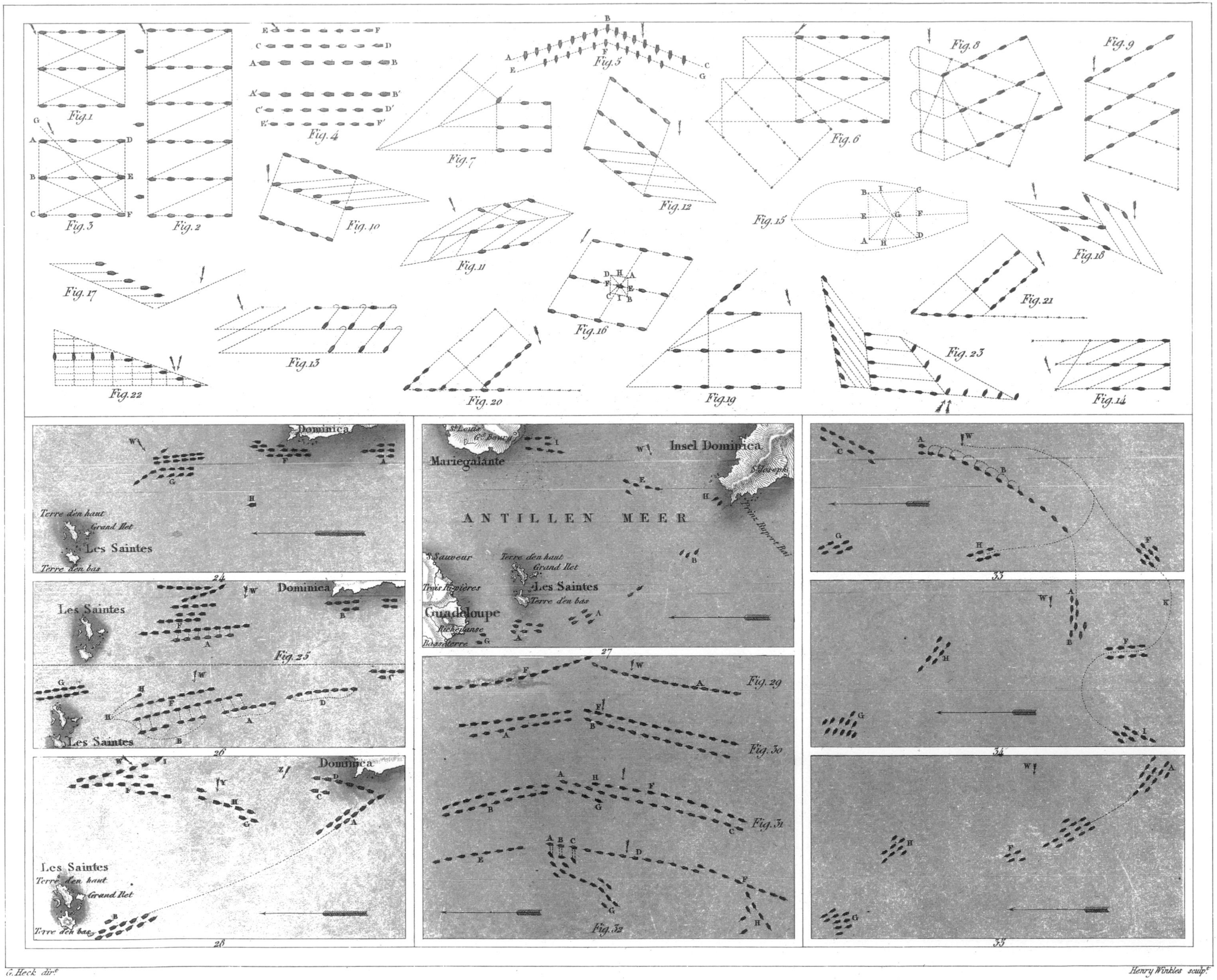
Fig. 1
Fig. 2
Fig. 3
Fig. 4
Fig. 5
Fig. 6
Fig. 7
Fig. 8
Fig. 9
Fig. 10
Fig. 11
Fig. 12
Fig. 13
Fig. 14
Fig. 15
Fig. 16
Fig. 17
Fig. 18
Fig. 19
Fig. 20
Fig. 21
Fig. 22
Fig. 23
Dominica
Terre d'en haut
Grand Ilet
Les Saintes
Terre d'en bas
24
Fig. 25
26
Insel Dominica
Mariegalante
ANTILLEN MEER
Guadeloupe
27
Fig. 29
Fig. 30
Fig. 31
Fig. 32
28
33
34
35
G. Heck dir.
Henry Winkles sculp.

 PLATE 345. ILLUSTRATING MANOEUVERS OF FLEETS

1 2 3

a 4 b

G. Heck dir.ᵗ Henry Winkles sculp.ᵗ

G. Heck dir.t

Henry Winkles sculp.t

PLATE 347. SHIPS IN DRYDOCK AND IN PORT

1

2

3

4

5

6

G. Heck dir.t

Henry Winkles sculp.t

Fig. 1
Themse
Süd Dock
Timber Dock
Westindische Docks (Ausfuhr)
Westindische Docks (Einfuhr)
Blackwall Eisenbahn
Bassin
Reservoirs
Fig. 2
Marine Arsenal
Artilleriepare
KRIEGSHAFEN
Bassins
Bagno
Fig. 3
Fig. 4
Fig. 5
Fig. 6
Fig. 7
Fig. 8
Fig. 9
Fig. 10
Fig. 11
Fig. 12
Fig. 13
Fig. 14
Fig. 15
Fig. 16
Fig. 17
Fig. 18
Fig. 19
Fig. 20
Fig. 21
Fig. 22
Fig. 23
Leucht ebene
G. Heck dir.
Henry Winkles sculp.

 PLATE 349. LIGHTHOUSES AND DOCKS

ARCHITECTURE

Captions to the Architecture Plates, 350–409

PLATE 350.
Ancient Indian Temples and Pagodas

Figure
1. Rock temple of Mavalipuram
2. Pagoda at Chalembaram
3. Pagoda at Tretshengur
4. Pagoda near Benares
5. Interior of the temple of Indra

6, 7. Grotto temples

PLATE 351.
Indian Temples at Ellora and Elephanta

Figure
1. Temple of Kailasa near Ellora
2. Temple of Indra Sabah at Ellora
3. Interior of the grotto temple on the island of Elephanta
4. Interior of the temple of Wisua Karmah at Ellora

PLATE 352.
Ancient Architecture and Sculpture

Figure
1, 2. Sculptures from Nineveh
3–11. Fragments from Persepolis
12. Tomb of Nakshirustam
13–15. Hindoo pillars

PLATE 353.
Egyptian Temples and Tombs

Figure
1. Temple of Antæopolis
2. Theatre in Antinoe
3. Ruins of Apollinopolis Magna
4. Temple of Carnak

5*a*. Temple of Tentyra
5*b*. Temple at Latopolis

6. Temple on the island of Philæ
7. Rock-cut tombs of Silsilis
8. Entrance to the temple of Typhon at Denderah

PLATE 354.
Temple, Palace, and Catacombs

Figure
1–6. Temple of Apollinopolis Magna
7. Plan of the Palace of Carnak
8–11. Details from the same
12. Catacombs at Thebes
13, 14. Catacombs of Alexandria

PLATE 355.
Pyramids and Monuments

Figure
1. Pyramid in Lake Mœris
2. Pyramids of Gizeh
3. Section of a pyramid at Memphis
4. Pyramid at Assur in Nubia
5. Colossi at Thebes
6. The Sphinx of Gizeh
7. Hall of the palace at Carnak
8. Entrance into the palace of Luxor
9. Propylæa on the island of Philæ

PLATE 356.
Illustrating General Considerations on Architecture

Figures 1–24.

PLATE 357.
Ancient Architecture

Figure
1. The Acropolis of Tiryns
2. Section of the same

3, 4. The Grottoes of Corneto

5. The Gate of the Lions at Mycenæ
6. Section through the same
7. Entrance of the Treasury of Atreus at Mycenæ
8. Section of the same

9–11. Plan and sections of the Giganteja on the Island of Gozzo

PLATE 358.
Architecture of Classical Greece

Figure
1. View of ancient Athens
2. Western front of the Parthenon
3. The temple of Theseus
4. The Tower of the Winds
5. The Choragian monument of Lysicrates
6. Temple of Segesta in Sicily

PLATE 359.
Classical Greek Temples

Figure
1, 2. Temple of Jupiter at Olympia
3–5. Temple of Theseus
6. Eastern front of the Parthenon
7. Plan of the Parthenon
8, 9. Temple of Minerva Polias, etc.
10–12. The Odeon in Athens
13, 14. Doric portico
15. Temple on the Ilissus
16. The temple of Diana in Eleusis
17. Temple of Cybele in Sardis
18, 19. Temple of Concordia in Agrigentum
20, 21. Temple at Pæstum
22, 23. Temple at Euxomus in Ionia
24–27. Temples at Pæstum

PLATE 360.
Greek and Roman Temples

Figure
1. The Acropolis of Athens
2. Temple of Jupiter Olympius in Athens, elevation
3. Temple of Jupiter Olympius in Athens, plan
4. Temple of Jupiter Olympius in Athens, section
5. Temple of Minerva Polias, Erechtheus, and the Hall of the Nymph Pandrosos in Athens (restored view)
6. Longitudinal section of the Parthenon in Athens

7, 8. Temple of Castor and Pollux in Rome
9–12. Temple of Faustina in Rome

13. Plan of the temple of Cybele in Sardis
14. Plan of the temple of Concordia in Agrigentum
15. Plan of the temple of Juno in Agrigentum

16, 17. Plans of Doric temples in Selinuntiæ

18. Plan of the temple of Ceres in Pæstum
19. Plan of the temple of Minerva in Sunium
20. Plan of the temple of Apollo at Bassæ

PLATE 361.
Greek Temples in Several European Countries

Figure
1, 2. Temple of Diana at Ephesus
3, 4. Temple of Apollo at Miletus
5, 6. Temple of Bacchus at Teos
7, 8. Temple of Diana in Magnesia
9. Ruins of the temple of Neptune at Pæstum
10, 11. Temple of Jupiter at Selinuntiæ
12. Temple of the Sun in Palmyra
13, 14. Temple of Nemesis at Rhamnus
15, 16. Temple of Portumnus at Ostia
17. Temple of Jupiter in Rome

PLATE 362.
Roman and Middle Eastern Architecture

Figure
1. Ruins of Baalbec
2. Plan of the temple of the Sun at Baalbec
3. Plan of the temple of Jupiter at Baalbec

4, 5. Temple of Concordia in Rome

6. Plan of the temple of the Sun in Palmyra
7. Plan of the temple of Mars in Rome
8. Plan of the temple of Portumnus in Ostia
9. Plan of the temple of Serapis in Pozzuoli
10. Plan of the temple of Augustus in Pompeii
11. Plan of the Rotunda on the Via Prænestina in Rome
12. Plan of the temple of Theseus in Athens
13. Plan of the temple of Jupiter in Ægina

14, 15. Portico of Metellus
16, 17. Forum of Nerva
18–22*ab*. Mausoleum at Halicarnassus

PLATE 363.
Roman Forum and Various Amphitheatres

Figure
1. The Forum Romanum
2. Amphitheatre of Flavius
3. Half ground plan of the Coliseum
4. Section of the Amphitheatre at Verona
5. Section of the Amphitheatre at Nismes

PLATE 364.
Greek and Roman Temples

Figure
1, 2. Temple of Neptune in Pæstum
3–5. Temple of Jupiter at Olympia

19. Portal of the Ecole des Beaux Arts in Paris
20. Triumphal arch of Alphonso I. in Naples

PLATE 392.
Renaissance Churches and Architectural Details

Figure
1–3. Church of the Redeemer in Venice
4–16. Church of St. Francis in Perugia
17. Plan of the church of St. Zacharias in Venice
18, 19. Monument of the Doge Vendramini in Venice
20–22. Monument of Louis XII. in St. Denis
23. Capital from the triumphal arch of Alfonso I. in Naples

PLATE 393.
Saint Peter's in Rome

Figures 1–4.

PLATE 394.
Italian Churches of the Middle Ages and Renaissance

Figure
1, 2. The church Della Superga in Turin
3, 4. The church of the Assumption in Genoa
5. The basilica in Vicenza
6. The church of Santa Maria del Fiore in Florence
7–9. The church San Pietro in Montorio in Rome
10. The church delle Figlie in Venice
11. The church of Trevignano

PLATE 395.
European Churches of Various Architectural Styles

Figure
1. Interior of St. Magdalene's church in Paris
2. The church of Notre Dame de Lorette in Paris
3, 4. The church of St. Gervais and St. Protais in Paris
5. The church of St. Paul and St. Louis in Paris
6, 7. The church of Mary Magdalene at Bridgenorth
8. All Saints church in Munich
9. The basilica St. Boniface in Munich
10. The church of San Giorgio Maggiore in Venice
11. The church of St. Francesco de la Vigna in Venice
12. The church of San Pietro in Montorio in Rome
13, 14. Chapel at Fresnes
15. Plan of the basilica Bibiana in Rome
16. Plan of the church of St. Agnes in Rome
17. Plan of the basilica Julia in Rome
18. Plan of the church St. Cosmo e Damiano
19, 20. Church Madonna degli Angeli in Rome
21, 22. The church of St. Cyriacus in Ancona

PLATE 396.
European Churches of the Sixteenth and Seventeenth Centuries

Figure
1–6. The Hotel des Invalides in Paris
7, 8. St. Isaac's church in St. Petersburg
9–11. The church of the Sorbonne in Paris
12–14. The church of the Assumption in Paris

PLATE 397.
European Churches of the Seventeenth and Eighteenth Centuries

Figure
1, 2. St. Magdalene's church in Paris
3–5. The Pantheon in Paris
6. Plan of Notre Dame de Lorette in Paris
7, 8. The Garrison church at Potsdam
9. The church of St. Ignatius in Rome
10, 11. The church of San Carlo alle Quattro Fontane in Rome
12. The bell tower of Palermo

PLATE 398.
Major European Cathedrals

Figure
1–3. St. Paul's church in London
4, 5. Church of St. Sulpice in Paris
6. Plan of Santa Maria del Fiore in Florence
7. Interior of the church of All Saints in Munich
8. Interior of the church in Faubourg Au in Munich

PLATE 399.
European Churches of Various Architectural Periods

Figure
1. Interior of the Invalides' church in Paris
2. Church of St. Louis in Munich
3. Werder church in Berlin
4. The chapel of St. Ferdinand at Sablonville
5. The church Santa Maria della Vittoria in Rome
6, 7. The church della Consolazione in Todi
8. Ground plan of a church in the form of a Latin cross
9. Plan of the church San Andrea in Mantua
10–12. The chapel of the Knights of Malta in St. Petersburg
13. The clock tower in Venice

PLATE 400.
Secular Architecture of the Renaissance and Baroque Eras

Figure
1–4. The palace of Caserta near Naples
5. Court of the Palazzo Saoli in Genoa
6. Plan of the palace of Laeken
7. Plan of the country seat of the duke of Argyle in Scotland
8–13. Markets

PLATE 401.
Palatial Architecture of Various Periods

Figure
1, 2. The Louvre in Paris
3. The papal Cancelleria in Rome
4. The papal palace in Rome
5. The Palazzo Paolo in Rome
6. The Palazzo Sora in Rome
7. The Palazzo Sacchetti in Rome
8. The Villa Medici in Rome
9. The Palazzo Giraud in Rome
10*a–c*. The Casa Silvestri in Rome
11. Ground plan of an antique Roman building

PLATE 402.
Palatial and Monumental Architecture of France and Germany

Figure
1. The palace of the Tuileries in Paris
2, 3. The navy department in Paris
4. The Luxembourg palace in Paris
5. The palace of Laeken
6. Plan of the Glyptothek in Munich
7–9. The column of the Place Vendôme in Paris
10*ab*, 11. The column of July in Paris
12, 13. The bell tower in Rome

PLATE 403.
Neo-Classical Architecture in France and Rome

Figure
1. The palace of Versailles
2. The battle gallery in the same
3. The Palazzo Doria Tursi in Genoa
4. The Fontana Paolina in Rome
5. The fountain of Marius
6–9. Doors from Roman palaces

PLATE 404.
Neo-Classical Architecture in Germany and Holland

Figure
1, 2. The Walhalla at Ratisbon
3*ab*. Candelabra from the same
4–6. The royal residence in Amsterdam
7. The city hall at Maestricht
8, 9. The town hall in Neuenburg

PLATE 405.
Public Buildings in the Neo-Classical Style

Figure
1. The Capitol at Washington
2. The Glyptothek in Munich
3. The edifice for exhibitions in Munich
4. The Exchange in New York
5–7. The Exchange in Paris
8, 9. Plans of the Exchange in Ghent
10. The University of Ghent
11. The Exchange in London

PLATE 406.
Monumental and Public Architecture of Various Periods

Figure
1. The triumphal arch in Paris
2, 3. The Paris observatory
4. The theatre at Dresden
5, 6. The theatre in St. Petersburg
7. St. Charles theatre in New Orleans
8. The Custom-house in New York
9. Plan of the Palazzo del Te in Mantua
10–12. Casino in Liège
13. The museum in Cassel
14. Old Exchange in Amsterdam
15*ab*. Plans of caravansaries
16*ab*, 17. Watchhouses
18. Plan of the prison in Aix

PLATE 407.
Commercial Architecture

Figure
1–4. Grain hall in Paris
5–7. Market of St. Germain in Paris

8. The market at Pavia
9, 10. The Magdalene market in Paris
11. Plan of the market in Pavia
12, 13. The Almeidan at Ispahan

PLATE 408.
Various European Prisons

Figure
1–14. The prison at Halle
15. Plan of the prison of Newgate in London
16–18. Plans of Prisons in Ghent, Milan, and Amsterdam

PLATE 409.
The Architecture of Bridges

Figure
1, 2. Bridge over the Rialto in Venice
3–6. Bridge at Ispahan
7. Bridge of Gignac
8–10. Bridges at Paris
11. Waterloo Bridge in London
12. Bridge of St. Maizence
13. Bridge of Kösen
14. Bridge of Zwetau
15. Bridge over the Taff
16. Bridge over the Melfa
17. Bridge of the Ticino
18. Bridge near Lyons
19, 20. Chinese bridges
21. Bridge of Toledo
22. The bridge of Colebrookdale

G. Heck dir.t Henry Winkles sculp.t

PLATE 350. ANCIENT INDIAN TEMPLES AND PAGODAS

G. Heck dir.

Henry Winkles sculp.

 PLATE 351. INDIAN TEMPLES AT ELLORA AND ELEPHANTA

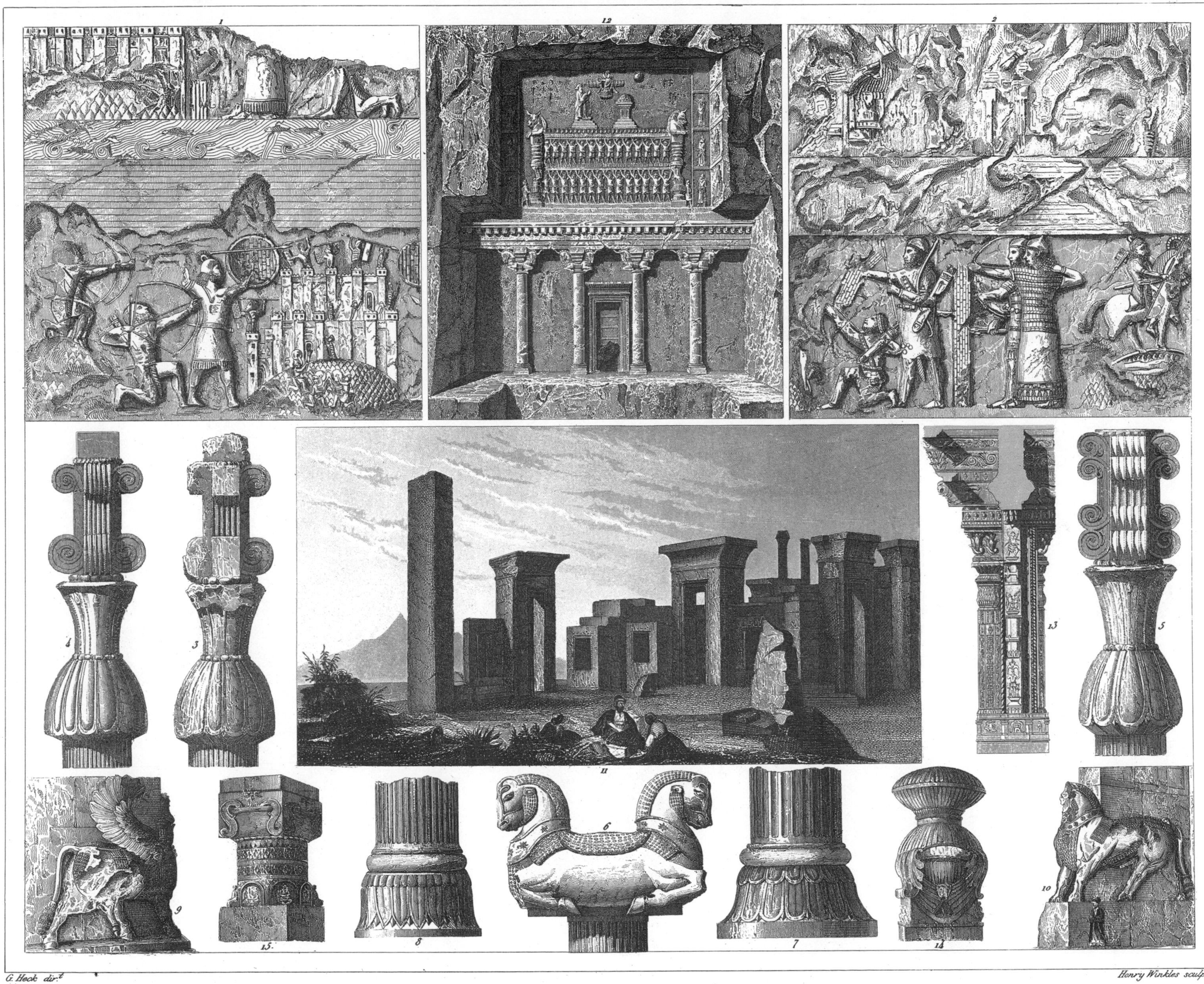

G. Heck dir.t

Henry Winkles sculp.t

PLATE 352. ANCIENT ARCHITECTURE AND SCULPTURE

G. Heck dir.t

Henry Winkles sculp.t

 PLATE 353. EGYPTIAN TEMPLES AND TOMBS

G. Heck dir.t

Henry Winkles sculp.t

Maasstab für Figur 2.

0 5 10 20 30 40 Métres

Maasstab für Figur 3 & 4.

0 5 10 15 20 25 30 Métres

PLATE 354. TEMPLE, PALACE, AND CATACOMBS

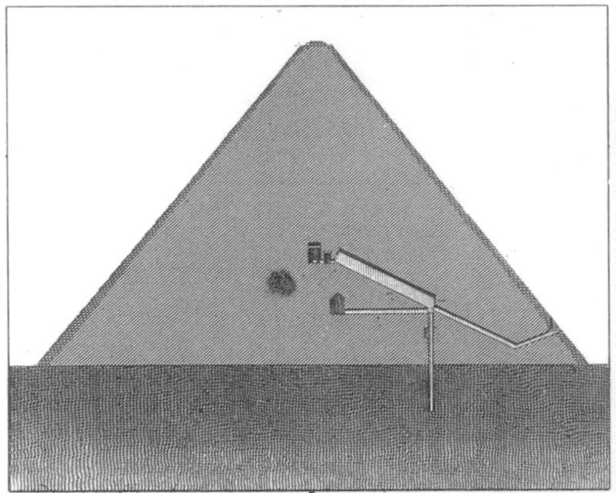

3

1

4

7

2

8

6

9

5

G. Heck dir.

Henry Winkles sculpt.

PLATE 355. PYRAMIDS AND MONUMENTS

PLATE 356. ILLUSTRATING GENERAL CONSIDERATIONS ON ARCHITECTURE

5
4
7
6
9
2
11
1
10
3
8
dir.t
Maasstab für Fig.10.
0 1 2 3 4 5 10 15 20 Metr.
Maasstab für Fig.8.
0 1 2 3 4 5 10 15 20 Metr.
Henry Winkles sculp.t
Maasstab für Fig.9
0 1 2 3 4 5 6 Metr.

Henry Winkles sculp.
G. Heck dir.

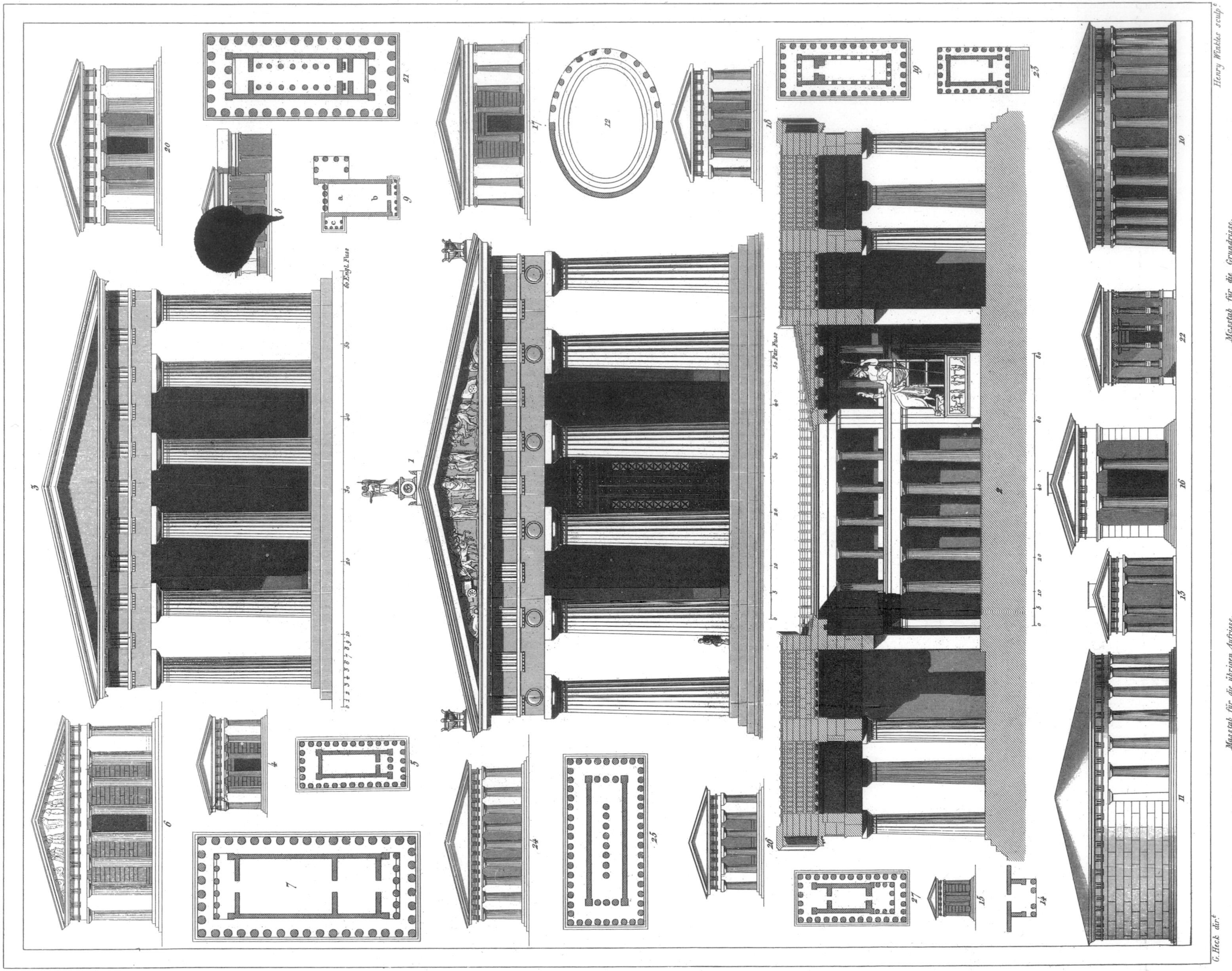
Henry Winkles sculp.t
G. Heck dir.t
Masstab für die Grundrisse
Masstab für die übrigen Aufrisse

 PLATE 359. CLASSICAL GREEK TEMPLES

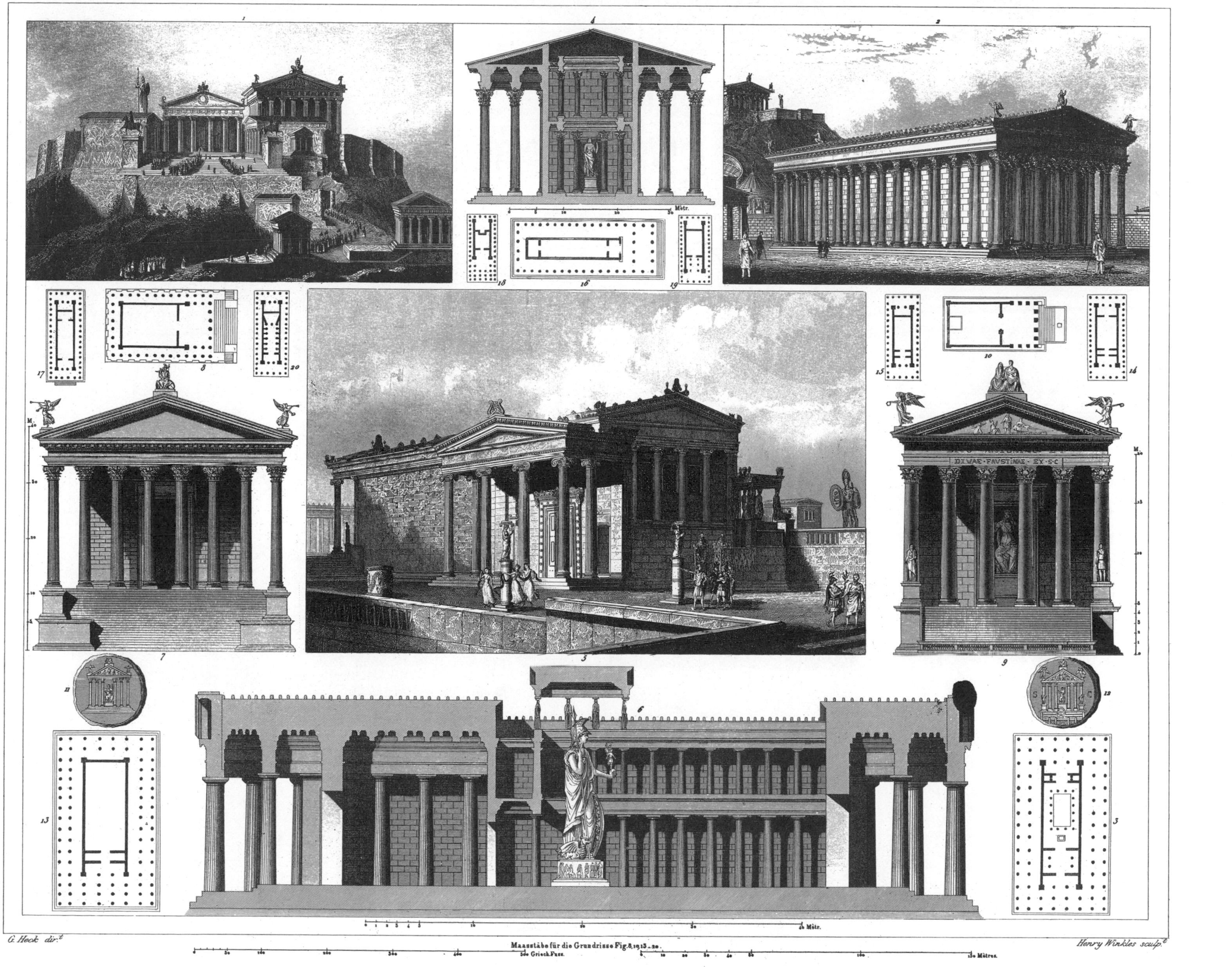
DIVAE·FAVSTINAE·EX·S·C
Mètr.
G. Heck dir.t
Henry Winkles sculp.t
Maasstäbe für die Grundrisse Fig. 8,13,15-20.
300 Griech.Fuss.
130 Mètres.

PLATE 360. GREEK AND ROMAN TEMPLES

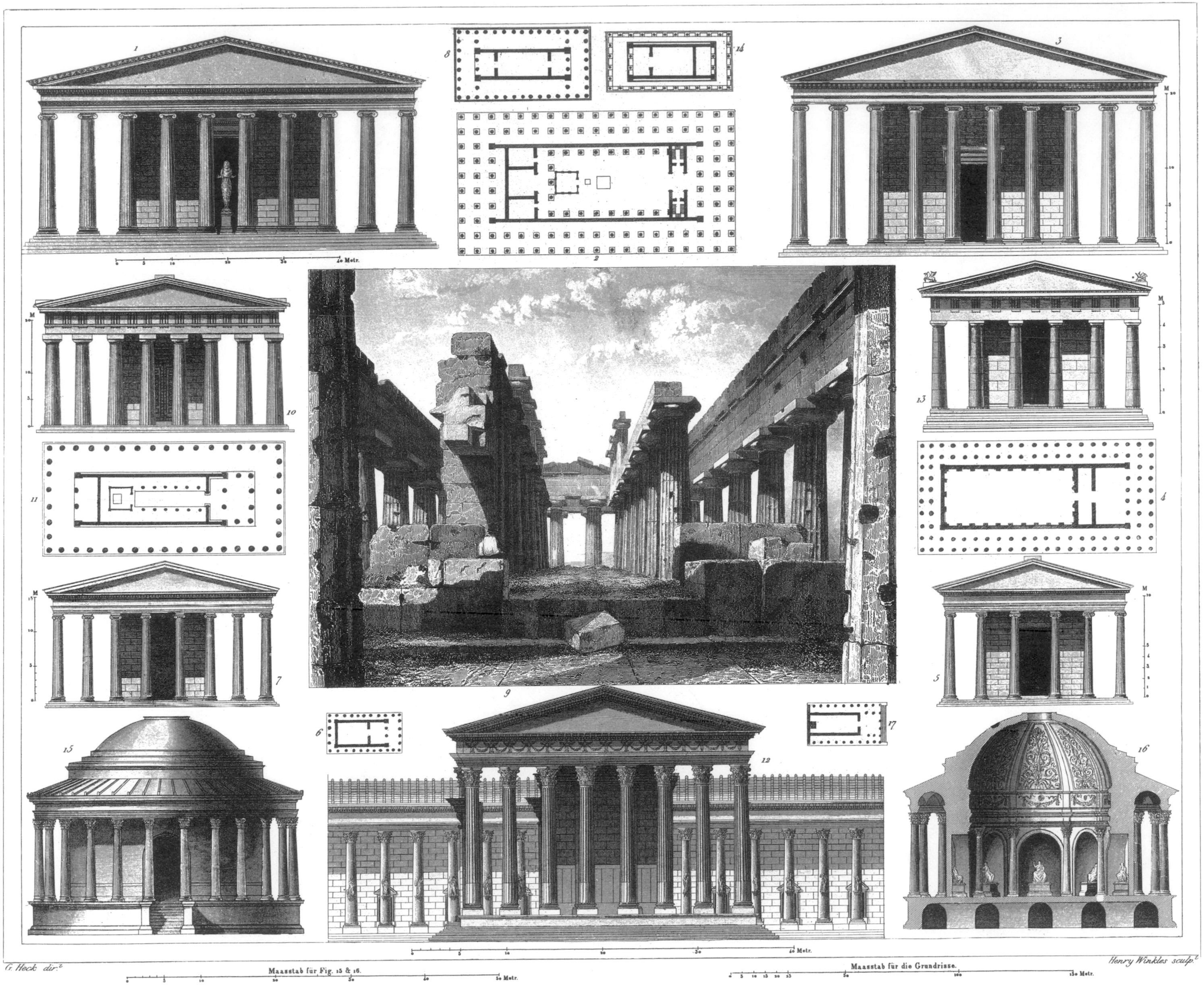

PLATE 361. GREEK TEMPLES IN SEVERAL EUROPEAN COUNTRIES

PLATE 362. ROMAN AND MIDDLE EASTERN ARCHITECTURE

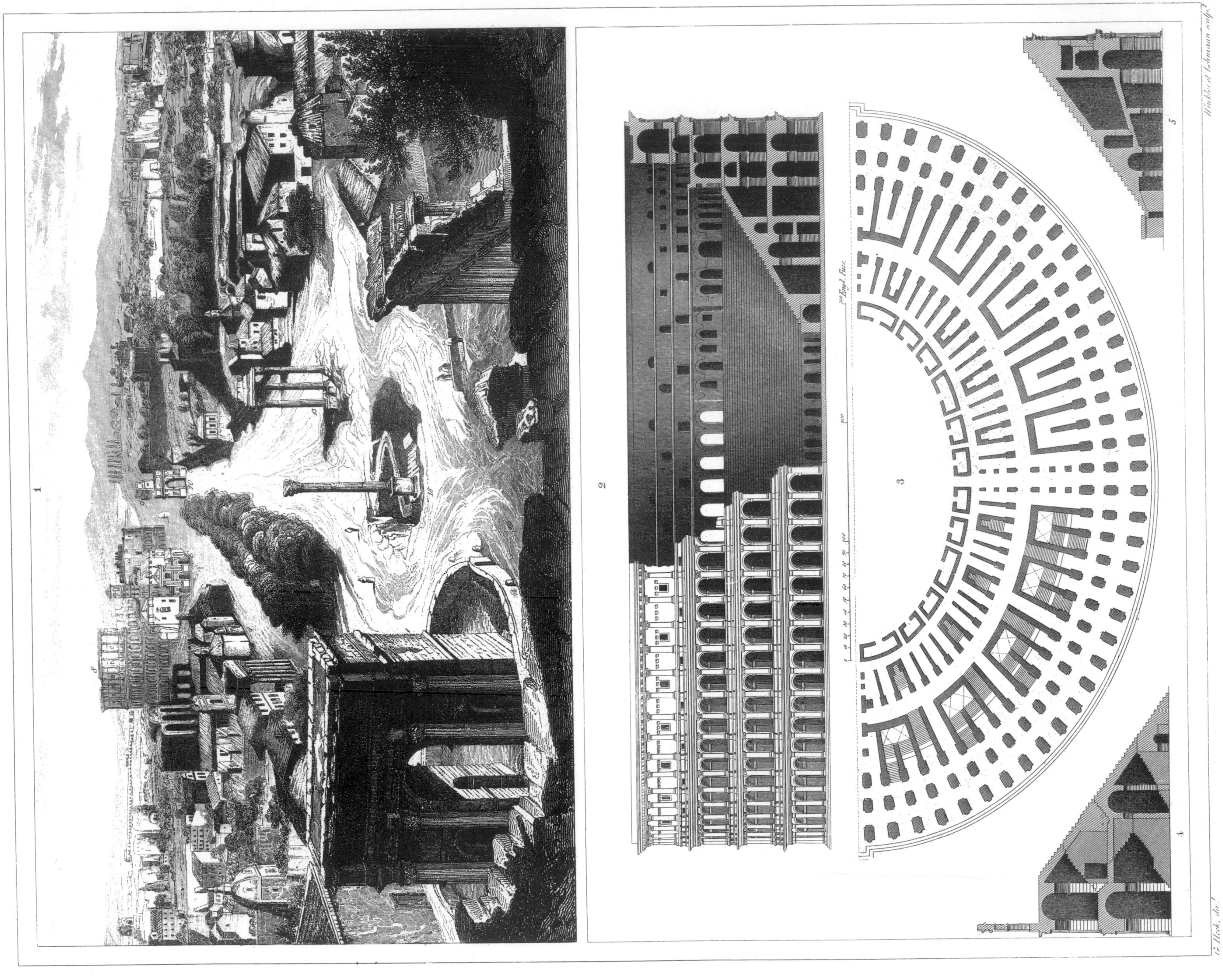

PLATE 363. ROMAN FORUM AND VARIOUS AMPHITHEATRES

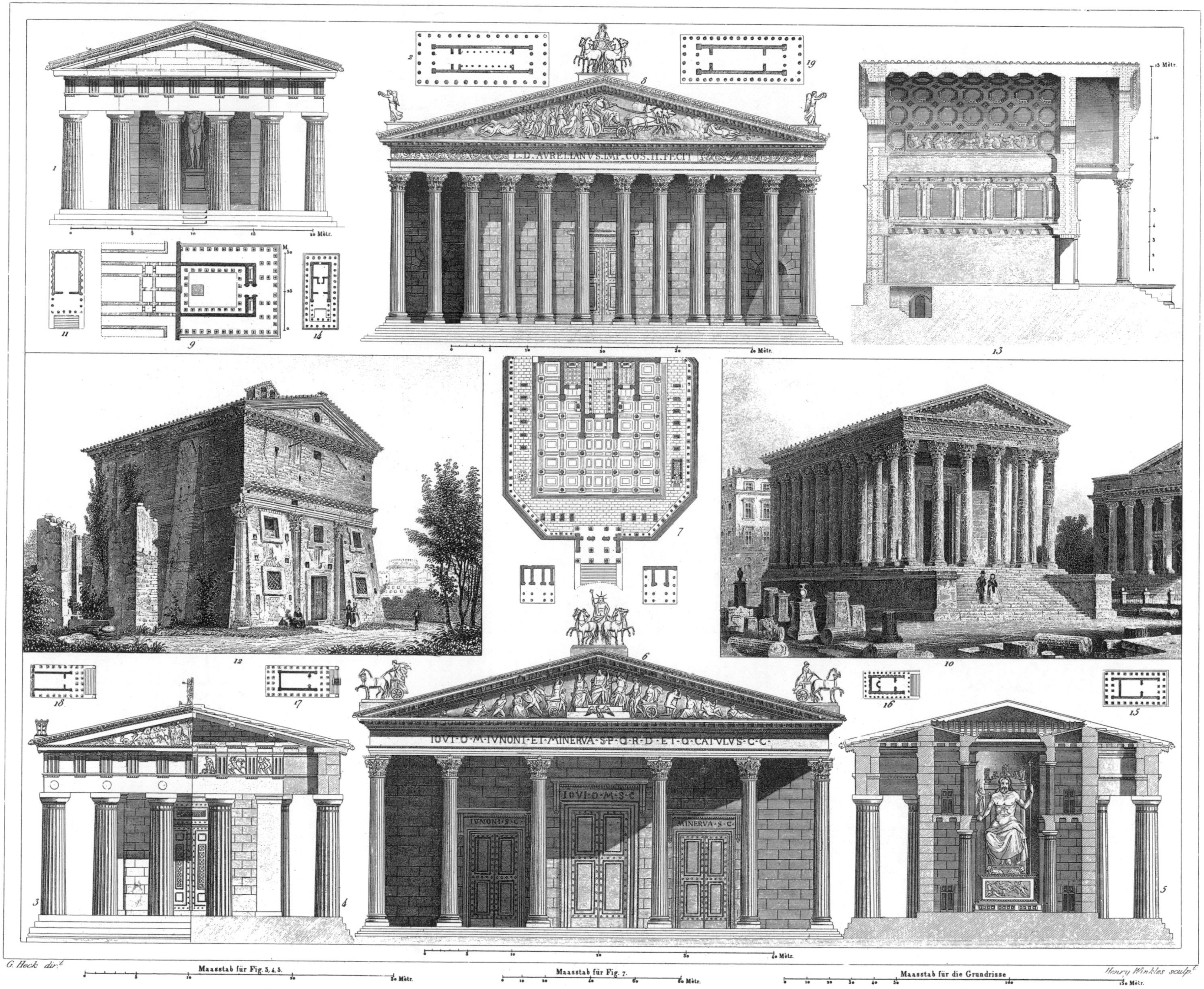
L·D·AVRELIANVS·IMP·COS·II·FECIT
IOVI·O·M·IVNONI·ET·MINERVA·S·P·Q·R·D·E·T·Q·CATVLVS·C·C·
IOVI·O·M·S·C
IVNONI·S·C
MINERVA·S·C
G. Heck dir.
Maasstab für Fig. 3, 4, 5.
Maasstab für Fig. 7.
Maasstab für die Grundrisse
Henry Winkles sculp.

PLATE 364. GREEK AND ROMAN TEMPLES

PLATE 365. TEMPLE AT BAALBEC AND OTHER GREEK AND ROMAN ARCHITECTURE

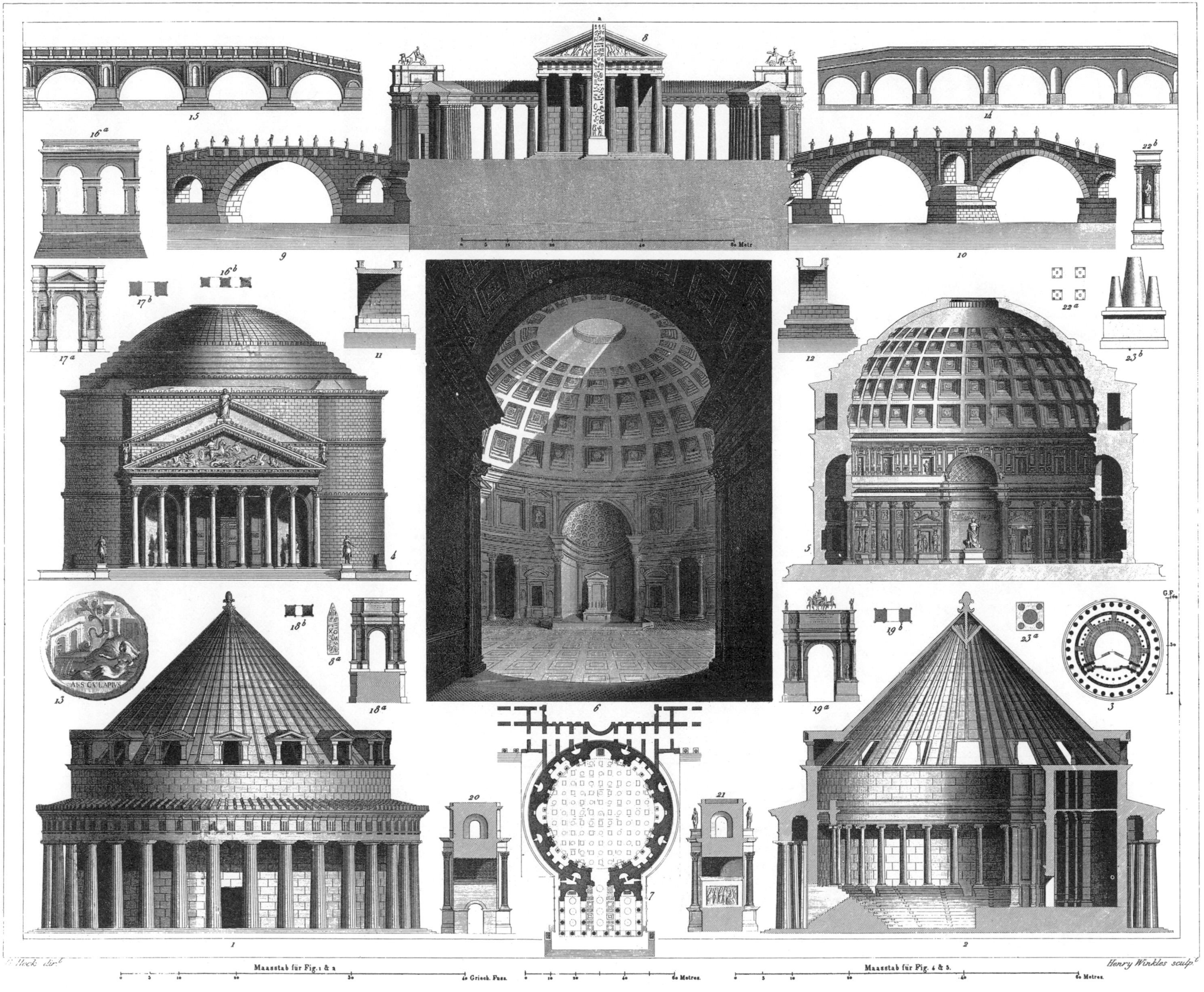

PLATE 366. MONUMENTAL AND TRIUMPHAL ARCHITECTURE IN GREECE AND ROME

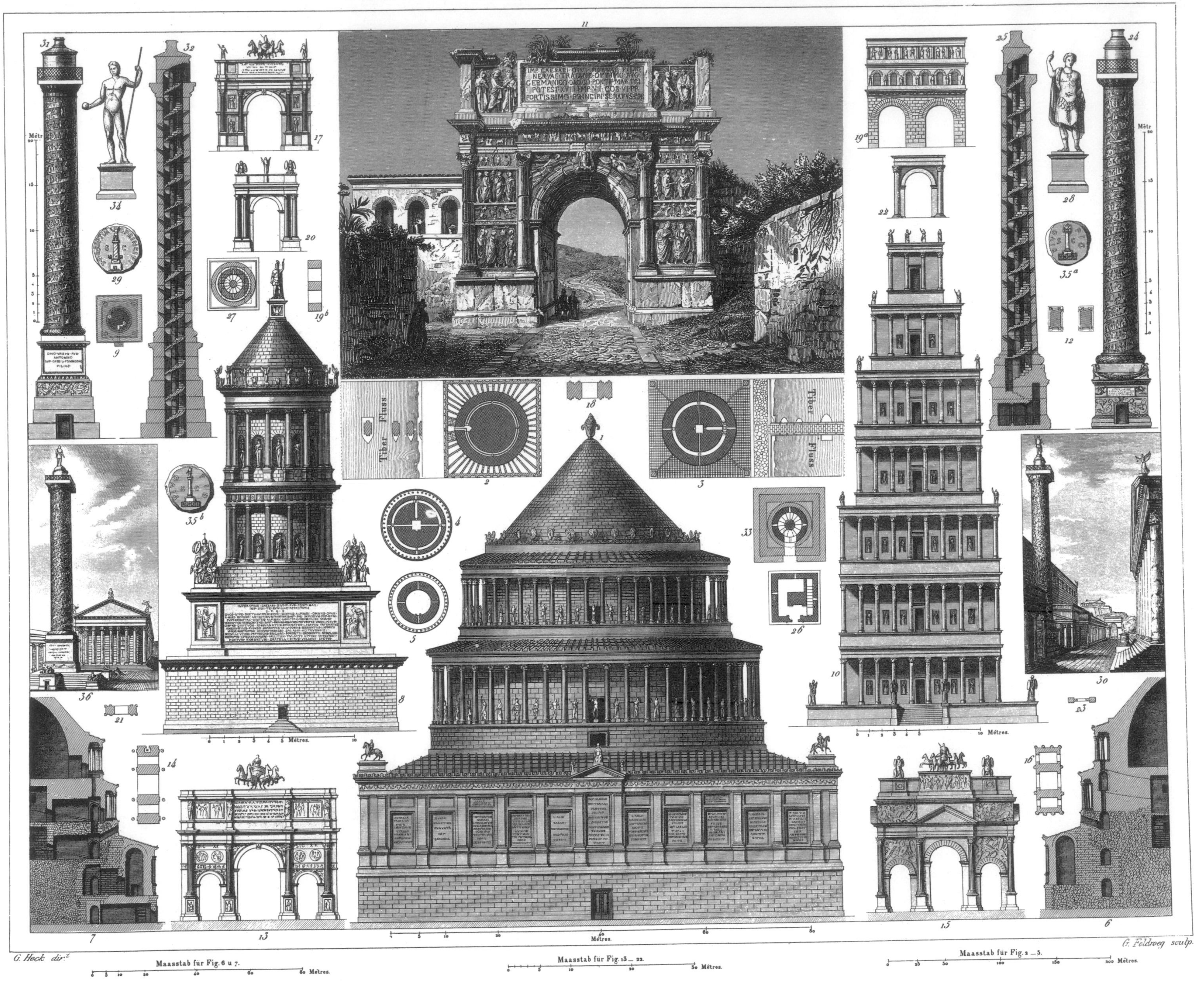

PLATE 367. ROMAN MEMORIAL AND CEREMONIAL ARCHITECTURE

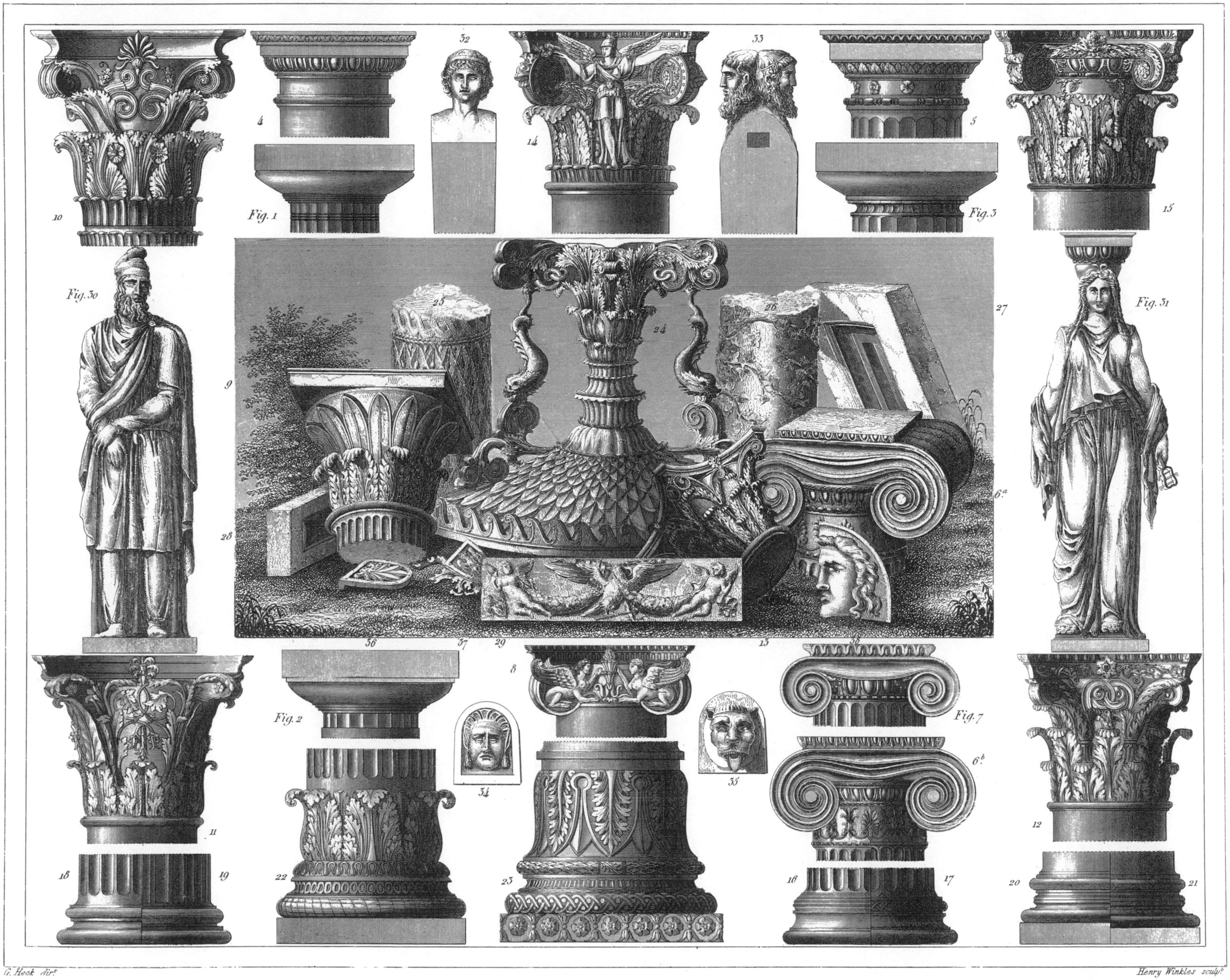

G. Heck dir.t Henry Winkles sculp.t

PLATE 368. GREEK AND ROMAN CAPITALS AND BASES

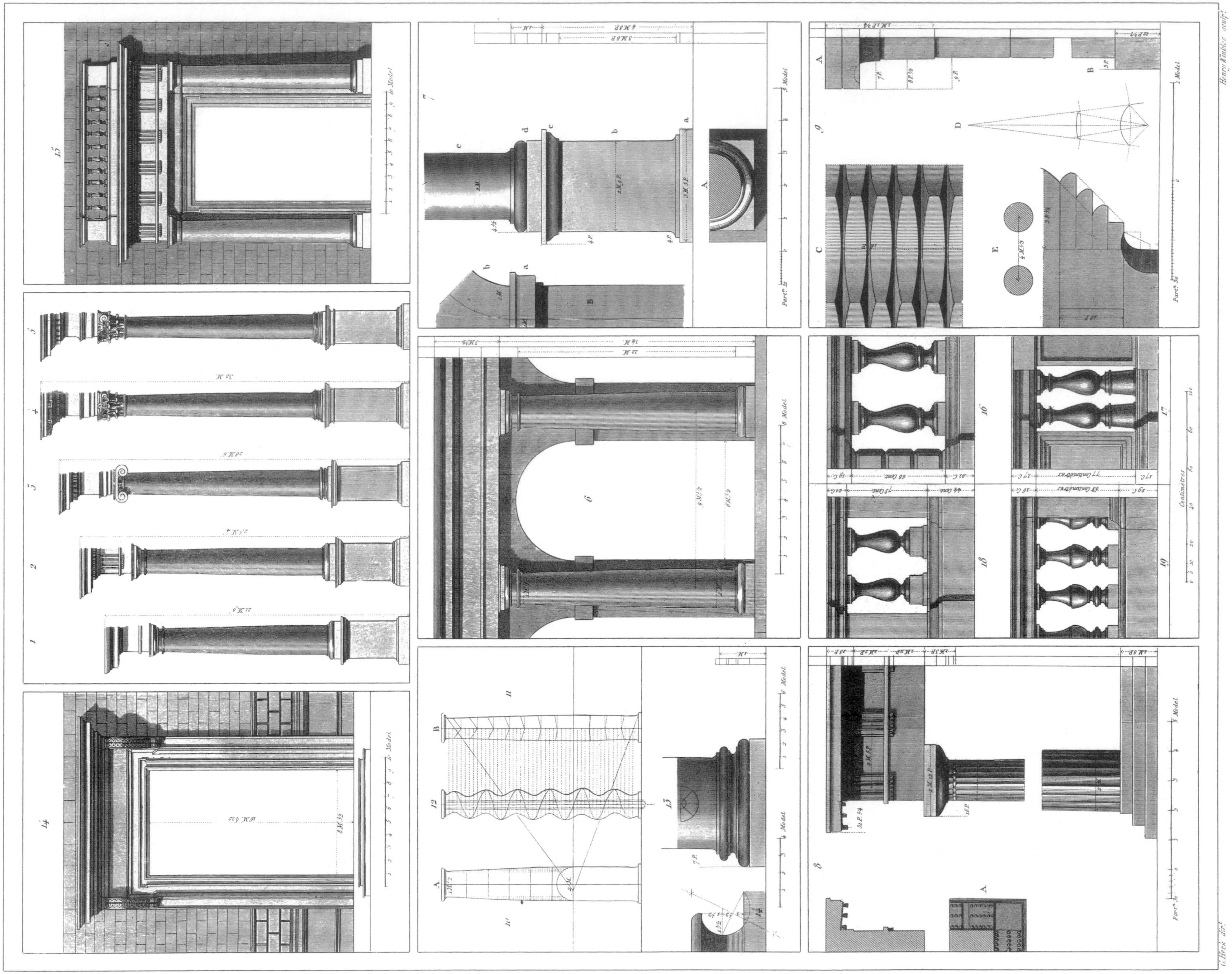

PLATE 369. CLASSICAL COLUMNS, DOORS, AND BALUSTERS

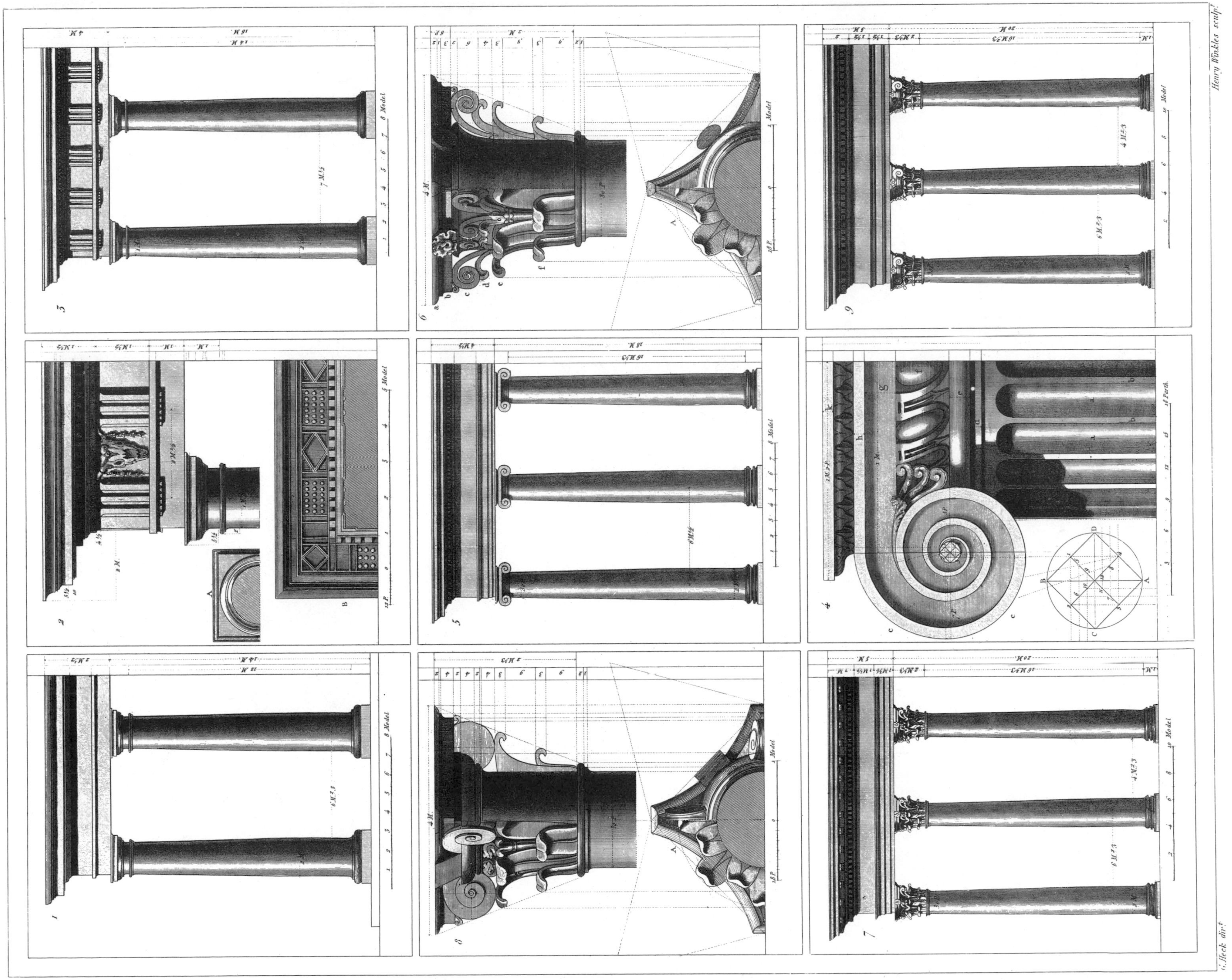
Henry Winkles sculp.
Heck dir.

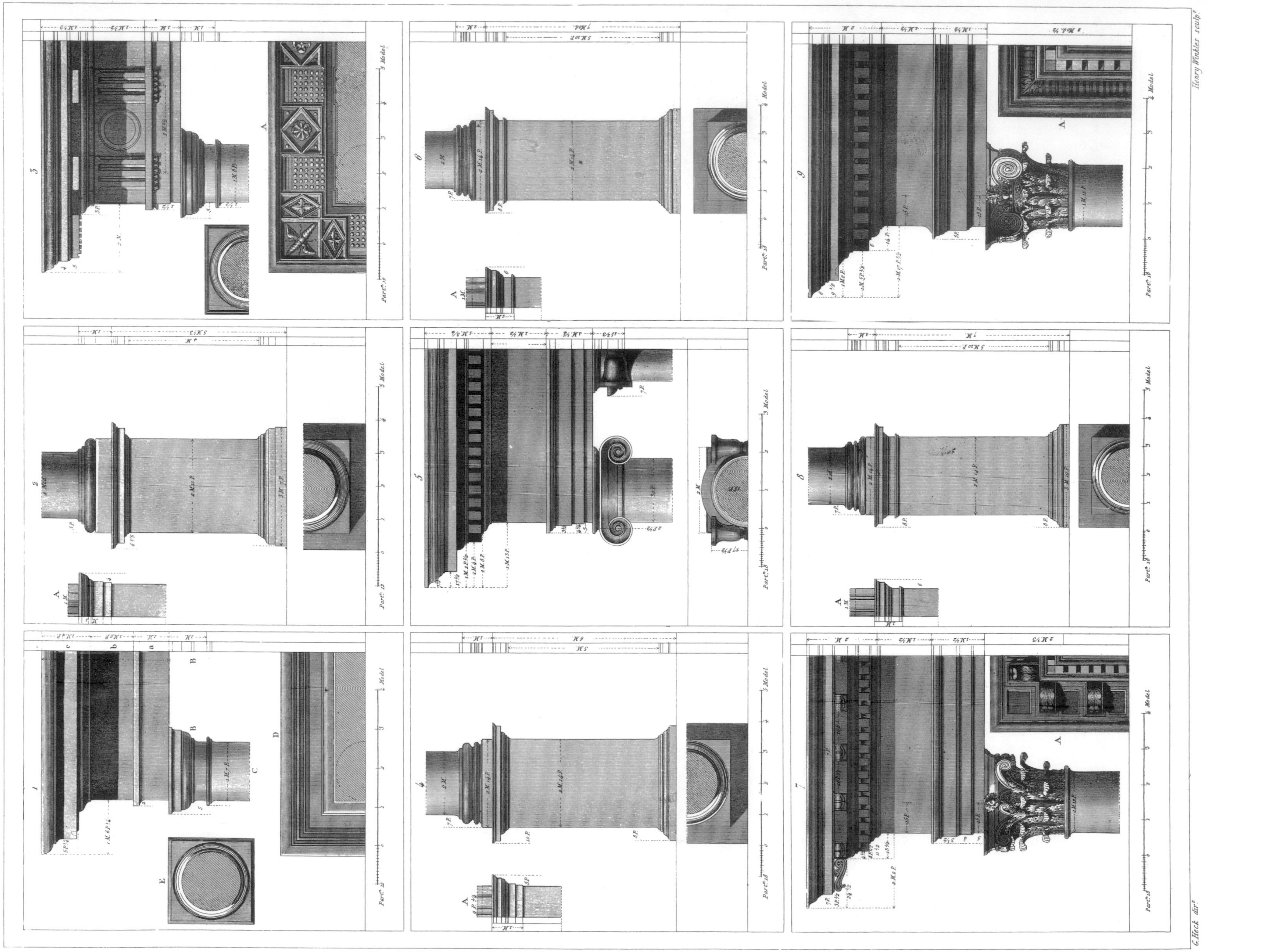

PLATE 371. CLASSICAL CAPITALS AND BASES

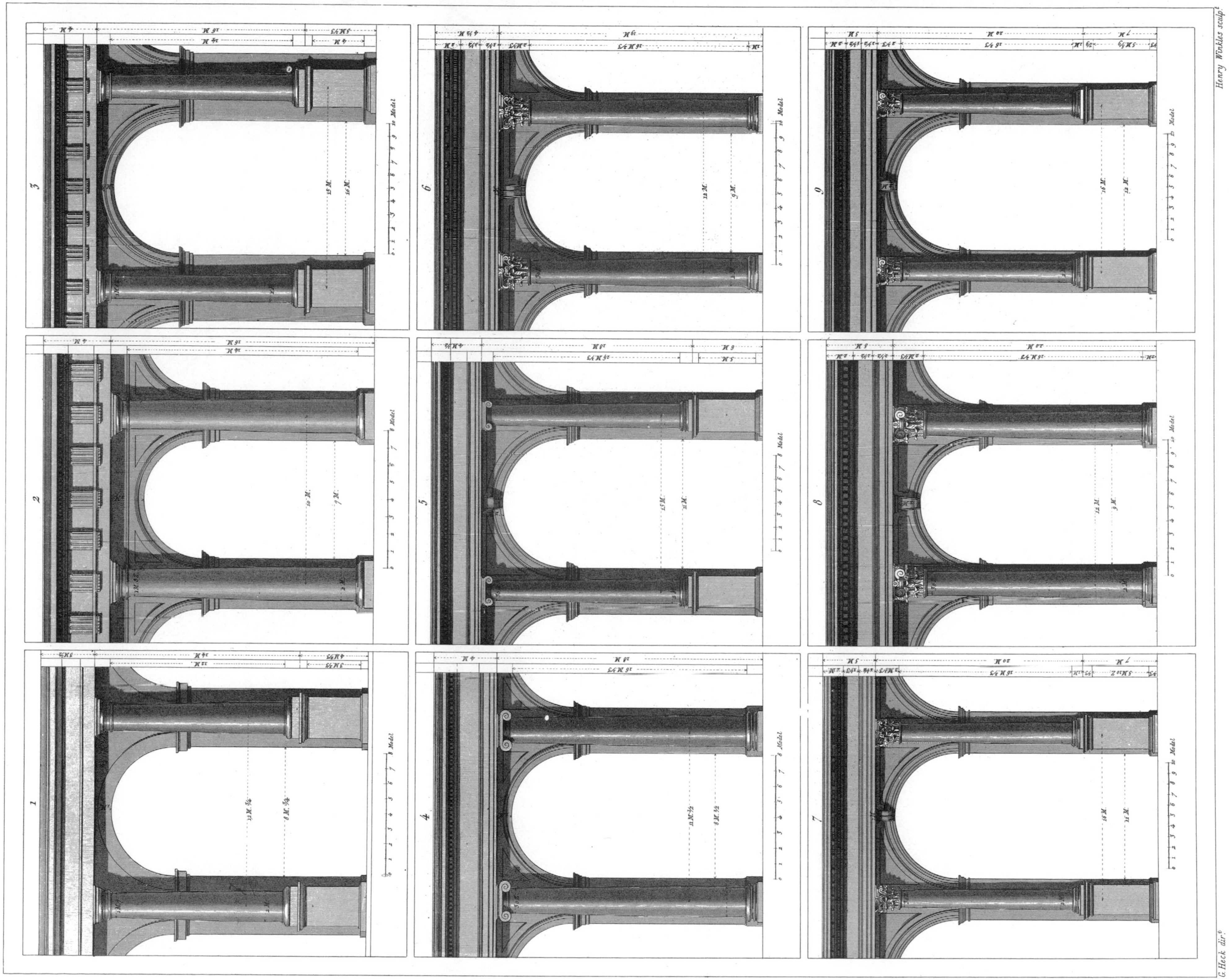

PLATE 372. CLASSICAL ARCADES

G. Heck dir.t Henry Winkles sculp.t

PLATE 373. PRIMITIVE STANDING STONE ARCHITECTURE OF WESTERN EUROPE

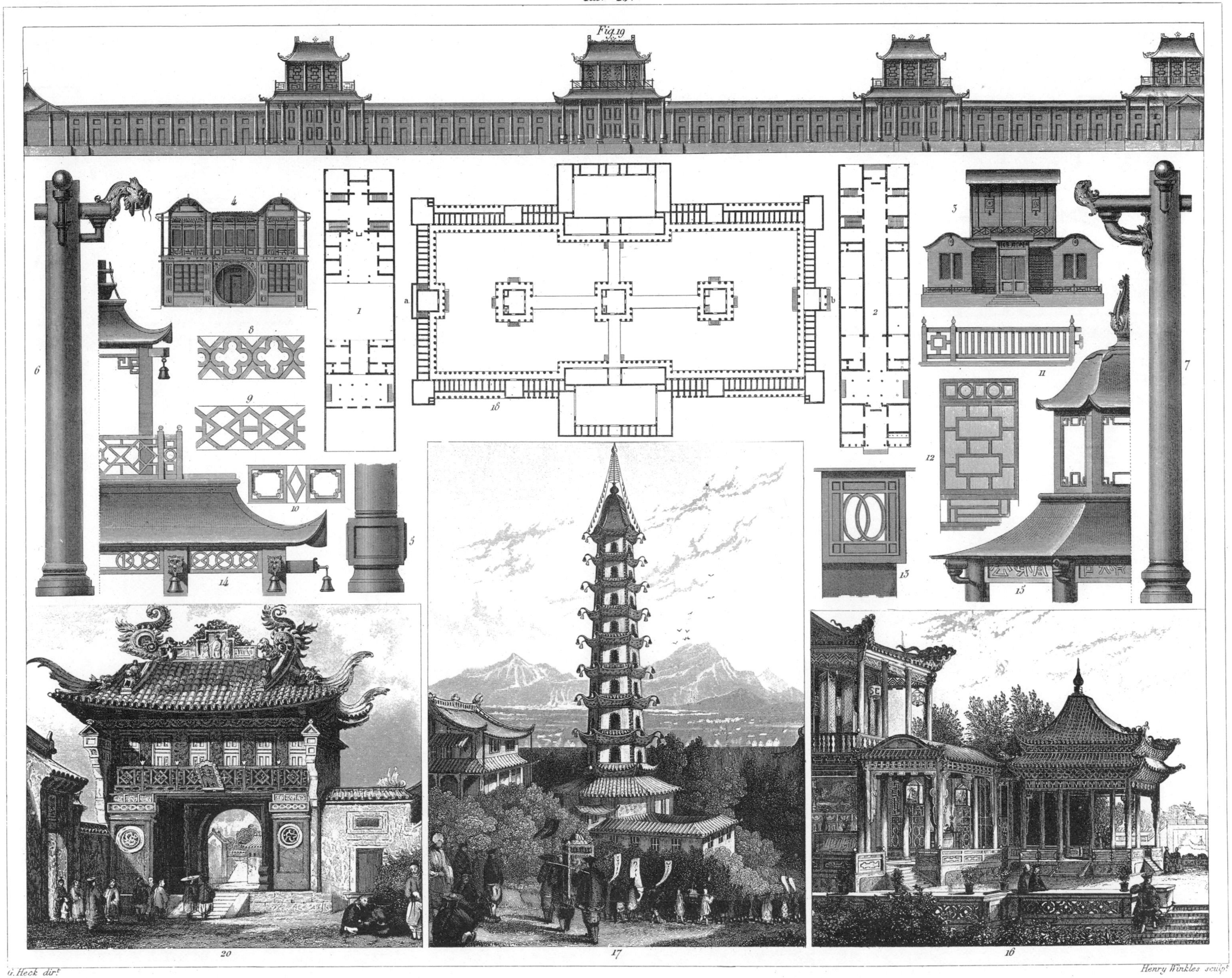
Fig.19
4
1
a
b
2
3
6
8
9
10
5
14
11
12
13
15
7
18
20
17
16

G. Heck dir.t Henry Winkles sculp.t

6

1

3

2

8

5

4

7

G. Heck dir.ᵗ Henry Winkles sculp.ᵗ

 PLATE 375. PRE-COLUMBIAN ARCHITECTURE OF CENTRAL AMERICA

G. Heck dir.t

Henry Winkles sculp.t

PLATE 376. EARLY CHRISTIAN ARCHITECTURE

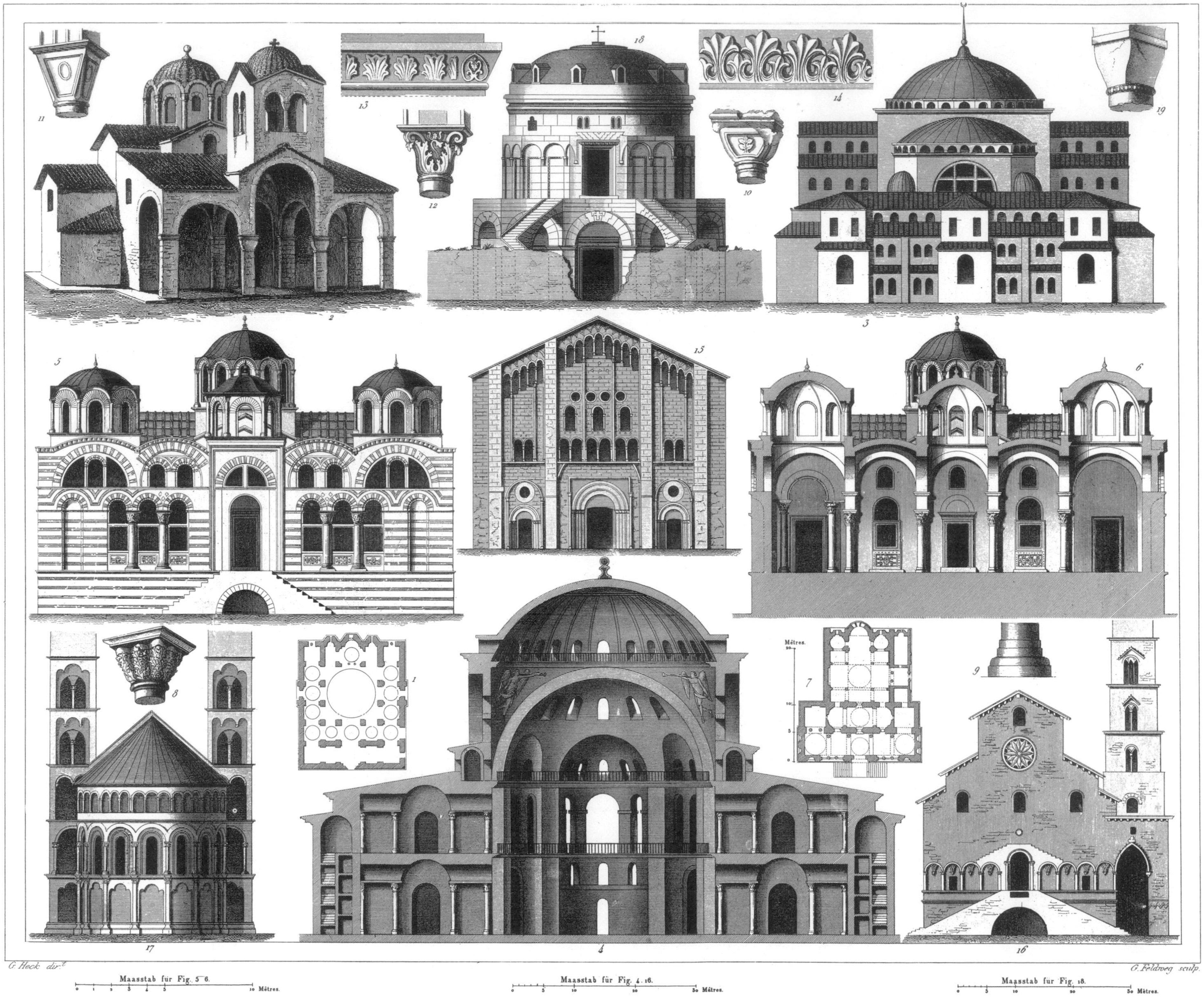

PLATE 377. BYZANTINE ARCHITECTURE

G. Heck dir.t

Henry Winkles sculp.t

PLATE 378. BYZANTINE ARCHITECTURE

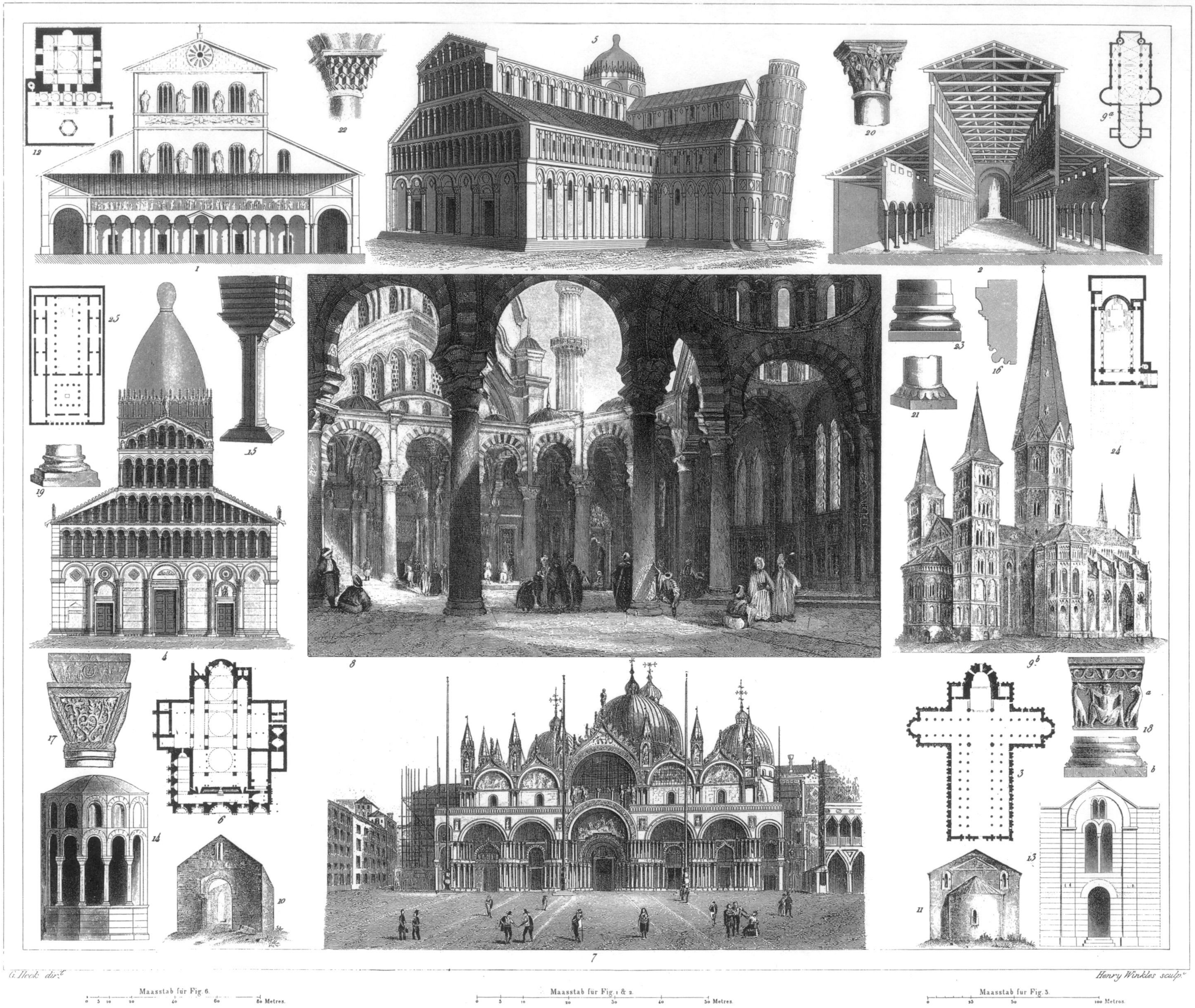

PLATE 379. BYZANTINE AND EARLY ROMANESQUE ARCHITECTURE

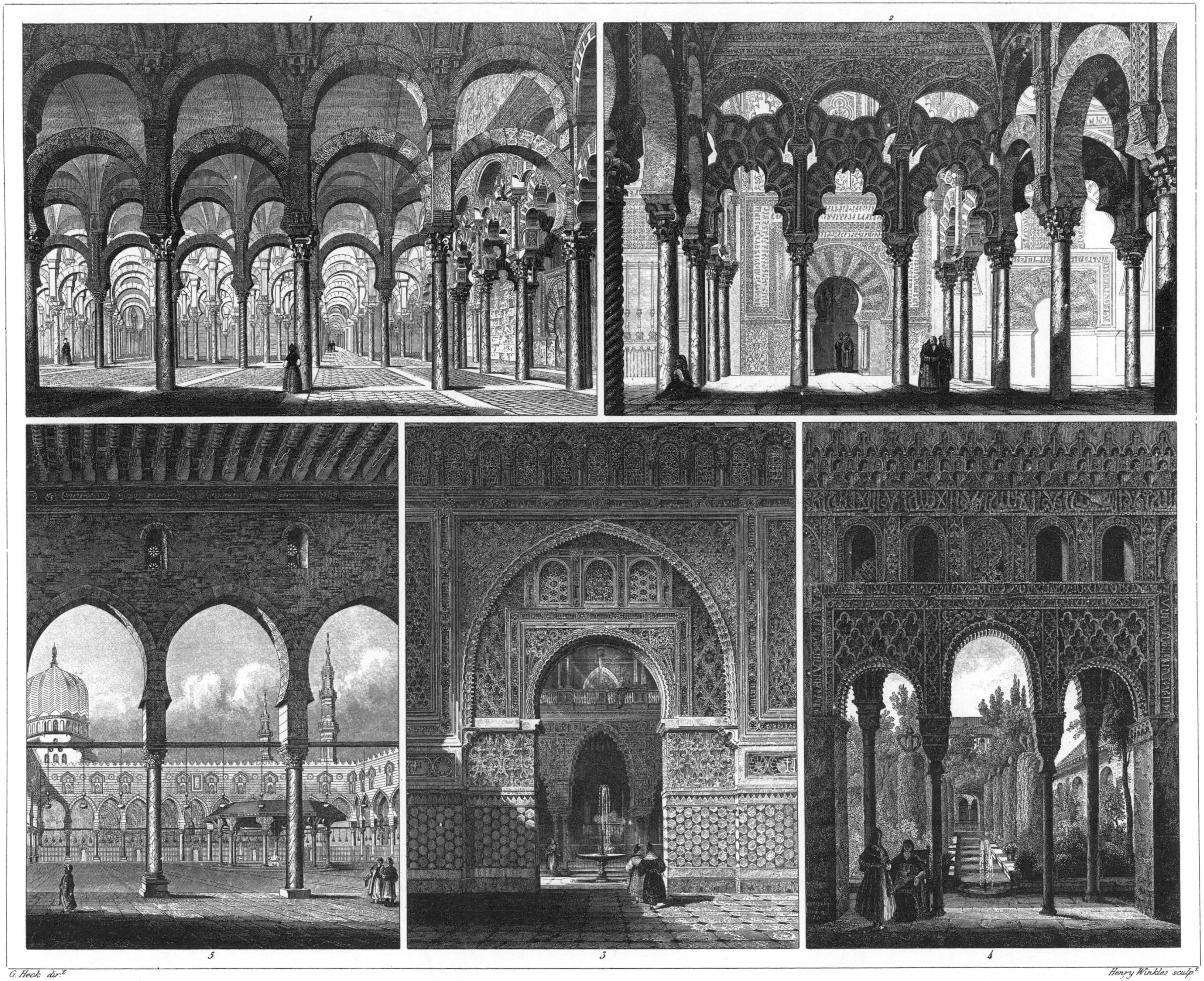

PLATE 380. ISLAMIC ARCHITECTURE

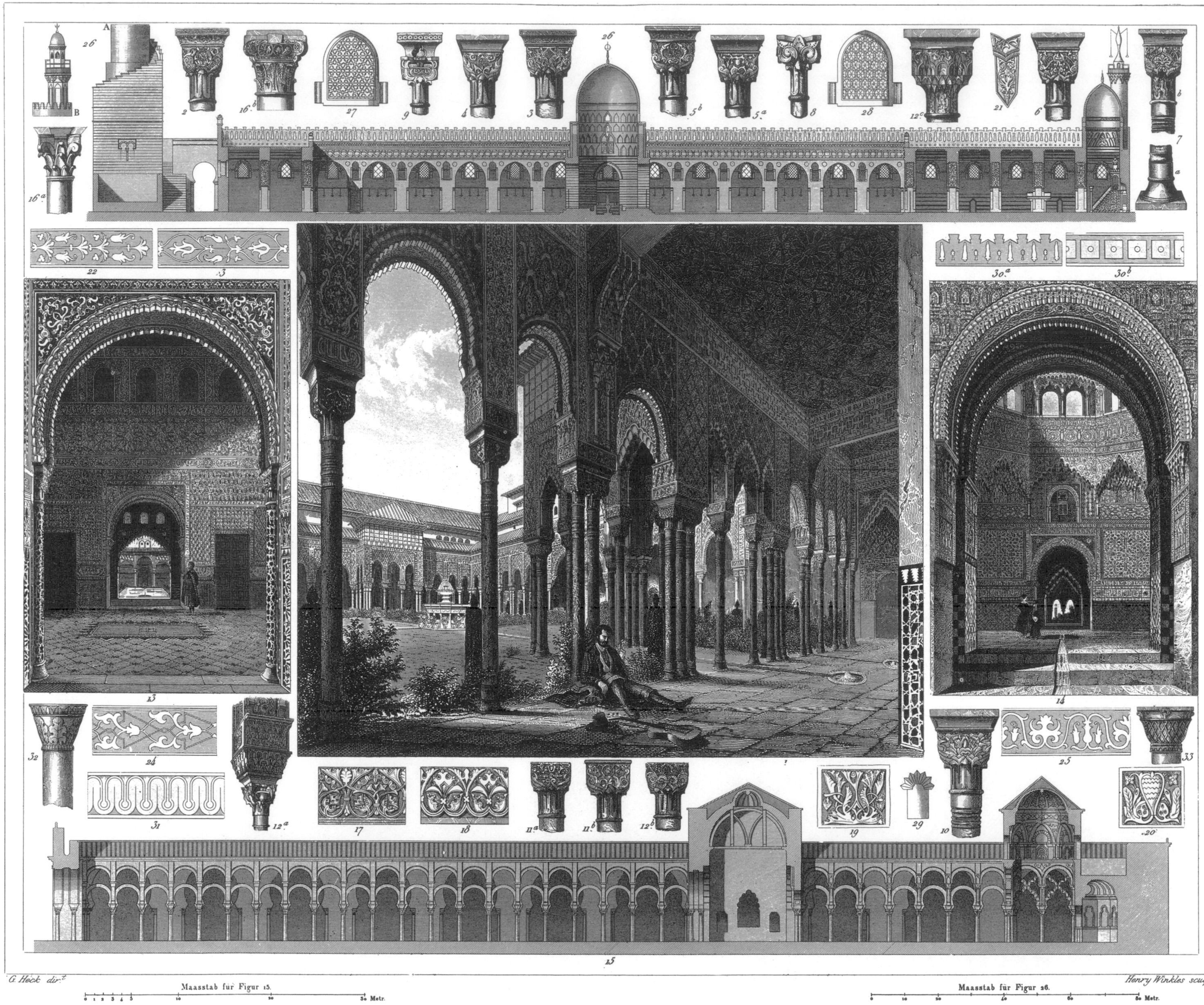

PLATE 381. ISLAMIC ARCHITECTURE

PLATE 382. ISLAMIC, INDIAN, AND EARLY ROMANESQUE ARCHITECTURE

 PLATE 383. COLOGNE CATHEDRAL; MEDIEVAL ARCHITECTURE

G. Heck dir.t

Henry Winkles sculp.t

Maasstab für Figur 16

0 50 100 200 300 400 Rh. Fuss

PLATE 384. VARIOUS ARCHITECTURAL STYLES OF THE MIDDLE AGES

G. Heck dir.t

Henry Winkles sculp.t

PLATE 385. VARIOUS ARCHITECTURAL STYLES OF THE MIDDLE AGES

PLATE 386. MEDIEVAL CATHEDRALS AND ARCHITECTURAL DETAILS

G. Heck dir.t F. Schmidt sculp. Dresden.

PLATE 387. MEDIEVAL CATHEDRALS AND ARCHITECTURAL DETAILS

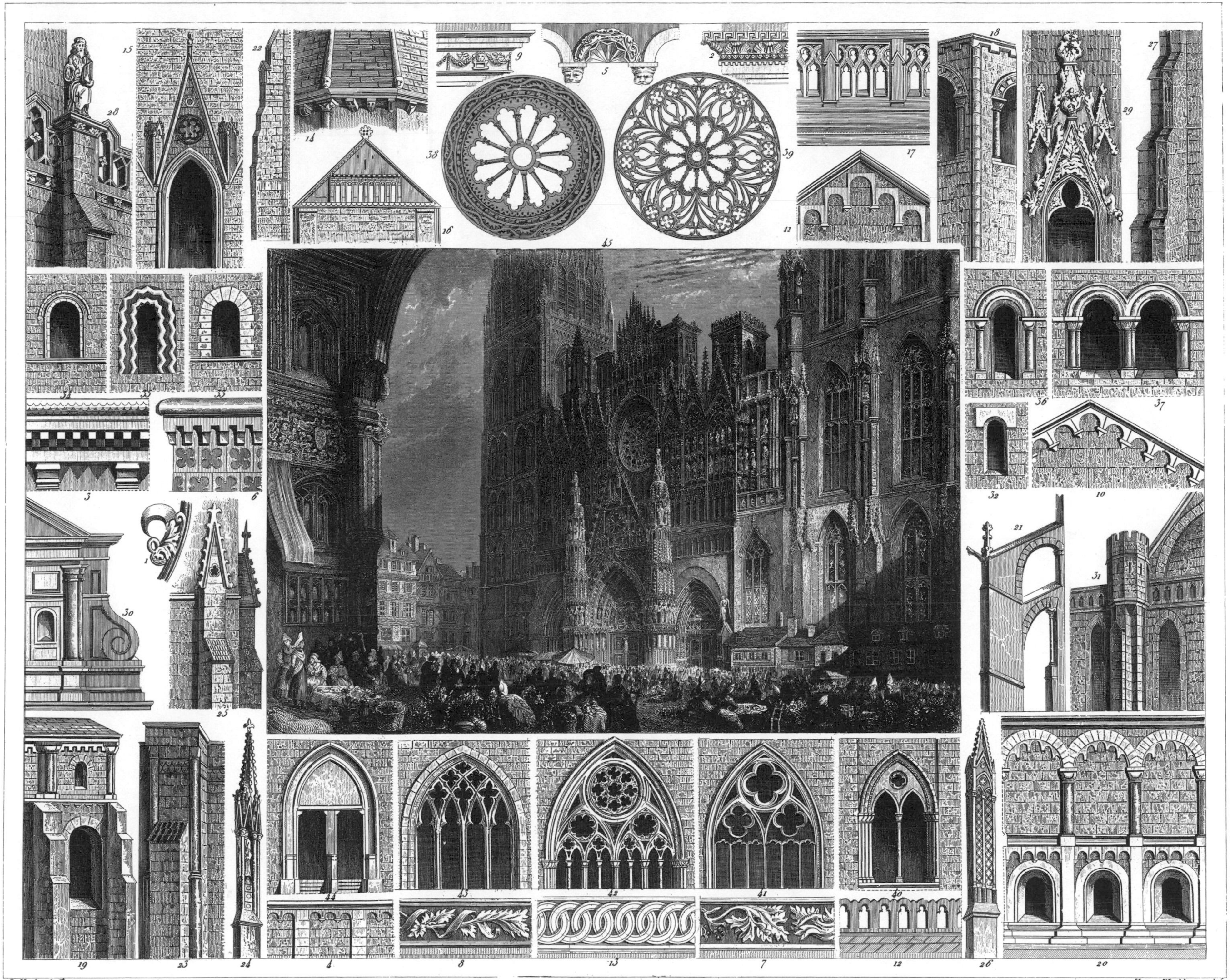

PLATE 388. CATHEDRAL OF ROUEN; ARCHITECTURAL DETAILS OF THE MIDDLE AGES

G. Heck dir.t Henry Winkles sculp.t

PLATE 389. ROMANESQUE AND GOTHIC ARCHITECTURE

PLATE 390. SCENES AND DETAILS OF GOTHIC CATHEDRALS AND ABBEYS

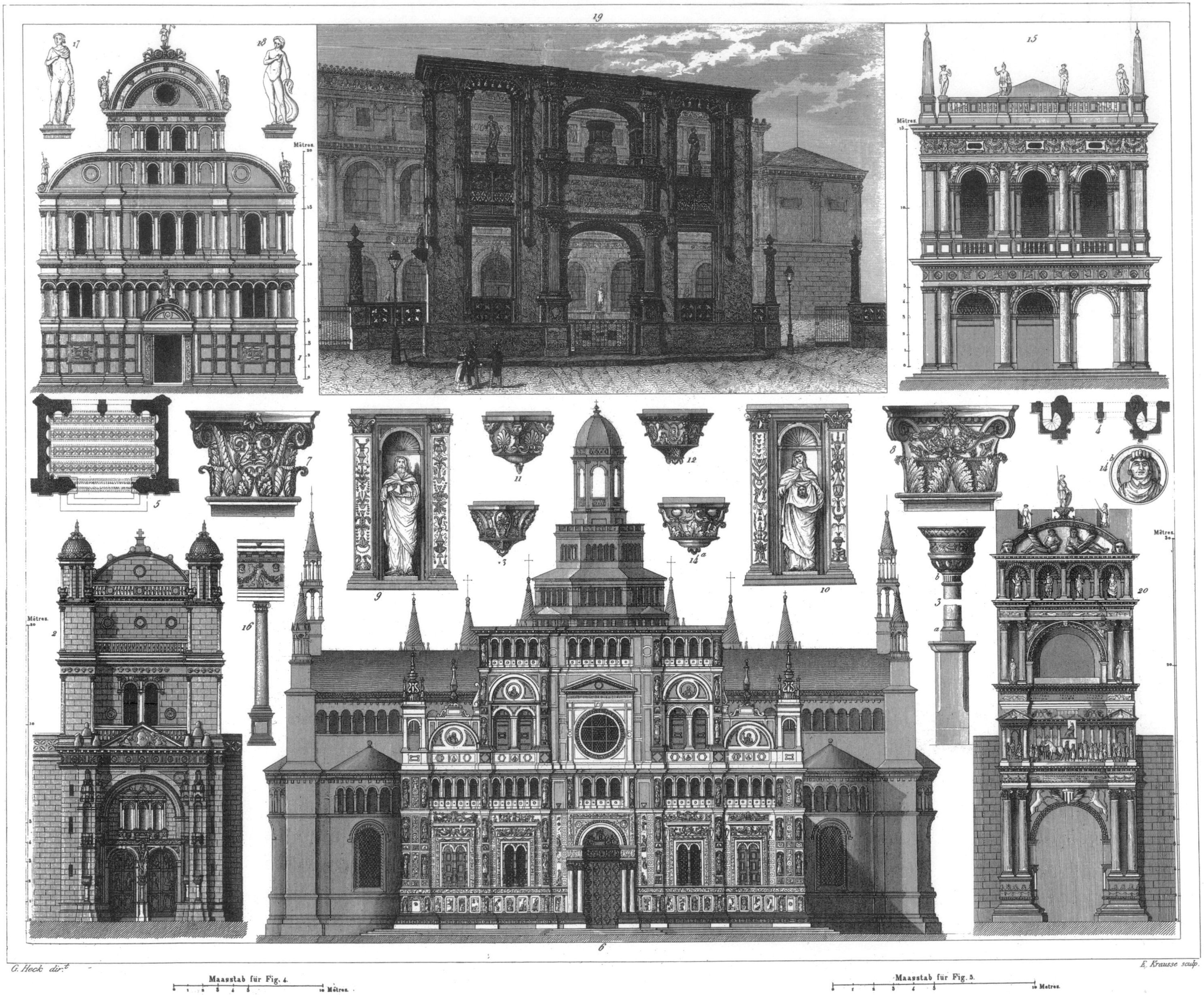

 PLATE 391. ECCLESIASTICAL AND SECULAR ARCHITECTURE OF THE RENAISSANCE

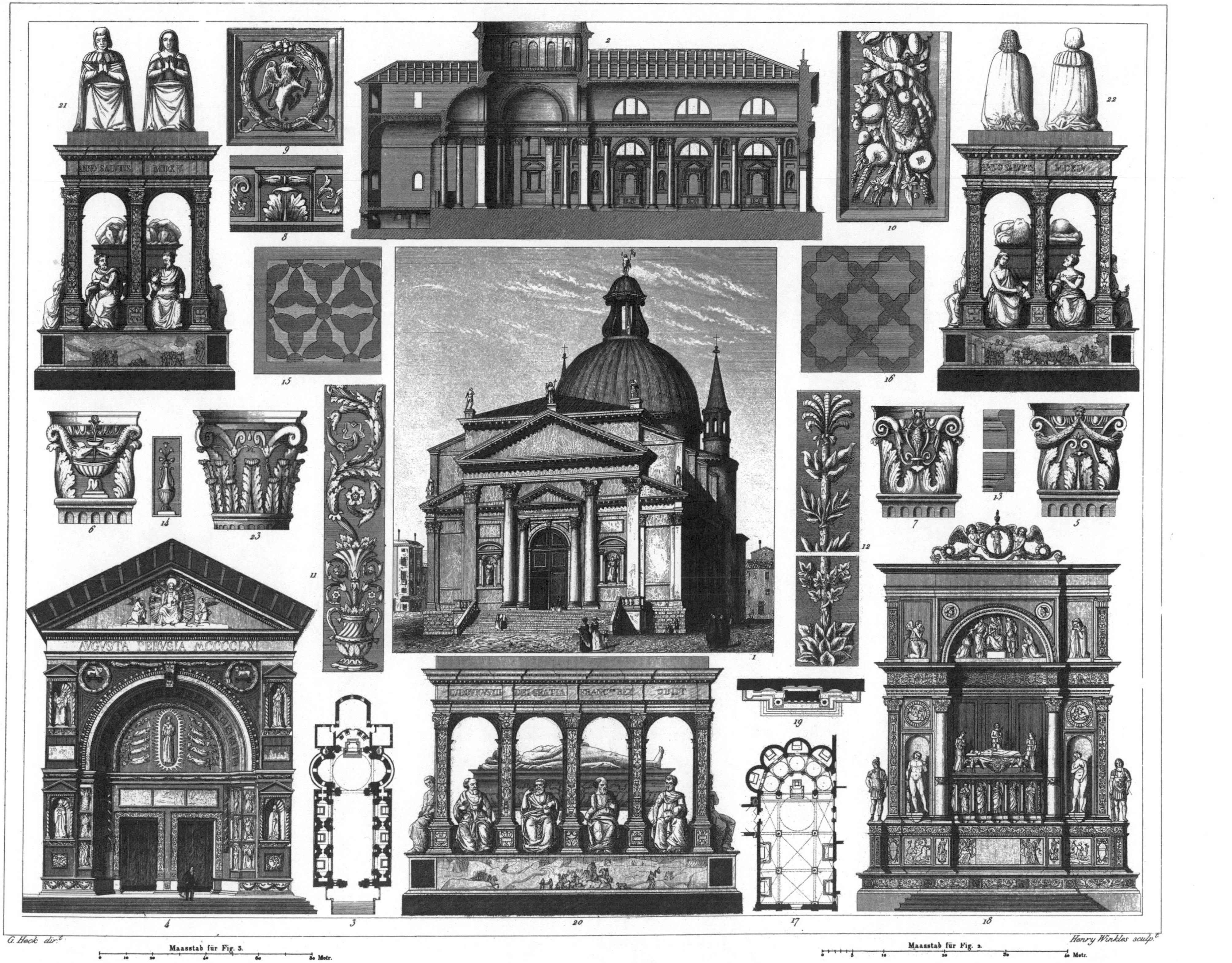

PLATE 392. RENAISSANCE CHURCHES AND ARCHITECTURAL DETAILS

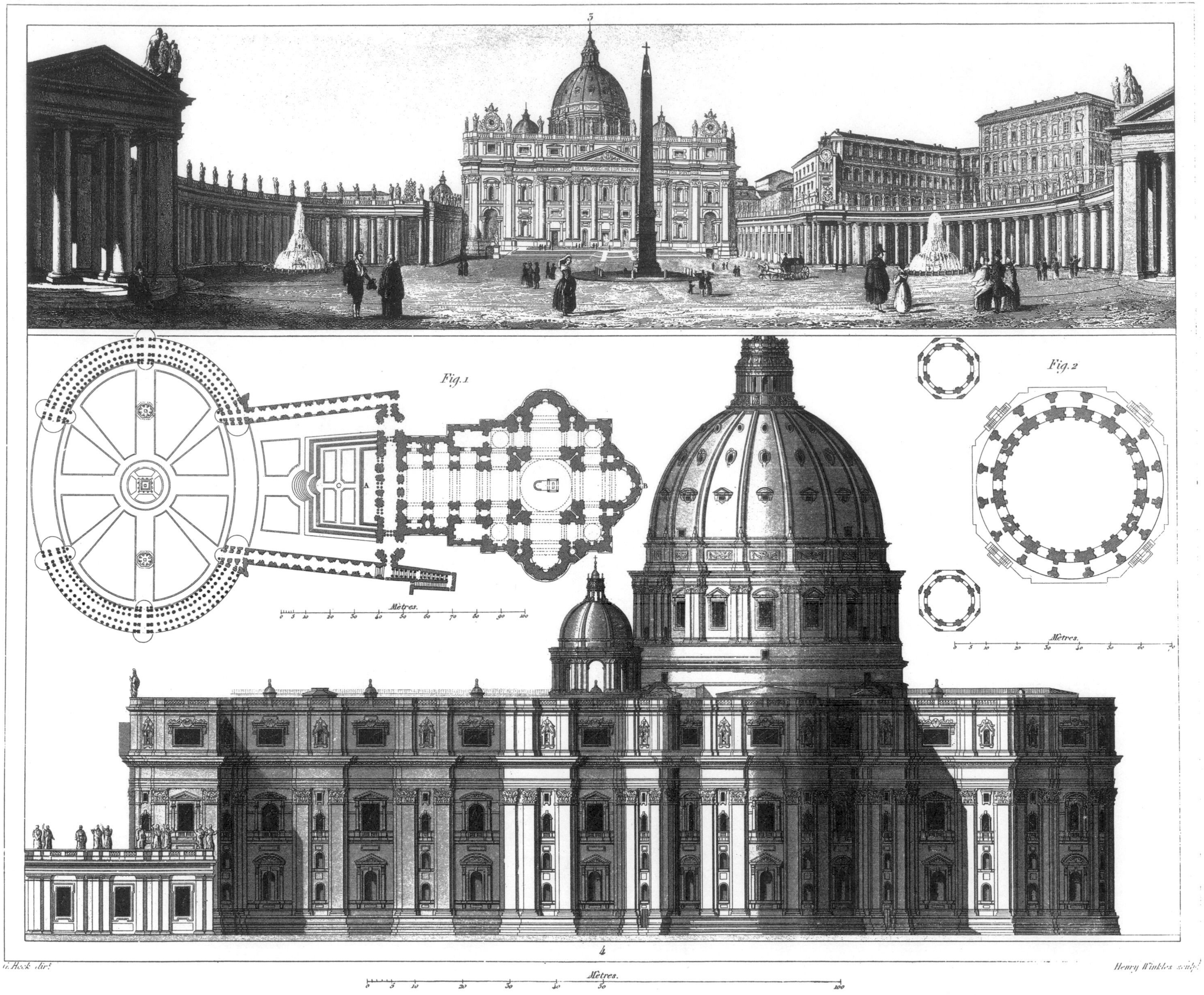
3
Fig. 1
A
B
Mètres.
0 5 10 20 30 40 50 60 70 80 90 100
Fig. 2
Mètres.
0 5 10 20 30 40 50 60 70
4
G. Heck dir.
Henry Winkles sculp.
Mètres.
0 5 10 20 30 40 50 100

 PLATE 393. SAINT PETER'S IN ROME

PLATE 394. ITALIAN CHURCHES OF THE MIDDLE AGES AND RENAISSANCE

 PLATE 395. EUROPEAN CHURCHES OF VARIOUS ARCHITECTURAL STYLES

PLATE 396. EUROPEAN CHURCHES OF THE SIXTEENTH AND SEVENTEENTH CENTURIES

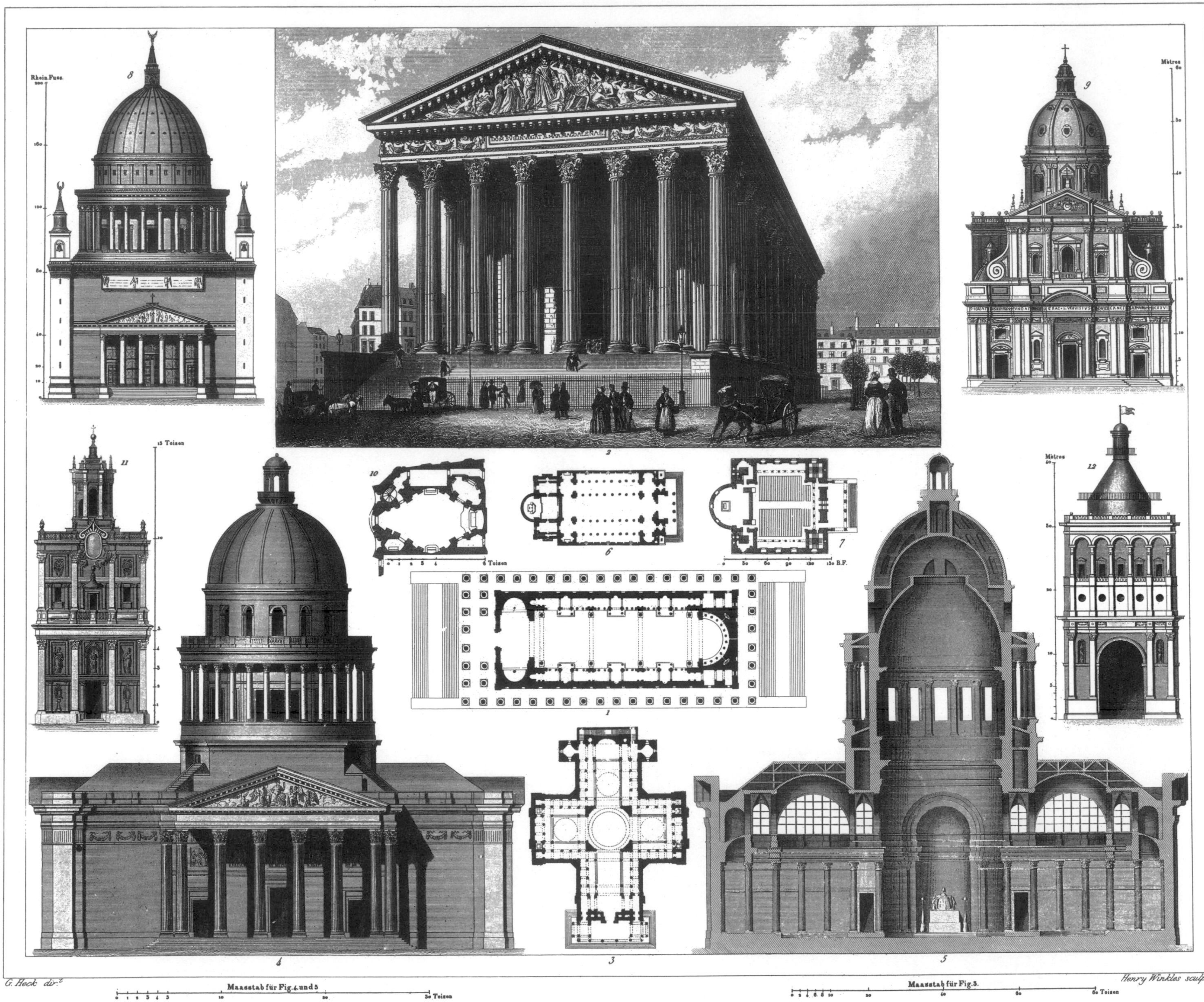

 PLATE 397. EUROPEAN CHURCHES OF THE SEVENTEENTH AND EIGHTEENTH CENTURIES

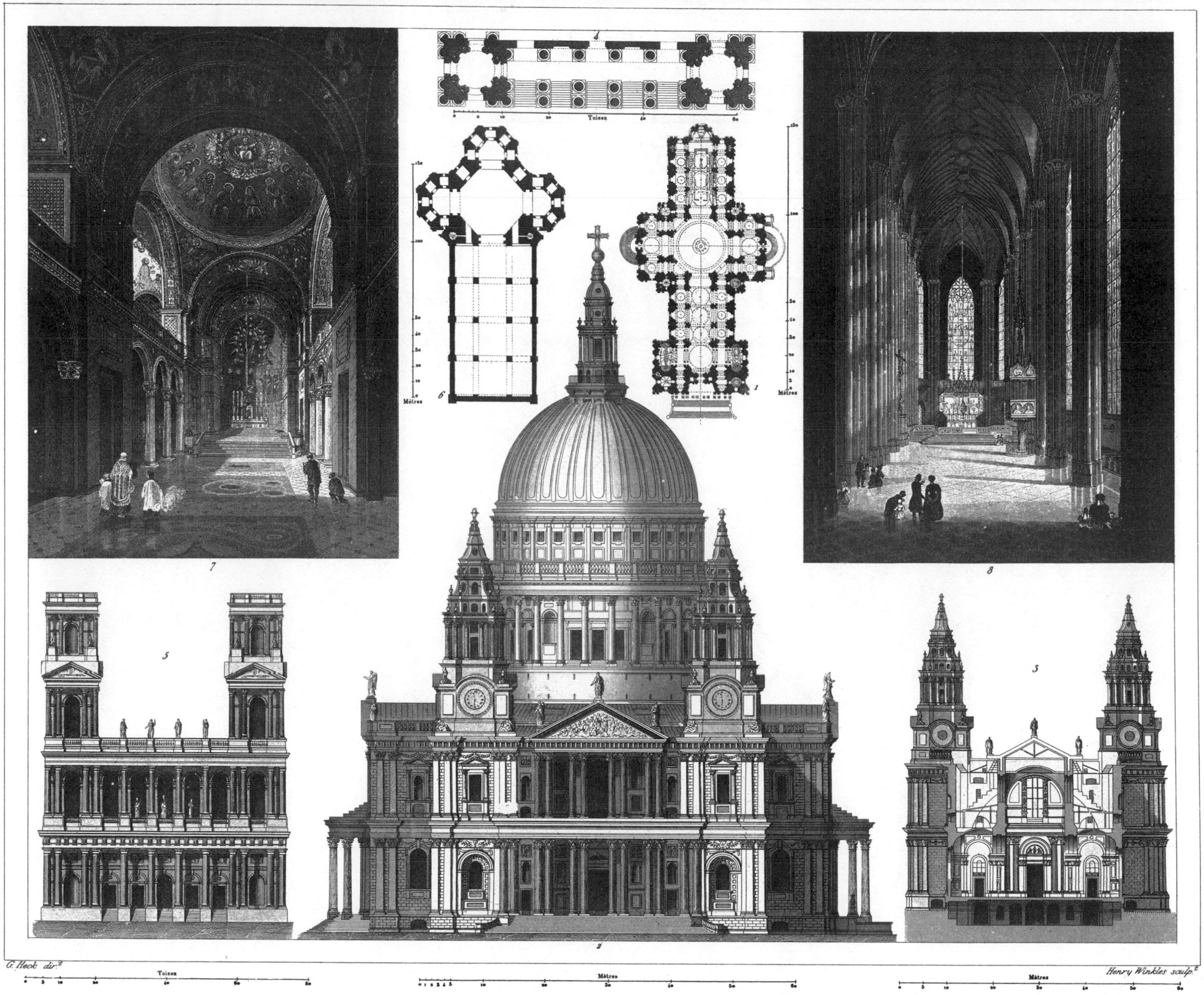
4
Toisen
6
Mètres
1
Mètres
7
8
5
3
2
G. Heck dir.
Toisen
Mètres
Henry Winkles sculp.
Mètres

PLATE 398. MAJOR EUROPEAN CATHEDRALS

PLATE 399. EUROPEAN CHURCHES OF VARIOUS ARCHITECTURAL PERIODS

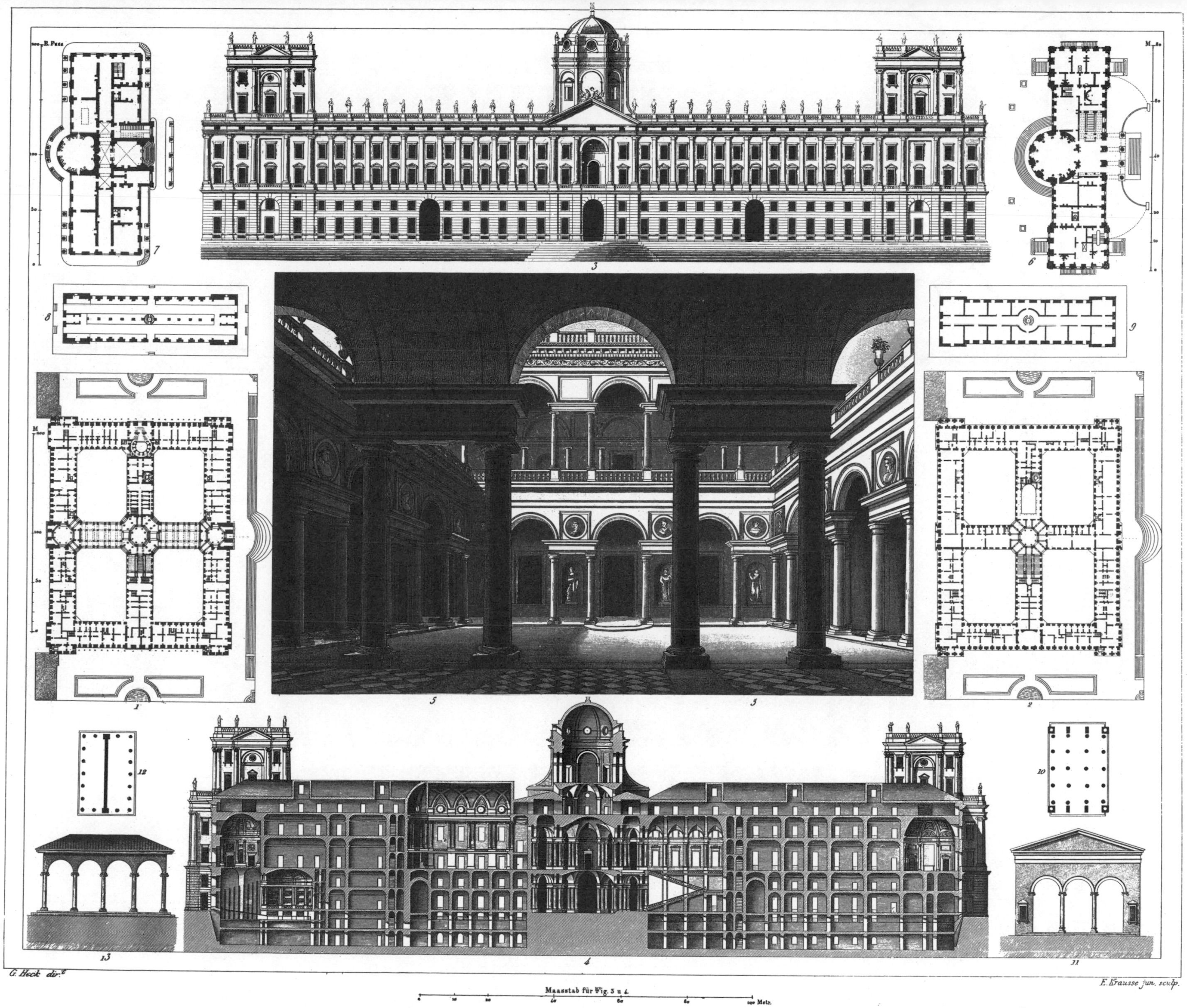

PLATE 400. SECULAR ARCHITECTURE OF THE RENAISSANCE AND BAROQUE ERAS

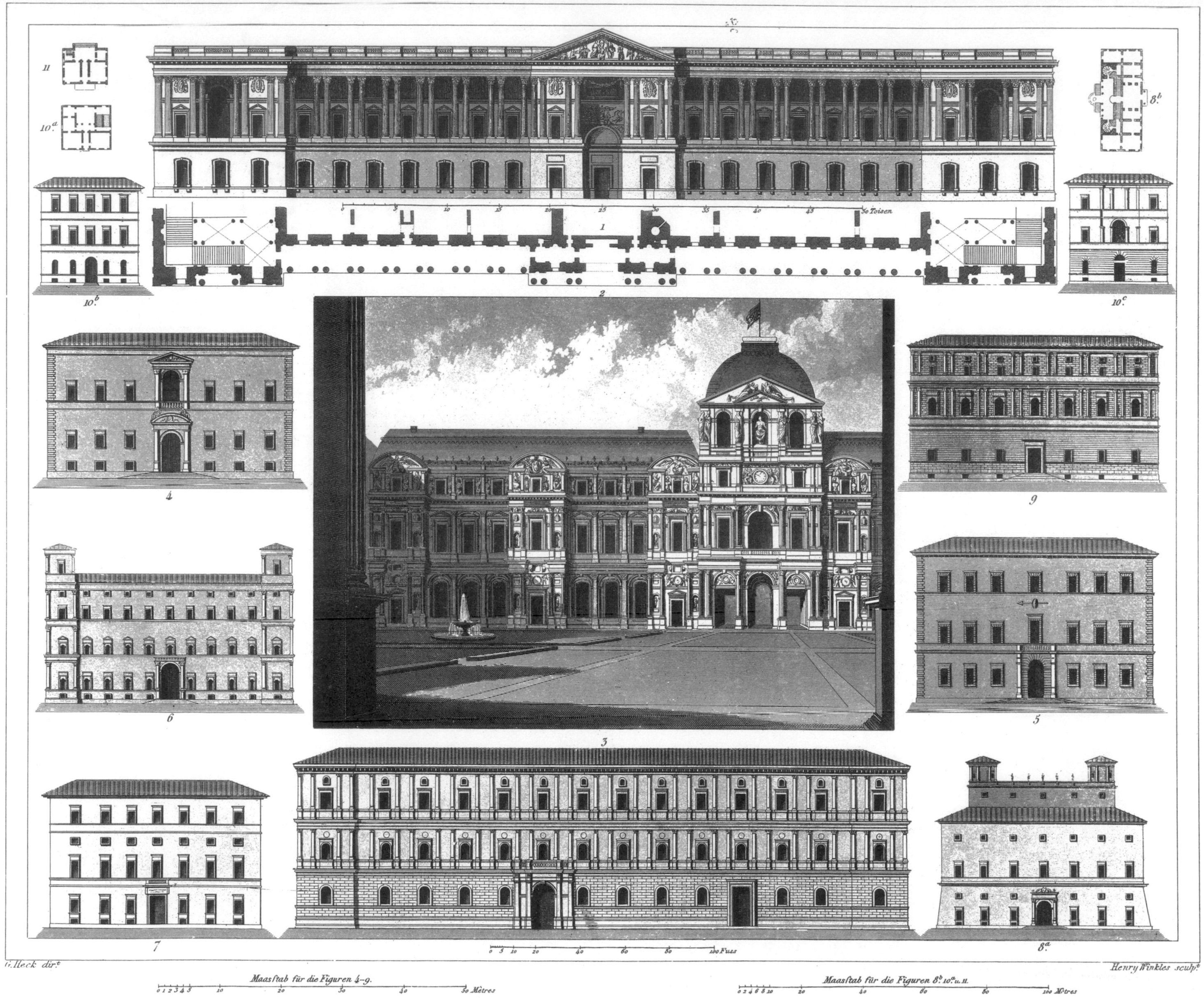

PLATE 401. PALATIAL ARCHITECTURE OF VARIOUS PERIODS

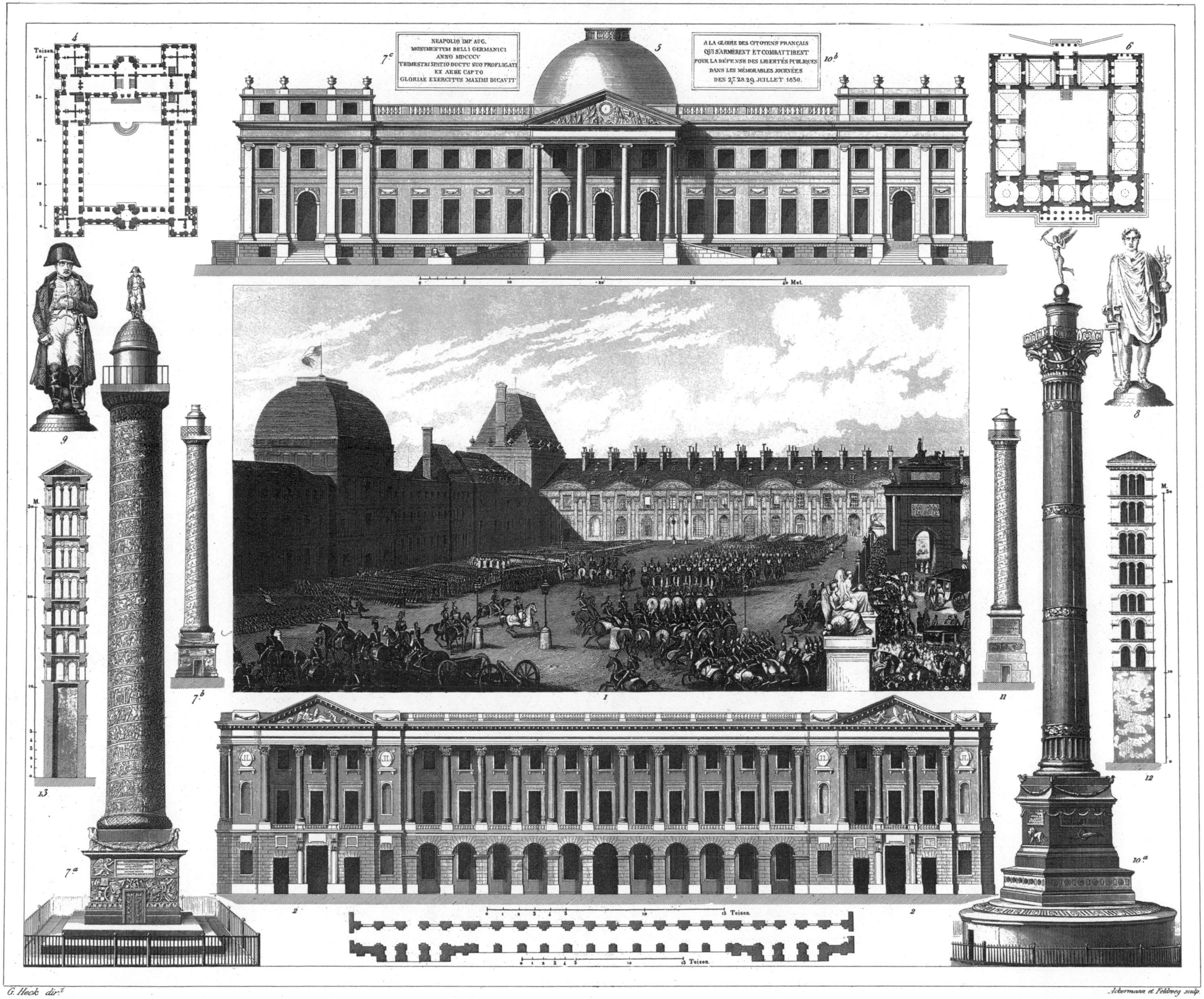

G. Heck dir.t *Ackermann et Feldweg sculp.*

PLATE 402. PALATIAL AND MONUMENTAL ARCHITECTURE OF FRANCE AND GERMANY

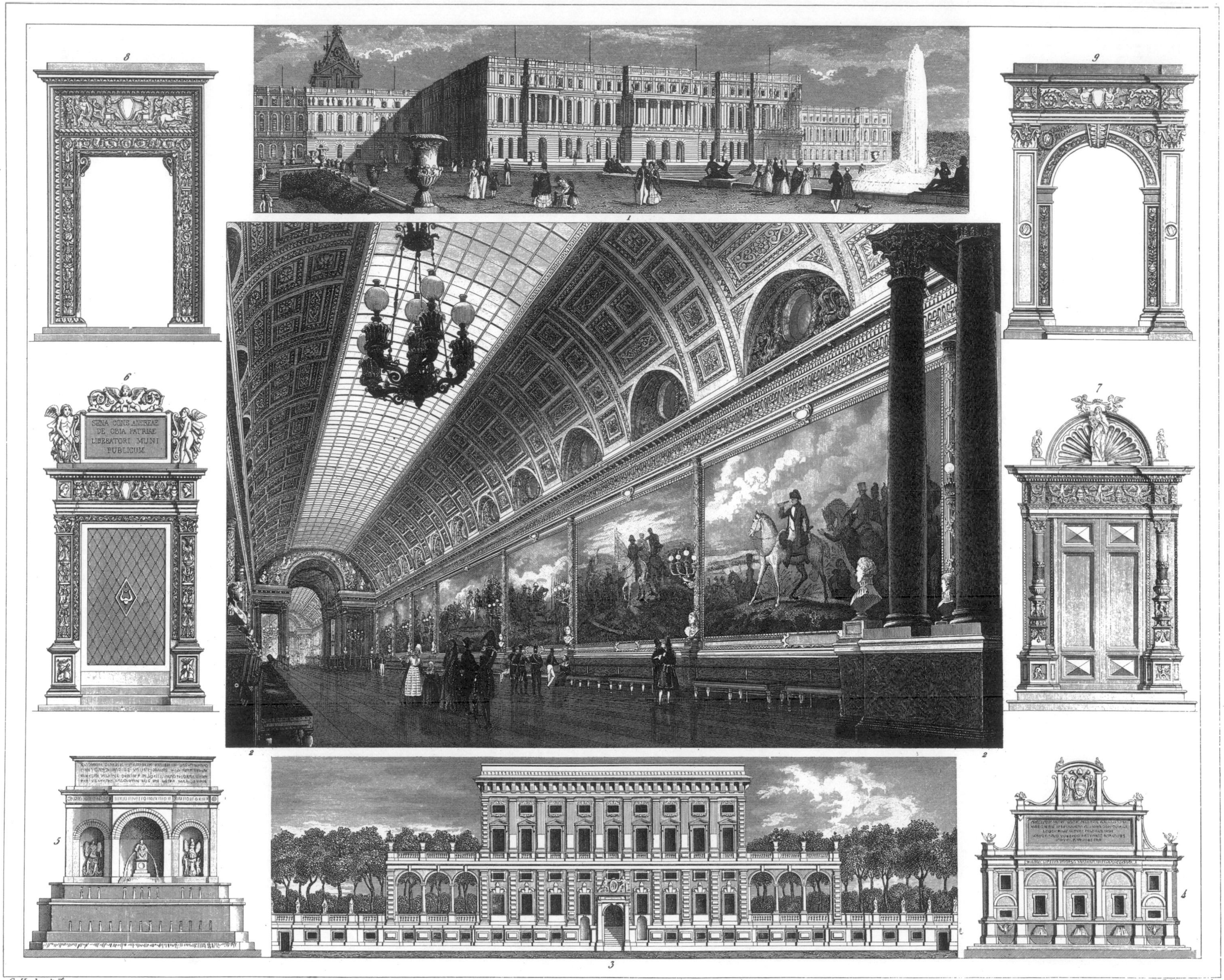

G. Heck dir.t

G. Feldweg sculp.

PLATE 403. NEO-CLASSICAL ARCHITECTURE IN FRANCE AND ROME

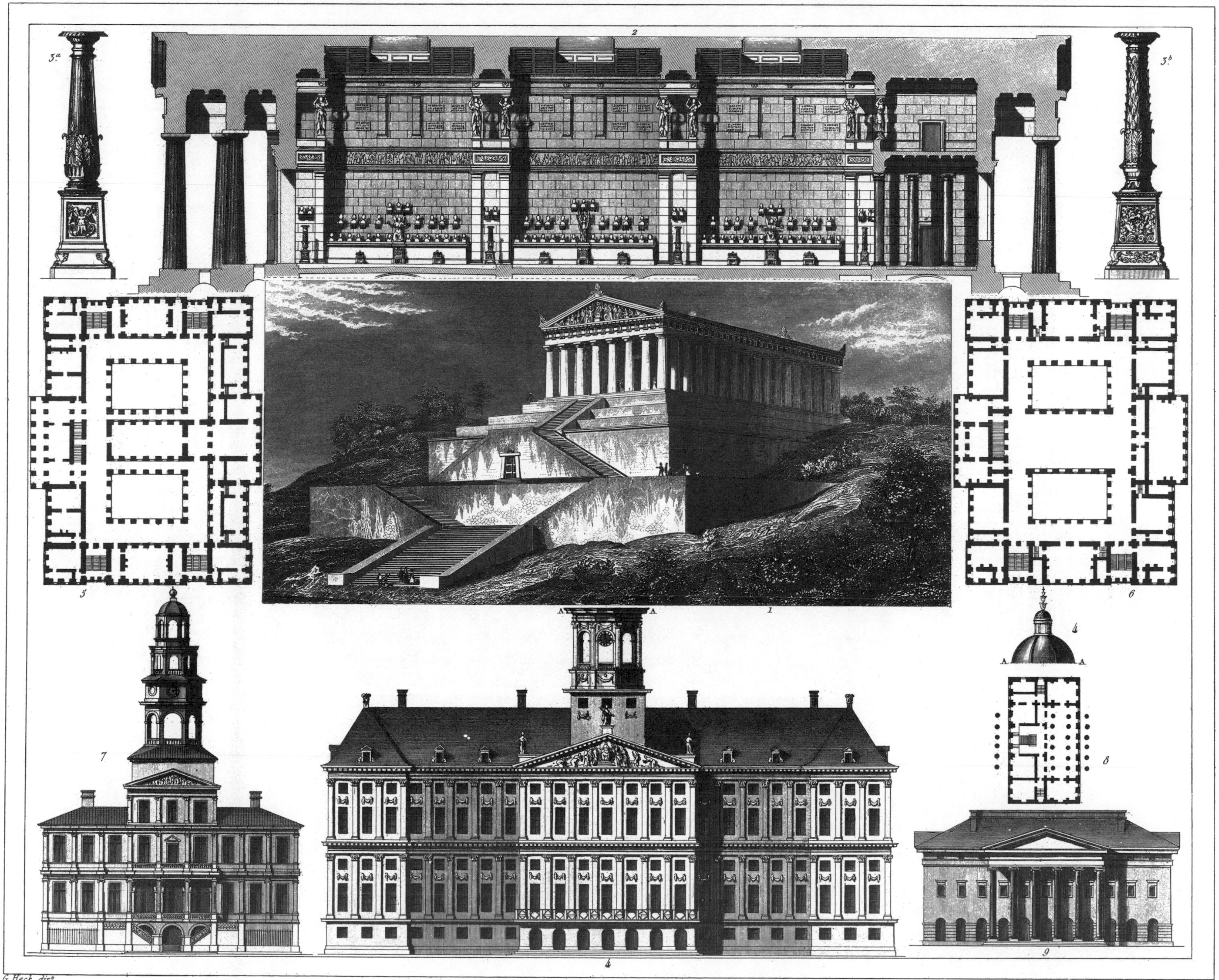

G. Heck dir.

Feldweg sculp.

PLATE 404. NEO-CLASSICAL ARCHITECTURE IN GERMANY AND HOLLAND

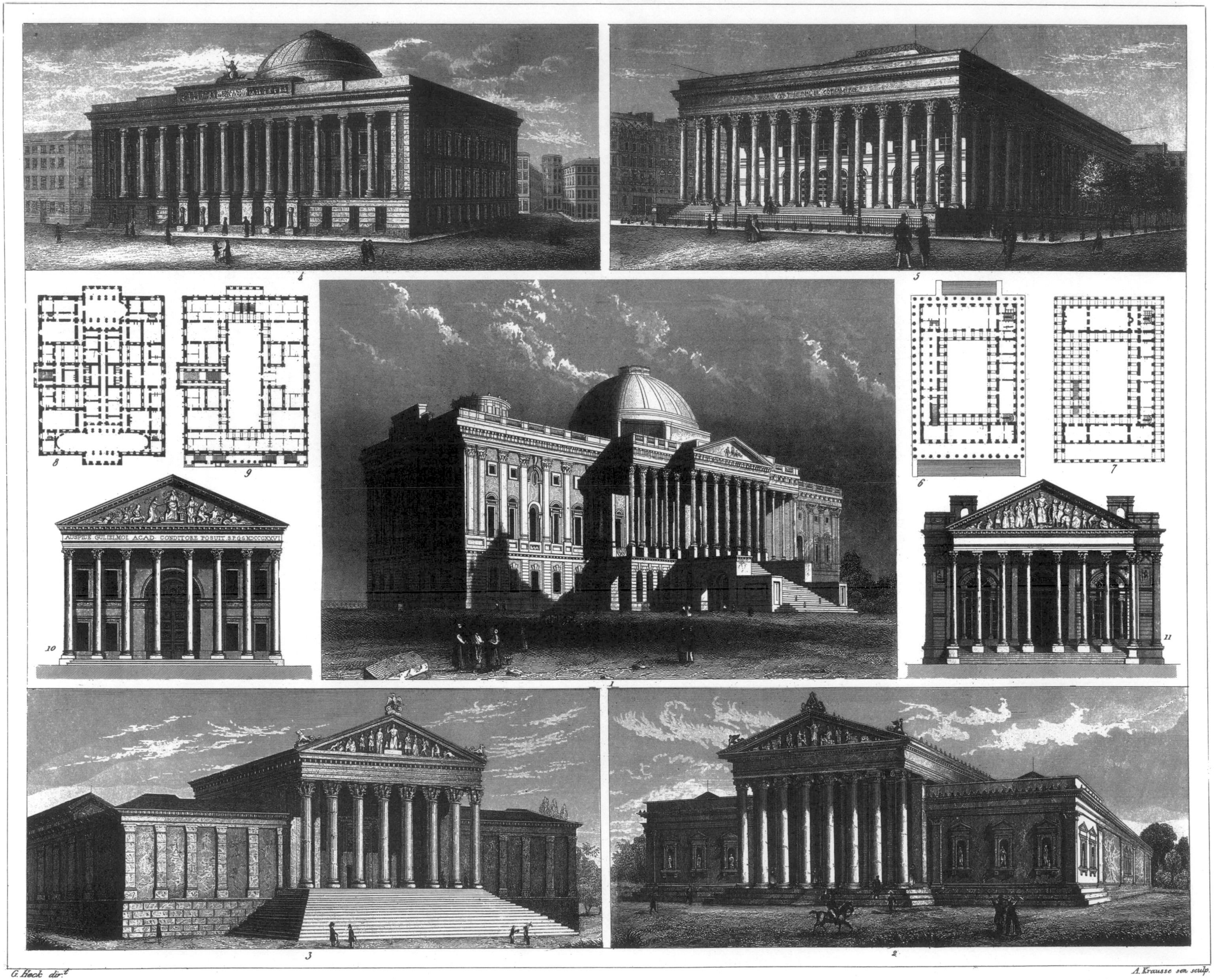

G. Heck dir.t A. Krausse sen. sculp.

PLATE 405. PUBLIC BUILDINGS IN THE NEO-CLASSICAL STYLE

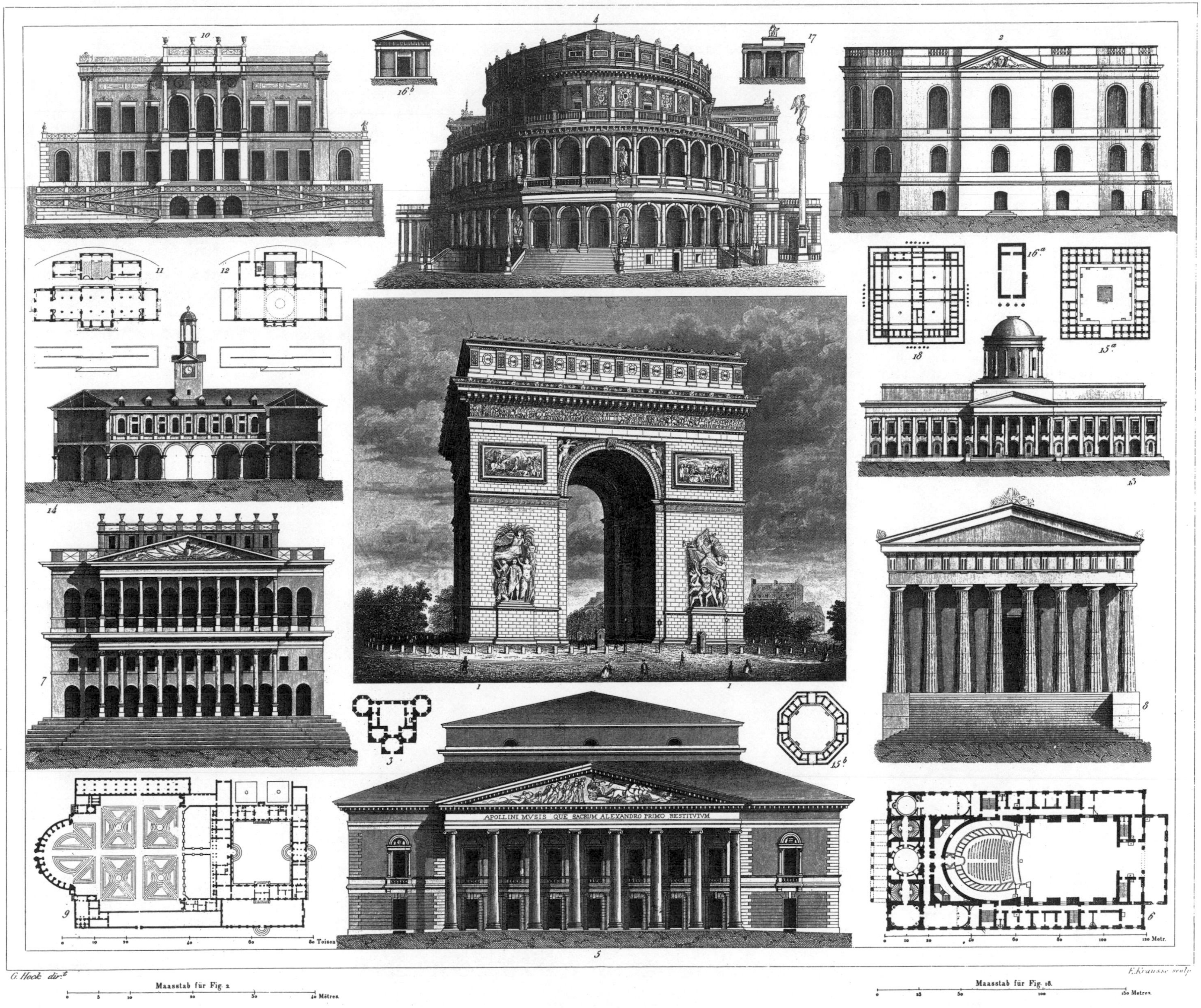

PLATE 406. MONUMENTAL AND PUBLIC ARCHITECTURE OF VARIOUS PERIODS

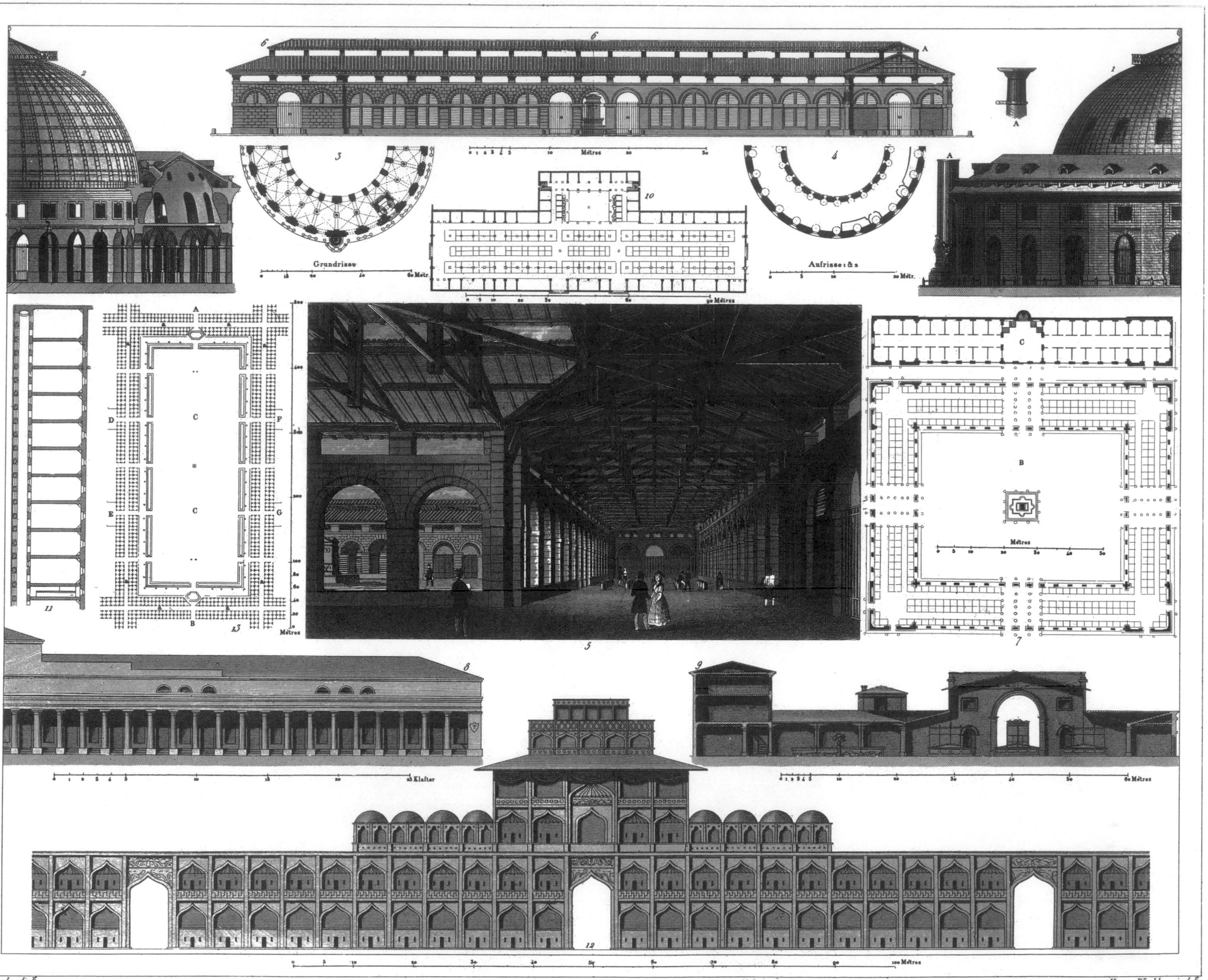

G. Heck dir.[t]

Henry Winkles sculp.[t]

PLATE 407. COMMERCIAL ARCHITECTURE

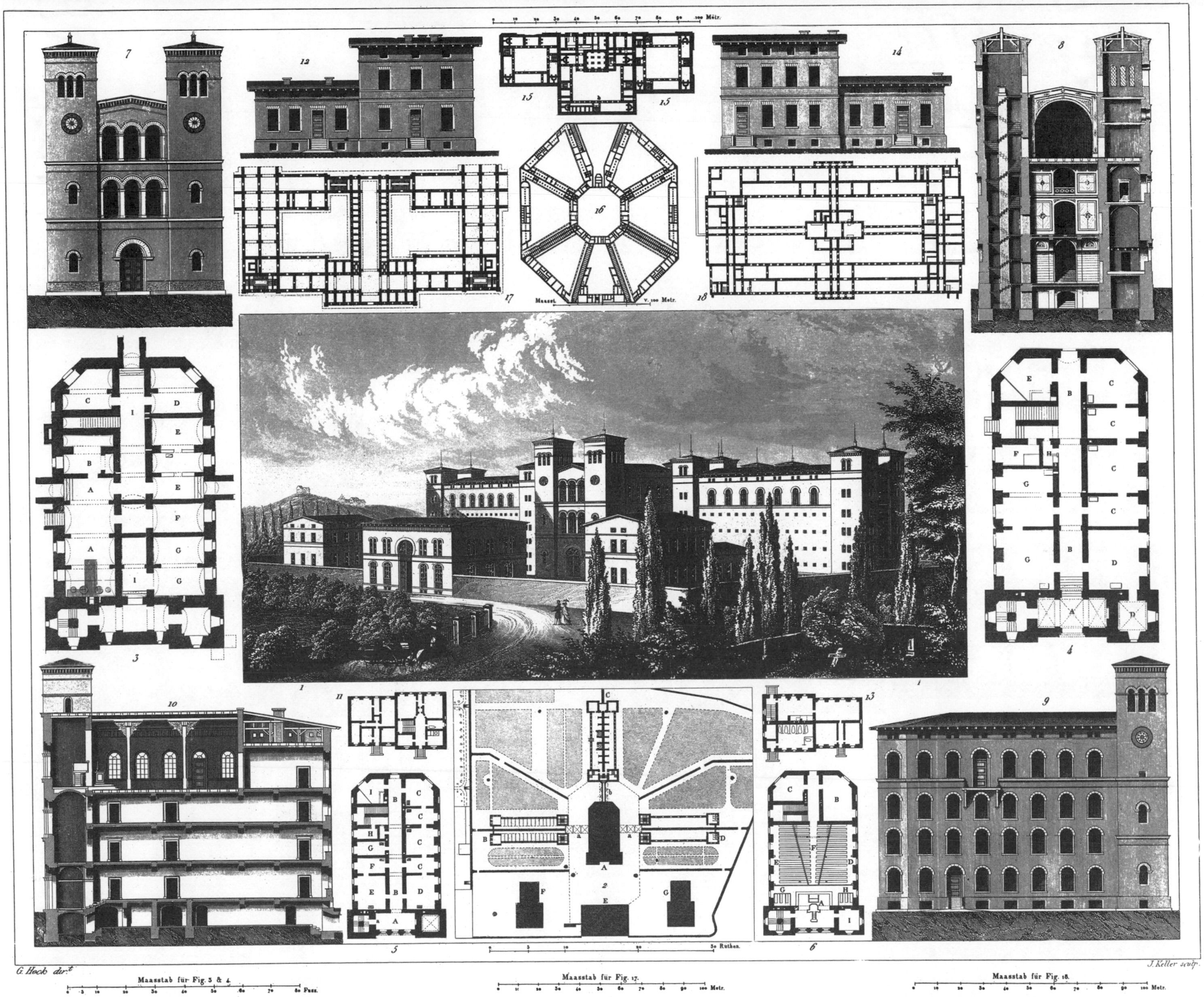
Maasst. v. 100 Metr.
G. Heck dir.t
J. Keller sculp.
Maasstab für Fig. 3 & 4.
Maasstab für Fig. 17.
Maasstab für Fig. 18.

G. Heck dir.t A. Krausse sen. sculp.

PLATE 409. THE ARCHITECTURE OF BRIDGES

MYTHOLOGY AND RELIGIOUS RITES

Captions to the Mythology and Religious Rites Plates, 410–439

PLATE 410.
Hindoo and Buddhist Symbols and Religious Implements

Figure
1*a*. Vishnu the Creator
1*b*. Brahm wrapped in the Maya
2. The Maya as Bhavani
3. Brahma, the creative power
4. Birth of Brahma
5. Siva, the destroying power
6. The Trimurti
7. The Lingam
8. The Hindoo symbol of wisdom
9. The figure Om or Aum
10. The Hindoo symbol of creation
11. Pracriti
12. The tortoise supporting the world
13. The seven celestial spheres
14. Siva Mahadeva
15. Parvati
16. Lakshmi or Sri
17. Siva as Rudra
18. Vishnu as man-lion
19. Surya, the god of the sun
20. Camadeva or Camos
21. Ganges, Jamuna, and Saraswadi
22. The giant Garuda
23. The giant Ravana
24. Buddhistic altar-piece
25–28. Buddhistic temple implements

PLATE 411.
Hindoo Penitents, Religious Figures and Paraphernalia; Mongolian Idols; Figures of Buddha

Figure
1. The Trimurti
2. Vishnu and Siva
3. Vishnu as a fish
4. Vishnu as a tortoise
5. Vishnu as a bear
6. Vishnu as a dwarf
7. Vishnu as Parasu Rama
8. Siva
9. Vishnu
10. Vishnu as Krishna
11. The nymphs of the Milk Sea
12. Vishnu as Kaninki or Katki
13. Siva as Hermaphrodite
14. Siva on the giant Muyelagin
15. Brahma and Saravadi
16. Buddha
17. Buddha-Surya
18. The Hindoo solar system
19. Mythic camel
20. Hindoo penitents
21–24. Hindoo sacrificial utensils
25–30. Mongolian idols

PLATE 412.
Religious Scenes and Figures of India and Central Asia

Figure
1–5. Hindoo idols
6. Vishnu on the giant Garuda
7. Indian idol of Astrachan
8. Buddha
9. A Brahmin
10–12. Hindoo ascetics
13–20. Idols of Lamaism
21. Mongolian Lama
22. Tartar Lama
23. Funeral of the Dalai Lama

PLATE 413.
Religious Scenes and Figures of the Far East

Figure
1. Allegorical pillar from Barolli
2. Chinese god of immortality
3, 4. Chinese idols
5. Worship at Honan
6. Chinese bonzes
7–13. Japanese idols
14, 15. Japanese house gods
16. Temple of Nitsirin at Honrensi
17. Temple at Foocoosaizi
18–32. Buddhistic temple implements
33–36. Buddhistic votive tablets

PLATE 414.
Rites and Religious Figures and Paraphernalia of the Far East

Figure
1. Worship of Fo in Canton
2, 3. Japanese idols
4. Temple of Miroc in Japan
5–10. Japanese idols
11. Chapel of the Cami at Givon
12, 13. The two Inari
14–17. The four Camini
18–36. Japanese temple utensils
37, 38. Japanese monks
39, 40. Buddhistic priests
41. Blind monk of Japan
42. Japanese nun and lay sister

PLATE 415.
Religious Scenes, Symbols, and Figures of China, Japan, and Indonesia

Figure
1–3. Japanese idols
4. Chief priest of the Tensjû
5. Priest of the same
6. High priest of Japan
7, 8. Buddhistic priests
9. Chinese procession
10. Chinese fanatic
11. Japanese procession
12–15. Japanese temple utensils
16, 17. Necklaces of the chief priest of the Tensjû
18–23. Javanese idols

PLATE 416.
Religious Scenes and Symbols of the Ancient Near East

Figure
1, 2. Persian processions
3. Persian Magi
4. Median high priest and Feruer
5. Persian fire worship and Feruer
6. Worship of the sun
7, 8. The priest kings
9. Sacrifice by Mithras
10, 11. Mythic animals
12*ab*. Persian coin
13. The celebration of the Darun
14. Idols of Afghanistan
15–17. Abraxas Gems

PLATE 417.
Egyptian Gods and Religious Symbols

Figure
1. Egyptian symbol of the sun
2. The All-seeing Eye
3–5. Sacred ships
6. Egyptian Amun
7. Nubian Amun
8. Kneph Mendes or Pan
9. Athor with the dove
10. Isis upon a lotus
11. Statue of Isis
12. Isis as a cow
13. Isis as a star
14. Isis nursing Osiris
15. Osiris upon a cow
16. Osiris with the serpent
17. Amun, Isis, and Osiris
18. Hermes as Ibis
19. Horus
20. The bull Apis
21. Typhon
22. Ailures
23. Serapis as the sun
24. Serapis and the seven planets
25. Harpocrates
26*ab*. Sacred jugs
27*a–c*. Egyptian family idols
28. The Sistrum
29. The sacred camel
30. The Egyptian zodiac
31. Priests and priestesses of Isis

PLATE 418.
Egyptian Religious Symbols and Tableaux

Figure
1. Kneph
2. Isis nursing Osiris
3. Isis nursing Horus
4. Osiris as a lion
5. Osiris as a bull
6. Anubis, Hermes, or Thot
7. Anubis and Isis
8. Anubis, Canop, and Horus
9. The wolf
10. The tribunal of the dead
11–14. Head-dresses of Egyptian idols
15, 16. Sacred jugs
17–19. Egyptian family idols
20, 21. Egyptian mythic animals
22. A sphinx
23. The Sistrum
24–28. Sacred vessels
29. Mystic procession
30, 31. Abraxas Gems

PLATE 419.
Sacrifice to Isis; Religious and Mythological Figures of Egypt

Figure
1. Head of Isis
2. Isis Pharia
3, 4. Statues of Isis
5, 6. Serapis and Isis
7. Statue of Serapis
8. Serapis on his throne
9. Isis nursing Horus
10, 11. Statues of Osiris
12, 13. Statues of Anubis
14. Statue of Harpocrates
15. Harpocrates on a ram
16. The Nile
17. The Nile key
18. Kneph as Agathodemon
19–22. Votive hands
23, 24. Sphinxes
25. The flower of the lotus
26–31. Egyptian priests
32–34. Egyptian priestesses
35. Sacrifice to Isis

PLATE 420.
Scene of Chinese Worship; Ancient Middle Eastern Deities and Idols; Norse Gods

Figure
1. Assyrian sacrifice
2. Syrian idol
3. The goddess Astarte

4. Phœnician Deities
5. Phœnician procession of the gods
6. Odin, Thor, Freyr, Tyr, and Loke
7–10. Odin
11*ab*. Norwegian idol
12. Ziselbog
13. Ipabog
14, 15. Slavonic idols
16. Nehalennia
17, 18. Runic stones
19. Runic calendar
20. Chinese worship

PLATE 421.
Figures and Scenes of Norse and Germanic Mythology

Figure
1. Frigga
2. Braga
3. Idunna
4. Freya
5. Heimdall
6. The tree Yggdrasill and the Norns
7. The Valkyræ
8. Triglav
9. Svantevit
10. Radegast
11. Prove
12. Siebog
13. Shvaixtix
14. Nirthus or Hertha
15. Flyntz
16. Magusanus
17. Alemanic idol
18. Germanic religious ceremony
19. Venus Anadyomene
20. The Gallic Isis

PLATE 422.
Deities and Religious Rites of the Norse, Gauls, and Celts

Figure
1. Odin the supreme
2. Thor the thunderer
3. Freyr, god of the sun
4. Freya with her maids
5. Njord, god of winds
6. Tyr, god of battle fields
7. Hermode the messenger
8. Aske and Emla, the first human beings
9. Radegast
10. Sieba, goddess of love
11. Podaga
12*ab*. Perkunust
13. Nemisa
14*a*. Sarmatian idol
14*b*. Silesian idol
15, 16. Northern idols
17, 18. Gallic Jupiter
19. Gallic Vulcan
20. Gallic Mercury
21. Hercules Saxanus
22. Gallic Diana
23. Mercury, Abelio, Vulcan, Ceres, and Minerva
24, 25. Druid and Druidess
26. Annual search for the mistletoe

PLATE 423.
Aztec and Mayan Religious Rites, Figures, and Artifacts

Figure
1–7. Mexican idols
8. Fragment of Aztek writing
9*ab*. Mexican priestess
10. The Mexican year
11. The Mexican almanac
12. Mexican altar top
13. Mexican sacrifice
14–19. Idols of Guatemala
20. Altar with idols
21–24. Sacrificial vessels of Guatemala
25–28. Idols of Yucatan
29. Sacrificial vase from Yucatan
30, 31. Abraxas Gems

PLATE 424.
Religious Rites and Figures of Ancient Greece and Rome

Figure
1, 2. Statues of Janus
2*ab*. Heads of Janus
3. Saturnus
4. Opis or Ops
5. Jupiter as Deus pater
6, 7. Hera
8. Hestia
9. Vesta
10. Diana
11. Apollo
12. Tages
13. Mars the advancing
14. Bellona
15. Hermes
16. Ancharia
17. Aphrodite (Venus)
18. Vertumnus
19. Pomona
20. Voltumna
21*ab*. Fortuna
22*ab*. Vejovis
23. Asclepios (Æsculapius)
24. Tyrrhenian Heracles
24*ab*. Sacred coin
25. The shield dance of the Salii
26*ab*. Demeter (Ceres)
27*ab*. Demeter and Zeus

PLATE 425.
Sacred Rites, Religious and Mythological Figures, and Religious Paraphernalia of Greece and Rome

Figure
1. Faunus
2. Nemesis
3. Proserpine
4. The genius of death
5, 6. Two heroes
7–9. Lares
10. Æon
11, 12. Cronos
13. Cronos and Rhea
14. Rhea
15. Atys
16*ab*. Attributes of Atys
17. The goat Amalthea
18. Jupiter Axur
19. Zeus Ammon
20. The Olympian Zeus
21. Zeus the Supreme
22. Zeus with the eagle
23. Hera suckling Ares
24. Bonus Eventus
25. Ceres Catagusa
26. Diana Lucifera
27–33*ab*. Grecian sacrificial vessels
34. The Augures

PLATE 426.
Legendary Scenes and Figures from Greek and Roman Mythology

Figure
1. Nux or Night
2. Cœlus
3. Rhea
4. Jupiter Axur
5. Zeus Hellenios
6. Jupiter receiving the homage of the gods
7, 8. Zeus as warrior
9. Pegasgian Zeus
10. Zeus carrying off Europa
11. Birth of Athene (Minerva)
12. Jupiter Conservator
13. Pelasgian Hera
14–17. Juno
18–21. Ares (Mars)
22. Mars Pacificus
23. Victoria (Nike)
24. Ganymede
25. Hebe
26. Apollo and Daphne
27. Sibylla
28. Apollo's raven
29. A sacrificial knife
30. The Delphian oracle

PLATE 427.
Classical Deities and Mythological Characters

Figure
1. Zeus
2. Zeus conquering the Titans
3. Europa on the bull
4. Zeus on the centaur
5. Ares and Aphrodite
6–8. Genii of Mars
9. Nymph of Artemis
10. The Dioscuri
11. Poseidon, Amphitrite, and Eros
12. Bacchanalian genii
13. Dionysos (Bacchus)
14. Apollo
15. Ariadne
16. Demeter (Ceres)
17–24. Roman sacrificial implements
25. The assembly of the gods

PLATE 428.
Greek and Roman Gods and Religious Paraphernalia

Figure
1. The twelve planet gods
2. Zeus, Hermes, and Aphrodite
3. Pallas Athene
4. Ceres (Demeter)
5. The muse Erato
6, 7. Flora
8. Fortuna
9. A naiad
10. Genii
11. The Seasons
12. Tritons
13. Bacchanalia
14. Priestess of Bacchus
15, 16. Priestesses of Ceres
17, 18. Grecian priest and priestess
19, 20. Altars
21–47. Sacrificial utensils

PLATE 429.
Greek Festival and Mythological Figures and Scenes

Figure
1. Argos guarding Io
2. Leda and the swan
3, 4. The Dioscuri
5. Leto (Latona)
6. Lunus
7. Apollo and Marsyas
8. Aurora
9. Artemis Locheia
10. Diana Lucifera
11. Artemis Soleia
12. Juno Sospita
13. Helios
14. Artemis (Diana)
15. Artemis and her nymphs
16. Mountain nymphs
17. Niobe
18. Amphion
19. Hermes the messenger
20. Hermes Agonios
21. Zeus with the eagle
22. Europa and the bull
23. The Panathanæan festival at Athens

PLATE 430.
Classical Legends and Mythological Figures

Figure
1. Artemis of Ephesus
2. Artemis Tauropolos
3. Artemis Selene
4. Hebe
5. Iris
6. Death of the children of Niobe
7. Nereus
8. Palæmon
9. Nereid

10. Taras
11. Poseidon
12. Poseidon and Pallas Athene
13. Hippocamp
14. River god and naiad
15*ab*. Nilus (the Nile)
16*ab*. Tibris (the Tiber)
17–19. Sirens
20. Artemis and Orion
21. Mænade
22. Hermes (Mercury)

PLATE 431.
Gods and Mythological Creatures

Figure
1. Hylas carried off by nymphs
2. Nereids
3. A Triton
4. Pelasgian Poseidon
5, 6. Statues of Poseidon
7, 7*a*. Neptune
8. Hippocamp
9. Melicertes (Palæmon)
10. Thetis
11. Hebe
12–15. The winds
16. Boreas bearing off Oreithyia
17. Hades (Pluto)
18*ab*. Proserpine (Persephone)
19. Sacrifice to Neptune

PLATE 432.
Gods and Mythological Characters

Figure
1. Hades (Pluto)
2. Zeus Ammon
3. Hades (Pluto)
4. Poseidon and Amymone
5*ab*. Nemesis
6. Hypnos (Sleep)
7. Thanatos (Death)
8, 9. Hypnos (Sleep)
10. The genius of sleep
11, 12. Persephone (Proserpine)
13. Hecate
14. Erinnyes or Eumenides
15. Prometheus
16. Pandora
17. The Dreams
18. Demeter and Triptolemus
19. Dionysos nursed by nymphs
20. Triumph of Poseidon and Amphitrite
21, 22. Tritons

PLATE 433.
Gods and Mythological Creatures and Figures

Figure
1. Pelasgian Demeter
2. Bust of Demeter
3. Ceres
4. Persephone
5. Procession of Dionysos and Ariadne
6. Triptolemus
7. Birth of Dionysos
8. Leucothea
9. The sacred lion
10*ab*. The sacred serpent
11. Dionysus and Faunus
12, 13. Dionysos
14. Ariadne
15. Indian Dionysos
16. Pan and Olympos
17*ab*. Pan and the Panic
18. Silenos
19. Hygeia
20. Hephæstos (Vulcan)
21. Telesphorus
22, 23. Hermes (Mercury)
24. Charon
25. Sisyphos, Lapithæ, and Tantalos

PLATE 434.
Gods and Mythical Characters

Figure
1. Faunus and a Bacchante
2, 3. Pan
4, 5. Dionysos
6. Dionysos of Naxos
7. The Dionysian mysteries
8. Apollo and Marsyas
9. Marsyas and Olympos
10–12. Silenos
13. Priapos
14–18. Heracles
19*a*. Persephone
19*b*. Dionysos Zagreus
20. Hephæstos (Vulcan)
21. Mount Parnassos

PLATE 435.
The Muses and Other Legendary Female Figures; Apollo and Dionysus

Figure
1. The nine Muses
2. The muse Calliope
3. The muse Clio
4. The muse Polyhymnia
5. The muse Euterpe
6*ab*. The muse Urania
7. The muse Thalia
8. Mnemosyne
9*a*. Flora
9*b*. Vestal virgin
10*a*. Aurora
10*b*. Medusa
11. Apollo and the Hours
12. Dionysos as god of the sun

PLATE 436.
Aphrodite and Other Goddesses and Gods

Figure
1. Artemis (Diana)
2. Hermes (Mercury)
3. A herma
4. Hermes the Eloquent
5. Hermes with the tortoise
6. Vesta
7–14. Pallas Athene (Minerva)
15. The Delphian Apollo
16. Antinous
17–25*a*. Aphrodite (Venus)
25*b*. Mars and Ilia
26. Aphrodite as goddess of matrimony
27. Mars the Avenger
28. Athene, Asclepios, and Hygeia
29. Asclepios and Hygeia
30. Venus Victrix
31. Birth of Aphrodite

PLATE 437.
Apollo; Sacrifice to Mars; Other Mythological Figures

Figure
1–4. Apollo
5. Dionysos and Apollo
6. Bust of Athene (Minerva)
7–12. Hermes (Mercury)
13. Silenos
14–18. Aphrodite (Venus)
19–21. The Graces
22. Hermaphrodites
23. Hymen
24. Asclepios
25. Melicertes (Palæmon)
26. The sacred bull of Dionysos
27. Sacrifice to Mars

PLATE 438.
A Sacrifice in Rome; Gods and Mythological Characters

Figure
1. Ariadne
2. Dionysian orgies
3–6. Eros (Amor)
7–10. Amor and Psyche
11. Statue of Psyche
12. The Graces
13. The Hours
14. Fides
15. Pax
16. Pietas
17. Pudor or Pudicitia
18. Concordia
19. Bonus Eventus
20. Spes
21. Astræa
22. A centaur
23. Sacrifice in Rome

PLATE 439.
Legendary and Mythological Scenes and Figures of Greece and Rome

Figure
1. Roman pontifex maximus
2. Roman augur
3. Guardian of the Sibylline books
4. Priest of Jupiter
5. Vestal virgin
6. Victimarius
7. The Suovetaurilia
8. Sacrificial tripod
9. Sacrificial horn
10. Gorgons
11, 12. Perseus
13*ab*. Medusa
14. Charybdis
15. Scylla
16. The nymph Circe
17. Minotaur
18*ab*. Sphinxes
19. A centaur
20. Œdipous slaying the sphinx
21–23. Giants
24. Allegorical representation of Atlas
25, 26. Bellerophon
27, 28. Amazons
29. Pygmies
30, 31. Pallor, Pavor

G. Heck dir.t — Henry Winkles sculp.t

PLATE 410. HINDOO AND BUDDHIST SYMBOLS AND RELIGIOUS IMPLEMENTS

G Heck dir.t Henry Winkles sculp.t

PLATE 411. HINDOO PENITENTS, RELIGIOUS FIGURES AND PARAPHERNALIA; MONGOLIAN IDOLS; FIGURES OF BUDDHA

PLATE 412. RELIGIOUS SCENES AND FIGURES OF INDIA AND CENTRAL ASIA

G. Heck dir.t Henry Winkles sculp.t

 PLATE 413. RELIGIOUS SCENES AND FIGURES OF THE FAR EAST

G. Heck dir.

Henry Winkles sculp.

PLATE 414. RITES AND RELIGIOUS FIGURES AND PARAPHERNALIA OF THE FAR EAST

G. Heck dir.[t]   Henry Winkles sculp.

PLATE 415. RELIGIOUS SCENES, SYMBOLS, AND FIGURES OF CHINA, JAPAN, AND INDONESIA

PLATE 416. RELIGIOUS SCENES AND SYMBOLS OF THE ANCIENT NEAR EAST

 PLATE 417. EGYPTIAN GODS AND RELIGIOUS SYMBOLS

G. Heck dir.[t] Henry Winkles sculp.[t]

PLATE 418. EGYPTIAN RELIGIOUS SYMBOLS AND TABLEAUX

 PLATE 419. SACRIFICE TO ISIS; RELIGIOUS AND MYTHOLOGICAL FIGURES OF EGYPT

G. Heck dir.t

Henry Winkles sculp.t

PLATE 420. SCENE OF CHINESE WORSHIP; ANCIENT MIDDLE EASTERN DEITIES AND IDOLS; NORSE GODS

G. Heck dr.[t]   W. Werner sculp.

PLATE 421. FIGURES AND SCENES OF NORSE AND GERMANIC MYTHOLOGY

PLATE 422. DEITIES AND RELIGIOUS RITES OF THE NORSE, GAULS, AND CELTS

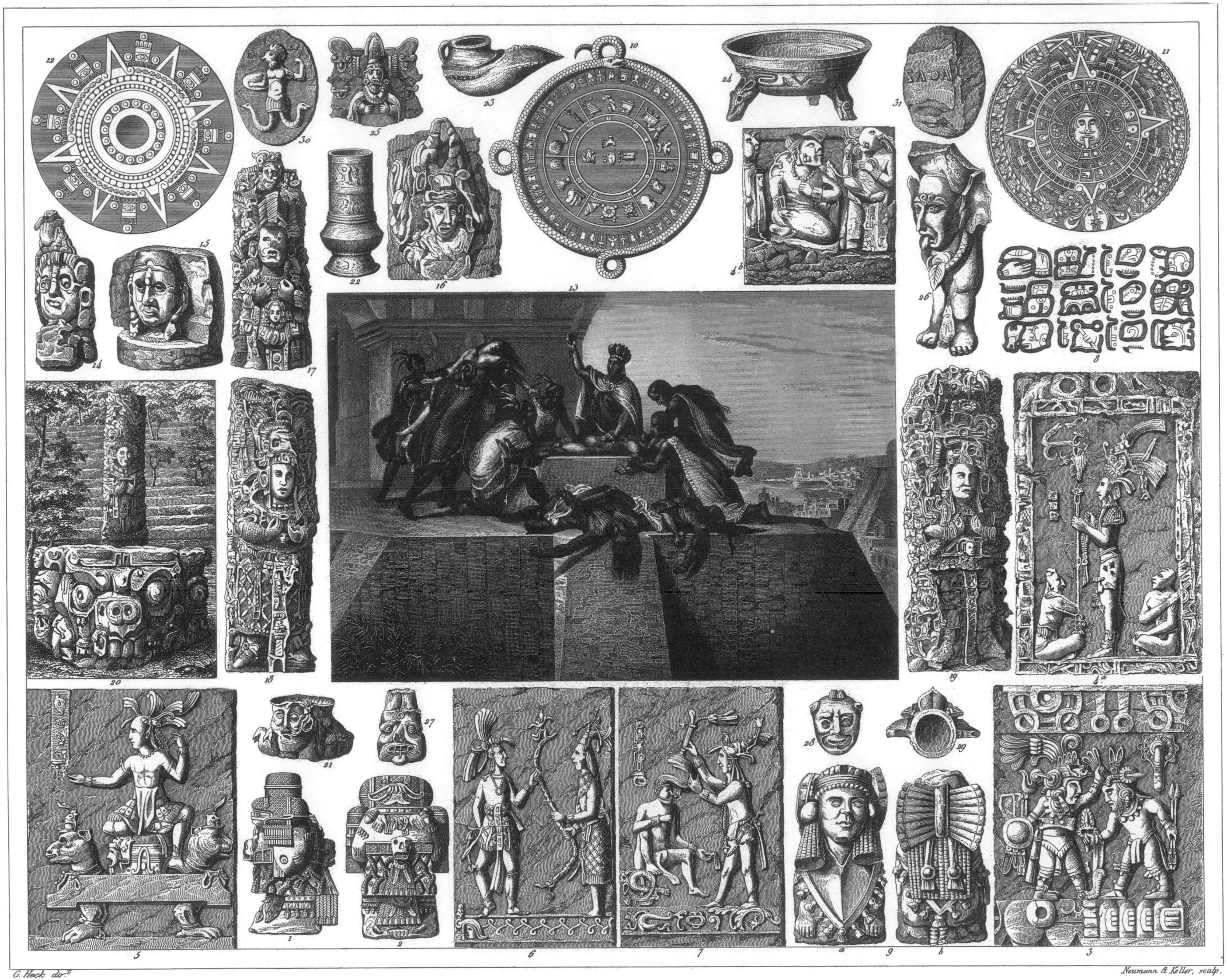

G. Heck dir.t Neumann & Keller, sculp.

PLATE 423. AZTEC AND MAYAN RELIGIOUS RITES, FIGURES, AND ARTIFACTS

G. Heck dir.t

W. Hohneck sculp.

PLATE 424. RELIGIOUS RITES AND FIGURES OF ANCIENT GREECE AND ROME

G. Heck dir.t

Henry Winkles sculp.t

PLATE 425. SACRED RITES, RELIGIOUS AND MYTHOLOGICAL FIGURES, AND RELIGIOUS PARAPHERNALIA OF GREECE AND ROME

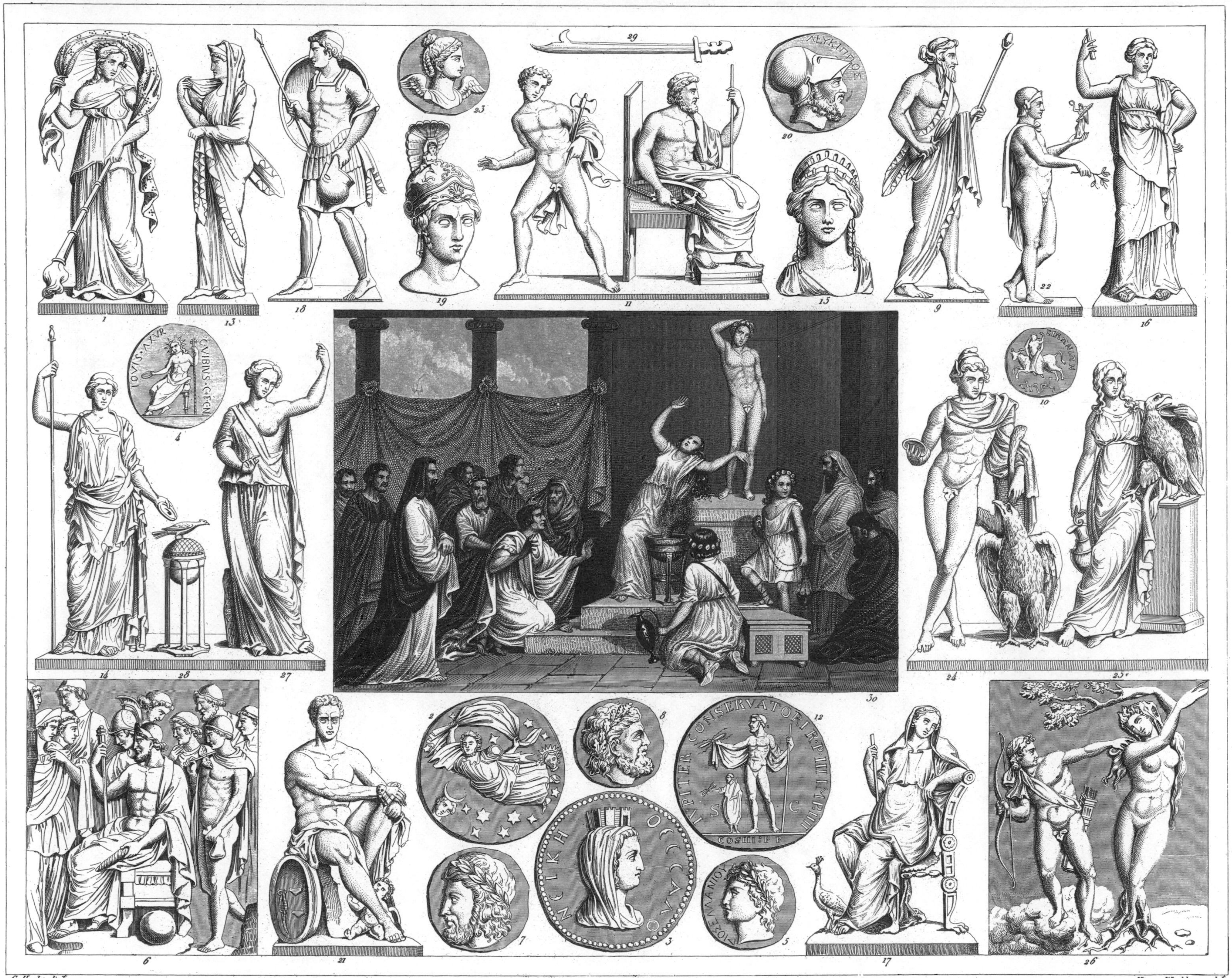

G. Heck dir.ᵗ Henry Winkles sculp.ᵗ

PLATE 426. LEGENDARY SCENES AND FIGURES FROM GREEK AND ROMAN MYTHOLOGY

G. Heck dir.t Ackermann sculp.t

 PLATE 427. CLASSICAL DEITIES AND MYTHOLOGICAL CHARACTERS

PLATE 428. GREEK AND ROMAN GODS AND RELIGIOUS PARAPHERNALIA

G. Heck dir.t Henry Winkles sculp.t

PLATE 429. GREEK FESTIVAL AND MYTHOLOGICAL FIGURES AND SCENES

G. Heck dir.t

Henry Winkles sculp.t

PLATE 430. CLASSICAL LEGENDS AND MYTHOLOGICAL FIGURES

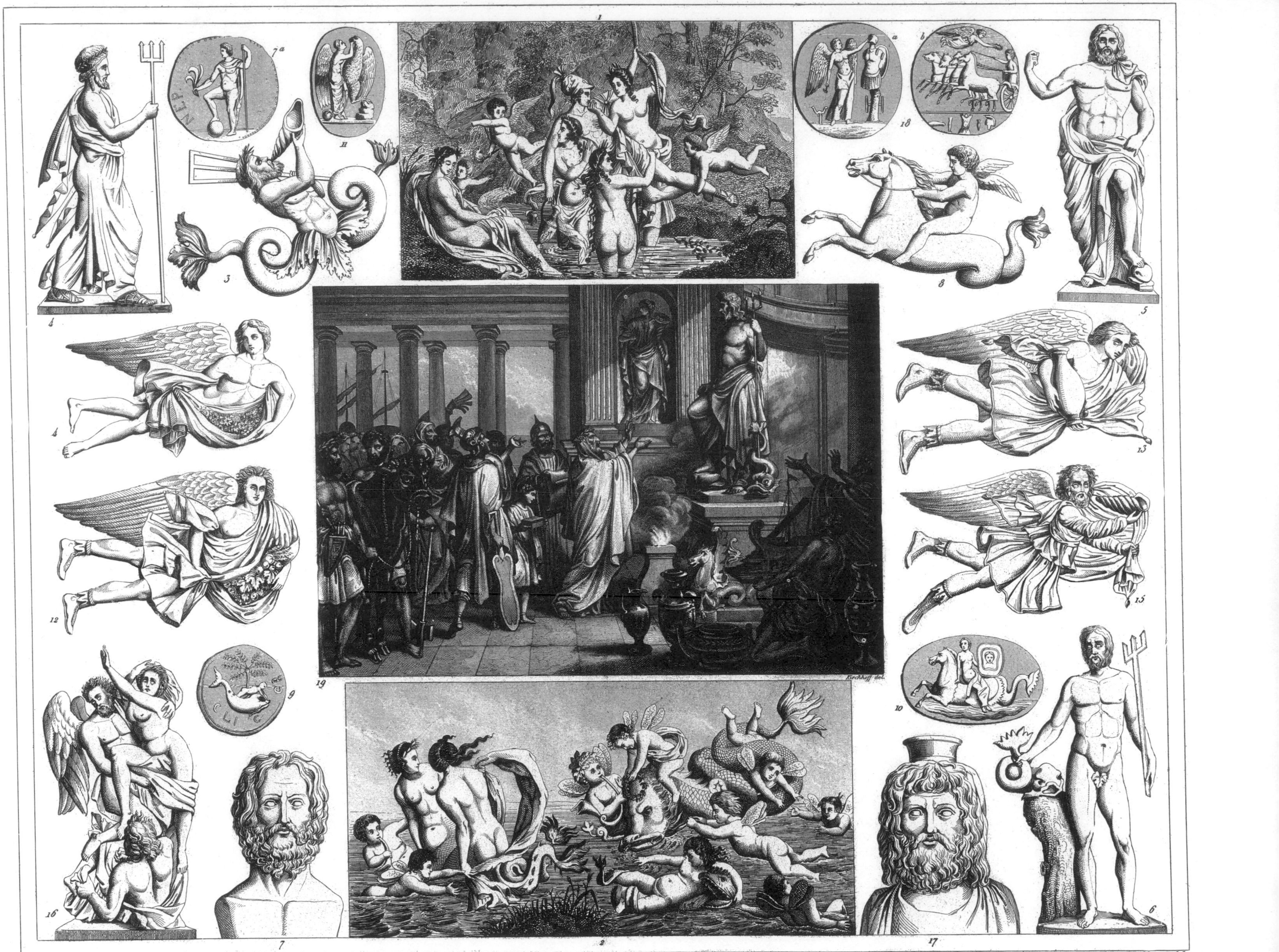

G. Heck dir.t   Henry Winkles sculp.t

PLATE 431. GODS AND MYTHOLOGICAL CREATURES

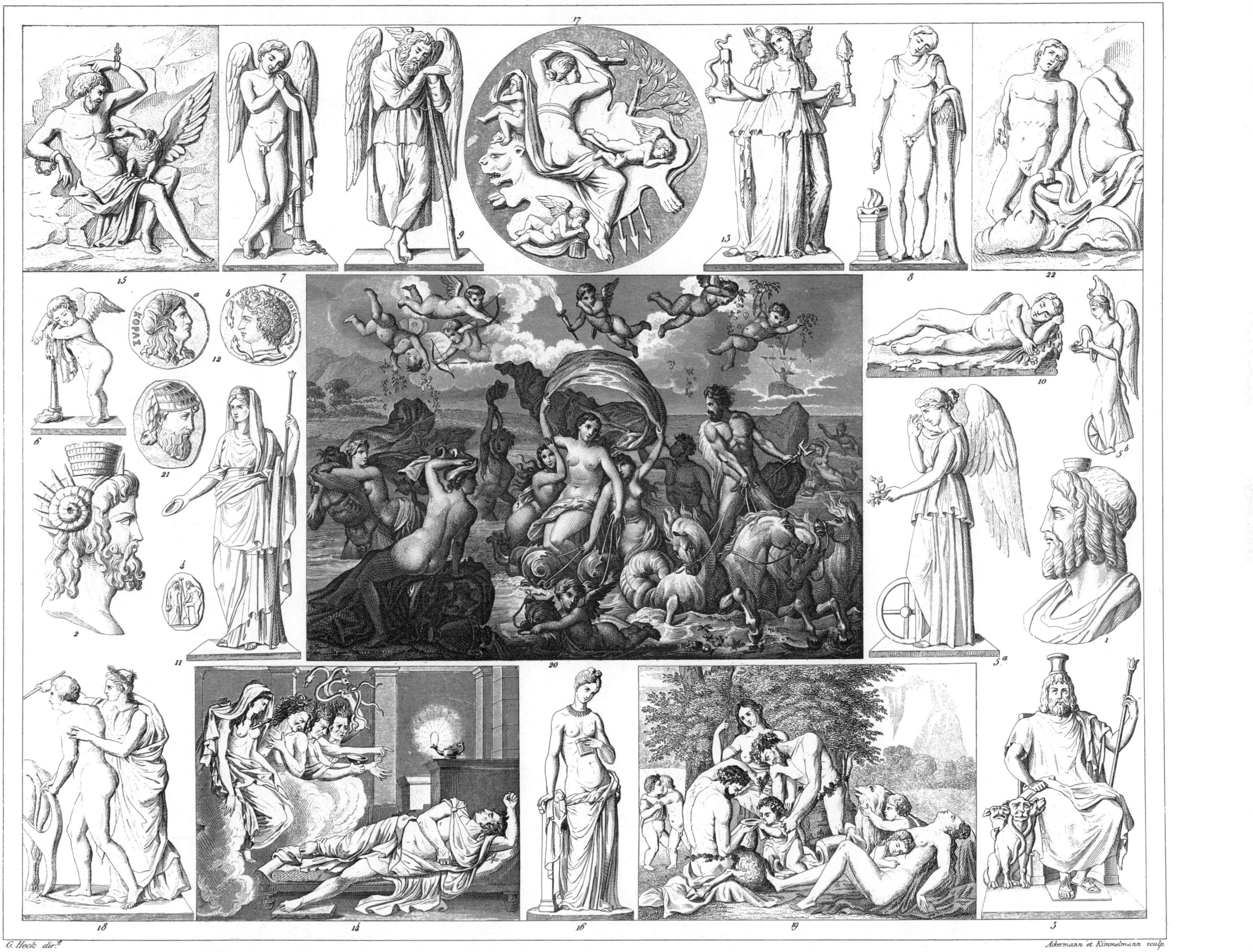

G. Heck dir.^t Ackermann et Kimmelmann sculp.

PLATE 432. GODS AND MYTHOLOGICAL CHARACTERS

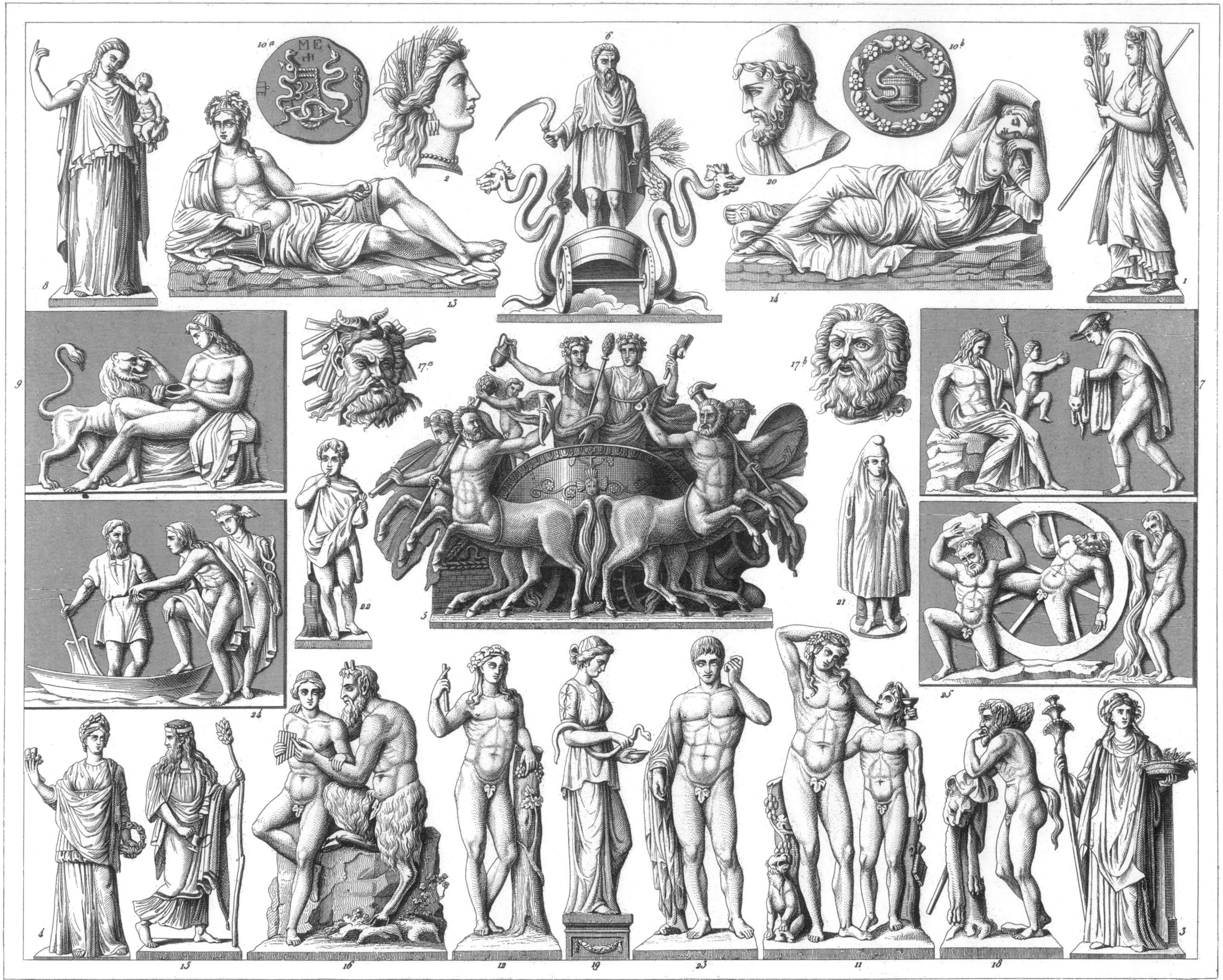

 PLATE 433. GODS AND MYTHOLOGICAL CREATURES AND FIGURES

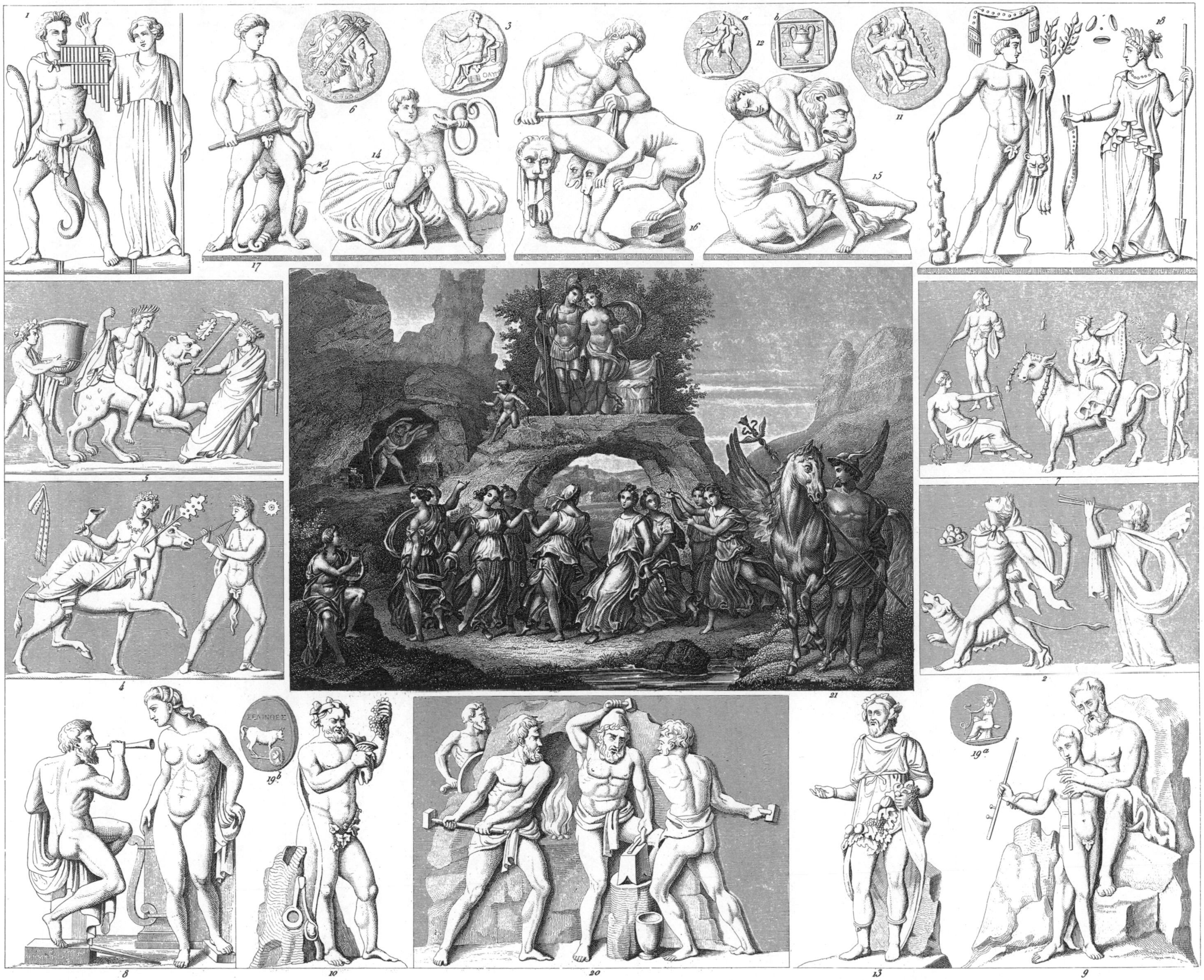

G. Heck dir.t

Ackermann & Schmidt sculp.

PLATE 434. GODS AND MYTHICAL CHARACTERS

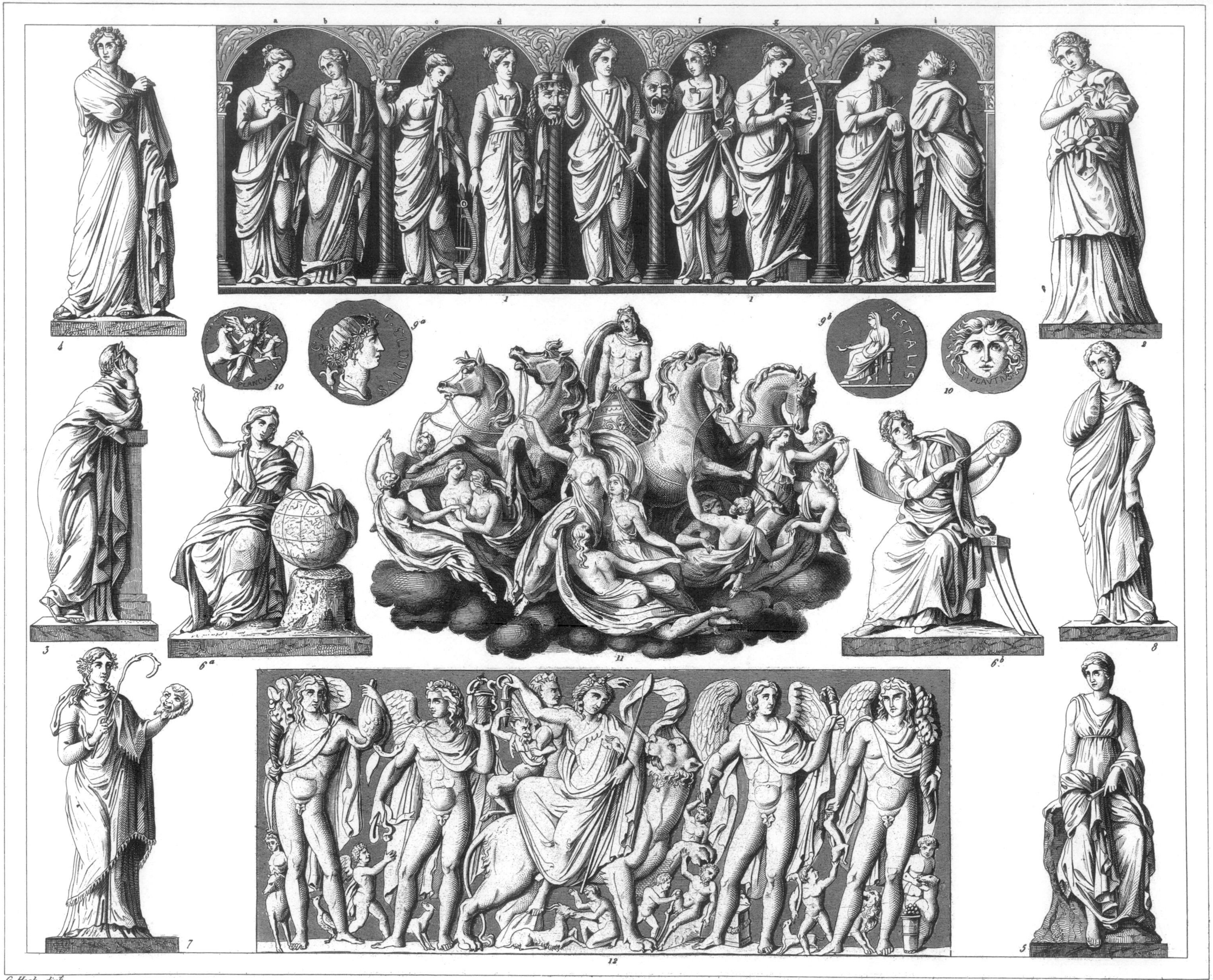
PLANCVS
C. CLODIVS
VESTALIS
PLAVTIVS

G. Heck dir.t

Kimmelmann sculp.

G. Heck dir.t

Ackermann & Werner sculp

PLATE 436. APHRODITE AND OTHER GODDESSES AND GODS

PLATE 437. APOLLO; SACRIFICE TO MARS; OTHER MYTHOLOGICAL FIGURES

G. Heck dir.t

Ackermann & Kimmelmann sculp.

PLATE 438. A SACRIFICE IN ROME; GODS AND MYTHOLOGICAL CHARACTERS

G. Heck dir.t Neumann et Werner sculp.

PLATE 439. LEGENDARY AND MYTHOLOGICAL SCENES AND FIGURES OF GREECE AND ROME

THE FINE ARTS

Captions to the Fine Arts Plates, 440–465

PLATE 440.
Ancient Sculpture

Figure
1. Bas-relief from the ruins of Persepolis
2. Trimurti from the temple of Elephanta
3. Bas-relief from Ellora
4. Bas-relief from Kenneri
5. Bust from Ægina
6. Mask from Selinuntiæ
7, 8. Etruscan bas-reliefs
9–11. Grecian sculptures of the second period
12. Bas-relief from Selinuntiæ
13, 14. Bas-reliefs from Xanthus

PLATE 441.
Ancient Sculpture

Figure
1–9. Egyptian statues
10. Façade of the temple of Hathor at Ipsambul
11, 12. Phœnician grave-stones
13. Numidian half-bust
14. Statue of Lakshmi from Bengalore
15. Statue from Isura
16–19. Persian sculptures

PLATE 442.
Greek and Roman Sculpture and Coins

Figure
1. Hercules's combat with Antæus
2. Aphrodite and Ares (Venus and Mars)
3. The reclining Hermaphrodite
4. Pallas, in the Villa Albani
5. Pallas with the serpent
6. The Farnese Flora
7. The wounded Amazon of Ctesilaus
8. The dancing Hours
9. Fragment of the frieze of the Parthenon
10. Fragment from the Capitoline Museum
11. Bas-relief from a tripod-stand in Dresden
12–17. Grecian portrait-busts
18–20. Grecian animal heads
21. The Gonzaga cameo
22–26. Grecian coins

PLATE 443.
Greek and Roman Sculpture

Figure
1. Phidias's statue of Pallas in the Parthenon in Athens
2. The Medicean Venus
3. The Venus of Melos
4. The Venus of the Dresden Museum
5. The Venus Victrix from Capua
6. The Capitoline Venus
7. Diana the Huntress in Paris
8. Statue of Sallustia Barbara Urbana with Eros, in Rome
9. Statue of Julia Soæmis in Rome
10. Sleep as a boy, in Dresden

PLATE 444.
Classical Sculpture

Figure
1, 2. The Farnese Hercules
3. The Torso Belvedere
4. The Borghese Gladiator
5. The Dying Gladiator
6. The Pallas from Velletri
7. Cupid and Psyche
8. Venus crouching in the bath
9. Statue of Adonis
10. Statue of Dionysus, in Paris
11. Statue of Bacchus, in Dresden
12. Statue of Cincinnatus in Paris
13. Boy extracting a thorn from his foot, in Rome

PLATE 445.
Classical and Classical Revival Sculpture

Figure
1. Statue of Antinous of Belvedere
2. The Apollo of Belvedere
3. Statue of a Faun
4. Statue of Germanicus, from the 15th century; it belongs to the period of the revival of art, but the sculptor is not known. It is preserved in the Louvre in Paris
5. Hercules with the boy Telephus on his arm, in Rome
6. Boy wrestling with a goose
7. Laocoön, in the Vatican
8. Statue of Meleager, in Rome

PLATE 446.
Renaissance Sculpture

Figure
1. Pietas Militaris, bas-relief in Rome
2. The restoration of the dead to life, bas-relief in the Vatican
3. Statue of a bishop, by Agostino and Angelo de Senis
4. Shrine of St. Peter the Martyr, by Giovanni Balducci
5–8. Four Caryatides from this shrine
9. Bust from a fountain at Siena, by Jacopo della Quercia
10. Bust of an apostle, by Andrea Verocchio
11. St. John the Baptist, by Donatello
12. St. George, by Donatello
13. Holy Virgin, by Giovanni da Pisa
14. Apollo and Daphne, by Lorenzo Bernini
15. The Angel of the Annunciation, by Francesco Mocchi
16. Perseus, by Benvenuto Cellini
17. Mercury, by Giovanni da Bologna
18. Bacchus and a Satyr, by Michael Angelo
19. Moses, by Michael Angelo
20. Morning and Evening, by Michael Angelo

PLATE 447.
Renaissance, Mannerist, and Neoclassic Sculpture

Figure
1. The Three Graces with the Urn, by Germain Pilon
2. The Fettered Slave, by Michael Angelo
3. The Penitent Magdalene, by Canova
4. The Dancing Girl, by Canova
5. Statue of Jason, by Thorwaldsen
6. Statue of Apollo, by Thorwaldsen
7. Statue of Cincinnatus, by Chaudet
8. Dancing Neapolitan, by Duret
9. Statue of Spartacus, by Fogatier
10. The Maid of Orleans, by the Duchess Marie of Orleans

PLATE 448.
Neoclassic Sculpture

Figure
1. Statue of Hebe, by Canova
2. Cupid and Psyche, by Canova
3. The Three Graces, by Canova
4. Statue of Venus, by Thorwaldsen
5. The Three Graces, by Thorwaldsen
6. Achilles and Briseis, bas-relief by Thorwaldsen
7–11. Fragments from the Procession of Alexander, bas-relief by Thorwaldsen

PLATE 449.
Heroic and Memorial Sculpture and Monuments

Figure
1. Statue of Admiral Duquesne, by Roguier
2. Statue of Bayard, by Montour
3. Statue of Du Guesclin, by Bridan
4. Statue of the great Condé, by Jean David
5. Statue of Mozart, by Schwanthaler
5*ab*. Bas-reliefs from the pedestal of the last-named monument, by Schwanthaler
6. Statue of Margrave Frederick, by Schwanthaler
7. Ino with the boy Bacchus, by Dumont
8. Leda and the Swan, by Seurre jeune
9. Statue of Bavaria, by Rauch
10. Statue of *Felicitas publica*, by Rauch
11. Monument to Marshal Saxe, by Pigalle
12. Monument to Robert Burns in Edinburgh

PLATE 450.
Nineteenth-Century Memorial and Ceremonial Sculpture

Figure
1. Statue of Otto the Illustrious, by Schwanthaler
2. Statue of Ludwig the Bavarian, by Schwanthaler
3. Statue of Gutenberg, by Jean David
4. Statue of Gutenberg, by Thorwaldsen
5, 6. Bas-reliefs from the pedestal of the last-named monument, by Thorwaldsen
7. Statue of Schiller, by Thorwaldsen

8, 9. Bas-reliefs from the pedestal of the last-named monument, by Thorwaldsen
10. Statue of General Kleber, by Ph. Gross
11. Monument to the Duchess of Saxe-Teschen, by Canova
12. The Death of Epaminondas, bas-relief by Jean David
13. Bellona, bas-relief by Chinard
14. Monument to Dugald Stewart in Edinburgh

PLATE 451.
Ancient Wall and Vase Painting

Figure
1, 2. Egyptian paintings
3–7. Etruscan vase-paintings
8, 9. Wall-paintings from Pompeii
10. Monochrome from Herculaneum
11. Achilles and Briseis, from Pompeii
12. Achilles at Scyros, from Pompeii
13, 14. Wall-paintings from the baths of Titus

PLATE 452.
Ancient Decorative Arts

Figure
1–4. Etruscan vase-paintings
5. Theseus, wall-painting from Herculaneum
6. Narcissus, wall-painting from Herculaneum
7. The Aldobrandini wedding
8. Fresco painting from the villa Pamfili
9. The Pythian Apollo
10. The Delphian Apollo
11, 12. Nymphs, from the Baths of Constantine
13, 14. Amorettes, from the same
15. Ceiling from the sepulchre of the Naso family
16. Masks, mosaic in the Vatican
17. Doves, mosaic in the Capitoline Museum
18. Relief-mosaic in Rome
19–22. Mosaic pavement

PLATE 453.
Ancient and Early Medieval Painting and Mosaics

Figure
1–3. Grecian vase-paintings
4. Wall-painting from the sepulchre of the Naso family
5ab. Miniature paintings of the 8th century
6. Mosaic from the Villa Albani
7. Mosaic from St. John's in the Lateran
8. Fragment from Trajan's column
9. Mosaic from Cosmedino
10. Mosaic from St. John's in the Lateran
11. Mosaic from Florence
12. Mosaic from St. Peter's in Rome

PLATE 454.
Italian Painting of the Renaissance

Figure
1. School of Athens, by Raphael
2. Madonna and Child, by Leonardo da Vinci
3. Ecce Homo, by Ludovico Cardi
4. St. Mark, by Fra Bartolomeo
5. St. Francis, by Guido Reni
6. The Entombment of Christ, by Caravaggio
7. Mary Magdalen and St. Francis of Assisi by the body of Christ, by Annibale Caracci
8. Joseph and Potiphar's wife, by Carlo Cignani
9. Praying Madonna, by Sassoferrato
10. Madonna, by Guido Reni
11. St. John the Baptist, by Guido Reni
12. Galathea, by Ludovico Caracci
13. Pluto, by Agostino Caracci

PLATE 455.
Italian Renaissance and Baroque Painting

Figure
1. St. Cecilia, by Raphael
2. Madonna and Child, by Raphael
3, 4. Fresco paintings by Raphael
5. The Distribution of the Holy Rosaries, by Carlo Maratti
6. Venus and Vulcan, by Giulio Romano
7. Madonna, by Annibale Caracci
8. Descent from the Cross, by Andrea del Sarto
9. Polyhymnia and Erato, by Pietro da Cortona
10. Euterpe and Urania, by Pietro da Cortona

PLATE 456.
Painting of the Sixteenth and Seventeenth Centuries

Figure
1ab, *2ab*. Fresco paintings, by Raphael
3. Raphael's portrait, by himself
4. The Adulteress before Christ, by Tintoretto
5. The Dying Magdalen, by Rustichino
6. Holy Family, by Francesco Albano
7. Charity, by Andrea del Sarto
8. Madonna, by Murillo
9. Vandyk's portrait, by himself
10. Passage of the Granicus, by Lebrun

PLATE 457.
Baroque and Mannerist Painting

Figure
1. Madonna and the Fathers of the Church, by Raphael
2. The Virgin Mary, by Fra Bartolomeo
3. Christ crowned with thorns, by Titian
4. Andromeda, by Francesco Furini
5. Offering brought to Æsculapius, by Guérin
6. Guido Reni's portrait, by himself
7. Assumption of St. Mary, by Rubens
8. Portrait of Rubens, by himself
9. The Adoration of the Shepherds, by Van der Werff
10. Youth with the Drinking-cup
11. Guitar-player, by Netscher
12. The Adoration of the Magi
13. Endymion, by Girodet-Trioson
14. Belisarius, by François Pascal Gérard

PLATE 458.
Illustrations of the Theory of the Art of Drawing

Figure
1–12. The eye
13–15. The nose
16–19. The mouth
20–27. The ear
28–31. The feet
32–39. The hands
40–45. Pictorial perspective

PLATE 459.
Illustrations of the Theory of the Art of Drawing

Figure
1–10. The head
11–14. The entire body
15, 16. Artistical Anatomy
17–21. The hands

PLATE 460.
Illustrations of the Theory of the Art of Drawing

Figure
1–11. Auxiliary lines
12–15. Proportions of the human body
16, 17. Proportions of the human face
18. Antique torso
19–21. Antique heads

PLATE 461.
Illustrations of the Graphic Arts

Figure
1. Etching on soft ground
2. Etching
3. Etching finished with the graver
4. Mezzotinto
5. Aquatint engraving
6. Stippling combined with line engraving
7, 8. Manner of holding the graver
7a. Engraver's easel
8a. Engraver's hand-vise
9. Manipulation of cutting stones
9a. Engraver's oil-rubber
10, 11. Tampons, or dabbers
12. Common ruler
13. Parallel ruler
14, 15. Scrapers
16. Burnisher
17. Rocking-tool or cradle
18. Roulette
19. Scratcher
20–22. Etching needles
23–26. Gravers
27. Callipers
28ab. Improved callipers
29, 30. Punches
31, 32. Engraver's anvil and hammer
33. Lines made by the cradle
34. Reducing frame
35. Frame for correctly observing curves on busts, etc.
36–38. Hands for engraving stamps

PLATE 462.
Alphabets of Various Languages for the Use of Engravers

* * The values of the letters in English characters are placed opposite them. It will suffice here to give the list of the languages whose superscriptions are in German. The only words that may require explanation are: *Kehlhauch*, guttural aspiration; *Kurz*, short; *Lang*, long; *Werth*, value; *Zahlwerth*, numerical value; and *Benennung*, name

The alphabets are: 1. Japanese; 2. Tamul; 3. Bugic (Malay); 4. Persian arrow-headed characters; 5. Hebrew; 6. Samaritan; 7. Pehlvi (Parthian); 8. Armenian; 9. Ancient Greek; 10. Modern Greek; 11. Coptic; 12, Gothic; 13. Etruscan; 14. Anglo-Saxon; 15. Runic.

PLATE 463.
Alphabets for Engravers

1. Magadha (older Sanscrit); 2.

Sanscrit; 3. Tibetan; 4. Arabic; 5. Ethiopian; 6. Syriac; 7. Zend; 8. Mongolian; 9. Russian; 10. Wallachian; 11. Serbian.

GLOSSARY

Bemerkungen, Observations; these are: **Jerr* adds to the force of the preceding consonant; ** *Jehr* softens the preceding consonant; ***The Serbian language is printed with Russian type, with the addition of *Jerr* and *Jehr*.

Interpuctionszeichen der Zendschrift, Punctuation marks of the Zend language.

PLATE 464.

Details Illustrating the Construction of Theatrical Buildings

Figures 1–33.

PLATE 465.

Details Illustrating the Construction of Theatrical Buildings

Figures 1–45.

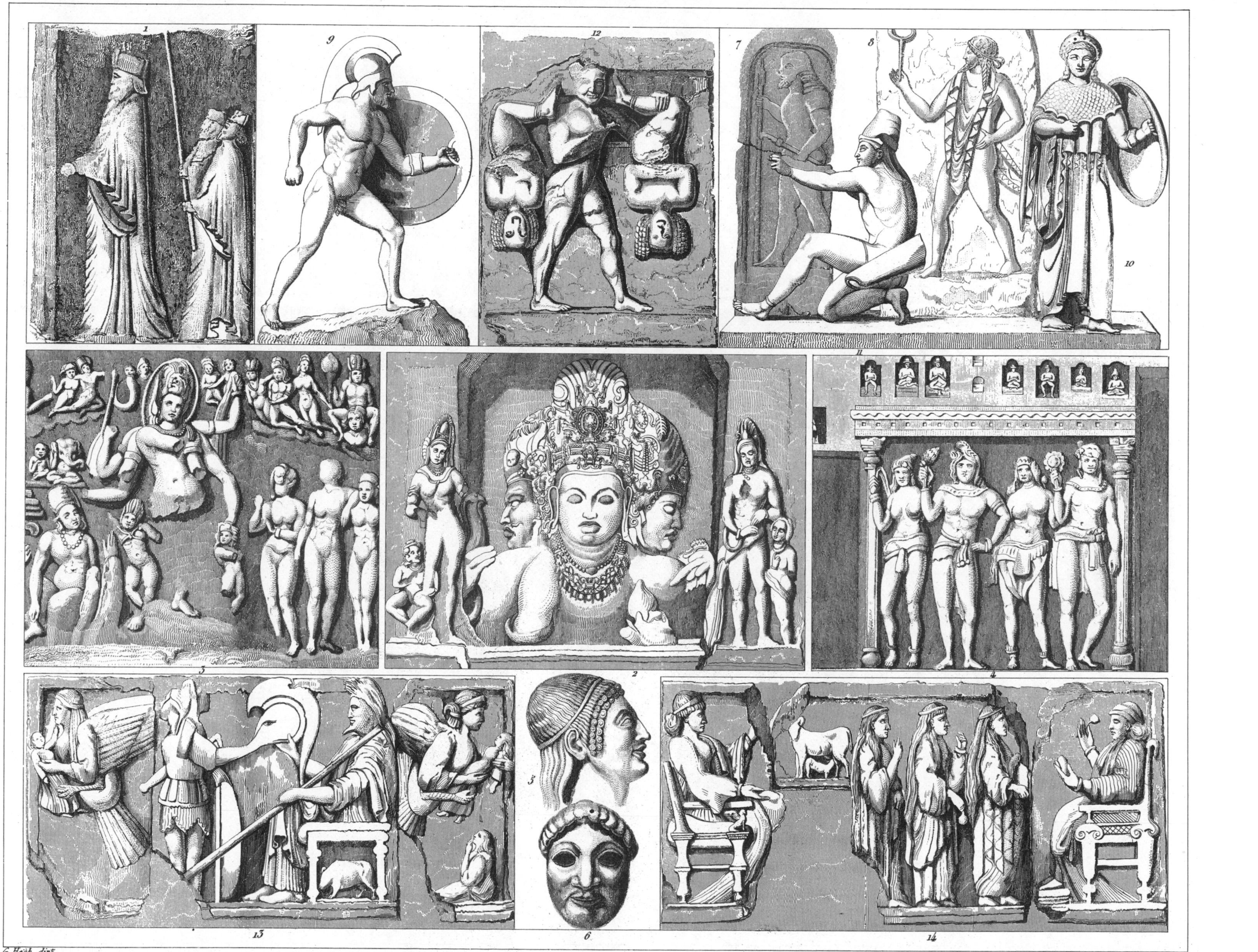

G. Heck dir. *Henry Winkles sculp.*

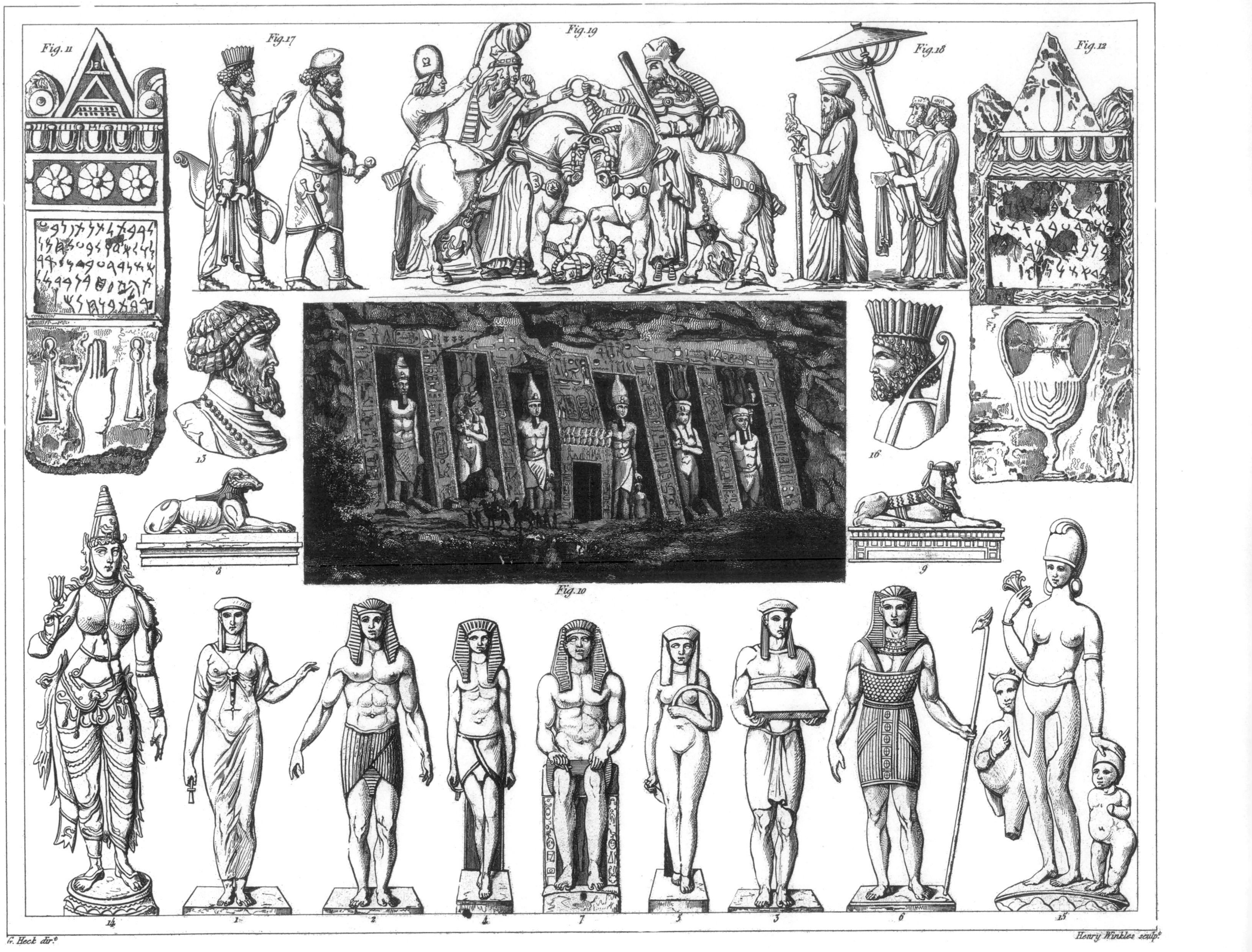
Fig. 11
Fig. 17
Fig. 19
Fig. 18
Fig. 12
13
16
8
9
Fig. 10
14
1
2
4
7
5
3
6
15

G. Heck dir.

Henry Winkles sculp.

G. Heck dir.t
Henry Winkles sculp.t

10
3
6
4
2
5
7
1
9
8
G. Heck dir.
Henry Winkles sculp.
Masstab für Figur 1.
0
5
10
15
20 Fuss

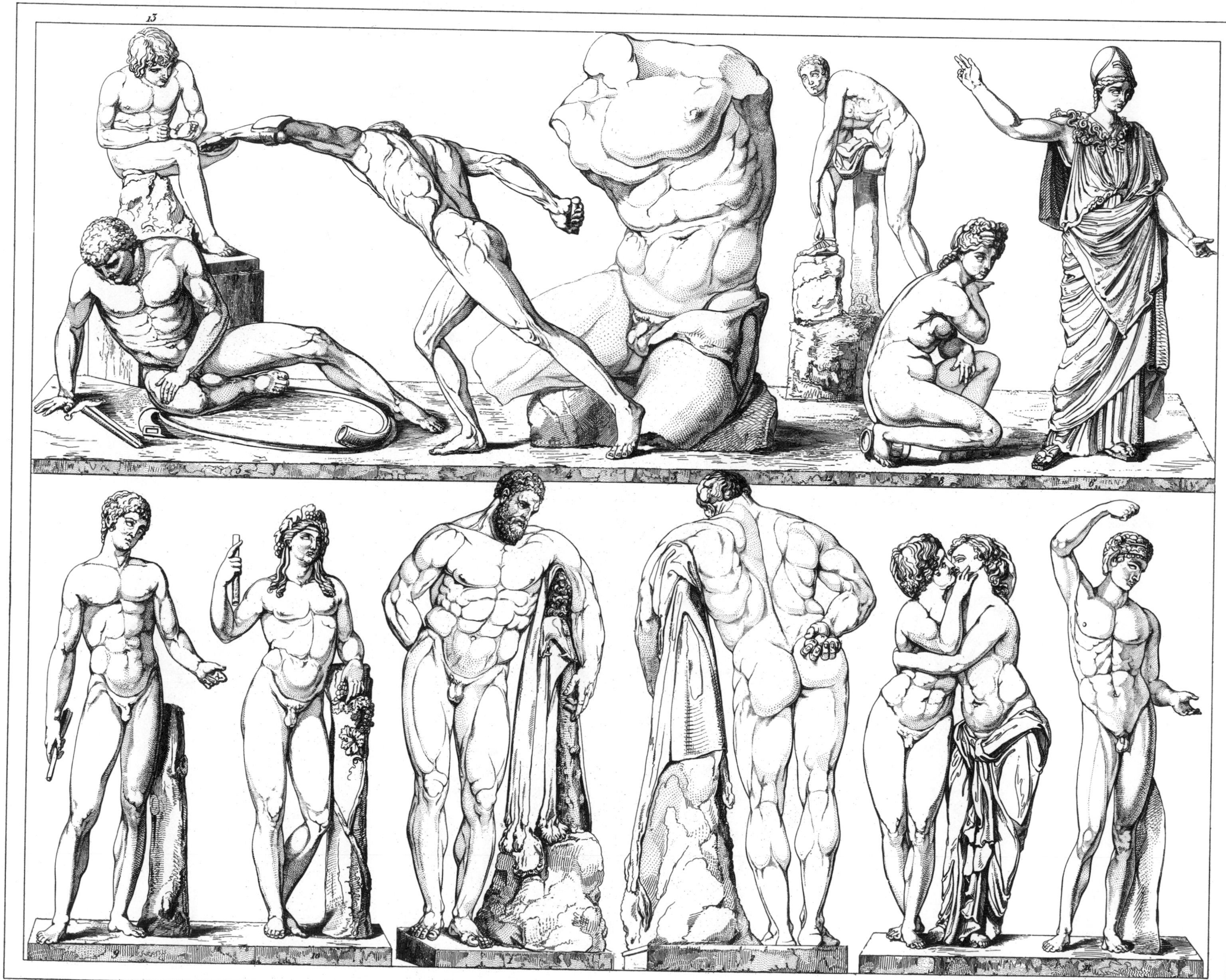

G. Heck dir.t

Henry Winkles scup.t

PLATE 444. CLASSICAL SCULPTURE

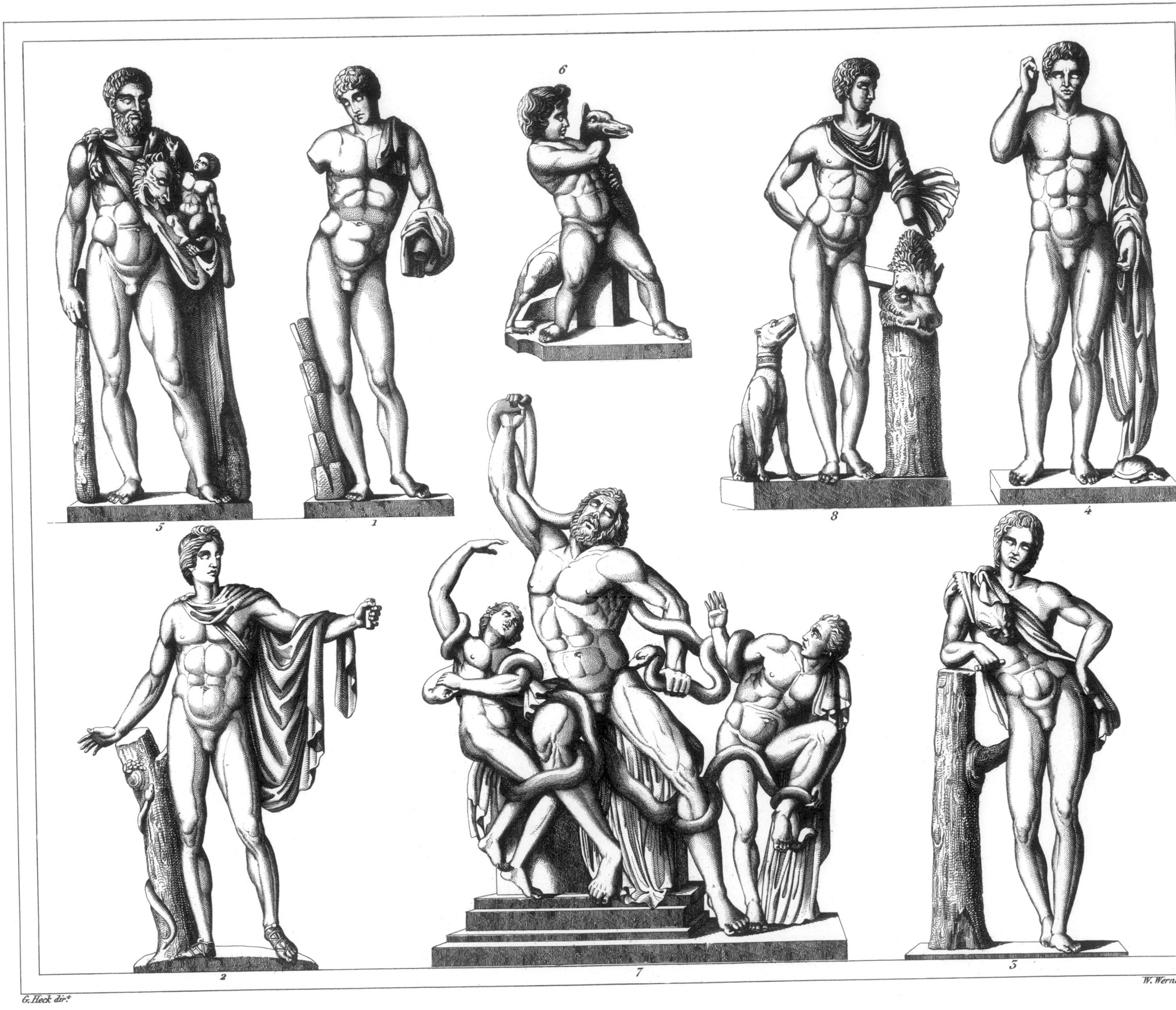

 PLATE 445. CLASSICAL AND CLASSICAL REVIVAL SCULPTURE

PLATE 446. RENAISSANCE SCULPTURE

G. Heck dir.^t Henry Winkles sculp.^t

 PLATE 447. RENAISSANCE, MANNERIST, AND NEOCLASSIC SCULPTURE

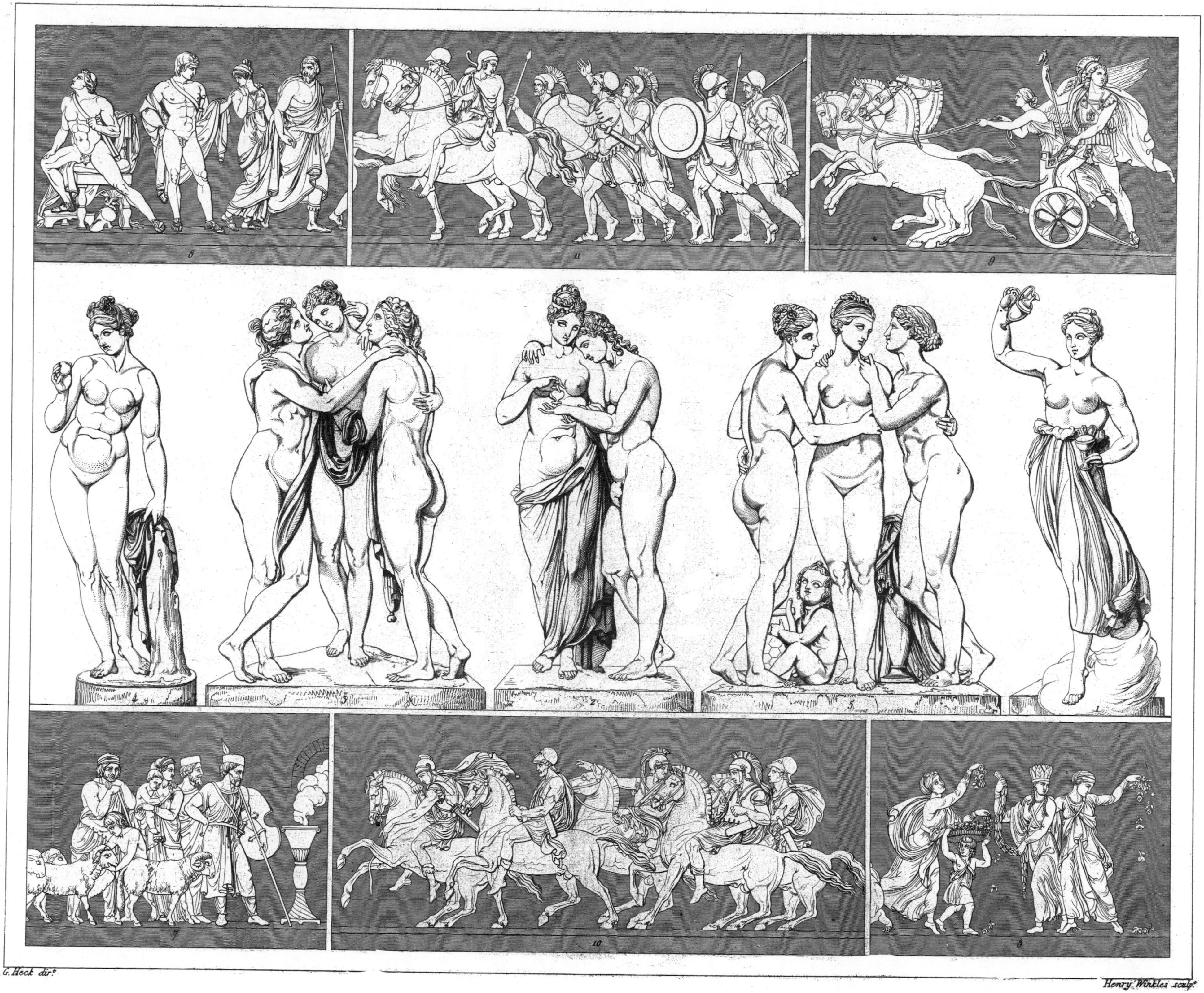

PLATE 448. NEOCLASSIC SCULPTURE

G. Heck dir.t

A. Krausse sen. sculp.t

PLATE 449. HEROIC AND MEMORIAL SCULPTURE AND MONUMENTS

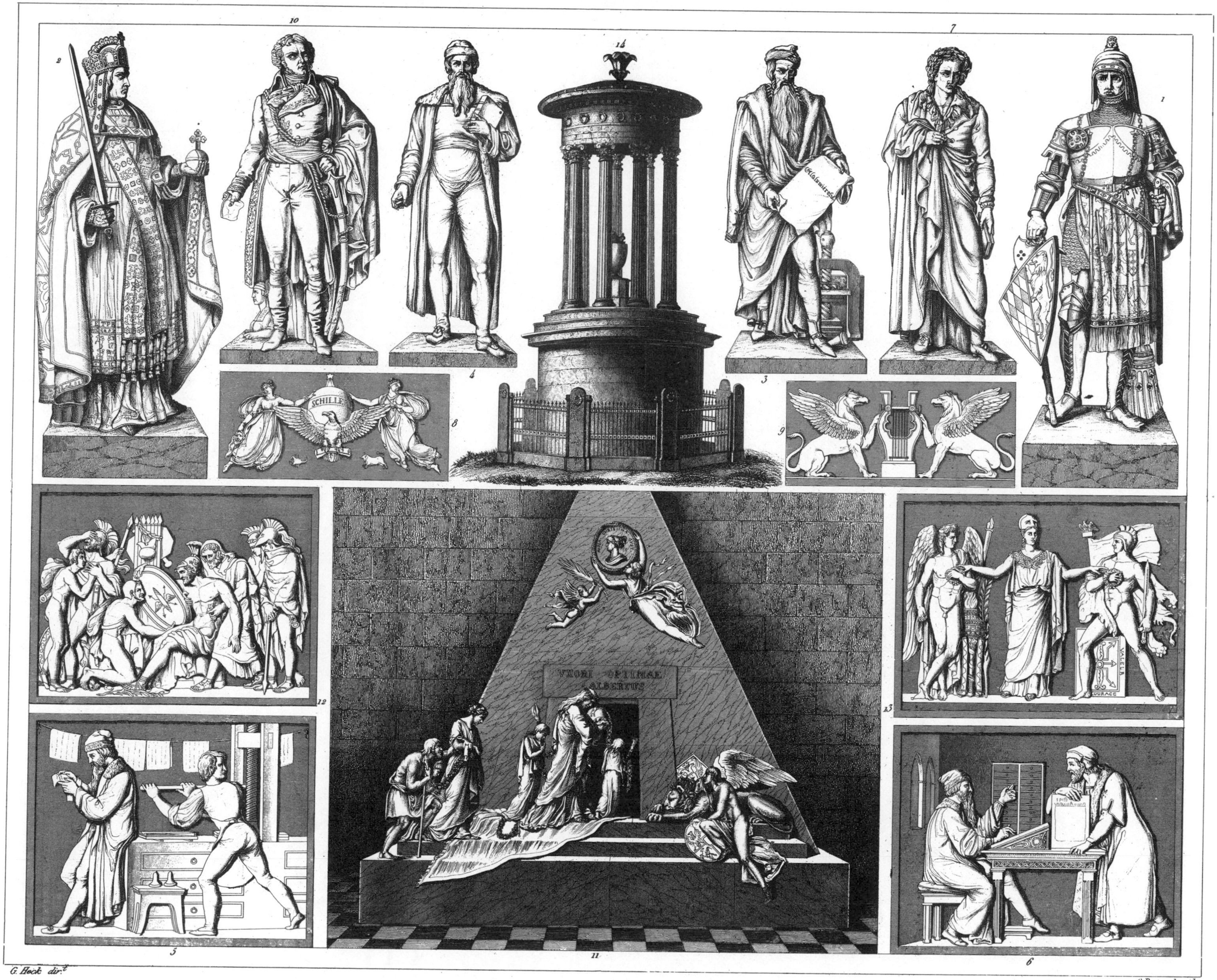
SCHILLER
VXORI OPTIMAE
ALBERTUS

G. Heck dir.[t] *C. Bertrand sculp.*

G. Heck dir.t

Feldweg sculp.

PLATE 451. ANCIENT WALL AND VASE PAINTING

G. Heck dir.t

W. Werner sculp.

PLATE 452. ANCIENT DECORATIVE ARTS

PLATE 453. ANCIENT AND EARLY MEDIEVAL PAINTING AND MOSAICS

G. Heck dir.t

W. Werner sculp.

PLATE 454. ITALIAN PAINTING OF THE RENAISSANCE

G. Heck dir.t   A. Krause sculp

PLATE 455. ITALIAN RENAISSANCE AND BAROQUE PAINTING

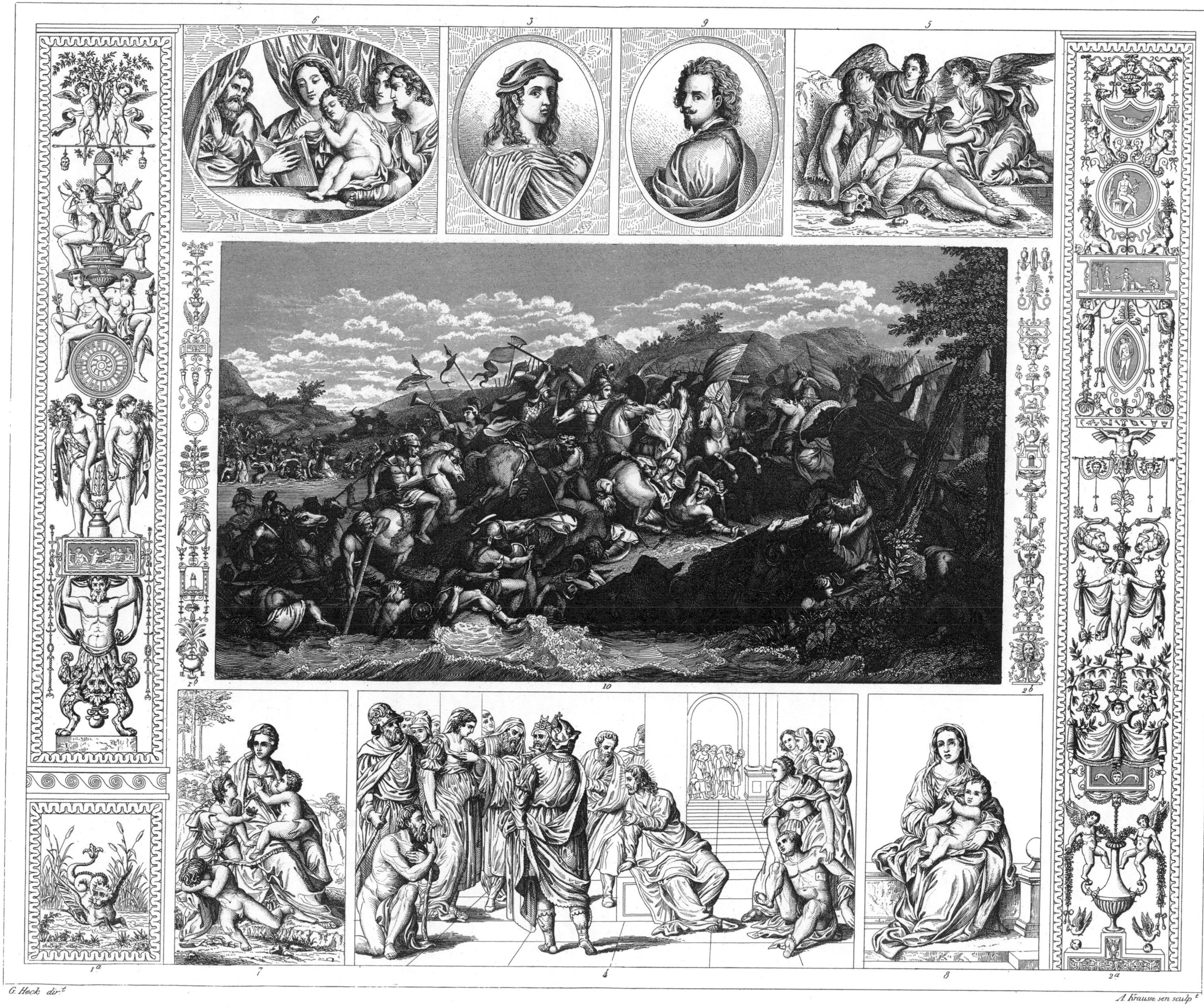

PLATE 456. PAINTING OF THE SIXTEENTH AND SEVENTEENTH CENTURIES

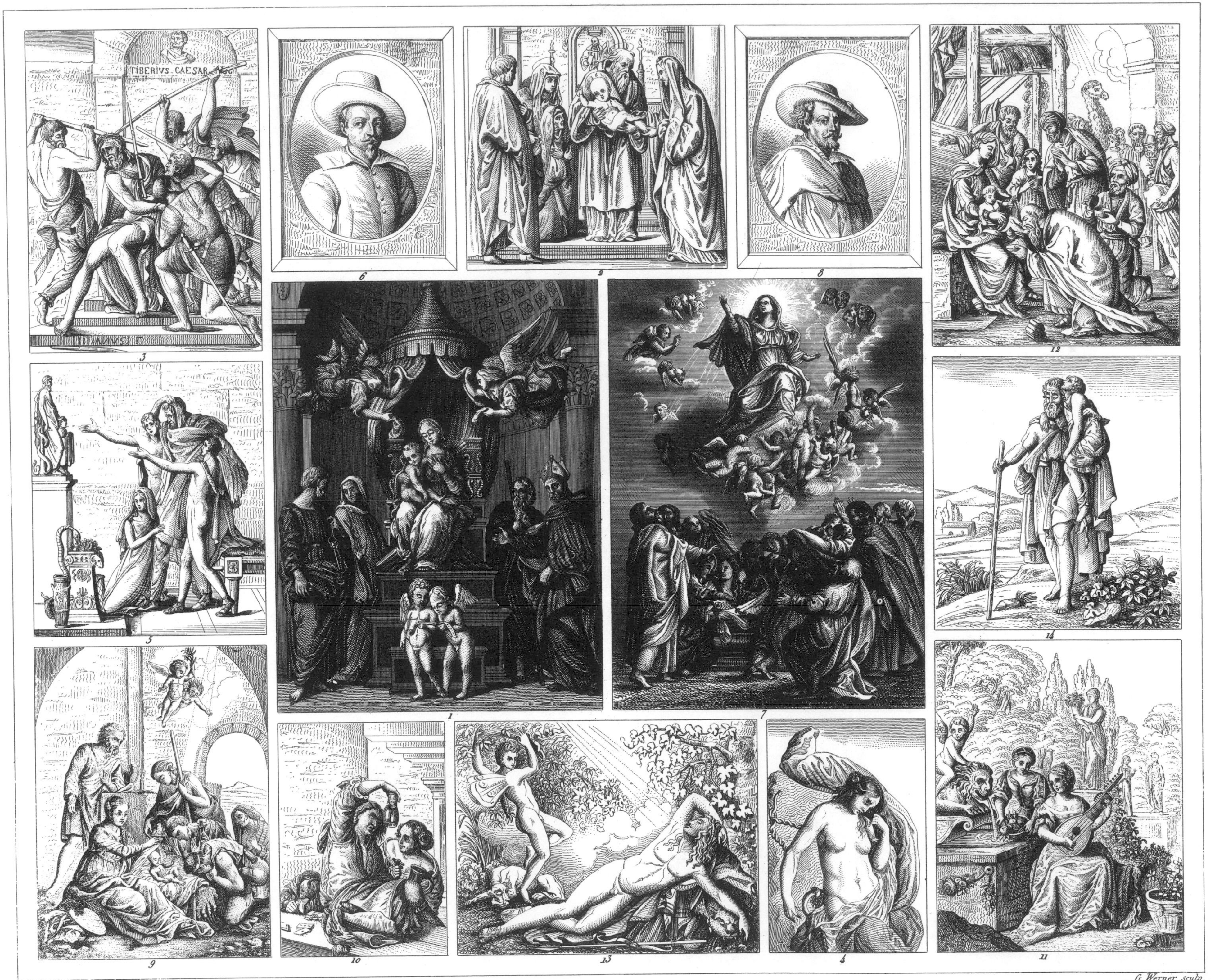

G. Heck dir.t G. Werner sculp.

 PLATE 457. BAROQUE AND MANNERIST PAINTING

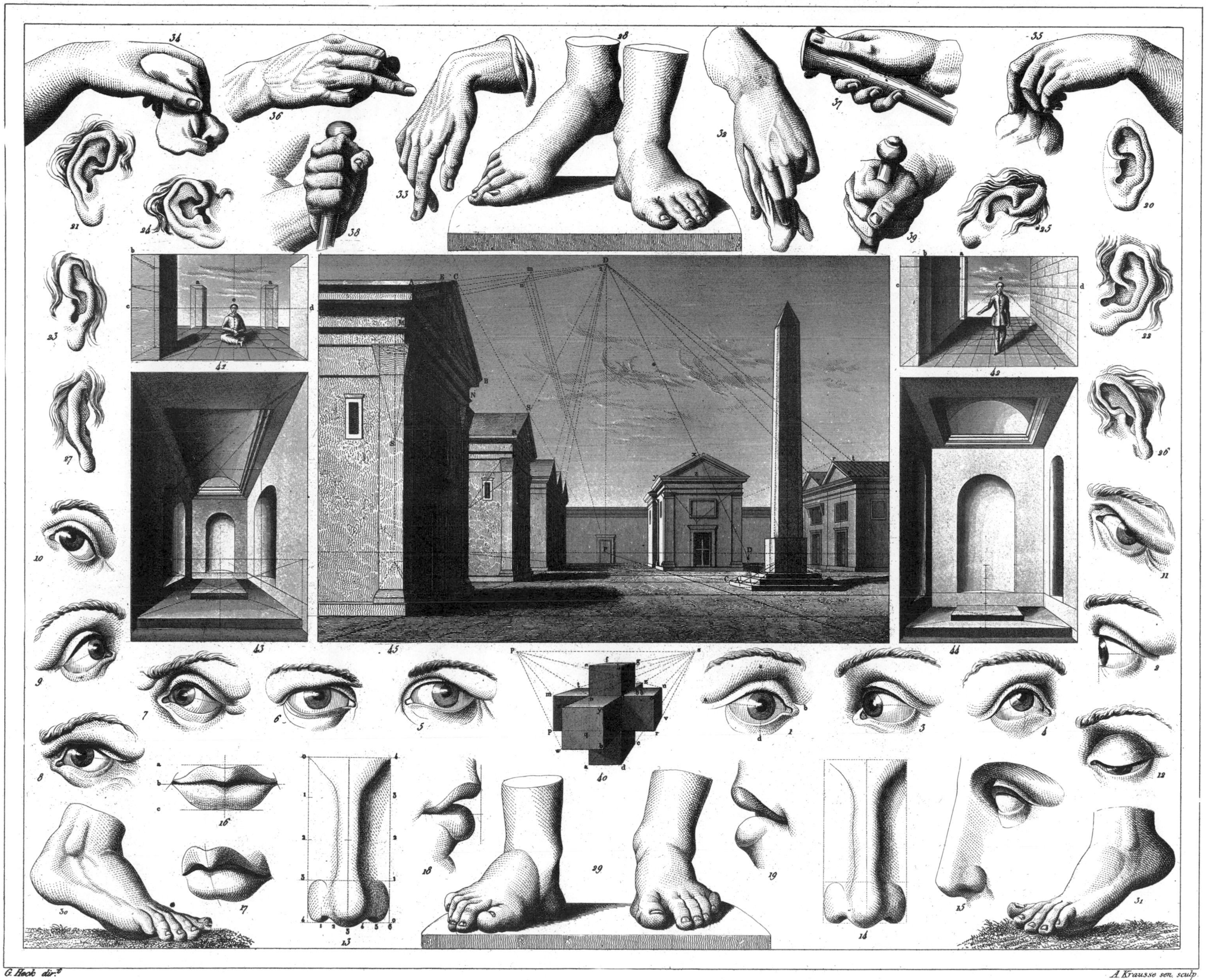

G. Heck dir.t A. Krausse sen. sculp.

PLATE 458. ILLUSTRATIONS OF THE THEORY OF THE ART OF DRAWING

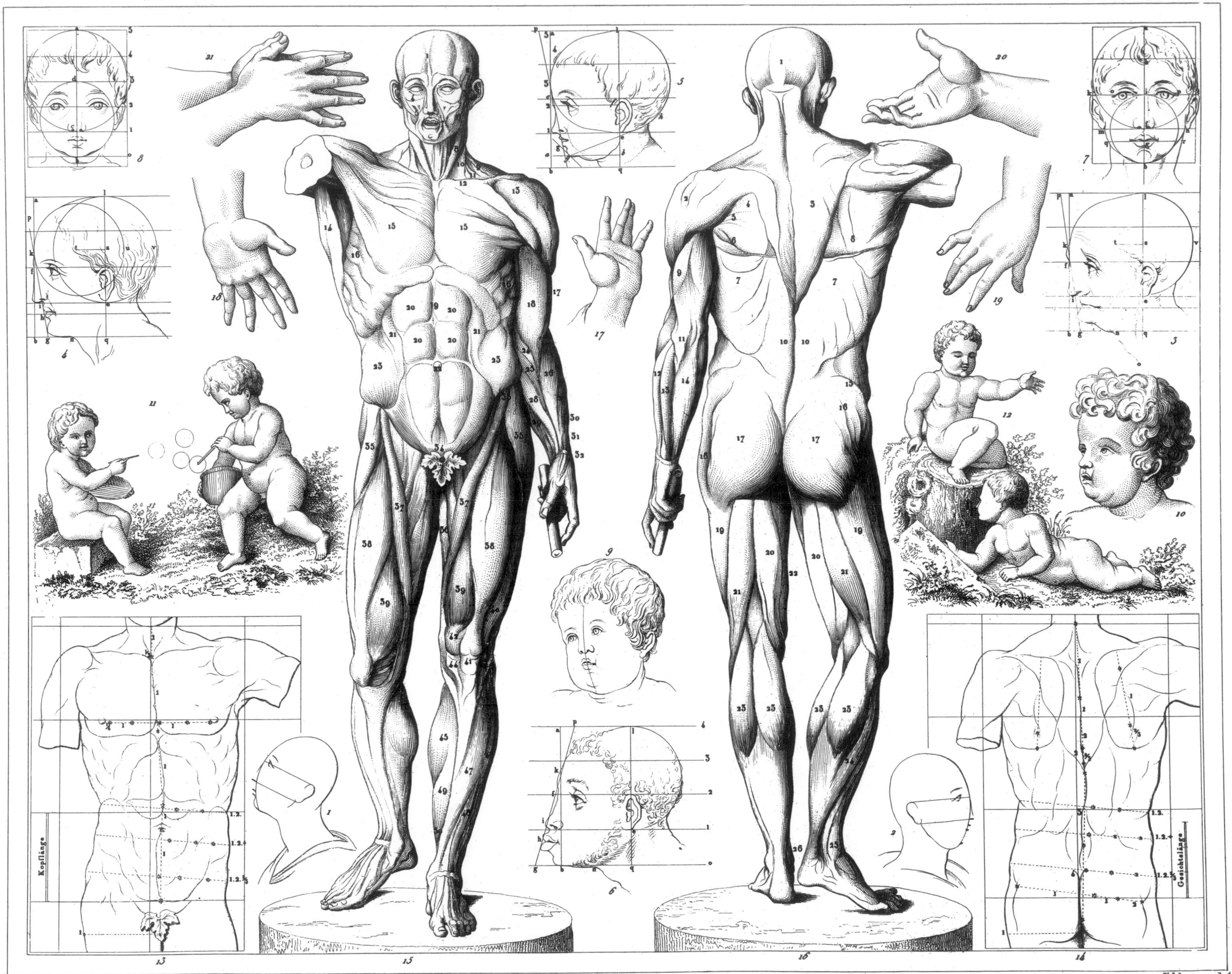

G. Heck dir.^t *Feldweg sculp.^t*

 PLATE 459. ILLUSTRATIONS OF THE THEORY OF THE ART OF DRAWING

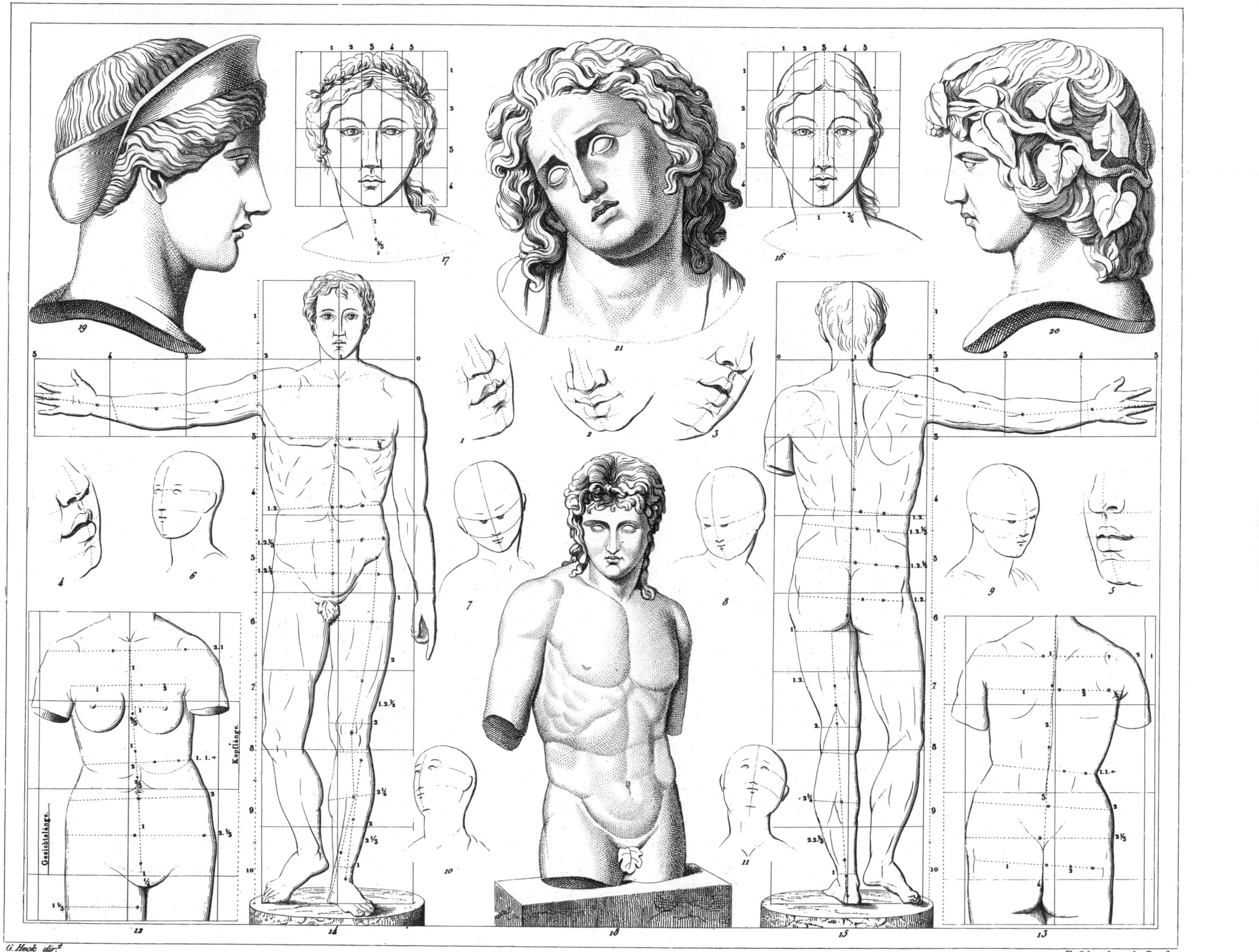

G. Heck dir.^t F. Schmidt sculp. Dresden

PLATE 460. ILLUSTRATIONS OF THE THEORY OF THE ART OF DRAWING

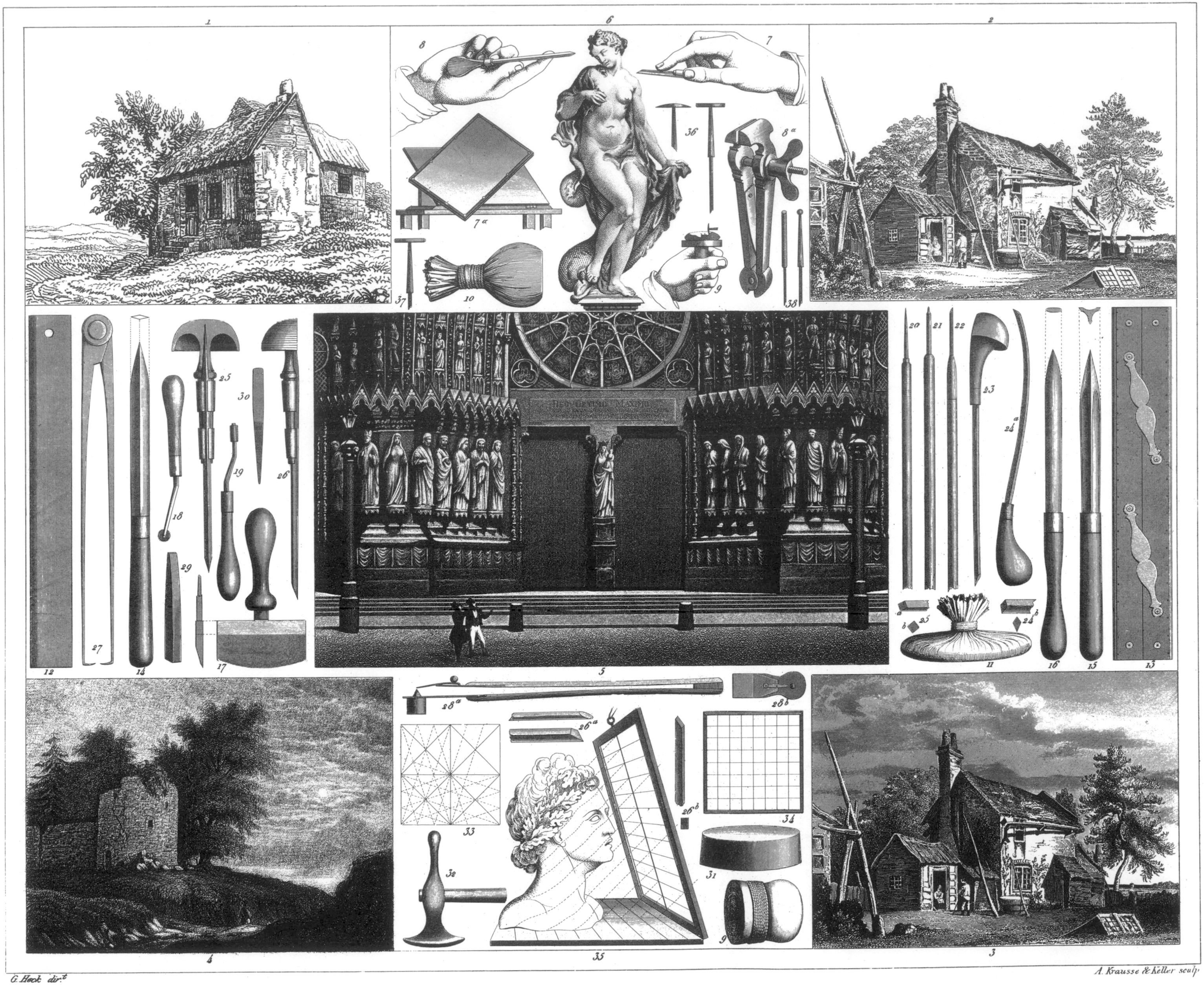

G. Heck dir.t

A. Krausse & Keller sculp.

 PLATE 461. ILLUSTRATIONS OF THE GRAPHIC ARTS

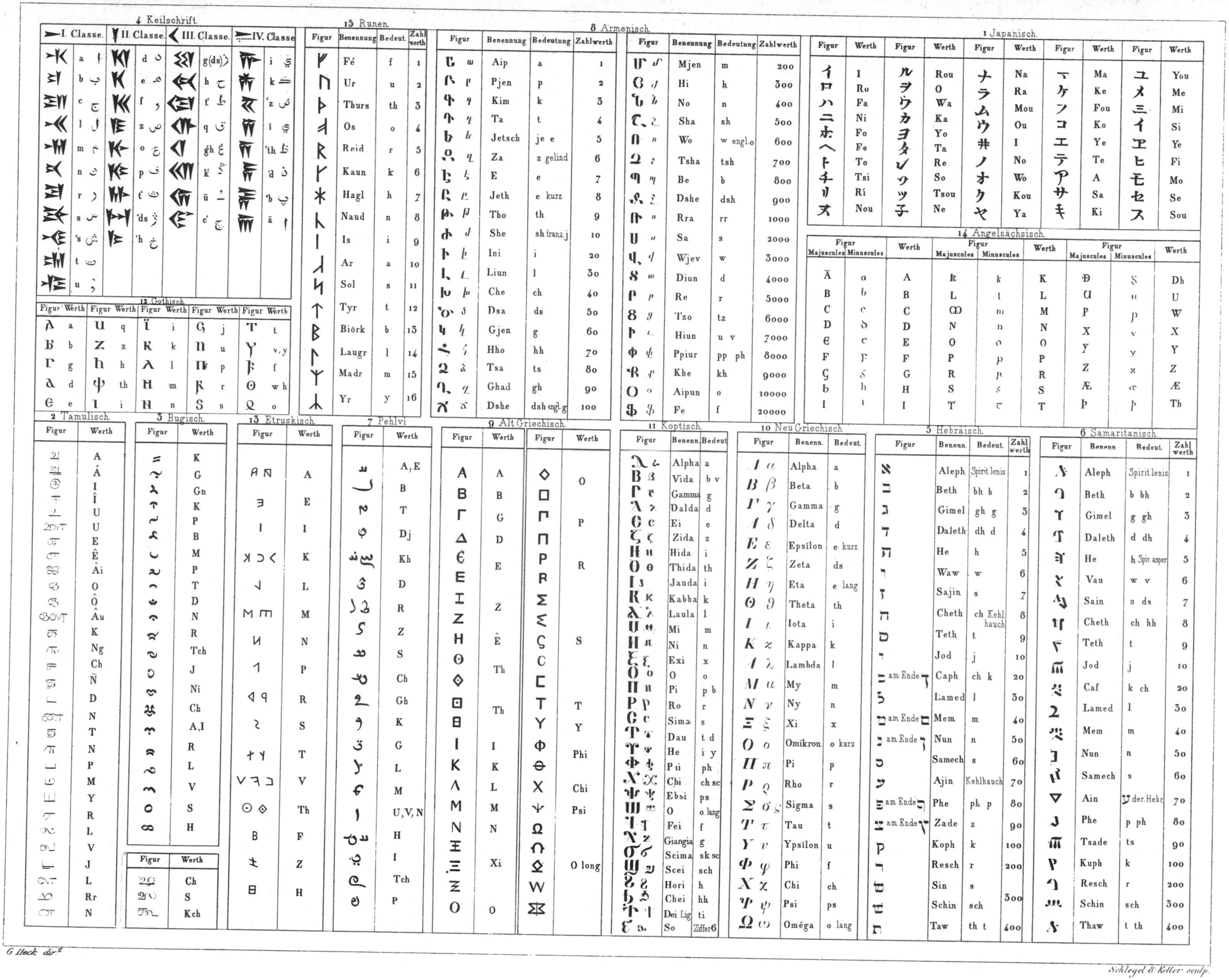

PLATE 462. ALPHABETS OF VARIOUS LANGUAGES FOR THE USE OF ENGRAVERS

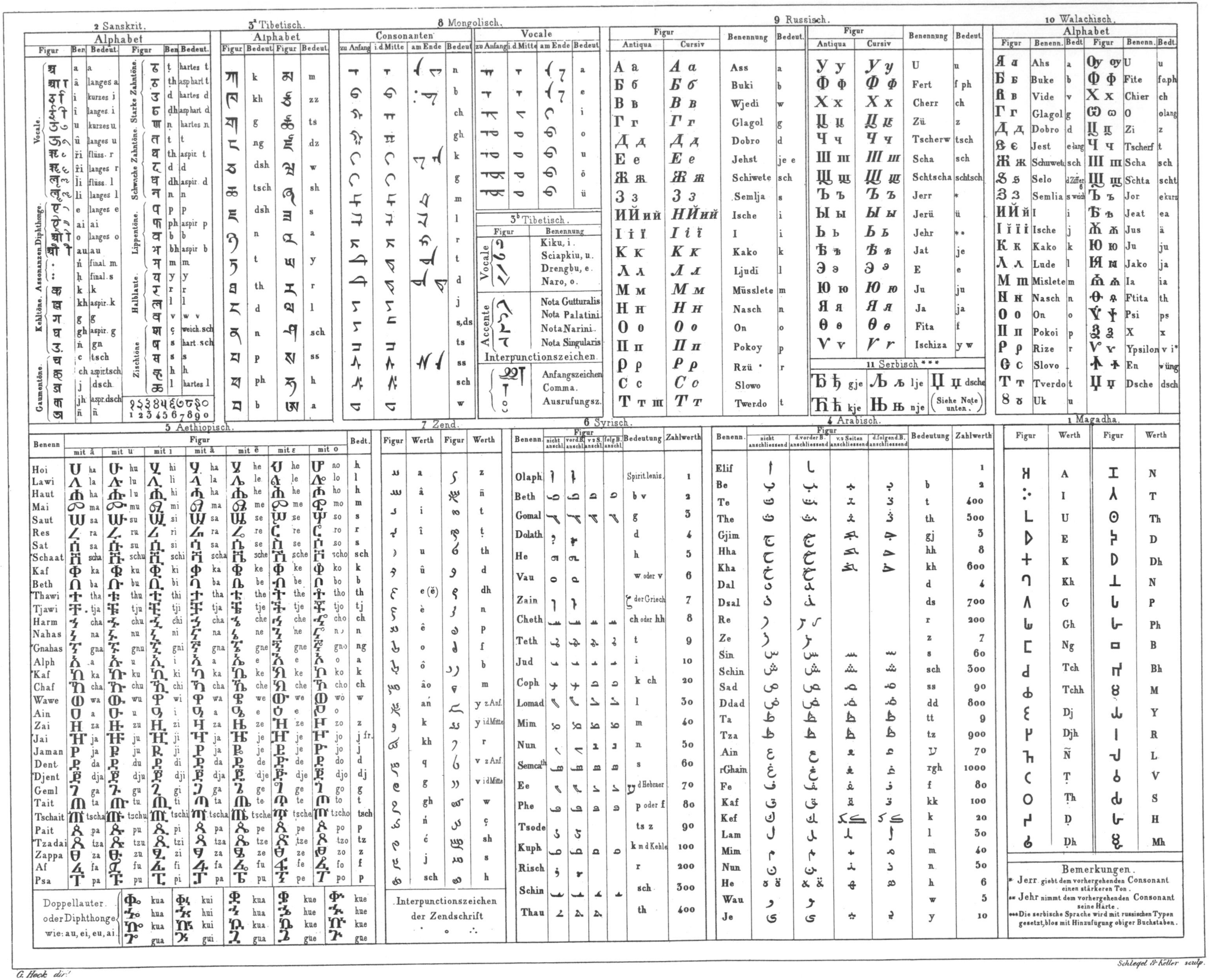
1 Magadha.
2 Sanskrit.
3a Tibetisch.
3b Tibetisch.
4 Arabisch.
5 Aethiopisch.
6 Syrisch.
7 Zend.
8 Mongolisch.
9 Russisch.
10 Walachisch.
11 Serbisch ***
Doppellauter oder Diphthonge wie: au, ei, eu, ai.
Interpunctionszeichen der Zendschrift
Interpunctionszeichen.
Bemerkungen.
* Jerr giebt dem vorhergehenden Consonant einen stärkeren Ton.
** Jehr nimmt dem vorhergehenden Consonant seine Harte.
*** Die serbische Sprache wird mit russischen Typen gesetzt, blos mit Hinzufügung obiger Buchstaben.
G. Heck dir.
Schlegel & Keller sculp.

PLATE 463. ALPHABETS FOR ENGRAVERS

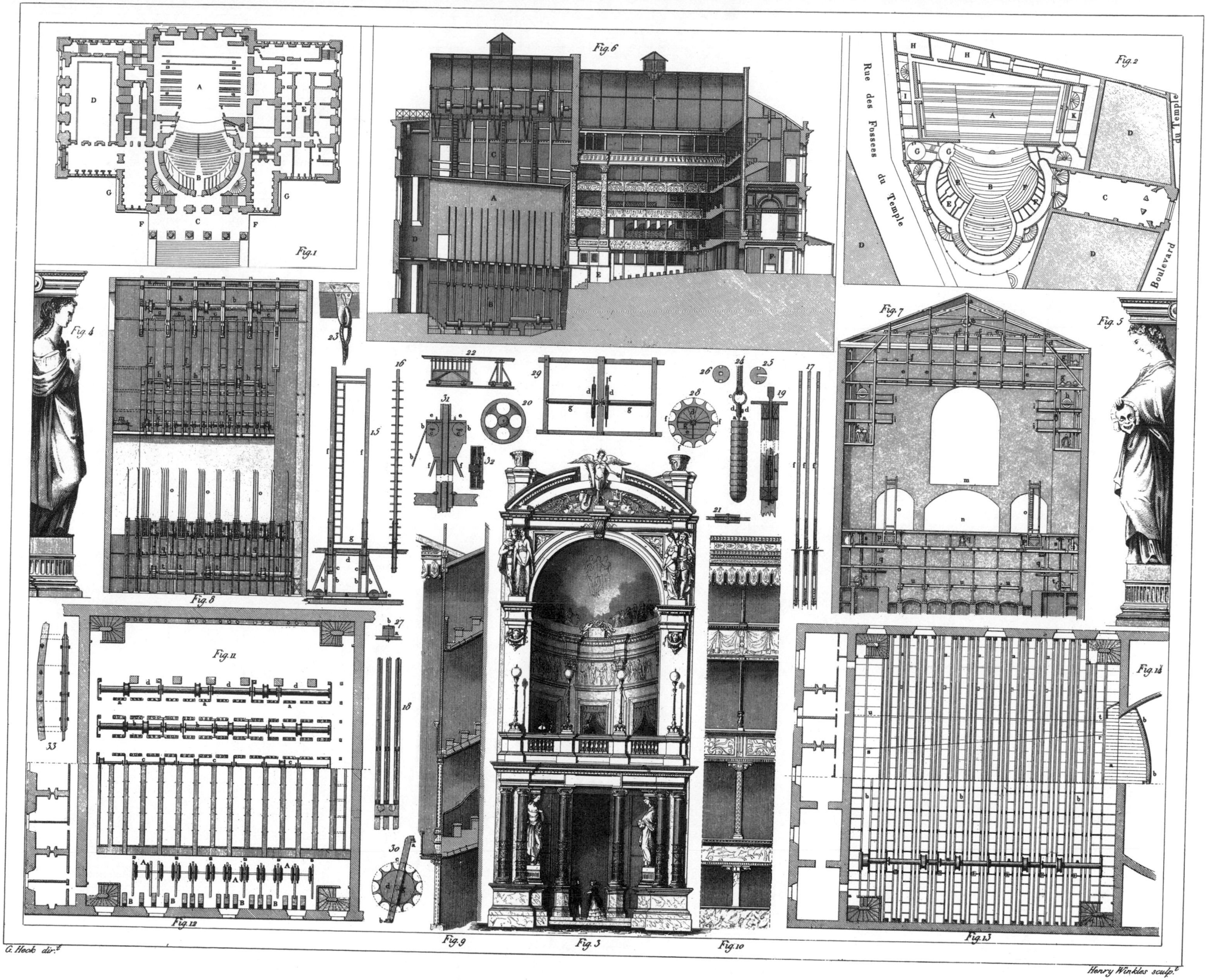

PLATE 464. DETAILS ILLUSTRATING THE CONSTRUCTION OF THEATRICAL BUILDINGS

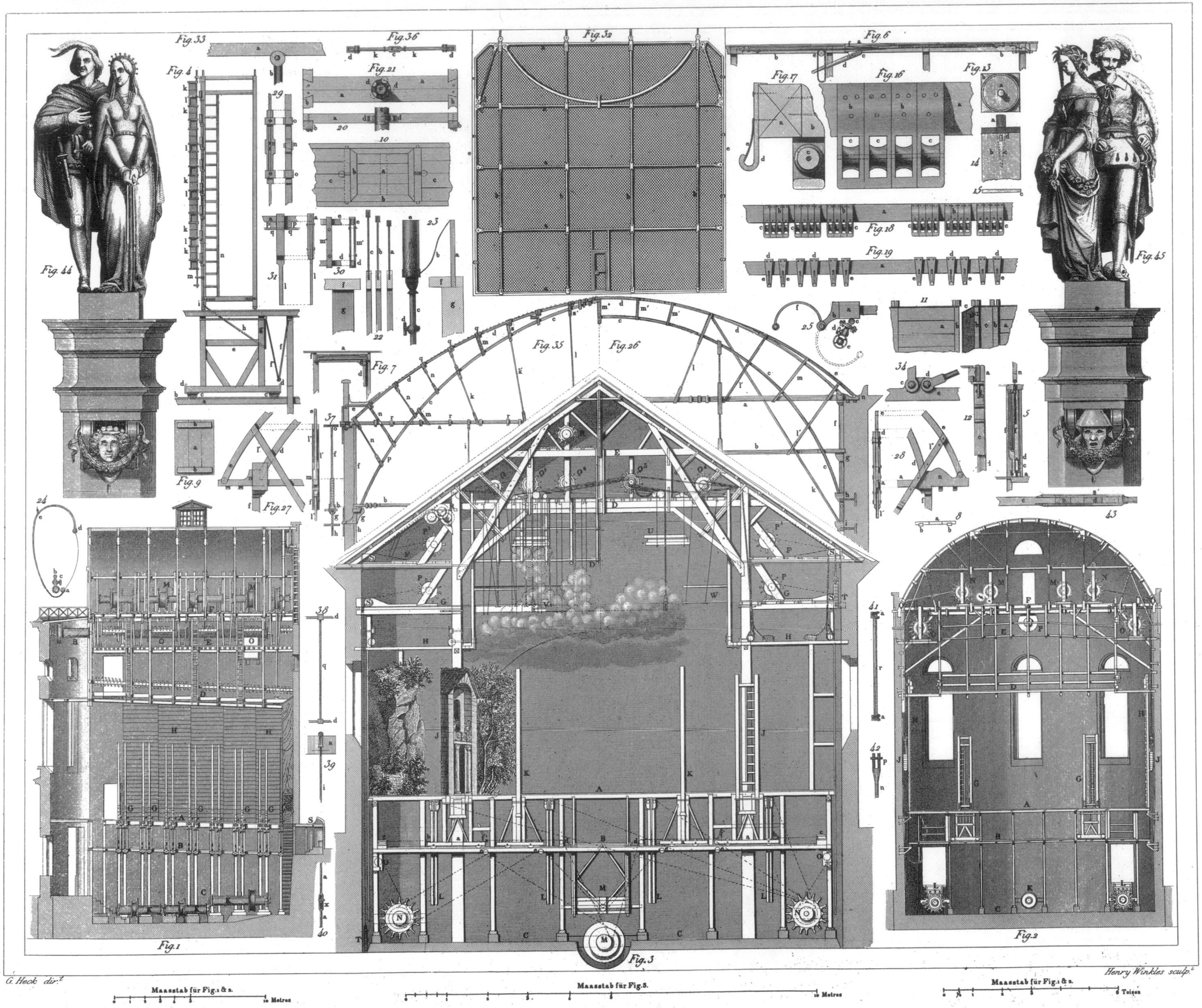

PLATE 465. DETAILS ILLUSTRATING THE CONSTRUCTION OF THEATRICAL BUILDINGS

TECHNOLOGY

Captions to the Technology Plates, 466–500

PLATE 466.
Construction of Streets and Roads; the Thames Tunnel

Figure
1–27. Illustrating the construction of streets and roads
28–34. Illustrating the Thames tunnel in London

PLATE 467.
Illustrating the Construction of Railroads

Figures 1–54.

PLATE 468.
Railroad Construction; Leipsic Station

Figure
1–29. Illustrating the construction of railroads
30. The Leipsic station of the Saxon and Bavarian railroad

PLATE 469.
Motive Power; Construction of Inclined Planes

Figure
1–6. Illustrating the motive power on railroads
7–15. Illustrating the construction of inclined planes

PLATE 470.
Construction of Locomotives and Railway Cars

Figure
1–8. Illustrating Stephenson's locomotive with variable expansion
9–28. Illustrating the construction of tenders and railroad cars
29. Interior of the Duke of Brunswick's car on the Brunswick railroad
30. Interior of Queen Victoria's car on the London and Dover railroad

PLATE 471.
Illustrating the Construction of Atmospheric Railroads

Figures 1–10.

PLATE 472.
Illustrating the Construction of Stone Bridges

Figures 1–23.

PLATE 473.
Illustrating the Construction of Wooden Bridges

Figures 1–45.

PLATE 474.
Illustrating the Construction of Iron Bridges

Figures 1–33.

PLATE 475.
Construction of Canals and Dams

Figure
1–28. Illustrating the construction of canals and dams
29. View of a chain of locks on the Rideau canal near Bytown in Canada

PLATE 476.
Canals and Aqueducts

Figure
1–5. Details from the Languedoc canal in France
6–8. The Cesse Aqueduct
9–11. The Croton Aqueduct of New York
12–18. Locks and weirs

PLATE 477.
Illustrating the Construction of Windlasses and Cranes

Figures 1–12.

PLATE 478.
Pumping Devices

Figure
1. A lift pump
2. A forcing pump
3–6. Stephenson's double action pump
7–9. Pump used in the mine Huelgoet in Normandy
10–12. Letestu's pump
13, 14. Jordan's hydraulic ram in Clausthal
15–21. Reichenbach's hydraulic ram in the saltworks at Illfang in Bavaria

PLATE 479.
Fire-Fighting Equipment

Figure
1, 2. The simplest construction of a fire-engine
3, 4. Portable fire-engine
5, 6. Pontifex's fire-engine
7–10. Repsold's fire-engine
11–15. Letestu's fire-engine
16–21. Common double-action fire-engine
22, 23. Bramah's fire-engine
24. Steam fire-engine
25–29. Apparatus to save persons and property at fires

PLATE 480.
Construction of Water-Wheels

Figure
1–18. Illustrating the construction of vertical water-wheels
19–29. Illustrating the construction of horizontal water-wheels

PLATE 481.
Illustrating the Construction of an American Grinding-mill

Figures 1–15.

PLATE 482.
Cotton Processing Equipment

Figure
1, 2. Cotton gin
3–5*a*. Wolf or willow
6. Spreading machine
7. Lap-machine
8–16. Carders and carding machines
17–20. Drawing frame
21–24. Roving frame

PLATE 483.
Wool Processing Equipment

Figure
1–7. Danforth's tube roving-frame
8–16. Self-acting mule
17–19. Washing-kettle
20, 21. Wringing-machine
22–24. Scales for weighing yarn
25, 26. Starching and steam drying apparatus
27–29. Press for packing yarn
30–33. Woollen willow

PLATE 484.
Weaving Equipment

Figure
1. Beaming for handweaving
2, 3. Warping-mill
4. Simplest loom
5–7. Power-loom
8, 9. Shuttle
10, 11. Jaw-temples
12, 13. Singing-oven
14, 15. Wash-wheel
16–19. Gassing-machine
20. Arrangement of spools
21. Lever of a power-loom
22. Batten of a power-loom

PLATE 485.
Minting Equipment

Figure
1, 2. Casting-machine of mints
3, 4. Rolling mill of mints
5, 6. Circular shears
7–9. Flattening-mill
10–14. Drawing machine of mints
15, 16. Coin-punch
17–20. Milling machine
21–37. Stamping machines

PLATE 486.
Minting

Figure
1. Stamping machine of the mint in Rio Janeiro

		VALUE*
2.	Persian gold piece of Imam Riza	$7 35
3.	East India Rupee Zodiac	6 20
4.	Gold piece of the East India Company	4 90
5.	Gold piece of the Dutch East India Company	4 90
6.	Double gold sovereign of Brabant of 1800	13 00
7.	Gold Sovereign of Brabant of 1796	6 50
8.	Belgian gold lion of 1790	9 00
9.	Danish Species Ducat	2 35
10.	Danish double Frederic d'or of 1828	7 90
11.	Austrian ducat of 1826	2 25
12.	Bavarian ducat of 1821	2 25
13.	Hamburg ducat of 1818	2 40
14.	Ducat of Electoral Saxony of 1797	2 25
15.	Ducat of Canton of Berne	2 15
16.	Carl d'or of the duchy of Brunswick, 1799	4 00
17.	Hanoverian double pistole, 1829	7 90

* Values as of mid-nineteenth century

18.	Wilhelm d'or of the Electorate of Hesse, 1829	4 00
19.	Royal Prussian double Frederick d'or, 1800	7 90
20.	Royal Prussian Frederick d'or, 1822	3 90
21.	Royal Wirtemberg Frederic d'or, 1810	3 90
22.	Sixteen franc piece or pistole of the Helvetic Republic, 1800	4 25
23.	Five guilder piece or imperial ducat of the grand duchy of Baden, 1827	2 35
24.	Ten guilder piece or Caroline of the grand duchy of Hesse, 1826	4 50
25.	Royal guinea of Great Britain, 1801	5 00

PLATE 487.
Coins of Various Nations

Figure		VALUE*
1.	English guinea of George III, 1793	$5 00
2.	English third of a guinea of George III, 1797	1 75
3.	English sovereign of Queen Victoria, 1845	4 85
4.	French Louis d'or of Louis XVI, 1797	3 75
5.	Napoleon d'or, 1813	3 85
6.	Italian double Napoleon d'or, 1814	6 50
7.	French Louis d'or of Louis XVIII, 1818	3 80
8.	French twenty franc piece, Louis Philippe, 1831	3 85
9.	French forty franc piece, 1848	7 70
10.	Half guinea of Ligurian republic, 1798	6 40
11.	Holland ducat, 1827	2 00
12.	Netherland five guilder piece, 1827	2 00
13.	Netherland ten guilder piece, 1825	4 00
14.	Milan zechino, Joseph II, 1784	2 25
15.	Maltese single Louis d'or, 1782	3 75
16.	Neapolitan twenty lire piece, Joachim Napoleon, 1813	3 75
17.	United States half-eagle of 1798	5 00
18.	Roman zechin of Pius VI, 1783	2 25
19.	Double Romana of Pius VII	7 70
20.	Scudo d'oro of the Roman republic, 1798	10 25
21.	Piedmontese *Doppia nuova* of Charles Emanuel, 1797	7 80
22.	Polish ducat, 1791	3 75
23.	Portuguese dobrao, 1725	27 50
24.	Portugalese, 1800	5 40
25.	Crusado nuovo of Maria I, 1790	2 60
26.	Russian ducat of Paul I, 1801	4 00
27.	Russian imperial of Catharine II, 1766	7 50
28.	Sardinian gold piece of 20 *lire nuove*, 1827	3 30
29.	Swedish ducat of Charles XIII, 1810	2 00
30.	Sicilian double oncia, 1752	8 00
31.	Spanish quadruple, 1801	16 00
32.	Tuscan ruspone of Ferdinand III, 1798	6 40
33.	Turkish zerma-hubzechino of Selim III	1 45
34.	Sequin or zechino of Selim III	1 45
35.	Venetian zechino	2 20
36.	Venetian gold ducat	3 30

* Values as of mid-nineteenth century

PLATE 488.
Mining

Figure
1. Exterior view of the mines of Falun in Sweden
2. Exterior view of the mines of Persberg in Sweden
3. Coal strata of Ronchamps
4. Coal strata of Newcastle-upon-Tyne
5–7. Slate quarries near Angers
8–11. Apparatus for blasting
12, 13. Boring apparatus
14–35. Miners' tools
36. Interior view of a coal mine at Newcastle-upon-Tyne

PLATE 489.
Mining

Figure
1–32. Illustrating the construction of levels and shafts
33, 34. Illustrating the ventilation of mines
35. Exhausting engine
36–39. Modes of descent and ascent in mines
40–43. Miners at work

PLATE 490.
Mining

Figure
1. Interior view of the mines of Persberg in Sweden
2. Interior view of the mines of Falun in Sweden
3, 4. Sections of mines
5. Two coal seams
6–9. Apparatus for boring
10. Mining by fire
11–26. Illustrating the construction of levels and shafts
27–35. Miners' tools for slate mines

PLATE 491.
Mining

Figure
1. Interior view of the salt mines of Wieliczka
2. Interior of the millstone quarry at Niedermendig
3–5. Interior plans of mines
6–10. Illustrating the ventilation of mines
11. Breathing tube
12. Davy's and Dumesnil's safety lamps
13–15. Anemometer
16–28. Means of transport of ores
29–34. Hydraulic ram at Huelgoet

PLATE 492.
Metal Milling

Figure
1–7. Open furnaces
8–14. Stack furnaces
15. Puddling furnace
16. Gold amalgam mill
17, 18. Tongs for handling crucibles
19. Interior of a blast furnace house
20. Tuyere chambers
21. Stamping mill

PLATE 493.
Metal Milling

Figure
1, 2. Stack furnaces
3. Reverberatory furnace
4–8. Crucible furnaces
9, 10. Tongs for handling crucibles
11. Heating chamber for hot-blast
12–22. Rollers for the final preparation of iron

PLATE 494.
Agriculture

Figure
1–17. Various ploughs
18–23. Various harrows
24–26. Drags and rollers
27–36. Sowing and planting machines
37, 38. Winnowing machine
39. Grain shock
40. Grain crusher
41. Straw cutter
42. Machine for cleaning flax
43. Machine for washing potatoes
44. Plan and elevation of a farmhouse with barn and stables attached

PLATE 495.
Agriculture

Figure
1–7. Illustrating the management of double crops
8–23. Agricultural tools
24. Thermometer used to indicate the temperature of heaps in which root crops are stored
25, 26. Grain stacks
27, 28. Clover frames
29, 30. Illustrating underground drainage
31. Stack of roots or fruits
32–34. Barns and threshing-floors
35–39. Apparatus for drying fruit
40, 41. Grain kilns
42, 43. Dairy
44, 45. Flax brake
46. English churn
47–49. Apparatus for making cider

PLATE 496.
Husbandry

Figure
1–8. Neat cattle
9–13. Sheep
14–17. Hogs
18–47. The horse

PLATE 497.
Agriculture

Figure
1–10. The economy of neat cattle
11–13. Sheep-folds
14–37. The management of silkworms
38–57. The management of honeybees

PLATE 498.
Hunting

Figure
1–56. Illustrating the art of hunting

PLATE 499.
Fishing

Figure
1–8. Illustrating fresh water fishing
9–14. Illustrating marine fishing

PLATE 500.
Fishing

Figure
1–3. Illustrating marine fishing

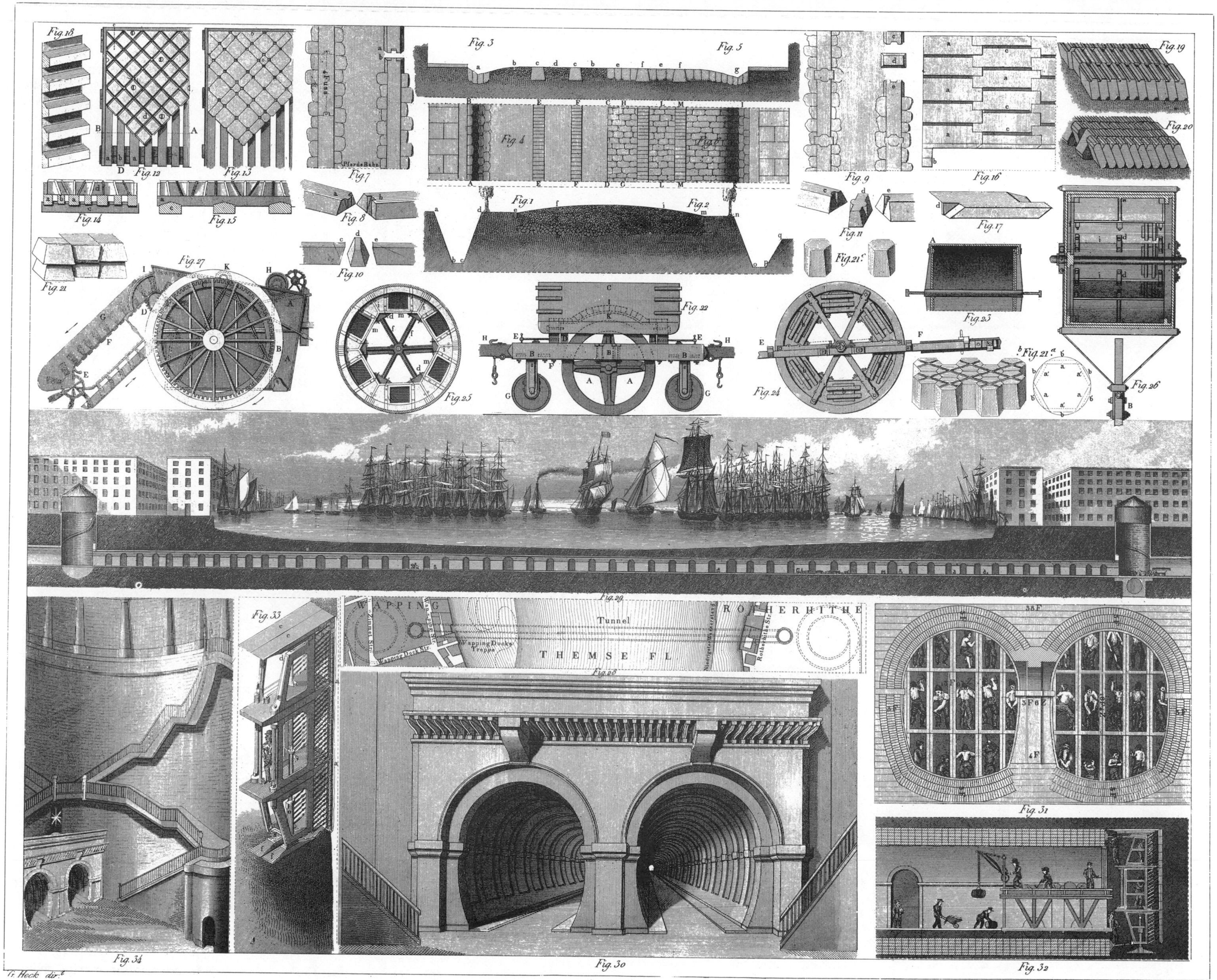

PLATE 466. CONSTRUCTION OF STREETS AND ROADS; THE THAMES TUNNEL

G. Heck dir.

Gust. Feldweg sculpt.

PLATE 467. ILLUSTRATING THE CONSTRUCTION OF RAILROADS

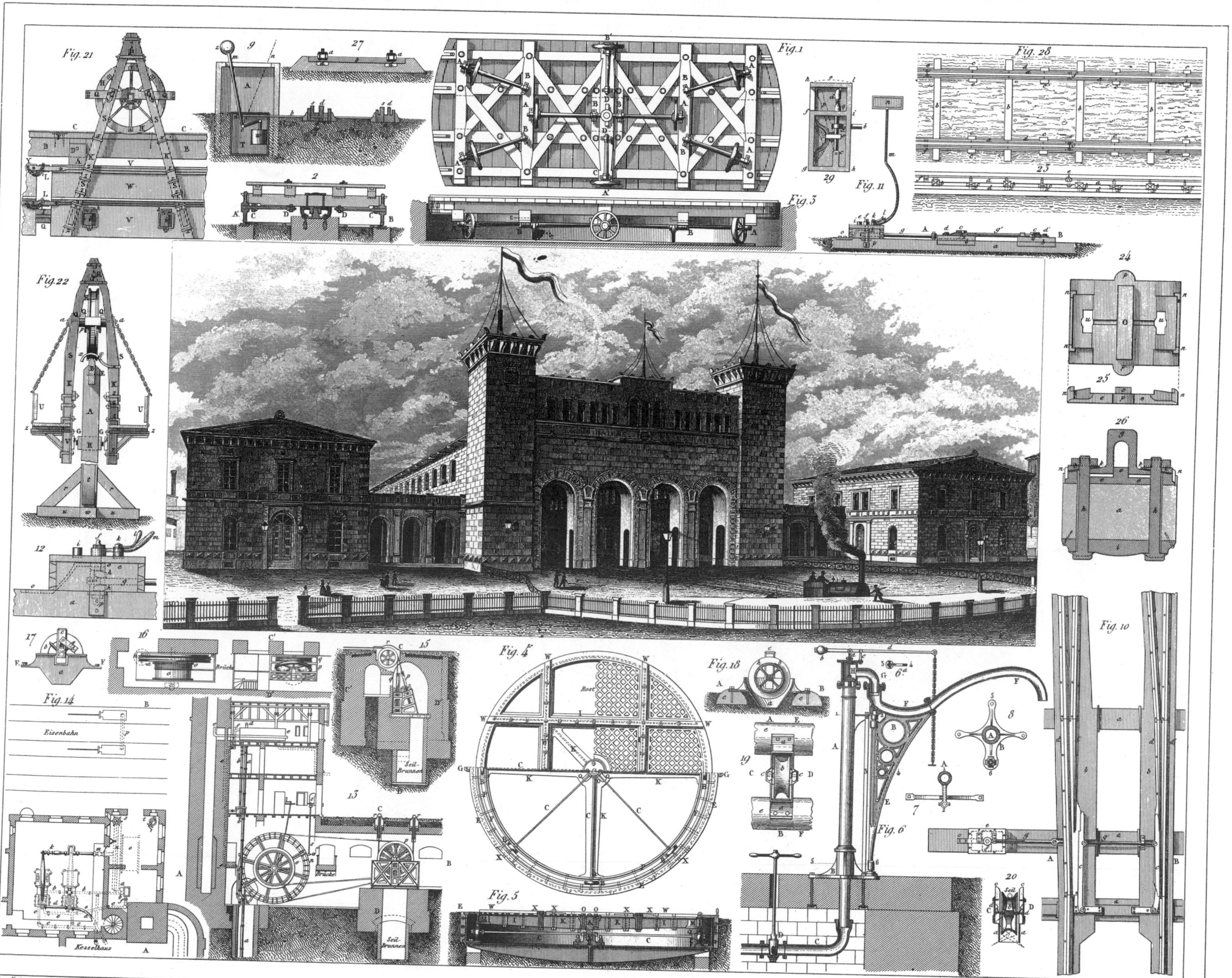
Fig. 21
Fig. 22
Fig. 1
Fig. 3
Fig. 28
Fig. 11
Fig. 10
Fig. 14
Eisenbahn
Fig. 4
Rost
Fig. 5
Fig. 6
Fig. 18
Seil-Brunnen
Kesselhaus
Brücke

G. Heck dir.

Henry Winkles sculpt.

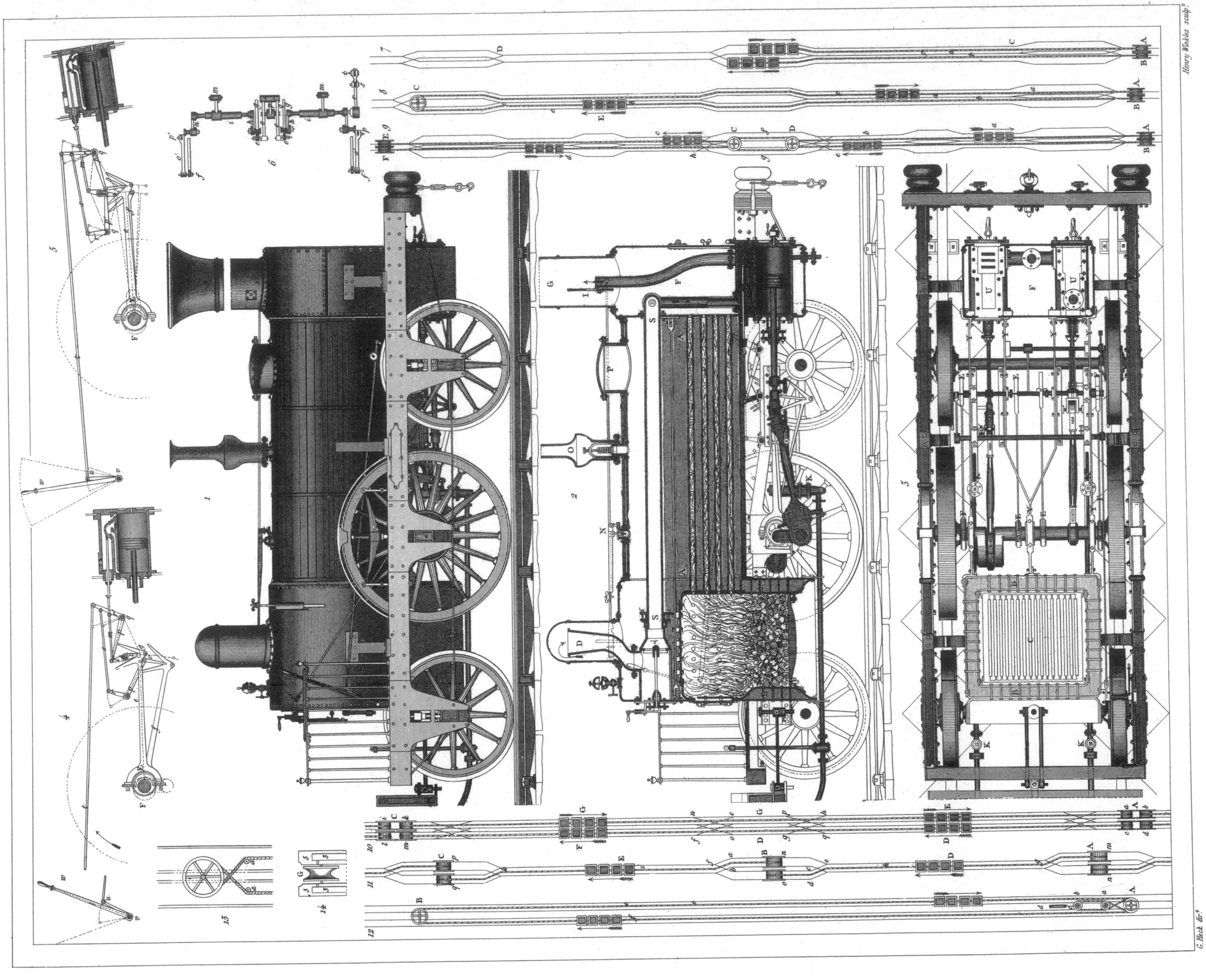

PLATE 469. MOTIVE POWER; CONSTRUCTION OF INCLINED PLANES

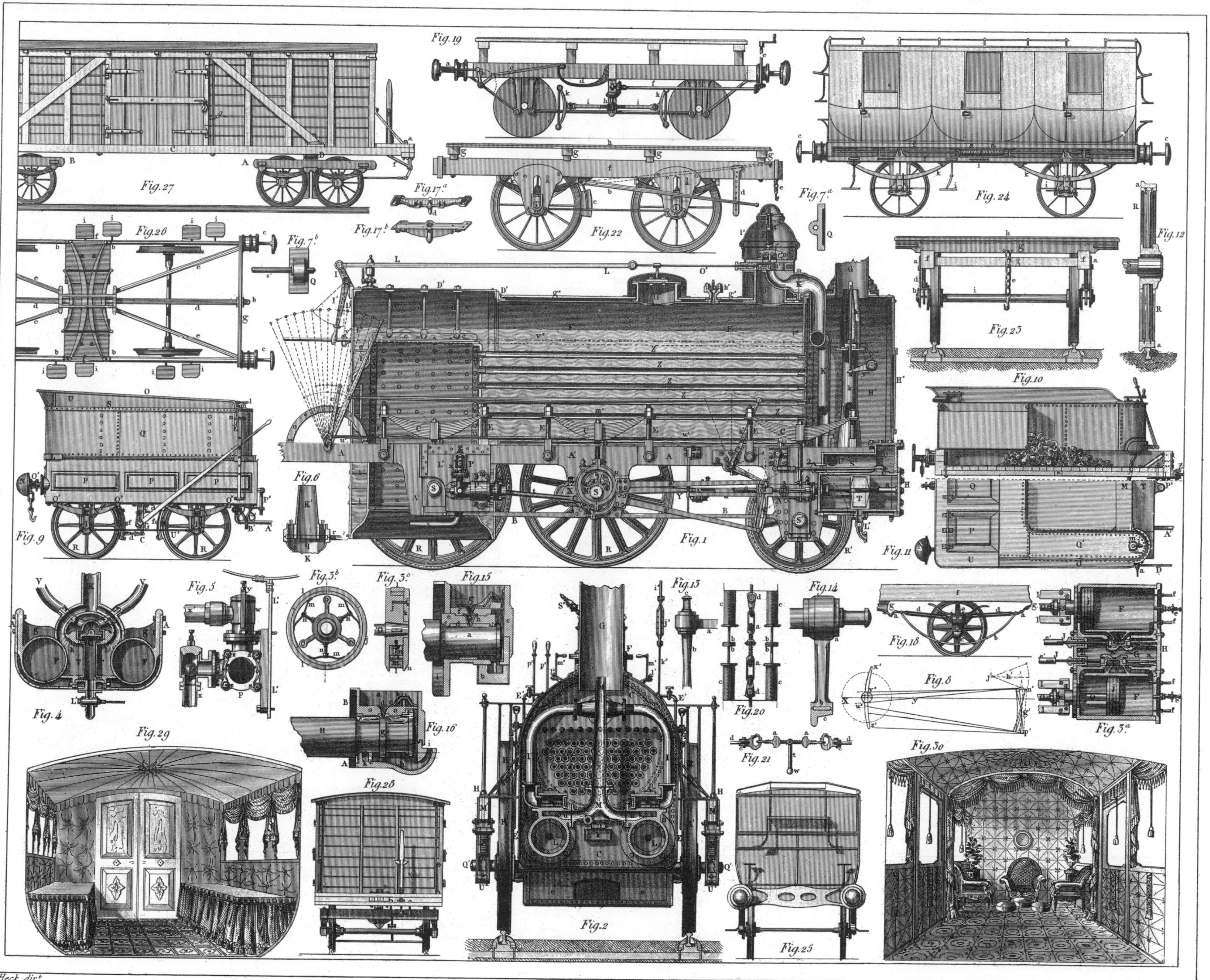

G. Heck dir.t

Feldweg sculp.t

PLATE 470. CONSTRUCTION OF LOCOMOTIVES AND RAILWAY CARS

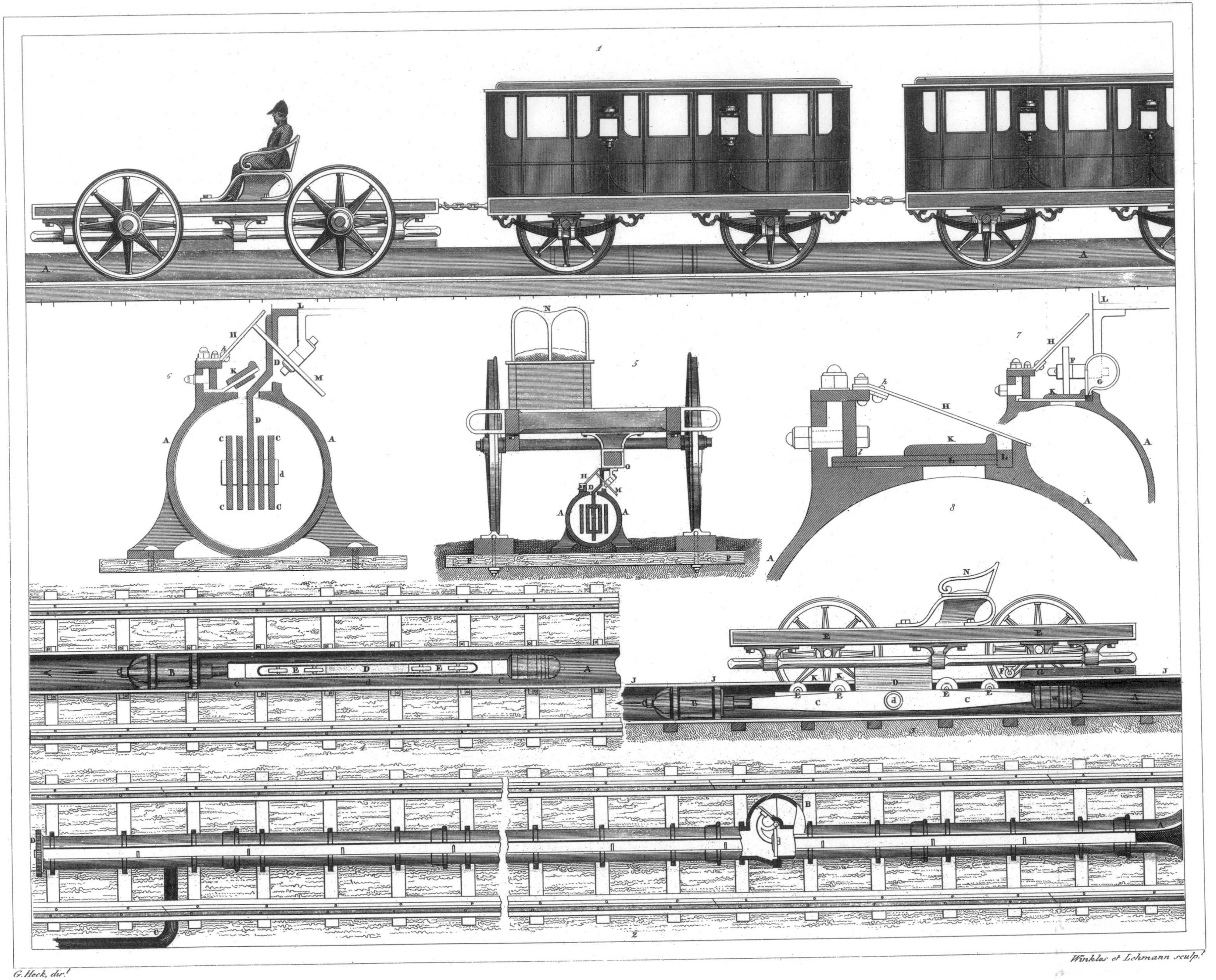

G. Heck, dir.

Winkles et Lehmann sculp.

PLATE 471. ILLUSTRATING THE CONSTRUCTION OF ATMOSPHERIC RAILROADS

G. Heck dir.t

Henry Winkles sculp.t

PLATE 472. ILLUSTRATING THE CONSTRUCTION OF STONE BRIDGES

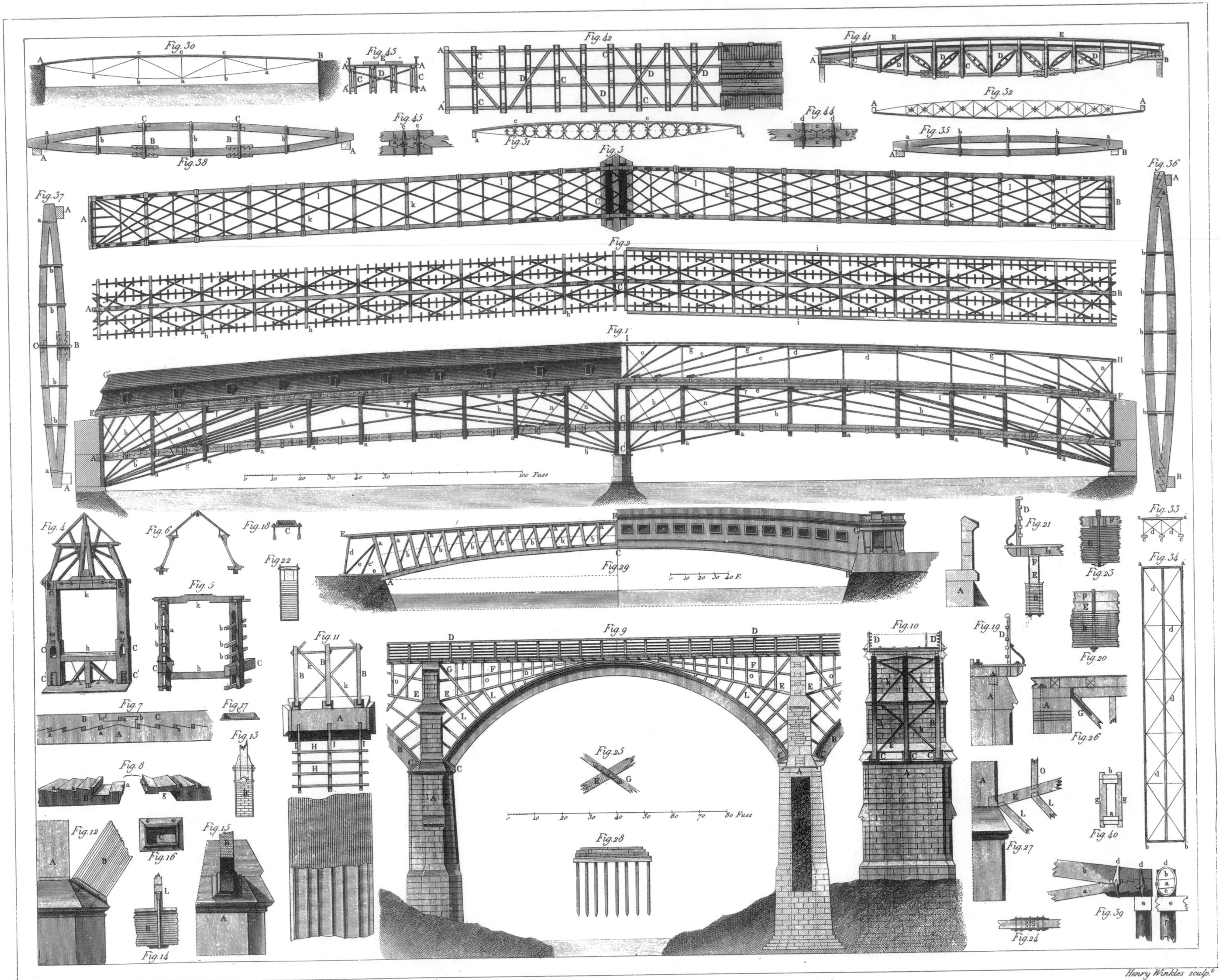

G Heck dir.t

Henry Winkles sculp.t

PLATE 473. ILLUSTRATING THE CONSTRUCTION OF WOODEN BRIDGES

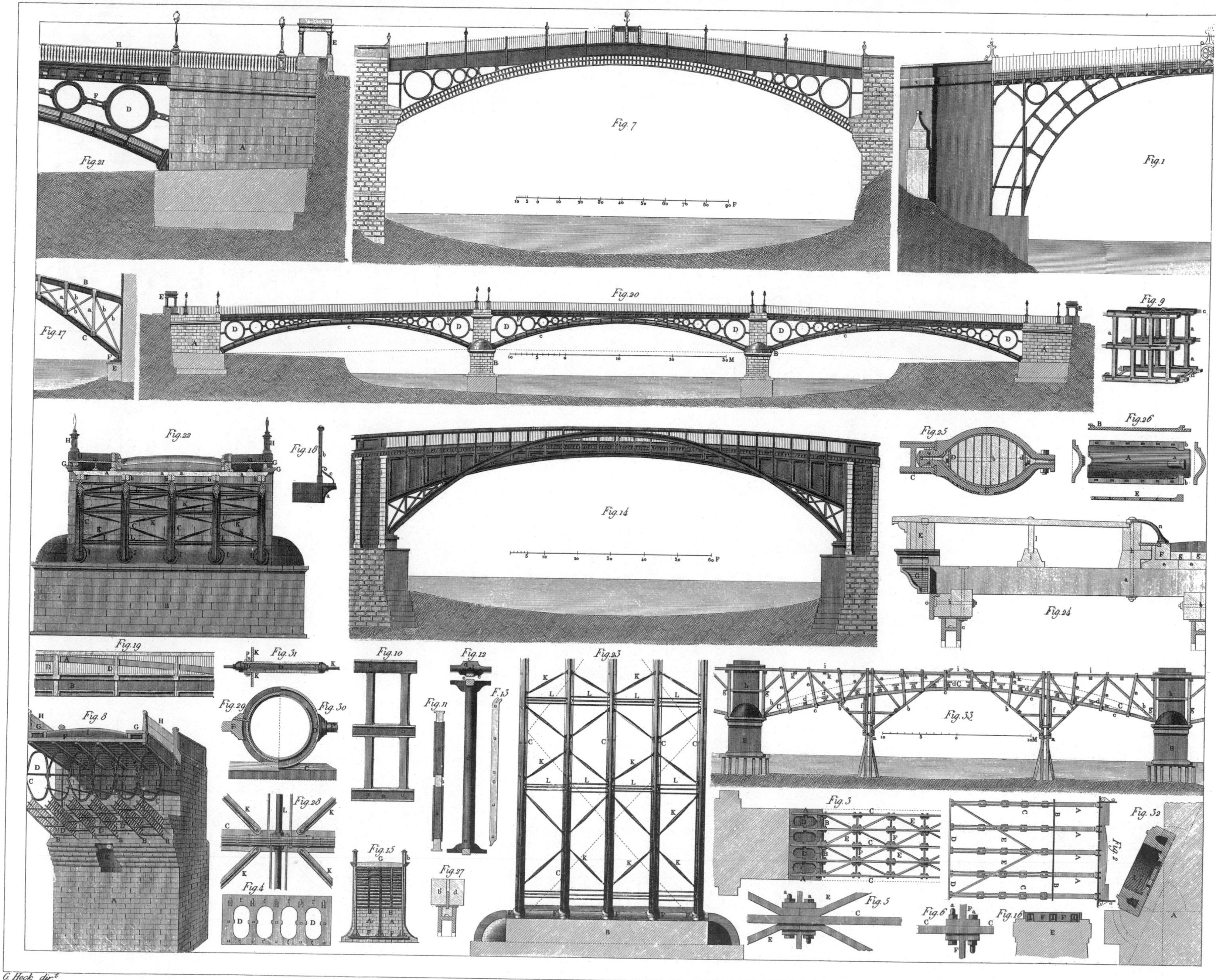

G. Heck dir.ᵗ

Henry Winkles sculpᵗ

PLATE 474. ILLUSTRATING THE CONSTRUCTION OF IRON BRIDGES

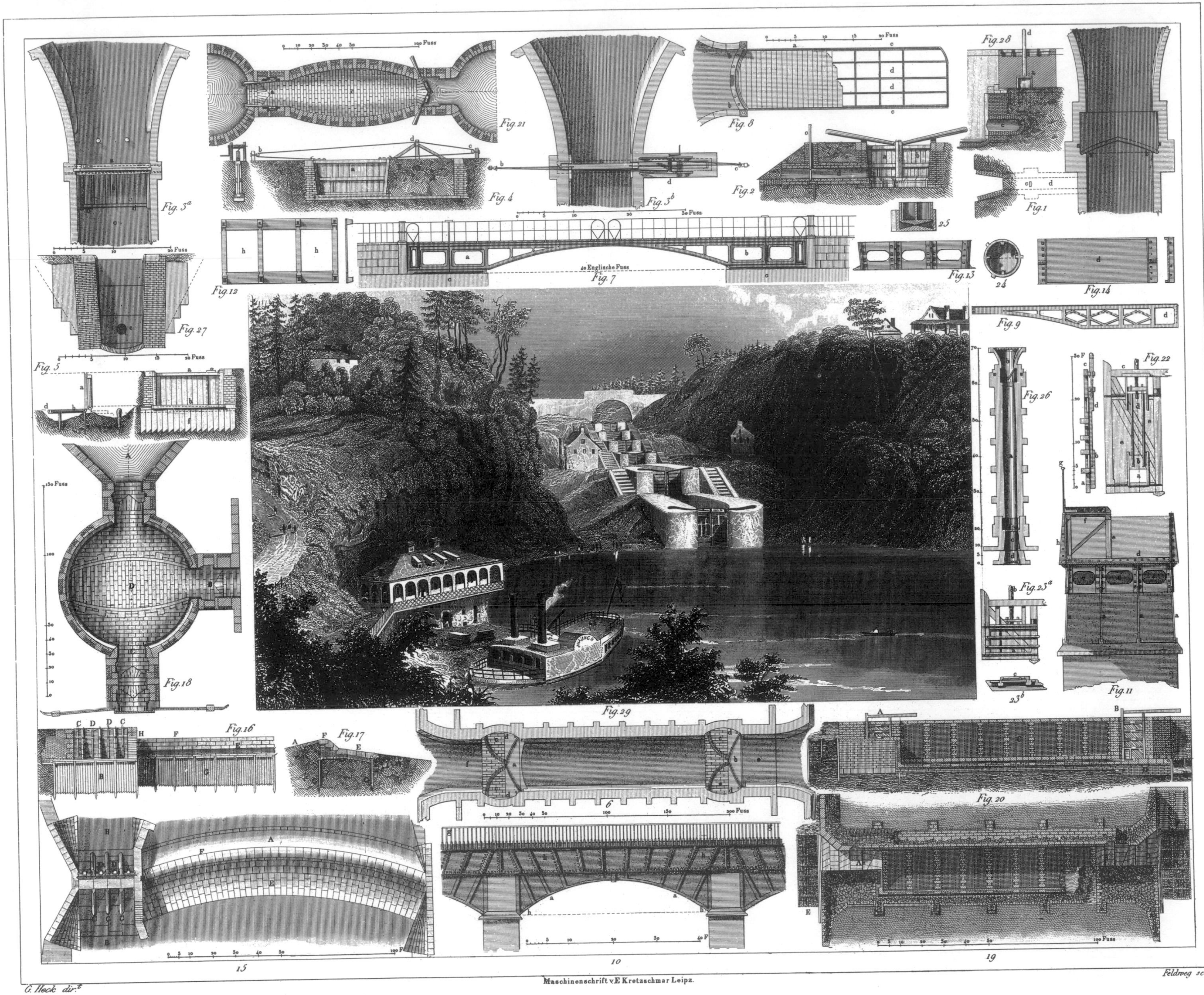

G. Heck dir.t Maschinenschrift v. E Kretzschmar Leipz. Feldweg sculp.

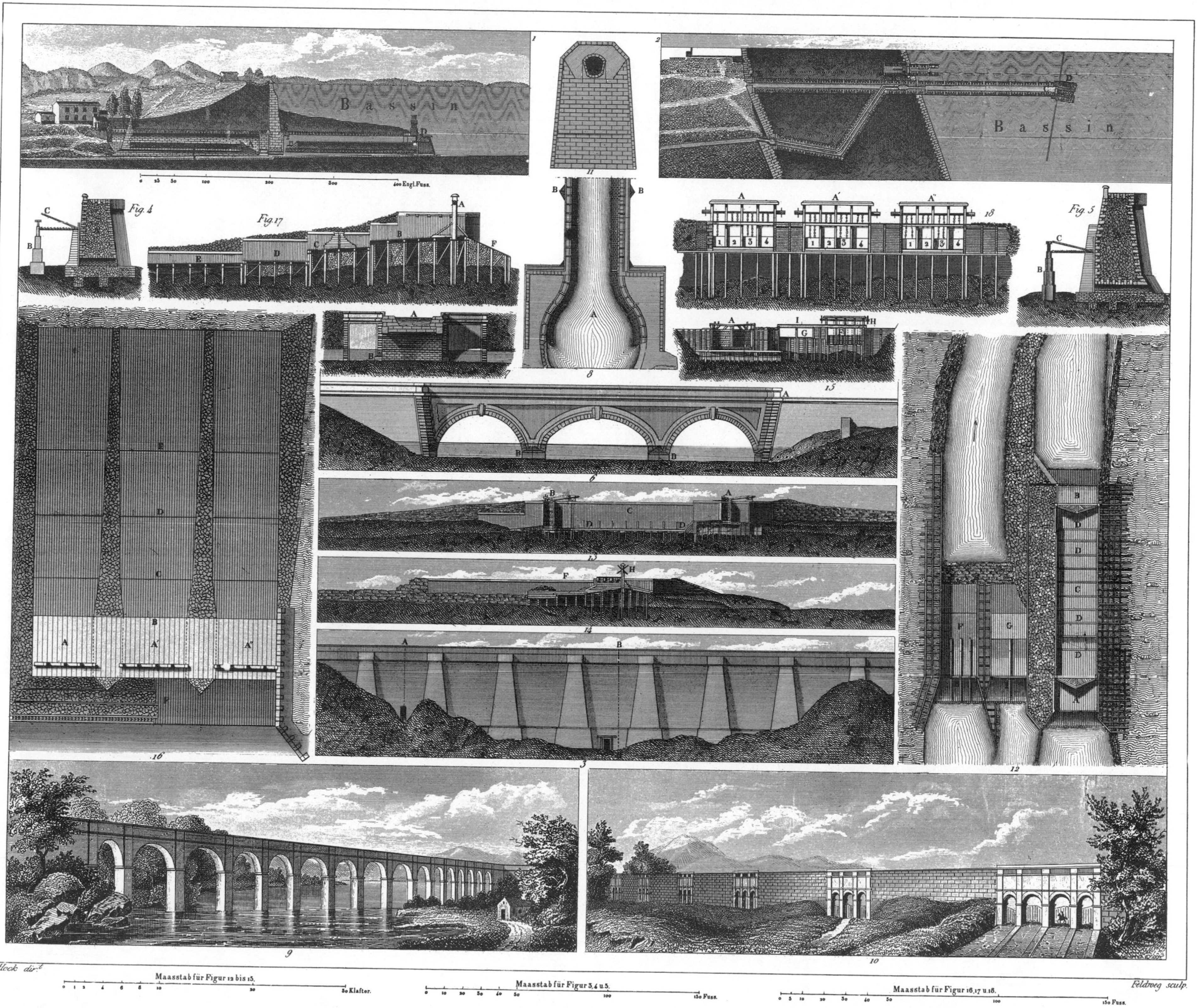
Bassin
0 25 50 100 200 300 400 Engl. Fuss.
Fig. 4
Fig. 17
Fig. 5
G. Heck dir.t
Maasstab für Figur 12 bis 15.
0 1 2 4 6 8 10 20 30 Klafter.
Maasstab für Figur 3, 4 u 5.
0 10 20 30 40 50 100 150 Fuss.
Maasstab für Figur 16, 17 u. 18.
0 5 10 20 30 40 50 100 150 Fuss.
Feldweg sculp.

PLATE 476. CANALS AND AQUEDUCTS

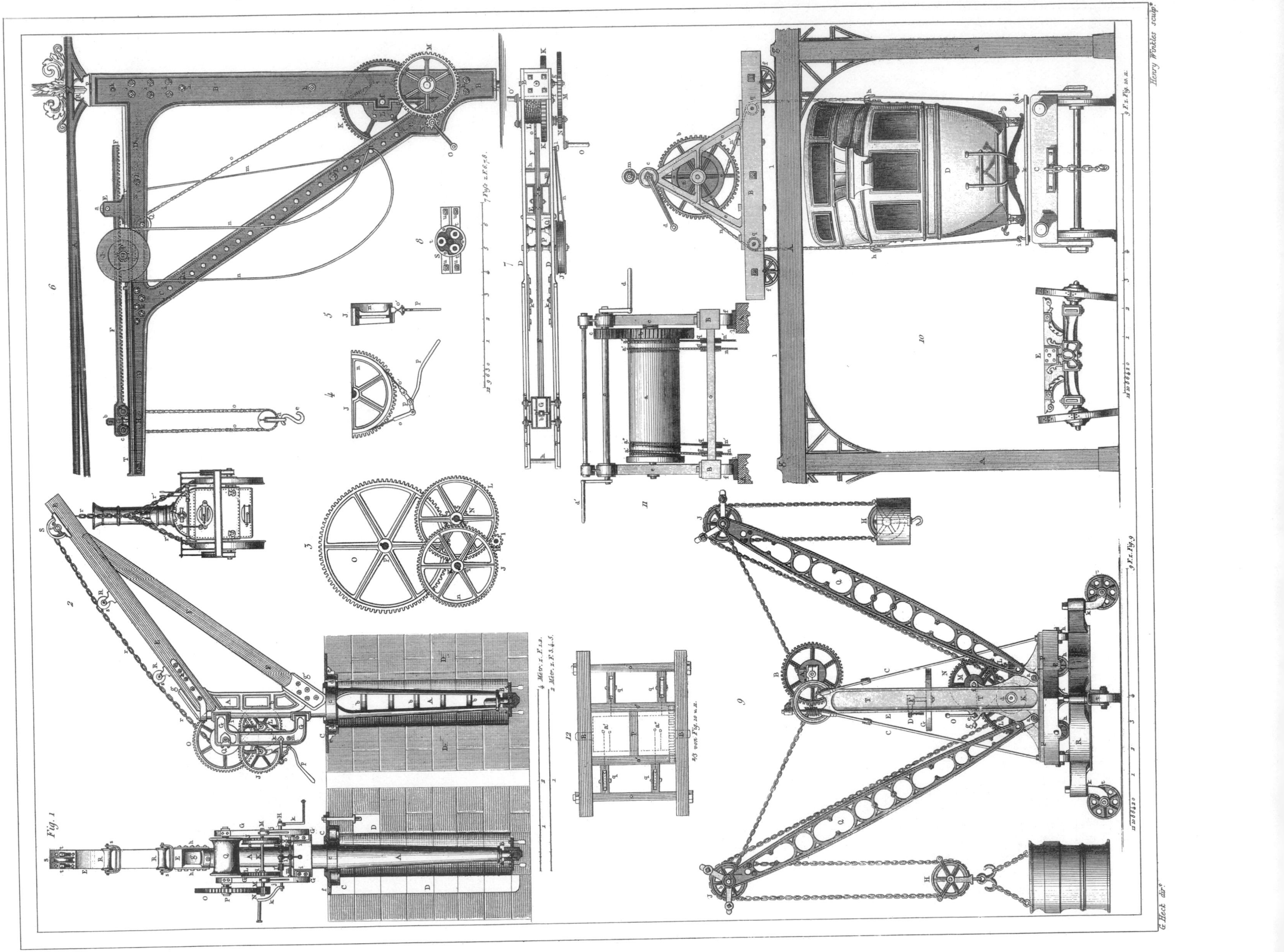

 PLATE 477. ILLUSTRATING THE CONSTRUCTION OF WINDLASSES AND CRANES

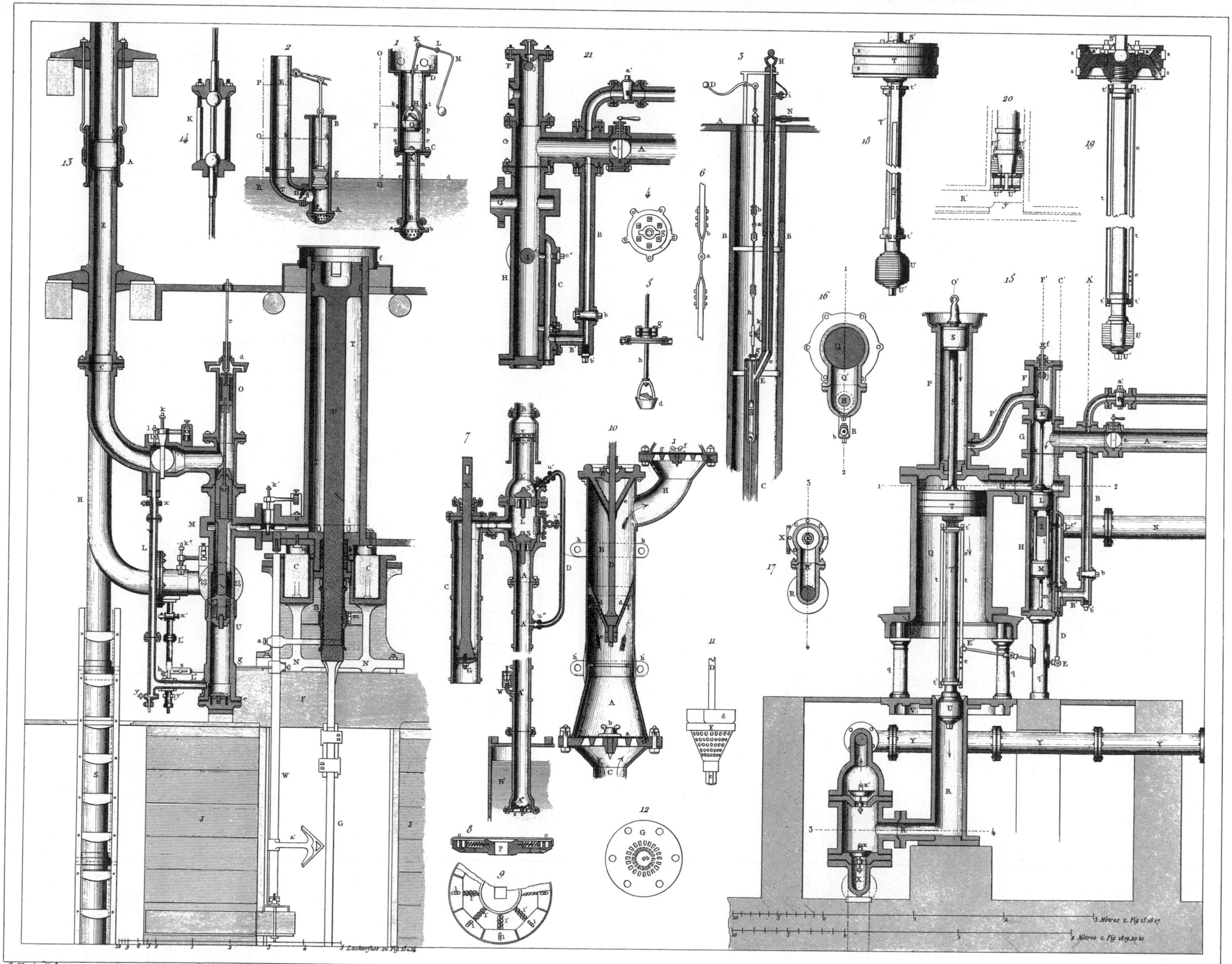

G. Heck dir.^t

Henry Winkles sculp.^t

PLATE 478. PUMPING DEVICES

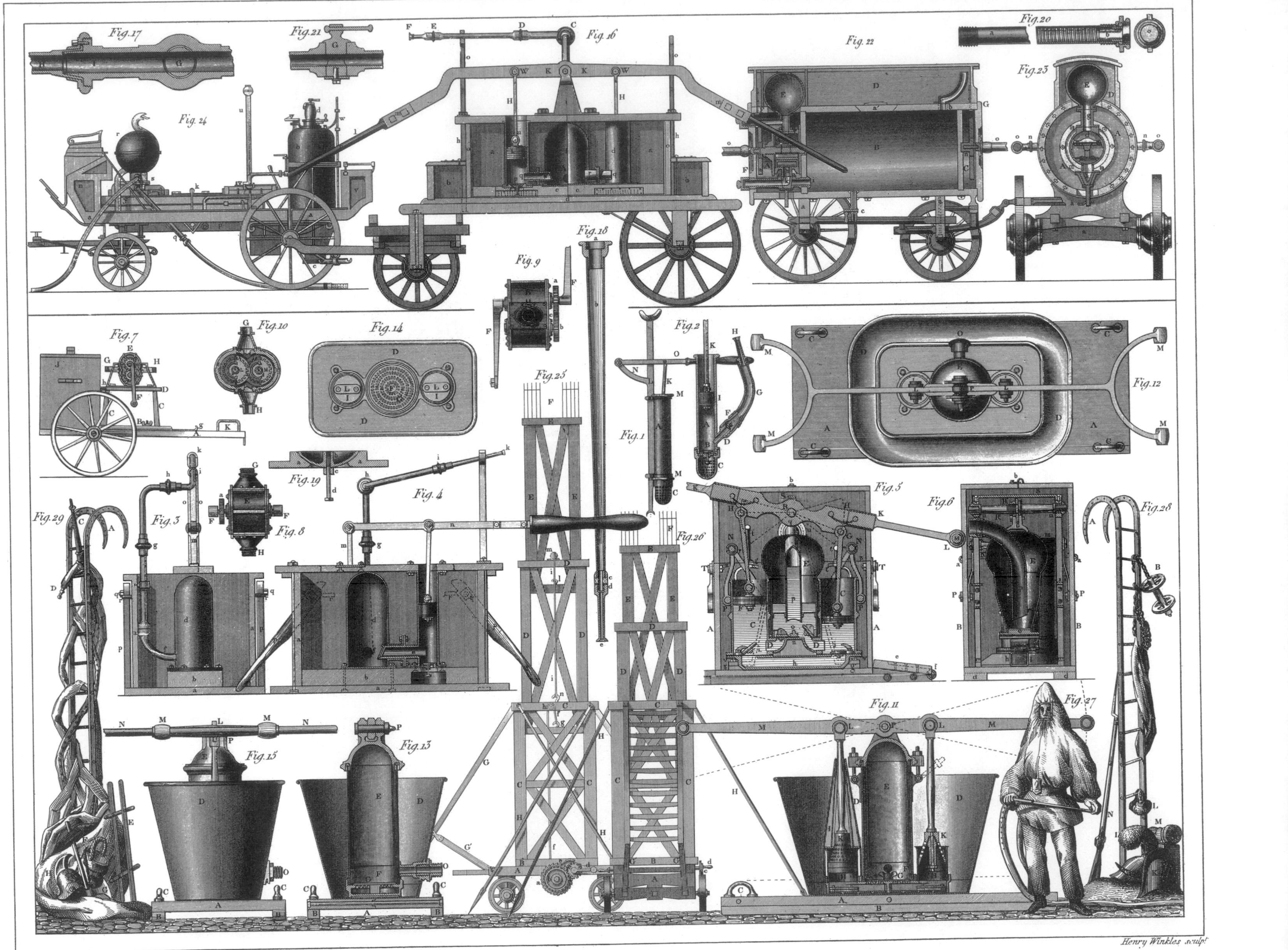

G. Heck dir.t

Henry Winkles sculp.t

PLATE 479. FIRE-FIGHTING EQUIPMENT

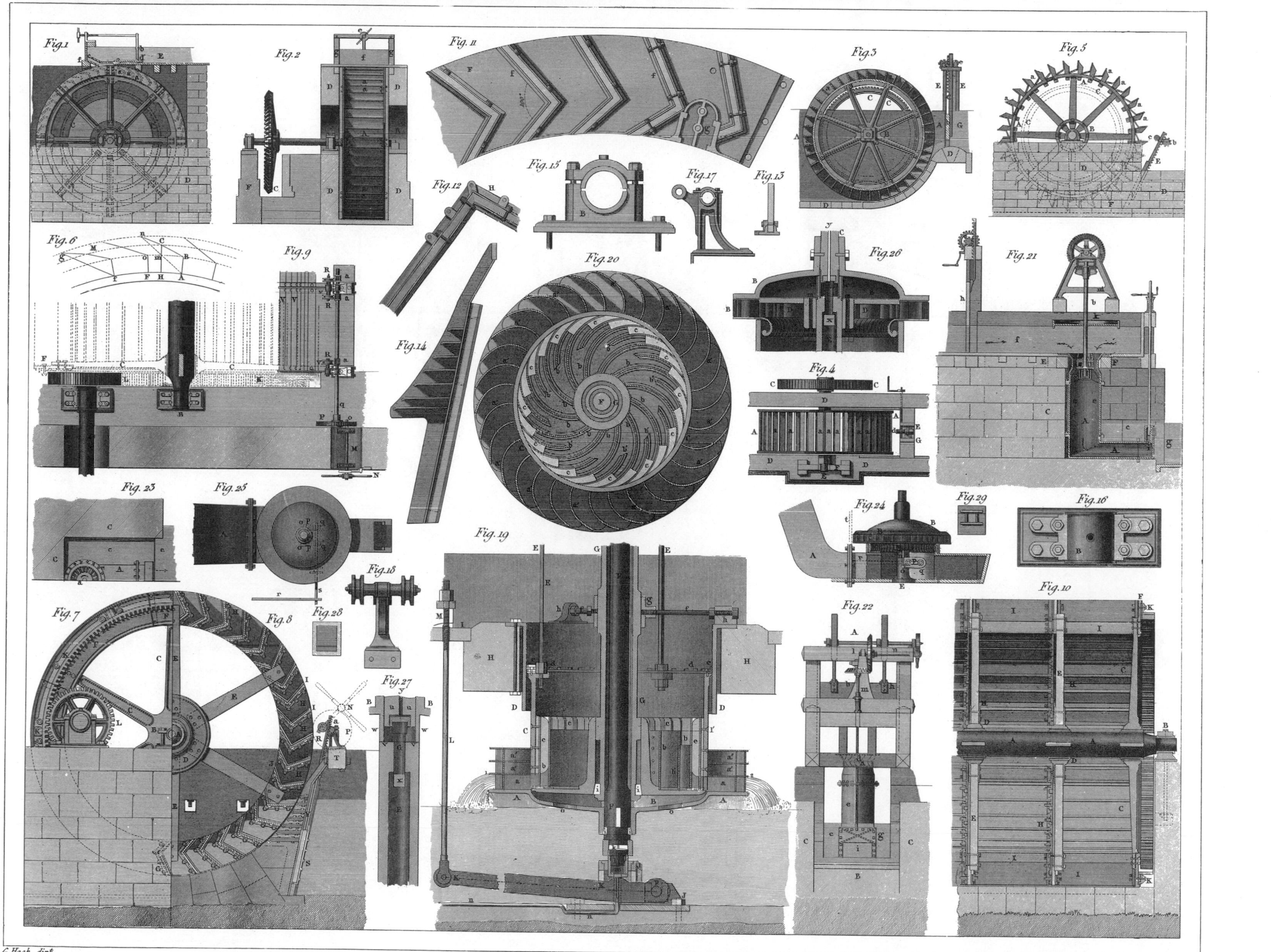

G. Heck dir.^t

Henry Winkles sculp.^t

PLATE 480. CONSTRUCTION OF WATER-WHEELS

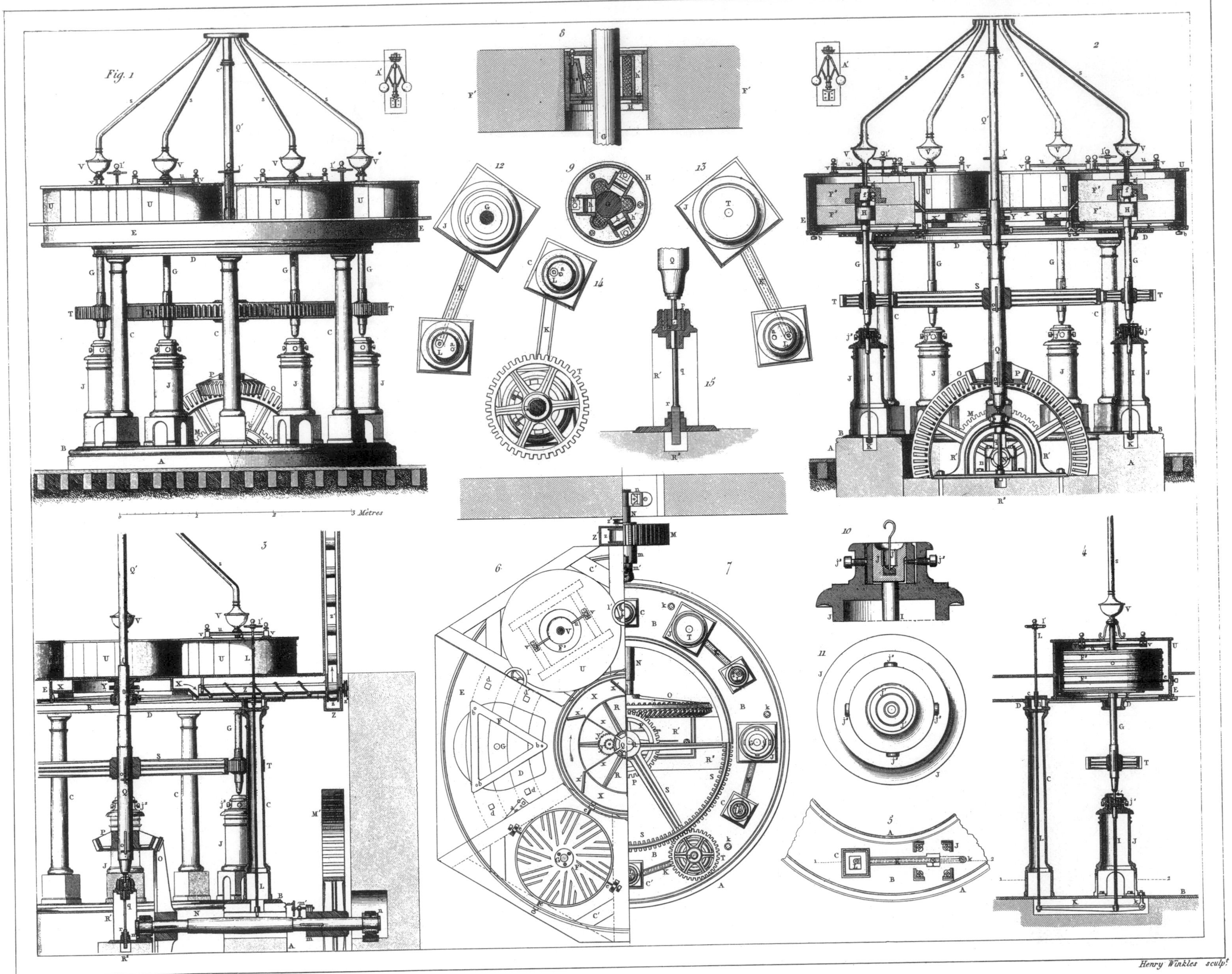

G. Heck dir.[t]

Henry Winkles sculp.[t]

PLATE 481. ILLUSTRATING THE CONSTRUCTION OF AN AMERICAN GRINDING-MILL

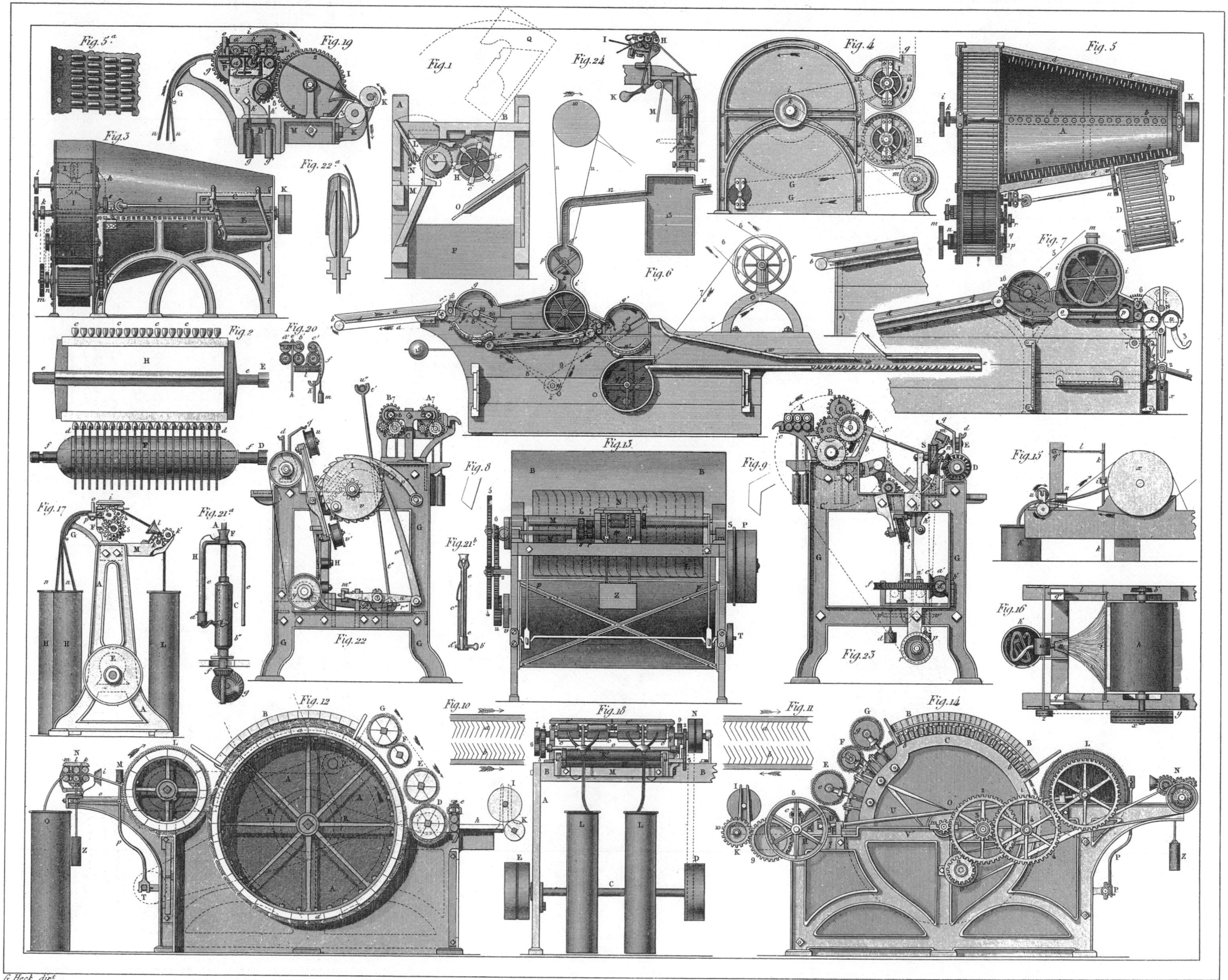

G. Heck dir.

Henry Winkles sculp.

PLATE 482. COTTON PROCESSING EQUIPMENT

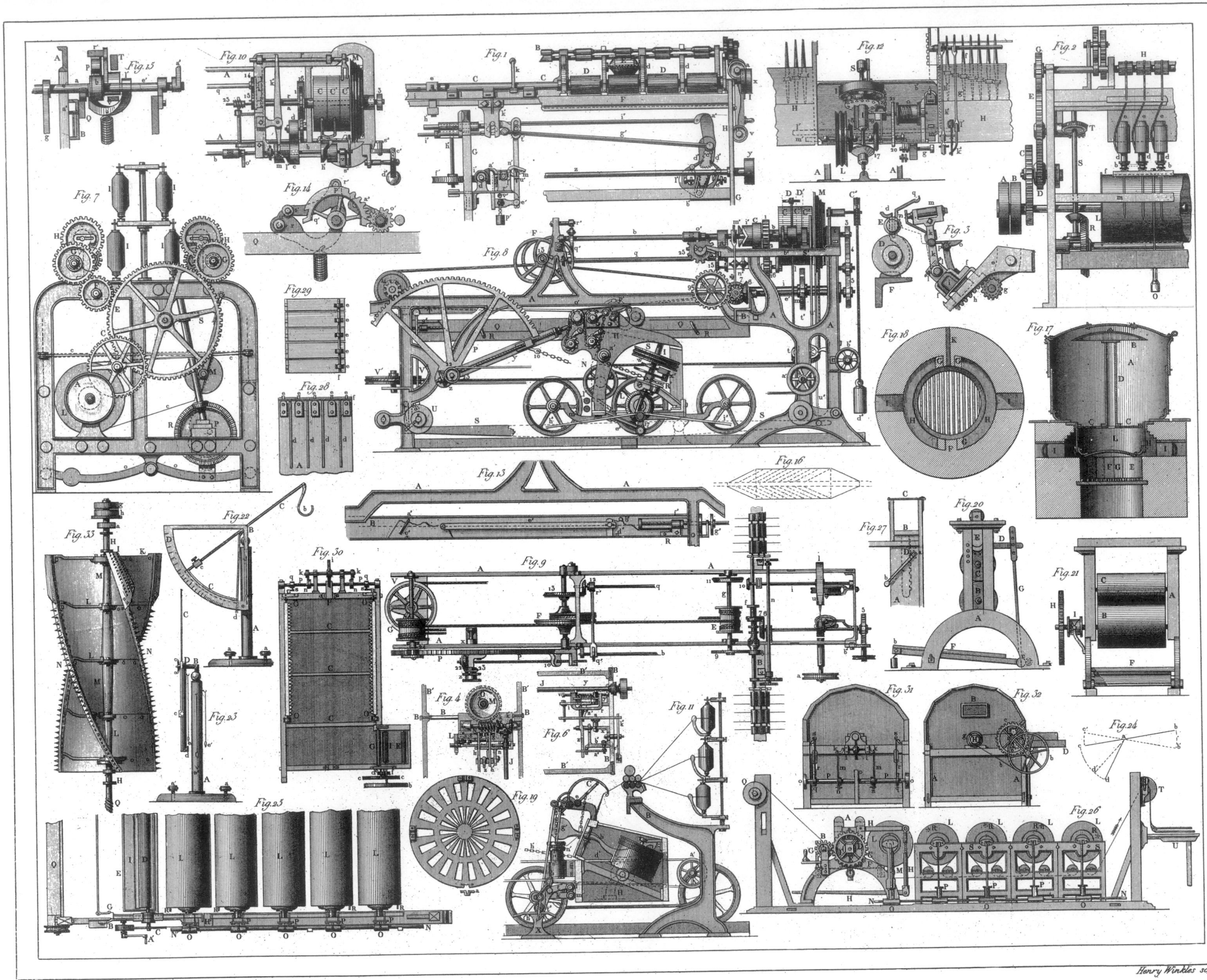

C. Heck dir.t

Henry Winkles sculp.t

 PLATE 483. WOOL PROCESSING EQUIPMENT

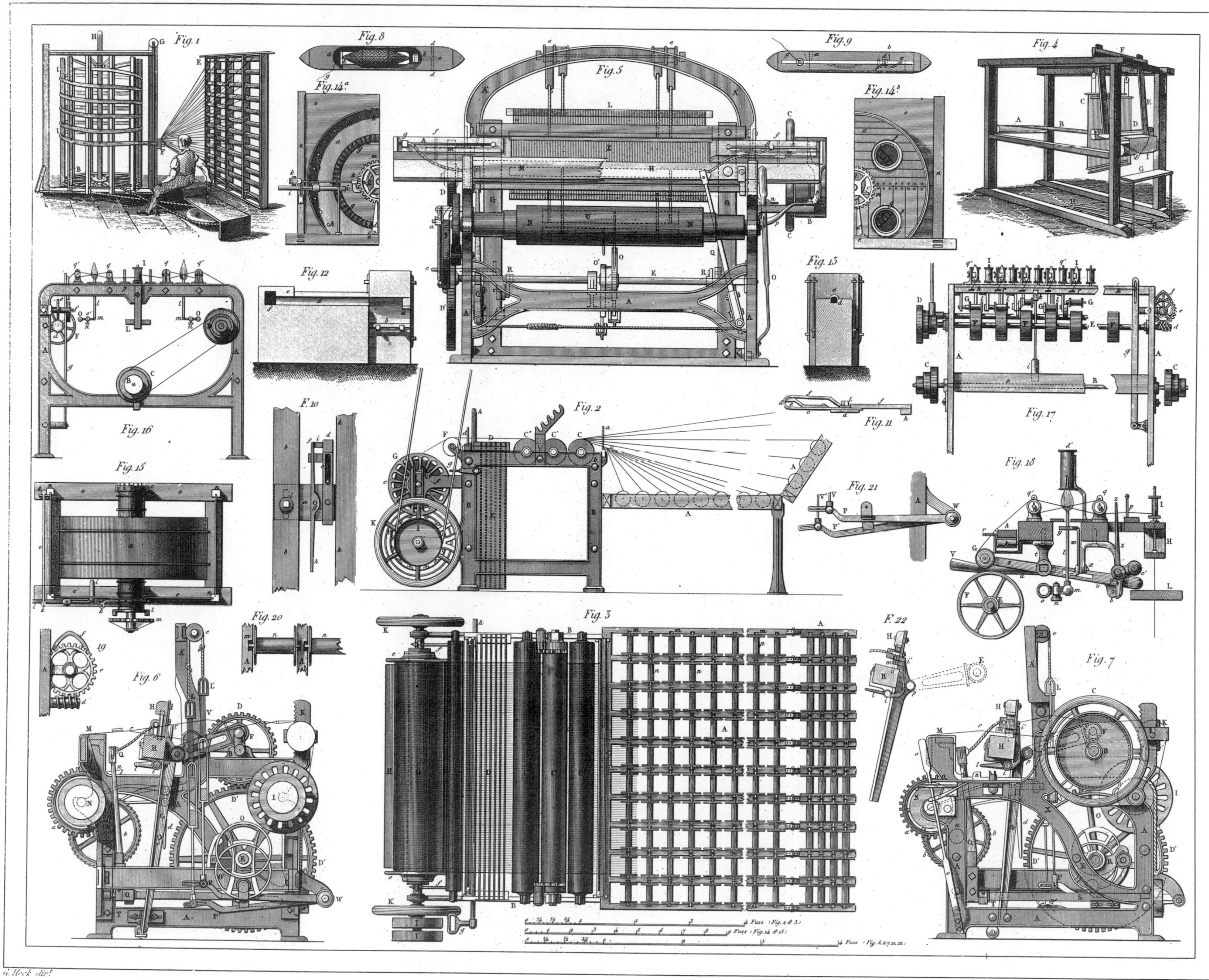

G. Heck dir.t

Henry Winkles sculp.t

PLATE 484. WEAVING EQUIPMENT

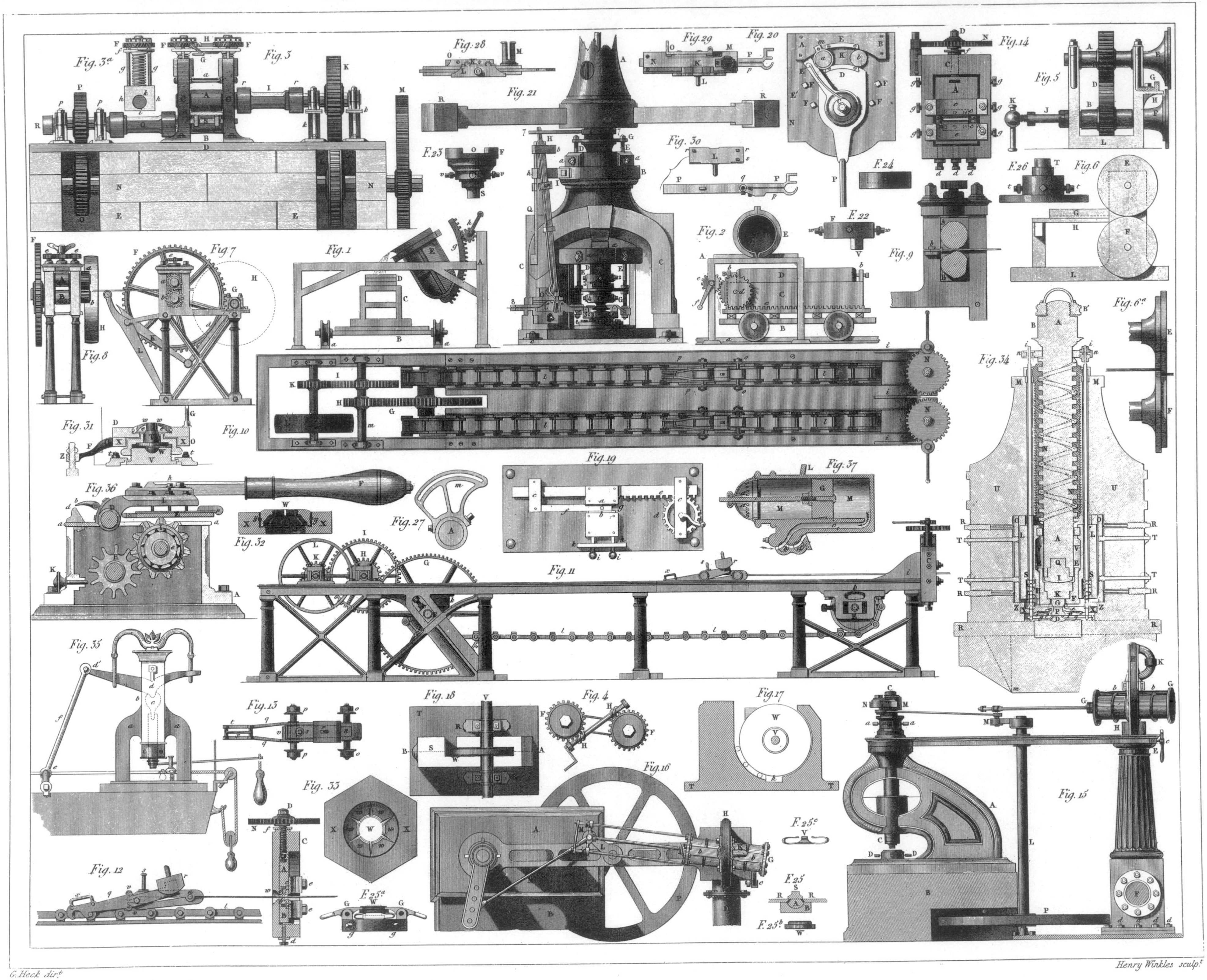

PLATE 485. MINTING EQUIPMENT

ENGLISH·EAST·INDIA·COMPANY
BOMBAY 1765
1797
MONETA·AVREA·DANICA
1·SPECIES DUCAT 23½ KARAT
FREDERICUS VI REX DANIÆ
NUMUS AUREUS HAMBURGENSIS
REPUBLICA BERNENSIS
BENEDICTUS SIT IEHOVA DEUS
1 DUCAT 1794
V THALER 1799
X THALER 1829
FRIDERICUS WÜRTEMB·REX
16 FRANKEN 1800
HELVETISCHE REPUBLIK
Fig. 1
Fig. 11
Fig. 12
Fig. 13
Fig. 15
Fig. 19
Fig. 21

G. Heck dir[t]

Henry Winkles sculp[t]

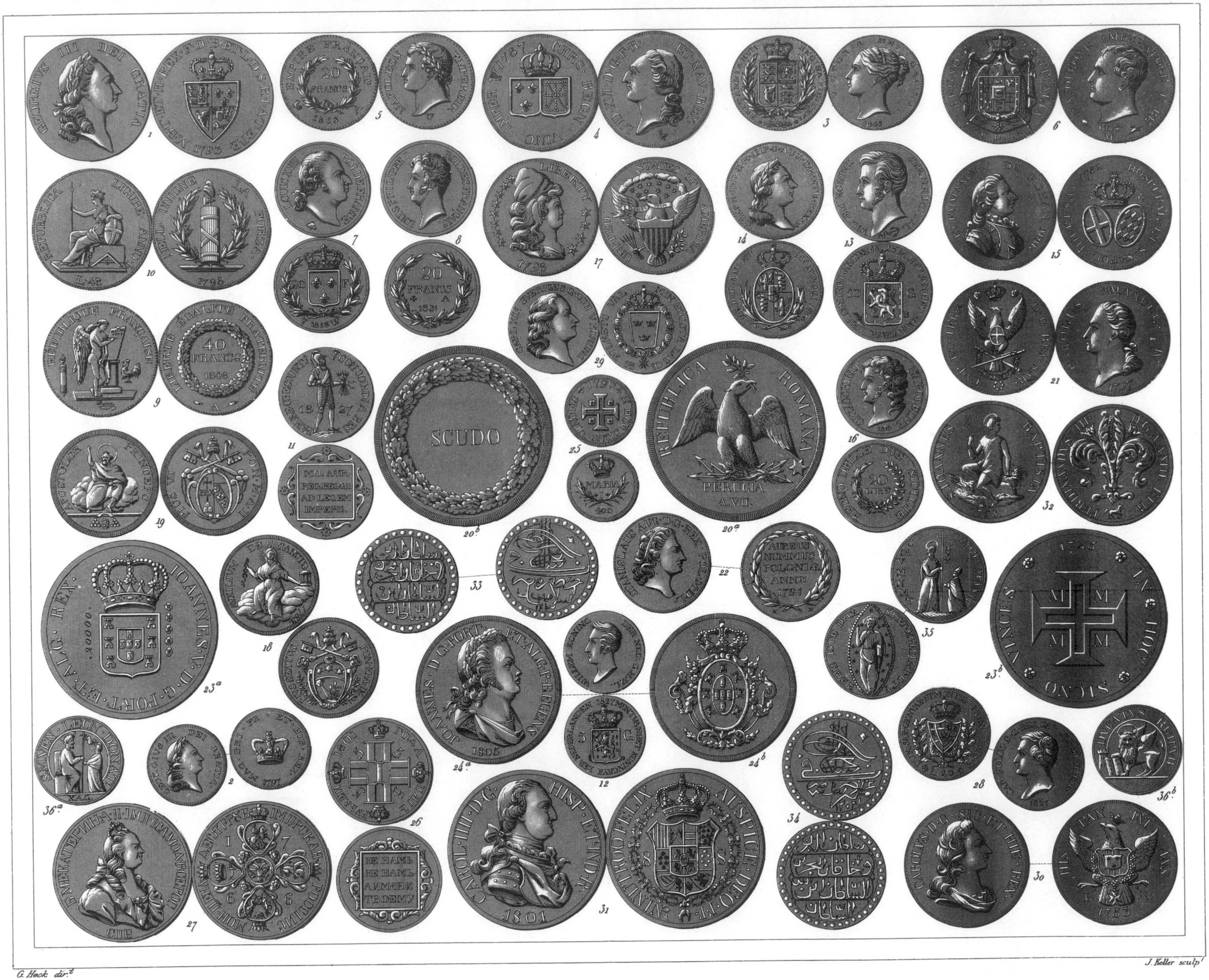

G. Heck dir.t

J. Keller sculp.t

 PLATE 487. COINS OF VARIOUS NATIONS

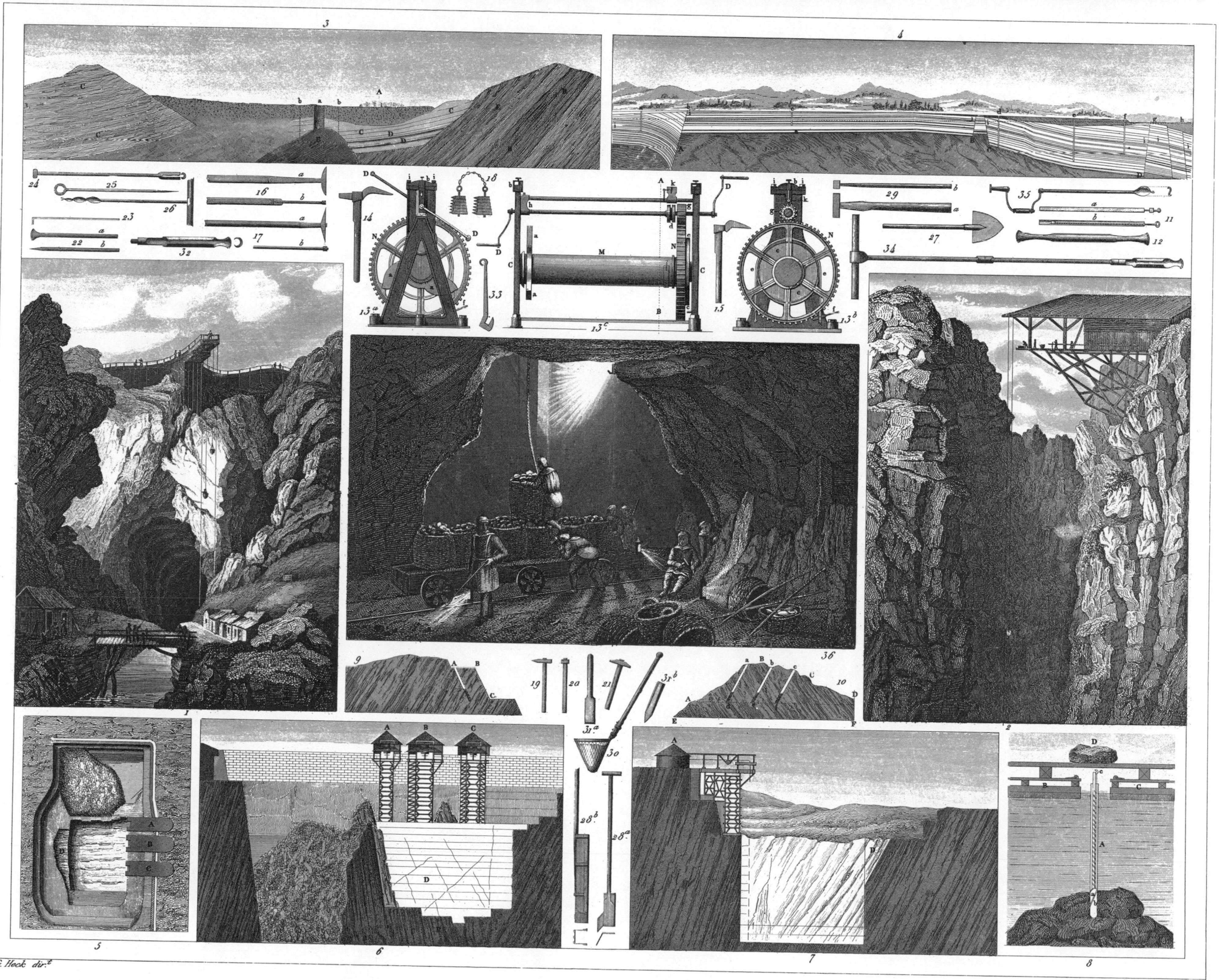

G. Heck dir.t

A. Krausse sen. sculp.

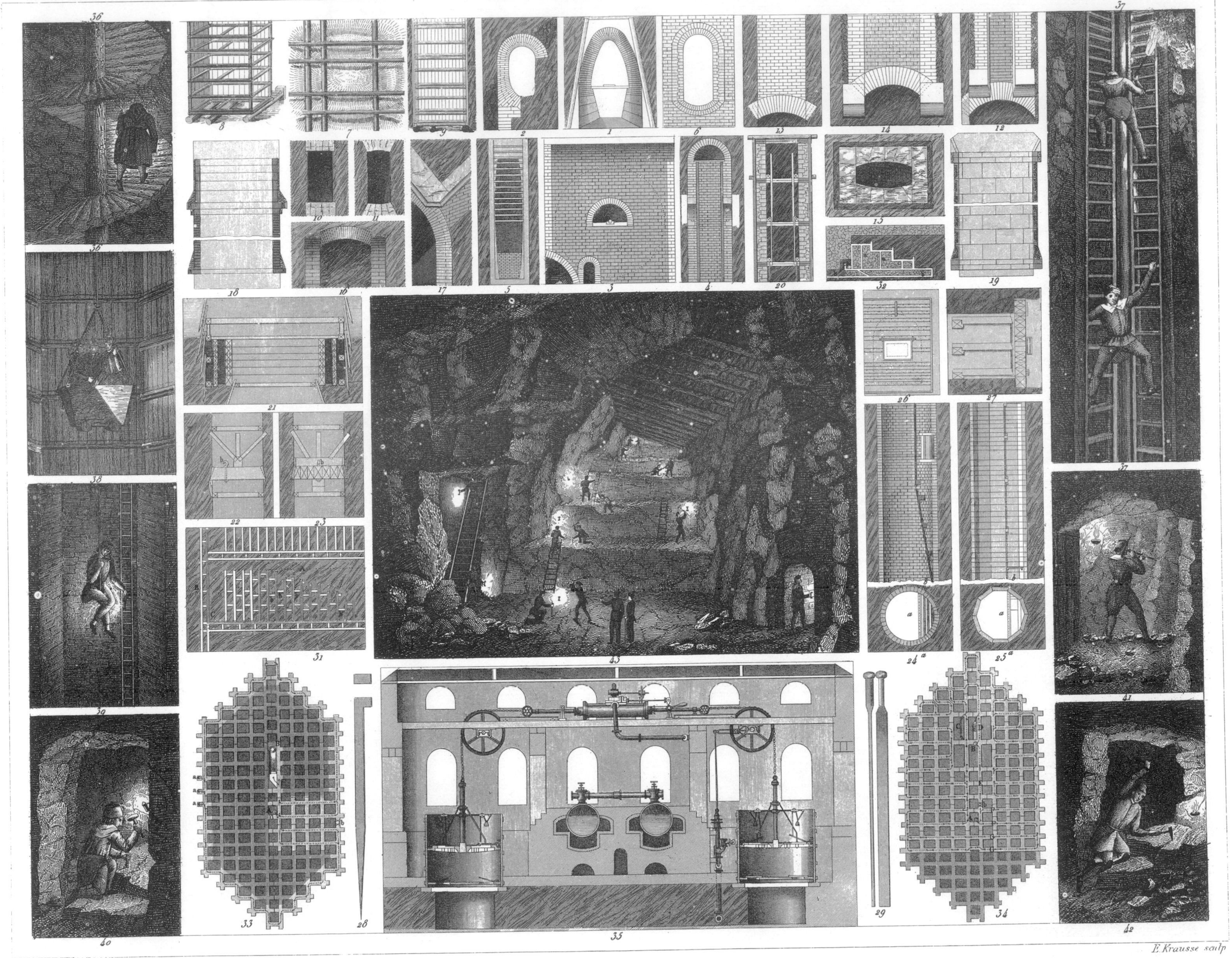

G. Heck dir.t F. Krausse sculp

G. Heck dir.t

G. Feldweg sculp

G. Heck dir.t A. Krausse sculp.

PLATE 491. MINING

G. Heck dir.t

E. Krausse sculp.

PLATE 492. METAL MILLING

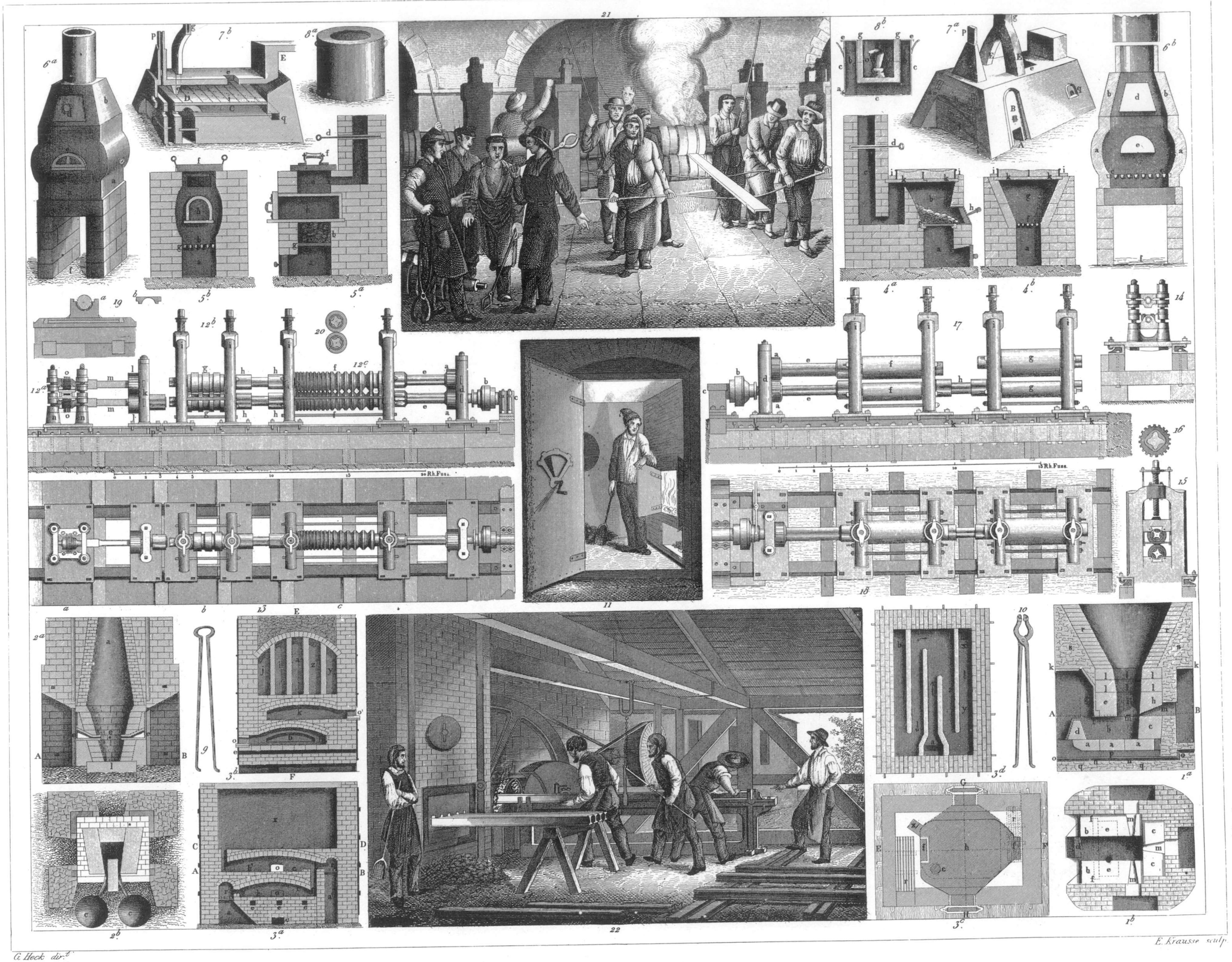

G. Heck dir.t E. Krausse sculp

 PLATE 493. METAL MILLING

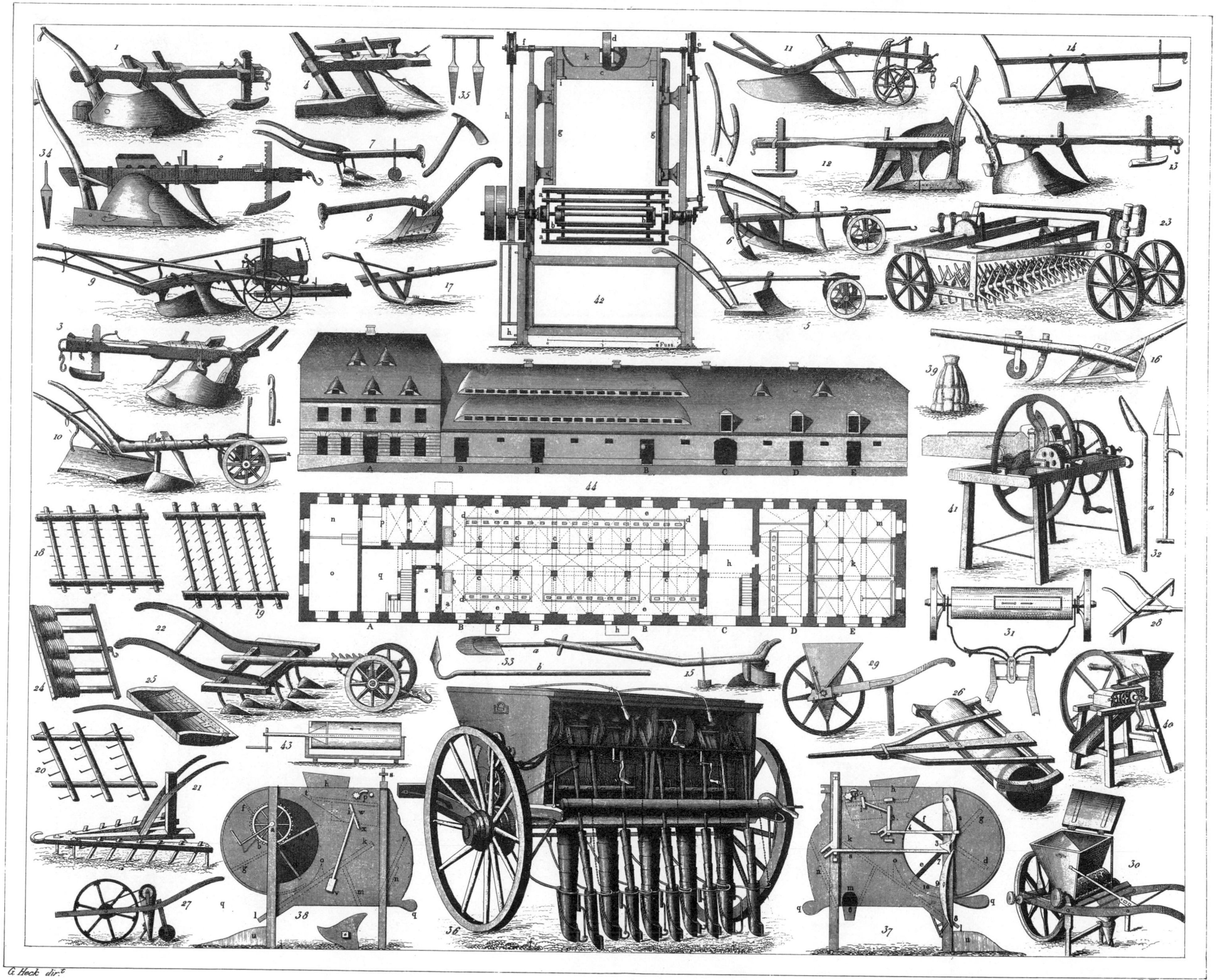

G. Heck dir.t

E. Krausse sculp

PLATE 494. AGRICULTURE

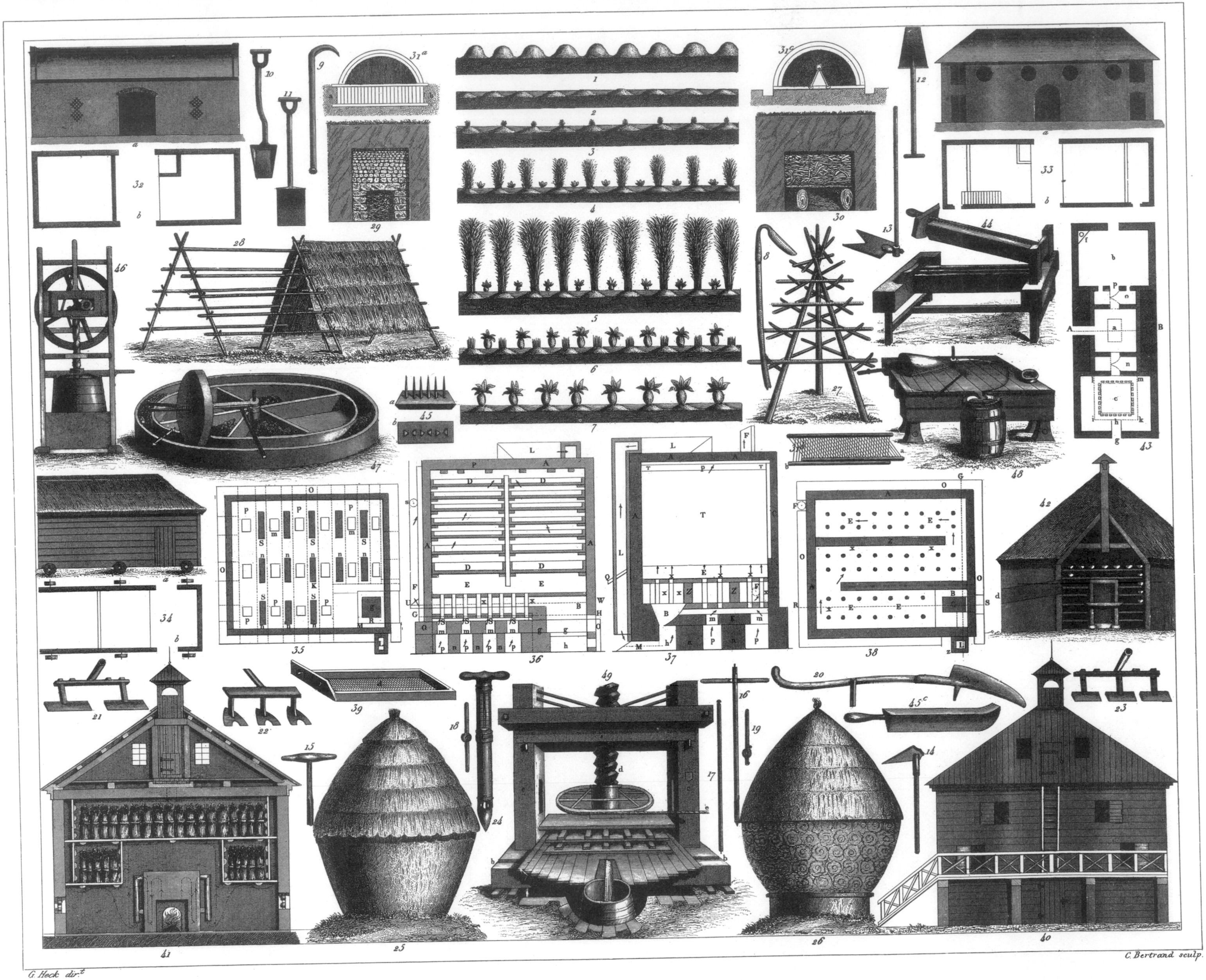

G. Heck dir.t

C. Bertrand sculp.

G. Heck dir.t

A. Krausse sculp.

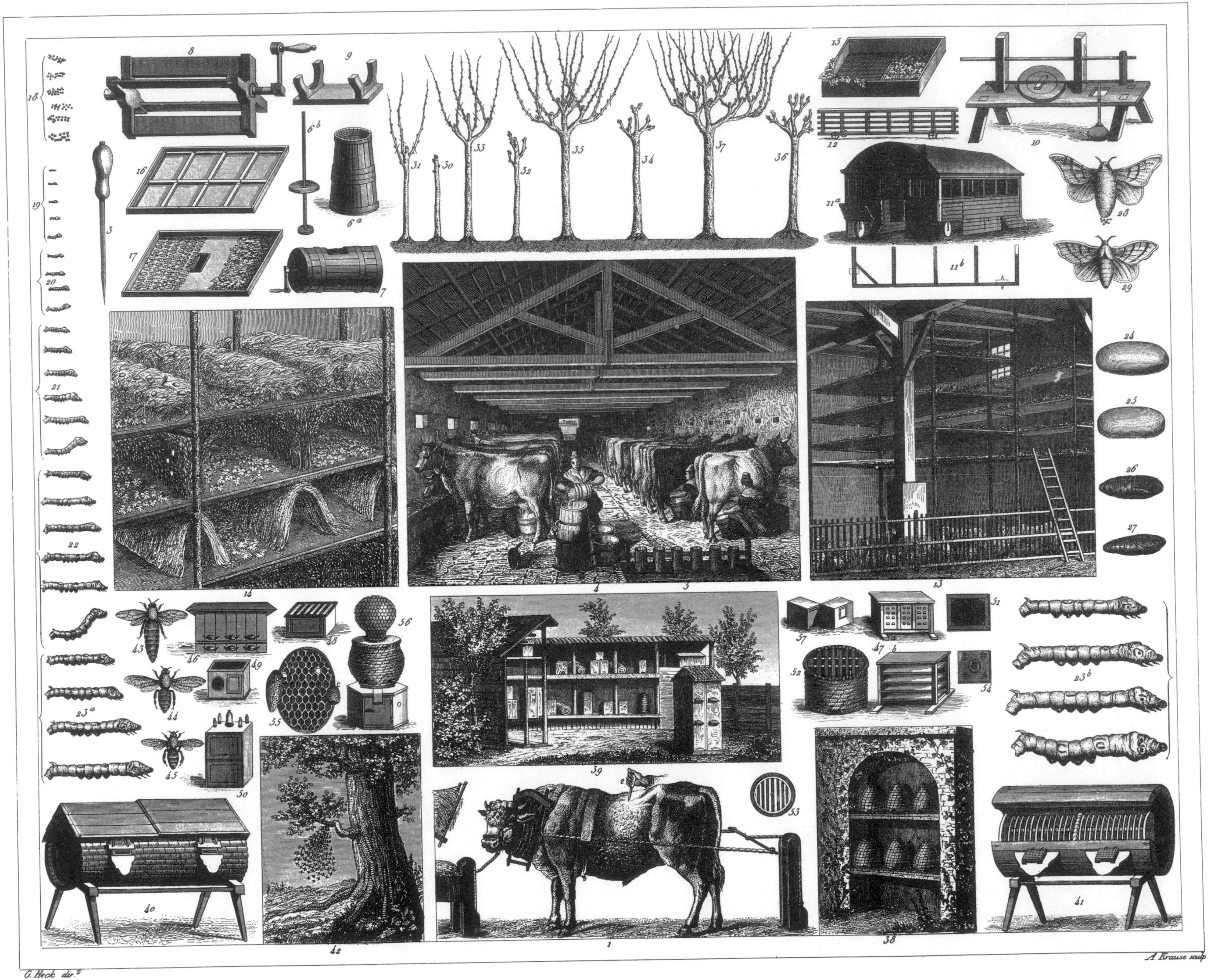
G. Heck dir.t
A. Krause sculp

G. Heck dir.t

G. Feldweg sculp

PLATE 498. HUNTING

G. Heck dir.t

G. Feldweg sculp

PLATE 499. FISHING

PLATE 500. FISHING